The Lord of glory

The Lord of glory

Day by day devotions with your children

Jim Cromarty

EP PUBLISHING WITH A MISSION

EP Books
Faverdale North, Darlington, DL3 0PH England
e-mail: sales@epbooks.org
www.epbooks.org

EP Books USA
PO BOX 614, Carlisle, PA 17013, USA
e-mail: usasales@epbooks.org
www.epbooks.us

Set in Bembo and Gill Sans Monotype.

British Library Cataloguing in Publication Data available

ISBN-10 0 85234 684 0
ISBN-13 978 0 85234 684 6

Printed and bound in the USA by Versa Print Inc., East Peoria, IL.

To Valerie, a faithful 'help meet' for fifty years

Contents

Preface

In my previous book of devotions I stressed the responsibility that God places upon parents to teach their children the glorious truths found in his Word. In earlier generations Christian parents daily gathered their families together to worship the living God. The Scriptures were read and God was glorified in prayer, and frequently in praise.

Today, in most families, even professing Christian families, the Bible is a neglected book, and the teaching of biblical truths is left to Sunday School teachers. Parents are generally more concerned that their children receive an education that will set them up for a life of financial reward.

Now education is of great importance in our society, but of greatest importance is having our descendants coming to saving faith. Thus parents, especially fathers, who are head of their household, should sincerely believe and implement the fundamental truth contained in the answer to the first question in the *Westminster Shorter Catechism*: 'What is the chief end of man?'

The answer is plain and profound: 'Man's chief end is to glorify God and to enjoy him for ever.'

No one will glorify and enjoy God until they know him intimately. Parents should be praying that God will bring about the new birth in the hearts of their children. While we acknowledge that salvation is the work of God, parents have been given the responsibility of teaching their children of the God who is the Creator and the God and Father of our Saviour, the Lord Jesus Christ.

My pastor, the Rev. George Ball, has written an introduction to this new book of devotions, which I beg you to read and implement.

This new writing is aimed to glorify Jesus Christ, my Lord and Saviour.

May God be pleased to bring our children and their descendants to saving faith. What a joy it would be if the head of the family could say with Joshua: 'as for me and my house, we will serve the LORD' (Joshua 24:15).

Jim Cromarty

Introduction

The well-being of the church should be a concern for every Christian believer. It should concern us that many of our young people have drifted away from the church or in some cases become merely nominal members. Why? There may be a number of reasons but surely one major reason must be the neglect of family worship. Not that I'm suggesting that this is the panacea for all our ills. You can have family worship without parental example. But where you have real, credible family religion, where the faith is not only talked about but also practised — this is a very powerful influence for good. Spurgeon remembered that his mother tearfully prayed over him, 'Lord, Thou knowest if these prayers are not answered in Charles's conversion, these very prayers will bear witness against him in the Judgement Day.' Spurgeon wrote: 'The thought that my mother's prayers would serve as a witness against me in the Day of Judgement sent terror into my heart.'

Many others can testify of the influence of family worship upon their lives. We all desire the growth of the church. One of the most effective means that the Lord gives us for the expansion of the church through the generations is family religion, where parents take time to lead the family before God in worship.

Those of us who are pastors must lovingly inform the families under our care of this obligation to worship God, not merely on the Lord's Day, but on all other days as well. The Lord said of Abraham, 'For I have known him, in order that he may command his children and his household after him, that they may keep the way of the Lord, to do righteousness and justice, that the Lord may bring to Abraham what he has spoken to him' (Genesis 18:19). It's ironic that much time and money is spent on the planning, building and maintaining of a house. By comparison very little is spent on the spiritual training of our most valuable assets. Thomas Brooks said, 'A family without prayer is like a house without a roof, open and exposed to all the storms of heaven.'

If you have not been in the habit of family worship, a good place to start would be in the Gospels, following the life, death and resurrection of Christ. 'The Holy Scriptures are able to make you wise for salvation through faith which is in Christ Jesus' (2 Timothy 3:15).

Jim Cromarty has again provided for us in his usual plain and pointed style another valuable resource, which if used in your family will be a great blessing. This book will help you discover more of the greatest living Person and lead you to the greatest activity of all — the worship of God.

Rev. George Ball
Pastor, *The Manning River Presbyterian Church*
of Eastern Australia

January

'Let this mind be in you which was also in Christ Jesus, who, being in the form of God, did not consider it robbery to be equal with God...' (Philippians 2:5-6).

Read: Isaiah 6:1-5

We are going to study the life, character and saving work of the Lord Jesus Christ, who came into this world to save sinners, but first we will look at the pre-incarnate Christ and some Old Testament prophecies that were fulfilled during Jesus' life. In our text we are called upon to be like Christ who, while he was God, humbled himself and became man to live and die to redeem his people. Our Saviour is God and man in one Person, which is something difficult for us to understand.

The passage of Scripture you have read from, Isaiah 6, is a description of the Lord before he became a man, and what a wonderful picture it is. For a time try to imagine God's throne room in heaven. Isaiah saw someone seated upon that throne. That Person was dressed in the glorious robes of his office. Human kings and queens, when dressed for formal occasions, usually wore the finest of clothing with a robe trailing behind them. Isaiah saw the same in his vision of the One sitting upon the heavenly throne, except the train of his robe filled the heavenly temple. We can only imagine the glory of the scene before the prophet.

The Lord, sitting in state, was surrounded by seraphs — angels of the highest order, servants ready to carry out God's commands. Even though they were sinless they dared not look upon God, but were always ready to carry out his every command. Those angels called out to one another:

> Holy, holy, holy is the LORD of hosts;
> the whole earth is full of his glory.

Did you notice that the word 'LORD' is in capital letters? Why? It is because the Jews feared writing God's revealed name, Jehovah.

However, you and I should recognize this name, because it tells us that the One sitting on the heavenly throne in regal splendour was the almighty, majestic Jehovah whose glory filled the whole universe.

This majestic God described by Isaiah was none other than our Saviour, Jesus Christ.

How do I know this? If you open your Bible and read John 12:37-41 you will find John's words referring to Isaiah. He wrote: 'Isaiah said this because he saw Jesus' glory and spoke about him.'

This is the One who humbled himself by leaving his heavenly glory to become a man and finally die on a cross to save his people. This was the greatest act of humility that could ever be. Christians are called to be humble people. Everything we are and ever shall be we owe to Jesus Christ.

THINGS TO DISCUSS WITH YOUR FAMILY

1. Why did Isaiah call the Lord 'the LORD of hosts'?
2. What was Satan's first sin? Read Isaiah 14:12-14.
3. What does it mean to be humble?

Meditation

Think for a time about Christ leaving the throne of his glory to become man, to suffer and die upon a cruel Roman cross in order to save sinners. This work shows the intensity of God's love for his people; that is, the love of the Father, Son and Holy Spirit.

Wise Words

Of all garments, none is so graceful, none wears so well, and none is so rare, as humility.   *J. C. Ryle*

'For by him [Christ] all things were created that are in heaven and that are on earth, visible and invisible, whether thrones or principalities or powers. All things were created through him and for him' (Colossians 1:16).

Read: Revelation 5:8-14

Some people believe that when they die they will become angels. This is not true!

There was a time when God alone existed. There was no universe as we know it. God — Father, Son and Holy Spirit — is eternal. It is impossible for our finite mind to understand how this could be — that the uncreated God always existed.

God is eternal. Every person who disbelieves this must believe that matter always existed or that at some point it came into existence.

We see the world in which we live, but there is another world in existence that you and I have not yet seen; that is the world of spirit-beings called angels. I have not seen an angel, but I have seen some illustrations of 'angels' drawn by people who have great imaginations. Their 'angels' are usually drawn wearing long white gowns and having wings.

Our text tells us that the Lord Jesus created everything — 'visible and invisible'. The 'invisible' creation is that of the angels who do not have bodies like ours. They have an invisible angelic body, but when they contacted humans they appeared in human form. In that body they talked, walked, sat and ate (see Genesis 18:1 – 19:1).

God did not need a creation, as Father, Son and Holy Spirit were in a perfect relationship. Yet in order to display God's glory the decision was made to create a world of angels and then our wonderful world. The angels are a fixed number as they do not die, nor do they marry and have children (Mark 12:25). In Psalm 68:17 we read they number 'twenty thousand, even thousands of thousands' about the throne of God.

We will later read about an angelic revolt in heaven. When angels were created they were to glorify God and be always ready to carry out his commands. When Adam and Eve were expelled from the Garden of Eden it was an angel who stood guard to prevent them returning and finding their way to 'the tree of life' (Genesis 3:24). It was an angel who appeared to Jesus when he was praying in the Garden of Gethsemane before his death (Luke 22:43). The writer to the Hebrews tells us that the angels are 'ministering spirits sent forth to minister to those who will inherit salvation' (Hebrews 1:14). God's angels have the task of protecting the saints from the demons. Have you ever thought as you sat down on the Lord's Day to worship God, that there are angels protecting the congregation from Satan and his evil followers? All of God's people could well have a personal angel standing guard at their side (Matthew 18:10).

When Jesus returns to this earth he will be accompanied by his 'mighty angels' (2 Thessalonians 1:7).

Remember that angels are created beings and are not to be worshipped.

THINGS TO DISCUSS WITH YOUR FAMILY

1. What did the angel guarding the entrance to the Garden of Eden have in his hand?
2. Is Jesus an angel? How do you know? Read Hebrews 1:5-14.
3. What is the role of the angels when a Christian dies? See Luke 16:22.

Meditation

Thank God for the angels who care for you and other Christians. Are you looking forward to meeting them one day?

Wise Words

Angels will never be kings. They will always be servants.
Andrew Bonar

'In the beginning was the Word, and the Word was with God, and the Word was God. He was in the beginning with God. All things were made through him, and without him nothing was made that was made' (John 1:1-3).

Read: Genesis 2:1-6

When I was a schoolteacher there were times I took my class outside our classroom to look at God's creation. We talked about all that God had made and considered it amazing that God, who is spirit, should make a world that can be seen and touched. We talked about the trees, grasses, flowers, rivers, hills and all the animals that are part of the creation. We also discussed our amazing bodies that worked so well.

We also thought about God who created the millions of colours about us, the taste we have in our foods and the great variety of smells that we can detect. To finish our nature wander we would all lie down on the grass and looking up into the heavens use our imaginations to describe what we could see in the many cloud formations.

Creation is amazing and reveals to us many things about our God. Think of his power in creating this world through Christ, his one and only Son. He simply gave the command and matter appeared out of nothing. If you read Genesis 1 you will find the order of creation. Not only is God's power seen in the work of creation, but we also see the wisdom of his plan. Everything created had a purpose and worked together in perfect harmony.

The Apostle John clearly wrote of Jesus: 'All things were made through him, and without him nothing was made that was made.' There are some religions which teach that the Lord Jesus was created, but John makes it perfectly clear that Christ created everything. He did not create himself!

In your reading you find that God rested on the seventh day. This was not a rest of doing nothing. The world had to keep functioning — the earth had to spin on its axis and circle the sun. Gravity had to continue or the world would fall apart. God's rest was like that of an artist who, when he has finished his masterpiece, stands back and looks it over. God did this on the seventh day, having already declared that his creation was 'very good' (Genesis 1:31).

Almighty God created this world to display his glory. Humans were created to magnify God and to enjoy and care for the creation.

Go outside now and look at God's world. Isn't it wonderful? I know it is!

THINGS TO DISCUSS WITH YOUR FAMILY

1. Who is the 'Word' of John 1:1?
2. For what purpose was this universe created?
3. In what ways does this world show the power and wisdom of God?
4. What do you think is the most unusual aspect of the universe in which we live?

Meditation

Look at some of the things that God created. Think about God's great power in creating this universe out of nothing.

Wise Words

Every one of God's great works is in its way *great*. All angels and all men united could not make one grasshopper. *William Plumer*

'How you are fallen from heaven, O Lucifer, son of the morning!' (Isaiah 14:12).

Read: Isaiah 14:12-15

Humility is that part of human nature that is frequently missing from most people. The most humble person who ever walked this earth was the Lord Jesus Christ. He who is Jehovah left heaven, was born to his mother Mary, grew up and finally died on a cruel Roman cross. This is the greatest act of humility the world has ever known. On one occasion while he was on earth, the Saviour who is called 'the KING OF KINGS AND LORD OF LORDS' (1 Timothy 6:15) carried out a most humiliating act — he knelt down and washed his disciples' feet (John 13:2-15). This was usually the work of the lowest slave.

Pride, the opposite of humility, is a curse and one of the worst of sins. Christians should always say with the Apostle Paul 'by the grace of God I am what I am' (1 Corinthians 15:10). Even our salvation is the gift of God. Everything we are or ever shall be is a gift of God. No one can boast about his or her achievements; all the glory must go to God!

The Bible contains many warnings about pride, all of which we should take notice: 'Pride goes before destruction, and a haughty spirit before a fall' (Proverbs 16:18); and 'A man's pride will bring him low...' (Proverbs 29:23). We have a proverb: 'Pride goes before a fall.'

Today's reading is about Lucifer, one of the most glorious of God's angels. Lucifer (meaning 'Day Star') is described in Ezekiel 28:15 as being 'perfect in your ways from the day you were created, till iniquity was found in you'. Despite being so glorious and good Lucifer was free to rebel as were Adam and Eve!

However, the time came when he was not satisfied with the position he held in heaven among the angels. He decided that he wanted to push God off heaven's throne and sit on it himself. Your reading outlines Lucifer's terrible sin — there are five 'I wills' to be found. The fifth one reads 'I will be like the Most High.' This is pride of the worst kind! How different he is from the Lord Jesus Christ who created him.

He was immediately to discover the truth of the proverb: 'Pride goes before destruction...' (Proverbs 16:18) for we read in verse 15 of today's reading: 'You shall be brought down to Sheol, to the lowest depths of the Pit.' Lucifer or Satan was to end up in the most terrible part of hell. No one tempted Satan to sin; he did it all himself and then came down to the earth to tempt Adam and Eve to sin against God their Creator. Pride was also mankind's sin.

Satan and the angels who followed him in his sin kept the world, with the exception of Israel and a few Gentiles, in spiritual darkness. Things changed when Christ came with the gospel and his saving work — the good news concerning salvation through faith in the Redeemer is being taught throughout the world. Satan and his demons today go about tempting individuals to sin. His power has been broken, but he is still causing great harm in the world. Today he is like a dog on a leash — his freedom is limited.

When our Saviour returns, Satan and all who follow him — demons and humans — will be cast into hell — 'the lake of fire' (Revelation 20:10-15).

I trust that you are a Christian, because then heaven will be your eternal home.

THINGS TO DISCUSS WITH YOUR FAMILY

1. Make a list of the names by which Satan is known. What do we learn about Satan's activity from each of these names?
2. Why do you think Satan tempted Adam and Eve to sin?
3. What is hell and what is its purpose? Read Revelation 20:10-15.

Meditation

Think about your life. Do you need to repent of pride?

Wise Words

Everyone proud in heart is an abomination to the LORD... *Proverbs 16:5*

'And the LORD God said, "It is not good that man should be alone; I will make him a helper comparable to him"' (Genesis 2:18).

Read: Genesis 2:8-25

There is no doubt that we live in an unhappy world. Humans fight and squabble, families are torn apart, and nations go to war with their neighbours, causing great destruction and heartache. Even the world itself is spoiled by the weeds that thrive in our gardens, and the thorns and prickles that hurt our hands and feet. Our text tells us that the day is coming when God will make a new world and this ruined world will be forgotten.

Things were not always like they are. God's creation through Christ was perfect in every respect. Adam was placed in the beautiful Garden of Eden. He was to cultivate it, but didn't have the problem of weeds to spoil it. He was surrounded by trees with the most delicious fruits and was told he could eat any except that of 'the tree of the knowledge of good and evil' which was found in the middle of the garden. Adam was not expected to water the garden as 'a mist went up from the earth and watered the whole face of the ground' (Genesis 2:6).

We are told that God came into the garden in the cool of the evening and walked about with Adam. This no doubt was Christ, sometimes called 'the Angel of Jehovah',[1] who took a human body for the occasion. There was perfect friendship between God and Adam. I can imagine Christ telling Adam all about the creation and what he was to do. Adam's heart should have been filled with love and gratitude towards God. Sin destroyed this relationship, but the day was to come when Jesus Christ would again enter the world as God and man in one Person. He paid the penalty for the sins of his people, making it possible for them to once again have that close relationship with God.

But there was work to be done — all the animals were paraded before Adam and to each one he gave a name. This must have been a taxing job! Try and imagine the hundreds of names Adam had to invent. He realized that while the animals had partners, he was alone. Nevertheless, God had no intention of leaving Adam without a partner. He had a plan to make Adam a perfect helper. After putting him to sleep he removed one of his ribs out of which he made a woman who was named Eve. Adam and Eve were naked and felt no shame. For a short time they enjoyed living in that perfect Garden of Eden which was indeed Paradise!

Today there is much unhappiness in many marriages, but God never intended it to be like that. Marriage can be a source of peace and contentment if God's laws are obeyed. Paul gave good advice to husbands and wives — 'Husbands, love your wives, just as Christ also loved the church and gave himself for her ... Wives, submit to your own husbands, as to the Lord' (Ephesians 5:22,25).

THINGS TO DISCUSS WITH YOUR FAMILY

1. On what day of the creation week was Adam made? Of what was he made?
2. Try and find out the meaning of 'Eve'.
3. What name was given to the tree bearing the forbidden fruit?
4. Think of some words that describe the Garden of Eden.

Meditation

Consider what it must have been like for Adam to walk and talk with the Son of God in the Garden of Eden.

Wise Words

The creation is both a monument of God's power and a looking-glass in which we may see his wisdom.

Thomas Watson

1. See Judges 13:21-23. Here the 'Angel of the LORD' is called God.

'And the LORD God commanded the man, saying, "Of every tree of the garden you may freely eat; but of the tree of the knowledge of good and evil you shall not eat, for in the day that you eat of it you shall surely die"' (Genesis 2:16-17).

Read: Genesis 3:1-13

There is no doubt we live in a world that is unsafe. Terrorists are willing to blow themselves to pieces in their plans to achieve their ends. Many of these people think they will be welcomed into Paradise because of their 'sacrificial' death. This belief is wrong as all unrepentant murderers will spend eternity in hell!

You have read of the grandeur of God's creation, but today you have read of the greatest vandal this world has known. I imagine that wherever you live you have people who murder and destroy the property of others. God's perfect world had been vandalized in the worst possible way and all of this has been caused by Adam and Eve who rebelled against God. They were clearly warned not to eat the fruit of the 'tree of the knowledge of good and evil'. They were told that disobedience meant death!

Satan was the evil malignant one who having revolted against God in heaven, then tempted Eve to eat of the forbidden fruit, which she did because the fruit looked attractive. Satan spoke to her through a serpent and said that God's words could not be believed. She believed the words that came from a snake and ate the fruit of the 'tree of the knowledge of good and evil'.

What would you, a sinner, do if when walking through the fields, a snake came up and spoke to you? I would get out of the way very quickly — snakes do not talk! Eve however believed the snake and ate the fruit. She then handed some to Adam, who seeing that Eve had not died also ate, believing that what the snake had said must have been true. Instantly both died spiritually and their bodies began the long journey that would end in physical death, burial and decay, returning to dust.

Adam knew what God had said and should have instantly stepped in and forbidden Eve to eat that special fruit, but he failed. This act of rebellion has brought death to every person, except Enoch and

Elijah. Adam and Eve were terrorists of the worst type. Their rebellion also ruined the physical world — they were vandals of the first order.

When confronted by God in the cool evening God demanded to know why they had made clothes of leaves. Adam then told what had happened. And when it was time to blame someone for what they had done, Adam blamed God — 'The woman whom *you* gave to be with me, she gave me of the tree, and I ate.'

What a mess Adam and Eve had made of God's perfect world! Every person who has ever lived, except the Lord Jesus, has inherited their sinful nature.

THINGS TO DISCUSS WITH YOUR FAMILY

1. What do you know of the serpent's character? Read 2 Corinthians 11:14 — 'And no wonder, for Satan himself masquerades as an angel of light.'
2. What are the two types of death that Adam's sin brought upon the world?
3. In what way was Adam the world's worst vandal?

Meditation

Think about the consequences of Adam's sin.

Wise Words

The wages of sin is death, but the gift of God is eternal life in Christ Jesus our Lord. *Apostle Paul*

'...the LORD God sent him out of the garden of Eden to till the ground from which he was taken' (Genesis 3:23).

Read: Genesis 3:14-24

Adam and Eve were about to suffer the consequences of their sin. We have already seen that the death sentence was passed upon our representatives in the Garden of Eden. There are many activities where we are represented by other people and what they do has an affect upon us. When the Australian cricket team won the 'Ashes' series we did not say, 'They won the Ashes!' but rather, 'We won the Ashes!'

The disease of sin was passed on to every person born into the world, with the one exception being the Lord Jesus Christ. We are all dead spiritually and need to be 'born again' in order to regain that close fellowship with God that Adam lost because of his sin. Without the new birth our destiny is hell.

As soon as we are born our bodies begin to move towards death and it is not only old people who die, but people of all ages. Our bodies suffer sickness, both physical and mental. Yet, sin brought more punishments than just spiritual and physical death.

The joy of gardening has become a problem. In the Garden of Eden all was perfect, but after Adam's sin God put a curse on the earth — thorns and thistles grew making gardening and farming hard work. After the day's work farmers come home tired, ready to have their meal and sleep. Work is hard and tiring!

Eve's punishment was the pain associated with giving birth. She would want to rule the home, causing arguments with her husband who was given the position of head of the house. Husbands and wives are to love each other and work together in harmony, but today, sad to say, nearly half of all marriages result in divorce.

Even the snake Satan used to tempt Eve to disobey God was punished. No longer would he and his offspring be proud creatures, but now they would slide about on their bellies and appear to be eating the dust of the ground. Down through the ages most people have feared snakes. Rarely do you hear of someone having a pet snake!

Sin caused great troubles for Adam and Eve, and this has continued throughout the ages. Today we are still suffering the consequences of Adam's and our own sins. The world is in a frightening mess.

To make matters worse for Adam and Eve, they were expelled from the Garden of Eden. To prevent them returning God placed cherubim at the eastern entrance to the garden. An unsheathed flaming sword also flashed about as a clear warning to Adam and Eve that neither they nor their descendants would ever re-enter that earthly Paradise. God was now guarding his Paradise from sinners.

THINGS TO DISCUSS WITH YOUR FAMILY

1. What are 'cherubim'?
2. What is 'spiritual death'?
3. What does it mean to be 'born again'? Read John 3:1-8 and Ezekiel 36:26-28.

Meditation

Spend some time thinking about the consequences of sin and God's punishment upon unrepentant sinners. Read John 3:16 and meditate upon God's wonderful gift to this world.

Wise Words

Sin has two great powers; it reigns and it ruins.

Anonymous

'For God so loved the world that he gave his only begotten Son, that whoever believes in him should not perish but have everlasting life' (John 3:16).

Read: Romans 3:9-20

Adam and Eve now knew they had a problem. There was no way they could regain their close fellowship with God. Outside the garden they had to work hard, and their lives would be filled with troubles and finally death. If unrepentant, their eternity would be spent in the place of God's eternal punishment.

However, God did not leave them without hope because he gave a promise which has been given a big name — 'Protevangelium' which means 'the first gospel proclamation'. We read God's words to Satan who had used the serpent to tempt Eve: 'I will put enmity between you and the woman, and between your seed and her Seed; he shall bruise your head, and you shall bruise his heel' (Genesis 3:15). For many years this promise was all they knew about God's salvation. Yet they knew that God would have the victory over Satan. It would be God who gave men and women the desire to destroy the evil one, but this was something they could never achieve alone. They needed help.

Eve had been tempted and succumbed to Satan's lies but she was assured now that her seed (descendant) would one day crush the serpent's head. Eve's offspring who loved God and hated sin would fight against Satan and his demons, but the promise points to just one of her 'seed' crushing the serpent's head.

God's words in Genesis 3:15 depict the battle between the serpent and his people. The serpent can only bite the heel, which can be cured, but when the serpent's head is crushed, his power is ended. This victory was the outcome of Christ's sacrificial death for the elect.

In the eyes of the world the church is only a 'little flock' (Luke 12:32) having very small power, but the promised 'Seed' would be victorious. One of the woman's children would have the total victory over Satan. Who could this be other than the Lord Jesus Christ who is both the servant of Jehovah and is God?

Adam and Eve had no knowledge when the victory would be won. We know that it was won by Christ during his life on earth which ended in his sacrificial death on the cross and resurrection. Adam and Eve may well have thought the one to overthrow Satan's power was their godly son Abel, but that was not to be. Satan had to be on guard all the time as he did not know who would attack and overthrow him.

As the years rolled by, God's prophets revealed more about the One who would destroy Satan and his followers, and in doing so showed God to be a God of grace, mercy and justice.

God's words to Adam and Eve would have given them hope. Despite their rebellion God would bring about a victory over the evil Satan who, through lies, had tricked God's first two humans to rebel against their Creator. We can only praise God for his goodness in saving a people. Are you one of those people? I pray that you are.

THINGS TO DISCUSS WITH YOUR FAMILY

1. What do you learn from John 3:16?
2. Who is God's one and only perfect Son?
3. When in his earthly life did our Saviour defeat Satan in a face to face battle? Read Matthew 4:1-11.

Meditation

Meditate for some time on why God, who is perfectly holy and hates sin, should bother to save sinners. If you are a Christian why should he have saved you?

A crushed head means utter defeat.   *H. C. Leupold*

Wise Words

'But God demonstrates his own love toward us, in that while we were still sinners, Christ died for us' (Romans 5:8).

Read: Isaiah 53

I was once asked to write my life story in three thousand five hundred words. There was a lot to say, but after much effort I achieved the set task. Obviously much was omitted and sometimes just several words described a lengthy part of my life. Isaiah wrote a biography of Christ (Isaiah 53), covering his life from the manger to his sacrificial death, in just twelve verses of Scripture.

The Jews misunderstood this passage and refused to believe it had any reference to the Messiah of God. The church leaders of Israel believed this and other sections of Scripture referring to the Servant of the Lord were spoken of Israel. Recently, when discussing today's reading with a Jewess I was told the passage described the suffering of the nation. Sadly the majority of the Israelites had it all wrong. When Jesus came they rejected the proposition that if he truly was the Messiah, he could not die. They saw their Christ as a great warrior King who would drive out the Roman occupying forces and rule as promised from the throne of David.

However, many times passages of Isaiah 53 were quoted in Scripture to support what was happening to Jesus. This gave added proof that he was the Messiah who had come to die and so save his people, both Jews and Gentiles.

The chapter speaks of the contempt in which he would be held by the people. He would be despised and rejected, to the extent that finally he was put to death on a Roman cross. The holy, compassionate Son of God was accused of being indwelt by God's great enemy Satan. Yet no one could accuse him of sin. He performed many great miracles and taught the people that salvation was not to be found in obedience to the law of God, but by faith in himself.

The Apostle Peter made great use of Isaiah 53 when he wrote of Christ's salvation (1 Peter 2:21-25). He pointed to those passages to show that Christ would die a sacrificial death which would deal with the sins of God's people. In part he wrote that Christ 'bore our sins in His own body on the tree, that we, having died to sins, might live for righteousness — by whose stripes you were healed' (1 Peter 2:24).

Isaiah foresaw that Jesus would die with wicked men, and yet in his death his body would be found with 'the rich'. This was fulfilled when Christ was crucified between two criminals, and later buried in a rich man's tomb.

Despite his rejection by the nation there were those who believed in him as the only way of salvation, and since the outpouring of the Holy Spirit millions worldwide have been brought into his kingdom. Isaiah prophesied this when he wrote that he would 'justify many'.

As we study the life of our Saviour we will see the words of Isaiah 53 fulfilled exactly. Memorize this chapter as it is a majestic prophecy of our salvation.

THINGS TO DISCUSS WITH YOUR FAMILY

1. Why was Jesus 'despised and rejected by men' (verse 3)?
2. Why in verse 7 is Jesus called a 'Lamb'?
3. In verse 10 we read 'it pleased the LORD to bruise him'. Why did God 'bruise' Jesus?

Meditation

Meditate upon the Lord's words in Matthew 20:28 — '...the Son of Man did not come to be served, but to serve, and to give his life a ransom for many'.

Wise Words

There is no death of sin without the death of Christ.
John Owen

'He came to his own and his own did not receive him' (John 1:11).

Read: Psalm 2

Val and I had a trip to Malaysia and on the plane we wondered how we would be recognized by the company that had organized our holiday. We arrived at 3:00 a.m. and after waiting for an hour or so in hot humid weather we finally made our way through the immigration section and faced a crowd of strange faces. We were becoming concerned about what we should do when suddenly a sign was held high — 'Cromarty'. We were found, welcomed and taken to our huge hotel where we had a lengthy rest, ready for our exciting adventures. When Jesus commenced his ministry, despite his majestic miracles, godliness and teaching the word of God, people failed to recognize who he was.

Jesus was born into a hostile world. Within a few months King Herod took action to have him killed by issuing orders for all babies in the Bethlehem region to be put to death. Mary and Joseph saved the life of Christ by fleeing to Egypt for safety. When Christ commenced his ministry, hatred very quickly raised its ugly head. The people refused to believe his words of invitation to eternal life — 'I am the way, the truth, and the life. No one comes to the Father except through me' (John 14:6).

As Jesus was not the type of Messiah the people expected, their attitude was expressed in one of Christ's parables: 'We will not have this man to reign over us' (Luke 19:14). The church rulers of Israel should have been models of love and compassion of both God and man, but they hated Christ to the extent that they wanted him put to death.

Following the raising of Lazarus who had been dead for over three days, the Jewish church leaders should have been rejoicing and praising God for the compassionate Lord of glory in their midst. Instead the chief priests and Pharisees met to make plans. John records, 'And one of them, Caiaphas, being high priest that year, said to them, "You know nothing at all, nor do you consider that it is expedient for us that one man should die for the people, and not that the whole nation should perish." Now this he did not say on his own authority; but being high priest that year he prophesied that Jesus would die for the nation, and not for that nation only, but also that he would gather together in one the children of God who were scattered abroad' (John 11:49–52).

The Jews did not have the power to execute anyone and called upon Pilate, Rome's appointed ruler in the area, to pronounce the death sentence upon Jesus. The prophecy of Psalm 2 was fulfilled: 'Why do the nations rage, and the people plot a vain thing? The kings of the earth set themselves, and the rulers take counsel together, against the LORD and against his Anointed, saying, "Let us break their bonds in pieces and cast away their cords from us."'

God's plan of salvation was being fulfilled perfectly. Always remember that our living God rules the affairs of this world.

THINGS TO DISCUSS WITH YOUR FAMILY

1. What groups of people planned the death of the Lord Jesus?
2. For whom did Christ die?
3. Why was it necessary to involve Pilate in Christ's death?

Meditation

Meditate upon Psalm 2:11: 'Serve the LORD with fear, and rejoice with trembling.'

Wise Words

It does not follow that because the death of Christ has a special application to the elect that it has no reference to the whole world. It is the ground on which salvation is offered to all who hear. The merit of Christ's death is immeasurable. *E. F. Kevan*

'And at the ninth hour Jesus cried out with a loud voice, saying, "Eloi, Eloi, lama sabachthani?" which is translated, "My God, my God, why have you forsaken me?"' (Mark 15:34).

Read: Psalm 22

I sometimes think about a day which will come upon me soon — the day of my death. The only event that will prevent me from dying is the return of the Lord Jesus. Only two humans escaped dying — Elijah and Enoch. God has made no such promise to me and I have no idea of the circumstances that will surround my death, but I have his promise that he will never leave me (Hebrews 13:5). I also know that when I face death God will give me the grace I need at that time.

God planned the life, death and resurrection of the Lord Jesus to the smallest detail and Psalm 22 gives us some glimpses of the events surrounding his death.

The author of the psalm, David, Israel's second king, knew what it was like to be persecuted and humiliated by his enemies, some being members of his family. This psalm shows David's dependence upon God in those difficult times and concludes with thanksgiving and praise for God's comfort and care. Yet there are portions of the psalm that can only refer to Christ Jesus, our Saviour.

Peter wrote of the prophets of old who 'prophesied of the grace that would come … searching what, or what manner of time, the Spirit of Christ who was in them was indicating when he testified beforehand the sufferings of Christ and the glories that would follow' (1 Peter 1:10,11). Our psalm attests to our Saviour's suffering.

Portions of Psalm 22 are quoted thirteen times in the New Testament and nine portions apply to Christ's suffering and atoning death. The opening words of the psalm, which are in today's text were spoken by Christ when he hung upon the cross. Darkness was falling and he was feeling the weight of the sins of his people on his sinless body, and suffering the wrath of God in their place. For a time the fellowship with his Father appeared to be broken and as he hung alone on the cross he cried out, not to his Father, but to God — 'My God, my God, why have you forsaken me?' (Mark 15:34).

Guided by the Holy Spirit David recorded material that must have appeared strange to him. Because of insufficient space I will mention just a couple — 'They pierced my hands and my feet.' This happened when Jesus had nails driven through his hands and feet, securing him to the accursed cross. In verse 18 we read of his clothing being divided among men by the casting of lots. The Apostle John records the soldiers dividing the Lord's clothing between them, but when it came to his tunic we read, 'They said therefore among themselves, "Let us not tear it, but cast lots for it, whose it shall be," that the Scripture might be fulfilled which says: "They divided my garments among them, and for my clothing they cast lots"' (John 19:24). All of Christ's humiliation, suffering and death were in the place of the elect. Did Jesus suffer for you?

THINGS TO DISCUSS WITH YOUR FAMILY

1. Make a list of David's worst enemies.
2. In what way did David's life symbolize that of the Lord Jesus?
3. Why did Jesus cry out, 'My God, my God, why have you forsaken me?' (Mark 15:34).

Meditation

Meditate upon Psalm 22:28 — 'For the kingdom is the LORD's, and he rules over the nations.'

Wise Words

The dying of the Lord Jesus rescues us from eternal death, whilst the doing of the Lord Jesus obtains for us eternal life.   *J. M. Killen*

'And I will make your descendants multiply as the stars of heaven; I will give to your descendants all these lands; and in your seed all the nations of the earth shall be blessed...' (Genesis 26:4).

Read: Galatians 3:5-18

Abraham is not a name frequently given to boys in the western world, but a great political leader was Abraham — 'Honest Abe'. Do you know who he was?

However, Abraham is mentioned in many places in the Bible; in fact in my Bible Abraham's name appears 253 times. He was called by God to leave his homeland — Ur of the Chaldeans — and with Sarah his wife and all of his possessions departed for the land of Canaan. He had never been to that country before, but when God spoke, he obeyed. This must have been a hard move for him as he, and those with him, had not worshipped Jehovah, but were idol worshippers. But when God sets his love upon a person amazing changes take place.

In fact God made a great covenant with Abraham, a promise that means something to me and all of God's people. Abraham and Sarah his wife were unable to have children. God appeared to him and promised him that the day would come when his descendants would be as numerous as the stars in the heavens (Genesis 15:5). He was also promised the land of Canaan as an everlasting possession (Genesis 17:8).

I wonder if Satan was listening to all that was said, especially when God later revealed to Abraham words concerning a special seed (descendant) who would be born? We read: 'In your seed all the nations of the earth shall be blessed...' (Genesis 22:18). In your reading from Paul's letter to the Galatians, you discover who would bring worldwide blessing: 'Now to Abraham and his Seed were the promises made. He does not say, "And to Seeds," as of many, but as of one, "And to your Seed," who is Christ.'

The Lord Jesus has saved people from all parts of the earth and from all ages. He has proved to be a great blessing to sinners who could not save themselves. In the book of Revelation (Revelation

7:9-10) we read about the great number of people who are re-deemed: 'After these things I looked, and behold, a great multitude which no one could number, of all nations, tribes, peoples, and tongues, standing before the throne and before the Lamb, clothed with white robes, with palm branches in their hands, and crying out with a loud voice, saying, "Salvation belongs to our God who sits on the throne, and to the Lamb!"'

Can you imagine Satan thinking, 'The Person I need to find and destroy will be a descendant of Abraham. By killing him he will be a blessing to no one!'?

Every person who has a saving faith in the Lord Jesus is part of Abraham's family. We read (Romans 4:11-12) that both the circum-cised (Jews) and the uncircumcised (Gentiles) have as their father, Abraham, who is 'the father of all those who believe...' Is Abraham your spiritual father?

THINGS TO DISCUSS
WITH YOUR FAMILY

1. List three promises God made to Abraham which are recorded in Genesis 17.
2. Who was Hagar?
3. Who was the special child promised to Abraham and Sarah?

Meditation

Meditate upon Genesis 17:7 — 'And I will establish my covenant between me and you and your descendants af-ter you in their generations, for an everlasting covenant, to be God to you and your descendants after you.'

Wise Words

The devil is a better theologian than any of us and is a devil still.   *A. W. Tozer*

37

'Abraham said, "My son, God will provide for himself the lamb for a burnt offering"' (Genesis 22:8).

Read: Genesis 22:1-19

It is a wonderful experience to be looking forward to the birth of a child, but a great sorrow when that child dies. Try and imagine how Abraham must have felt when God told him to sacrifice his son.

Abraham and Sarah now had a baby son, just as God had promised, and he was given the name Isaac which means 'laughter'. This name would be a continual reminder that the aged Sarah had laughed when she heard the angel say that she would give birth to a baby. She laughed because she was ninety years old — well past the age of having a child, and did not believe what she heard the angel say to her husband, Abraham.

When Isaac was born Satan knew that it would be one of his descendants who would be his mortal enemy. Nevertheless God was to test Abraham's faith and told him to take Isaac to Mount Moriah and there offer him as a sacrifice to God. Abraham did everything as God had commanded. The writer to the Hebrews wrote: 'By faith Abraham, when he was tested, offered up Isaac, and he who had received the promises offered up his only begotten son, of whom it was said, "In Isaac your seed shall be called," concluding that God was able to raise him up, even from the dead...' (Hebrews 11:17-19).

On the way to Mount Moriah when Isaac asked his father about the lamb that would be needed for the sacrifice Abraham replied: 'My son, God will provide for himself the lamb for a burnt offering.' Arriving at Mount Moriah, Isaac allowed his father to bind him and place him on the altar, ready to be sacrificed. Abraham raised the knife to kill his son, but heard the voice of God calling, 'Do not lay a hand on the boy.' God now knew that Abraham would obey him even in the most difficult times.

I wonder what Satan thought of the events that day. He probably did not know what we know — that God's one and only Son, the Lord Jesus Christ would be offered as an atoning sacrifice for sinners. God so greatly loved the world that he gave his Son, the Lord Jesus, to die on a cross to pay the penalty for sin. What a sacrifice this was! God did provide the 'Lamb' for the sacrifice. When John the Baptist saw Jesus approaching him on the day of his baptism he called out: 'Behold! The Lamb of God who takes away the sin of the world!' (John 1:29). At that moment Satan knew who was his enemy and began planning his death. The sacrificial death of Christ proved to be Satan's downfall, as in his sacrifice, he was the Saviour of sinners throughout the world.

Again we find in the Old Testament another clue to the One who would save the elect of all ages and places.

THINGS TO DISCUSS WITH YOUR FAMILY

1. What city was built in the region of Mount Moriah?
2. Why was Abraham known as 'the friend of God'? (James 2:23).
3. How can sinners become 'friends' of the Lord Jesus? Read John 15:14.

Meditation

Read and think about the gift of God to sinful people as we are taught in John 3:16 — 'For God so loved the world that he gave his only begotten Son, that whoever believes in him should not perish but have everlasting life.'

Wise Words

The only life that counts is the life that costs.   *F. Wood*

'The LORD is a man of war; the LORD is his name' (Exodus 15:3).

Read: Joshua 5:13 - 6:5

When we make a study of the history of our world we find it is continual war. While some nations may be experiencing a peaceful time there are wars raging in other parts of the world. We like to think that we were the victors against the might of Hitler and the Japanese in World War II, but really there are no true victors in war as both sides suffer great losses of people and property.

The history of Israel recorded in the Old Testament does not speak of any lengthy periods of peace. Again and again God's people were forced to take up arms to defend themselves against violent enemies. Israel was Satan's enemy as he knew that one day Messiah would be born to a Jewish virgin and he was determined to do all he could to prevent this from happening.

Moses had successfully overthrown the power of Pharaoh and after forty years of wandering in the desert Joshua was given the privilege of leading the nation into Palestine. The first city to be attacked was the walled army post of Jericho. Israel's spies had secretly been in the city where they met and were helped by Rahab who became an ancestor of the Lord Jesus. God had promised to fight with his people and the time had come for the battle to commence.

However, as Joshua was looking towards the city he saw a 'Man' standing before him with a sword in his hand. When he asked if he was an enemy or friend, Joshua was told, 'No, but as Commander of the army of the LORD I have now come.' Joshua immediately bowed down to the ground and worshipped the warrior who stood before him.

This almighty warrior had come with God's plans which if carried out would result in the destruction of Jericho and the defeat of the occupying soldiers. In Joshua 6:2 we read that this 'Man' spoke to Joshua and his name was 'LORD' — Jehovah. The One speaking to him was the second Person of the Godhead, Christ, the Mediator between God and man. He was there to ensure Israel's victory! Had he not overthrown Pharaoh's armies in the Red Sea?

Our text tells us that 'the LORD is a man of war' — he fights for his people. The spiritual war that started with Lucifer's heavenly rebellion continued on earth and with the advent of the Lord Jesus, Satan did all he could to destroy the Son of God. The battle that took place was a battle to death. When Satan saw Jesus die, he and his demon army must have rejoiced, but all too soon they were to learn that Christ was victorious. He rose from the tomb having defeated the power of death and having saved his people by paying their penalty for sin.

Jesus is Jehovah — a man of war. Today he is destroying the kingdom of Satan and bringing citizens into the kingdom of God, again showing that he has all power in heaven and on earth. When he returns in majestic glory, warfare will be ended and his people will enjoy his presence for ever, and praise Jehovah — Father, Son and Holy Spirit.

THINGS TO DISCUSS WITH YOUR FAMILY

1. Why was Jesus able to defeat Satan and save his people?
2. Make a list of five victories Jesus had over Satan.
3. Discuss the scene of Christ's victory over Satan as described in Revelation 20:10.

Meditation

Meditate upon the all powerful Saviour who is 'a man of war'.

Wise Words

The death of Jesus was the decisive defeat of 'the ruler of this world' — the devil. And as Satan goes, so go all his fallen angels. All of them were dealt a decisive blow of defeat when Christ died. *John Piper*

 'The angel of the LORD encamps all around those who fear him, and delivers them' (Psalm 34:7).

Read: Judges 6:11-24

One night the missionary John Paton and some friends were surrounded by cannibals who had decided to kill and eat God's servants. Suddenly, amid all the shouting, quietness descended and the natives melted away into the surrounding bush. Years later when John questioned the chief why they had departed he was asked, 'Who were all those men surrounding the mission house — they were armed and we had no hope of getting to you?' All John could assume was that the Lord had sent his mighty angels to protect them from their murderous foe.

In the Old Testament we frequently read of an angel called 'the Angel of the LORD'. Who was this special, great angel? It was the pre-incarnate Jesus Christ, the Lord of glory in his role as Mediator between God and man. In your reading, the Angel of the LORD appeared to Gideon and in the conversation that followed the One who spoke to him was 'the LORD'. The Angel of the LORD is God — Jehovah. It was Christ, the second Person of the Godhead, who spoke to Gideon.

When Hagar took Ishmael and ran away from Sarah, she was met by the Angel of the Lord (Genesis 16:7) who told her to return to her mistress. We read: 'Then she called the name of the LORD who spoke to her, YOU-ARE-THE-GOD-WHO-SEES; for she said, "Have I also here seen him who sees me?"' (Genesis 16:13). Hagar knew she had been spoken to by Jehovah.

In 1 Chronicles 21:16 David faced the Angel of Jehovah and with the elders fell face downwards on the ground. It is then re-corded that David spoke to 'God' (1 Chronicles 21:17) — 'Let your hand, I pray, O LORD my God...' Here as elsewhere the Angel of the Lord is called by God's holy name — Jehovah.

When Moses approached the burning bush we are told that 'the Angel of the LORD appeared to him in a flame of fire from the midst of the bush' (Exodus 3:2). Then we read that the Angel of the LORD bore the name 'LORD' (Exodus 3:4) and spoke to Moses saying, "'I am the God of your father — the God of Abraham..." And Moses hid his face, for he was afraid to look upon God' (Exodus 3:6).

We could turn to many places in the Old Testament where the Angel of the LORD took an active part in the affairs of this world. The LORD walked with Adam in the Garden of Eden (Genesis 3:8). The Angel of the LORD defeated the Assyrian army in one night by killing one hundred and eighty-five thousand soldiers (2 Kings 19:35).

Our Saviour is almighty, because he is Jehovah God, and he will ensure the eternal security of his people. He is the only 'Mediator between God and men' (1 Timothy 2:5).

THINGS TO DISCUSS WITH YOUR FAMILY

1. Who is the one and only Mediator between God and man?
2. Who was 'the Angel of the LORD'?
3. Try and prove that the Angel of the LORD is God.

Meditation

Meditate upon the words of Isaiah 44:6 — 'Thus says the LORD the King of Israel, and his Redeemer, the LORD of hosts: "I am the First and I am the Last; besides me there is no God."'

Wise Words

Our narrow thoughts can no more comprehend the Trinity in Unity than a nutshell will hold all the water in the sea. *Thomas Watson*

'The LORD your God will raise up for you a Prophet like me from your midst, from your brethren. Him you shall hear...' (Deuteronomy 18:15).

Read: Deuteronomy 18:15-22 and John 1:19-21

Just as we often look back in history, the Jews looked back to the time of Moses as being one of the most glorious times in their history. Moses was considered the greatest of the prophets, as the law had been revealed to them through him. Moses had seen God's glory and when he came down from Mount Sinai his face glowed so much that the people could not bear looking at him. At first Moses didn't understand why the people were so fearful, but all was well when he covered his face with a veil (Exodus 34:35).

Many times God revealed more of his law to Moses, who on one occasion gave the prophecy that is our text. The Israelites longed for the fulfilment of this prophecy because they knew it spoke of Messiah who would come to his people as their eternal king and Saviour. God's prophecy through Moses concerning the new Prophet was completely fulfilled in the Lord Jesus. He revealed God his Father to his disciples and the people of Israel. The gospel was spread throughout the world and Gentiles were added to the church in big numbers.

It was Jesus, the Messiah, who was the final Prophet. The author of Hebrews wrote: 'God, who at various times and in various ways spoke in time past to the fathers by the prophets, has in these last days spoken to us by his Son, whom he has appointed heir of all things, through whom also he made the worlds; who being the brightness of his glory and the express image of his person, and upholding all things by the word of his power, when he had by himself purged our sins, sat down at the right hand of the Majesty on high' (Hebrews 1:1-3). His teaching, recorded by the authors of the New Testament should be prayerfully read again and again.

The demons, who all hate God, now had another clue concerning the One who would trample their leader's head into the dust.

Satan was gradually putting together a picture of his enemy, whom he hoped one day to destroy.

When John the Baptist began to prepare the way for Jesus, many Jews thought that he was the Messiah. That was why the church leaders from Jerusalem asked him the question: 'Are you the Prophet?' (John 1:21). John denied this. He knew that his cousin, Jesus, was 'the Prophet' foretold by Moses.

As you read the Bible always remember that you are reading God's message to you concerning his Son, the Lord Jesus. Don't ever allow your Bible to sit on a shelf gathering dust. It should be the most read book that you own. At least once a day read your Bible, and don't be just a New Testament Christian, but read the whole Bible! If you don't own a copy of the Scriptures and your mum and dad can't afford to purchase one, ask your pastor and I'm sure he will get one for you.

THINGS TO DISCUSS WITH YOUR FAMILY

1. Why was Moses so greatly respected by the Jews?
2. Where was Moses buried and who buried him? Read Deuteronomy 34:4-8.
3. In what ways was Jesus Christ like the great Moses?

Meditation

For a time think about the majesty and glory of the Saviour.

Wise Words

The words of Moses about Jesus the Prophet give us three major truths to consider ... He was sent by God ... He was like Moses ... He was from the people.

Roger Ellsworth

'For indeed Christ, our Passover, was sacrificed for us' (1 Corinthians 5:7b).

Read: Exodus 12:21-30

The story of the Passover night is always exciting to read as it reminds us that God can and does save his people. Satan didn't understand that the events of the Passover night pointed to the saving work of Jesus. He didn't understand that Christ would die a cruel death on a cross, in the place of sinners. He didn't understand that the use of the blood of the lamb on the Passover night pointed to the shed blood of Christ. Had he understood God's plan of salvation he would have attempted to prevent Christ being crucified. Satan as a detective made a great blunder concerning the sacrificial death of Jesus, having failed to comprehend what we read in the New Testament: '…without [the] shedding of blood there is no remission' (Hebrews 9:22).

The Old Testament temple worship required the continual sacrifice of animals for sin. Blood had to be shed as that was God's only way of salvation. This indicated that the Saviour's death would be violent.

On the night of the Passover the lamb was killed and its blood collected by the head of the house who painted the outside section of the door posts and the wooden beam above the door so that the blood could be clearly seen by those outside. That night the Angel of the LORD killed the eldest child in every family living in Egypt — except in those houses where the lamb's blood had been placed on the door frame. What the people inside the house couldn't see was visible to the Angel who passed over those homes marked with blood.

In the New Testament we are told that just as the blood of the lamb, seen by the Angel, resulted in the saving of the eldest child in each family, so also God's only Son, Jesus Christ our Saviour, shed his blood in order to save his people. Christ was both the sacrifice for sins and the Priest to carry out the sacrifice. Because he died in the place of the elect, on the Day of Judgement the anger of God towards sinners will pass over those for whom Christ died.

Each year at the time of the Passover each Jewish family killed a lamb and ate the Passover meal. This was one wonderful opportunity for the parents to teach their children what the Passover meant. In the Christian church we don't celebrate the Jewish Passover in order to remember our Saviour's death for his people. His death is remembered in the Lord's Supper.

Jesus Christ is truly our Passover, sacrificed for us. Can you say and mean the same?

THINGS TO DISCUSS WITH YOUR FAMILY

1. Describe the lamb that was killed on that first Passover. (Read Exodus 12:1-6.)
2. In what way is the Lord Jesus our Passover?
3. On what day do the Jews celebrate the Passover? See Leviticus 23:5-6. What name do Gentiles give to the time of the Passover?

Meditation

Think for a while how you would have felt if you were in a house on the Passover night, knowing what was to take place and having seen your father paint the lamb's blood on the door frame. Remember that the lamb died in the place of the eldest child in the family.

Wise Words

In forty years I have not spent fifteen waking minutes without thinking of Jesus.   *C. H. Spurgeon*

'All we like sheep have gone astray; we
have turned, every one, to his own way;
and the LORD has laid on him the iniquity of us all' (Isaiah 53:6).

Read: Leviticus 16:15-28; 23:26-32

When we pray we ask that our sins be forgiven. We know we
will be forgiven because of Christ's atoning death. We know
that 'without shedding of blood there is no remission' (Hebrews
9:22). In the days before the Lord's sacrifice on Calvary the priests
of Israel were obliged to carry out daily, weekly and annual sacrifices
for sin. Animals were killed and blood was shed. Yet the writer to
the Hebrews said, 'it is not possible that the blood of bulls and goats
could take away sins' (Hebrews 10:4).

While the animal sacrifices didn't gain forgiveness, they pointed
to the atoning sacrifice of the Lord Jesus when he died on the cross
at Calvary carrying his people's sins.

The Day of Atonement was Israel's greatest time of sacrifice,
for it was on the tenth day of the seventh month, Tishri, that the
high priest made a sacrifice for his own sins and then went into the
holy place where he alone was allowed to go. Inside that holy place
he sprinkled blood on the mercy seat on the top of the Ark of the
Covenant, for the sins of the people. This was Israel's annual sacrifice
for sins.

Many sacrifices required the priest to place his hands on the
sacrificial animal, signifying the transfer of his sins to the sacrificial
animal who would then die in his place. On the Day of Atonement
the High Priest took two goats. One was sacrificed for the sins of
the people; the second however was treated differently. The priest
placed his hands upon the animal's head signifying the transferring
of the nation's sins to the beast, which was then taken out into the
wilderness and sent away.

When Jesus died upon the cross the Apostle Peter wrote that he
'bore our sins in his own body' (1 Peter 2:24). The Apostle Paul said
that God 'made him who knew no sin to be sin for us' (2 Corinthians 5:21). Christ's sacrifice does not have to be repeated annually

because of the value of the One who was sacrificed. The Person who died on that Roman cross was Jesus Christ, the Son of God, and his atoning sacrifice marked the sins of all his people, 'Paid in full!'

The writer to the Hebrews said, 'But this Man, after he had offered one sacrifice for sins for ever, sat down at the right hand of God' (Hebrews 10:12). Never again is a sacrifice for sins needed. When Jesus died, the curtain in the temple was torn, exposing the Holy of Holies for all to see. The penalty for sin was paid and never again was it necessary to sacrifice animals. Jesus, the Lamb of God and our High Priest, saved his people, passed into the true 'Holy of Holies' and 'is seated at the right hand of the throne of the Majesty in the heavens' (Hebrews 8:1).

The Day of Atonement was finished and would never again play a part in the worship of God.

THINGS TO DISCUSS WITH YOUR FAMILY

1. What was the Day of Atonement?
2. What was the duty of the High Priest on that day?
3. In what way is Jesus Christ our High Priest?

Meditation

Meditate upon the words of Hebrews 7:25 — 'Therefore he is also able to save to the uttermost those who come to God through him, since he always lives to make intercession for them.'

Wise Words

A religion that costs nothing is worth nothing.

J. C. Ryle

 'The Son of Man must suffer many things, and be rejected by the elders and chief priests and scribes, and be killed, and be raised the third day' (Luke 9:22).

Read: Daniel 7:9-14

One of the best known stories in the Bible is that of Daniel in the lions' den. I loved hearing that story when I was young and I still do. It is a story of faith in the face of death and also of the almighty power of God who turned some ferocious lions into lovely pussy cats. Daniel was given many prophecies concerning the Lord Jesus and we should know them all.

In today's reading we have both the judgement scene, and the Lord Jesus receiving his kingdom. Satan and his demons knew that they would one day face the judgement of God. They would suffer eternal punishment because of their sinfulness. They hated God's Judge, the Lord Jesus. Those of the human race who died without a saving faith in the Saviour faced the same judgement — they also would hate Christ.

Daniel prophesied that the One who approached God to receive his eternal kingdom was known as 'the Son of Man'. This name was claimed by the Lord Jesus. In fact the name 'Son of man' is found more times than the 'Son of God' in the New Testament. In my New Testament the term 'son of man' is found eighty-eight times and 'son of God' just forty-six times.

The Pharisees and other students of the Old Testament knew Daniel's prophesies and understood that their Messiah would use the title 'Son of Man', but when Jesus did so they wanted him killed.

They didn't want him as their Messiah as they expected a warrior king to arrive, who would overthrow their Roman rulers and take his seat upon the throne of David. No doubt Satan and his demons understood what Daniel had written and looked for the person to claim that name for himself. Jesus used the title of himself when speaking of his saving work: 'For the Son of Man has come to save that which was lost' (Matthew 18:11).

Daniel's prophecy was fulfilled in Christ who was both God and man in one Person. Jesus Christ being perfect man was able to pay the penalty for sins. To satisfy God's justice a sacrifice of supreme value had to be made. Only Christ could make such a perfect offering.

The Lord Jesus, 'the Son of God' and 'the son of man', was the perfect sacrifice for sin and the perfect Mediator. He is able to represent his people before his Heavenly Father, because he is God. We must always give thanks to God if we are citizens of that eternal kingdom. We shall enjoy the presence of God and all the saints in the new heavens and new earth for ever.

Truly all believers can say: 'The best is yet to be!'

THINGS TO DISCUSS WITH YOUR FAMILY

1. In your reading, who is described as 'The Ancient of Days'? See Daniel 7:13.
2. What punishment did God inflict upon the Jews because they crucified his Son?
3. In Daniel 7:28 we read that Daniel's 'thoughts greatly troubled [him]'. Why?

Meditation

Think about this question: What will Christ's kingdom be like? Whom do you look forward to seeing? Why?

Wise Words

The old book always proves true. It truly portrays Christ, and we can rest on what it says — not only with regard to time, but also with regard to eternity. *Stuart Olyott*

'Therefore the Lord himself will give you a sign: Behold, the virgin shall conceive and bear a Son, and shall call his name Immanuel' (Isaiah 7:14).

Read: Matthew 1:18-25

A couple of years after Val and I were married the doctor announced that a baby was on the way. It was an exciting time, but as with many other babies there was nothing unusual and we just waited for the infant's arrival. Everything about Mary's conception of the baby Jesus was miraculous.

Isaiah was writing about a very unhappy time for the people of Judah. They were ruled by wicked king Ahaz, who had turned them away from the worship of Jehovah. His father Jotham was a godly ruler as was his son, Hezekiah. Of his ways we read: 'Ahaz was twenty years old when he became king, and he reigned sixteen years in Jerusalem; and he did not do what was right in the sight of the LORD his God, as his father David had done. But he walked in the way of the kings of Israel; indeed he made his son pass through the fire … And he sacrificed and burned incense on the high places, on the hills, and under every green tree' (2 Kings 16:2-4).

He ruled at the time when Assyria was the emerging world power. Israel and Syria wanted Judah to join them in an effort to overthrow their Assyrian overlords, but Ahaz refused and soon faced the armies of Israel and Syria. A call for Assyrian help was refused.

The outcome was total defeat for Judah. One hundred and twenty thousand brave soldiers were killed and two hundred thousand men, women and children were taken captive with a large amount of treasures. Judah was being punished because they had turned away from the worship of Jehovah. Ahaz then commenced to worship the gods of Damascus, believing they were more powerful than the true God, having given the victory to Israel and Syria.

He 'gathered the articles of the house of God, cut in pieces the articles of the house of God, shut up the doors of the house of the LORD, and made for himself altars in every corner of Jerusalem' (2 Chronicles 28:24).

The LORD spoke to Isaiah: "'Go out now to meet Ahaz, you and Shear-Jashub your son" ... Moreover the LORD spoke again to Ahaz, saying, "Ask a sign for yourself from the LORD your God; ask it either in the depth or in the height above."

'But Ahaz said, "I will not ask, nor will I test the LORD!"'

Then came God's wonderful prophecy: 'Hear now, O house of David! Is it a small thing for you to weary men, but will you weary my God also? Therefore the Lord Himself will give you a sign: Behold, the virgin shall conceive and bear a Son, and shall call his name Immanuel' (Isaiah 7:3,10-14).

The ungodly Ahaz refused to obey God and ask for a 'sign'. Despite his refusal to obey, God gave him a 'sign' which was so very special. A virgin would give birth to a very special 'Son'.

Here we have another prophecy concerning the coming Christ. I wonder if Satan understood what God meant?

THINGS TO DISCUSS WITH YOUR FAMILY

1. Who was the virgin who gave birth to Christ?
2. What is the meaning of 'Immanuel'? Check the Bible footnote for Isaiah 7:14.
3. What was the meaning of Isaiah's first son's name? See Isaiah 7:3.

Meditation

Think of the incomprehensible miracle of a virgin giving birth to Christ.

Wise Words

The God who took a motherless woman out of the side of a man took a fatherless man out of the body of a woman. *Matthew Henry*

'But you, Bethlehem Ephrathah, though you are little among the thousands of Judah, yet out of you shall come forth to me the One to be the ruler in Israel, whose goings forth have been from old, from everlasting' (Micah 5:2).

Read: Luke 2:1-7

Many cities and most towns scattered throughout the world are unknown unless there is something special about them. I live in Wingham. It is a small country village having a population of just over five thousand citizens. We have a small hospital, primary and secondary schools, a swimming pool and a small shopping centre. However the many visitors to the town come to see a colony of fruit bats that live all summer in a small area of rain forest.

If you ever visit Australia be sure to drive to a very small coastal village called Pebbly Beach, south of Sydney. Why should you visit this place? Because at Pebbly Beach the local kangaroos enjoy the ocean. They are known to hop into the water and then surf to the shore on the incoming waves. This is most unusual as kangaroos are land animals and not fond of water!

I'm sure very few people would have known that there was a place named Bethlehem, except for the fact that it was Christ's place of birth. Through the prophet Micah the people of Israel were clearly told that their Messiah would make the town very well-known throughout the world.

King David, the second king of Israel, was born in Bethlehem, but a greater King would come from that town. The Jews eagerly awaited the coming of Messiah, and yet when he was born in Bethlehem he was despised by his people and finally put to death on a Roman cross.

How often it is that God chooses the smallest and weakest places and people for himself. Bethlehem was a small village yet it would become famous because his Son would be born there of a virgin. The name 'Bethlehem' means 'House of Bread' and 'Ephrathah' means 'Fruitful'. From here would come 'the Bread of Life' (John 6:48), who would be very fruitful, gathering many sons and daughters of God into his kingdom.

We have a great, almighty and wise God who not only planned where his Son would be born, but also had the power and wisdom to bring his plan to fruition. Now Satan had another clue concerning the One who would save God's people. I imagine Satan and his evil angels — demons — looked at every clue God revealed concerning his Son as he wanted to prevent God's saving plan from coming to fruition. Satan was like a private detective using every revealed clue, but we know that he failed to disrupt God's plan to redeem his people.

The One spoken of in our text is 'eternal'. He had no beginning or end because he is God. Isn't it wonderful that the eternal Son of God, born at Bethlehem calls his people 'brethren' (Hebrews 2:11)?

Are you numbered among those Christ calls 'brethren'?

THINGS TO DISCUSS WITH YOUR FAMILY

1. Find out all you can about Bethlehem, including its place on a map of Israel.
2. What were the circumstances that ensured Christ's birth in Bethlehem?
3. Why do you think Bethlehem was chosen by God to be the birthplace of his Son?

Meditation

Think about Christ coming into this sinful world as a perfect man in order to save sinners from God's anger. If you are a Christian, why did he come to save you?

Wise Words

What an honour to be acknowledged as a brother by him who is the Everlasting! *Dr Theo Laetsch*

'But when the fulness of the time had come, God sent forth his Son, born of a woman, born under the law' (Galatians 4:4).

Read: Daniel 9:24-27[2]

Daniel is one of the best known characters of the Old Testament. We have already read of him being protected by God when he was placed in a den of lions. He was one of God's faithful servants who foretold the time of Christ's birth and death.

The passage of the Scriptures that you have read has presented difficulties to all who study the chapter, but one thing is clear — the Israelites living at the time of Christ's birth lived in an age of great expectation. In verse 24 there is mention made of 'seventy weeks' (really seventy sevens). This has been understood to mean weeks of years, the seventy weeks meaning four hundred and ninety years.

This period of time has been divided into sections. It commences with the commandment to 'restore and build Jerusalem'. The decree of Artaxerxes I in the seventh year of his reign (457 BC) which is found in Ezra 7:12-26, relates to the rebuilding of Jerusalem and the temple, which was to take forty-nine years (seven sevens). This was certainly a troublesome time for those involved in the reconstruction work.

There follows a period of sixty-two sevens (434 years) during which Daniel records nothing of great importance happening. It is during the seventieth week that Christ would be 'cut off'. Christ preached the good news for just over three years at which time the Jews — God's covenant people — had him put to death on a cross. Daniel explained the purpose of that cruel death when he wrote: 'And after the sixty-two weeks [sixty-nine in all] Messiah will be cut off, but not for himself.' Christ's crucifixion certainly brought to an end the sacrificial system of the Old Testament and achieved salvation for his people.

As the time prophesied by Daniel grew nearer many Israelites were filled with great anticipation that the coming of Messiah would soon take place. Four hundred and eighty-three years (sixty-nine sevens) had passed and there was the hope that the coming King would re-establish the kingdom of Israel. Messiah, the descendant of David, would take his promised seat upon David's throne and drive out Israel's enemies. While the time of Messiah's coming was correct, the activity expected of Messiah was incorrect. Yes, Jesus would establish his kingdom of citizens from all ages and all places throughout the world, but it would be a spiritual kingdom made up of all who looked to him for salvation.

Satan, God's great enemy, was determined to prevent Christ from establishing the kingdom of God and was devising his strategies to ruin God's plans in every way he could, including the death of the Lord Jesus.

THINGS TO DISCUSS WITH YOUR FAMILY

1. What are we taught in Daniel 9:25?
2. Describe the Kingdom that was established by Christ.
3. For whom was Messiah 'cut off'?

Meditation

Consider the courage shown by Daniel during the time of the Babylonian and Persian Empires. How could he remain so faithful to God?

Wise Words

God has a timetable in world history, and he is working carefully according to that plan. *James Montgomery Boice*

2. For a better understanding of Daniel's prophecy, read Boice, J., *Daniel. An Expositional Commentary,* Ministry Resources Library, USA, 1989; Young, E. J., *The prophecy of Daniel,* W. B. Eerdmans Publishing Co., USA, 1975; and Olyott, S., *Dare to stand alone,* Evangelical Press (Welwyn Commentary Series), England, 1995.

 'When Israel was a child, I loved him, and out of Egypt I called my son' (Hosea 11:1).

Read: Matthew 2:7-23

It is usually pleasant to reminisce about the time when we were young. My children remember moving home several times because as a schoolteacher I was transferred to other schools. Such moves involved a lot of packing, but for the girls it was always an adventure.

Matthew records a big move in the life of Jesus and his family. Jesus was only a baby when he was taken to Egypt to escape the clutches of King Herod who had decreed the death of all babies, two years old and under, who were living in the region of Bethlehem. You have read the events that caused Herod to make such a shocking decree and the way in which God ensured that Jesus was not killed by that wicked King's soldiers.

Behind Herod's terrible action was God's great enemy, Satan, who wanted Jesus killed. The whole history of mankind is a battle between God and Satan, but despite Satan's apparent victory when Christ was crucified, it was God who was victorious. It is Satan and his followers, both demons and sinful men and women who will be punished eternally in the raging fires of hell.

The unusual part of the events that took place was that prophecy was being fulfilled. Herod's actions didn't catch God unawares, but were part of God's eternal plan concerning his beloved Son. God instructed Joseph to take Mary and the baby Jesus and escape to Egypt where they would find safety. We should remember that Joseph had made Egypt a safe haven for his father and family when the seven years of drought destroyed the crops. While there, the children of Israel grew into a nation, but Pharaoh refused to allow them to leave for the Promised Land of Canaan, which God had given them as a homeland.

God instructed Moses to say to Pharaoh, 'Israel is my son, my firstborn. So I say to you, let my son go that he may serve me' (Exodus

4:22-23). In our text Hosea uses the same expression concerning Israel, but Matthew declares that prophecy was being fulfilled when an angel of God appeared to Joseph in a dream instructing him to return to Israel — 'Out of Egypt I called my Son.' Herod had died and it was safe for Jesus to be brought back to the land of his birth.

The nation of Israel was a 'type' of God's only begotten Son, Jesus Christ.

Today the true Israel of God is the church of the redeemed. There are not two churches — one of Old Testament saints and another of New Testament saints. The division between Jew and Gentile has been broken down and the church is one united body of believers (read Ephesians 2:11-22).

When you read the Old Testament look out for those parts that speak of our Saviour.

THINGS TO DISCUSS WITH YOUR FAMILY

1. Why did Herod want Jesus killed?
2. In what way could Israel be called God's son?
3. How do people become citizens of today's Israel of God?

Meditation

Jesus, Mary and Joseph were immigrants in Egypt. Meditate upon the way Christians should treat needy immigrants — Zechariah 7:10: 'Do not oppress the widow or the fatherless, the alien or the poor.'

Wise Words

It was Israel out of which Christ, according to his human nature, would come forth. Had Israel been destroyed in Egypt, the Messianic prophecies would not have been fulfilled. It is therefore very true, indeed, that when Israel was effectually called out of Egypt, Christ, too, was called out. *William Hendriksen*

'Behold, I will send you Elijah the prophet before the coming of the great and dreadful day of the LORD' (Malachi 4:5).

Read: Isaiah 40:1-8

When victorious generals leading their forces returned to Rome it was the practice of the government to prepare the way. This meant that workmen repaired the roadway upon which the soldiers would march. Holes and gullies had to be filled in with stones and soil and ridges were cut away in an effort to make the road level. The land on each side of the roadway was cleared so that citizens could stand, watch and cheer the brave men who had won the victory. At one stage, in the early days of Rome, generals were obliged to disband their army before entering the city. To do otherwise was considered an act of war, but times changed and the returning victorious generals with their men were permitted to enter Rome to the cheers and praise of the people.

In like manner, God had determined to prepare the way for the coming of the Lord Jesus. The prophet Isaiah drew a verbal picture that the people could easily understand: 'The voice of one crying in the wilderness: Prepare the way of the LORD; make straight in the desert a highway for our God. Every valley shall be exalted, and every mountain and hill shall be made low; the crooked places shall be made straight, and the rough places smooth.'

Some people believe that this prophecy is about a resurrected Elijah who will return to the world to announce the second coming of the Lord Jesus. This is not so, as Matthew very clearly points out that the one spoken of is none other than John the Baptist. Matthew quoted the words we have read in Isaiah 40:3 and applied them to John who went about preaching: 'Repent, for the kingdom of heaven is at hand!' (Matthew 3:2).

Elijah of the Old Testament was a great prophet who courageously faced the wicked King Ahab to tell him: 'As the LORD God of Israel lives, before whom I stand, there shall not be dew nor rain these years, except at my word' (1 Kings 17:1). The prophet immediately departed. It was through him that God broke the power of Ahab and his disgraceful wife, Jezebel, who had turned her husband and the people away from serving and worshipping Jehovah, the living God. John the Baptist lived in the wilderness regions as did the 'Elijah' of the Old Testament.

Satan would have known this prophecy and must have commenced looking for the person who would prepare the way for Christ, God's only Son.

All Christians are to be like Elijah and stand firm for their faith in the Saviour. We are to call upon people to repent of their sins and live a life of faith in Jesus Christ.

Do you?

THINGS TO DISCUSS WITH YOUR FAMILY

1. Discuss Elijah's first recorded words to King Ahab — 1 Kings 17:1 — 'As the LORD God of Israel lives, before whom I stand, there shall not be dew nor rain these years, except at my word.'
2. Where did Elijah overthrow the prophets of Baal?
3. What do you think Ahab and Jezebel thought of Elijah?

Meditation

Think for a time about Elijah's faithfulness to God, despite the threat to his life.

Wise Words

Sin and hell are married unless repentance proclaims the divorce. *C. H. Spurgeon*

'For as Jonah was three days and three nights in the belly of the great fish, so will the Son of Man be three days and three nights in the heart of the earth' (Matthew 12:40).

Read: Jonah 1:14 – 2:10

When I was young we used to have secret signs that we used with our friends. I can't see the purpose in those signs, but they were good fun. Today there are some adult groups that have signs that are used to let others know they are comrades.

When Jesus made his public appearance he performed many miracles, but they were of no use to hardened unbelievers who attributed his power to Satan. He was not the Messiah they expected. The Jews were expecting a warrior Christ who would gather an army and drive out the occupying Roman forces.

Jesus showed compassion to those who sought him out, believing that he was a great prophet sent by God. John the Baptist had spoken out, bearing witness to God's word to him concerning Jesus who was 'the Lamb of God who takes away the sin of the world!' (John 1:29).

Jesus had preached the way of salvation which was so different to that taught by the church leaders. He preached salvation by faith in himself, not by works of obedience to the law of God and the multitude of rules and regulations enacted by the scribes and Pharisees.

In the Old Testament we find the historical story of Jonah, and I can well imagine that no one believed that God's discipline of the disobedient prophet symbolized a major event in the life of the Lord Jesus.

The Jews demanded that Christ give them a 'sign' to prove that he was Messiah. Already they had seen and heard so much and didn't believe. Another 'sign' would make no difference, but Jesus obliged them by saying that he would give them the sign of Jonah the rebellious prophet of old. That sign we find in today's text, and it was fulfilled when Jesus rose from the tomb after being dead for three days and nights (according to the Jewish method of time). It is worth noting that Jesus believed the story of Jonah to be a historical fact and not a story told to teach some spiritual truth.

The Pharisees and scribes who 'politely' spoke to him were great hypocrites and Jesus rebuked them saying they were part of that 'adulterous generation'. They had turned away from the living God to serve gods of their own making, thus breaking the sacred bond that had existed between God and themselves. The people of Nineveh had repented and believed Jonah's message from God, but the Jews were too hard hearted to believe what Jesus had to say.

The leaders of the church organized the death of their Messiah, and when he rose from the dead, fulfilling the 'sign of the prophet Jonah' they still didn't believe. Christ's body didn't see corruption and death could not hold him.

This is our Saviour. He today holds all power in heaven and on earth — praise the Lord!

THINGS TO DISCUSS WITH YOUR FAMILY

1. Why did Jonah run away from the land of Israel?
2. How did God discipline Jonah for his rebellion?
3. Was Jesus' death on the cross the punishment of God? How could this be?

Meditation

Meditate upon the words of Romans 14:9 — 'For to this end Christ died and rose and lived again, that he might be Lord of both the dead and the living.'

Wise Words

The resurrection of Christ and the fact of the empty tomb are not part of the world's complex and continuing mythologies. This is not a Santa Claus tale — it is history and it is reality. *A. W. Tozer*

'But I have a greater witness than John's;
for the works which the Father has
given me to finish — the very works
that I do — bear witness of me, that the
Father has sent me' (John 5:36).

Read: Luke 7:11-23

There are people today who claim to be able to perform miracles
and this has been the situation down through the ages. Yet none
of these 'miracle workers' are able to produce one marvel every time
they want. Some of those performing 'miracles' make no claim to be
Christians. What then is there about Christ's actions that give proof
that he is the Messiah?

The people expected a warrior Messiah who would sit on the
throne of David, but when the compassionate Jesus arrived he was
rejected. The prophet Isaiah foretold that among other characteristics Christ would perform great miracles that would bear witness to
his claim to be the Son of God. In Isaiah 35:5-6 we read, 'Then the
eyes of the blind shall be opened, and the ears of the deaf shall be
unstopped. Then the lame shall leap like a deer, and the tongue of
the dumb sing.'

Every time Jesus said he would perform a miracle it came to
pass. The Old Testament prophets who performed miracles didn't do
so on their own initiative, but were either directed by God to do so
or prayed for the gift to perform it. Not so with Jesus. On his own
authority he spoke and the miracle occurred.

Your reading today included the Lord raising a widow's son
simply by touching the coffin and saying, 'Young man, I say to you,
arise.' Now the man was dead and couldn't hear Christ's command,
but life flowed back into his body and he sat up. Jesus healed the
blind, the deaf, the sick and cast out demons all by the power of
God, for he was God and man in one Person and was filled with the
Holy Spirit.

When John the Baptist was locked away in prison facing death
he began to doubt if Jesus was the Messiah and sent two disciples to
question the Lord. Jesus said to them, 'Go and tell John the things
which you hear and see: the blind see and the lame walk; the lepers

are cleansed and the deaf hear; the dead are raised up and the poor have the gospel preached to them' (Matthew 11:4-5). Other believers asked, 'When the Christ comes, will he do more signs than these which this Man has done?' (John 7:31).

Christ's power over physical and mental illness and Satan and his demons symbolized his victory over Lucifer which culminated in his atoning death upon the cross.

THINGS TO DISCUSS WITH YOUR FAMILY

1. In what way did Christ's miraculous healings fulfil the prophecy of Isaiah recorded in Matthew 8:17 — 'He himself took our infirmities and bore our sicknesses'?
2. How did Jesus' miracles help prove he was the Messiah?
3. Why didn't the Lord's miracles convince the people of Israel to follow him?

Meditation

Meditate upon Christ's words when he raised Lazarus — 'Now when he had said these things, he cried with a loud voice, "Lazarus, come forth!" And he who had died came out bound hand and foot with graveclothes, and his face was wrapped with a cloth. Jesus said to them, "Loose him, and let him go"' (John 11:43,44).

Wise Words

The miracles were to the gospel as seals are to a writing.
William Gurnall

'I am the good shepherd. The good shepherd gives his life for the sheep' (John 10:11).

Read: Isaiah 40:1-17

When our children were growing up it was a pleasant time for all of us. We all had our difficulties at times, but when we get together each year it is great to sit and talk about those good days. We laugh about many activities — some of which Val and I had no idea had happened. Several times we were unable to discover the culprit to some mischief — but now the guilty one owns up and there is usually a lot of laughter. One of my daughters tells me she was never smacked and the girls often talk about their mother being a 'lovely, gentle and kind person'. I guess many children think particularly of their mother in these terms.

We have looked at the Lord Jesus and the almighty power he had for he is God — the mighty God. We have looked at Isaiah's vision of Christ seated upon the heavenly throne of his glory surrounded by the mighty seraphim who called to one another, 'Holy, holy, holy is the LORD of hosts; The whole earth is full of his glory!' (Isaiah 6:3). Today's reading speaks of Christ, the second Person of the Godhead and is a display of his almighty power. He 'has measured the waters in the hollow of his hand'. Then we read, 'Behold the nations are as a drop in a bucket … all nations before him are as nothing.'

In the midst of the description of Messiah's infinite power and majesty we find a most wonderful passage — 'He will feed his flock like a shepherd; he will gather the lambs with his arm, and carry them in his bosom, and gently lead those who are with young.' This is Jesus, our Saviour who humbled himself to come into this world to save his 'flock'.

In Psalm 23:1 David wrote, 'The LORD is my shepherd' and Jesus said, 'I am the good shepherd. The good shepherd gives his life for the sheep' (John 10:11). Jesus compared himself to Israel's 'shepherds' who were miserable failures. They were 'blind leaders of the blind' (Matthew 15:14). Instead of showing the people the way of salvation they proudly taught that obedience to the law of God and their own laws would result in salvation. The distressed people knew they couldn't keep God's laws perfectly and the burden placed upon them by the Pharisees was an impossible one.

Jesus called sinners to himself and said that simple faith was the way of salvation. As the 'good shepherd' the Lord gently led his flock and gave them rest, just as David wrote, 'He makes me to lie down in green pastures; he leads me beside the still waters' (Psalm 23:2). As a 'good shepherd' he took special care of those who were weak in faith and those young ones who loved him. Paul saw the power of God displayed in his own weakness for Jesus said to him, 'My grace is sufficient for you, for my strength is made perfect in weakness' (2 Corinthians 12:9).

So often Jesus showed his compassion in his miracles. This is our almighty Saviour God and we can rejoice because of his infinite power, seen in his 'arms' of compassion that save and protect his 'flock'.

THINGS TO DISCUSS WITH YOUR FAMILY

1. What did Jesus mean when he said, 'My sheep hear my voice, and I know them, and they follow me' (John 10:27)?
2. Make a list of Christ's acts of compassion to you.
3. What was Christ's greatest act of mercy?

Meditation

Meditate upon John 10:28 — 'And I give them eternal life, and they shall never perish; neither shall anyone snatch them out of my hand!'

Wise Words

Our total welfare is the constant concern of God's loving heart. *W. J. White*

'And when he heard that it was Jesus
of Nazareth, he began to cry out and
say, "Jesus, Son of David, have mercy on
me!"' (Mark 10:47).

Read: 2 Samuel 7:4-17

Blindness is a terrible affliction. What a tragedy it is not to be able
to see the glorious creation in which we live. Our text includes
words spoken by blind Bartimaeus who knew that Jesus was passing by. He realized that this was his opportunity to be healed as he
no doubt had heard of the many miracles the Lord had performed.
Despite the crowds telling him to be quiet he called out louder than
ever, hoping to attract the Lord's attention. You should notice the
title that Bartimaeus gave Jesus — 'Son of David'.

Saul, Israel's first king was dead and now God's man sat upon
the throne of the nation. He was visited by the prophet Nathan who
delivered a promise made by God to David. He had wanted to construct a permanent building in Jerusalem that would be the LORD's
dwelling place, but Nathan told him that this was not to be. David's
kingship was marked by warfare and when peace was established his
son Solomon would construct a temple to be the permanent place
where the LORD would meet with his people.

David accepted God's decree that he would not build the Lord's
house, but was given a wonderful promise. Nathan said, 'Also the
LORD tells you that he will make you a house … And your house and
your kingdom shall be established for ever before you. Your throne
shall be established for ever.' God would build a 'house' for him —
his kingdom would be for ever and his throne would be eternal.
This raised the question — Who would be the eternal King to sit
on David's throne?

In Isaiah 9:7 we are given a description of the Messiah: 'Of the
increase of his government and peace there will be no end, upon
the throne of David and over his kingdom, to order it and establish
it with judgement and justice from that time forward, even for ever.
The zeal of the LORD of hosts will perform this.'

When Gabriel appeared to Mary with the news that she would bear the Messiah, he said, 'And behold, you will conceive in your womb and bring forth a Son, and shall call his name JESUS. He will be great, and will be called the Son of the Highest; and the Lord God will give him the throne of his father David ... [and] will be called the Son of God' (Luke 1:31-32,35). Mary's son, Jesus, would sit on David's throne.

For a long time the Jews expected the Messiah to be king, reigning on the throne of David. Jesus acknowledged that the scribes said that the Christ was 'the Son of David' (Mark 12:35). Jesus accepted the name 'Son of David' as correctly applying to himself and didn't silence those who used it of him. The Apostle Paul preached that Jesus was a descendant of David (Acts 13:22-23).

God decreed that Jesus Christ, a descendant of David, was the eternal King.

THINGS TO DISCUSS WITH YOUR FAMILY

1. In what way did God make an eternal 'house' for David?
2. Who built the great temple?
3. Why was Jesus called 'Son of David'?

Meditation

Meditate upon the words of Ezekiel 34:23 — 'I will establish one shepherd over them, and he shall feed them — my servant David. He shall feed them and be their shepherd.'

Wise Words

The degree to which our King's shout is known in our churches and congregations is vitally related to our personal relationship and obedience to him.   *Derek Prime.*

A king riding a donkey?

'Rejoice greatly, O daughter of Zion! Shout, O daughter of Jerusalem! Behold, your King is coming to you; he is just and having salvation, lowly and riding on a donkey, a colt, the foal of a donkey' (Zechariah 9:9).

Read: Matthew 21:1-11

When we read of the military victories of Alexander the Great we picture him riding a great horse, because he was one of the first military leaders to make use of horses in battle. They were swift and strong and soldiers could quickly move from place to place causing great confusion among the enemy. On the other hand the greatest King of all ages, the Lord Jesus, entered his capital city in the most humble manner — he rode upon a donkey — a beast of burden.

In the midst of outlining God's judgement on some nations Zechariah devoted a short passage to the first coming of Jesus. It must have seemed unusual to those who studied the Scriptures. Sure, they expected a King to come from God, but a warrior King — riding a horse ready for battle!

After David's rule, the kings of Israel rode horses as a mark of their kingship and power, but Jesus was the 'Prince of Peace' (Isaiah 9:6). Our Messiah rode into Jerusalem on a young, unbroken donkey. His humble entrance into the city a few days before his crucifixion gave further proof to the purpose of his life — 'For even the Son of Man did not come to be served, but to serve, and to give his life a ransom for many' (Mark 10:45).

Jesus knew the prophecy of Zechariah and as part of his obedience to his Father had to ensure it was fulfilled. Had this event not taken place it would have shown that Jesus was not the Messiah.

It was what many call 'Palm Sunday' and Christ was about to enter Jerusalem. He sent two disciples to Bethphage where they, in a miraculous way, found a donkey for him to ride. In recording the event Matthew quoted the words found in our text as being fulfilled. The disciples sat their Lord on the donkey, and as he rode towards the city the crowds who knew who he was, and were also on their way to Jerusalem for the Passover spread their clothing and palm branches on the roadway before him.

Then they cried out, 'Hosanna to the Son of David! Blessed is he who comes in the name of the LORD! Hosanna in the highest.' Portion of their cry came from Psalm 118:26. The words shouted out were a clear recognition that Jesus was the Messiah; yet a few days later the same crowd was calling out, 'Crucify! Crucify!' I trust that you are not fickle like the members of that great crowd, but rather are faithful followers of Christ the Saviour of sinners.

THINGS TO DISCUSS WITH YOUR FAMILY

1. What is the meaning of 'Hosanna'?
2. How did Zechariah know what to write concerning this event?
3. What did the chief priests and scribes think of the people saying, 'Hosanna to the Son of David!' (Matthew 21:15)?

Meditation

Meditate upon Paul's words concerning Christ: 'And being found in appearance as a man, he humbled himself and became obedient to the point of death, even the death of the cross' (Philippians 2:8).

Wise Words

He [Jesus] is gentle and merciful, bringing salvation, and demanding both faith and then obedience from his potential subjects. Sadly, they do not know the time of their visitation (Luke 19:41-44). *John Legg*

71

'Even my own familiar friend in whom I
trusted, who ate my bread, has lifted up
his heel against me' (Psalm 41:9).

Read: Matthew 26:14-16; 27:3-10

Earlier in my life I had a friend who at a crucial time turned
against me. What went wrong I was never able to discover, but
eventually we went our own ways. Jesus suffered the tragedy of a
disciple betraying him for thirty pieces of silver — the value of a
slave that was gored by an ox (Exodus 21:32).

In Zechariah 11:12-13 we read of the value placed upon the
prophet as a 'shepherd' of Israel —'Then I said to them, "If it is
agreeable to you, give me my wages; and if not, refrain." So they
weighed out for my wages thirty pieces of silver. And the LORD said
to me, "Throw it to the potter" — that princely price they set on
me. So I took the thirty pieces of silver and threw them into the
house of the LORD for the potter.' This, Matthew tells us, was the
money Judas received for betraying Christ.

Matthew then quoted a portion of Jeremiah 19:1-11 where we
are told that land was purchased as a burial plot. It is unusual that
only the name of Jeremiah is mentioned but this was not an uncommon practice when two quotes were linked together; the more
senior prophet was often alone recorded.

Despite this issue that theologians have written much about,
we have prophecies concerning Christ's betrayal by one who was a
trusted friend. Yet Jesus knew from the start that Judas would betray
him. Judas was a thief and pilfered the money bag which he looked
after — he was the treasurer for the Lord and his disciples. He loved
money and while we never find any hatred shown by Judas to the
Lord, he took the opportunity to get thirty pieces of silver for pointing out Jesus in the darkness of night.

When Jesus was taken captive Judas was sorry for what he had
done and when he wanted to return the money to the priests they
refused to accept it — they saw it as blood money. Throwing it on
the floor of the temple Judas went out and committed suicide.

The money was used to purchase land to be used for the burial of foreigners visiting Jerusalem. In Jeremiah's day this piece of land was called 'Valley of Slaughter' (Jeremiah 19:6). It became known as the 'Field of Blood' as recorded by Matthew.

Again we find a prophecy concerning the Lord Jesus being fulfilled. This shows us that it is God who rules this world and brings to pass all that he has ordained. The whole of Scripture revolves on the saving work of the Son of God, Christ our Redeemer. May none of you ever betray our compassionate Redeemer.

THINGS TO DISCUSS WITH YOUR FAMILY

1. Why did Judas betray Jesus?
2. How did Judas betray Jesus?
3. What use was made of the betrayal money?

Meditation

Meditate upon Christ's words concerning Judas: 'Woe to that man by whom the Son of Man is betrayed! It would have been good for that man if he had never been born' (Mark 14:21).

Wise Words

We cannot read hearts and, while deeply saddened, we should never be utterly surprised when people give up their profession of faith and even turn into opponents of Christ. *John Legg*

'Indeed the hour is coming, yes, has now come, that you will be scattered, each to his own, and will leave me alone' (John 16:32).

Read: Matthew 26:30-35; 47-56

There are many times in our life when we need the company of friends. When facing a hospital stay involving surgery, it is comforting to have a close friend holding our hand and helping to calm us. The best comfort of all is that which comes from the presence of our Saviour, the Lord Jesus Christ. Recently at our Bible study we looked at the words of Psalm 4:8 and all agreed they would be comforting words when we were about to die — 'I will both lie down in peace, and sleep; for you alone, O LORD, make me dwell in safety.'

Jesus had been betrayed by Judas Iscariot. After the Passover meal the Lord left for the Garden of Gethsemane, on the Mount of Olives, to spend some time in prayer, preparing for the terrible ordeal that was to envelop him. This was a time when the comforting presence of the disciples who loved him could have provided some support, but he said to them, 'All of you will be made to stumble because of me this night, for it is written: "I will strike the Shepherd, and the sheep of the flock will be scattered."'

Again we have a prophecy from the Old Testament which foretold an event that must have been impossible for Zechariah to fully understand. His full statement was, '"Awake, O sword, against my Shepherd, against the Man who is my Companion," says the LORD of hosts. "Strike the Shepherd, and the sheep will be scattered"' (Zechariah 13:7).

The swords signified that what was to take place was a judicial act, for the sword spoke of a judge exercising the death penalty, causing the shedding of blood. Christ's death was the judicial act of God upon the sin-bearer, who suffered death in the place of his people.

The sword was to be used by Jehovah (Isaiah 53:4,6) on 'the Man who is [my] Companion' (Zechariah 13:7). The one to be punished was Jesus Christ who is God and man in one Person. He is God in flesh and blood. John writing of Christ using the name 'the

Word' says, 'And the Word became flesh and dwelt among us' (John 1:14).

When the soldiers, led by Judas, arrived under cover of darkness to arrest Jesus, the disciples were filled with fear. Despite Peter's initial reaction of drawing his sword and cutting off one person's ear, the disciples turned and ran to save their lives. Our text describes this happening. They didn't want to end up on a cross beside Jesus and showed that at that time they were cowards. The prophecy of Zechariah was fulfilled to the letter.

Again this shows us that God is in control of this world's affairs for he brings to pass everything he had foretold. Jesus would be without the comforting presence of those who should have been faithful 'sheep'. May we be courageous servants of the Lord Jesus.

THINGS TO DISCUSS WITH YOUR FAMILY

1. From Scripture prove that Jesus Christ is God and man in one Person.
2. What is meant by Christ's death being a judicial act by God?
3. Why did the disciples desert Jesus in his hour of great need?

Meditation

Meditate upon Daniel 9:26 concerning Christ: 'Messiah shall be cut off, but not for himself.'

Wise Words

Faithfulness to God is our first obligation in all that we are called to do in the service of the gospel.

Iain H. Murray

February

 'Then they spat in his face and beat him; and others struck him with the palms of their hands, saying, "Prophesy to us, Christ! Who is the one who struck you?"' (Matthew 26:67-68).

Read: Isaiah 50:1-9

Our newspapers and TV report many criminal cases that have been heard by a judge and jury. If a person is convicted of a crime we expect that they will receive punishment, but frequently the cry goes up, 'The punishment didn't suit the crime! The criminal only received a slap on the wrist when he should have been sentenced to a term in jail.'

God's law insisted that sentences for crimes be just and fair. We read, 'life shall be for life, eye for eye, tooth for tooth, hand for hand, foot for foot' (Deuteronomy 19:21). In some parts of the world a thief is punished by the cutting off of his hand. That is not a just or biblical punishment.

As we read through the Old Testament we find a large number of prophecies concerning the Lord Jesus Christ, many dealing with his trial and subsequent death. Isaiah 50 deals with our Saviour's obedience to God, which was perfect in every respect. We also read words concerning his trial and illegal punishment, 'I gave my back to those who struck me, and my cheeks to those who plucked out the beard; I did not hide my face from shame and spitting.'

The members of the Sanhedrin were unable to produce witnesses to the Lord having committed any crime. He had never broken God's law, as this was part of his saving work — the elect need the righteousness of God to enter heaven. The writer to the Hebrews said, 'Pursue peace with all people, and holiness, without which no one will see the Lord' (Hebrews 12:14). When Jesus was dragged before Pilate and the Roman governor the crowds demanded that he be put to death by crucifixion. Pilate investigated the claims of the members of the Jewish Council and concluded, 'You take him and crucify him, for I find no fault in him' (John 19:6). Pilate even 'took water and washed his hands before the multitude, saying, "I am innocent of the blood of this just Person"' (Matthew 27:24).

Jesus was handed over to the soldiers who very cruelly abused him, fulfilling the prophecy in Isaiah 50:6. Every time another prophecy is fulfilled it adds proof that Christ was the Messiah, sent by God, to his covenant people. Fulfilled prophecy also gives proof that the Scriptures are the inspired words of the living God, who has the almighty power to bring to pass everything he has ordained.

Jesus was whipped until the blood flowed from the wounds, he was spat upon, his face was slapped and some cruel men plucked handfuls of hair from his beard. This is a most unjust treatment of a man who was perfectly innocent of any crime. Always remember that all Jesus suffered was for his sinful people, so that they all might take their place in the kingdom of God and there glorify and enjoy him for ever. Will you be there?

THINGS TO DISCUSS WITH YOUR FAMILY

1. Why was Jesus so cruelly treated by those wicked men?
2. How is it possible for prophecy to be fulfilled?
3. What was the significance of Pilate washing his hands before he handed Jesus over to the Jews to be crucified?

Meditation

Meditate upon the sufferings of Jesus in order to sincerely repent of your sins and serve him more faithfully.

Wise Words

We cannot wash our hands of our responsibility for the death of Christ, for he died because of us.   *John Legg*

'And as Moses lifted up the serpent in the wilderness, even so must the Son of Man be lifted up, that whoever believes in him should not perish but have eternal life' (John 3:14-15).

Read: Numbers 21:4-9

I don't like snakes! Many years ago while I was in the hospital a snake bite victim was placed in the bed beside me. He was a farmer who had stood on a 'red-belly black snake' while rounding up the cows for milking. He had been given anti-venom but was violently ill. About three o'clock in the morning he hopped out of bed and said, 'I'm OK now. I'm going home to milk the cows.' Suddenly the matron appeared and very soon the farmer was back in bed, complaining bitterly that he should be at home helping his wife in the dairy.

In today's reading, the children of Israel were on their way to the Promised Land after more than four-hundred years of slavery in Egypt. Sadly, they soon became discouraged and started complaining to Moses about what they believed was God's lack of care for them. They were rebels at heart — sinners who had no thankfulness for the LORD who had brought them out of Egypt.

God was determined to punish the sin that was in the camp and sent a plague of 'fiery serpents' that bit many of the people causing widespread death. When the people repented, Moses pleaded with God to take away the snakes. God told Moses to mould a brass serpent and place it on a pole where everyone could see it. The people were told that if they were bitten they were to look to the serpent and immediate healing would follow.

This historical incident pointed to the saving work of the Lord Jesus Christ. When talking to Nicodemus, Jesus made reference to the serpents and spoke the words that are in our text. This would have reminded Nicodemus that God punished sin but also provided a way of salvation. Just a look at the brass serpent was the anti-venom to save life.

We are all sinners because of Adam's sin in the Garden of Eden, when Adam listened to Satan talking to him through the serpent.

We know the terrible distress that sin has caused, and without a Saviour we face a Christless eternity. God provided the answer to sin by having his beloved Son die a sacrificial death, bearing the sins of his people. Moses' brass serpent provided physical healing, but Christ provides spiritual healing and eternal life to all who believe in him.

Isaiah quoted God's words which we must obey, 'And there is no other God besides me, a just God and a Saviour; there is none besides me. Look to me, and be saved, all you ends of the earth! For I am God, and there is no other' (Isaiah 45:21-22).

As we trace the life of Christ, remember that if you look to the Saviour, with a repentant heart, eternal life will be yours.

THINGS TO DISCUSS WITH YOUR FAMILY

1. List some Old Testament historical events that spoke of Christ.
2. Why did God send the serpents among the Israelites when they were in the desert?
3. What did God mean when he said, 'Look to me, and be saved' (Isaiah 45:22)?

Meditation

Meditate upon the Saviour on the cross. Did he bear your sins?

Wise Words

Jesus came not only to teach but to save, not only to reveal God to mankind, but also to redeem mankind for God. *John Stott*

'For you will not leave my soul in Sheol, nor will you allow your Holy One to see corruption' (Psalm 16:10).

Read: Acts 2:22-36

Most people who stand beside a grave and watch the coffin being lowered go away thinking that is the end of the person being buried. They believe he is gone for ever, never to be seen again. And this is what it really looks like. Walk about a cemetery and ask yourself, 'Is it possible that those buried here will ever rise from the dead?'

Our text was written by David almost three-thousand years ago. In the midst of writing about God's care of those who trusted in him, he says something that was not true of himself — 'For you will not leave my soul in Sheol, nor will you allow your Holy One to see corruption' (Psalm 16:10). We know that these words do not apply to any human who has died, for within a few short years of death, the body returns to the earth from which it came. Following his sin the LORD very bluntly said to Adam, 'For dust you are, and to dust you shall return' (Genesis 3:19).

Of whom then was David writing? In his first sermon after the outpouring of the Holy Spirit on the Day of Pentecost, Peter gave the answer to this question — David was speaking of the Messiah, the Lord Jesus Christ, whom Israel and the Romans had crucified. Peter quoted David's words in Psalm 16 and said they could not apply to David as his tomb and remains were still with them. David had not been resurrected, and his body was still in the grave.

Peter quoted David who 'spoke concerning the resurrection of the Christ, that his soul was not left in Hades, nor did his flesh see corruption'. He went on to say, 'This Jesus God has raised up, of which we are all witnesses.' All of the apostles and others, including over five hundred on one occasion saw the risen Christ. Three days after his death he was seen and there was no sign of any corruption. Thus Jesus fulfilled the words of prophecy found in Psalm 16.

In future devotions concerning the death and resurrection of our Redeemer remember Psalm 16, for it is further proof that Jesus was the Messiah, promised by God. And we have the assurance that just as Jesus was raised from the dead so also shall we one day rise again. From our last resting place the Lord will gather together all our elements and give us glorified bodies that are perfect beyond anything we can imagine. Our perfected souls which have been with Christ in heaven will once again be united with our bodies that have been glorified.

The grave and corruption is not the end as far as we are concerned. All mankind will rise again to face the judgement of Christ. Are you ready for that day?

THINGS TO DISCUSS WITH YOUR FAMILY

1. How was it possible that David could write of the resurrection of Christ?
2. What was David writing about when he used the word 'Sheol'?
3. What does the resurrection of Christ mean to you?

Meditation

Mediate upon Paul's words in 1 Corinthians 15:21 — 'For since by man came death, by Man also came the resurrection of the dead.'

Wise Words

The Gospels cannot explain the resurrection; it is the resurrection which alone explains the Gospels.

John S. Whale

'And Jesus came and spoke to them, saying, "All authority has been given to me in heaven and on earth"' (Matthew 28:18).

Read: Isaiah 9:1-7

Something that should be precious to each of us is our character. Solomon wrote, 'A good name is better than precious ointment' (Ecclesiastes 7:1). I agree! What do people say about us when they speak to other people? In the passage of Scripture you have read, Isaiah describes the character of the Messiah. Later in our devotions, you will see these aspects of his divine nature shining brightly.

Isaiah tells us that a 'Child is born,' indicating that the One spoken of is a human baby boy, but he is also a 'Son' who is given to us. We know that this is God's Son, for we read in John 3:16, 'For God so loved the world that he gave his only begotten Son, that whoever believes in him should not perish but have everlasting life.' We are also told that 'God, who at various times and in various ways spoke in time past to the fathers by the prophets, has in these last days spoken to us by his Son' (Hebrews 1:1-2).

This 'Child' was born to be a ruler as he would carry the authority of God's government upon his shoulders. For this reason Christ was, as our text states, given all authority in heaven and on earth. His kingdom is not of this world (John 18:36), but exists in the hearts of his people.

Isaiah gives this ruling 'Son' the title 'Wonderful Counsellor'. Jesus is a statesman of almighty power and majestic wisdom. Of him Isaiah wrote, 'The Spirit of the LORD shall rest upon him, the Spirit of wisdom and understanding, the Spirit of counsel and might, the Spirit of knowledge and of the fear of the LORD.' Through his atoning death and resurrection he established the kingdom of God and today is governing that kingdom with power and wisdom. He doesn't need human advisors, but cares for all citizens of his kingdom with compassion. God's kingdom grows as members bear witness to Christ's saving power and the Holy Spirit renews the hearts of sinners. Jesus is a 'Wonderful Counsellor'.

Isaiah went further and said that he has the character of 'Mighty God'. Literally the words are 'God-hero'. This man-child is not just human, he is also God. Of Jesus Christ, the Apostle John wrote, 'In the beginning was the Word, and the Word was with God, and the Word was God ... And the Word became flesh and dwelt among us, and we beheld his glory, the glory as of the only begotten of the Father, full of grace and truth' (John 1:1,14).

The Messiah is God in flesh and blood and could say, 'I and my Father are one' (John 10:30). As the Mighty God he could say to his disciples, 'I have overcome the world' (John 16:33). The inspired psalmist wrote of the Messiah, 'Your throne, O God, is for ever and ever' (Psalm 45:6). In Hebrews, the writer says, 'But to the Son he [God] says: "Your throne, O God, is for ever and ever..."' (Hebrews 1:8). This is Christ, our Saviour. The Jews refused to acknowledge these characteristics of the humble Jesus who perfectly displayed that he is God in the flesh.

THINGS TO DISCUSS WITH YOUR FAMILY

1. How can it be said that Jesus is called 'Mighty God'?
2. Of what kingdom is Jesus the Ruler?
3. In what way is Jesus a 'Wonderful Counsellor'?

Meditation

Meditate upon Jesus being called 'Mighty God'.

Wise Words

Christ contains in himself the totality of divine powers and excellencies. *George Barlow*

'As a father pities his children, so the LORD pities those who fear him' (Psalm 103:13).

Read: Isaiah 9:1-7

When I was attending Teachers' College, Val and I saw the film, *The Student Prince* many times. We enjoyed the story, but more so the singing of Mario Lanza. There are several books I have read many times. All Christians need to read and reread the Bible. Why? Because God speaks to us through the Scriptures. Today you have again read the passage from Isaiah because it is a glorious prophecy concerning Jesus Christ. We have looked at several aspects of his wonderful character, especially that he is both God and man in one Person.

Next, we read that he is called 'Everlasting Father' which would be better translated as 'Father for ever'. We must not confuse the name 'Father' with that of the Heavenly Father of the Godhead. There we have three Persons, Father, Son and Holy Spirit. The title here given to Christ is that he will act as a Father to the members of his kingdom. This is expressed in our text — God acts as a Father to those who fear him.

Isaiah wrote of God's judgement upon Israel, yet could say, 'You O LORD are our Father; our Redeemer from Everlasting is your name' (Isaiah 63:16). Our Redeemer God is the Good Shepherd who cares for his sheep. In the kingdom that he has established he will act with loving care to all citizens as a loving father cares for his children. In this sense Jesus Christ is 'Father for ever'.

Our Saviour is also called 'Prince of Peace'. When the 'Child' was born, heaven's angels sang to some shepherds 'Glory to God in the highest, and on earth peace, goodwill toward men!' (Luke 2:14). From the very start our Saviour was associated with 'Peace'.

The kingdom of which he is the governor has been established by peaceful means, not with weapons of carnal warfare. The blood that was shed to establish the kingdom was that of Christ who died on the cross, bearing the sins of the elect. In his atoning, sacrificial death he established peace between God and man. The Apostle Paul wrote, 'Therefore, having been justified by faith, we have peace with God through our Lord Jesus Christ' (Romans 5:1).

The Prince of Peace broke down the wall that divided Jews from Gentiles, thus establishing peace in the church. Again Paul wrote, 'For he himself [Jesus] is our peace, who has made both one, and has broken down the middle wall of separation' (Ephesians 2:14). The kingdom of which Christ is the Lord 'is not food and drink, but righteousness and peace and joy in the Holy Spirit' (Romans 14:17).

Christ's kingdom consists of people who should be living at peace with each other and with God. The life of Jesus demonstrates these glorious aspects of his character.

THINGS TO DISCUSS WITH YOUR FAMILY

1. In what way is Jesus Christ the 'Prince of Peace'?
2. In what way is Christ a 'Father' to his people?
3. How can you become a member of the kingdom of God?

Meditation

Meditate upon the words of Isaiah 11:6-9 — 'The wolf also shall dwell with the lamb, the leopard shall lie down with the young goat, the calf and the young lion and the fatling together; and a little child shall lead them. The cow and the bear shall graze; their young ones shall lie down together; and the lion shall eat straw like the ox. The nursing child shall play by the cobra's hole, and the weaned child shall put his hand in the viper's den. They shall not hurt nor destroy in all My holy mountain...'

Wise Words

The kingdom of God is like a grain of mustard seed, not like a can of nitro-glycerine. *J. B. Thomas*

 '...the gospel, which has come to you, as it has also in all the world, and is bringing forth fruit...' (Colossians 1:5-6).

Read: Galatians 3:26 – 4:7

The birth of a baby is always an exciting time for expectant parents — I know because we have four daughters in our family. We prepared for the new arrival with clothes, suitable toys, a bassinet and plenty of nappies.

When the time had come for the Son of God to make his entrance into the world, he came as a baby, not as a mighty warrior. We have looked at some prophecies concerning Christ who would come to save sinners, but the Pharisees and many others had misinterpreted what should have been clear to them. For thousands of years people had longed for the coming of Messiah, and at last the prophecy made to Adam and Eve was about to be fulfilled: 'And I will put enmity between you [Satan] and the woman, and between your seed and her Seed; he shall bruise your head, and you shall bruise his heel' (Genesis 3:15).

God had determined the exact moment for the Lord Jesus to preach the good news concerning salvation through faith in himself. The apostles and others preached the gospel and within a few years the Apostle Paul could write the words of our text: '...the gospel, which has come to you, as it has also in all the world, and is bringing forth fruit...' (Colossians 1:5-6).

This raises the question: 'Why was the time of God's action perfect?' We know that God makes no mistakes in fulfilling his plans.

I believe there are sound reasons that the gospel was preached when it was.

It was during the time of the greatest empire the world had known. Rome ruled the known world, both land and sea. The Romans were road builders and soon highways stretched throughout the Empire, making it possible for merchants and travellers to move about in comfort. The roads were well made, and in parts of Europe men and women still travel on roadways constructed two-thousand years ago.

Not only were the roads well built, but the Roman soldiers also made sure that it was safe to walk along the highways. They stood guard at regular intervals preventing thieves from attacking travellers. It is easy to imagine Paul, Peter and other Christian teachers safely taking the gospel to the outposts of the Roman Empire. Their main danger came from the Jews.

Another reason for the ease of the spread of the gospel was the use of the Greek language. The empire preceding Rome was that of Alexander the Great which was founded by his father, Phillip of Macedon. Under Alexander's rule, Greek became the language of the known world. The Jews translated the Old Testament into Greek (known as the Septuagint) so that the Israelites living away from their homeland could read and study God's Word. The New Testament was written in Greek in order to be read throughout the Roman Empire.

The time was right for the advent of the Messiah and the preaching of the gospel throughout the world. God's plans are always perfect because of his great wisdom and power. We have a majestic God!

THINGS TO DISCUSS
WITH YOUR FAMILY

1. What is the greatest empire the world has ever known?
2. Who is the King of God's kingdom?
3. Who was the Roman emperor at the time of Christ's birth?

Meditation

For a few minutes sit and think about the spread of the gospel. What were the reasons for Christ's entrance into the world at that time?

God has no problems, only plans.   *Corrie ten Boom*

Wise Words

'For indeed he does not give aid to angels, but he does give aid to the seed of Abraham' (Hebrews 2:16).

Read: Hebrews 2:5-18

It is hard to comprehend that in the unseen world about us there is a host of angels, carrying out the commands of God. Many people believe that God has assigned a special angel to watch over them during their life.

The writings of the Old Testament point to the coming of the Lord Jesus and the salvation of men, women, boys and girls, but not the redemption of Satan and the angels who followed him in his deliberate, sinful attempt to dethrone God. We do not know the number of angels who followed Satan, but we are given a clue that one third, puffed up with pride, attempted to throw God off his heavenly throne. In Revelation 12:3-4 we read of Satan, the 'great, fiery red dragon' who 'drew a third of the stars of heaven and threw them to the earth'. Their sin was doomed to failure from the very beginning, and they were overcome with fear when they faced Christ during his time on earth.

Christ was born to a virgin and as the God-man he would be crucified and die, bearing his people's sins, not the sins of fallen angels.

This gives us another reason to thank God and praise his name for our salvation. What a terrible state we would be in if Christ had paid the penalty for the sins of the fallen angels instead of us. We would be eternally lost without any hope of redemption. However, for some reason, known only to God, he planned the salvation of sinful men and women. I often wonder why this was God's plan but I know that the Lord Jesus died to save all believers. I can only thank him for his amazing grace.

Maybe God by-passed the fallen angels because Satan sinned without anyone tempting him. In the Garden of Eden, Adam and Eve did not act alone in their sin, but were enticed by Satan to doubt

God's Word. Whatever the reason for God's decision to save sinful humanity, we should praise and glorify him for what he has done.

What a wonder it is that God has written in the Lamb's book of life the names of his people. Is your name there? If you have truly repented of your sins and are trusting Christ alone for your salvation, be thankful, for your name has been inscribed in God's book.

Jesus did not live and die just to save a few, but a great number of sinners — '…a great multitude which no one could number, of all nations, tribes, peoples, and tongues…' (Revelation 7:9).

Christians are 'of the seed of Abraham', who live by faith in Christ their Redeemer. May we always praise God that his plan of salvation was for repentant men and women. If you are a Christian give thanks for what God — Father, Son and Holy Spirit — has done for you.

THINGS TO DISCUSS WITH YOUR FAMILY

1. Jesus tasted death for everyone (Hebrews 2:9). What does this mean?
2. What is the eternal end for the fallen angels? Read Revelation 20.
3. In Hebrews 2:18 we read that Jesus 'is able to aid those who are tempted'. What does this mean?

Meditation

Think for a time of what our situation would have been had God decided to save the fallen angels and not sinful men, women, boys and girls. Consider the debt of gratitude and love we owe him.

Wise Words

I believe Satan to exist for two reasons: first, the Bible says so; and second, I've done business with him.

D. L. Moody

'And being found in appearance as a man, he humbled himself and became obedient to the point of death, even the death of the cross' (Philippians 2:8).

Read: Philippians 2:5-11

The cross of Christ is central to our salvation. As we meditate upon his sacrificial death we see that this was the lowest point in his humiliation. Do you remember Isaiah 6:1-4, where Isaiah records his vision of Christ seated upon his royal, heavenly throne, surrounded by seraphim who cried out to one another: 'Holy, holy, holy is the LORD of hosts; the whole earth is full of his glory'?

In Revelation 5:12-13, we read of the resurrected Christ in heaven, surrounded by angels and saints who praise him: 'Worthy is the Lamb who was slain to receive power and riches and wisdom, and strength and honour and glory and blessing … Blessing and honour and glory and power be to him who sits on the throne, and to the Lamb, for ever and ever.'

The majestic Son of God humbled himself and entered this sinful world as a baby. He had a human body, yet was without sin. Reading the Gospels we see the way wicked men and women treated him. Some of his family didn't understand him; the Pharisees and other leaders of the church rejected him as their Messiah, and finally the people demanded that Pilate order his crucifixion.

As Christ walked the roads of Israel, with perspiration on his body and covered in dust blown by hot winds, he didn't look like the LORD of Glory. He had nowhere to regularly lie down in comfort; he grew weary and faced cruelty from most of the Jews. He felt sorrow and wept. He had left his royal throne and while on earth he certainly didn't look like the heavenly King. The writer to the Hebrews spoke of Christ's humility (Hebrews 2:7). For a time the angels who glorified him must have been amazed, for we read of Jesus: 'You made him a little lower than the angels.' A footnote gives an alternative rendering: 'You made him *for a little while* lower than the angels.'

Carrying the sins of his people, he was whipped by the Roman soldiers and tormented by the Romans and the Jews. Then he was stripped of his clothes and nailed to that rough, wooden cross where he died. I never cease to be amazed that as he hung there naked, bleeding from the whipping, the crown of thorns upon his head and the nail holes in his hands and feet, a thief who was nailed to a cross beside him said: 'Lord, remember me when you come into your kingdom.' To this Jesus replied, 'Assuredly, I say to you, today you will be with me in Paradise' (Luke 23:42-43). He recognized Jesus as being a King, Immanuel — 'God with us'! So amazing!

What an act of humiliation by our Saviour!

THINGS TO DISCUSS WITH YOUR FAMILY

1. In what ways did Christ humble himself?
2. When did his humiliation come to an end?
3. Jesus died upon the cross. What do you think was the first step in his glorification?
4. When, during his earthly life, did Jesus display his majestic glory? Read Matthew 17:1-13.

Meditation

Think for a moment about the humiliation of Christ. Why was this necessary? Did he suffer for you?

There is a fountain filled with blood
    Drawn from Immanuel's veins;
And sinners, plunged beneath that flood,
    Lose all their guilty stains.

William Cowper

Wise Words

 'But the angel said to him, "Do not be afraid, Zacharias, for your prayer is heard; and your wife Elizabeth will bear you a son, and you shall call his name 'John'"' (Luke 1:13).

Read: Luke 1:5-25

Some time ago we looked at the text: 'Behold, I will send you Elijah the prophet before the coming of the great and dreadful day of the LORD' (Malachi 4:5). You also read a portion of Isaiah 40, which prophesied the coming of one whose work it was to prepare Israel for the advent of the Lord Jesus Christ. We now come to the fulfilment of that prophecy.

It was John the Baptist who fulfilled the words of Isaiah — 'The voice of one crying in the wilderness: "Prepare the way of the LORD, make his paths straight"' (Matthew 3:3).

John's work was to arouse the interest of the people in the coming Messiah and to call them to repent of their sins. As they became aware of their desperate plight before God they would, by God's grace, seek salvation. Many thought that by obedience to God's law they would be rewarded with eternal life. There were others who saw this as hopeless because they knew they could not perfectly keep God's law. They began searching for the promised Messiah through whom they could be saved.

The aged Zacharias and his wife Elizabeth had no children and were past childbearing age. Nevertheless, by God's almighty power, there was to be a miracle in their life — in old age they would have a son who would be named 'John'. An angel brought the good news to disbelieving Zacharias. The angel declared: 'He will also go before him in the spirit and power of Elijah, "to turn the hearts of the fathers to the children," and the disobedient to the wisdom of the just, and to make ready a people prepared for the Lord' (Luke 1:17).

Mary, Christ's mother, and Elizabeth were relatives, and it is likely that Jesus knew John as they grew up. John was to prepare the people to recognize Jesus as the Christ.

We don't read anything about Satan attempting to have John killed, so it is possible that at first he was unaware of John's special task. Later, when John commenced calling the people to repentance and openly recognized Jesus as the Messiah, Satan stirred King Herod's wife to have John beheaded.

Zacharias and Elizabeth were given a wonderful duty — to raise the one who would proclaim Christ to the nation. They were a godly couple. Zacharias was a priest who served in the temple. We can learn one great truth from today's reading, and that is to believe all that God has said to us, all that is recorded in the Bible. Zacharias was disciplined for his disbelief. May this not be said of us.

THINGS TO DISCUSS WITH YOUR FAMILY

1. What special work in the temple was given to Zacharias?
2. In Luke 1:15 we have a description of John. What two things would make him 'great'?
3. In what way was Zacharias punished for disbelieving what the angel said?
4. Name the angel who appeared to Zacharias.

Meditation

For a time think how Zacharias must have felt when the angel appeared to him.

Wise Words

The unbelieving believer robs himself of God's blessings, while the unbeliever robs himself of eternity in heaven with God. *Roger Ellsworth*

95

'Behold a virgin shall be with child, and bear a Son, and they shall call his name "Immanuel," which is translated, "God with us"' (Matthew 1:23).

Read: Luke 1:26-38

I have never knowingly been visited by an angel, but each Lord's Day I imagine God's angels surrounding the congregation during our time of worship. They may be there to keep Satan and his demons out of the way, so we can worship the God we love, in spirit and truth.

In our reading we find the fulfilment of one of the most wonderful prophecies of the Old Testament — the announcement to Mary that she would become the mother of the Messiah. Christ was to be born to a virgin, just as Isaiah had proclaimed (Isaiah 7:14). The promise given to Adam and Eve in the Garden of Eden (Genesis 3:15) was soon to become a reality.

The great angel Gabriel appeared to Mary with God's Word that she would give birth to a Son who was to be the Saviour of sinners. Mary was a descendant of King David as was Joseph, her future husband. This fact was also prophesied, but she lived in Nazareth and Micah had foretold that the Messiah would be born in Bethlehem (Micah 5:2). God would show his almighty power in bringing this prophecy to fulfilment also.

Of all the virgins in Israel, why did God choose Mary to be Jesus' mother? Gabriel's recorded words to Mary give us the clue to the answer: 'Rejoice highly favoured one, the Lord is with you … you have found favour with God' (Luke 1:28,30). Obviously Mary was a young woman who was a true believer, and showed her love of God by obedience to his law. God had planned to place his Son in a family that would teach him about his Heavenly Father, and guide him in living a holy life. What a great privilege it is to be born into such a family. If this has happened to you then thank God for your parents.

Mary was betrothed to a godly man, Joseph, who was a carpenter by trade. The custom in Israel was for a couple to become betrothed (engaged) for about a year, after which they would begin living as a married couple. Mary was to have a baby who didn't have a human father. Her pregnancy would be a miracle of the Holy Spirit, and her infant was to be the 'Son of God' (Luke 1:35). Jesus would be both God and man in one Person and the Saviour of all who believe. In heaven he would stand before his Father as his people's Advocate. As God and perfect man he would be the only possible Mediator between God and sinners.

Mary graciously accepted all that Gabriel revealed to her.

There was one problem — what would people think, including Joseph her intended husband, when it was found out that she was expecting a baby while unmarried?

THINGS TO DISCUSS WITH YOUR FAMILY

1. In Matthew 1:1-16 we are given the ancestry of the Lord Jesus. Find out something about Salmon and Rahab (verse 5).
2. Do you think Satan was aware of Gabriel's words to Mary? Why?
3. Discuss Mary's character. Why did Gabriel say of her: 'Blessed are you among women' (Luke 1:28)?

Meditation

Think about Gabriel's revelation to Mary in Luke 1:31: 'And behold, you will conceive in your womb and bring forth a Son, and shall call his name JESUS.'

Wise Words

When Jesus came to earth he did not cease to be God; when he returned to heaven he did not cease to be man. *Anonymous*

'She shall bring forth a Son, and you shall call his name JESUS, for he will save his people from their sins' (Matthew 1:21).

Read: Matthew 1:18-25

When Joseph found out that Mary was expecting a baby, he must have been very upset. Mary probably told him of Gabriel's visit to her and what he had said. Even then he couldn't believe that any woman who was a virgin could become pregnant by the Holy Spirit. He loved Mary and didn't want her to become the talk of Nazareth, where the people would accuse her of immorality. He believed that she had been unfaithful to him and so could not take her to be his wife. He was thinking of sending her away to have the baby and then divorcing her.

No doubt anxiety filled his mind day and night, but it soon ended when the great angel, Gabriel, was ordered by God to appear to him in a dream and explain the situation. He was told that what had happened to Mary was the fulfilment of Isaiah's prophecy: 'Behold, a virgin shall be with child, and bear a Son, and they shall call his name Immanuel.' Isaiah had prophesied the Messiah's virgin birth and we can only wonder what thoughts must have filled Joseph's mind. His Mary was to give birth to the long awaited Messiah, and they would give him the name 'JESUS' which means 'Saviour'. He was also told that Jesus would save 'his people from their sins'.

Christian readers, think for a moment of the emotions felt by both Joseph and Mary when they realized the part they would play in God's plan of salvation. It was this 'JESUS' who was to be the Saviour of the world. No longer was Joseph thinking about a quiet divorce; he immediately married her. However, they did not live as a married couple until after the birth of our Saviour. Later, they were to have other children who grew up with their half-brother, Jesus.

Part of Gabriel's message to Joseph that often raises questions is that the baby was to be called 'Immanuel'. This word means 'God with us' and describes the divine nature of the Lord Jesus. Mary's Son was God in flesh and blood. Often names were not used in everyday conversation, but were explanations of the person's character. Isaiah later said that the Messiah would be called, 'Wonderful, Counsellor, Mighty God, Everlasting Father, Prince of Peace' (Isaiah 9:6), which are descriptions of Christ's character.

Satan was unaware of Joseph's dream and didn't realize that Mary's baby, of whom Joseph was the 'foster father', was the Messiah. As we progress in our devotions we will come to the place where Satan discovered who the Messiah was and then made every effort to put Jesus to death — again a great blunder!

THINGS TO DISCUSS
WITH YOUR FAMILY

1. In what way was Mary's conception unusual?
2. In Luke 3:23-38 we find the ancestry of Joseph. Was he descended from King David?
3. What was Joseph's occupation?

Meditation

Consider Joseph's thoughts when he realized that he and Mary would be responsible for the care of Christ. Pray for spiritual guidance in caring for your own family.

Wise Words

The virgin birth is the guarantee of salvation for God's people, for, apart from this kind of birth, it is difficult to understand how Christ could be their Saviour.

William Hendriksen

'Then she spoke out with a loud voice and said,"Blessed are you among women, and blessed is the fruit of your womb!"' (Luke 1:42).

Read: Luke 1:39-45

The news of the forthcoming birth of a baby quickly spreads and friends and relatives join in the happiness.

The angel Gabriel had revealed to Mary that her aged relative, Elizabeth, was expecting a very special child. Her pregnancy was miraculous. Mary decided to visit Elizabeth, who, we are told, lived in a city of Judah, possibly in Hebron.

As they were greeting one another, the baby in Elizabeth's womb gave a noticeable movement. It is normal for babies of this age to move about, but there was something very different this time. It was as if her baby recognized the presence of another baby in a nearby womb — that of the Saviour, Jesus Christ. We are also told that the Holy Spirit filled Elizabeth's heart and she spoke wonderful words of praise. The Holy Spirit revealed to her that Mary's baby was 'Lord', but not just 'Lord' but '*my* Lord'. She recognized that Mary's baby was the promised Messiah. He was the One who would 'bruise' Satan's 'head' (Genesis 3:15). At that time Mary and Elizabeth knew something of which Satan was unaware.

In verse 45 of our reading, Elizabeth spoke of Mary's faith in what God had revealed to her. Gabriel's revelation concerning the virgin birth and who it was that she carried in her womb, required great faith in Mary's heart. May you and I have a saving faith in Jesus, the living Saviour. He is the One who carried our sins to the cross and there suffered our hell. Our saving faith is more precious than the most valuable treasures on earth. If you are a Christian, then always thank God for his gift of salvation.

The true value of our faith will be revealed to the world on Judgement Day, when the books are opened and we, individually, stand before Jesus Christ, the Judge. Those who lived, unconcerned about their spiritual welfare, will realize how foolish they have been as they pass into a Christ-less eternity.

From our reading we see the joy when those two saints met. You and I should endeavour to associate with likeminded people — those who put Christ first in their lives. We can be a means of blessing and joy when we visit other Christians, especially those who for one reason or another are unable to attend worship and other Christian gatherings. There are many godly men and women living in homes for the aged, or living alone who would love a visit from other Christians. Make an effort to visit those people; pray and read the Scriptures with them, and you will discover that not only will they be blessed, but you also will be greatly encouraged.

THINGS TO DISCUSS WITH YOUR FAMILY

1. Find Hebron on a map. There should be one in the back of your Bible.
2. Elizabeth's baby was to play a special role in the life of Jesus. What was that role?
3. What are we taught in Galatians 6:10? 'Therefore, as we have opportunity, let us do good to all, especially to those who are of the household of faith.'

Meditation

Try and imagine how Elizabeth felt during Mary's visit. Also meditate upon the family into which God placed his Son.

Wise Words

Men and women will learn on the Day of Judgement, if they have never learned before, how true are the words, 'Blessed are they that believed.' *J. C. Ryle*

'And Mary said: "My soul magnifies the Lord, and my spirit has rejoiced in God my Saviour"' (Luke 1:46-47).

Read: Luke 1:46-56

Mary, having been welcomed to Elizabeth's home with a welcome inspired by the Holy Spirit, responded with words of praise to God, using expressions showing that she knew the words of the Old Testament. We should be students of the Old and New Testaments as they are God's words to us. It is sad that we live in an age where the Bible is readily available but little read. Even many professing Christians have little real understanding of God's Word and have no regular Bible reading. Have you ever read through the Bible? Maybe you just read parts of the New Testament but not in a systematic or regular way. We should not only read the Scriptures but meditate upon what we have read, and pray for a clear understanding.

From Mary's words we also see that she was a humble woman. She could have been proud but she saw her 'lowly state'. We too should be humble people, able to say with the Apostle Paul: 'But by the grace of God I am what I am' (1 Corinthians 15:10). All of our abilities are God's gift to us, and all that we possess is due to his kindness.

Mary acknowledged her need of a Saviour. She spoke of God being her Redeemer and said: '...my spirit has rejoiced in God my Saviour'. Christians should always praise God that he has saved them from eternal punishment. Like Mary, we must thank God for everything — food on the table, a warm bed, a house in which to live, loved ones, and most of all, a Saviour.

What a joy it is to be able to say: 'You will cast all our sins into the depths of the sea' (Micah 7:19). Our Heavenly Father has blotted out our transgressions. We can praise God with the psalmist: 'As far as the east is from the west, so far has he removed our transgressions from us' (Psalm 103:12).

Thanking God should be our daily delight. Not only have Christians been forgiven, but we are clothed in Christ's righteousness, without which we would not be allowed to enter heaven. Mary knew this and blessed God for his goodness. The writers of the New Testament also devoted many words of gratitude to God for his kindness. Have you this reason for thanking God? Mary would have known God's promise to Abraham: 'In your Seed all the nations of the earth shall be blessed' (Genesis 22:18). The promised 'Seed' rested in her womb.

Mary acknowledged that God ruled the affairs of mankind. It is he who 'put down the mighty from their thrones, and exalted the lowly'.

Mary spent what must have been three enjoyable months with Elizabeth! I trust you are also able to spend spiritually rewarding times with Christian friends.

THINGS TO DISCUSS WITH YOUR FAMILY

1. Who are the 'fathers' spoken of in Luke 1:55?
2. What promises did God make to Abraham?
3. Use four words to describe Mary's words of praise.

Meditation

Meditate upon Luke 1:50 — 'And his mercy is on those who fear him from generation to generation.'

Wise Words

Promises are, in fact, the manna that we should daily eat, and the water that we should daily drink as we travel through the wilderness of this world.   *J. C. Ryle*

'When her neighbours and relatives heard how the Lord had shown great mercy to her, they rejoiced with her' (Luke 1:58).

Read: Luke 1:57-66

We must remember that Elizabeth's husband, Zacharias, had been unable to speak since the day Gabriel had revealed to him that he and his wife, both past childbearing years, were about to have a very special child. Life must have been rather difficult for him. There was great rejoicing when Elizabeth held her baby in her arms and no doubt, with Zacharias, glorified God for his wonderful gift. We are told that their relatives and neighbours praised God with them.

The Scriptures teach us plainly that Christians should 'rejoice with those who rejoice, and weep with those who weep' (Romans 12:15). This is a Christian responsibility and privilege.

On the eighth day after their baby's birth, Zacharias and Elizabeth took him to be circumcised, as God required of all male members of the covenant nation. When the parents were asked the name they were to give their child, Elizabeth replied, 'John'. This was unusual as everyone expected him to be named Zacharias, after his father. Zacharias asked for writing material and indicated that he agreed with what his wife had said — 'His name is John.' At that moment the Lord restored Zacharias' speech. Immediately, Zacharias began to glorify God.

You and I should always be ready to thank God for all his marvellous gifts to us. Think about your body and thank God if you can speak, hear, read, write and move about. Bless God for your daily food, a bed upon which to rest and a house in which to live. Thank God for your loved ones and friends, but most of all praise him for the gift of his Son. And when, like Zacharias, you face hard times and temptations, turn to the Lord, for he knows our suffering. The writer to the Hebrews tells us: 'For we do not have a High Priest who cannot sympathize with our weaknesses, but was in all points tempted as we are, yet without sin. Let us therefore come boldly to the throne of grace, that we may obtain mercy and find grace to help in time of need' (Hebrews 4:15-16).

Anxious times are usually times when we grow in the grace and knowledge of God.

People living nearby were aware of God's miracle in giving Zacharias and Elizabeth a baby, and the question must have been asked: 'What kind of child will this be?'

We know that John was to be the one to prepare the way for the coming of the Lord Jesus: 'The voice of one crying in the wilderness: Prepare the way of the LORD; make straight in the desert a highway for our God' (Isaiah 40:3). John was the 'Elijah' prophesied by Malachi (4:5). John was well taught by his parents and as he grew he lived a hard life, which was preparation for the future (Luke 1:80).

THINGS TO DISCUSS WITH YOUR FAMILY

1. Was John to be a priest? Why?
2. We read in Luke 1:66: 'And the hand of the Lord was with him.' What does this mean?
3. What can you learn from God in times of trials and difficulties?

Meditation

Think for a time about Zacharias and Elizabeth's praise and thankfulness to God. For what can you give thanks to God?

Wise Words

What God did for the son of Zacharias, he can do for our boys and girls.   *J. C. Ryle*

'And you, child, will be called the prophet of the Highest; for you will go before
the face of the Lord to prepare his ways'
(Luke 1:76).

Read: Luke 1:67-80

People, especially in the Western world, are greatly privileged because they have access to the Bible, both Old and New Testaments. The Old Testament contains many prophecies concerning the promised Messiah, but I often wonder to what extent the Jews understood those prophecies. As we read the Gospels we discover that the nation had largely misinterpreted the nature and work of the Messenger of the LORD.

In Zacharias' words concerning his son and the Lord Jesus, we see a man worshipping God not only for the promised Messiah, who was soon to appear, but also that his son, John, would prepare the people for his coming. We have read words that came from the heart of a man who was faithful to God.

Zacharias praised God for bringing to pass what he had foretold. In like manner you and I should understand that God will fulfil all that he has declared will take place. The greatest event yet to be realized is the return of Christ to gather his people together. Then will follow the judgement by the Lord Jesus of every person who has ever lived. There is to be a day when the saints will inhabit the new heavens and new earth for ever. There will also be a hell in which everyone who had no saving faith in the Redeemer will be found. Christians can truly praise God as 'the best is yet to be'! The day will come when we will see our Saviour face to face. We should be praying that he will soon come.

Zacharias glorified God for the imminent redemption of God's people by the One descended from King David. He specifically makes mention of Abraham as it was from that patriarch that God would bring forth a 'Seed' who would prove to be a blessing to people worldwide. That 'Seed' is the Lord Jesus whose life and death would bring about the forgiveness of the sins of all true believers.

The final words of Zacharias' praise speak of his son, John, who would announce the advent of Christ. The world lived in spiritual darkness and we read those wonderful words of Christ's saving work: 'To give light to those who sit in darkness and the shadow of death, to guide our feet into the way of peace.'

John the Baptist proved himself to be a faithful servant of God, despite the hatred shown him by Herod and many leaders of the church.

THINGS TO DISCUSS WITH YOUR FAMILY

1. List four promises made to Abraham.
2. What hope for the future was given in Luke 1:78-79?
3. Who is referred to by the word 'Dayspring' ('Rising Sun' in NIV) found in verse 78?

Meditation

Consider the important work of John the Baptist as he prepared the people for the revelation of the Messiah.

Let us never rest till the Spirit witnesses with our spirit that our sins are forgiven us — that we have passed from darkness to light, and that we are actually walking in the narrow way, the way of peace. *J. C. Ryle*

Wise Words

'And she brought forth her firstborn Son, and wrapped him in swaddling cloths, and laid him in a manger, because there was no room for them in the inn' (Luke 2:7).

Read: Luke 2:1-7

In Paul's first letter to Timothy, we read that God appeared in a body (1 Timothy 3:16). The time had come for the Second Person of the Godhead to fulfil all the prophecies found in the Old Testament concerning his saving work. We face the mystery that God, clothed in perfect human flesh and blood, was born of a virgin. Every person who is a Christian must, with true joy, praise and give thanks to God for all that Christ has done for his people.

Micah had prophesied where Christ would be born: 'But you, Bethlehem Ephrathah, though you are little among the thousands of Judah, yet out of you shall come forth to me the One to be ruler in Israel, whose goings forth have been from of old, from everlasting' (Micah 5:2). Satan must not have realized the truth of these words, as he was not waiting to destroy Christ at the moment of his birth.

The problem for this prophecy was that Mary and Joseph lived in Nazareth. Nevertheless, we know that our God is in control of all the affairs of heaven and earth. His plan was fulfilled through the Roman Emperor, Caesar Augustus, who ordered that a census be made throughout his empire, in order that taxes could be more efficiently collected. This meant that Mary and Joseph had to travel to the city of Bethlehem, as they were descendants of King David.

This journey of about ninety miles must have been difficult for Mary, who was due to give birth to her first baby. Despite it being summertime, the journey on donkeys had to be made as ordered by Augustus. Arriving at an overcrowded Bethlehem, they could not find any suitable accommodation. Joseph found a stable where animals were kept, possibly a big cave, and there Mary gave birth to her promised child. There was no palace room, or costly bassinet, or doctor present with all the attire that normally go with the birth of royalty. The One who is called 'the KING OF KINGS AND LORD OF LORDS' (Revelation 19:16) began his humble life in a stable, his bed being a feeding trough. This baby was 'the Son of God' and 'the Son of man' in one Person. Then we read those triumphant words: 'and you shall call his name JESUS, for he will save his people from their sins' (Matthew 1:21).

THINGS TO DISCUSS
WITH YOUR FAMILY

1. What does the name 'Jesus' mean? What is the English equivalent for the name 'Jesus'?
2. Jesus was to 'save his people from their sins'. What does this mean?
3. Discuss the teachings of Micah 5:2 — 'But you, Bethlehem Ephrathah, though you are little among the thousands of Judah, yet out of you shall come forth to me the One to be Ruler in Israel, whose goings forth are from of old, from everlasting.'

Meditation

Consider the kingdom of which Jesus is 'KING OF KINGS AND LORD OF LORDS' (Revelation 19:16). What part do you have in that kingdom? If you are a Christian then thank God for your heavenly citizenship.

Wise Words

O come to my heart, Lord Jesus!
    There is room in my heart for thee.
Emily E. Elliott

'Glory to God in the highest, and on earth peace, good will toward men' (Luke 2:14).

Read: Luke 2:8-20

While most Israelites didn't praise God for the coming of the Messiah, nor was there widespread awareness of the birth of the Redeemer, God sent his angel to some shepherds to tell them the good news. The shepherds were caring for their flocks during the night when, without warning, the announcement was made: 'Do not be afraid, for behold, I bring you good tidings of great joy which will be to all people.' They revealed that Christ the Saviour had been born.

It must have been summer as the shepherds would have had their sheep in the warm fold had it been winter. I can imagine they needed to be told, 'Do not be afraid,' as I know I would have been amazed had I been with those shepherds. What we should notice is that this announcement was made to humble shepherds who were working during the night. There was no public announcement made to the rulers of the land or the church officials; there was no great celebration of the event which would affect people worldwide. The One who would bruise the head of Satan had been born, and of this birth even Satan and his demons appeared unaware.

We should forever thank God as the nobodies of this world become 'somebodies' in Christ's kingdom. We read: 'Listen, my beloved brethren: has God not chosen the poor of this world to be rich in faith and heirs of the kingdom which he promised to those who love him?' (James 2:5). And again we find: 'For you see your calling, brethren, that not many wise according to the flesh, not many mighty, not many noble, are called. But God has chosen the foolish things of the world to put to shame the wise, and God has chosen the weak things of the world to put to shame the things which are mighty; and the base things of the world and the things which are despised God has chosen, and the things which are not, to bring to nothing the things that are, that no flesh should glory in his presence' (1 Corinthians 1:26-29).

The angels who had no need of a Redeemer spoke words of praise to God for what had taken place. They witnessed Christ becoming a true man and commencing his work of salvation. God's prophecies, which had been delivered to the prophets, were being fulfilled before their eyes. The darkness of sin would soon be dispelled and the light of salvation spread worldwide. The wonder of the work of salvation filled the hearts of the angels with praise to God:

> Glory to God in the highest,
> And on earth peace, good will toward men!

At once, the shepherds made their way to Bethlehem to see the baby.

Having seen the child, they told other people in the crowded city; however, the Scriptures do not record that crowds of people visited Mary and her newly born infant. Mary and Joseph listened to all that the shepherds had seen, and heard and meditated upon them.

The shepherds returned to their flocks glorifying God; with hearts filled with joy, they rejoiced at what they had seen and heard. Let our hearts be filled with joy as we learn about the Son of God who came into this world to save sinners.

We have so much for which to magnify our God.

THINGS TO DISCUSS WITH YOUR FAMILY

1. When was Christ's birthday? Give a reason for your answer.
2. Why did Christ enter this world as a baby?
3. Why do you think God uses the 'nobodies' of the world to accomplish his purposes?

Meditation

What thoughts do you think might have gone through the shepherds' minds following the angel's announcement?

Wise Words

Creation glorified God, but not so much as redemption.

J. C. Ryle

'And when eight days were completed for the circumcision of the Child, his name was called Jesus, the name given by the angel before he was conceived in the womb' (Luke 2:21).

Read: Luke 2:22-24 and Leviticus 12:1-8

Circumcision of all the male babies born to Jewish parents was mandatory. It was the covenant sign, cut into the flesh of the baby on the eighth day, to identify God's people. God's great promise to Abraham and his descendants was 'to be God to you and your descendants after you' (Genesis 17:7). All male converts to Judaism were also to be circumcised. This meant blood was shed (see Genesis 17:7-15). Today this is not required of covenant children and adults, as baptism replaces it. In the times of the Old Testament we should note that circumcision of baby girls was not required by God's law. Today some religious groups carry out this cruel practice, which has no religious significance at all.

On the eighth day, Jesus was circumcised by a priest and this identified him as a member of God's covenant people. Jesus was both God and man, and, as our Saviour, obeyed God's law perfectly. This was necessary so that the righteousness given his people would be perfect. Without perfect obedience to God, there would be no hope for their salvation. Mary and Joseph obeyed God's command given through Gabriel and named their baby 'Jesus'(Luke 2:21).

Mary was not permitted to take part in religious activities for a time. Then she was to make a 'sin offering'. Normally this meant the sacrifice of a lamb, after which the priest would pronounce her to be 'clean'. We read that those who were poor and couldn't afford a lamb were to offer 'a pair of turtledoves or two young pigeons' (Luke 2:24; cf. Leviticus 12:2,8), which Mary and Joseph did. This sin offering shows us that Mary was a sinner who acknowledged her need of a Saviour (Luke 1:47).

Our Lord didn't live the life of the rich. He wasn't born in a castle with all the privileges of the well-to-do. No! His mother and Joseph were poor people, but they were godly! Jesus didn't wear the clothes of the rich, nor have a soft feather bed and pillow on which to sleep. There were times when he had nowhere to lay his weary head, except on the hard, rocky ground. Frequently his time of prayer was in an open field or garden.

Jesus was the most humble man who ever lived and set a pattern of living that we should follow. We have nothing of which to be proud, as everything we have is the gift of God. We can only say with the Apostle Paul: 'But by the grace of God I am what I am...' (1 Corinthians 15:10). What a debt of gratitude we owe to our Heavenly Father!

THINGS TO DISCUSS WITH YOUR FAMILY

1. Why was Jesus circumcised?
2. What replaced circumcision following Christ's resurrection and ascension into heaven?
3. What was one of Christ's final instructions to his disciples? See Matthew 28:19.

Meditation

Think about the meaning of your baptism.

Wise Words

Christ took our flesh upon him that he might take our sins upon him. *Thomas Watson*

'Lord, now you are letting your servant
depart in peace, according to your word;
for my eyes have seen your salvation…'
(Luke 2:29-30).

Read: Luke 2:25-35

It is always a happy experience to show a newly born baby to
friends and relatives. Usually pleasant comments are passed and
frequently gifts are given to the infant.

While Joseph and Mary and the baby Jesus were in Jerusalem
they were met by Simeon, an aged man. He was a godly man who
was anxiously awaiting not just the birth of the Lord Jesus, but for
the day when he would see him. When God revealed to him that
Christ was in the temple, he went there, and seeing the young family asked that he might hold the infant in his arms. It was the Holy
Spirit who led him to Christ.

We can only try and imagine the joy that filled his heart as he
held the little child close to his heart and spoke words of praise to
God and a prophecy concerning the work of Christ. He thanked
God that soon the gospel would be known worldwide and Gentiles would flow into his kingdom. Christians who are reading these
words must praise God that the gospel spread throughout the world,
making it possible for you and me to have a saving knowledge of
Christ. Simeon saw the baby as the One who would be 'A light
to bring revelation to the Gentiles'. All who trust Christ for their
salvation should thank God for the truth of these words spoken by
Simeon.

Having seen Jesus with his own eyes, Simeon said that he was
ready to die. His words show that God's peace filled his heart and
mind. He was saved by the blood that the Saviour would soon shed
on the cross at Calvary. Death held no fears for him — his destiny
was Paradise with Christ and all the holy angels and saints of all ages.
Often we hear people saying that they look forward to death as they
will see their loved ones again. This might be so, but all Christians
should be looking forward to death primarily as it will mean seeing
Christ *face to face* and being able to thank him for their salvation. Like

Paul we should be able to say concerning the day of our death: 'For to me to live is Christ, and to die is gain' (Philippians 1:21).

Mary and Joseph were amazed at what Simeon said. He had some special words for Mary: '...a sword will pierce through your own soul also...' (Luke 2:35). Mary's heart would be broken one day in the future. This of course was when her son was brutally nailed to a cross and left to die, bearing God's punishment for the sins of his people.

Death is the last enemy and we should prepare for that event. It will certainly take place, unless Christ returns before we die. Our preparation is made when we come to trust our eternal security to Christ. Death, then, is the doorway into heaven. Pray for the Holy Spirit to dwell in your heart and give you spiritual peace. Then you can face death with confidence.

THINGS TO DISCUSS WITH YOUR FAMILY

1. What is the meaning of Luke 2:34? 'Then Simeon blessed them, and said to Mary his mother, "Behold, this Child is destined for the fall and rising of many in Israel..."'
2. The Holy Spirit was active in Simeon's life. In what way is the Holy Spirit active in your life?
3. Why would Mary and Joseph 'marvel' at Simeon's words?

Meditation

What thoughts do you think went through Simeon's mind as he held Jesus in his arms?

Wise Words

Christ was indeed the glory of Israel.   *J. C. Ryle*

'She gave thanks to the Lord, and spoke of him to all those who looked for redemption in Jerusalem' (Luke 2:38).

Read: Luke 2:36-38

The story of Anna occupies just three verses in the Scriptures, but there is much we can learn about this godly woman. The life she lived was her testimony that she loved God. Christians should let their life speak to all who know them, that they are members of the heavenly kingdom.

Anna's name means 'grace' or 'favour'. Today there are many girls named 'Anna' or 'Grace'. She was the daughter of Phanuel which means 'The appearance of God'. Her family was part of the tribe of Asher, which was one of the 'lost' tribes — a tribe that failed to return in large numbers after the Babylonian captivity.

She was an aged woman who had been a widow for many years. Her husband, whose name we do not know, died after just seven years of marriage. Anna was probably well over one-hundred years old, having been a widow for eighty-four years.

We are told that she was a prophetess who spent her time serving God by working in the temple. She may have helped keep the building clean and tidy, but Luke tells us that she spent much of her time in fasting and prayer. Today, prayer is so often neglected by professing Christians, but when we read biographies of great saints we find that prayer was a major part of their lives. Martin Luther, whose time was filled with Christian work, spent hours in prayer each day. He claimed that it was the time spent praying that made it possible for him to carry out his calling from God.

God's law didn't require fasting during prayer time, but Anna found that she could devote uninterrupted periods upon her knees when she didn't have to cook meals. This is a lesson for you and me. We must spend time talking to our Heavenly Father. To lay aside cooking and eating allows more time for prayer and is worthy of our consideration for special times of self denial.

Anna eagerly awaited the coming of the Messiah. She must have spent much time in the temple telling the people who came to worship that the Messiah would soon come. She was doing a work like that of John the Baptist. She had been anxiously awaiting the appearance of Christ, and we can only try to imagine the excitement and godly joy that must have filled her heart when she carried the Lord Jesus in her arms. She had been longing and praying for the coming of Christ.

She gave thanks to God for that great privilege. She could now announce to Israel that the One she had been speaking of had arrived. She could speak to the temple worshippers of redemption through Christ the Saviour. May you and I follow in her footsteps and bear witness to the Lord Jesus who is our Redeemer.

THINGS TO DISCUSS WITH YOUR FAMILY

1. Why are some of the tribes of Israel called 'the lost tribes'?
2. What do we learn from the way Anna worshipped and served God?
3. What do we learn from Hebrews 9:28? 'Christ was offered once to bear the sins of many. To those who eagerly wait for him he will appear a second time, apart from sin, for salvation.'

Meditation

How would you have felt if you had had the privilege of holding the baby Jesus in your arms?

Wise Words

Anna had learned how to crucify the flesh in order to serve God more acceptably.   *Herbert Lockyer*

'And when they had come into the house, they saw the young Child with Mary his mother, and fell down and worshipped him' (Matthew 2:11).

Read: Matthew 2:1-12

When our babies came home from the hospital we usually had many visitors who wanted to see them and give some little gift to make caring for them easier. It seems that this has always been so.

Our Saviour was visited by wise men from the east. Their names and homeland we are not told, but we find from this historical event that God's people are found everywhere, even in the most unexpected places. One great example is Abraham who was called by God to be his servant; he lived among people who had no real knowledge of the LORD.

Once, my wife and I visited Hong Kong and there met several Christians who knew my brother (who was then a minister in Victoria). In the midst of a people who had no real interest in Christianity, we found Christians. I went to a shop to have some silk shirts made, and when I was asked my occupation I told the shopkeeper that he wouldn't understand, but I said that I was a Christian minister. He took hold of me and said, 'Brother, we are both lovers of the Lord Jesus Christ.' At once, showing love to a Christian brother and sister, he halved the price of the shirts and gave my wife a lovely length of silk for a dress — and there was no cost to a 'Christian brother'.

The wise men must have had a knowledge of the Scriptures, especially the writing of Daniel, and were anxiously awaiting the birth of the Messiah. When God made them aware that Jesus was born in Bethlehem they set out on the journey to Israel. It would have been a long, uncomfortable trip that cost them a great deal. Upon arriving in Bethlehem they asked King Herod where the baby could be found.

They had purchased costly gifts for the baby — gold, frankincense and myrrh. We are not told how many wise men made the journey to Bethlehem, but frequently people say there were three, because there were three gifts for the Lord. We do know that they followed a star that came to a stop above the house where Jesus was found.

These men had only read of the coming Messiah, but their faith in God and his revelation was strong, and they rejoiced to see the baby. They bowed down before the infant and worshipped him. This act of faith is similar to that of the thief upon the cross who prayed to Christ who was on a cross beside him. That thief believed that the bleeding, dying, mocked Person beside him was really a King who had a kingdom. He asked the Lord for a place in his kingdom. Christ certainly didn't look like a King as he hung upon that cross. Neither did the baby, held in the arms of a poor young woman, who, with her husband, was resting in a stable. That baby was completely dependent upon his mother's care in order to live, yet they worshipped him as their Messiah. What great faith!

THINGS TO DISCUSS WITH YOUR FAMILY

1. Why had the wise men come to Bethlehem?
2. What can be said about their faith?
3. In what way had God revealed to them the place where Jesus was to be found?

Meditation

Give some thought to the feelings of the wise men when they came into the presence of the baby Jesus.

Wise Words

The Lord Jesus has many 'hidden ones' like these wise men. *J. C. Ryle*

'Behold an angel of the LORD appeared to Joseph in a dream, saying, "Arise, take the young child and his mother, flee to Egypt, and stay there until I bring you word ..."' (Matthew 2:13).

Read: Matthew 2:13-15; 19-23

Some months after Jesus' birth, efforts were made to have him killed. We will look at the wicked King Herod later, but let us now consider the wisdom and majesty of Jesus' Heavenly Father.

After the visit by the wise men who had come from an eastern country, we now find God revealing to Joseph the necessity of escaping from Israel to Egypt, and remaining there until it was safe for the family to return.

God knew that Herod was about to give the order to kill all the young children, two years of age and under, who lived in and about Bethlehem. Jesus had entered the world to save sinners, which involved his sacrificial death when aged thirty-three and a half years. God had determined that his Son would die, but not at the hands of Herod's soldiers, and God's plans are unalterable.

Being a poor couple, Joseph and Mary gathered their few possessions together and with Jesus left Bethlehem for Egypt, where they would be safe from Herod.

This event was the fulfilment of a prophecy found in Hosea 11:1: 'When Israel was a child, I loved him, and out of Egypt I called my son.' This statement referred to God's salvation of his covenant nation; when under the leadership of Moses, the nation left slavery in Egypt and slowly made its way to the Promised Land. Moses and Aaron were told to say to Pharaoh: 'Israel is my son, my firstborn. So I say to you, "let my son go that he may serve me"' (Exodus 4:22-23). God called the nation of Israel his 'son'.

Now we find God's only Son living in Egypt to escape the clutches of vile King Herod. Satan was unaware who the Messiah was, but knew that he had been born in Bethlehem.

Joseph, having been visited by an angel, set out with Mary and Jesus for the safety of Egypt. What happened during their time in what was once the place of slavery for Israel we do not know. Just as

God had announced to Moses that the time had come for Israel to leave Egypt for the Promised Land, so God's angel told Joseph when it was time to take his family back to Israel and settle in Nazareth.

Today there are many aliens settling in our lands, and I hope we treat immigrants fairly as I believe the Egyptians helped Joseph and his family. We are told: 'You shall not oppress a hired servant who is poor and needy, whether one of your brethren or one of the aliens who is in your land within your gates' (Deuteronomy 24:14).

From his birth Christ suffered the anger of God's covenant people; he suffered from the hands of Herod in having to flee Bethlehem.

THINGS TO DISCUSS WITH YOUR FAMILY

1. Why did God call Israel his 'son'?
2. In what way was Jesus God's Son?
3. What can you do to help immigrants settle into their new homeland?

Meditation

Consider the difficulties faced by Joseph and his family as they made their way to Egypt.

Wise Words

Greatness and riches are a perilous possession for the soul.   *J. C. Ryle*

'Go and search diligently for the young Child, and when you have found him, bring back word to me, that I may come and worship him also' (Matthew 2:8).

Read: Matthew 2:1-23

Whenever King Herod is mentioned, most people immediately associate him with the murder of the young children living in and about Bethlehem. He wanted to ensure that Christ was killed. We also become aware that Satan was again at work, using Herod to try and kill Jesus, and so destroy God's plan of salvation. Herod gave the appearance of being a godly man as he had the temple built in Jerusalem. This building gave him the title 'Herod, the Great'. The wise men had sought help from King Herod concerning the place of Christ's birth in order to find him, present him with gifts and to worship him. It was the chief priests and the scribes who gave them the information they needed. The people who should have been in Bethlehem worshipping the young baby did nothing. It was those men from the East who sacrificed their time and finances to find the Messiah.

Herod hated the idea that the King of Israel had been born. He lied to the visitors and asked them to return and tell him where the child could be found. He claimed that he wanted to visit the Saviour and worship him. In reality, he wanted to murder the Messiah. God would never allow this to happen and warned the wise men of Herod's plans.

Herod's wicked action fulfilled the prophecy of Jeremiah: 'A voice was heard in Ramah, lamentation, weeping, and great mourning; Rachel weeping for her children, refusing to be comforted, because they were no more' (Matthew 2:18; cf. Jeremiah 31:15).

The one who gave the order to kill the young children was soon to face his own death. He found out the truth of the word of God, written by the author of Hebrews: 'And as it is appointed for men to die once, but after this the judgement...' (Hebrews 9:27). What a terrible judgement Herod faced, as he was responsible for the death of so many covenant children. In his Gospel, Luke warned those who were considering harming young covenant children and new-born Christians: 'It would be better for him if a millstone were hung around his neck, and he were thrown into the sea, than that he should offend one of these little ones' (Luke 17:2).

Herod would have known the commandment: 'You shall not murder' (Exodus 20:13). The mouth of hell was open to receive that enemy of God. He was ripe for judgement.

Upon Herod's death an angel told Joseph it was safe to return to Israel with his family. Again the Scripture was fulfilled when the family made their home in Nazareth.

THINGS TO DISCUSS WITH YOUR FAMILY

1. What prophecy was fulfilled when Joseph and his family made their home in Nazareth? See Matthew 2:23.
2. What prophecy was fulfilled when Joseph and his family departed Egypt for Israel?
3. In what way was Herod a great hypocrite?
4. Discuss the words of Jeremiah 31:15.

Meditation

Consider the care that God showed for Jesus Christ, his Son.

Wise Words

The Lord Jesus comes down from heaven to save sinners, and at once we are told that Herod the king 'seeks to destroy him'. *J. C. Ryle*

'And the child grew and became strong in spirit, filled with wisdom; and the grace of God was upon him' (Luke 2:40).

Read: Luke 2:39,40

We are not told much concerning Christ as a young child, but we catch glimpses of his life in various places in the Scriptures.

Luke makes no mention of Joseph and his family escaping to Egypt. We do know that Joseph settled in the city of Nazareth in order that prophecy would be fulfilled: 'He shall be called a Nazarene' (Matthew 2:23). Nazareth was not a large city, but a country town and it was there that Jesus lived for almost thirty years. There were much larger cities in the region, but Christ was a most humble Person, and even the place chosen as his home was in a small, unknown town.

Christ learned a trade. We are told that Joseph, who was believed to be his father, was a carpenter, and that, by trade, Jesus also was a carpenter, Matthew 13:55 — a lowly occupation for God's Son. When he was preaching in a synagogue the people were surprised at his knowledge and asked the question: 'Is this not the carpenter, the Son of Mary, and brother of James, Joses, Judas, and Simon? And are not his sisters here with us?' (Mark 6:3).

Mary and Joseph spent much time teaching him the Scriptures, which the Holy Spirit used to awaken his mission in life, which was to save sinners. As the Saviour's knowledge grew, we are told he also became very wise. During all of his growing years he lived a life of perfect obedience to his Heavenly Father, and to Mary and Joseph as well. Luke tells us that Jesus was 'subject' to Mary and Joseph (Luke 2:51). He did not curse when he hurt himself, nor was he involved in the use of the vulgar language he must have heard from those around him; no, the Holy Spirit kept him free from sin.

Jesus would have been taught the Ten Commandments that God had handed to Moses. He lived according to that law which included: 'Honour your father and your mother...' (Exodus 20:12).

There may have been times when he was mocked by other children because of his perfect obedience to his parents, and because he didn't become involved in any sinful activity other children enjoyed. Christ was different to all other children — he was sinless and for that we can praise God. Luke tells us that Jesus 'increased in wisdom and stature, and in favour with God and men' (Luke 2:52). Part of Jesus' humility was laying aside the knowledge he had as God, and growing in knowledge and understanding as others, Philippians 2:6-8. He knows what it is like to grow in knowledge and wisdom. This does not mean that Jesus was a weakling; we are told that he grew 'strong in spirit' (Luke 2:40).

THINGS TO DISCUSS WITH YOUR FAMILY

1. Where on your map is Nazareth?
2. What is meant by 'wisdom'?
3. Jesus 'grew strong in spirit'. What does this mean?

Meditation

Consider the feelings of Mary, Joseph, and their family as Jesus grew up.

Wise Words

Nazareth was esteemed of small account, and so were its citizens, the Nazarenes. *William Hendriksen*

'And he said to them, "Why is it that you sought me? Did you not know that I must be about my Father's business?"' (Luke 2:49).

Read: Luke 2:41-52

All adult covenant males were obligated to be in Jerusalem for the celebration of three historical feasts — the Passover, Pentecost and Tabernacles, but things had changed. It was usual that all males visit Jerusalem to celebrate at least one of the feasts, usually the Passover. Our reading gives us the picture of a godly family who regularly made its way to Jerusalem for Passover celebrations. This would have been a long and tiring journey for a family with young children. Jesus was twelve years old when Joseph and Mary went up to Jerusalem according to custom. In Jerusalem they would celebrate the night when the Angel of the LORD passed over the homes displaying the blood of the lamb. They would also thank God for Moses, who led the nation as it made its way to the Promised Land.

Travelling homeward from the Passover festival, with hundreds of worshippers, it was usual for the women and children to lead the way, the men following. It is easy to understand how Jesus was missed. Possibly, Mary thought he was with the men and Joseph expected him to be with his mother. When they realized he was missing they returned to the city and found him in the Temple asking questions of the religious scholars. The normal way of teaching then was by teachers and students asking and answering questions. Those with Jesus that day were amazed at his intelligence.

Seeing her Son, Mary rebuked him for causing her and Joseph some concern. Jesus' reply teaches us several great truths. First, we find from Jesus' answer, 'Did you not know that I must be about my Father's business?' that he recognized a special relationship between himself and God. God was his unique, 'Heavenly Father'.

Secondly, we find that Jesus knew that his life was to be one of obedience to his Heavenly Father. It was right for him to be in Jerusalem for the Passover and to be in the Temple with the church leaders, learning all he could about his covenant God.

We are told that Joseph and Mary didn't comprehend what he meant when he answered them, despite all that Gabriel had revealed twelve years before. Our reading concludes by telling us that Christ grew physically, and in knowledge and wisdom, and 'in favour with God and men'. He was a popular, godly young man.

Christian parents should pray that their children might be like the Saviour, and devote time to the study of God, his law and the way of salvation.

THINGS TO DISCUSS
WITH YOUR FAMILY

1. In what way is God, Jesus' Father?
2. What happened in Jerusalem during the time of the Passover?
3. In what way can you be like the twelve-year-old Jesus?

Meditation

Give some thought to how you can be about God's business.

Wise Words

Let [children] remember that if they are old enough to do wrong they are also old enough to do right; and that if they are able to read storybooks and to talk, they are also able to read their Bibles and pray. *J. C. Ryle*

'As it is written in the Prophets: "Behold,
I send my messenger before your face,
who will prepare your way before you.
The voice of one crying in the wilderness: 'Prepare the way of the LORD; make
his paths straight'"' (Mark 1:2–3).

Read: Matthew 3:1-12

The time had arrived for John the Baptist to commence his work
preparing Israel for the arrival of the long-awaited Christ. The
people were ruled by Rome, and Roman soldiers walked the streets
of Jerusalem exercising the power of the greatest empire in the
world. The truth of God concerning salvation was not being taught
by the leaders of the church. The influential Pharisees taught that
salvation was to be earned by obedience to the law of God, as well
as the many laws they had introduced. There can be no doubt that
the people lived in spiritual darkness.

Then there appeared a rugged looking man, John, the son of
Elizabeth and Zacharias, a priest. This meant that John was also a
priest. He was to 'bear witness of the Light, that all through him
might believe' (John 1:7). It was Jesus Christ who was the 'Light of
the world' (John 9:5).

To ordinary people, John must have appeared to be an uncul-
tured person. We are told that he 'was clothed with camel's hair and
with a leather belt around his waist, and he ate locusts and wild
honey' (Mark 1:6). Yet this wild–looking man had a message from
God: 'Repent for the kingdom of heaven is at hand!'

There was nothing new in John's preaching. In many places in
the Old Testament, the people were called to turn from their sins.
The Saviour proclaimed the same message as did the disciples. The
message of the Apostle Paul was a godly sorrow for sin and a saving faith in Jesus. We read his words: 'but [God] commands all men
everywhere to repent…' (Acts 17:30); and 'so they [Paul and Silas]
said, "Believe on the Lord Jesus Christ, and you will be saved, you
and your household"' (Acts 16:31).

Today this message is proclaimed by men in the pulpits of
evangelical churches. The *Westminster Shorter Catechism* defines saving repentance as follows (Question 87): 'Repentance unto life is

a saving grace, whereby a sinner, out of a true sense of his sin, and apprehension of the mercy of God in Christ, doth, with grief and hatred of his sin, turn from it unto God, with full purpose of, and endeavour after, new obedience.'

John also, with very plain words, rebuked the Pharisees and the Sadducees for leading the people astray: 'Brood of vipers! Who has warned you to flee from the wrath to come?' Those who expressed their repentance were baptized.

John told the people to prepare for the coming of Christ, and declared that while *he* baptized with water, *the Saviour* would baptize with the Holy Spirit. If Jesus is your Lord and Saviour, you have been baptized with God's Spirit.

THINGS TO DISCUSS WITH YOUR FAMILY

1. What illustration did John use to show the greatness of Christ when compared to himself?
2. Describe John's character.
3. In what region did John do most of his preaching and baptisms? Why?

Meditation

Give some consideration to the task that God had given John. How did he prove himself faithful? Think about the responsibilities God has given you and what you have done to carry them out.

Wise Words

John saw in his desert surroundings much that symbolised his nation's calamity and which lent colour to his solemn warnings of impending doom. *Herbert Lockyer*

'He said, "I am the voice of one crying in the wilderness: 'Make straight the way of the LORD'"' (John 1:23).

Read: John 1:19-28

How many times have you been asked to fill in forms giving information about yourself and your family. Government departments want to know so much about you, and this information is stored somewhere on computer files. We are told that the information is secure from prying eyes, but every now and again information is accidentally made public. In recent years, and for the second time, the Australian Government has raised the question about a card to be carried by Australian citizens. This card would contain information about the citizen carrying it.

John the Baptist didn't have to carry a card indicating who he was, but he was faced by a group of priests and Levites who wanted to know who he was. The leaders of the church saw something unusual in John and in the message he preached. The question asked of him was really, 'Are you the long awaited Messiah, promised by God?'

John was very honest and stated plainly that he was not the Christ, or the prophet Elijah they believed would come before him (see Malachi 4:5). He also declared that he was not 'the prophet' whose coming had been prophesied by Moses (see Deuteronomy 18:15-18).

John then stated that he was the one foretold in Isaiah 40:3. He gave his questioners a clear indication of who he was and the work he was to carry out. He was the one to announce the imminent appearance of Christ, the Son of God.

The unusual part of John's preaching was the fact that he was 'baptising' those who claimed they had repented of their sins. This baptism was an acknowledgement that the one being baptized had repented, and so was cleansed of their sin. John went on to state that the Christ would baptize, but in a totally different way. John baptized with water while Christ baptized with the Holy Spirit. Holy Spirit baptism brought about the new birth, which is known as 'regeneration'.

John, a most humble man, recognized the infinite superior nature of Christ. He said he was not even worthy to loose the Lord's sandals.

Just as the Australian Government has a record of every citizen of our nation, so our God has a record of every person who is a citizen of heaven. Is your name written in Christ's book of life? If you have been baptized by the Holy Spirit, you are numbered among God's people. Eternal life is yours!

THINGS TO DISCUSS WITH YOUR FAMILY

1. John the Baptist was a priest. How could this be?
2. What was the theme of John's preaching? Read Matthew 3:2.
3. What was the difference between the work of John and Jesus?

Meditation

Meditate upon Mark 12:30-31 — "'And you shall love the LORD your God with all your heart, with all your soul, with all your mind, and with all your strength.' This is the first commandment. And the second, like it, is this: 'You shall love your neighbour as yourself.'"

Wise Words

We have no true religion about us, until we cast away our high thoughts, and feel ourselves sinners.

J. C. Ryle

'And suddenly a voice came from heaven, saying, "This is my beloved Son, in whom I am well pleased"' (Matthew 3:17).

Read: Matthew 3:13-17

In the Christian church there are two sacraments — baptism and the Lord's Supper. Both are reasons for spiritual joy and thanksgiving. I am confident that when you have attended a baptism, you saw happiness in the faces of everyone present. Usually baptisms are just of one or two people, but in Acts 2:41 we read of about three thousand people being baptized when they confessed their faith in the Lord Jesus. The apostles worked hard that day.

Your reading tells of the Saviour making his public appearance and commencing his work as Messiah. John didn't want to baptize Jesus, as he knew that the baptism of our Lord was far superior to his water baptism — Christ would baptize with the Holy Spirit. However, Jesus insisted saying: 'Permit it to be so now, for thus it is fitting for us to fulfil all righteousness.' Jesus was to obey perfectly God's law; so the question is: 'What law was Jesus obeying in his baptism?'

Christ approached John for baptism when he was thirty years old. This was the age when priests took up their priestly duties (see Numbers 4:3,47). At that time there was to be a purification ceremony carried out by a priest (Numbers 8:6-7). John the Baptist was a priest, having inherited that position from his father. Christ's baptism was the formal proclamation of God's Son commencing his priestly duties; he was of the order of Melchizedek and not of Aaron (Psalm 110:4; Hebrews 7:11-28).

What a glorious event. Our Redeemer was not only commencing his High Priestly duties, but would become the sacrifice for sin. He would become sin for his people and in their place suffer God's anger; he would suffer hell for his people! For his three and a half years of public ministry, as the substitute of his elect, he perfectly obeyed God's law, as he did all his life, in order to provide the holiness they needed to enter heaven.

Baptism is a vital part of the Christian life, for we have the command of our Saviour to his disciples: 'And Jesus came and spoke to them, saying, "All authority has been given to me in heaven and on earth. Go therefore and make disciples of all the nations, baptising them in the name of the Father and of the Son and of the Holy Spirit, teaching them to observe all things that I have commanded you; and lo, I am with you always, even to the end of the age. Amen"' (Matthew 28:18-20).

THINGS TO DISCUSS WITH YOUR FAMILY

1. What did Jesus mean when he said he had to be baptized to 'fulfill all righteousness'? (Matthew 3:15).
2. Why were three thousand people baptized on the Day of Pentecost? (See Acts 2.)
3. Where was Jesus baptized? Why there?
4. What is the meaning of 'Melchizedek'?

Meditation

Meditate upon the words of our text: 'And suddenly a voice came from heaven, saying, "This is my beloved Son, in whom I am well pleased"' (Matthew 3:17).

Wise Words

Grace, and grace alone, is the cause of our salvation.

J. K. Davies

 'And the Holy Spirit descended in bodily form like a dove upon him, and a voice came from heaven which said, "You are my beloved Son; in you I am well pleased"' (Luke 3:22).

Read: Matthew 3:13-17

Recently one of my granddaughters applied for work with a firm of solicitors. With her application for the position, she had to send in references from people who knew her well. After interviews she was given a position and commenced doing secretarial work. Once, when I wrote a reference for a young man seeking an important job, I received a phone call from the prospective employer who wanted to ask questions about the person. Employers want to employ the most qualified people they can find.

In our last devotion, we looked at the reason for John's baptism of Jesus. The Son of God was about to commence his high priestly work of salvation. It was important for John the Baptist to know who was the long awaited Messiah, as he was to prepare his way by pointing the people to him. There had been some who falsely claimed to be the Christ, but God was to announce in an audible and visible way who was his Son. There would be no mistaking the identity of Christ as far as John was concerned.

John was baptizing at the Jordan River where there were many springs of fresh water. He was anxiously awaiting the coming of the Messiah. God had revealed to him that he would know who the Christ was as he would see the Holy Spirit descending upon him like a dove. When this happened he and those present knew that the Person being baptized was the Messiah.

There was a further confirmation that Jesus was the Son of God. God spoke aloud to those who were present: 'This is my beloved Son, in whom I am well pleased.' Such a baptism has never been repeated. As you read today's passage, you will have noticed that the three Persons of the Godhead were involved. Christ was baptized with the Holy Spirit and his Heavenly Father spoke. God's eternal plan of salvation was now to commence with Jesus as the prophet, priest and king of his people. He would be acknowledged as the mediator between God and man, being God and man in one Person.

What happened that day was confirmation that Jesus was the Messiah. John could confidently direct his congregations to Jesus as the Saviour of the world. Christ's saving work had commenced!

THINGS TO DISCUSS WITH YOUR FAMILY

1. What was the significance of God's spoken words at Christ's baptism?
2. Name one other time God spoke from heaven acknowledging Jesus to be his Son.
3. What does 'Messiah' mean?

Meditation

Think for a time about Mark's description of Jesus' baptism — 'And immediately, coming up from the water, he saw the heavens parting and the Spirit descending upon him like a dove. Then a voice came from heaven, "You are my beloved Son, in whom I am well pleased"' (Mark 1:10-11).

Wise Words

The admission of every new member into the visible church, whether young or grown up, is an event which ought to excite a lively interest in a Christian assembly; it is an event that ought to call forth the fervent prayers of all praying people.   *J. C. Ryle*

March

'Then Jesus was led up by the Spirit into the wilderness to be tempted by the devil' (Matthew 4:1).

Read: Matthew 4:1-11

Every day we face the temptations of the evil one. Some time ago my wife made a plate of delicious looking muffins. As she put them out to cool she looked at me and said: 'These are for supper after our church service. Please do not take any; I will make more later for us.' I was happy to reply, 'It's all right Val, they are safe with me.'

As I walked by the plate, the muffins smelled more delicious; it was so tempting, and at last I took one, saying to myself, 'Val will never notice.' I was right — Val made no comment about the missing muffin. Still, I had broken my word to her and certainly God was aware of what I had done. I later confessed.

Jesus had been baptized and the Holy Spirit now filled him beyond measure. In the power of God's Spirit he could confront his and our great enemy — Satan. Many people deny the existence of Satan, but the Scriptures teach that he is the mortal enemy of God and his people. It was the devil who led the angelic rebellion against God's rule. It was Satan who tempted Adam and Eve to sin. It is Satan and his army of demons who cause all the world's heartaches.

The time had arrived for Christ to face Satan. This confrontation was not of Satan's choosing, for we read that our Saviour was led into the wilderness by the Holy Spirit.

Three times Satan tempted Christ, yet despite having gone without food for forty days he stood his ground against the evil one. Temptation is not sin. It is succumbing to temptation that is sin. We should note that Christ's temptation is different to that which we suffer. He was sinless and his temptations came from outside of himself. Our temptations are difficult to resist because we have a sinful nature which is inclined to sin. Of course Christians have a different nature, but temptations come from both within and without and we fall so easily. The Apostle Paul knew the battle Christians experience when tempted. He wrote: 'For the good that I will to do, I do not do; but the evil I will not to do, that I practice. Now if I do what I will not to do, it is no longer I who do it, but sin that dwells in me. I find then a law, that evil is present with me, the one who wills to do good. For I delight in the law of God according to the inward man. But I see another law in my members, warring against the law of my mind, and bringing me into captivity to the law of sin which is in my members. O wretched man that I am! Who will deliver me from this body of death?' (Romans 7:19-24).

Paul knew that victory over temptation was only possible through the Lord Jesus. May you and I know the same great truth.

THINGS TO DISCUSS WITH YOUR FAMILY

1. What is temptation?
2. Is temptation sin? How do you know this?
3. What did Paul think about God's law? Read Romans 7:12 and Psalm 19:8. What is your attitude towards God's law?

Meditation

Meditate upon the way sin grieves the Holy Spirit. Thank God for all Christ has done for you.

Wise Words

To be tempted is in itself no sin; it is the yielding to temptation, and the giving it place in our hearts, which we must fear. *J. C. Ryle*

'Be sober, be vigilant; because your adversary the devil walks about like a roaring lion, seeking whom he may devour. Resist him, steadfast in the faith, knowing that the same sufferings are experienced by your brotherhood in the world' (1 Peter 5:8-9).

Read: Luke 4:1-13

Val and I have our Bible reading and prayer together each day after breakfast. In some of my other books you will have read about our faithful Maltese dog named Wags. When he hears us start reading the Scriptures he gives a soft bark which means he wants to be with us. Each day he comes and sits on Val's lap during the time of our devotions. He must like something about the soft voice we use when reading the Scriptures and praying.

Val and I have discussed the way we deal with temptations and have decided that first of all we should keep away from places that cause temptation. We agreed that when we are tempted we should follow the pattern set by Christ in his confrontation with Satan in the wilderness — meditate upon the Word of God. We would think of the majesty and holiness of God and the loving kindness of Christ in bearing our sins on the cross. We'd also give thanks to the Holy Spirit for our new hearts and giving us the strength to fight against sin.

Christ was tempted to turn a stone into bread and so provide food for his body. The Lord's reply was to quote words found in the Old Testament: 'It is written, "Man shall not live by bread alone, but by every word of God."'

Satan's second temptation was to offer Jesus the glory of ruling the nations if he would bow down and worship him. Again the Saviour's reply was from Scripture: 'Get behind me, Satan! For it is written, "You shall worship the LORD your God, and him only you shall serve."'

The third temptation questioned whether Christ was the Son of God. The Lord was taken to the top of the temple where Satan tempted him to jump — the Scriptures promised God's protective care of Messiah. Satan quoted Scripture, but again the Lord replied with Scripture: 'It has been said, "You shall not tempt the LORD your God."'

Satan then left Jesus, his temptations having been a failure. The first Adam had given way to Satan's lies, but Jesus, the second Adam, was victorious. This victory set the pattern for every confrontation between Christ and the evil one.

And just as our Saviour was victorious, so can we be. James wrote: 'Resist the devil and he will flee from you' (James 4:7). We can have the victory, but this requires effort. We do not have to fight alone for we read concerning Christ: 'For in that he himself has suffered, being tempted, he is able to aid those who are tempted' (Hebrews 2:18). The One who has all power and authority in heaven and on earth fights at our side. May we always pray for his help when we are tempted. Freedom from sin can be ours!

THINGS TO DISCUSS WITH YOUR FAMILY

1. Why does Satan tempt people to sin?
2. What can Christ's people do to have success over temptations?
3. Jesus didn't sin. Why not?

Meditation

Think of the holiness of our Saviour. What does this mean to you?

Wise Words

He who was 'full of the Holy Spirit' was yet not ashamed to make the Holy Scripture his weapon of defence and his rule of action.   *J. C. Ryle*

'Behold! The Lamb of God who takes away the sin of the world' (John 1:29).

Read: John 1:29-34

There are more sheep in Australia than there are people. Sheep stations provide wool for the clothing industry worldwide. Years ago it was said that Australia's overseas income came largely from the export of wool. With the invention of refrigeration Australia now exports many tons of lamb and mutton to a hungry world.

When they were young, my wife and her brother had two pet lambs which they fed with milk in a baby's bottle. One lamb often went out of his way to 'bunt' Val and Lindsay and on one occasion it broke Lindsay's collarbone when it knocked him off his tricycle.

During the time before the Lord's sacrificial death, lambs were needed for sacrifices. At the Passover many thousands were slaughtered by the priests and then eaten at the Passover meal. The family looked back to the night when God opened the doors of slavery in Egypt and gave his people their freedom. It was the blood from the lamb which marked the homes of the Israelites. When the Angel of the Lord came to kill the eldest child in each family, he passed over those homes that had the lamb's blood on the door posts and above the door. The Passover lamb symbolized the true 'Lamb of God' — the Lord Jesus Christ, who in his death would pay God the penalty owing for sin.

Abraham had, in obedience to God's command, taken his son Isaac to Mount Moriah where he was to sacrifice him to the LORD. When Isaac asked where was the lamb for the sacrifice, his father replied: 'My son, God will provide for himself the lamb for a burnt offering' (Genesis 22:8). This God did when a lamb was found in a thicket. This symbolized the one, true offering for sin which was the sacrificial death of Christ, God's only begotten Son.

Christ was the true Lamb symbolized by the morning and evening temple sacrifices. Isaiah prophesied of Jesus — 'He was led as a lamb to the slaughter...' (Isaiah 53:7).

John, when he saw Jesus approaching him after his wilderness temptations, knew who it was and was able to say: 'Behold! The Lamb of God who takes away the sin of the world.' He had seen the Holy Spirit descend like a dove upon the Saviour and had heard God's words spoken to his Son.

And what a 'Lamb'! The One standing before John was God's only Son, the 'son of man' who became sin for his people and paid their debt for their sin, imposed by their Heavenly Father.

Isaiah wrote of you and me: 'All we like sheep have gone astray; we have turned, every one to his own way…' However there is salvation to be found in 'the Lamb of God,' the Lord Jesus Christ. Has God's Lamb dealt with your sins?

THINGS TO DISCUSS WITH YOUR FAMILY

1. Why did John call Jesus 'the Lamb of God'?
2. In Revelation 5:6 we read of a Lamb. In the previous verse the Lamb is called 'the Lion of the tribe of Judah'. How can this be?
3. In what way was Christ like the Passover lamb? Read Exodus 12:5.

Meditation

For a time consider the way in which the saving work of our Saviour was similar to that of the sacrificial lamb.

Wise Words

At the inauguration of his public ministry, Jesus was given one of the most striking and frequently used of his titles. He was called 'the Lamb of God'.   *Gordon J. Keddie*

'And he said to them, "Come and see"'
(John 1:39).

Read: John 1:35-42

I am sure that many of you are like me and often don't hear what a speaker says. It is only when the words are spoken two or three times that we know what is being said. People have told me that I have selective hearing — I only hear what is of interest to me. Today I have an excellent excuse — I'm not wearing my hearing aid.

In your reading you should have noticed that John the Baptist repeated what he had said before to his disciples: 'Behold the Lamb of God.' This time two of his disciples, Andrew and probably John, the author of the gospel, understood what was said and followed Jesus. When the Saviour asked them, 'What do you seek?' they replied by asking him where he was staying as they had questions to ask of the One they called 'Rabbi' — 'Teacher'. They had become aware that Jesus was God's Messiah, 'the Lamb of God who takes away the sin of the world' (John 1:29).

It was about 4.00pm and with his heart bursting with great joy and thanksgiving, Andrew immediately set out to tell his brother Simon of his great discovery. It is true that when we fall in love with someone we have the desire to tell someone of that love. When we become Christians we have the same impulse to tell others of the Redeemer who loved us and saved us from the penalty owing because of our sins. We should be praying that God might give us such a zeal for Christ as filled the heart of Andrew. And what an announcement he made to Simon: 'We have found the Messiah.' All Christians have a duty to tell others of Christ and his salvation freely offered to sinners. We must not leave this work to the minister and other office bearers of the congregation.

When Jesus met Simon he knew his character — impulsive, unstable and outspoken. Yet he foresaw Peter's death upon the cursed cross because of the growth of a strong, courageous faith in Christ. Thus Jesus gave him a new name — 'Cephas,' which in Greek was

Petros (Peter). Cephas meant a 'stone' or part of a bigger rock. Jesus could see what God's grace would accomplish in Peter's life.

The disciples had to be taught about Christ and his saving work and this is what is expected of all Christians in their dealings with young believers. Christ's command to the disciples before his ascension into heaven was: '"Go therefore and make disciples of all the nations, baptising them in the name of the Father and of the Son and of the Holy Spirit, teaching them to observe all things that I have commanded you; and lo, I am with you always, even to the end of the age." Amen' (Matthew 28:19-20).

Are you growing in your knowledge of your Saviour?

THINGS TO DISCUSS WITH YOUR FAMILY

1. Why would Andrew and his friend (John?) be so excited?
2. Why did Andrew want to tell Simon about the Person he had found?
3. How would John the Baptist have felt losing his disciples?
4. Find out all you can about Andrew.

Meditation

Remember the time when you became a Christian. Pray that you might recapture that feeling of wonder and thanksgiving.

Wise Words

Was what they [John's disciples] were seeking the removal of sin by this Lamb of God? Was it, accordingly, salvation full and free, entrance into the kingdom? Whatever it was, he was (and is) able to supply. *William Hendriksen*

 'Nathanael answered and said to him, "Rabbi, you are the Son of God! You are the King of Israel!"' (John 1:49).

Read: John 1:43-51

We are not all converted to Christ in the same way. When I was growing up I was taken to Sunday School and worship each Lord's Day. My brother and I had no choice in the matter — we had to go with our parents. I was not a Christian when I set out to take up my first teaching appointment in the country, but I took my Bible with me. When I arrived at the home where I was to have a room I was asked if I had a 'Protestant' Bible with me. When I replied, 'Yes,' I was told that I was not to take it into the house. I did take my Bible inside and began to seriously read, praying that God would give me an understanding of what I read and why the 'Protestant' Bible was hated so greatly.

We have seen how Andrew and his friend were directed to Jesus by John the Baptist. God uses many pathways to draw a sinner to his Son and we now find others coming to faith in Christ by a different way. It is the same Holy Spirit, acting in his sovereign power that brings sinners to saving truth and gives the new birth. The ways are different, but the end is the same — repentance and faith in Christ.

The Lord Jesus commanded Philip: 'Follow me.' At once he found his friend, Nathanael — possibly Bartholomew — and told him the exciting news that he had found the Messiah, spoken of by Moses and the prophets. Nathanael questioned whether the Messiah could come from Nazareth, but followed Philip to meet Jesus.

When the Lord met him he heard words about himself that made him aware that this was indeed the Christ. Who but the Son of God could have seen him 'under the fig tree' without being present. Nathanael was probably well schooled in the Old Testament and knew the words of Proverbs 15:3: 'The eyes of the LORD are in every place, keeping watch on the evil and the good.' We should all remember this truth.

Nathanael, knowing that Christ stood before him, spoke the words in our text: 'Rabbi, you are the Son of God! You are the King of Israel.' He knew the Old Testament prophecies concerning the Messiah. The Lord's reply confirmed what Nathanael knew as he called himself 'The Son of Man,' the title Daniel had given to the coming Saviour (Daniel 7:13). Christ also made a statement that has caused difficulty in interpretation: 'And he [Jesus] said to him, "Most assuredly, I say to you, hereafter you shall see heaven open, and the angels of God ascending and descending upon the Son of Man."' These words remind us of Jacob's vision recorded in Genesis 28:12.

The first 'you' is singular and obviously was spoken to Nathanael, but the second 'you' is plural. There is no recorded incident in the New Testament of what Christ described. Possibly the Lord spoke of an event yet to happen, when every eye would see him descending in holy, majestic glory at his second coming. He will be accompanied by his mighty angels obeying his every command. What a day it will be!

THINGS TO DISCUSS WITH YOUR FAMILY

1. Discuss Jacob's vision recorded in Genesis 28:10-22.
2. How can you witness to others of the Lord's saving work?
3. Discuss the return of Christ, our Redeemer.

Meditation

Give thanks to the God of all grace for sending his Son into the world to save sinners.

Wise Words

The point for Nathanael was that because Jesus is the Son of God, he was also the King of Israel. As such, he was therefore Nathanael's sovereign Lord. He is also your Lord... *Gordon J. Keddie*

'Jesus said to her, "Woman, what does your concern have to do with me? My hour has not yet come"' (John 2:4).

Read: John 2:1-12

Weddings are usually times of much happiness, not just for the bride and groom, but for all the friends and relatives who have gathered to celebrate the joyful occasion. It is a tragedy that in our western society over 50% of marriages end in divorce. Val and I can still remember the day we were married almost fifty years ago in 1958. I've lost much of my hair, what's left is greying and I'm bigger around the waist, but Val's looks haven't changed much, although the grey hair is shining through. During all those years we have supported one another in our Christian life, for we are 'heirs together of the grace of life' (1 Peter 3:7).

God's advice to every unmarried Christian is this: 'Do not be unequally yoked together with unbelievers. For what fellowship has righteousness with lawlessness? ... Or what part has a believer with an unbeliever?' (2 Corinthians 6:14-15). Christians marry Christians. It is wiser to remain single than marry an unbeliever.

Jesus, his mother and his disciples were invited with others to a marriage in Cana. Towards the end of the celebrations the wine ran out which meant much embarrassment to the one who had organized the feast. Mary, thinking this was the opportunity for her Son to reveal to those present that he was the Messiah, drew the situation to his attention. Christ's reply may seem disrespectful. He didn't address Mary as his mother but said: 'Woman, what does your concern have to do with me? My hour has not yet come.' 'Woman' was the same term he used to address his mother from the cross (John 19:26). It was a term of respect, but a gentle rebuke to her followed. Jesus told Mary that she was not to make demands of him. He was to be fully committed to the work of his 'Heavenly Father'. His reply also explains that it was not yet the moment for him to be revealed to people far and wide by his miracles. He then performed the miracle without any publicity.

Mary then quietly told the servants to do as her Son told them. Maybe she expected him to give them money to buy some wine, but left what was to happen in Jesus' hands.

Our Lord ordered that the big pots, normally used for washing, be filled with water. Then the servants were told to take the drink to the master of ceremonies who was delighted with the wine. He said: 'Every man at the beginning sets out the good wine, and when the guests have well drunk, then the inferior. You have kept the good wine until now!' Those who witnessed Christ's miracle saw something of the majestic glory of the Son of God.

It is worth noting that Jesus drank fermented wine and this was not sinful. Wine is the gift of God to mankind (Psalm 104:15). It is the abuse of strong drink that is sinful (Proverbs 23:29-35; Ephesians 5:18).

All Christians can look forward to sitting with the Redeemer on the day of the great marriage feast in Paradise (Revelation 19:9). This will be a time of great rejoicing.

THINGS TO DISCUSS WITH YOUR FAMILY

1. Discuss the teaching of Proverbs 20:1 — 'Wine is a mocker, strong drink is a brawler, and whoever is led astray by it is not wise.'
2. Wine is one of God's good gifts to mankind which has been made a stumbling block to many. Can you think of another of God's gifts to us that has been spoiled by sin?
3. Why did Jesus refer to his mother as 'Woman'?

Meditation

Give some thought to the effect of Christ's miracle upon those who were at the wedding.

Wise Words

I never see a sign 'Licensed to sell spirits' without thinking that it is a licence to ruin souls.

Robert Murray M'Cheyne

149

'Jesus answered and said to them, "Destroy this temple, and in three days I will raise it up"' (John 2:19).

Read: John 2:13-22

Sometimes we hear people saying of their church building, 'Oh, it's only a place to keep us out of the weather.' They seem to have no special regard for the building in which they meet with the saints to worship God. Now, I know that there is no special place where we must go to worship God, but our church building is special to me. It is the place where each Sunday I meet with others to glorify God. There the Scriptures are read, a sermon is preached, prayers are made and God is praised in song. Our church building is a place where we can have a time of fellowship and encourage one another in our Christian life. Many testify that it was in that church building that they were born again and became citizens in the kingdom of God. It is a building that is kept in good repair and cleaned regularly.

It was the time of the Passover and Jesus was in Jerusalem in obedience to God's law. First, he visited the temple and there in the courtyard for the Gentiles he saw the priests and others selling cattle and birds for use in sacrifices. He also saw money changers exchanging the currency of Israel for foreign coins. What he saw annoyed him! The place of sacrifice and worship was being used as a place of commerce. At once he made a whip and hunted the animals and the traders from the temple area. In righteous anger he tipped over the tables being used by those exchanging foreign coins for the local currency.

Can you imagine the scene — animals and people were avoiding Christ's whip, while others crawled about trying to gather their money that lay scattered about on the floor. Clearly the words of the Saviour could be heard: 'Take these things away! Do not make my Father's house a house of merchandise!' His words reminded his disciples of a passage from Psalm 69:9: '... zeal for your house has eaten me up'. Psalm 69 is a Messianic Psalm which contains several prophecies concerning Christ and is quoted seven times in the New Testament.

Christ was also fulfilling words found in Malachi 3:1: '...And the Lord, whom you seek, will suddenly come to his temple, even the Messenger of the covenant, in whom you delight. Behold, he is coming.'

When the priests and others demanded a sign to prove he had a right to do what he had done, Jesus replied: 'Destroy this temple, and in three days I will raise it up.' Jesus spoke of his body and his resurrection after being crucified and lying in a tomb for three days. Some time later Jesus said this sign was the sign of Jonah: 'A wicked and adulterous generation seeks after a sign, and no sign shall be given to it except the sign of the prophet Jonah' (Matthew 16:4).

Christian readers, our body is also a temple for Paul wrote: '...do you not know that your body is the temple of the Holy Spirit who is in you...' (1 Corinthians 6:19). We must keep it clean from sin.

THINGS TO DISCUSS WITH YOUR FAMILY

1. What was the 'Passover'?
2. What sinful activities were being carried out in the temple?
3. Psalm 69:9: '...zeal for your house has eaten me up'. What does this mean?
4. Is anger a sin? Why do you give that answer? See Ephesians 4:26.

Meditation

Meditate on the holiness of God our Saviour — 'But you are holy, who inhabit the praises of Israel' (Psalm 22:3).

Wise Words

Today's church ... has no more solemn duty than to maintain purity of doctrine.   R. B. *Kuiper*

'You believe that there is one God. You
do well. Even the demons believe —
and tremble!' (James 2:19).

Read: John 2:23-25

At Cana Jesus had performed a great miracle which confirmed to
his disciples that he was from God and that he was the Christ
for whose coming the nation longed. However, he was not the warrior King who would drive out the Roman occupation force and
re-establish the visible kingdom of the great King David of old.

The miracles performed by our Saviour demonstrated his almighty power, majesty and glory. Today we have people talking
about 'miracles' that happen. Recently (2006) the newspapers and
TV reported a 'miracle' that occurred in Beaconsfield, a small town
in Tasmania, Australia. The town was unknown to most people until
it was reported that three men were trapped, a kilometre under-
ground, in a gold mine. There had been a small earthquake which
caused a fall of rocks and while most miners were able to escape to
a safe area three men were missing. One body was soon found and
it was expected that the other two men had also been killed. The
miners began using explosives and digging machinery to make their
way through to the area where it was expected the bodies would be
found. One miner, against orders, made his way into the area of the
rock fall and there heard the two trapped miners calling out, warning that the explosives could possibly cause another rock fall. When
it was known that the men were alive a rescue plan was put into
operation. They were trapped in a small steel cage and for days food
and drink were passed to them through a small tunnel, only several
centimetres in diameter.

Many people throughout Australia began praying for the rescue
of the men and two weeks after the rock fall the rescuers finally
completed a one metre diameter tunnel that came up beside the
men. The newspapers and TV gave a lot of publicity to what was
called a 'miracle'. Sadly, I haven't heard of any people coming to saving faith in Christ because of this 'miracle'.

Jesus performed miracles during the time of the Passover and we are told that 'many believed in his name when they saw the signs which he did'. This belief was not saving faith. Our omnipotent Saviour knew the hearts of those who 'believed'. We read in 1 Kings 8:39 that only God can see into the hearts of men: '...for you, only you, know the hearts of all the sons of men'. Jesus saw that they wanted him as their king because of what he could provide for them. God alone appointed him King (Psalm 2:6), not fickle men and women.

Jesus wouldn't trust himself to these people, and he didn't need their wavering testimony to declare who he was. There is a faith that does not save. Our text shows us that the very demons 'believe' that there is a God, yet they tremble in fear as their 'belief' is not a saving faith. In our next devotion we will learn that saving faith comes from God.

THINGS TO DISCUSS WITH YOUR FAMILY

1. Read and discuss one of the most frightening passages of Scripture — Matthew 7:21-23.
2. Why did many people 'believe' in Jesus at the time of the Passover?
3. Why didn't their 'belief' last? Read Matthew 13:1-23.

Meditation

Think for a time on the all knowing Christ who can see into your heart. Only he can cleanse from sin. If you are a Christian give him thanks for your saving faith.

Wise Words

Jesus had not come into the world to ride to the heights of earthly kingship on the backs of the mob. He had come as Immanuel — 'God with us' — to confront the basic problem of the human race, namely, the fact of the universal fallenness of human nature. *Gordon J. Keddie*

'Jesus answered and said to him, "Most assuredly, I say to you, unless one is born again, he cannot see the kingdom of God"' (John 3:3).

Read: John 3:1-10

Much had been happening in Jerusalem at the time of the Passover. Jesus had cleansed the temple of the money changers and cattle traders and performed many miracles. The people in Jerusalem thought that he could be the Messiah, but their belief didn't last and they returned to their old ways. One man, a Pharisee named Nicodemus, wanted to know who Jesus was and decided to visit him one night and find out all he could about this miracle worker.

Australia, like many western countries, has many citizens who have been adopted into the population. To be a citizen of Australia a person must be born in the country or be granted citizenship. Millions of migrants have become wonderful citizens, pledging loyalty to their new nation.

Now Nicodemus wanted to question Jesus, but he found Jesus speaking to him about the way of salvation. The Lord told him that to become a citizen of the kingdom of God he needed to be 'born again'.

Nicodemus, by his reply, showed that he had no idea what Jesus was speaking about. I can imagine him smiling and asking, 'How can a man be born when he is old? Can he enter a second time into his mother's womb and be born?' He was saying that what Christ had said was an impossibility. Jesus went on to explain that being 'born again' was a spiritual rebirth, which was the sovereign work of God, the Holy Spirit.

Almost every person born is a citizen of Satan's kingdom and will one day reap the wages of sin — death, both physical and spiritual. To become a member of the Kingdom of God, the Holy Spirit must bring about a spiritual change. Nicodemus should have known this because we read in Ezekiel 36:26-27, 'I will give you a new heart and put a new spirit within you; I will take the heart of stone out of your flesh and give you a heart of flesh. I will put my Spirit within you and cause you to walk in my statutes, and you will keep my judgments and do them.' Nicodemus was a learned Pharisee yet he was a stranger to salvation and to an understanding of how God saved his people. He was one of the 'blind leaders of the blind' (Matthew 15:14).

Jesus told him that the work of the Holy Spirit in bringing about the new birth was mysterious, something like the breezes that blow. Where they came from and where they went people could not tell. In the same way the 'new birth' is the sovereign work of the Holy Spirit. Nevertheless, like a breeze that cannot be seen, we see its effects. The moving clouds, smoke and leaves of the trees are evidence of the wind blowing. So also the work of the Holy Spirit can be seen in the life of the person 'born again'. Are you born again?

THINGS TO DISCUSS WITH YOUR FAMILY

1. Discuss the evidence of the new birth as found in Galatians 5:22-23. 'But the fruit of the Spirit is love, joy, peace, longsuffering, kindness, goodness, faithfulness, gentleness, self-control.'
2. What is meant by being 'born again'?
3. From where does saving faith in Christ come? Read Ephesians 2:8-9: 'For by grace you have been saved through faith, and that not of yourselves; it is the gift of God, not of works, lest anyone should boast.'

Meditation

Mediate upon Paul's words: 'Or do you not know that your body is the temple of the Holy Spirit who is in you, whom you have from God, and you are not your own?' (1 Corinthians 6:19).

Wise Words

We are dead until made alive, blind until given sight; we are at war with God until we are reborn as his adopted children of faith. *Gordon J. Keddie*

'For God so loved the world that he gave his only begotten Son, that whoever believes in him should not perish but have everlasting life' (John 3:16).

Read: John 3:11-21

Nicodemus had more to learn from Jesus that night. He possibly had seen Christ performing great miracles and cleansing the temple from its irreligious activities. He had been instructed concerning the need to be born again, which was the work of the Holy Spirit. Christ was to now explain something more of the way of salvation which flowed from the grace and love of God. Someone once wrote that 'Love is the queen of God's grace' — how true.

Love is a very important part of human life. For a family to function well there must be love. Between husband and wife there is a special love. As we grow we find that it is easy to love nice people who show love towards us. Yet most people find it difficult, if not impossible, to love the unlovely. Few people would go out of their way to help a person who was drunk, swearing, covered in his own filth and asking for help.

God's love is so different to human love for we read in Romans 5:8, 'But God demonstrates his own love towards us, in that while we were still sinners, Christ died for us.' God loves the unlovely and how we should praise him for that!

Nicodemus was rebuked by the Lord for failing to believe the most basic truth of salvation — the 'new birth'. The Saviour went on to say that he would find great difficulty comprehending his next teaching — 'the Son of Man' had come down from heaven, not to judge the world, but to save sinners.

Nicodemus was told an unpalatable truth, that the Son of God, who spoke to him would be lifted up on a cross and there bear the anger of God for the sins of all who repented and had saving faith. Paul wrote of Christ: 'For he (God) made him (Christ) who knew no sin to become sin for us, that we might become the righteousness of God in him' (2 Corinthians 5:21).

We come to the words of our text, John 3:16, possibly the best known verse in the Bible. These words were to show Nicodemus the immensity of God's love for mankind. God so greatly loved his creation, despite the damage done by sin, that he 'gave' his Son to redeem all those who 'believed' in him. Faith in the Lord Jesus is the only way into heaven. Eternal life is God's gift to all those who trust their everlasting well-being to his Son.

Those who have no interest in Christ stand before God already condemned. Their destiny is eternal hell. They love their sins and unrighteousness and despise the Heavenly Father's love.

Nicodemus was taught very clearly that salvation is the work of the Godhead, Father, Son and Holy Spirit. He no doubt left Christ that night, confused, but later we see a change in his attitude towards the Lord. With Joseph of Arimathea he asked Pilate for Christ's body and helped give the Lord a respectful burial.

We are all taught that God's only way of salvation is a saving 'belief' in the Redeemer, Jesus Christ.

THINGS TO DISCUSS
WITH YOUR FAMILY

1. Learn by heart the words of John 3:16.
2. Discuss God's love for sinners, especially the elect.
3. What is the source of saving faith. Read Ephesians 2:8.

Meditation

Give some thought to Romans 5:8 — 'But God demonstrates his own love towards us, in that while we were still sinners, Christ died for us.'

Wise Words

The faith which justifies is not the faith which includes charity (love), but the faith which lays hold on Christ.
Martin Luther

'That at the name of Jesus every knee should bow, of those in heaven, and of those on earth, and of those under the earth, and that every tongue should confess that Jesus Christ is Lord' (Philippians 2:9-11).

Read: John 3:22-36

If you want to see men and women exhibiting their pride, power and arrogance listen to or watch meetings of parliament. I enjoy watching 'Question Time' at our Federal Parliament in the hope of finding out what is the state of our nation. I am so often disgusted with the behaviour of our parliamentary members who exhibit rudeness and pride in their speaking. On occasions members are ordered out of sittings because of extreme rudeness, but pride is the order of the day, even with some men and women who profess saving faith.

The only way to humble these people is to vote them out of parliament!

The disciples of John the Baptist were proud of their Rabbi and some were very much offended when they learned that more people were flocking to hear Christ's preaching than they were to John. There had been some discussion among John's disciples about the superiority of John's 'purification' or his baptism. When they heard that Christ's disciples were also baptising repentant sinners they were greatly concerned.

John was a most humble man who acknowledged that Christ was far superior in every respect to himself. He declared that Jesus was, 'The Lamb of God who takes away the sin of the world' (John 1:29). He told his listeners that he was the one God ordained to prepare the way for the coming Messiah. He then said, 'It is he who, coming after me, is preferred before me, whose sandal strap I am not worthy to loose' (John 1:27). John baptized with water, but Christ did so with the Holy Spirit.

The popularity that then surrounded Jesus was exactly as he had expected: 'This was he of whom I said, "He who comes after me is preferred before me, for he was before me"' (John 1:15). In all that John said, he demonstrated a true humility and joy in seeing Jesus' popularity increase. He saw himself as the 'friend' (John 3:29) of the Christ, who had come to save his bride, the church.

The more we learn about our Saviour the more our love for God increases. We have no reason for pride because we are what we are only by the grace of God. Christ demonstrated the greatest act of humility that the world has ever known. Paul wrote of the Lord: 'who, being in the form of God, did not consider it robbery to be equal with God, but made himself of no reputation, taking the form of a bondservant, and coming in the likeness of men. And being found in appearance as a man, he humbled himself and became obedient to the point of death, even the death of the cross' (Philippians 2:6-8).

Today Christ rules this world with supreme power. Before his ascension to heaven he told his disciples, 'All authority has been given to me in heaven and on earth' (Matthew 28:18). Our humility should be clearly visible to others.

THINGS TO DISCUSS WITH YOUR FAMILY

1. Jesus was 'Immanuel'. What does this mean?
2. Why did people flock to hear John the Baptist speak?
3. In John 3:36 we read of the way of salvation. What is it?

Meditation

Give some thought to the majesty and holiness of the Lord Jesus Christ. What effect should this have upon you?

Wise Words

The way to true honour is to be humble.   *J. C. Ryle*

'Now Jacob's well was there. Jesus therefore, being wearied from his journey, sat
thus by the well. It was about the sixth
hour' (John 4:6).

Read: John 4:1-6

Most decisions that you and I make are the result of events that
happen in our life. When we make decisions we should not
act upon impulse, but only after prayer and serious consideration,
using our God given intelligence. I'm sure that if people thought
prayerfully about their selection of a marriage partner there would
be fewer divorces. Young people should also give serious thought
to their careers. Wise advice is given to Christians in Isaiah 28:16,
'Whoever believes will not act hastily.'

Because of events happening in Jerusalem Jesus decided to set
off for Galilee, passing through Samaria. This was the normal route
for travellers returning home after the feast days. The way was usually dusty and tiring to the travellers and when Jesus reached Jacob's
well, near the city of Sychar, his disciples left their weary Lord while
they went to the city to buy some food.

Jesus had decided to leave Jerusalem because of the activities of
the Pharisees. John the Baptist had been arrested and imprisoned
(Matthew 4:12) and the Pharisees and members of the Sanhedrin
were showing an unhealthy interest in Christ. Even at that early time
in his ministry they were suspicious of him and wanted his ministry
ended. However our Redeemer knew that 'his hour had not yet
come'. Much had yet to be done before his sacrificial death. And on
his walk to Galilee there was a Samaritan woman who needed to
hear the gospel.

A tired Jesus rested at Jacob's well, and from this incident we
learn that he was not just God, but true, sinless man. He grew weary, was thirsty and often had no soft bed on which to sleep. He
depended upon others for his food and clothing, and experienced
the temptations of Satan and his demons. He knew what pain and
death were like and experienced the distress of being deserted by his
friends when he needed them most. On the cross he suffered the

punishment of hell owing to his people because of their sins. May all my readers never experience this eternal horror.

Because Christ was truly man and experienced the pains that we experience (except sin), he is the perfect High Priest, just as the writer to the Hebrews wrote: 'For we do not have a High Priest who cannot sympathize with our weaknesses, but was in all points tempted as we are, yet without sin. Let us therefore come boldly to the throne of grace, that we may obtain mercy and find grace to help in time of need' (Hebrews 4:15-16).

Here is your invitation to go to the Redeemer with confidence when you experience joy or pain. Remember to thank Christ for his many blessings, and seek his promised help when you are in need.

THINGS TO DISCUSS WITH YOUR FAMILY

1. Who was Jacob?
2. How do you know that Jesus was a perfect man? Why was he called 'Adam'? Read 1 Corinthians 15:45-49.
3. Joseph's tomb was near Jacob's well. Who was Joseph?

Meditation

Consider how important it is for our Saviour to be a true man, yet without sin.

Wise Words

To say that the Virgin Mary, or any one else, can feel more sympathy for us than Christ, is ignorance no less than blasphemy.   *J. C. Ryle*

'Jesus answered and said to her, "Whoever drinks of this water will thirst again, but whoever drinks of the water that I shall give him will never thirst"' (John 4:13-14).

Read: John 4:7-26

How things have changed! Once people were contented to turn on the tap and drink the water that came from the local dam. Today it is usual to see people getting about with a bottle of water in one hand and a mobile telephone in the other. No longer are many people satisfied with tap water, but believe that bottled spring water is good for their health and better tasting than dam water. It is interesting to note that more people suffer tooth decay today because bottled water contains no flouride! When I was young we drank water that was stored in tanks that caught the rain that fell on the house roof.

Jesus, while he was sitting at Jacob's well, was approached by a Samaritan woman who had come to get a supply of water. Jesus knew who the woman was and all about her life. When she came close to him, he asked her to give him a drink of water. Now Jesus knew the woman's character, but didn't rebuke her for her sins. He wanted to teach her about the new birth. He spoke to her in a friendly manner and we should learn from this to be pleasant when introducing people to the gospel. We should be courteous in what we say and do. The woman wanted water and this was used by Christ as a point of contact.

Jesus had something to give the woman that was more precious than all the treasures of this world — eternal life. The great Augustine once said, 'Our hearts are restless until they find their rest in thee (Christ).' The Samaritan woman didn't have peace of heart and Jesus offered her 'living water'. This was the new birth which would be given when the Holy Spirit entered her heart. Christ's 'living water' gives spiritual peace, love of God and joy because our sins are pardoned. God is at peace with us and we with him. Christ's spiritual water gives eternal life and the desire to tell others of our salvation.

Jesus then awakened the woman's sinful heart by asking her to call her husband. She had been married many times and was then just living with a man. When the Lord showed her that he knew all about her, she realized that she was not speaking to any ordinary person but one who could see into her heart (1 Samuel 16:7). When she admitted her sin the discussion turned to worship and the Messiah.

The Samaritan woman was told two great truths: first, that the One speaking to her was the Christ; and second, the true worship of God didn't depend upon being offered in a special place. She was told: 'God is Spirit, and those who worship him must worship in spirit and truth.' We reverence God with our mind and heart. Do you?

THINGS TO DISCUSS WITH YOUR FAMILY

1. Find Samaria on a map in the back of your Bible.
2. What do you think was the 'living water' that Christ offered to the woman?
3. What does it mean to 'worship in spirit and truth'?

Meditation

Give some thought to Christ's words: 'I who speak to you am he' (John 4:26).

Wise Words

Jesus' approach to the woman at the well showed her that she needed heart surgery, not a bandage! Evangelism is not the peddling of vitamins and health food. It is a trip to the hospital's emergency department for lifesaving care by the best doctor in the world. *Gordon J. Keddie*

'Come and see a Man who told me all things that I ever did. Could this be the Christ?' (John 4:29).

Read: John 4:27-30; 39-42

Usually when something exciting happens to us we want to tell others about it. When I was teaching, often on Monday morning I would tell my class about my Saturday fishing trips, especially describing the big fish I had caught. I can remember when I became a Christian and told so many people about the gracious, saving work of the Lord Jesus. I remember cutting a text out of red reflective tape and sticking it to the back of my car. The text read: 'Believe on the Lord Jesus Christ, and thou shalt be saved, and thy house' (Acts 16:31).

The Samaritan woman had met the Saviour who told her very plainly that he was the Messiah for whom the people longed. Now she had great news for the people who lived in Sychar. She had gone to Jacob's well to get water for the members of her family and was returning with a new heart. She had experienced what Christ had told Nicodemus was essential for salvation — she was 'born again'.

It is true that when a person has been given saving faith their desire is to follow Christ and tell others of his glory and salvation. They want their friends and relatives to also come to saving faith. More than all else Christians wish to see men and women glorifying God.

The Samaritan woman had seen her sins and found that salvation was only possible through faith in the Lord Jesus Christ, who stood before her. She was so excited about her changed heart that she forgot about getting water from the well and quickly went to Sychar to tell the citizens about the Messiah. Getting the water was important, but now she had something more important — she had been awakened to great spiritual truths.

The number one priority in the Christian's life is to glorify and love God totally. Do you remember Christ giving the first and greatest commandment: '"And you shall love the LORD your God with all your heart, with all your soul, with all your mind, and with all your strength." This is the first commandment' (Mark 12:30). Our life's priorities change after the new birth.

The question all Christians should ask themselves is: 'Do I talk to others about my Saviour?' We have such a wonderful story to tell!

Christ stayed with the people of Sychar for two days and preached to them the good news of salvation. Many came to saving faith through the woman's witness, but others were saved when they actually heard Christ call them to repentance and saving faith.

One day Christians will meet that woman of Samaria. What a joy that will be.

THINGS TO DISCUSS WITH YOUR FAMILY

1. Who were the Samaritans?
2. What witnessing to Christ's salvation is being carried out by the members of your congregation?
3. What can you do to make Christ better known in your community?

Meditation

Meditate upon Luke 19:10 — '...the Son of Man has come to seek and to save that which was lost'.

Wise Words

One single soul saved, shall outlive and outweigh all the kingdoms of the world.   *J. C. Ryle*

'Then I said, "Behold, I come; in the scroll of the book it is written of me. I delight to do your will, O my God, and your law is within my heart' (Psalm 40:7-8).

Read: John 4:31-38

I spent twenty-seven years as a school teacher, teaching young people how to live in this modern world. I gave them information that would be useful as they continued their studies and when they finally looked for work. However I had no real idea of what jobs would be available to them when they finished their studies. I also spoke to them of their need to make peace with God through the Lord Jesus Christ. I taught in that era when teachers could speak about Christ. Today things have changed and very few public schools allow educators to mention the name of Christ.

Jesus was a teacher who instructed his disciples about his Heavenly Father and the way of salvation. He also told them something they found difficult to believe — that he would one day die upon a cross where he would pay the penalty for the sins of his people.

When his disciples returned from Sychar they offered Jesus some food to eat, but he told them that his 'food' was to 'do the will of him who sent [him] and to finish his work'. Jesus likened his great saving work to food he would consume. Often we read of Christ's words just before his crucifixion, concerning his obedience to his Father: 'Father, if it is your will, remove this cup from me; nevertheless not my will, but yours, be done' (Luke 22:42).

Jesus told the disciples of a work they had to carry out, and that was the immediate preaching of the gospel. Pointing to the growing crops he told his disciples that the harvest was four months away. He likened the people from Sychar to a ripe harvest ready to be gathered. It is true that all Christians are spiritual sowers, labourers or harvesters. Some Christians are all three, which one we are is in the purpose of God. We read these truths in Psalm 126:5-6 — 'Those who sow in tears shall reap in joy … bringing his sheaves with him.'

The disciples saw many Samaritans won into the kingdom of Christ that day and realized preaching about Christ was to be their lifelong duty. The same is true of Christians — we must bear spiritual fruit — the fruit of the Spirit, doing good and witnessing to the glory of our Saviour. Can you say with the psalmist: 'I delight to do your will, O my God, and your law is within my heart'? (Psalm 40:8). We show our love of Christ by obeying his commands. Those who are called to the ministry of the word are precious people to repentant sinners. We should give them the respect and honour which is due to them.

Jesus obeyed his Father perfectly. On the cross he confidently said, 'It is finished!' (John 19:30). May all Christians take note of Ecclesiastes 9:10 — 'Whatever your hand finds to do, do it with your might...' Look at the needy fields about you and obey Christ's command to spread the 'seed' which is God's Word and that with the prayer that the Holy Spirit will bring salvation.

THINGS TO DISCUSS WITH YOUR FAMILY

1. What is the fruit of the Spirit? Read and discuss Galatians 5:22-23 — 'But the fruit of the Spirit is love, joy, peace, longsuffering, kindness, goodness, faithfulness, gentleness, self-control.'
2. What work is Christ carrying out today in heaven?
3. After the Judgement Day what will Christ do with his kingdom? Discuss 1 Corinthians 15:24.

Meditation

Meditate upon the words of Matthew 10:32-33 — 'Therefore whoever confesses me before men, him I will also confess before my Father who is in heaven. But whoever denies me before men, him I will also deny before my Father who is in heaven.'

We may eat to live, but we must not live to eat.

Gordon J. Keddie

Wise Words

'Now after John was put in prison, Jesus came to Galilee, preaching the gospel of the kingdom of God, and saying, "The time is fulfilled, and the kingdom of God is at hand. Repent, and believe in the gospel"' (Mark 1:14-15).

Read: John 4:43-45

It is often true that our family members and close friends fail to recognize those qualities in us that bring praise from others. Maybe they know us too well and can see our many frailties. In Australia it is commonly said that people are ever ready to 'knock down tall poppies'. When they read in the papers or see on the TV of the fall of some well-known person there is often the feeling of, 'It serves them right.'

In Jerusalem Jesus had carried out some great miracles and cleansed the temple causing people to ask, 'Who is this man who can do such marvellous things?' Many believed in him, but the Pharisees and leaders of the church began to hate him. John the Baptist was in jail and people were scheming to end Christ's ministry.

Christ made his way to Galilee because he knew 'that a prophet [had] no honour in his own country'. Those who grew up with him in Nazareth must have seen his perfection of character and life. Sometimes people don't like these qualities because they lack them themselves.

Why did Christ then go to Galilee? He went there to avoid the popularity that would cause the church leaders to plan his death. Christ had a work to do and as a prophet he had much to teach both his disciples and the populace. The time for his death was still years away.

You and I are called to honour and glorify our Lord and Saviour Jesus Christ. We are also to respect and appreciate those faithful pastors who teach us the truth. The Apostle Paul wrote of them: 'For "whoever calls on the name of the LORD shall be saved." How then shall they call on him in whom they have not believed? And how shall they believe in him of whom they have not heard? And how shall they hear without a preacher? And how shall they preach unless they are sent? As it is written: "How beautiful are the feet of those who preach the gospel of peace, Who bring glad tidings of good things!'" (Romans 10:13-15).

As we read in Hebrews 1:1-2, God spoke to the world through his Son, the greatest prophet of all times. 'God, who at various times and in various ways spoke in time past to the fathers by the prophets, has in these last days spoken to us by his Son...'

Today you and I can read the words of God's Son. God still speaks to us through his Word and we should continue to pray for the Holy Spirit to give us spiritual insight into all we read in the Scriptures.

THINGS TO DISCUSS WITH YOUR FAMILY

1. Why do you think Christ was not honoured in his homeland?
2. How should we treat those put over us by God — parents, school teachers, government and spiritual teachers?
3. How does God speak to you today?

Meditation

Think for a time of the majesty, glory, holiness, mercy, love and grace of God in Christ.

Wise Words

I do not know how a preacher can be much blessed of God who does not feel an agony when he fears that some of his hearers will pass into the next world impenitent and unbelieving. *C. H. Spurgeon*

'Jesus said to him, "Your son lives." And he himself believed, and his whole household' (John 4:53).

Read: John 4:46-54

There is no doubt that the words of Job are true: 'Yet man is born to trouble, as the sparks fly upward' (Job 5:7). We usually think our difficulties and sadnesses are unique, until we meet someone else in a worse situation. I suffer from chronic back pain and take morphine, but my problem is nothing compared to those whose back injury means they are confined to a wheelchair. Many of our difficulties are medical, but praise God we have doctors, nurses and hospitals who can usually give some relief of the symptoms. Often they are able to cure the problem entirely.

Soon after his arrival in Galilee Jesus was approached by a distressed royal official whose son was critically ill. The nobleman knew his only hope was with Christ, the worker of miracles. We see the faith of this man who believed Christ only had to speak to carry out the healing.

Today we have the Scriptures which are frequently used by the Holy Spirit to bring sinners to saving faith in Christ, the Saviour. In his High Priestly prayer Christ prayed for all 'who would believe in [him]' through what was revealed in the Scriptures (John 17:20).

We also learn from this incident that the rich and upper classes of this world are not exempt from troubles. So often people look at these people and think that all is well with them. Yet all humanity suffer trials and tribulations but often it is the poor who can say, 'Amen,' to the words of Ecclesiastes 5:12 — 'The sleep of a labouring man is sweet, whether he eats little or much; but the abundance of the rich will not permit him to sleep.'

We also note from this incident that the nobleman and his household came to believe in Jesus. It is frequently in the hard times, when all else has failed, that sinners turn to Jesus and say with the psalmist, 'It is good for me that I have been afflicted, that I may learn your statutes' (Psalm 119:71).

We should also remember that it is not just the aged who die. Children die before their parents in some situations, and from this we learn the vital importance of teaching our young ones about the Saviour. We must pray for our children and direct them to Christ because we do not know what tomorrow will bring.

Jesus is the greatest spiritual healer of all times. In him alone is to be found forgiveness of sins and the imputed righteousness we need to enter heaven. Jeremiah (8:22) asked the question: 'Is there no balm in Gilead, is there no physician there?' Sinners of all ages must understand that Christ is the healing balm of Gilead. To him they must go to obtain healing for their sin.

Today is the day of salvation, and let us never forget this.

THINGS TO DISCUSS WITH YOUR FAMILY

1. What responsibilities do parents have for their children?
2. What is the meaning of Proverbs 15:16 — 'Better is a little with the fear of the LORD, than great treasure with trouble'?
3. How can everyone prepare for their death?

Meditation

For a moment consider how the nobleman would have felt about the Saviour who had healed his son.

Wise Words

The miraculous is absolutely basic to Christianity.

E. H. Andrews

'And he began to say to them, "Today this Scripture is fulfilled in your hearing"' (Luke 4:21).

Read: Luke 4:16-21

When I was growing up our family were weekly attenders at our local church. I know that my brother and I were not happy with that regular routine as we had many other things that we would rather have been doing. When young we didn't understand much of what was said by the minister and the time dragged. We longed to see the service ended so we could get outside and talk with our friends. Yet the truth was faithfully preached week after week and as we grew older it began to make sense. I was not a Christian then, but I had my Bible and read it frequently. I still have my first copy of the Scriptures. The pages are loose and passages I came to love are well marked.

Jesus went to Nazareth, and as was his custom he attended worship at the local synagogue. Usually it was the Pharisees and scribes who taught the people, but their understanding of the way of salvation was limited and there was little true spiritual blessing.

Jesus was asked to preach, but first he read from Isaiah chapter 61. Then rolling up the scroll he preached a sermon that those present would never forget.

There is a message here for you and me — don't neglect the regular attendance at worship. The writer to the Hebrews rebuked those who were giving up attending worship: 'And let us consider one another in order to stir up love and good works, not forsaking the assembling of ourselves together, as is the manner of some, but exhorting one another, and so much the more as you see the Day approaching' (Hebrews 10:24-25). What a spiritual tragedy it would be for the Holy Spirit to carry out a work of grace on the assembled congregation and you were absent! Worship should be a time to praise God and give thanks for our salvation. It is a time to be edified through the preaching of God's truth as well as encouraging one another in our spiritual walk.

We should prepare for worship by spending time in prayer, asking for spiritual blessings from our Lord. Prayer should be made for the minister that God would give him words that, under the power of the Holy Spirit, will edify everyone present. Do you pray for the unconverted in the congregation? After the service you should talk with each other, especially the young people, and testify to the work of grace in your heart. We should not just be seat warmers!

The Spirit of God was upon Jesus for we read, 'God anointed Jesus of Nazareth with the Holy Spirit and with power' (Acts 10:38). He had a knowledge of the Scriptures beyond that of the scribes and Pharisees, yet had never attended their dead theological schools. Having read the Scriptures Christ made the thrilling announcement of our text, 'Today this Scripture is fulfilled in your hearing.' Christ announced that he was God's Prophet, Priest and King.

THINGS TO DISCUSS WITH YOUR FAMILY

1. What did Christ mean when he claimed he would preach 'deliverance to captives'?
2. Discuss the teaching of today's text.
3. What was a synagogue?

Meditation

Meditate upon Isaiah 61:1-2 quoted by Jesus — 'The Spirit of the LORD GOD is upon me, because the LORD has anointed me to preach good tidings to the poor; he has sent me to heal the brokenhearted, to proclaim liberty to the captives, and the opening of the prison to those who are bound; to proclaim the acceptable year of the LORD.'

Wise Words

Worship comes before service, and the King before the King's business. *Anonymous*

'Then he said, "Assuredly, I say to you, no prophet is accepted in his own country"' (Luke 4:24).

Read: Luke 4:22-32

I have already mentioned that Australians are well known for knocking down 'tall poppies'. Often well-known people are hounded by reporters who do all they can to discover something about the person which results in the downfall of their popularity. Many people then openly say, 'Pride goes before a fall.' Mr Bond, the wealthy businessman, rode the waves of popularity when his sailing boat defeated the USA in the 'America's Cup' sailing race. People cheered his success, but few were concerned when he ended up in jail for illegal business transactions. Instead of sadness there was a sense of satisfaction seeing him disgraced.

Often it is those who know us best who are the most critical. They know us 'warts and all', and delight in talking about the 'warts', usually because they are envious of our Christian character. It is true that so often 'familiarity breeds contempt'.

Jesus had just announced that he was the Christ, and instead of praise the congregation asked, 'Is not this Joseph's son?' They could not point to any flaw in his character or works, but they looked upon him as just a man who from a lowly family had done some miracles. They wanted to see more done in their locality. However, Jesus knew their hearts and reminded them that 'no prophet is accepted in his own country'.

The Saviour went on to tell them of the great works of God done for Gentiles. He spoke of Elijah and God's blessing upon the Gentile widow living in Sidon. He reminded them that in the days of Elisha it was a Gentile, Naaman, who had been healed of leprosy, not an Israelite. The congregation was furious at Christ's preaching. They would not accept the electing love God had for the world of both Jew and Gentile. We should read and meditate often upon the words of John 3:16-17 — 'For God so loved the world that he gave his only begotten Son, that whoever believes in him should not perish but have everlasting life. For God did not send his Son into the world to condemn the world, but that the world through him might be saved.'

The congregation tried to kill Jesus by throwing him over a cliff, but they failed. The people had treated the King of Glory with contempt. What about us? We have so many spiritual blessings. In our homes we all have more than one Bible. Australia still enjoys freedom of worship and freedom to witness to the saving grace of God in Christ. So many despise these precious gifts of God. May we all make use of them to glorify God and display the saving power of Christ to a lost generation. The day may come for us, as it already has in some places where freedom of worship is curtailed, except in the government approved building. Legislation is even envisaged in Australia that will prevent the open preaching of Christ for fear of insulting members of other religions.

The members of the congregation that heard Christ's gracious words missed the opportunity to glorify God for the gift of his Son, the Saviour of sinners, worldwide. May we never make that mistake.

THINGS TO DISCUSS WITH YOUR FAMILY

1. Why do you think the congregation wanted Christ to perform miracles for them, just as he had done elsewhere?
2. Was Christ Joseph's son? Who was he?
3. Find out all you can about Naaman. Read 2 Kings Chapter 5.

Meditation

Meditate upon God's gift of his Son to save sinners throughout the world. Had you lived in the time of the Old Testament in some Gentile land, you would have limited knowledge of the true God. Praise God for the privileges you enjoy today.

Wise Words

A stone in the heart is worse than one in the kidneys.
Thomas Watson

'The people who sat in darkness have seen a great light, and upon those who sat in the region and shadow of death Light has dawned' (Matthew 4:16).

Read: Matthew 4:13-16

The word 'repentance' has special significance to me for two reasons. First, the second small one-teacher school to which I was appointed was 'Repentance Creek'. The school population numbered just 28 children spread over all primary grades. Second, it was the place where I came to a saving knowledge of Christ.

Jesus had commenced his preaching ministry and we read in Matthew 4:17 the summary of his sermons — 'Repent for the kingdom of God is at hand.' What then is repentance?

No one can truly repent and turn from their sins until they have a change of heart — they must be born again which is the sovereign work of God's Holy Spirit. In 2 Corinthians 7:10 the Apostle Paul wrote, 'For godly sorrow produces repentance leading to salvation, not to be regretted; but the sorrow of the world produces death.' Many people regret something they have done and make an effort not to make the same mistake a second time. A child caught taking a biscuit without permission may be truly sorry they were caught, but possibly will do the same the next day.

Godly repentance, which leads to salvation has several important elements: first, there is a true, godly sorrow for sin; second, there is sincere confession to God of those sins; third, the repentant sinner turns away from the life of sin; fourth, there is a heartfelt hatred of sin and love of God's law; and finally there is restitution if that is possible.

This was the message that Christ, the 'light of the world' preached to the people living in the region about Capernaum. He described these people as a 'people who sat in darkness'. Many were Gentiles who served pagan gods, and they, with their Jewish neighbours, were to hear of the grace, love and mercy of God whose Son would die a sacrificial death bearing his people's sins. Spiritual light had dawned on those people — a 'Light' which is perfectly holy and gives great spiritual joy to all who truly repent and trust their eternal security to Christ.

Despite the Lord's presence very few people believed in his claims to be the Messiah who would save all who came to him in repentance. The kingdom of God was close to them all, but few entered. Later Christ spoke of the judgement of God that would fall upon the people of the region. We read his words recorded in Matthew 11:23: 'And you, Capernaum, who are exalted to heaven, will be brought down to Hades; for if the mighty works which were done in you had been done in Sodom, it would have remained until this day.'

Have you repented of your sins?

THINGS TO DISCUSS WITH YOUR FAMILY

1. What is the 'kingdom of God'?
2. Find Capernaum on a map.
3. What does the Apostle John mean by the expression, 'God is light and in him is no darkness at all'? (1 John 1:5).

Meditation

Think about the great blessings the people of Capernaum could have received from God if only they had repented and believed the gospel. Thank God for your blessings, spiritual and material.

Wise Words

Our repentance needs to be repented of, and our tears washed in the blood of Christ.   *George Whitefield*

'And Jesus said to Simon, "Do not be
afraid. From now on you will catch
men"' (Luke 5:10).

Read: Luke 5:1-11

In my younger days I spent a lot of time fishing, particularly out
at sea. There is no doubt that the big fish are to be found in the
ocean in deeper water than found in rivers and lakes. Still, there
were times when I came home with an empty bag. In our reading
we notice that Simon and others had been fishing all night and had
caught nothing. They were on the shore, busy cleaning their nets
when they saw Christ surrounded by 'multitudes' of people wanting
to see miracles and hear what he had to say.

Because of the crowds, Jesus had Peter launch his boat and an-
chor it out from the land. He used the boat as his pulpit from which
to preach. Many faithful ministers have used unusual pulpits when
church buildings were closed to them. Whitefield and the Wesley
brothers preached from paddocks, horseback, from carriages, in the
fields, the streets and family homes. We should be ready to take every
opportunity to speak of Christ and the gospel of salvation — in the
bus, train, car, at work, school, and play — anywhere there is someone who is ready to listen to the good news we have experienced
in Christ.

When Christ ordered Simon to try again for fish in the deep
water, the fishermen knew that was foolish. As experienced fishermen they knew that during daytime it was a waste of time to fish
in the deep water, but as their Master had given the command they
obeyed. May this be said of all of us. Jesus said, 'If you love me, keep
my commandments' (John 14:15). Simon's obedience was an act of
faith and with his workers he caught such a haul of fish that the nets
almost broke and the boats almost sank.

Our Lord knew where the fish were and as the One who created all things, directed the fish to the spot where Simon was to
lower his nets. As true man, Christ's knowledge and power was limited, but at times he exercised his divine powers of omnipotence and
omniscience. We should always remember that our Saviour is both
God and man in one Person. Paul wrote of Christ: 'For in him dwells
all the fullness of the Godhead bodily' (Colossians 2:9).

For a moment Simon glimpsed the glory, majesty, holiness and kingly powers of his Lord and falling before Christ who was sitting in the boat, cried out, 'Depart from me, for I am a sinful man, O Lord!'

It is true that the closer we are to our holy, merciful Saviour, the more we become aware of our sins and the debt of gratitude we owe our Redeemer.

Christ then told Simon of the great work that lay before him and the other disciples — they would become fishermen of sinners, and by preaching the gospel win people into the kingdom of God. Simon, Nathaniel, John and James packed up their fishing equipment and followed Christ. If needed we must be ready to sacrifice everything, even life itself, to follow the Saviour.

THINGS TO DISCUSS WITH YOUR FAMILY

1. What is the meaning of 'omniscience'?
2. Why did Simon become so conscious of his sinful nature?
3. What do your sins teach you?

Meditation

Meditate upon Proverbs 9:10 — 'The fear of the LORD is the beginning of wisdom, and the knowledge of the Holy One is understanding.'

Wise Words

If ever the Divine appeared on earth, it was in the Person of Christ.   *Johannes Von Goethe*

'So they were all amazed and spoke among themselves, saying, "What a word this is! For with authority and power he commands the unclean spirits, and they come out"' (Luke 4:36).

Read: Luke 4:31-37

We live in a world where so few know much about the Lord Jesus Christ. The Bible stories we grew up with are today not known by the majority of young people. Few know the story of Daniel in the lions' den or the reason for the death of Christ upon the cross. Easter and Christmas are just words that describe enjoyable holidays, chocolates and presents. Generally the voice of the church and Christians are not heard because we keep quiet.

Jesus was the greatest preacher the world has known. He had the truth to expound which he did with authority. He was filled with the Holy Spirit and in the power of God called people to repentance and faith. The disciples were pupils in the Redeemer's school and they had much to learn.

In today's reading we again see the almighty power of our Saviour. By just speaking he was able to drive demons from people who were possessed by the evil spirits. Here and elsewhere we learn something of the character of Satan and his demon followers. They are intelligent and know the Scriptures. In the wilderness temptations Satan was able to accurately quote passages of the Old Testament. They know the truth about God, but their knowledge is not a saving knowledge. In his epistle James warned those who thought a knowledge of God was sufficient for salvation: 'You believe that there is one God. You do well. Even the demons believe — and tremble!' (James 2:19).

In our reading we learn of a demon who knew who it was that ordered him out of a man. He said, 'Let us alone! What have we to do with you, Jesus of Nazareth? Did you come to destroy us? I know who you are — the Holy One of God!' The title 'Holy One' had been used by David in Psalm 16:10 where he wrote of Christ. The demons know the teaching of the Scriptures.

What about Christians today? Do we know the Scriptures as we should? Do you read your Bible daily and spend time praying with your family? Do you have time set aside when you praise your Redeemer and read his word in a systematic way? The Bible talks about 'justification'. This is the most fundamental teaching concerning salvation, which all Christians should understand. Do you?

Let every Christian spend time reading and meditating upon the word of God and commit to memory the truths of Scripture.

Again we have seen the almighty power of our Saviour. There is no doubt that the healings became well known in the region where Jesus walked. Our Lord has almighty power because he is God.

THINGS TO DISCUSS
WITH YOUR FAMILY

1. Who is Satan?
2. How was it that Christ had power over the de-
    mons?
3. Should Christians fear Satan and his demons?
    Why? Read 1 Peter 5:8 — 'Be sober, be vigilant;
    because your adversary the devil walks about like
    a roaring lion, seeking whom he may devour.'

Meditation

Meditate upon the almighty power exercised by Christ
both in heaven and when on this earth.

Wise Words

When Satan fell he may have lost his innocence but he
did not lose his intelligence. *Trevor Knight*

'He himself took our infirmities and bore our sicknesses' (Matthew 8:17).

Read: Luke 4:38-41

In our reading we find that Simon (Peter), who had invited Jesus to his home, was married. We today live in a world where marriage is ignored by so many and frequently treated with contempt. Men and women just 'live together' without having made any public declaration of their love for one another or making their relationship legal in the eyes of the law. Now there is a push for legislators to recognize 'same sex marriages'. How we must stand firm for the truth of the Scriptures. Divorce is rife and sadly many who take a vow 'for better or worse' turn away from what they have promised.

Peter's mother-in-law was very ill with a high fever. At once our Redeemer, having been asked to heal her, did so by speaking. This was just another mighty act of Christ in his healing ministry. Our Saviour is most compassionate and in his saving work carried our sins to the cross and there suffered the hell deserved by his people. He suffered and because of his first-hand knowledge of the effects of sin, including death, displays mercy time and again to those who suffer illness.

He saw the terrible effects of sin when he stood before the tomb in which the body of his dear friend Lazarus had been placed. Surrounded by mourners we read John's words: 'Jesus wept' (John 11:35). This is the shortest verse in the Bible! Our hearts should be filled with joy because we have such a merciful Lord.

Many others were brought to Jesus while he was in Simon's home and he healed them all. He cast out demons from those who were demon-possessed which again shows us that Satan and his evil followers were a defeated foe. The demons knew who it was who had such power over them as many cried out, 'You are the Christ, the Son of God!' Jesus ordered them to refrain from saying who he was.

We should be aware of those people and sects who look upon marriage as being less holy than remaining single. Paul wrote, 'Now the Spirit expressly says that in latter times some will depart from the faith, giving heed to deceiving spirits and doctrines of demons, speaking lies in hypocrisy, having their own conscience seared with a hot iron, forbidding to marry, and commanding to abstain from foods which God created to be received with thanksgiving by those who believe and know the truth' (1 Timothy 4:1-3).

The Church of Rome, which forbids its priests to marry, should recognize that Peter, the person they claim was their first pope, was married and took his wife with him on his preaching journeys (1 Corinthians 9:5). In Hebrews 13:4 we read, 'Marriage is honourable in all, and the bed undefiled.' Jesus put his seal of approval on marriage when he attended the wedding ceremony at Cana. Don't be led astray by false teaching — pray for discernment.

THINGS TO DISCUSS WITH YOUR FAMILY

1. What responsibilities do members of a family have? Read Ephesians 5:22 – 6:4.
2. Why did Christ order the demons to refrain from calling out who he was?
3. What are demons?

Meditation

Consider the spiritual blessings that can be enjoyed in a Christian marriage. Pray for God's grace to be a godly family member.

Wise Words

As God by creation made two of one, so again by marriage he made one of two.   *Thomas Adams*

 'Let us go into the next towns, that I may preach there also, because for this purpose I have come forth' (Mark 1:38).

Read: Luke 4:38-41

I have a friend who spends at least an hour in private, personal devotions every day after he gets out of bed. In order to prevent interruptions from the telephone and noise generally, he made himself a 'prayer closet' under his house. It's a small room with a light and on the wall he has maps showing him where those missionaries he prays for are serving the Lord. His prayer life puts me to shame. God has blessed him with the gift of prayer.

Our Lord was a man of prayer and we frequently read of him getting away by himself and there in solitude praying to his Heavenly Father. He was often up before the break of day to commune with his Heavenly Father. His prayers show us that he trusted his Heavenly Father implicitly and always bowed before his will. His prayers were times of thanksgiving and glorification.

Take time to read the following short passages of Scripture that teach us about the Lord's prayer life:

a.   Christ prayed during his baptism, Luke 3:21.
b.   Prayed before choosing his disciples, Luke 6:12.
c.   In the Garden of Gethsemane Jesus submitted to God's will, Mark 14:32.
d.   The Lord prayed at the time of his transfiguration, Luke 9:29.
e.   Jesus wept and prayed at the tomb of Lazarus, John 11:41.
f.   Our Saviour prayed while in agony on the cross, Luke 23:34.

We are urged to spend time in prayer and Jesus gave his disciples what is called 'The Lord's Prayer' (Matthew 6:9-13) which is better called 'The Disciples' Prayer' because it was never prayed by our Redeemer.

Jesus also expressly announced the important purpose of his incarnation — to preach the gospel concerning sin and the only way of salvation. In Luke 4:43 it is recorded that Christ also preached 'the kingdom of God'. The people who heard Jesus should have realized that he was the prophet prophesied by Moses (Deuteronomy 18:15).

For three and a half years he would preach the gospel — delivering captives from the dominion of sin; and giving spiritual light to the spiritually blind. This is what your minister does week after week. You should always thank God for his work, and that of other faithful preachers. Pray for your pastor's family; support your minister in every way you can (including making sure he is paid well), and always remember that preaching is central in public worship. It is more important than the sacraments of baptism and the Lord's supper.

Think hard about Paul's words: 'How beautiful are the feet of those who preach the gospel of peace, who bring glad tidings of good things!' (Romans 10:15).

THINGS TO DISCUSS WITH YOUR FAMILY

1. If you don't have regular family and personal devotions start now.
2. Learn by heart 'The Lord's Prayer'.
3. What is the 'kingdom of God' and how do sinners gain entrance?
4. How can you assist your minister and all who preach the gospel in your land and overseas?

Meditation

Consider the sacrifices your pastor has made to care for your congregation. Thank God for him and pray for God's blessing to be upon him and his service for the Lord.

Wise Words

To be prayerless is to be Christless, Godless, and in the high road to destruction.   *J. C. Ryle*

'Then a leper came to him, imploring him, kneeling down to him and saying to him, "If you are willing, you can make me clean"' (Mark 1:40).

Read: Mark 1:40-45

Leprosy is a cursed disease as it eats away the nerves of the body, destroying feeling. Then when particularly the feet or hands are hurt, sores form. Without treatment the festering sores eat away the flesh causing problems with walking and using the hands.

In Australia there are very few cases of this terrible disease. Nevertheless many Christians are involved in leprosy societies that raise money for hospitals, medical personnel and people working to make the life of lepers easier. Some ladies in our congregation spend a lot of time knitting cotton bandages for use by lepers.

In the Old Testament days leprosy was incurable and Israel's law demanded that lepers lived an isolated life away from their families and friends: 'Now the leper on whom the sore is, his clothes shall be torn and his head bare; and he shall cover his moustache, and cry, "Unclean! Unclean!" He shall be unclean. All the days he has the sore he shall be unclean. He is unclean, and he shall dwell alone; his dwelling shall be outside the camp' (Leviticus 13:45-46).

The leper in our reading was convinced that Christ could heal him of his terrible disease and made his way to the great Healer. Our text tells us what he did and said. Then we read words that showed the mercy and compassion that filled the heart of our Saviour. He reached down, touched the person who was 'unclean' and said, 'I am willing; be cleansed.' Instantly the man was completely healed! His skin was again soft, firm and white.

Our Lord came into this world of sin and distress to deal with sin and its consequences. In this and other examples of Christ's healings we see the loving compassion of our Redeemer. What a wonderful and majestic Saviour Christ is. Here and elsewhere we see examples of his almighty power.

From this incident we should all learn that we are to be like the Lord. We must show compassion for those in need — even the unlovely and those who are looked upon as 'unclean' by the citizens of this world. Our hearts must love God and our fellow man. Not only must we wish the best for the down and out person, but we must give whatever help we can. The Apostle Paul wrote: 'Therefore, as we have opportunity, let us do good to all, especially to those who are of the household of faith' (Galatians 6:10).

Jesus then told the healed leper to refrain from telling people how he had been made well. Instead he was to go to the priests in Jerusalem and carry out the instructions of Moses so that he could once again become a member of the community and live with his family. This involved a sacrifice and the formal declaration by the priest, after careful physical examination, that the leper was cleansed (Leviticus 14:1-7). Jesus obeyed God's law perfectly so that his people might have his righteousness put to their account. What a glorious Saviour we have!

THINGS TO DISCUSS WITH YOUR FAMILY

1. Discuss the problems faced by the leper when he found he had leprosy.
2. Why did Jesus heal people?
3. What responsibility do we have to those who are ill?

Meditation

Sin is like leprosy in that it makes us unclean. Give thanks to God for providing a way of spiritual cleansing.

Wise Words

Jesus Christ is not only the Son of God mighty to save, but the Son of man able to feel.   *J. C. Ryle*

'...but that you may know that the Son of man has power on earth to forgive sins...' (Mark 2:10).

Read: Mark 2:1-12

Most of us have many friends, but very few that we can call 'bosom' pals. My closest friend is my wife, Val. She knows me very well, tolerates my peculiarities and faults and still loves me. My children also fall into this group. I have many people I call friends, but during my entire life have only had several people who were 'soul' mates.

Jesus was in Capernaum again. The house in which he was staying was filled with friends, disciples and others, including some scribes, who were there to see the show. It is sad but people can hear the gospel preached week after week and still turn their backs upon the Saviour. The Apostle Paul wrote of the word he preached: 'To the one we are the aroma of death to death, and to the other the aroma of life to life' (2 Corinthians 2:16). In Proverbs 28:14 we read of the danger of a hardened heart: 'Happy is the man who is always reverent, but he who hardens his heart will fall into calamity.' It is the 'new birth' that removes the heart of stone and replaces it with a heart of flesh (Ezekiel 36:26).

Our reading is about a sick man whose friends were determined to somehow get him to Jesus so that he might be healed. When Jesus saw the faith of the sick man he said, 'Son, your sins are forgiven you.' Why did he say this? It was because the man saw his sins and wanted to be at peace with God. He had heard the gospel before and had repented. The words he first heard from Christ gave him peace of heart — his sins had been forgiven.

Instead of great rejoicing from the scribes, they were critical of the Lord's statement. To them Jesus was just a man who had no authority to forgive anyone. They knew that forgiveness was the prerogative of God alone. They objected to Christ's compassion. They were legalists and demanded that people simply obey both the law of God and all the human laws that had been made. Jesus knew what was going on in their minds and asked what was easier to say, '"Your sins are forgiven you," or, "Arise, take up your bed and walk"?'

The scribes were to find that Christ's miracle was more difficult to their understanding as anyone could say that sins were forgiven. Now they would discover that Jesus, by healing the sick man, had the power and right to forgive sins. After all he was 'the Son of Man' — the Messiah. And remember that when God forgives our sins they are gone for ever. We read in Psalm 103:12: 'As far as the east is from the west, so far has he removed our transgressions from us.'

I'm sure that the sick man would often thank God for his paralysis as that sickness was used to draw him to Christ and salvation.

Let us be like the friends of the sick man and 'turn away from evil and do good' (1 Peter 3:11). And praise God for the hard times that come our way, for that is God calling us to walk closer to himself. It is in the good times that we so often drift away from our Lord to serve self.

THINGS TO DISCUSS WITH YOUR FAMILY

1. Who were the scribes?
2. What do you think about the sick man's friends?
3. Make a list of ways you can serve God by doing 'good'.

Meditation

What does it mean to you to know that God does forgive sins because of what Christ has done? If you are a Christian thank God for your salvation.

Wise Words

It is shallow nonsense to say God forgives us because he is love. The only ground upon which God can forgive us is the cross. *Oswald Chambers*

'When Jesus heard it, he said to them, "Those who are well have no need of a physician, but those who are sick. I did not come to call the righteous, but sinners, to repentance"' (Mark 2:17).

Read: Mark 2:13-17

Most people find taxation time unpleasant. It is that time of the year when we carefully work out the amount of tax we must pay the government out of our wages. This is to be done with great care and accuracy for we read God's command: 'Render therefore to all their due: taxes to whom taxes are due, customs to whom customs, fear to whom fear, honour to whom honour' (Romans 13:7).

Jesus was to add another disciple to his band and this time he called 'Levi' who was one of the hated tax collectors. Levi is best known by his name 'Matthew' which means 'Gift of Jehovah'. He worked for the Romans, collecting taxes from merchants who travelled the busy highway from Syria to Egypt. Many tax collectors overcharged and became wealthy men. The Jews hated them for this form of theft, and as members of God's covenant people believed they should not have agreed to work for their Gentile overlords.

Seeing Matthew at work and knowing that he was to become a disciple we read that Jesus 'called' him. Possibly Matthew knew well what Christ was teaching and was aware of his own sinful character. Yet Christ came at a time when he wasn't seeking the Lord.

Now if you are a Christian rejoice because at some point in your life the Holy Spirit 'called' you to follow Jesus. The *Shorter Catechism*, Question 31, defines an effectual call in the following words: 'Effectual calling is the work of God's Spirit, whereby, convincing us of our sin and misery, enlightening our minds in the knowledge of Christ, and renewing our wills, does persuade and enable us to embrace Jesus Christ, freely offered to us in the gospel.' Calling is the first step in God's plan that ends in glorification (Romans 8:29-30) — life for ever with Jesus.

Immediately after Matthew was called by Jesus, he followed his Saviour. He then gave a great feast for Christ and his disciples which gave the scribes and Pharisees present the opportunity to complain to the disciples: 'How is it that he eats and drinks with tax collectors and sinners?' Matthew is put into a category with sinners generally, but Jesus, when he heard their criticisms, replied that it was tax collectors and sinners who needed spiritual healing, not self-righteous scribes and Pharisees as they were. Jesus was there to save sinners, the spiritually lost, those burdened with their sins, those who walked in spiritual darkness.

Our terrible spiritual disease is sin and it is Christ, God's spiritual physician, who can give healing. The first step to recovery is repentance and asking for forgiveness, and that through the Saviour. Christ is a tender Redeemer who saves sinners. The self-righteous believe they have no need of spiritual healing as they can be their own doctors. Their end is hell.

We should mix with unsaved sinners, not to copy their sinful ways, but to direct them to the physician of spiritually sick souls, for he has the much needed balm of Gilead.

THINGS TO DISCUSS WITH YOUR FAMILY

1. Jesus spoke of 'tax collectors' (publicans). What was their work?
2. What means does God use to 'call' people to Christ?
3. Try and work out the steps in God's dealing with those he saves. Read Romans 8:28-30.

Meditation

Meditate upon your spiritual state now. Do you need to thank God for calling you to faith in Christ or must you pray for the Holy Spirit to awaken you to your spiritual sickness?

Happy are they who have found out their souls' disease! Let them know that Christ is the very Physician they require, and let them apply to him without delay.

J. C. Ryle

Wise Words

'These things I have spoken to you, that in me you may have peace. In the world you will have tribulation; but be of good cheer, I have overcome the world' (John 16:33).

Read: Mark 2:18-22

Often when I visit my doctor he asks me to get on the scales, after which he tells me I need to lose weight. His comment is that my weight problem is due to what goes into my mouth and that I should give up eating chocolate and other sweet foods. Sometimes I diet and get rid of some of the fat, but it doesn't always last.

It is hard to find an explicit command in the Old Testament that God's people should fast. It is possible that fasting was carried out on the Day of Atonement. As we read the Old Testament we find that there were times when people fasted, usually during times of trouble when time was devoted to prayer. In Christ's day the Pharisees made a big thing of fasting. In a story Jesus told he had the Pharisee say, 'I fast twice a week' (Luke 18:12). Of course the Pharisees made sure they had downcast faces to let others know they were going without food as a spiritual exercise. Christ didn't condemn the practice but laid down some plain rules for those who fasted. In the Sermon on the Mount he said, 'Moreover, when you fast, do not be like the hypocrites, with a sad countenance. For they disfigure their faces that they may appear to men to be fasting. Assuredly, I say to you, they have their reward. But you, when you fast, anoint your head and wash your face, so that you do not appear to men to be fasting, but to your Father who is in the secret place; and your Father who sees in secret will reward you openly' (Matthew 6:16-18).

John's disciples questioned why Christ's disciples didn't fast. His reply indicated that his disciples didn't need to do so — they had no reason to do so as Christ, the Bridegroom of the church, was with them and preaching the good news of God's kingdom. John's disciples had reason to fast as their teacher was either locked up in jail or had been put to death.

Jesus was teaching his disciples that Old Testament ways of worship were coming to an end. With his saving work on the cross and his resurrection there was no reason for sadness, but joy. Christ had overcome the world, his people had spiritual peace and could rejoice. The reason for fasting was finished. To introduce this into New Testament worship was like patching old clothing with new cloth — the new tears away from the old; or putting new wine in old leather wineskins bursts the 'bottle' as the wine ferments.

In Galatia the Jews wanted to unite obedience to God's law, especially circumcision with saving faith, believing both were necessary for entrance into the Lord's kingdom, but Paul said that this was not to be! Today some churches mingle ritual with the gospel. With the destruction of the temple Israel's ritualistic way of worship was ended.

We have no command to fast, but may do so if we want to devote time to prayer without the need to cook and eat meals. We have every reason to praise God for all that Christ has done for us.

THINGS TO DISCUSS WITH YOUR FAMILY

1. What was Jesus teaching in Matthew 6:16-18?
2. Can you think of any time you could have a fast for spiritual reasons? Discuss those times.
3. What was Jesus teaching in Mark 2:22?

Meditation

Meditate upon John 4:24 — 'God is Spirit, and those who worship him must worship in spirit and truth.'

Wise Words

Nothing prepares the heart more for the worship of the Lord than to contemplate his beauty and perfection.
Frank Gabelein

'Afterward Jesus found him in the temple, and said to him, "See, you have been made well. Sin no more, lest a worse thing come upon you"' (John 5:14).

Read: John 5:1-15

We need to thank God for giving us scientists, doctors and nurses who care for the sick. In the world today great discoveries are being made that help control disease and sickness. I take morphine daily for pain control and it is most effective. I thank God for this great drug. Nevertheless there is a side effect that I experience — it makes me itch! At home I have a back scratcher ready to rub those hard to reach places.

Sickness is the result of sin and death is the last enemy to be destroyed (1 Corinthians 15:26). All of the saints can look forward to the new heavens and earth as there 'God will wipe away every tear from their eyes; there shall be no more death, nor sorrow, nor crying. There shall be no more pain, for the former things have passed away' (Revelation 21:4).

While in Jerusalem for one of the feast days requiring the presence of all male members of the nation Jesus saw a man who had been ill for thirty-eight years. The circumstances are strange, but the man had no hope of being healed as he didn't have anyone to help him into the pool when the angel stirred the water.

Once again we read of the compassion of our Saviour. He didn't need to help the man into the water, but spoke to him telling him to stand up, roll up his mattress and walk. When the man obeyed the Lord's prescription he was instantly and completely healed. And we are told that it was the Sabbath day. Our God is a God of mercy in dealing with sinners. Micah wrote of Jehovah: '...he delights in mercy. He will again have compassion on us, and will subdue our iniquities. [He] will cast all our sins into the depths of the sea' (Micah 7:18-19).

The man had no idea who had healed him and later when Jesus met him he was told, 'Sin no more, lest a worse thing come upon you.' Apparently the man's illness was the result of a particular sin and he was warned by the Lord of his danger. This is true of some sins today. The drunk who smashes his car into a post and is seriously injured can blame the alcohol. Some serious sexual diseases are the result of promiscuity. In 1 Corinthians 11:30 we read that many in the Corinthian congregation were ill and some had died because of their abuse of the Lord's Supper. They had been judged by God for their sin. But not all sickness is due to a particular sin. On one occasion the disciples asked the Lord about a blind man: 'Rabbi, who sinned, this man or his parents, that he was born blind?' We should note Christ's reply before we blame sick people for committing some particular sin — 'Neither this man nor his parents sinned, but that the works of God should be revealed in him' (John 9:2-3).

Micah's words describe what the Lord requires of us: 'And what does the LORD require of you but to do justly, to love mercy, and to walk humbly with your God?' (Micah 6:8).

THINGS TO DISCUSS WITH YOUR FAMILY

1. Did the man break God's law by carrying his bed on the Sabbath? Read Jeremiah 17:21.
2. How should Christians spend the Lord's Day?
3. The healed man was warned that sin could cause worse problems than the illness he had. What could be worse? Read Matthew 5:29.

Meditation

Give thanks to God for those who help the sick and pray for opportunities to give help to people in need.

Wise Words

All disease is primarily the result of sin, but not always directly so. *Anonymous*

'But Jesus answered them, "My Father has been working until now, and I have been working"' (John 5:17).

Read: John 5:16-18

The Lord's Day has always been a special day in my life, even before I became a Christian. As a youngster I was not allowed to play sport on Sundays as it was to be a day of rest and worship. We milked the cows, but there was no other work done on the farm, except when it was a necessity such as in times of flood. The cows had to be milked twice a day no matter what day of the week it was. In those days most people respected the Lord's Day whether they were Christians or not. On Sunday almost everyone on the surrounding farms attended church. Today it is different!

Jesus faced great opposition from the church leaders for two basic reasons. It was claimed that he failed to keep the Sabbath law. The same people considered that his claim to be God by what he preached was blasphemous.

The fourth commandment reads: 'Remember the Sabbath day, to keep it holy. Six days you shall labour and do all your work, but the seventh day is the Sabbath of the Lord your God. In it you shall do no work' (Exodus 20:8-10). Obviously the Sabbath which was a creation ordinance (Genesis 2:1-3) was not the day for ordinary work. Later the seventh day rest became associated with redemption (Deuteronomy 5:15).

The Jews willingly rescued an animal that had fallen into a pit on the Lord's Day (Luke 14:5). Nor did they object when Christ reminded them they fed and gave food to their animals on the Sabbath day (Luke 13:15). As it was right to do good and show mercy to animals on the seventh day, why should they accuse him of sin when he healed a sick human made in God's image?

Jesus reminded his hearers that God's rest on the seventh day was not one of inactivity, as he controlled and governed the universe every day. If he did not, the world would be chaotic. By claiming that God was his Father and he worked in unison with God, the

Jews rightly deduced that Christ was claiming equality with his Father. This was a claim to be God and would not be tolerated by his hearers.

The Scriptures plainly teach that Christ is God and man in one Person. In 1 Timothy 3:16 we read: 'And without controversy great is the mystery of godliness: God was manifested in the flesh...' The Apostle Paul wrote of Jesus: 'For in him dwells all the fullness of the Godhead bodily...' (Colossians 2:9).

So great was their hatred of Jesus, that persecution became more rife and plans were being made to have him killed. Jesus' claim to be God demands one of two responses — either belief or rejection. The same is true today.

THINGS TO DISCUSS WITH YOUR FAMILY

1. Why does the church gather for worship on the Lord's Day?
2. List some works of mercy that can be done on the Lord's Day.
3. Prove that Jesus is God. Read John 1:1-2 and Hebrews 1:8.

Meditation

Meditate upon the sanctity of the Lord's Day as a 're-demption ordinance' and not a creation ordinance as was the Jewish Sabbath.

Wise Words

Remember, Christ was not a deified man, neither was he a humanised God. He was perfectly God and at the same time perfectly man. *C. H. Spurgeon*

'…all should honour the Son just as they honour the Father. He who does not honour the Son does not honour the Father who sent him' (John 5:23).

Read: John 5:19-23

When I come to portions of the Bible that I find difficult to comprehend I sit and think and then make use of my commentaries. Too many Christians complain that the Scriptures are too difficult to understand and they neglect important sections that teach great truths. The passage you read today is one such section.

Ryle wrote of our reading: 'These verses begin one of the most deep and solemn passages in the gospels. They show us the Lord Jesus asserting his own divine nature, his unity with God the Father, and the high dignity of his office.'[1] What then is Jesus teaching about himself?

First, he is one with his Heavenly Father. Whatever the Father does, so also does the Son. Jesus is claiming to be of the same essence as God which means equality with God. As God is omnipotent, omniscient and omnipresent, so also is Christ, God's Son.

As God gives life to the dead so also does the Son. In creation Christ gave life, and in redemption he gives spiritual life without which no one would be saved. We are told of Christ that 'In him was life, and the life was the light of men' (John 1:4). It is our Saviour who has 'the keys of Hades and Death' (Revelation 1:18). Elsewhere we are told that it is the Spirit who gives life (2 Corinthians 3:6). Paul also wrote 'of God who gives life to all things' (1 Timothy 6:13). The Jews rightly deduced that Christ was claiming to be God.

Second, we read that 'the Father loves the Son'. In the unity of the Godhead there is a holy affection that is beyond our comprehension, but again that special love places Jesus in a position of honour and glory.

Third, the Father has given the Son the 'duties' of God. God raises the dead, but this is the work of the Redeemer also in conjunction with the Holy Spirit. The spiritually dead are 'born again' by the Holy Spirit in conjunction with the Son. On the day of

Christ's second coming he will raise the dead. This is the work of God who said, 'Then you shall know that I am the LORD, when I have opened your graves, O my people, and brought you up from your graves' (Ezekiel 37:13).

Fourth, Christ is judge of mankind. Writing to the Romans (2:16) Paul said, 'God will judge the secrets of men by Jesus Christ.' In Athens Paul said, 'God commands all men everywhere to repent, because he has appointed a day on which he will judge the world in righteousness by the Man whom he has ordained' (Acts 17:30-31). As the Mediator between God and man, and the One who saved sinners he is the perfect judge before whom all will one day stand.

Because of Christ's divine glory we are to give him the honour due to his holy name. Failure to honour God's Son is to dishonour his Heavenly Father. One great work of the Holy Spirit is to glorify Christ (John 16:14), and God is pleased when his Son is glorified. The majority of the Jews failed to do this. The same is true today. May we bring glory to our Redeemer in everything we say and do.

THINGS TO DISCUSS WITH YOUR FAMILY

1. Discuss Isaiah 6:1-4 in the light of John 12:37-41.
2. Discuss Colossians 2:9 — 'For in him [Jesus] dwells all the fullness of the Godhead bodily.'
3. How can we honour Christ?

Meditation

Give some thought to the glory of Jesus Christ, our Saviour — the Son of God and the Son of man in one Person.

Wise Words

Such knowledge is too wonderful for me; it is too high, I cannot attain it. *King David*

1. Ryle, J. C., *Short Expository Readings of the Gospel of St John*, William Hunt and Co., London, 1884, p.79.

April

'Most assuredly, I say to you, he who hears my word and believes in him who sent me has everlasting life, and shall not come into judgement, but has passed from death into life' (John 5:24).

Read: John 5:24-30

I sometimes sit and think about questions that are beyond my understanding. Try thinking about the eternity of God's existence. If you deny that God is eternal try meditating upon the other alternative — that dead matter is eternal and somehow has evolved into the universe about us. After a time the mind becomes confused.

Our reading opens with Jesus telling his hearers if only they would believe in the reality of the God who sent him into the world, and the gospel he preached they would be blessed with eternal life. Eternal life does not just speak of an endless existence, but also the wonderful quality of that existence. It is worth meditating on the wonder of Paradise.

Sinners must hear and believe. In John 10:27-30, Christ describing his followers as sheep said, 'My sheep hear my voice, and I know them, and they follow me. And I give them eternal life, and they shall never perish; neither shall anyone snatch them out of my hand. My Father, who has given them to me, is greater than all; and no one is able to snatch them out of my Father's hand. I and my Father are one.' The way of salvation is to hear the gospel, believe all things concerning Christ and then to follow him faithfully.

In our reading Christ plainly declares that just as his Heavenly Father has life in himself, so also has the Son, and he thus can give life to the spiritually dead. What almighty power is exercised by our Saviour in the salvation of sinners! Christ's servants are made spiritually alive by the work of the Holy Spirit bringing about the new birth. Paul wrote that 'having been justified by faith, we have peace with God through our Lord Jesus Christ...' (Romans 5:1). Later he wrote: 'There is therefore now no condemnation to those who are in Christ Jesus, who do not walk according to the flesh, but according to the Spirit' (Romans 8:1).

Christ also has the power to raise the dead which he will do when he comes a second time to gather together the saints and commence the great judgement. Faith in Christ is the only way to prepare for that awesome event.

God will also judge mankind through Christ, 'because he is the Son of Man'. The second Person of the Godhead humbled himself and became man and died on a cross as the sin-bearer of his people. Now he is the one exalted beyond anything we can comprehend. Paul wrote of our Lord's exaltation in Philippians 2:9-11: 'Therefore God also has highly exalted him and given him the name which is above every name, that at the name of Jesus every knee should bow, of those in heaven, and of those on earth, and of those under the earth, and that every tongue should confess that Jesus Christ is Lord, to the glory of God the Father.' Because Christ shares our nature he is the perfect judge.

THINGS TO DISCUSS
WITH YOUR FAMILY

1. Would you agree that the second coming of Christ will be public, audible and visible? Read and discuss 1 Corinthians 15:52; Revelation 1:7; and 1 Thessalonians 4:16-17.
2. What we have read concerning Christ proves that he is God. Do you agree? Why?
3. Why is Christ most fitted to be Judge of mankind?

Meditation

Consider the wonder and glory of the new heavens and earth and your place in it.

Wise Words

Whatever their trials, believers will persevere. They will never perish. Faith that fades was never true faith ...
Gordon J. Keddie

'For if you believed Moses, you would believe me; for he wrote about me' (John 5:46).

Read: John 5:31-47

In court cases today evidence is needed before a jury can make a decision concerning the guilt or innocence of a person. Recently a man was found guilty of murder despite the lack of eyewitnesses and the body of the missing person. All the evidence was scientific and circumstantial. In Israel of old two or more eyewitnesses were needed before a person could be convicted of a crime which carried the death penalty (see Deuteronomy 17:6-7; 19:15).

Now Christ's testimony about himself didn't need corroboration, but for the sake of the Jews he now called witnesses to validate all of his claims to be the Son of God with almighty power and glory.

First he called upon the words of John the Baptist who plainly said of him, 'Behold! The Lamb of God who takes away the sin of the world! ... And I have seen and testified that this is the Son of God' (John 1:29,34). However, Christ had a far superior witness to his divinity than a man.

He pointed to the great miracles that he had performed. They were witnesses to the fact that he was the Christ, sent into the world by God. Later Jesus said that his Heavenly Father worked through him: 'Do you not believe that I am in the Father, and the Father in me? The words that I speak to you I do not speak on my own authority; but the Father who dwells in me does the works ... believe me for the sake of the works themselves' (John 14:10-11).

The Father had spoken from heaven when Christ was baptized. Luke recorded the event: 'And the Holy Spirit descended in bodily form like a dove upon him, and a voice came from heaven which said, "You are my beloved Son; in you I am well pleased"' (Luke 3:22).

Christ spoke of the Old Testament, especially the writings of Moses, as they also testified of him. The Jews were to understand that the study of the Scriptures do not give eternal life, but are a means of grace, used by God to bring people to saving faith in his Son. In Genesis 3:15 Moses wrote of a descendant of Adam and Eve who would defeat Satan. Abraham was told that 'In your Seed all the nations of the earth shall be blessed...' (Genesis 22:18). In Deuteronomy 18:15 Moses wrote: 'The LORD your God will raise up for you a Prophet like me from your midst, from your brethren. Him you shall hear...' Yet, hearing they didn't believe and considered Jesus a false Christ, a blasphemer and worthy of death.

The same is true of the vast majority of the world's inhabitants today. False Christ's are more readily acceptable than Jesus Christ, the Son of God. This will climax in the worship of the antichrist at the end of time.

We must all read the Bible with a prayer that we might understand. Paul wrote: 'But the natural man does not receive the things of the Spirit of God, for they are foolishness to him; nor can he know them, because they are spiritually discerned' (1 Corinthians 2:14). As we read our Bibles we must pray for the Holy Spirit to change our hearts and give us a spiritual discernment of what we read.

THINGS TO DISCUSS WITH YOUR FAMILY

1. Who do you believe Jesus Christ is? Why?
2. Today, who or where can you find true witnesses that Christ is the Son of God?
3. What can you learn from the Bereans concerning the use of your Bible? Read Acts 17:10-11.

Meditation

Meditate upon 1 Corinthians 2:14 — 'the natural man does not receive the things of the Spirit of God, for they are foolishness to him.'

Wise Words

But men stand still, and will not stir hand or foot to get life. And this is the whole reason why many of the lost are not saved. *J. C. Ryle*

'And he said unto them, "The Sabbath was made for man, and not man for the Sabbath: Therefore the Son of Man is Lord also of the Sabbath"' (Mark 2:27-28).

Read: Matthew 12:1-8

At the time when our Lord walked the earth, the church rulers had made Sabbath observance a difficult issue. Not only did they expect the people of Israel to obey what the fourth commandment taught, but also the scores of laws they had devised in an effort to ensure the Sabbath was kept as they understood the Scriptures. The same applies today in some circles. I know of one family where objections were raised because a family member had picked a lettuce for lunch. Her parents looked upon that as work and a breaking of the Christian Sabbath.

Now our Lord faced objections from the Pharisees because his disciples ate some corn seed which they gathered as they walked through a corn field. Christians need to take note of Christ's words as they set the pattern for our observance of the Lord's Day.

First, we are taught that a weekly rest day was made for the benefit of man. It was never intended to be a burden. Christ did not abolish the Sabbath and treat all days alike as some would have us believe. He did however reject all the manmade laws that hedged the Sabbath, making it a burden.

Second, we are taught here and elsewhere that works of necessity and mercy may be carried out without sin. Christ healed on the Sabbath — an act of mercy. He reminded the people that they fed their animals and rescued those that had fallen into a pit on the Sabbath, again without sin.

Third, there are acts of necessity that could be done on the Sabbath — and on the Lord's Day. In this category was the matter of eating food that was necessary for the health of the body. Indeed the Old Testament law permitted those who were hungry to eat from their neighbour's corn: 'When you come into your neighbour's standing grain, you may pluck the heads with your hand, but you shall not use a sickle on your neighbour's standing grain' (Deuteronomy 23:25). The law didn't restrict this to the six weekly working days.

I have been told that the actions of the disciples was unnecessary as they wouldn't have starved to death by waiting a few hours until the Sabbath day ended. However, the disciples 'were hungry' and did what was a necessity — they ate the food that was available.

Christ reminded the Pharisees that the priests who worked in the temple each Sabbath day did so without breaking God's law. He also told them of King David who, with his men ate the 'showbread' which was in the temple. This bread was not for ordinary use, but was used by David as an act of necessity.

Jesus declared to the Pharisees that 'One greater than the temple' was in their presence and that he was the Lord of the Sabbath. He rightly interpreted the fourth commandment for us all. May we never be ashamed of a right use of the Lord's Day.

THINGS TO DISCUSS WITH YOUR FAMILY

1. What did Jesus mean when he said that he was 'Lord even of the Sabbath'?
2. Why is the first day of the week called 'the Lord's Day'?
3. Discuss the statement in 'Wise Words'.

Meditation

Meditate upon today's text and what it should mean to all Christians.

Wise Words

'It is lawful to do well,' and show mercy; but to give the [Lord's Day] to idleness, pleasure-seeking, or the world, is utterly unlawful. It is contrary to the example of Christ, and a sin against a plain commandment of God.

J. C. Ryle

'Of how much more value is a man than a sheep? Therefore it is lawful to do good on the Sabbath' (Matthew 12:12).

Read: Matthew 12:9-14

Recently an Australian was sentenced to twelve months in jail for cruelty to a cat. He deserved the punishment and many people thought he should have received a more lengthy time in jail. Occasionally, to everyone's disgust, a murderer is given a suspended sentence. Human life is greatly undervalued in some circles.

In our previous reading Jesus quoted Hosea 6:6 which reads: 'For I desire mercy and not sacrifice.' Jesus was so different to the cold, unmerciful Pharisee legalists. A man with a withered hand was in the synagogue. He had probably spent many years begging and his future was bleak. In this incident we again glimpse more of the character of Jesus.

Christ is a compassionate Saviour who knew the law of God; after all he was the One to give it to Moses. In this healing he displayed love and mercy to the deformed man. The Pharisees of that day had no problems with rescuing a sheep that had fallen into a hole, regardless what day it was. Such an act was one of mercy to the animal. The Pharisees also believed that medical help could only be given to a person if it was needed to prevent death. Everything on the Sabbath was to be done within the confines of their interpretation of God's law and the laws they had enacted.

Jesus asked the question, 'Of how much more value is a man than a sheep?' We are of infinitely more value than animals, for man was created in the image of God and capable of a personal relationship with his Creator and Redeemer. Of such value is man that Christ came into the world to bring about God's plan of salvation. God loved his creation and would save human sinners. What love!

Jesus knew that God's law encouraged works of necessity and mercy and was about to heal the unfortunate man. He would show mercy and answer the Pharisee's question, 'Is it lawful to do good on the Sabbath?' They were waiting, hoping Christ would heal the man. This would give them more evidence that Jesus was not the Christ, but an impostor. Silence reigned as Christ told the man with the withered hand, 'Stretch out your hand.' Obedience would result in healing and despite the fact that holding out his hand was painful, he believed that Jesus could heal him.

When Jesus healed the man the Pharisees inwardly rejoiced. They were filled with rage while Jesus was filled with compassion. Plans were then made with the ungodly Herodians to have Jesus killed. Yet, this was not possible as their Roman overlords alone had the authority to have a person put to death. The ordinary Jews who witnessed the healing would have objected to the plans of the Pharisees and Herodians. It was not yet God's time for Christ's sacrificial death.

THINGS TO DISCUSS WITH YOUR FAMILY

1. In what way did the attitude of the Pharisees reflect the words of Psalm 2:1-3?
2. Discuss the many ways in which you are of more value than your family pet. Read Matthew 10:31.
3. Why did John call the first day of the week 'the Lord's Day'? See Revelation 1:10.

Meditation

Meditate upon the compassion shown by Jesus to the physically sick. Consider Christ's spiritual care and compassion to you.

Wise Words

Observe [the Pharisees'] cruelty; they took counsel, not to imprison or banish [Christ], but to destroy him, to be the death of him who came that we might have life.

Matthew Henry

'Behold my Servant, whom I have chosen; my Beloved, in whom my soul is well pleased: I will put my Spirit upon him, and he shall show judgement to the Gentiles' (Matthew 12:18).

Read: Matthew 12:14-21

How common it is for humans to hold in contempt those who do good. They are looked upon as 'Goody Goodies', who should be ignored. The most glorious Man who ever lived was put to death and today is still treated as a nobody by the ungodly.

The Pharisees and Herodians were making plans to have Christ 'who is holy, harmless, undefiled, separate from sinners, and has become higher than the heavens' (Hebrews 7:26) put to death. They wanted to rid the world of the most compassionate Man who ever graced this earth.

But what's new? The human heart in its natural state thinks the same of the Lord Jesus and his followers. Christians worldwide have been persecuted and murdered by ungodly men and women for just one reason — they love God and are servants of God's only Son, Jesus Christ. Jesus knew this would happen and prayed for his disciples: 'I have given them your word; and the world has hated them because they are not of the world, just as I am not of the world' (John 17:14). Today is no different so we should be praying for those Christians and congregations experiencing persecution and hatred in every nation.

Jesus was God's Servant to bring salvation to all people — to the Jew first and then the Gentiles. How true are his words: 'And in his name the Gentiles will trust.' God's justice would be seen in the sacrificial and substitutionary death of Christ. How we should praise God for this! While Jesus warned those who heard him preach and saw his miracles not to spread the news about him, the day was coming and now is when the gospel was taken worldwide. With the great outpouring of the Holy Spirit on the day of Pentecost the gospel began its journey into the furthermost corners of the earth.

We should note the difference between Christ's nature and that of the Pharisees. Unlike the latter, Christ was not a troublemaker, arguing and causing tumults and disruption to Israel. Jesus was gentle as we read: 'A bruised reed he will not break, and smoking flax he will not quench.' These are encouraging words to those of small faith, who see themselves as the least of the saints and sometimes doubt the reality of their faith. Jesus lovingly cares for his weak sheep. When we are downcast we should go to Jesus our Redeemer. He does not despise any of his people, but loves and cares for them all.

Think on these words that are found in Isaiah 40:10-11: 'Behold, the LORD GOD shall come with a strong hand, and his arm shall rule for him ... He will feed his flock like a shepherd; he will gather the lambs with his arm, and carry them in his bosom, and gently lead those who are with young.' How unlike the Pharisees.

THINGS TO DISCUSS WITH YOUR FAMILY

1. The Pharisees were 'legalists'. What does this mean?
2. Are we to obey God's law today? Read John 14:15 and Romans 7:12,16,22.
3. How can you help those Christians who are being persecuted because they love God and serve the Lord Jesus?

Meditation

Meditate upon the words quoted from Isaiah 40:10,11.

Wise Words

It should be a standing maxim in our religion — a spark is better than utter darkness; and little faith is better than no faith at all. *J. C. Ryle*

'And when it was day, he called his disciples to himself; and from them he chose twelve whom he also named apostles' (Luke 6:13).

Read: Luke 6:12-16

During our life we usually have many people we call friends, but there are very few we can call 'soul mates'. David and Jonathan were such for we read in 1 Samuel 18:1: '...the soul of Jonathan was knit to the soul of David, and Jonathan loved him as his own soul.' My wife is my best 'soul mate', but during my entire life only two others outside the family fall into this category of friends.

The time had come for Jesus to pick twelve men from the many disciples who followed him, to be his close friends. They would have the privilege of being taught by him and of taking the gospel to sinners worldwide. These twelve he called 'apostles' which meant they were chosen and would be sent out on a special mission on the authority of Christ. They would also be accountable to the Lord for all that they did in his name. They were disciples or students in the Lord's school.

We should notice that before Jesus announced the names of the twelve he spent the night on a mountainside praying to his Heavenly Father. Prayer was so important to our Saviour and sets a pattern for the Christian's life. A prayerless person is not a Christian. We must set aside some time each day when we can pour out the thoughts of our heart to our Heavenly Father. We must praise God, petition our God and offer thanksgiving for all that our Lord has done for us.

The twelve disciples, recorded by Luke were: 'Simon, whom he also named Peter, and Andrew his brother; James and John; Philip and Bartholomew; Matthew and Thomas; James the son of Alphaeus, and Simon called the Zealot; Judas the son of James, and Judas Iscariot who also became a traitor.'

Of the twelve there were three close friends, Peter, and the brothers John and James. Of these three there was John, who had a special friendship with the Saviour. Jesus was truly a man and needed friendship as we all do. In Proverbs 17:17 we read of a good friend's nature — he 'loves at all times'. We find many statements about friends, but one that stands out is 'there is a friend who sticks closer than a brother' (Proverbs 18:24). The greatest friend of all Christians is the Lord Jesus Christ who said: 'You are my friends if you do whatever I command you' (John 15:14).

Christ's disciples were largely unschooled men who had a working background, but they had a zeal for their Saviour and turned the world upside-down with the gospel they preached. Yet, among the twelve was Judas Iscariot, the traitor who betrayed the Lord to the authorities and played a part in bringing about his death. Jesus could see into his heart and knew what he would do. It is possible that not every person in a congregation is a Christian. Let us make sure that we are united to Christ by a God-given faith.

THINGS TO DISCUSS
WITH YOUR FAMILY

1. Of whom is Psalm 109:1-8 speaking?
2. What do you look for in the character of people you want as friends?
3. In Proverbs 18:24 we read: 'A man who has friends must himself be friendly...' What are you being taught here?

Meditation

Consider the friendship that exists between God and yourself.

Wise Words

Christians may not see eye to eye, but they can walk arm in arm. *Anonymous*

'And the whole multitude sought to touch him, for power went out from him and healed them all' (Luke 6:19).

Read: Luke 6:17-19

We must ensure that we are associated with a congregation of God's people where the truth is faithfully preached week after week — our eternal security depends upon it. Even with the high cost of travel and sometimes the need to travel many miles we must be ready to make sacrifices in order to sit under a godly ministry. Do you?

Jesus had come to preach about the kingdom of God and the only way of gaining admission. With his newly ordained twelve disciples, Christ came down from the mountainside to a level spot where he healed many who were sick and those who were demon possessed. Satan was very active while Christ walked the earth and many unfortunate people had lost their sanity because of demon possession. However, praise God, One with greater power was present, and he healed those who were ill and dealt powerfully with Satan and his demon followers. In fact those needing healing realized they only had to touch the Lord to be made well. We can only be humbled at the Lord's almighty power and glorify him for all that he did and does today for his people.

Our Lord again displayed his compassion and mercy to those in need of help. This was so unlike the cold hard Pharisees who showed no compassion for those in need of physical and spiritual help. They had made their rules and treated law breakers with utter contempt.

The King had been preaching about the need of repentance, but now he was to teach those who had repented concerning their lifestyle as citizens of the kingdom of God. The greatest prophet who ever graced the earth was about to speak. He had no pulpit in a building where everyone could sit in comfort out of the weather, so he found a place on the mountainside where he could be clearly heard. Three groups of people surrounded him — the twelve, other disciples and then the crowds who had come to be healed and hear what he had to say. No doubt Pharisees and scribes were present, hoping to see and hear something they could use to have Jesus put to death by the civil authorities.

In Proverbs 8 we read of 'Wisdom' and we discover that this title belonged to the Christ. We read: 'The LORD possessed me at the beginning of his way, before his works of old. I have been established from everlasting, from the beginning, before there was ever an earth … When he prepared the heavens, I was there' (Proverbs 8:22-27). In verses 1 and 2 of this chapter we read: 'Does not wisdom cry out, and understanding lift up her voice? She takes her stand on the top of the high hill…' Christ was fulfilling those words as he sat on the mountainside and commenced to preach about the kingdom of which he was King.

Let us learn from this sermon and live out what is taught.

THINGS TO DISCUSS
WITH YOUR FAMILY

1. What is wisdom? How can we get it? Read James 1:5.
2. Can you think of one woman who deliberately touched the hem of Christ's tunic in the hope of being healed? What does this say about her faith in Christ? Read Matthew 9:20-22.
3. What do these healings teach us about the almighty power of our Saviour?

Meditation

For a time try and visualize the scene as Christ took his seat ready to preach 'the Sermon on the Mount'.

Wise Words

Wisdom opens the eyes both to the glories of heaven and to the hollowness of earth.   *J. A. Motyer*

'Blessed are the poor in spirit, for theirs is the kingdom of heaven' (Matthew 5:3).

Read: Matthew 5:1-12   .

Not far from where we live there is a group of people who have established an 'alternative society' which is largely based upon communal living and the use of illegal drugs. The members of the group dress differently to the people living in the region and work to make their own clothing and grow the food that is needed. Throughout the world there are many of these groups in existence. In reality there are only two great world groups — the kingdom of the world and the kingdom of God. It is those who are members of the kingdom of heaven who are really the world's 'alternative society'.

In Christ's sermon on the mount our Saviour outlines the character of those belonging to God's alternative society. As we work through the sermon you will be able to look at your own life and ask the questions — Does this describe my character? Am I truly a member of the kingdom of heaven?

Jesus commences his sermon by saying 'Blessed,' or 'Happy' are those who are 'poor in spirit'. Christians are people who are humble and see themselves insignificant in the eyes of the world. When considering the majesty and glory of God they see themselves as unworthy, sinful people whose confidence is centred upon God in Christ. They are so different to the proud, arrogant, self-sufficient Pharisees who considered themselves so much better than others. The 'poor in spirit' is the tax collector in the Lord's parable of the tax collector and the Pharisee. Of one man we read: 'And the tax collector, standing afar off, would not so much as raise his eyes to heaven, but beat his breast, saying, "God, be merciful to me a sinner!"' (Luke 18:13). This was the man who was 'poor in spirit'.

In Christ's letter to the church at Laodicea he pointed out that despite the church being wealthy and believing it could do what it wanted in its own strength and influence, repentance and humility were needed before it was rich in God's eyes.

Those who are 'poor in spirit' are members of the 'kingdom of heaven', but we have the promise, 'And whoever exalts himself will be humbled, and he who humbles himself will be exalted' (Matthew 23:12). In the parable of the tax collector and the Pharisee we read of the humble tax collector, '…this man went down to his house justified rather than the other; for everyone who exalts himself will be humbled, and he who humbles himself will be exalted' (Luke 18:14).

It is usually the proud and powerful who rule the kingdoms of this world, but the day will come when they are humbled by the almighty hand of God.

Despite our circumstances in life we should have the spirit of Job, who when he lost everything was able to say, 'Naked I came from my mother's womb, and naked shall I return there. The LORD gave, and the LORD has taken away; blessed be the name of the LORD' (Job 1:21). May we be able to say the same.

THINGS TO DISCUSS WITH YOUR FAMILY

1. What does it mean to be 'poor in spirit'?
2. How do we gain entry into the kingdom of God?
3. Can wealthy people be 'poor in spirit'?

Meditation

Meditate upon Paul's words in Philippians 4:13 — 'I can do all things through Christ who strengthens me.'

Wise Words

If you lay yourself at Christ's feet he will take you into his arms. *William Bridge*

'Blessed are those who mourn, for they shall be comforted' (Matthew 5:4).

Read: Psalm 51

I've often heard a minister conducting a funeral take for his address the words of our text and use them to describe those who were mourning the loss of a dear one. God does comfort his people but this is not the meaning Christ gave to this beatitude.

It is most unusual to read words that tell us that the person who mourns is happy. Mourning here is a spiritual mourning over one's sins. In our world there are so few who acknowledge their sins as an offence against a holy Jehovah, before whose Son everyone will stand on the great Judgement Day. The world does not look at sins that way, but rather as simple faults or bad habits. Only the worst of sins appear wicked in the eyes of the world — the sin of vicious murder, for example.

All who have been convicted by the Holy Spirit see their sins in the first place as being as an offence against God. Pride, unbelief, hatred, theft, coveting, immorality of both the body and the heart and failure to love both God and man are offences against God's holy law. The Apostle Paul saw his sin and wrote, '…Christ Jesus came into the world to save sinners, of whom I am chief' (1 Timothy 1:15).

This was a godly sorrow over his sins. God had been offended. King David was the same. He had stolen Uriah's wife and then to cover up his evil deed had arranged for Uriah's death on the battlefield. I often thought that David's action was first and foremost an evil deed against Uriah, but later I came to understand who he had offended in the first place. We read, 'Against you [God], you only, have I sinned, and done this evil in your sight — that you may be found just when you speak, and blameless when you judge.'

God hates sin 'and is angry with the wicked every day' (Psalm 7:11).

To truly mourn over your sins and seek forgiveness from God results in peace with God. Paul wrote of his state before God: 'O wretched man that I am! Who will deliver me from this body of death?' (Romans 7:24). He was spiritually comforted by his Saviour and could write: 'I thank God — through Jesus Christ our Lord! ... There is therefore now no condemnation to those who are in Christ Jesus' (Romans 7:25; 8:1).

Repentant sinners can glorify God and rejoice as '...the blood of Jesus Christ his Son cleanses us from all sin' (1 John 1:7). In Isaiah 61:1,2 we read of the effects of the saving work of Christ: 'the LORD has anointed me to preach good tidings to the poor; he has sent me to heal the broken-hearted, to proclaim liberty to the captives ... to comfort all who mourn...' Our sins are covered by our Saviour's imputed righteousness.

What joy is ours when we become a citizen in the eternal kingdom of heaven of which we read: 'Behold, the tabernacle of God is with men, and he will dwell with them, and they shall be his people ... And God will wipe away every tear from their eyes; there shall be no more death, nor sorrow, nor crying. There shall be no more pain, for the former things have passed away' (Revelation 21:3-4).

THINGS TO DISCUSS WITH YOUR FAMILY

1. Should we mourn over others' sins and the state of the world?
2. Simeon waited for the 'consolation of Israel' (Luke 2:25). What does this mean?
3. How does God comfort his mourning people?

Meditation

Meditate upon the meaning of the expression — Christ's 'imputed righteousness'.

Wise Words

The Lord Jesus calls those 'blessed' who mourn ...
These are they who trouble themselves more about sin than about anything on earth.   *J. C. Ryle*

'Blessed are the meek, for they shall inherit the earth' (Matthew 5:5).

Read: Psalm 37:1-20

I love the words of Isaiah 40:9-17. In the midst of describing the almighty power and authority of our God he describes the LORD's meek nature towards his covenant people. Read and meditate upon this passage of Scripture and you will love God more than ever. Sadly we are part of the world where the prevailing philosophy is: 'Might is right!' and 'Power comes from the muzzle of the gun!' Today such people and nations rule the earth and are treated with healthy 'respect' by those who have no power.

We all should take note of Christ's words: 'For what will it profit a man if he gains the whole world, and loses his own soul?' (Mark 8:36). These are fearful words to the rich and powerful who live for their own glory and strength.

In God's redeemed society it is the meek who are happy and will one day inherit the earth. The meek are those who humbly submit themselves to God and his law and accept his providence for them knowing that 'all things work together for good to those who love God, to those who are the called according to his purpose' (Romans 8:28). They are patient when provoked, suffer silently and are always ready to forgive. The meek are gentle in their relationships with others. The world sees meekness as a sign of weakness and timidity and a readiness to allow others to walk over them; such is not so. It is the meek who know how to control their strength because meekness is not weakness.

Moses was the meekest man of his age. This was learned the hard way when he resorted to human effort to lead a rebellion of the Israelite slaves against their Egyptian overlords (Acts 7:24-25). Years later he returned to Egypt a meek and humble man, dependent upon his brother Aaron to be his spokesman.

We have read before that Jesus was a meek man — 'He was oppressed and afflicted, yet he did not open his mouth; he was led like a lamb to the slaughter, and as a sheep before her shearers is silent, so he did not open his mouth' (Isaiah 53:7). He was strong but didn't use his strength to save himself from the cross. Christians are also meek. With the new birth comes a new character displaying the fruit of the Spirit — 'love, joy, peace, long-suffering, kindness, goodness, faithfulness, gentleness [and] self-control' (Galatians 5:22-23). The Apostle Paul urged Timothy (and all Christians) to 'pursue righteousness, godliness, faith, love, patience [and] gentleness' (1 Timothy 6:11).

Those who are meek of character have the assurance that they will inherit the new earth. Christ was possibly thinking of David's words in Psalm 37:11 — 'the meek shall inherit the earth, and shall delight themselves in the abundance of peace.' The Apostle Peter wrote: 'Nevertheless we, according to his promise, look for new heavens and a new earth in which righteousness dwells' (2 Peter 3:13). This is the land of the meek where the redeemed will worship God as 'kings and priests' (Revelation 5:10).

THINGS TO DISCUSS WITH YOUR FAMILY

1. Describe a 'meek' person.
2. What is necessary for a person to become meek in every respect?
3. In what way did Jesus exhibit meekness? Read Isaiah 53:7.

Meditation

Meditate upon the tenderness of God in Isaiah 40:11: 'He will feed his flock like a shepherd; he will gather the lambs with his arm, and carry them in his bosom, and gently lead those who are with young.'

The meek 'are never losers in the long run'. *J. C. Ryle*

Wise Words

 'Blessed are those who hunger and thirst for righteousness, for they shall be filled' (Matthew 5:6).

Read: Psalm 84

Job asked the question, '… how can a man be righteous before God?' (Job 9:2). The Pharisees had not only asked that question but believed they had the answer — if they obeyed God's law he would look upon them as holy people and welcome them into Paradise.

Martin Luther knew what God had said: 'Pursue peace with all people, and holiness, without which no one will see the Lord' (Hebrews 12:14). He hungered and thirsted after righteousness that would give him peace with God, but did it the wrong way. He believed that it was by works he could find spiritual peace. However, the day came when the Holy Spirit opened his mind to understand that there was nothing he could do to gain the righteousness he needed to enter heaven. Like the Apostle Paul he came to acknowledge that it was God who gave holiness to his people, and that holiness came from Christ, who on behalf of his people perfectly obeyed God's law.

Paul wrote of the end of his search for holiness: 'But indeed I also count all things loss for the excellence of the knowledge of Christ Jesus my Lord, for whom I have suffered the loss of all things, and count them as rubbish, that I may gain Christ and be found in him, not having my own righteousness, which is from the law, but that which is through faith in Christ, the righteousness which is from God by faith' (Philippians 3:8-9). Sins are forgiven and we bask in the glorious truth of 'THE LORD OUR RIGHTEOUSNESS' (Jeremiah 23:6).

This is the imputed righteousness put to our account in the court of heaven the day we believed in Christ as our Lord and Saviour. As sinners who acknowledged our sins before a holy God, our thirst for justifying righteousness ended with the gift of saving faith.

Then we commenced the sanctifying walk of holiness. Jesus entered this world to save his people from their sins. In part this means victory over sin. This is the work of the Holy Spirit, and God has already laid down the pathway that his people must walk. We read in Ephesians 2:10 — 'For we are his workmanship, created in Christ Jesus for good works, which God prepared beforehand that we should walk in them.' As the Psalmist wrote: 'As the deer pants for the water brooks, so pants my soul for you, O God' (Psalm 42:1), so our longing is to walk closely with our God and be moulded into the likeness of Jesus Christ our Redeemer. This is the 'ministry of the Spirit' (2 Corinthians 3:8).

This growth in holiness has ever been the plan of God for Christians. Paul wrote '… God from the beginning chose you for salvation through sanctification by the Spirit and belief in the truth…' (2 Thessalonians 2:13).

Our hunger and thirst for righteousness will be satisfied when we enter the new heavens and new earth in which is perfect righteousness. What joy awaits those who hunger and thirst for righteousness. We read: 'They shall neither hunger anymore nor thirst anymore; the sun shall not strike them, nor any heat; for the Lamb who is in the midst of the throne will shepherd them and lead them to living fountains of waters. And God will wipe away every tear from their eyes' (Revelation 7:16-17).

THINGS TO DISCUSS WITH YOUR FAMILY

1. How can we maintain our hunger and thirst for righteousness?
2. What is justification?
3. Explain the process whereby a Christian can be conformed to Christ's image.

Meditation

Consider the thanksgiving you owe God for Christ's imputed holiness.

Wise Words

Sow holiness and reap happiness.   *George Swinnock*

'Blessed are the merciful, for they shall obtain mercy' (Matthew 5:7).

Read: Matthew 18:21-35

It is wonderful to be surrounded by family members all of whom show love and compassion when a member is in need. I thank God that I have been blessed with such a family group. While it's usually easy to help those we love, God has demonstrated mercy in a most amazing way. He provides rain for the just and the unjust and makes the sun rise on everyone.

The greatest act of mercy however is seen in God's salvation of sinners. Paul wrote in Romans 5:8: 'But God demonstrates his own love toward us, in that while we were still sinners, Christ died for us.' Here is mercy in Christ's sacrificial death to save sinners. God's compassion for helpless sinners has resulted in the bestowal of eternal life on all who believe in Christ. God has made that 'belief' possible by sending the Holy Spirit into sinners' hearts and bringing about the new birth and saving faith.

Our Saviour continues to display his compassion for we read in Hebrews 2:17-18: 'Therefore, in all things he had to be made like his brethren, that he might be a merciful and faithful High Priest in things pertaining to God, to make propitiation for the sins of the people. For in that he himself has suffered, being tempted, he is able to aid those who are tempted.' Day after day we receive spiritual and material blessings from our forgiving Saviour.

In turn we are to show mercy to everyone. Paul wrote: 'Therefore, as we have opportunity, let us do good to all, especially to those who are of the household of faith' (Galatians 6:10). God delights to see acts of compassion carried out by Christians. We can rejoice in the words of 2 Samuel 22:26: 'With the merciful you will show yourself merciful.' This is what we are taught in today's reading about the unmerciful servant. That man had been shown great mercy, but he wouldn't show a small act of pity to one of his workers. Consequently the anger of his master fell upon him.

We live in a world of cruelty, despair and sadness. True believers are to reach out to help those who are hurting. Sometimes we read of wonderful acts of compassion by people who are not Christians and we are put to shame. God's command through Hosea is plain: 'For I desire mercy and not sacrifice…' (Hosea 6:6). The cold hearted Pharisees and Scribes failed in this area — we must not. When we show kindness we must do so with a cheerful disposition. Paul wrote — 'he who shows mercy, [must do so] with cheerfulness' (Romans 12:8). This is one way of showing our love of God; it is our response to the love he has shown us by sending Jesus to save us.

There is a Day of Judgement coming when our Christian life will be closely examined by Jesus, the Judge. We are told that the books will be opened, 'And the dead were judged according to their works, by the things which were written in the books' (Revelation 20:12). How will things go with you on that day? God does not forget any act of compassion (Proverbs 19:17). Jesus said: '… inasmuch as you did it to one of the least of these my brethren, you did it to me' (Matthew 25:40). We have a merciful Saviour who will reward every act of love done by his people.

THINGS TO DISCUSS WITH YOUR FAMILY

1. Why does God expect us to show mercy to others?
2. What are we taught in James 2:13 — 'For judgement is without mercy to the one who has shown no mercy. Mercy triumphs over judgement'?
3. List and discuss five acts of mercy carried out by our Lord.

Meditation

Meditate upon God's mercy to sinners as seen in Romans 5:8.

Wise Words

Jesus takes to heart the sufferings of his friends.
William Hendriksen

'Blessed are the pure in heart, for they shall see God' (Matthew 5:8).

Read: Matthew 23:13-28

It is impossible to see God with our physical eyes for we are told that 'God is spirit.' Yet I am always amazed and encouraged by Job's words, 'For I know that my Redeemer lives, and he shall stand at last on the earth; and after my skin is destroyed, this I know, that in my flesh I shall see God, whom I shall see for myself, and my eyes shall behold, and not another' (Job 19:25-27).

The Pharisees believed that they could successfully approach God through their ceremonial activities and obedience to the law. They neglected the 'inner man'. What was needed was a change of heart. In Psalm 24:3-4 we read: 'Who may ascend into the hill of the Lord? Or who may stand in his holy place? He who has clean hands and a pure heart, who has not lifted up his soul to an idol, nor sworn deceitfully.' Obtaining a 'pure heart' is the sovereign work of the Holy Spirit. This has always been so as Christ told Nicodemus who should have known what Ezekiel had written: 'I will give you a new heart and put a new spirit within you; I will take the heart of stone out of your flesh and give you a heart of flesh. I will put my Spirit within you and cause you to walk in my statutes, and you will keep my judgements and do them' (Ezekiel 36:26-27). This is the new birth which effectively removes a sinner from the kingdom of the world and makes him a citizen of the alternative society — the kingdom of God. The new heart is an act of God's abounding grace. If you are a Christian, praise God!

God looks upon the heart and sees the motives for all that we do. The Pharisees simply observed people's actions and made judgements accordingly. They should have known the Lord's words to Samuel: 'For the Lord does not see as man sees; for man looks at the outward appearance, but the Lord looks at the heart' (1 Samuel 16:7).

All who are pure in heart grow closer to God as each day passes. Daily our sins are washed and we, by God's grace, walk the narrow way that leads to life eternal. Our prayer time and study of the Scriptures should be times of rich fellowship with the God we love, and who loves us. Like Job we long to gaze upon our God. We should rejoice in David's words in Psalm 17:15 — 'As for me, I will see your face in righteousness; I shall be satisfied when I awake in your likeness.' The Apostle John wrote likewise: '... when he is revealed, we shall be like him, for we shall see him as he is' (1 John 3:2). Just as Moses had asked God, 'Please, show me your glory' (Exodus 33:18). Paul looked forward to that day and wrote: '... now we see in a mirror, dimly, but then face to face' (1 Corinthians 13:12).

In the new heavens and earth the covenant promise given to Abraham will become a reality — 'And there shall be no more curse, but the throne of God and of the Lamb shall be in it, and his servants shall serve him. They shall see his face, and his name shall be on their foreheads. There shall be no night there: They need no lamp nor light of the sun, for the Lord God gives them light. And they shall reign for ever and ever' (Revelation 22:3-5). Hallelujah!

THINGS TO DISCUSS WITH YOUR FAMILY

1. What are we taught in Psalm 51:7? 'Wash me, and I shall be whiter than snow.'
2. What is a pure heart and how do sinners get one?
3. How can a believer deal with his sinful heart?

Meditation

Meditate upon Jeremiah 17:9 — 'The heart is deceitful above all things, and desperately wicked; who can know it?'

Wise Words

Those that are acquainted with God and Christ are already in the suburbs of life eternal. *Matthew Henry*

'Blessed are the peacemakers, for they shall be called sons of God' (Matthew 5:9).

Read: Colossians 1:15-23

Each day we turn on the TV and most of the news is war, killings and other acts of hatred. We live in a world where arguments are so often solved by the use of force and the defeat or death of the weakest. I was appointed Principal of a school because the person previously nominated rejected the offer as he was disputing with members of his family who lived in the area.

But what a privilege it is to be called 'sons of God'. One of the most prominent features of Christians is that they are 'peacemakers'. Are you?

Jesus Christ, God's only true Son, bears the title 'Prince of Peace' (Isaiah 9:6). He was the God appointed One to establish harmony between God and man, and between Christians of all nations. Our reading contains the wonderful words concerning the work of Christ. God's saving plan was: '…to reconcile all things to himself, by him, whether things on earth or things in heaven, having made peace through the blood of his cross.…' Our God is 'the God of peace' (Romans 15:33); Christ is 'the Lord of peace' (2 Thessalonians 3:16); the Holy Spirit gives 'righteousness and peace and joy' (Romans 14:17); and the gospel is the 'gospel of peace' (Ephesians 6:15).

Christians in turn become peacemakers because they have become 'sons of God'. Of ministers of the gospel Paul writes: 'How beautiful are the feet of those who preach the gospel of peace, who bring glad tidings of good things!' (Romans 10:15). Every Christian is an ambassador for Christ urging sinners to be reconciled to God through the Lord Jesus (2 Corinthians 5:20).

Christ prayed for unity between believers, that 'all may be one, as you, Father, are in me, and I in you, that they also may be one in us, that the world may believe that you sent me' (John 17:21).

Yet the gospel of our Lord produces hatred in the hearts of so many unbelievers. They cannot stand the gospel or the Christ of the gospel. Of this loathing Christ said, 'Do you suppose that I came to give peace on earth? I tell you, not at all, but rather division' (Luke 12:51). This hatred, however, comes from the ungodly who loathe being reminded that they are sinners who need the Saviour.

There are professing Christians who harm the church by introducing teaching that causes division. Of such people we are told: 'Reject a divisive man after the first and second admonition, knowing that such a person is warped and sinning, being self-condemned' (Titus 3:10).

Judgement Day will reveal who are 'sons of God'. All things and people who offend will be cast into the bottomless pit, and 'then the righteous will shine forth as the sun in the kingdom of their Father' (Matthew 13:43). Good things are in store for the redeemed.

THINGS TO DISCUSS WITH YOUR FAMILY

1. Discuss Paul's words to Timothy concerning prayer 'that we may lead a quiet and peaceable life in all godliness and reverence' (1 Timothy 2:2).
2. In what way can you help establish peace in your family or community?
3. Today, who is trying to establish peace between the world's nations? Will they succeed?

Meditation

Pray for harmony in your family and your church congregation.

Wise Words

Christians — At peace with God and thus themselves filled with sweet peace, they live at peace if possible with all men and work to keep and make peace wherever peace is threatened.   *R. C. H. Lenski*

'Blessed are those who are persecuted for righteousness' sake, for theirs is the kingdom of heaven' (Matthew 5:10).

Read: Hebrews 11:32-40

Generally in the western world nobody really cares much about the church. Christians are tolerated provided they are not too outspoken about Christ and the gospel. We are largely ignored because we are not different from our ungodly neighbours. Most Christians have good jobs, nice homes and cars, happy families and all the possessions that are found in the homes of those who have no interest in Christ, the Redeemer.

When the church makes a stand against immorality and ungodly laws the world rises up in opposition and demands that Christians keep their thoughts to themselves. In many other parts of the world the Christian church, which is the bride of Christ, is hated and its members are sometimes treated with a contempt which ends in martyrdom. Paul's words concerning the ungodly are true — '... the carnal mind is enmity against God; for it is not subject to the law of God, nor indeed can be. So then, those who are in the flesh cannot please God' (Romans 8:7-8).

The Jews of old had rejected God's prophets and treated his Son with hatred which ended in his death upon the cross. He warned his disciples to expect the same — 'Remember the word that I said to you, "A servant is not greater than his master." If they persecuted me, they will also persecute you. If they kept my word, they will keep yours also. But all these things they will do to you for my name's sake, because they do not know him who sent me' (John 15:20-21).

Jesus warned his listeners, 'Woe to you when all men speak well of you...' (Luke 6:26). Trials are not signs of God's displeasure with his people, but rather are the proof of the world's hatred of the Christ of the gospel. God uses the world's assaults to purify and strengthen the faith of his people. As James writes (James 1:2-4): 'My brethren, count it all joy when you fall into various trials, knowing that the testing of your faith produces patience. But let patience have its perfect work, that you may be perfect and complete, lacking nothing.' The Apostle Peter wrote wonderful words of encouragement to persecuted Christians: 'Beloved, do not think it strange concerning the fiery trial which is to try you, as though some strange thing happened to you; but rejoice to the extent that you partake of Christ's sufferings, that when his glory is revealed, you may also be glad with exceeding joy. If you are reproached for the name of Christ, blessed are you, for the Spirit of glory and of God rests upon you. On their part he is blasphemed, but on your part he is glorified' (1 Peter: 4:12-14).

Great blessings are in store for suffering Christians, all of which are of grace and beyond anything we can ever imagine. Paul wrote: 'For I consider that the sufferings of this present time are not worthy to be compared with the glory which shall be revealed in us' (Romans 8:18). He also wrote: 'For our light affliction, which is but for a moment, is working for us a far more exceeding and eternal weight of glory' (2 Corinthians 4:17). We can but praise our God of grace.

THINGS TO DISCUSS WITH YOUR FAMILY

1. What are we taught in Romans 8:28?
2. Why does the world hate the Church?
3. Is there a place for retaliation when Christians are being killed for their faith?

Meditation

Meditate upon a fact that frequently the church grows in times of persecution. Why?

Wise Words

The fire of God can't be damped out by the waters of man's persecution.   *A. W. Tozer*

'Let your light so shine before men, that they may see your good works and glorify your Father in heaven' (Matthew 5:16).

Read: Matthew 5:13-16

On a recent stay in hospital I was restricted to a diet with no salt. I found this difficult as I enjoy the flavour of salt. When I was young, salt was important to preserve food as we didn't have a refrigerator, just an ice chest. The ice man came every week and delivered a huge block of ice for our cooler. It was an exciting day when Mum and Dad bought a refrigerator.

Christ now is telling members of the kingdom of heaven to live a consistent godly life and act as light and salt in their community. This was not the life of obedience to win the favour of God as the Pharisees believed, but to live in accordance with God's laws to please him, whose Spirit had brought about their new birth.

Salt was important to the people of Christ's age as it acted as a preservative and to give flavour to food. The world owes God a great debt of gratitude because of the presence of the saints who act as salt and make every effort to preserve communities from falling further into sin and chaos. We are to stand firm on questions of morality and use our influence with our rulers to enact legislation that is in accordance with the law of God.

The everlasting covenant is called 'a covenant of salt' (Numbers 18:19) and this covenant is the gospel which acts as a purifying and preserving agent in our community. Paul even wrote: 'Let your speech always be with grace, seasoned with salt' (Colossians 4:6). Our every word should encourage peaceful, godly living. As members of God's kingdom we are to be different to the citizens of the world. Tertullian wrote: 'But it's mainly the deeds of love so noble that leads many to put a brand on us: "See how they love one another."'

We are to be like light in this world. Our Saviour said of himself: 'I am the light of the world. He who follows me shall not walk in darkness, but have the light of life' (John 8:12). The purpose of a light is to drive away darkness and expose danger. Christians are to be winsome, attractive and godly, exposing the world's wickedness. We are to let the world see our godly acts, done out of love for Christ, and through them encourage unbelievers to turn to the Redeemer.

Christians are created for good works just as Paul wrote: 'For we are his workmanship, created in Christ Jesus for good works, which God prepared beforehand that we should walk in them' (Ephesians 2:10). Let us unashamedly do our works of righteousness in Christ's name so that the world 'may, by [your] good works which they observe, glorify God in the day of visitation' (1 Peter 2:12).

Failure to act as salt will mean being cast away from Christ and being of no use. Failure to shine will cause what little light we have to flicker and die. Let us not be like the Pharisees, but live to the glory of God.

THINGS TO DISCUSS WITH YOUR FAMILY

1. In what way can you act as salt in your community?
2. Does the light of God shine in your congregation?
3. If you were accused of being a Christian would there be sufficient evidence to prove you guilty?

Meditation

Meditate upon the words of Psalm 18:28 — 'For you will light my lamp; the LORD my God will enlighten my darkness.'

Wise Words

Ignorance of the nature and design of the law is at the bottom of most religious mistakes.   *John Newton*

'For I say to you, that unless your righteousness exceeds the righteousness of the scribes and Pharisees, you will by no means enter the kingdom of heaven' (Matthew 5:20).

Read: Matthew 5:17-20

The picture Christ painted about not 'destroying' the law of God was that of a house or tent being pulled down. The Pharisees believed that Jesus was not living in accordance with the will of God as revealed in the Law (the Pentateuch) and the Prophets (the remainder of the Old Testament). Today we have some professing Christians who are convinced that they no longer must obey God's commands — they believe that faith in Christ is all that is needed to ensure their salvation. This is not so, as the faith that saves results in a life of righteousness. We read in James 2:26 — 'For as the body without the spirit is dead, so faith without works is dead also.'

The Pharisees had misunderstood God's law and its place in salvation. Jesus obeyed God's precepts because he loved God and was filled with the Holy Spirit. He could do no other but obey the ordinances that he had given to Moses and the Prophets.

In the Old Testament we read of Christ and the law: 'He will magnify the law and make it honourable' (Isaiah 42:21). In Psalm 40:8 we read of Messiah's attitude: 'I delight to do your will, O my God, and your law is within my heart.' Christ obeyed every aspect of God's law on behalf of his people. He fulfilled all the prophecies made concerning him. The ceremonial law was ended with his sacrificial death.

The Apostle Paul declared that God's law was good and wrote: 'For I delight in the law of God according to the inward man' (Romans 7:22). Every Christian says the same because love of God's law is one of the marks of the new birth. Of the new covenant Jeremiah quoted God's word: 'I will put my law in their minds, and write it on their hearts; and I will be their God, and they shall be my people' (Jeremiah 31:33).

Jesus declared that our righteousness must exceed that of the law-obeying hypocritical Pharisees and Scribes. It is done in two ways: first, the righteousness of Christ is put to our account in the court of heaven. God looks upon his people through Christ and accepts us as perfectly righteous in his sight.

Secondly, Christians obey God for the right reason; not out of the desire to keep the law and win favour with him, but because they love the Lord. Jesus said, 'If you love me, keep my commandments' (John 14:15).

Obedience to God's word is one of the marks that we are citizens of God's kingdom. The Apostle John wrote in 1 John 2:3-6: 'Now by this we know that we know him, if we keep his commandments. He who says, "I know him," and does not keep his commandments, is a liar, and the truth is not in him. But whoever keeps his word, truly the love of God is perfected in him. By this we know that we are in him. He who says he abides in him ought himself also to walk just as he walked.'

Paul wrote that faith in Christ establishes the law (Romans 3:31). Let us always live to the glory of God and obey our Saviour's commandments as acts of love.

THINGS TO DISCUSS WITH YOUR FAMILY

1. What is an antinominian?
2. Why should you obey God's law?
3. Why did Jesus obey his heavenly Father's law?

Meditation

Thank God for his law that showed sinners their sin.

Wise Words

The Old Testament is the gospel in bud. The New Testament is the gospel in full flower.   *J. C. Ryle*

You shall not murder

'You shall not take vengeance, nor bear any grudge against the children of your people, but you shall love your neighbour as yourself: I am the LORD' (Leviticus 19:18).

Read: Matthew 5:21-26

Daily we hear of the terrible happenings throughout the world. News headlines are usually devoted to murders and killings. It is sad, but human life is considered cheap. This is not true as all life comes from God, and men and women are made in his likeness — human life is precious for this reason alone!

The Pharisees and other teachers of the law had taught that only deliberate acts of killing were condemned in the commandment, but they had overlooked the law of love that was clearly taught in the Old Testament. In Leviticus 19:16-18 we read — 'You shall not go about as a tale bearer among your people; nor shall you take a stand against the life of your neighbour: I am the LORD. You shall not hate your brother in your heart… You shall not take vengeance, nor bear any grudge against the children of your people, but you shall love your neighbour as yourself: I am the LORD.'

Jesus was simply expounding what the Pharisees and Scribes should have known. The Apostle John reiterated Christ's words — 'Whoever hates his brother is a murderer, and you know that no murderer has eternal life abiding in him' (1 John 3:15).

Jesus went on to caution his congregation that belittling comments about others were not to be spoken. Calling a person 'Raca' — brainless — and 'fool' — stupid or idiot — came from a hateful, impure heart. There were times when Christ showed righteous anger and used the word 'fool'. How can this be? It was because they weren't bitter words coming from a sinful heart, but the words of a pure heart hurt by wickedness and sin. Sinful anger that leads to bitter words is in its very nature 'murder'.

Jesus told his listeners that peace with God and their fellow man was essential before God would accept their worship. Cain found that his offering to God was unacceptable because he did 'not do well' (Genesis 4:7). Cain's pride and hatred of his brother resulted in murder. God told the Jews that because of their sin he would not accept their offerings (Amos 5:22). Jesus taught the same in the Sermon on the Mount. The one who caused the offence was to make peace with his offended brother before he presented an acceptable offering to God. People were to be peacemakers and those who established peace from a regenerate heart were the ones who would 'see God'.

The Apostle John wrote: 'If someone says, "I love God," and hates his brother, he is a liar; for he who does not love his brother whom he has seen, how can he love God whom he has not seen? And this commandment we have from him: that he who loves God must love his brother also' (1 John 4:20-21). A person with a heart consumed by hatred towards another person travels the broad way that ends in hell.

If you have hatred in your heart, go to Christ in true repentance and ask for forgiveness.

THINGS TO DISCUSS
WITH YOUR FAMILY

1. What are you taught in Proverbs 21:23? 'Whoever guards his mouth and tongue keeps his soul from troubles.'
2. How do you think the Pharisees would react to these words of Christ? Why?
3. What should you do if you have upset someone by some hurtful words you have spoken?

Meditation

Meditate upon Proverbs 24:29 — 'Do not say, "I will do to him just as he has done to me; I will render to the man according to his work."'

Wise Words

Hate is too great a burden to bear.   *Martin Luther*

'You shall not commit adultery' (Exodus 20:14).

Read: Matthew 5:27-30

Today, in the western world marriage break-ups are common. This is not just among worldly people, but also amongst Christians. In many countries almost 50% of all marriages end up in divorce. Frequently the cause of the divorce is that one marriage partner has committed adultery and so broken the solemn promise they made when married.

Marriage is a lifelong contract between a man and a woman where the two partners become 'one flesh' (Genesis 2:24). We read, 'Marriage is honourable among all, and the bed undefiled; but fornicators and adulterers God will judge' (Hebrews 13:4). Unfaithfulness is condemned.

Again Christ faced the hardhearted Pharisees who believed themselves innocent of the sin of adultery. Again they failed to understand that adultery could be a sin of the heart without the physical act. Malachi rebuked the hardhearted Jews who divorced their wives making it possible to marry a 'new, pretty, young model' — 'the LORD has been witness between you and the wife of your youth, with whom you have dealt treacherously; yet she is your companion and your wife by covenant' (Malachi 2:14). The divorce was the result so often of lusting after another woman. In Proverbs the people were clearly told: 'And rejoice with the wife of your youth... and always be enraptured with her love' (Proverbs 5:18,19). We are to be content with the marriage partner God has given us.

Jesus was looking at the heart where sin so often starts and is then fed through the eyes. The Apostle Peter knew that people had 'eyes full of adultery' (2 Peter 2:14). Job knew the danger of this. He acted to avoid lust in the heart: 'I have made a covenant with my eyes; why then should I look upon a young woman?' (Job 31:1). The Psalmist knew the danger of a sinful heart — 'the LORD will not hear' (Psalm 66:18).

All who are members of God's new society must remember that we glorify God with our body (1 Corinthians 6:20). This means a life of holiness, where by the grace of God we 'put to death the deeds of the body' (Romans 8:13).

Jesus instructs us to get rid of every temptation to commit adultery. He does this by saying we might need to pluck out our eyes or cut off our hands and feet in order to escape sin. He is really telling us to turn off that lustful TV show and to avoid places and things that stir immorality in the heart. This may mean no more visits to the beach on hot days because of the skimpy clothing of the bathers — or in some places, nudity on the beach.

We live in a permissive society, but let us take our stand for God's morality and fight the good fight of faith, again for the glory of God.

THINGS TO DISCUSS WITH YOUR FAMILY

1. What are you taught in Colossians 3:5? 'Therefore put to death your members which are on the earth: fornication, uncleanness, passion, evil desire, and covetousness, which is idolatry.'
2. What does it mean that Job made a covenant with his eyes (Job 31:1)? 'I have made a covenant with my eyes; why then should I look upon a young woman?'
3. What led to David's sin with Bathsheba? Read 2 Samuel 11:1-5.

Meditation

Meditate upon Ephesians 5:23-32 where the church is described as the bride of Christ.

Wise Words

What lust is so sweet or profitable that it is worth burning in hell for? *William Gurnall*

'Therefore a man shall leave his father and mother and be joined to his wife, and they shall become one flesh' (Genesis 2:24).

Read: Matthew 5:31-32

In Australia divorce is common and can be obtained for no reason at all.

Jesus now deals with the issue of divorce as it was being taught by the Pharisees who believed they understood the law of God as given to Moses. They were of the same opinion as many modern legislators, and taught that divorce could be had for any reason. One rabbi taught that a man could give his wife a bill of divorce if he wanted to marry a younger woman. He even went on to say that a wife's bad breath was sufficient reason for a divorce.

Moses had written that a man could divorce his wife if he found some 'uncleanness' in her but divorce was not God's original plan for marriage. In Eden, Adam and Eve became 'one flesh'. That union could only be broken by death. When sin entered the world because of the hardness of the fallen human heart, divorce was regulated by God's law (Matthew 19:8). In Malachi 2:16 we read: 'For the LORD God of Israel says that he hates divorce.' This was what Jesus was reiterating.

Unlike the Pharisees, Christ taught that divorce was permissible for one particular reason — adultery. Elsewhere Paul added desertion by an ungodly marriage partner, but he taught that normally marriages could only be ended by the death of one partner (Romans 7:2,3).

Jesus was rebuking the Pharisees who concentrated their attention on divorce, whereas Christ taught the sanctity of marriage. He also taught that forgiveness was far better than divorce. The Lord was concerned about the protection of the innocent woman who was cast aside by a cruel, hard-hearted husband. Christ used God and his relationship with his covenant people, Israel, as the example married people should follow, even when adultery marred the marriage relationship. Again and again Israel committed spiritual adultery by turning away from the LORD to worship the gods of the surrounding nations. Jeremiah quotes God's words to Israel — "'but you have played the harlot with many lovers; yet return to me,' says the LORD' (Jeremiah 3:1).

The Apostle Paul, in Ephesians 5:22-33, wrote of the marriage relationship which was based upon mutual love. Husbands were commanded to love their wives just as Christ loved the church. Wives were instructed to submit to their own husbands just as the church submitted to their Lord and Bridegroom, Jesus Christ. Christ's words to the Pharisees regarding divorce explained the sanctity of the marriage relationship which was not to be broken for frivolous reasons. Nevertheless, let us never think that divorce is the unforgivable sin. Unjust divorces require repentance and prayer for forgiveness.

THINGS TO DISCUSS WITH YOUR FAMILY

1. What makes a good marriage?
2. Who should Christians marry? Read 2 Corinthians 6:14 — 'Do not be unequally yoked together with unbelievers. For what fellowship has righteousness with lawlessness?'
3. Why did God permit divorce? How does divorce fit in with God's original intention of marriage?

Meditation

Think about the type of person you should marry and/ or ask God for guidance to become a better spouse.

Wise Words

God is the witness to every marriage ceremony, and will be the witness to every violation of its vows.

Thomas V. Moore

'You shall not take the name of the LORD your God in vain, for the LORD will not hold him guiltless who takes his name in vain' (Exodus 20:7).

Read: Matthew 5:33-37

Today we frequently hear people expressing themselves using an oath. Often they use the name of God or Christ in a blasphemous manner without any intention of carrying out what they have promised. Oaths are just part of some people's everyday speech.

Now the Pharisees faced the matter of oath-taking in the light of the third commandment. They taught that any oath taken in the name of the LORD was binding and had to be performed but oaths uttered in everyday speech using different words were not binding. Again the Pharisees were playing with words — to them the important word in the oath was that of 'LORD'.

Oaths were part of Old Testament life, but God established rules. Moses wrote in Leviticus 19: 12 — 'You shall not swear by my name falsely; nor shall you profane the name of your God: I am the LORD.' We read in Numbers 30:2 of the sanctity of an oath: 'If a man makes a vow to the LORD, or swears an oath to bind himself by some agreement, he shall not break his word; he shall do according to all that proceeds out of his mouth.' The people were also instructed that they were not to delay carrying out any vow they had made. Failure to fulfil the vow was sin (Deuteronomy 23:21).

Oath-taking was permissible. We read that God himself had sworn oaths in his own name. God swore to Abraham that he and his descendants would be greatly blessed because of his willingness to sacrifice Isaac to the LORD (Genesis 22:16-17). In Psalm 132:11 we read that God had sworn vows to David.

Jesus, in his sermon, was rebuking the Pharisees who taught that vows not taken in the name of the Lord need not be kept. Apparently it was common to swear by 'Jerusalem', 'heaven and the earth'. But the Lord taught that these were the property of the Creator and oaths sworn upon them were as binding as the oaths sworn in the King's great name.

Jesus went on to say that we are not to make vows in everyday speech for such blasphemes the name of God. Our Saviour calls for truthfulness in all that we say. Our 'Yes' or 'No' is binding and to be trusted because true believers do not practise deceit.

There is a place for the taking of an oath in some formal situations such as when being married. Christ did so when the High Priest demanded, 'I put you under oath by the living God: Tell us if you are the Christ, the Son of God!' Jesus said to him, 'It is as you said' (Matthew 26:63-64). The writer to the Hebrews (6:16) permitted an oath to end a dispute and Paul had no problem calling upon God as his witness (2 Corinthians 1:23). May we not be known for blasphemous statements in our speech, or being untrue to our word.

THINGS TO DISCUSS WITH YOUR FAMILY

1. What was the teaching of the Pharisees concerning the making of vows?
2. What did Jesus teach concerning the making of a vow?
3. Why should a 'Yes' or 'No' be sufficient when we make a promise to someone?

Meditation

Meditate upon the assurance that God will fulfil all of his promises. 'For all the promises of God in him are Yes, and in him Amen, to the glory of God through us' (2 Corinthians 1:20).

Wise Words

My future is as bright as the promises of God.

Adoniram Judson

22 April   Retaliation or turn the other cheek?

 'I gave my back to those who struck me, and my cheeks to those who plucked out the beard; I did not hide my face from shame and spitting' (Isaiah 50:6).

Read: Matthew 5:38-42

Some people unfortunately have a quick temper. My wife, Valerie, tells our grandson that there are times when he should count to ten before he says or does something he will later regret. Maybe there are times when we need to count to one hundred and think before we act.

The Pharisees were sticklers for the law and taught that when a person was offended it was right to retaliate — 'an eye for an eye and a tooth for a tooth'. However, the law of Israel did not have a place for personal vengeance and required strict justice when a decision was handed down from the court. It was the judge who gave 'eye for eye, tooth for tooth, hand for hand, foot for foot...' (Exodus 21:24). Where the death penalty was the appropriate punishment determined by the judge, the person convicted was taken outside the camp and stoned to death by the people — not only by the offended person.

The law of Moses forbade personal vengeance — 'You shall not take vengeance, nor bear any grudge against the children of your people, but you shall love your neighbour as yourself: I am the LORD' (Leviticus 19:18).

Jesus was reaffirming the role of the civil magistrate which was ordained by God for the well-being of society. Paul, writing to the Romans, said, 'Let every soul be subject to the governing authorities.... For rulers are not a terror to good works, but to evil... if you do evil, be afraid; for he does not bear the sword in vain; for he is God's minister, an avenger to execute wrath on him who practises evil' (Romans 13:1,4).

Christ, in this sermon, rebuked the spirit of vengeance that the Pharisees taught. He even said that the open-handed slap on the cheek, which was an insult, was to be ignored. Indeed the law of love taught that the one insulted in that way should turn the other cheek.

This was the Christian way — 'Blessed are the peacemakers...' Jesus urged the people to refrain from going to civil courts over minor matters. We are to do the same and be like the Redeemer who accepted the harsh treatment handed out to him. He also said that when the Roman soldiers conscripted a citizen to carry supplies they should do more than ordered. People were to show kindness to those in need and not seek revenge or strict justice. Jesus was simply teaching what was written in Proverbs 25:21-22 — 'If your enemy is hungry, give him bread to eat; and if he is thirsty, give him water to drink; for so you will heap coals of fire on his head, and the LORD will reward you.' As Christians we are to show love and kindness to the ungrateful and in doing so display our love of God.

Nevertheless, there are times when we must go to the police for protection. We have every right to repel an invading army. But in everything we do, let us always act in love 'for our citizenship is in heaven' (Philippians 3:20).

THINGS TO DISCUSS WITH YOUR FAMILY

1. Discuss the words of Proverbs 25:21,22. What do they teach us?
2. What is the 'law of love'?
3. What is your contribution to peace in your family?

Meditation

Meditate upon Proverbs 25:28 — 'Whoever has no rule over his own spirit is like a city broken down, without walls.'

Wise Words

The only people with whom you should try to get even are those who have helped you.   *John E. Southard*

'But I say to you, love your enemies…'
(Matthew 5:44).

Read: Matthew 5:43-48

The world needs constant doses of love. Our world is in a mess and instead of things improving most people despair for they see the world becoming worse. How often we hear the comment, 'I fear for the days of my children and grandchildren. Things are bad now, but the future looks worse. I thank God I won't be here to see it.'

The hard-hearted Pharisees were teaching as one commandment, several statements of the Old Testament. Clearly the Scriptures taught 'love'. We read in Leviticus 19:18, 'You shall not take vengeance, nor bear any grudge against the children of your people, but you shall love your neighbour as yourself: I am the LORD.' The commandment was plain — love your neighbour.

Then they read in Deuteronomy 23:3: 'An Ammonite or Moabite shall not enter the assembly of the LORD; even to the tenth generation none of his descendants shall enter the assembly of the LORD for ever.' To the Pharisee this meant one could hate his enemy, yet they were clearly told: 'If you meet your enemy's ox or his donkey going astray, you shall surely bring it back to him again' (Exodus 23:4). Proverbs 25:21-22 taught that genuine love was to be shown to everyone, even those considered to be an enemy — 'If your enemy is hungry, give him bread to eat; and if he is thirsty, give him water to drink; for so you will heap coals of fire on his head, and the LORD will reward you.'

Jesus stressed that love was needed in all relationships. He used God as the example of One who displays amazing grace and love to those who are his enemies. Mankind is in a state of rebellion, yet he continues to provide the much needed rain and sunshine.

The Apostle Paul wrote of God's love to fallen humanity: 'But God demonstrates his own love toward us, in that while we were still sinners, Christ died for us' (Romans 5:8). The saints are to conquer any hatred of the heart towards those who have hurt them. We are to pray for those people, do good to them and bless them always remembering that as Jesus was being put to death he prayed for those carrying out the sentence of the earthly court: 'Father, forgive them, for they do not know what they do' (Luke 23:34). Could you do this?

The Apostle Peter summarized our relationship with other people — have 'compassion for one another; love as brothers, be tender-hearted, be courteous; not returning evil for evil or reviling for reviling, but on the contrary blessing...' (1 Peter 3:8,9).

We are called to live a life of Christian love. Peter wrote of God, '... as he who called you is holy, you also be holy in all your conduct, because it is written, "Be holy, for I am holy"' (1 Peter 1:15,16). Love and holy living is the heart attitude of the citizens of God's redeemed society. As Christians we must excel in our demonstrations of love to all, even to those who hate us. We must love both God and our fellow man and continually walk in the footsteps of our Saviour, the Lord Jesus Christ. 'Love does no harm to a neighbour; therefore love is the fulfilment of the law' (Romans 13:10).

THINGS TO DISCUSS WITH YOUR FAMILY

1. Discuss Romans 5:10 — 'For if when we were enemies we were reconciled to God through the death of his Son, much more, having been reconciled, we shall be saved by his life.'
2. What is there in our lives that we should hate?
3. Why should you love your fellow man?

Meditation

Meditate upon Corrie Ten Boom who forgave the Nazi guards who abused her in the German concentration camp. Could you do the same?

Wise Words

Love is service rather than sentiment. *John Stott*

'Take heed that you do not do your charitable deeds before men, to be seen by them. Otherwise you have no reward from your Father in heaven' (Matthew 6:1).

Read: Matthew 6:1-4

In many countries the government has taken over the works that once were the responsibility of the church. Aged people receive pensions and often the church neglects giving help believing they have all they need. Yet, often it is just these people who do need assistance. A person I know very well is frequently visiting the home of an aged person to replace broken light bulbs. Age has prevented them doing what was once a simple operation. Others may need firewood cut or the lawn mowed. There is still a multitude of good deeds that can be done for these people.

Now the Pharisees were hypocrites of the first order. A hypocrite was the actor in the Greek play who wore a mask in order to take on the appearance of another person. The Pharisees did the same. They acted like godly people — not out of love of God, but rather to receive the praise of onlookers. Of them Spurgeon wrote: 'A penny in one hand and a trumpet in the other is the posture of a hypocrite.'

There are people today, and some claim to be Christians, who are the Pharisees of our age. They ensure the world sees their actions as they seek praise. Many times there are telethons for a good cause and some people give just to hear their name broadcast on the TV. I often wonder if they all give their promised donation to the cause.

Others say nothing, but secretly are proud of what they have done. Our good works must be the action of a generous heart that wants to see God glorified. Luke records Christ's words: 'But love your enemies, do good, and lend, hoping for nothing in return; and your reward will be great, and you will be sons of the Most High. For he is kind to the unthankful and evil' (Luke 6:35).

Jesus said that all hypocrites already 'have' their reward. The Greek word translated 'have' was a word taken from business life and meant 'Paid in full and this is the receipt.' It meant the debt had been paid and nothing more was to be added. It refers to those who have received their praise from man for their 'good' works, but they will not receive anything from God on the Judgement Day when the books are opened. What had been done for others to gain the praise of man will have beside it 'Paid in Full'.

God's people are to make sure that their good works come from a pure heart in order that God may have the praise. A new, regenerate heart is the reason for works of righteousness, not the expected praise of man.

I trust that we can all say amen to the answer to Question 1 of the *Shorter Catechism* — 'Man's chief end is to glorify God and enjoy him for ever.'

THINGS TO DISCUSS WITH YOUR FAMILY

1. What are we taught in Question 1 of the *Shorter Catechism?*
2. What are we taught in Galatians 6:10? — 'Therefore, as we have opportunity, let us do good to all, especially to those who are of the household of faith.'
3. Is there a contradiction between Christ's teaching in today's reading and what we have already read in Matthew 5:15? Discuss.

Meditation

Consider — 'Do I do good works for the praise of man or of God?'

Wise Words

When we take least notice of our good deeds ourselves, God takes most notice of them.   *Matthew Henry*

'But you, when you pray, go into your room, and when you have shut your door, pray to your Father who is in the secret place; and your Father who sees in secret will reward you openly' (Matthew 6:6).

Read: Matthew 6:5-8

The Lord is once again rebuking the Pharisees for their way of prayer. They were proud men who delighted in people regarding them as super godly people. Frequently they made sure they were in a public place when it was time for prayer and there with bowed heads gave every impression that they were the greatest of saints. Jesus told a parable that illustrated their pride — 'Two men went up to the temple to pray, one a Pharisee and the other a tax collector. The Pharisee stood and prayed thus with himself, "God, I thank you that I am not like other men — extortioners, unjust, adulterers, or even as this tax collector. I fast twice a week; I give tithes of all that I possess."

'And the tax collector, standing afar off, would not so much as raise his eyes to heaven, but beat his breast, saying, "God, be merciful to me a sinner!"

'I tell you, this man went down to his house justified rather than the other; for everyone who exalts himself will be humbled, and he who humbles himself will be exalted' (Luke 18:10-14).

Which one is you?

Times haven't changed as even today we sometimes find people who make sure that at prayer meetings they pray using their most religious voice and right words for lengthy periods. Godly Charles Spurgeon once said, 'I never pray for more than ten minutes and never go ten minutes without prayer.' Like Mr Spurgeon we are to 'pray without ceasing' (1 Thessalonians 5:17). But unlike the Pharisees our prayers must come from a heart that loves God and has no interest in the praise of others. Jesus said we should go into our 'room' and there in private pour out our heart to God. The word translated 'room' means a storehouse where precious items are kept. Surely the secret place of prayer is a storehouse of precious spiritual blessings. It is one of the places where our hunger and thirst for spiritual food is satisfied, and where the Holy Spirit gives us peace of heart.

There are times when our heart is overburdened with difficulties and we cannot find the right words to use in prayer, but again God comes to our rescue: 'Likewise the Spirit also helps in our weaknesses. For we do not know what we should pray for as we ought, but the Spirit himself makes intercession for us with groanings which cannot be uttered. Now he who searches the hearts knows what the mind of the Spirit is, because he makes intercession for the saints according to the will of God' (Romans 8:26-27).

God knows our needs, but has ordained prayer as the means of bringing our petitions before him. Christians, give time daily to communion with your God. Praise your Saviour and give thanks for all that he has done for you.

THINGS TO DISCUSS WITH YOUR FAMILY

1. What is wrong with the prayers of the heathen?
2. In whose name must we pray in order to have our prayers reach God?
3. What did Jesus mean when he said — 'If you ask anything in my name, I will do it'? (John 14:14). Compare this with John 15:16.

Meditation

Meditate upon your family's spiritual needs and pray that God will bless each member.

Wise Words

When we shoot an arrow, we look to the fall of it; when we send a ship to sea, we look for the return of it; when we sow a seed, we look for a harvest; and so when we sow our prayers into God's bosom, shall we not look for an answer? *Richard Sibbes*

'In this manner, therefore, pray: Our Father in heaven, hallowed be your name' (Matthew 6:9).

Read: Psalm 93

We come to what is called 'The Lord's Prayer' which I believe should be known as the 'Disciples' Prayer'. It was never prayed by our Saviour, but was given as an example of what should be included in prayer. Often congregations say this prayer as a matter of form, but we must always remember that any approach to God must come from the heart and be offered in the name and merit of our Redeemer, who is the only Mediator between God and man (1 Timothy 2:5). Our prayers should always include, 'Not my will, but yours, be done' (Luke 22:42).

The prayer opens by acknowledging that we are approaching God who is our Father. As Creator, God is the Father of all mankind — 'But now O Lord, you are our Father; we are the clay, and you our potter; and all we are the work of your hand' (Isaiah 64:8). All mankind are 'his offspring' (Acts 17:28). However God is in a very special way 'Father' to all who believe. Through saving faith in Jesus, we're adopted into the family of God. Paul wrote: 'And because you are sons, God has sent forth the Spirit of his Son into your hearts, crying out, "Abba Father"' (Galatians 4:6). He is our 'dear Father'. That God is Father of his people is not just a revelation of the New Testament, but was known in Old Testament times. In Jeremiah 3:4 we read: 'Will you not from this time cry to me, "My father, you are the guide of my youth?"' Christians should forever praise God for the new birth which is the sovereign act of God the Holy Spirit by which we 'become children of God' (John 1:12).

The 'Disciples' Prayer' commences with words of praise to God our Father — 'Hallowed be your name.' The Scriptures are full of words of praise to God glorifying his amazing grace. Peter wrote: 'that in all things God [is to] be glorified through Jesus Christ, to whom belong the glory and the dominion for ever and ever. Amen' (1 Peter 4:11).

The answer to Question 1 of the *Shorter Catechism* reads: 'Man's chief end is to glorify God and enjoy him for ever.' Our Saviour lived to have God's name respected. Before his crucifixion he prayed, "'Father, glorify your name."' Then a voice came from heaven, saying, "I have both glorified it and will glorify it again"' (John 12:28). We do the same, saying, 'Amen' to the words of Psalm 86:12: 'I will praise you, O Lord my God, with all my heart, and I will glorify your name for evermore.'

We have every reason to praise our God. His character is perfect in every way. The answer to Question 4 in the *Shorter Catechism* declares — 'God is a Spirit, infinite, eternal, and unchangeable, in his being, wisdom, power, holiness, justice, goodness and truth.' This is my God; is he yours?

He is omnipresent — everywhere at all times, but we read God's word that tells us his throne is in heaven — 'Heaven is my throne, and earth is my footstool' (Isaiah 66:1). In prayer we approach a majestic heavenly Father who loves sinners. Despite his holiness and our sinfulness we are invited to approach him with 'boldness' (Hebrews 4:16) knowing that he delights to bless his people.

THINGS TO DISCUSS WITH YOUR FAMILY

1. In what way is Christ's sonship different to that of his people?
2. What does the word 'hallow' mean? See our text.
3. Discuss the glory of God.

Meditation

Meditate upon the revealed majesty of God, our heavenly Father.

Wise Words

The Lord's Prayer (as indeed every prayer) is a letter sent from earth to heaven.   *Matthew Henry*

'Your kingdom come. Your will be done, on earth as it is in heaven' (Matthew 6:10).

Read: Revelation 21:1-8 and 22-27

Our world is in a terrible state. Wars with killings and destruction of property are widespread, murder is commonplace, families are torn apart by unfaithfulness and Christians find the way of life of so many to be a cause of distress. And people ask, 'What is the answer to the world's problems?' I know the answer — It is a turning to the Lord Jesus Christ in true repentance and a saving faith in the Saviour. Then it is to live in accordance with God's law — 'You shall love the LORD your God with all your heart, with all your soul, with all your strength, and with all your mind,' and 'your neighbour as yourself' (Luke 10:27).

This section of the 'Disciples' Prayer' is missionary orientated. It is a prayer that the kingdom of Satan might become the kingdom of God; that sinners might become citizens of God's society. Before ascending into heaven Jesus gave his disciples their working orders: 'Go into all the world and preach the gospel to every creature' (Mark 16:15). After the day of Pentecost when the Holy Spirit fell upon the disciples they commenced preaching a risen Christ with great power and courage. Within a few years the Apostle Paul could write that the gospel had 'in all the world [brought] forth fruit' (Colossians 1:6). The kingdom of God was growing and God's law was being lived out throughout the world.

In heaven God's will is perfectly obeyed. After Christ's resurrection Satan was thrown out of heaven, a defeated enemy (Revelation 12:7-11). On earth 'the devil walks about like a roaring lion, seeking whom he may devour' (1 Peter 5:8). All of God's people have turned from their sinful ways and 'live according to God in the spirit' (1 Peter 4:6). The devil cannot 'devour' them. Jesus came to this world to save sinners. This was not just to save them from the penalty owing to God because of their sins, but to save them from committing sins.

Despite our desire to live a holy life there is a struggle going on within our heart. Paul wrote of the struggle he experienced — 'For what I am doing, I do not understand. For what I will to do, that I do not practise; but what I hate, that I do... For the good that I will to do, I do not do; but the evil I will not to do, that I practise...' (Romans 7:15,19). With Christ there is forgiveness and we live in that age where God said, 'All shall know me, from the least of them to the greatest' (Hebrews 8:11).

There is a day coming when Christ returns and after the judgement there will be a 'new heavens and a new earth in which righteousness dwells' (2 Peter 3:13). Then there will be perfect righteousness — no sin or anything which causes hurt or distress. How we should look forward to that day of which Paul wrote: 'Then comes the end, when he delivers the kingdom to God the Father, when he puts an end to all rule and all authority and power. For he must reign till he has put all enemies under his feet. The last enemy that will be destroyed is death. For "He has put all things under his feet." But when he says "all things are put under him", it is evident that he who put all things under him is excepted. Now when all things are made subject to him, then the Son himself will also be subject to him who put all things under him, that God may be all in all' (1 Corinthians 15:24-28).

THINGS TO DISCUSS WITH YOUR FAMILY

1. Why should we pray: 'Come, Lord Jesus!' (Revelation 22:20)?
2. What can you do to extend the kingdom of God on earth?
3. Today, where are saved sinners to be found?

Meditation

Meditate upon the glory of God's eternal kingdom.

Wise Words

Earth has no sorrow that heaven cannot heal.

Thomas Moore

'Give us this day our daily bread' (Matthew 6:11).

Read: Psalm 104:10-30

In most places in the western world there is an abundance of food, and for this we should thank God. Last night I had a delicious piece of steak for tea and was conscious that in many places people went to bed hungry. I can only praise God for his goodness to me and enjoy what he has provided.

The first petitions of the 'Disciples' Prayer' dealt with God's glory and kingdom, but now we look at a fundamental need of all people — their daily bread. We are body and soul and our body is not to be despised. Our body, if we are believers, is 'the temple of the Holy Spirit' (1 Corinthians 6:19) despite our sin. When Christ returns there will be the resurrection and all of the saints shall receive new bodies like that of the Lord Jesus. Thus we are to care for our body and this means providing it with food.

This portion of the prayer is not asking for a life of luxury. In Proverbs 30:8-9 we read wise words concerning our prayer for food: 'Give me neither poverty nor riches — feed me with the food allotted to me; lest I be full and deny you, and say, "Who is the LORD?" Or lest I be poor and steal, and profane the name of my God.' We ask for a necessity — our daily bread.

I am not to sit back and wait for God to drop food onto my table, but work to produce the food my family and I need each day. In their desert wanderings God provided manna — food from heaven for his people. They still had to work for that food. Each day, except on the Sabbath, the people went about gathering what was needed for the family to eat. God provides the rain and the sunshine that are needed to make the crops grow, but work is needed to produce that food. We are advised in Proverbs 6:6-8 — 'Go to the ant, you sluggard! Consider her ways and be wise, which, having no captain, overseer or ruler, provides her supplies in the summer, and gathers her food in the harvest.'

There is a warning to those who will not work for their daily bread — 'Don't expect others to provide you with food!' Paul wrote: 'If anyone will not work, neither shall he eat' (2 Thessalonians 3:10).

We must always thank God for our daily food for he is the ultimate source of our daily meal just as James wrote: 'Every good gift and every perfect gift is from above, and comes down from the Father of lights' (James 1:17). The Psalmist wrote words of thanks to God for his bounty: 'He causes the grass to grow for the cattle, and vegetation for the service of man, that he may bring forth food from the earth, and wine that makes glad the heart of man, oil to make his face shine, and bread which strengthens man's heart' (Psalm 104:14,15).

Always thank God for his provision of your 'daily bread'.

THINGS TO DISCUSS
WITH YOUR FAMILY

1. What are we taught in 1 Corinthians 10:31 — 'Therefore, whether you eat or drink, or whatever you do, do all to the glory of God'?
2. In what way does God provide you with your daily food?
3. Travelling through the wilderness, how did God provide manna for the Sabbath day? See Exodus 16:13-31.

Meditation

Meditate upon God's goodness in the provision of your daily food, even in difficult times.

Wise Words

Hearty thanks must be given to God: such as cometh not from the roof of the mouth but the root of the heart. *John Trapp*

'And forgive us our debts, as we forgive our debtors' (Matthew 6:12).

Read: Matthew 18:21-35

'Please forgive me,' are sometimes difficult words to say to another person. It can also be hard for some people to reply, 'I do forgive you.' I have heard some people say, 'I will never forgive you for what you have done to me.' That is an ungodly thing to say and should never be said by a professing Christian.

Our sins caused such a rift between God and man that not only could we not overcome that separation, but we weren't interested in establishing harmony with our Creator. However, thanks be to our God for although he was the offended One, he did all that was necessary to re-establish peace between himself and the elect. This he did through the sacrificial, saving work of his Son. Now, when sinners are awakened to their sinful state before God, and the eternal punishment that is their destiny, they can seek forgiveness. Forgiveness is theirs if they come with a repentant heart, acknowledging that Jesus is the only way of salvation and trusting their eternal welfare upon the Saviour who delights to save lost sheep.

God's forgiveness is final and total. Repentant sinners can face the Day of Judgement with a confidence that 'there is therefore now no condemnation to those who are in Christ Jesus, who do not walk according to the flesh, but according to the Spirit' (Romans 8:1). Our sins will never be brought up against us to condemn us. They have been dealt with and are gone for ever. Micah wrote: 'You will cast all our sins into the depths of the sea' (Micah 7:19) and the Psalmist wrote: 'As far as the east is from the west, so far has he removed our transgressions from us. As a father pities his children, so the LORD pities those who fear him' (Psalm 103:12-13). God's forgiveness means we have 'passed from death into life' (John 5:24).

The day we confessed saving faith in Christ we were justified in the courts of heaven and all of our sins, past, present and future, were blotted out. But daily we must confess breaking God's law and seek his forgiveness. When Jesus washed his disciples' feet we read his words to Peter who had refused to allow Christ to wash his dirty feet, 'He who is bathed needs only to wash his feet, but is completely clean; and you are clean...' (John 13:10). Here Christ taught the necessity of daily confession of our sins. And praise God we read elsewhere: 'If we confess our sins, he is faithful and just to forgive us our sins and to cleanse us from all unrighteousness' (1 John 1:9). We have a glorious, merciful Saviour! Praise God!

Nevertheless, our sins will never find forgiveness with God unless we have forgiven those who have offended us. Christ reaffirms this: 'For if you forgive men their trespasses, your heavenly Father will also forgive you. But if you do not forgive men their trespasses, neither will your Father forgive your trespasses' (Matthew 6:14-15).

The parable you read today teaches this very clearly. We are to repeatedly forgive those who seek our pardon (Matthew 18:22). This does not mean that we should not take care to prevent the same offence happening again. The repentant thief who has broken into our home might confess and ask for forgiveness. We forgive as God requires, seek restitution and then put security locks on our doors. Our forgiveness must come from a purified heart that shows Christian love to the one who has caused the offence.

THINGS TO DISCUSS
WITH YOUR FAMILY

1. Should you forgive the unrepentant?
2. Psalm 51 is David's prayer for forgiveness. Discuss verse 5 of this psalm.
3. What wondrous transaction concerning sin and righteousness took place on the cross?

Meditation

Consider the wonder of God forgiving your sins. Why should he do this for you?

Wise Words

Ours is the religion of the forgiven.   *Theodore Williams*

259

'And do not lead us into temptation, but
deliver us from the evil one' (Matthew
6:13).

Read: James 1:1-18

God does not tempt anyone to commit sin. We are responsible
for our sins and on Judgement Day unrepentant sinners will be
punished for breaking God's holy law. They will not be able to point
the accusing finger at God and say, 'You're to blame for my wickedness.'

The 'Disciples' Prayer' returns to our spiritual need and it is a plea
to God that he will preserve us from the danger of daily temptations.
Again it is the desire of the renewed heart to turn from sin and live
a life of holiness in order to show our love for our Redeemer. The
regenerate heart hates sin and temptations to break God's law! One
great spiritual danger is the world, and the Apostle John warns us: 'Do
not love the world or the things in the world.... For all that is in the
world — the lust of the flesh, the lust of the eyes, and the pride of
life — is not of the Father but is of the world' (1 John 2:15-16). It is
Satan who uses the things of the world with which to tempt us. The
Apostle Peter instructs us, 'Be sober, be vigilant; because your adversary the devil walks about like a roaring lion, seeking whom he may
devour' (1 Peter 5:8). Satan is our enemy!

We must avoid those situations that tempt us to disobey God.
The Psalmist gives wise instruction in Psalm 1:1: 'Blessed is the man
who walks not in the counsel of the ungodly, nor stands in the path
of sinners, nor sits in the seat of the scornful.'

There are times when God puts us in situations to both test the
genuineness of our faith and to strengthen that faith. In all of these
situations we are assured that 'God is faithful, who will not allow you
to be tempted beyond what you are able, but with the temptation
will also make the way of escape, that you may be able to bear it'
(1 Corinthians 10:13). It is reason for great joy when we stand firm
against wickedness and our faith is strengthened to face new temptations. God has promised that when tempted his grace will be freely

available to give us the victory. If we fail, the fault is ours for not using the spiritual weapons God has abundantly given us. You will discuss these when answering Question 1.

We read in the Bible of the faith of the redeemed being tested. Peter failed miserably in one test (Mark 14:66-72). The faith of Abraham was tested when God commanded him to sacrifice his son, Isaac. He set out to obey God's instructions, believing that if necessary Jehovah would raise his promised son from the dead. When God saw his faith, Isaac was released, and a sheep provided for the sacrifice.

God has promised us victory over Satan. In his letter to the Romans Paul wrote: 'And the God of peace will crush Satan under your feet shortly' (Romans 16:20). When we pray the words of our text we must do so from the heart that fully trusts God to preserve us. We should praise God in the Psalmist's words: 'The LORD shall preserve you from all evil; he shall preserve your soul' (Psalm 121:7). Praise God for his goodness to repentant sinners.

THINGS TO DISCUSS WITH YOUR FAMILY

1. What weapons has God given you to defeat temptations? Read Ephesians 6:10-17.
2. Who is 'the evil one'? Where did he come from? Read Isaiah 14:12-15 and Genesis 3:1-15.
3. What is temptation and is there sin in just being tempted?
4. When Jesus was tempted by Satan what weapon did he use to repel him? Read Matthew 4:1-11.

Meditation

Think upon the following — 'God tests us to help us stand. Satan tempts us to make us fall.'

Sin stamps the devil's image on a man.   *Thomas Watson*

Wise Words

261

May

'For yours is the kingdom and the power and the glory for ever. Amen' (Matthew 6:13b).

Read: Psalm 27

There are times when I sit and contemplate the glory of God. One night I was alone in my small boat, fishing out in the ocean. I remember that night well as it was the time when the American astronauts were returning home in their crippled spaceship which was short of oxygen. The sky was dark and clear and above I could see the multitude of stars that city people can't see because there is so much light. I was struck with the majesty of the God who created everything. What wisdom, power, glory and majesty were revealed in the expanse above me.

The 'Lord's Prayer' concludes with a wonderful doxology reflecting the glory of God. The words of our text are similar to those spoken by David, king of Israel: 'Yours, O LORD, is the greatness and the power and the glory and the majesty and the splendour, for everything in heaven and earth is yours. Yours, O LORD, is the kingdom; you are exalted as head over all. Wealth and honour come from you; you are the ruler of all things. In your hands are strength and power to exalt and give strength to all. Now, our God, we give you thanks, and praise your glorious name' (1 Chronicles 29:11-13, NIV).

There are places in the Scriptures that reveal the majestic glory of God. One place is Daniel 4:34-35 where King Nebuchadnezzar regained his sanity and praised God, saying, 'For his dominion is an everlasting dominion, and his kingdom is from generation to generation. All the inhabitants of the earth are reputed as nothing; he does according to his will in the army of heaven and among the inhabitants of the earth. No one can restrain his hand or say to him, "What have you done?"'

Our God is omnipotent. He rules this world which by his almighty power he created, simply by speaking all things into existence. He is a saving God who through the sacrificial work of his Son has redeemed a people to himself. What wisdom and glory is seen in this plan of redemption! The saints should be humble people who give God the praise and glory due to his wondrous name. We must remember God's words, 'And I will not give my glory to another' (Isaiah 48:11).

Our God is matchless in holiness as was sung by the children of Israel: 'Who is like you, glorious in holiness, fearful in praises, doing wonders?' (Exodus 15:11). Isaiah had a vision of Christ upon the throne of God, before whom the all powerful, holy angels sang: 'Holy, holy, holy is the LORD of hosts; the whole earth is full of his glory!' (Isaiah 6:3). Like the Psalmist our desire is to praise God more and more each day (Psalm 71:14) and the more we learn about him the more our hearts will be filled with love and praise.

As we discover more about our God let us offer 'the sacrifice of praise ... that is, the fruit of our lips, giving thanks to his name' (Hebrews 13:15). Amen, what a majestic God we have.

THINGS TO DISCUSS WITH YOUR FAMILY

1. What does 'doxology' mean?
2. For what reason should you thank God?
3. Read and discuss Psalm 24:7-10.

Meditation

Go outside one night and gaze up into the clear dark sky and meditate upon the power, wisdom and majesty of the One who created all of it. Psalm 19:1 — 'The heavens declare the glory of God; and the firmament shows his handiwork.'

Wise Words

God is incomparable as he is immutable. He is infinitely farther above the tallest archangel than that archangel is above a worm. *William S. Plumer*

'Consecrate a fast, call a sacred assembly; gather the elders and all the inhabitants of the land into the house of the LORD your God, and cry out to the LORD' (Joel 1:14).

Read: Matthew 6:16-18

Today fasting is rare in the Christian church. The only fasting we read about is when people give up eating meals in order to lose weight. I have tried this many times.

We have read Christ's words of warning about fasting as the Pharisees did. Jesus was outlining the differences between members of the Kingdom of God and the schools of the Pharisees and scribes and stressing the one essential difference — that Christ's people have been born again. Gone is the stony, cold heart and in its place is a compassionate, loving one. The motivating force for the activities of the redeemed is that new, pure heart that loves God and wants the Saviour glorified.

We read that fasting was practised for spiritual reasons in Old Testament times. It was normally accompanied with prayer. When the ark of the covenant was about to be returned to its resting place in Israel we read of the nation: 'And they fasted that day, and said, "We have sinned against the LORD"' (1 Samuel 7:6). Prayer and confession of sin went hand in hand with fasting. When David faced the death of his child after his adultery with Bathsheba, and the murder of her husband, Uriah, we read, 'David therefore pleaded with God for the child, and David fasted and went in and lay all night on the ground' (2 Samuel 12:16). Again, going without meals was associated with prayer.

In Acts 13:2-3 we read of Saul and Barnabas being set apart for a special work. We read: 'Then, having fasted and prayed, and laid hands on them, they sent them away.'

The Pharisees made much of fasting as to them it was just another act of pride. They made sure they had a downcast look with some ashes on their face and clothing. They knew that all who saw them would admire their religiosity. Their pride would be satisfied for a time. Christ's parable of the tax collector and the publican reveals the attitude of the Pharisees to their public displays of false humility (Luke 18:10-14).

Every person who decides to fast should note the words of Jeremiah who was warned by God not to pray for the people of Israel: 'Do not pray for this people, for their good. When they fast, I will not hear their cry...' (Jeremiah 14:11-12).

Fasting is an acceptable secret practice in all ages when it is linked to some legitimate spiritual activity. Maybe you will want time to pray, praising God, confessing your sins, interceding for some special reason and reading your Bible. It could be a wise move to fast, saving time from cooking meals and devoting that time to the Lord. But always the reason for this must come from a pure heart and must not include showmanship to attract the praise of others. It is a means of withdrawing from the things of the world and helps us set our minds on heavenly matters.

THINGS TO DISCUSS WITH YOUR FAMILY

1. Why did Jesus fast before his wilderness temptations? (Matthew 4:2).
2. Does fasting only involve going for a time without food? See 1 Corinthians 7:5.
3. Give some reasons why you might fast.

Meditation

Set aside some time confessing your sin and thanking God for his many blessings.

Wise Words

That there is a close connection between fasting and spiritual meditation and contemplation is widely recognised. *William Hendriksen*

'Do not overwork to be rich; because of your own understanding, cease! Will you set your eyes on that which is not? For riches certainly make themselves wings; they fly away like an eagle toward heaven' (Proverbs 23:4-5).

Read: Matthew 6:19-24

'He has a hole in his pocket' is a common expression describing a person who is always broke despite earning good wages. Maybe there are times when we say this about ourselves. Nevertheless, I hope that we are not people who live for the things of this world. Some people use their eyesight to gather wealth yet they are spiritually blind.

Jesus in our passage states plainly that there are two pathways before every person upon the earth — the highway to heaven or the broad way that ends in hell. Many who travel the broad way do so because they have an all consuming passion to store away more of the world's goods. Judas is an example of a person who loved money so much that he stole what belonged to his fellow disciples and the Lord, while pretending to be an honest, upright disciple of Christ. His destiny was eternal damnation.

Again the Lord deals with another issue that stems from the state of the heart. All who are born again use their money for legitimate activities. Finances are necessary to purchase food and satisfy our bodily needs, but Jehovah our God controls the affairs of our life.

Jesus explained that there is no real security in wealth as it can vanish in a moment. Many people have lost their wealth because they invested in 'get-rich' schemes run by 'con-men'. Because of an economic disaster many have lost their fortunes. Then there are those who break into homes and steal everything; or the house catches on fire and all is lost. In Christ's day, frequently it was moths who ruined clothing that had been purchased as a form of investment. Others found their costly metal purchases lost their value when rust set in and ruined the item.

Then of course age itself steals from us all. Many things we valued and used when young have no value to us as we grow older. Finally death steals away all of our earthly possessions. Job put it plainly:

'Naked I came from my mother's womb, and naked shall I return there. The LORD gave, and the LORD has taken away; blessed be the name of the LORD' (Job 1:21).

The Apostle Paul once considered his life as a Jew and Pharisee to be the most important thing in his life, until with a change of heart he was brought to faith in Christ. Then he simply stated what he thought of those things — 'But indeed I also count all things loss for the excellence of the knowledge of Christ Jesus my Lord' (Philippians 3:8).

Christians have a wealth that the world does not comprehend. We have our names written in the Lamb's Book of Life, a home in Paradise, peace of heart here and now, and no fear of death or facing Christ on the Day of Judgement. Praise the Lord!

THINGS TO DISCUSS WITH YOUR FAMILY

1. What did Paul mean when he wrote: 'Set your mind on things above, not on things on the earth' (Colossians 3:2)?
2. Can you think of any saints who were very wealthy? What was their attitude towards wealth?
3. What are heavenly 'treasures'?
4. Is it sinful to be rich in this world's goods?

Meditation

Meditate upon the priorities you have set yourself. Should the list be altered?

Wise Words

Many a man's gold has lost him his God.

George Swinnock

'But seek first the kingdom of God and his righteousness, and all these things shall be added to you' (Matthew 6:33).

Read: Matthew 6:25-34

Tension and worry are the cause of many of the illnesses of this age. People want more and more of the world's goods. This all consuming passion can cause illness which for many ends in death at an early age. Jesus has something important to say to such people.

We all need clothes to wear, food to eat, a home in which to live and loving relationships with God and our fellow man. An ample supply of these things makes life pleasant, yet in reality all we are doing is pampering the body.

Our Lord tells us to look about us and observe how God has made provision for all the creatures in his creation. Each morning while the farmer is hard at work producing food, the animals and birds are eating what God has so richly provided for them. Humans are of more value than any animal because we were created in the image of God, capable of a loving relationship with the Creator. We must be content with the food God provides for us, yet many are not satisfied and want only the very best.

Clothing is needed, but many people are concerned with what they perceive as the need of more and better clothing. Again God provides what we need. Jesus said, 'Look at the flowers. They are most colourful; in fact their clothing is far superior to the clothing worn by the earth's richest people.'

Worry is not a method to gain the things we want, but rather it tears us apart. Christ has instructed us to put our needs in the right order. First we need peace with God, and that is only possible through a saving faith in the Lord Jesus. Then other things will fall into place and God will provide us with our daily needs. That does not mean we just sit and wait for food and clothing to fall from heaven; it means we work to earn wages to be used to purchase what we need. Solomon was asked by the LORD what he wanted. He was at peace with God and, knowing his own weakness and that material possessions would not make him a better ruler, asked for wisdom. God granted his prayer and then gave him material blessings as well: 'And I have also given you what you have not asked: both riches and honour…' (1 Kings 3:13).

Paul compared spiritual activities to bodily exercise and wrote: 'For bodily exercise profits a little, but godliness is profitable for all things, having promise of the life that now is and of that which is to come' (1 Timothy 4:8).

Instead of worry which causes tension, make sure you are right with God and then work to satisfy your material needs. Be willing to sacrifice your material comforts in the service of Christ. He has made a wonderful promise to his people, 'Assuredly, I say to you, there is no one who has left house or parents or brothers or wife or children, for the sake of the kingdom of God, who shall not receive many times more in this present time, and in the age to come eternal life' (Luke 18:29-30). Let us trust Christ's precious promises.

THINGS TO DISCUSS WITH YOUR FAMILY

1. Discuss the world's trinity of cares — eat, drink and wear.
2. Is worry a sin? Why?
3. Instead of worrying about food on the table to-morrow, what should we do?

Meditation

Meditate upon 1 Timothy 6:17 — 'Command those who are rich in this present age not to be haughty, nor to trust in uncertain riches but in the living God, who gives us richly all things to enjoy.'

Wise Words

Nothing influences a man so much as that which he calls his own. *C. H. Spurgeon*

'There is one Lawgiver, who is able to save and to destroy. Who are you to judge another?' (James 4:12).

Read: Matthew 7:1-6

Life is full of making decisions in the light of the available evidence. Yet there are some people who often make the statement 'Judge not, that you be not judged' without realizing that they are making a judgement.

Jesus rebuked the Pharisees and others who make unfair deductions without considering the available evidence. Their sin was the proud, censorious criticism they made of others, not realizing that when they condemned another person they were acting contrary to God's commandments. In his epistle, James takes up this matter with the warning that we are not to speak evil of another person because to do so breaks God's 'royal law' which is, 'You shall love your neighbour as yourself' (James 2:8). To break this law by unjust criticism of another person is to effectively say, 'I don't agree with God's law of love. I am now the lawgiver and my law is to make unjust, censorious criticisms of other people' (see James 4:11-12).

Christ was not forbidding the making of fair determinations, after all, he did so on many occasions. In our reading he called some people 'dogs' and 'pigs' which was a harsh judgement upon wicked people, but Christ was aware of all the facts and made righteous judgements. The Pharisees were included in the 'pigs' and 'dogs' as they persecuted the righteous and trampled the pure teaching of Christ into the mud of their own making.

So often the very subject of criticism is found in the life of the one making the judgement. Paul warns such people: 'Therefore you are inexcusable, O man, whoever you are who judge, for in whatever you judge another you condemn yourself; for you who judge practise the same things. But we know that the judgement of God is according to truth … And do you think this, O man, you who judge those practising such things, and doing the same, that you will escape the judgement of God?' (Romans 2:1-3). Jesus said that we must look at the evidence when making decisions: 'Do not judge according to appearance, but judge with righteous judgements' (John 7:24).

Paul wrote that we are to make judgements in spiritual matters: 'Test all things; hold fast what is good. Abstain from every form of evil' (1 Thessalonians 5:21-22). The noble Bereans were commended for doing this when Paul preached (Acts 17:11). With so much false spiritual teaching about today we should carefully carry out what John said in 1 John 4:1: 'Beloved, do not believe every spirit, but test the spirits, whether they are of God; because many false prophets have gone out into the world.' Also the day is coming when the saints will be involved in making determinations that have eternal consequences. We read: 'Do you not know that the saints will judge the world?... Do you not know that we shall judge angels?' (1 Corinthians 6:2-3).

May we always exercise that 'royal law' when we judge the actions of others.

THINGS TO DISCUSS WITH YOUR FAMILY

1. What is Christ teaching when he speaks about a 'log' being in a person's eye?
2. Is there a 'log' in your eye when you make judgements? Discuss this matter.
3. What do we use in order to make righteous judgements?

Meditation

Meditate upon God's eternal judgement of you. Why has he made this judgement?

Wise Words

Love should be the silver thread that runs through all your conduct.   *J. C. Ryle*

'If you then, being evil, know how to give good gifts to your children, how much more will your Father who is in heaven give good things to those who ask him!' (Matthew 7:11).

Read: Matthew 7:7-11

Prayer is hard work. We have so much to do each day that often prayer is well down the priority list. This should never be, for prayer is communication with God. When we read the Scriptures God speaks to us, and we should constantly be speaking to our heavenly Father.

Why should we pray? After all, God knows our every need. The answer is quite simple — God has ordained prayer as the means by which we make our needs known. Prayer is an acknowledgement by Christians that there is a God in heaven who listens and answers prayers. James wrote, '… you do not have because you do not ask' (James 4:3).

God gives many blessings to people generally without their asking. The rain falls on the just and the unjust and the sun shines on everyone. However, there are some blessings, especially spiritual blessings, that are the result of sincere prayer. Yet we must always remember that every blessing is the outcome of the grace of a loving, merciful God. Our God is rich in mercy and all who realize their need of a Saviour are invited to call upon him just as Paul wrote: 'For whoever calls upon the name of the LORD shall be saved' (Romans 10:13).

Jesus in our reading outlines the kindness of parents to their children when they came asking for help. He then declares that our heavenly Father will give precious gifts in response to the prayers of his people. Luke records words of great encouragement to people who are sincerely seeking Christ, the Redeemer: 'If you then, being evil, know how to give good gifts to your children, how much more will your heavenly Father give the Holy Spirit to those who ask him!' (Luke 11:13).

In your reading Christ reminds us that the humble, sincere person who is seeking blessings from God should be persistent in his prayers. We are told to 'come boldly to the throne of grace, [in order to] obtain mercy and find grace to help in time of need' (Hebrews 4:16). This should remind you of that widow who constantly appeared before an unjust judge with her plea for justice. Finally the judge, who didn't want to hear her petition, heard what she had to say just to have peace (Luke 18:2-8).

Our God is our heavenly Father who cares for his adopted children. In fact the Psalmist writes words of great encouragement: 'When my father and my mother forsake me, then the LORD will take care of me' (Psalm 27:10). God does not forget his people and is ever ready to pour blessings upon them. God said, 'Can a woman forget her nursing child, and not have compassion on the son of her womb? Surely they may forget, yet I will not forget you. See, I have inscribed you on the palms of my hands…' (Isaiah 49:15-16). Let us approach God with a pure sincere heart and wait to be blessed according to his will.

THINGS TO DISCUSS WITH YOUR FAMILY

1. God does not answer the prayers of every person. Why not? Read Isaiah 1:15 and Zechariah 7:9-14.
2. What is prayer?
3. Why should our prayers be made in the name of Jesus Christ? See 1 Timothy 2:5 and John 14:6.

Meditation

Meditate upon the blessings you need from your heavenly Father. Now pray for them with a humble spirit and pure heart.

Wise Words

Those blessings are sweetest that are won with prayers and worn with thanks. *Thomas Goodwin*

'Therefore, whatever you want men to do to you, do also to them, for this is the Law and the Prophets' (Matthew 7:12).

Read: Romans 13:8-10

Someone once wrote: 'Christian love is the queen of all grace.' This is so true. I'm sure that we would all agree with today's text which is often put: 'Do unto others as you would have them do to you.' Putting it into practice can present difficulties to many people, especially to those who have been offended by the actions of another.

In this brief verse Christ is giving a positive commandment, 'Do good to all people', which means that we are to show Christian love to every person, even our enemies. Why should we act in this way? Jesus said that this was the teaching of the law and the prophets who spoke the very words of God to a sinful society. Because it is God's law we are obliged to obey. Our obedience must be the consequence of our love of God and our fellow man, not just because it is God's law.

Christ was confronted by a Scribe who wanted to test his understanding of the Scriptures and asked the question, 'Which is the first commandment of all?'

Jesus answered him, 'The first of all the commandments is: "Hear, O Israel, the LORD our God, the LORD is one. And you shall love the LORD your God with all your heart, with all your soul, with all your mind, and with all your strength." This is the first commandment. And the second, like it, is this: "You shall love your neighbour as yourself." There is no other commandment greater than these' (Mark 12:28-31). Our dealings with our fellow man must be seasoned with Christian love.

We cannot expect good things from God unless we extend true blessings to others. But what is to be our response to those who have hurt us in some way? The answer is clear: 'Do to them what you would like them to do to you.' Jesus elsewhere said, 'Love your enemies, do good to those who hate you, bless those who curse you, and pray for those who spitefully use you' (Luke 6:27,28). This involves self denial to unworthy people.

The Apostle Paul wrote extensively on Christian love and his teachings in this area should fill our thoughts at all times. He wrote, 'Love suffers long and is kind; love does not envy; love does not parade itself, is not puffed up; does not behave rudely, does not seek its own, is not provoked, thinks no evil; does not rejoice in iniquity, but rejoices in the truth; bears all things, believes all things, hopes all things, endures all things...' (1 Corinthians 13:4-7).

Our responsibility to our 'neighbour' is summed up in the words of our text. That God may recognize any good in our actions, what we do must be the outworking of saving faith in our heart — 'But without faith it is impossible to please him, for he who comes to God must believe that he is, and that he is a rewarder of those who diligently seek him' (Hebrews 11:6).

May we be faithful, obedient servants of the Lord Jesus.

THINGS TO DISCUSS WITH YOUR FAMILY

1. Think of some person who doesn't like you; how are you to deal with his feelings?
2. Learn the text by heart and discuss how you can implement it in your everyday life.
3. What does Paul mean in his words '...work out your own salvation with fear and trembling; for it is God who works in you both to will and to do for his good pleasure' (Philippians 2:12-13)?

Meditation

Meditate upon Matthew 5:39-41 — 'But whoever slaps you on your right cheek, turn the other to him also. If anyone wants to sue you and take away your tunic, let him have your cloak also.'

Wise Words

What is hateful to you do not do to anyone else. This is the whole law; all the rest is only commentary.

Rabbi Hillel

'Jesus said to him, "I am the way, the truth, and the life. No one comes to the Father except through Me"' (John 14:6).

Read: Matthew 7:13,14

How often we complain about the state of our roads. Motorists pay heavy taxation when they purchase their cars and then on the oil and petrol needed to keep them functioning smoothly, but so often all of those taxes are not used to maintain roads. Too often alternative routes are difficult to travel.

Jeremiah wrote God's words: 'Thus says the LORD, "Behold, I set before you the way of life and the way of death"' (Jeremiah 21:8). Jesus now taught the same in what is the concluding section of the Sermon on the Mount.

The narrow way is all about Jesus, our Redeemer. Our text tells us that he is the way, and elsewhere he said — 'I am the door. If anyone enters by me, he will be saved...' (John 10:9). The doorway is opened by the Holy Spirit when he brings about the new birth in the sinner's heart and gives saving faith in the Lord Jesus. Paul put it this way: 'For by grace you have been saved through faith, and that not of yourselves; it is the gift of God, not of works, lest anyone should boast' (Ephesians 2:8-9). Then commences the journey of faith, repentance, confession, hatred of sin, self denial, obedience and the love of God and man. The narrow way is fenced by God's law of which the redeemed can say with David, 'Therefore I love your commandments more than gold, yes, than fine gold!' (Psalm 119:127).

The destination of the narrow way is heaven. Again the godly David was able to write of his great hope, which is the hope of every Christian — 'And I will dwell in the house of the LORD for ever' (Psalm 23:6). Sadly there are only few who tread the narrow pathway.

In Proverbs 16:25 we read: 'There is a way that seems right to a man, but its end is the way of death.' This was the way of the Pharisees and the vast majority of mankind. All mankind, with the revealed exceptions of Jesus, John the Baptist and Jeremiah, are born on the broad way and continue walking that way until they see the futility of their life and turn to Christ for salvation.

The broad way has a wide gate which allows its travellers to take whatever they want with them — pride, sin, love of self and the world. The broad way has no fences as it is the way of spiritual ignorance and permissiveness. Paul, writing to the Ephesian Christians, said the broad way was the way 'in which you once walked according to the course of this world, according to the prince of the power of the air, the spirit who now works in the sons of disobedience, among whom also we all once conducted ourselves in the lusts of our flesh, fulfilling the desires of the flesh and of the mind, and were by nature children of wrath, just as the others' (Ephesians 2:2-3).

The broad way is the way of death and we read of those who travel that way, 'And the smoke of their torment ascends for ever and ever; and they have no rest day or night…' (Revelation 14:11). The Psalmist said of these ungodly travellers, that they 'shall perish' (Psalm 1:6b). Which roadway are you travelling?

THINGS TO DISCUSS WITH YOUR FAMILY

1. How do you get onto the narrow way?
2. The Pharisees taught that obedience to God's law was the way to heaven. What did Paul say of that way? Read Galatians 1:6-9.
3. 'I live by the golden rule and will one day get to heaven.' Discuss this statement.

Meditation

Meditate upon the narrow way and its destiny.

It is scarcely possible in most places to get anyone to attend a meeting where the only attraction is God.

A. W. Tozer

Wise Words

'Beloved, do not believe every spirit, but test the spirits, whether they are of God; because many false prophets have gone out into the world' (1 John 4:1).

Read: Matthew 7:15-20

I sometimes open my books about the Jehovah Witness sect and am amazed at the number of prophecies that were made and never came to pass. Despite this so many deluded people follow the broad way, ignorant of God's warning: 'When a prophet speaks in the name of the LORD, if the thing does not happen or come to pass, that is the thing which the LORD has not spoken; the prophet has spoken it presumptuously; you shall not be afraid of him' (Deuteronomy 18:22). In fact God's law to Israel was that these people were to be put to death (Deuteronomy 18:20).

Paul warned the Ephesian elders of false prophets and we should take careful note of his words, 'For I know this, that after my departure savage wolves will come in among you, not sparing the flock. Also from among yourselves men will rise up, speaking perverse things, to draw away the disciples after themselves' (Acts 20:29-30). The great danger to the church comes from within when smooth talkers start preaching a different gospel and lead many astray. These people commence their teachings with fine words and doctrines that seem to be the truth, but soon false teaching becomes their message and many follow their heresy. Paul warns of these people: 'Now I urge you, brethren, note those who cause divisions and offences, contrary to the doctrine which you learned, and avoid them. For those who are such do not serve our Lord Jesus Christ, but their own belly, and by smooth words and flattering speech deceive the hearts of the simple' (Romans 16:17-18). In many churches there is no preaching of God's wrath, his holiness and justice.

Many of these false prophets are worldly people who wallow in their pride. Their 'church services' are little more than concerts entertaining the congregation with supposed healings, slayings in the Spirit, melodious choirs and claims that they alone teach the truth. Some even say that there is no salvation outside of their particular system of beliefs. The greatest false prophet is the Antichrist who has been established by Satan as his representative on earth. We are told to beware of Satan and his human teachers. Paul wrote, 'For such are false apostles, deceitful workers, transforming themselves into apostles of Christ. And no wonder! For Satan himself transforms himself into an angel of light. Therefore it is no great thing if his ministers also transform themselves into ministers of righteousness, whose end will be according to their works' (2 Corinthians 11:13-15).

Christ's people must cling to the teaching of Scripture so they can exercise discernment. A true prophet and teacher is one who loves God and his fellow man and delights in the law of God. His teaching glorifies God because it is based upon the Lord's word and not his own. He invites sinners to turn to Christ in true repentance and faith. Such pastors are followers of the greatest prophet of all — the Lord Jesus Christ.

THINGS TO DISCUSS WITH YOUR FAMILY

1. Paul wrote much about the 'man of sin' (2 Thessalonians 2:1-12). Who is this evil man?
2. What can you do to prevent being led astray by false teachers? Read 1 Thessalonians 5:21.
3. How should you witness to Jehovah's Witnesses and members of other cults?

Meditation

Meditate upon the traits of a true teacher of God. Is your pastor such a minister of righteousness? If so, thank God and pray for the man God has placed over you spiritually.

Wise Words

Sound doctrine and holy living are the marks of true prophets.   *J. C. Ryle*

'Not everyone who says to me, "Lord, Lord," shall enter the kingdom of heaven, but he who does the will of my Father in heaven' (Matthew 7:21).

Read: Psalm 119:41-48

I believe that these are some of the most fearful words that professing Christians find in the Scriptures. It deals with people who truly believed they were travelling the narrow way, only to discover on Judgement Day that their faith was false. John Bunyan wrote of these people and their end: 'Then I saw that there was a way to hell, even from the gates of heaven, as well as from the city of destruction.'

Christ is answering the question found in Psalm 15:1, 'LORD, who may abide in your tabernacle? Who may dwell in your holy hill?' He is telling us about those who have no place in the kingdom of God.

The first group are those spoken of by Christ in Luke 6:46: 'But why do you call me "Lord, Lord" and not do the things which I say?' Many people of all ages have believed they were saved simply because they professed faith in Christ, but James give the serious warning — 'For as the body without the spirit is dead, so faith without works is dead also' (James 2:26). Words are not enough, although Jesus said to his disciples shortly before his crucifixion, 'You call me Teacher and Lord, and you say well, for so I am' (John 13:13). But more than words are needed — what is required is a new heart producing the fruit of the Spirit and works of faith. Jesus later told a parable about two sons whose father instructed them to start work in the vineyard. One said he would, but did nothing, the second said he wouldn't, but repented and set to work doing as his father had asked. It was the repentant son who was praised by Christ (Matthew 21:28-32).

First let us look at our lives and search for the fruit of the Spirit — 'love, joy, peace, long-suffering, kindness, goodness, faithfulness, gentleness, self-control' (Galatians 5:22-23). This fruit must be present to some extent in every Christian. There are also the works of faith of which Paul wrote, 'For we are his workmanship, created in Christ Jesus for good works, which God prepared beforehand that we should walk in them' (Ephesians 2:10).

Jesus was again looking at the lifestyle of the Pharisees who had the reputation of being the most godly people in Israel. Later the Lord warned the people not to imitate those proud people — '... they say and do not do' (Matthew 23:3).

How do you know that you are a Christian? The Apostle John gives one clue that perfectly fits the teaching of our text. He wrote, 'Now by this we know that we know him, if we keep his commandments' (1 John 2:3). If we are not living a godly life then 'Lord, Lord,' are very hollow words indeed.

May we all examine our life to ensure we never hear Christ's words of condemnation: 'I never knew you; depart from me, you who practise lawlessness.'

THINGS TO DISCUSS WITH YOUR FAMILY

1. What are the great commandments? Read Matthew 22:37-39.
2. What type of faith is a saving faith?
3. What are some of the ways we can do God's will?

Meditation

Meditate upon the genuineness of your faith and the majesty of Jesus in whom you have faith.

Wise Words

The Day of Judgement will reveal strange things. The hopes of many who were thought to be great Christians while they lived will be utterly confounded. The rottenness of their religion will be exposed and put to shame before the whole world. *J. C. Ryle*

'Many will say to me in that day, "Lord, Lord, have we not prophesied in your name, cast out demons in your name, and done many wonders in your name?"' (Matthew 7:22).

Read: Matthew 24:4-25

I'm sure that as we meditate upon the day when we will appear individually before God's Judge, the Lord Jesus Christ, there is a degree of concern in our hearts. During our lifetime we have largely controlled our activities, but on that day we will obey the orders of the Judge. Christians can face Judgement Day with confidence because we have already been pardoned, but still there is the unknown to face.

Jesus speaks not just of people who confess him as Lord and do not carry out his commandments, but also of those who confess him as their Lord and perform great wonders. Jesus warned the disciples about such people during the events leading up to the destruction of Jerusalem by the Roman armies in AD 70. Many false Christs would arise and lead many astray.

Today is no different. We are forewarned by Paul, 'For Satan himself transforms himself into an angel of light. Therefore it is no great thing if his ministers also transform themselves into ministers of righteousness, whose end will be according to their works' (2 Corinthians 11:14-15). These people will be able to carry out mighty deeds, but lack a transformed heart. Again the Apostle Paul wrote, 'Though I speak with the tongues of men and of angels, but have not love, I have become sounding brass or a clanging cymbal. And though I have the gift of prophecy, and understand all mysteries and all knowledge, and though I have all faith, so that I could remove mountains, but have not love, I am nothing' (1 Corinthians 13:1-2).

Today we have great showmen who perform 'slayings in the Spirit,' healings and other great 'miracles'. We must be wary of these people, for much of their teaching is not entirely biblical. The Apostle Paul warned us of the Antichrist who would do great wonders: 'The coming of the lawless one is according to the working of Satan, with all power, signs, and lying wonders, and with all unrighteous deception among those who perish, because they did not receive the love of the truth, that they might be saved' (2 Thessalonians 2:9-10). The 'lawless one' and his organization will perform great wonders and we must be on guard. Paul went on to say that God detests all who show an interest in Satan's man. We read, 'And for this reason God will send them strong delusion, that they should believe the lie, that they all may be condemned who did not believe the truth but had pleasure in unrighteousness' (2 Thessalonians 2:11-12).

We must compare the teaching of church leaders with that found in the Scriptures and when we find significant differences have nothing to do with them.

THINGS TO DISCUSS WITH YOUR FAMILY

1. The Apostle John wrote, 'Dear friends, do not believe every spirit, but test the spirits to see whether they are from God' (1 John 4:1). How can you 'test the spirits'?
2. How can you determine if a person is a Christian or not?
3. Why was Judas called 'the son of perdition'? (John 17:12).

Meditation

Are you able to say 'Amen' to Paul's words in Philippians 1:20 — '... now also Christ will be magnified in my body, whether by life or by death'?

Wise Words

A man may be a preacher, may have gifts for the ministry, and an external call to it, and perhaps some success in it, and yet be a wicked man; may help others to heaven, and yet come short himself. *Matthew Henry*

'Unless the Lord builds the house, they labour in vain who build it' (Psalm 127:1).

Read: Matthew 7:24-29

A section of our retirement home is built on a cement slab. At the time the builder told me that sandy soil was best for a concrete block. To put a cement floor on clay soil sometimes results in cracking as the clay shrinks and expands according to the weather. Our reading tells us that the wise builder constructed his home on rock as sand was dangerous in flood times. Christ was saying that it was foolish to build in a sandy creek bed because floods would destroy the house.

Our Saviour was concluding his Sermon on the Mount and this short parable summarized what he had been saying. He had been rebuking the Pharisees whose teaching concerning salvation was like the builder who built his house on the creek bed. On the Day of Judgement their hope would come to nothing, because good works, pride and self satisfaction cannot save anyone. Even during our lifetime people find that a life built on self is of little or no value when hard times come. Self righteousness bars the door to the Saviour!

Jesus concluded that the wise person built his hope for eternity upon a solid foundation which was God alone. It is faith in Jesus that turns away the anger of an offended God. Peter's confession of faith in Christ was declared to be the rock upon which the church was being built. He said: 'You are the Christ, the Son of the living God' (Matthew 16:16). The Apostle Paul said to the Philippian jailer, 'Believe on the Lord Jesus Christ, and you will be saved, you and your household' (Acts 16:31). To the Romans he wrote, '… if you confess with your mouth the Lord Jesus and believe in your heart that God has raised him from the dead, you will be saved' (Romans 10:9).

Both builders had the desire to build. One used the easy way wanting quick results. The other took time and spent his money and energy building on rock which proved effective when the storm came.

Jesus is the Rock of our salvation and our eternal security is to be found in him. Paul wrote in 1 Corinthians 3:11: 'For no other foundation can anyone lay than that which is laid, which is Jesus Christ.'

Christ's sermon is a spiritual feast which we should read again and again and ask ourselves, 'Have I been born again? Are my good works motivated out of love for God and my neighbour?' Saving faith is always accompanied by practical obedience.

Is it true of us what we read in James 1:22, 'Be doers of the word, and not hearers only, deceiving yourselves'? Christ continued to condemn the Pharisees and all like them for their pride in what they did. The most fundamental matter is the new birth when the Holy Spirit gives us a heart of flesh in place of our natural heart of stone. We can fool others and even ourselves, but it is God who can see into the heart.

May each one of us be humble, repentant sinners who cling to Christ alone for our salvation.

THINGS TO DISCUSS WITH YOUR FAMILY

1. Is your life built on 'the Rock'?
2. The Pharisees were spiritually lost. Why?
3. What does this parable teach you?

Meditation

Thank God for what you have been taught in Christ's 'Sermon on the Mount'.

Wise Words

What costs little is worth little.   *Anonymous*

'And it happened, when the king of Israel read the letter, that he tore his clothes and said, "Am I God, to kill and make alive, that this man sends a man to me to heal him of his leprosy?"' (2 Kings 5:7).

Read: Matthew 8:1-4

Many members of our congregation belong to the Leprosy Mission. These people pray for lepers and for those who work with the sufferers of that terrible disease. They also work to raise money to purchase what is needed to help make life easier for the sick. Much time is devoted to knitting cotton bandages and beanies that the doctors can use with their patients.

Jesus was on his way to Capernaum after preaching and was followed by his disciples and a big crowd of people. There was one person close by who had probably heard Christ's preaching and knew of the Lord's healing ministry. This man was a leper, an outcast from society who had been declared to be 'unclean' by the priest. The doctors of the day made no effort to treat lepers as the disease was believed to be a punishment from God. When Miriam rebelled against Moses' leadership, she was punished with leprosy. When Moses interceded with God on her behalf the Lord healed her (Numbers 12:10-16).

When the king of Syria sent Naaman, the commander of his army, who suffered from leprosy, to the King of Israel asking that he be healed, the king was distressed. He knew that God alone could bring about a healing and asked Elisha the prophet to deal with Naaman. After he was healed Gehazi, Elisha's servant, tried to obtain the payment that his master had refused. God punished him by giving him and his descendants Naaman's disease.

When a person had symptoms of leprosy they had to face a priest who, if he confirmed the disease, ordered the person away from civilization. Lepers were to make sure that people knew they carried the disease by shouting, 'Unclean!'

The leper in our reading saw his only hope of cure as coming from Christ. He believed that Jesus could cleanse him because he recognized in the Lord what so many didn't see — that he was God, for only God could heal him. He also acknowledged that everything depended upon Christ who had the authority to say, 'Yes' or 'No' to his plea.

Jesus did the unthinkable to the people surrounding him — he put out his hand and touched him. Immediately the man had flesh like that of a newborn baby. Jesus, in order to perfectly obey the law, told the man to go to the priest (Leviticus 14:1-9) so he could be declared cleansed and again mix with society. We can only imagine the man rushing off to Jerusalem to obtain a certificate of cleansing.

We see the compassion of our Lord in dealing with that man, who because of his disease had lost everything he held dear. Others would not have touched him, fearing contamination, but this could not be so with Jesus 'who is holy, harmless, undefiled, separate from sinners' (Hebrews 7:26). Jesus gave his disciples, who acted in his name, the power to perform miracles: 'Heal the sick, cleanse lepers, raise the dead, cast out demons' (Matthew 10:8). What awesome power was in the hands of our compassionate Messiah.

THINGS TO DISCUSS WITH YOUR FAMILY

1. What is leprosy?
2. In what way was leprosy like sin?
3. How did the leper show his humility?

Meditation

Meditate upon the sentiment of Isaiah 1:18, "'Come now, let us reason together," says the LORD. "Though your sins are like scarlet, they shall be as white as snow; though they are red as crimson, they shall be like wool.'"

Wise Words

God has two hands, a right hand of mercy and a left hand of justice. *John Boys*

'And I say to you that many will come from east and west, and sit down with Abraham, Isaac, and Jacob in the kingdom of heaven … There will be weeping and gnashing of teeth' (Matthew 8:11-12).

Read: Matthew 8:5-13

Life in the army must be difficult and dangerous, especially when soldiers are part of an occupying force. In many places the local citizens would be ready to rid themselves of their enemy.

The centurion in this incident was a commander of the Roman army stationed at Capernaum and would have been involved in the protection of King Herod. He was respected by many Jews as he was a convert to their faith and had used some of his money to build a synagogue. God was fulfilling his promise concerning the work of Christ, 'I will also give you as a light to the Gentiles, that you should be my salvation to the ends of the earth' (Isaiah 49:6). In the days of the Old Testament some Gentiles had come to saving faith, but soon the gospel would be preached worldwide. With their rejection of Jesus and his crucifixion the Jews lost their privileged place in God's purposes and their failure became 'riches for the Gentiles' (Romans 11:12).

This centurion knew of Christ. He had possibly heard him preach and seen his miracles and called him, 'Lord'. He was a compassionate man who had a young servant who was seriously ill and close to death. He knew that Christ had the power to heal the sick and saw this as his only hope for his worker.

He was a rich and powerful man, but a humble person as well. He considered himself unworthy to have Jesus come to his home. Nevertheless, he was used to giving orders and having servants and soldiers obey his every command. Jeremiah had written of God's omnipresence, '"Am I a God near at hand," says the LORD, "and not a God afar off? … Do I not fill heaven and earth?" says the LORD' (Jeremiah 23:23-24). The centurion's request of Christ was an acknowledgement that he was God and that distance didn't matter — all that was necessary was a word.

Jesus saw the compassion, love and faith of this centurion and spoke words of assurance, 'Assuredly, I say to you, I have not found such great faith, not even in Israel.' Christ then went on to say that the day was at hand when the Gentiles would be brought into the kingdom in great numbers because the Jews would continue to reject Jesus as Messiah. We should praise God that we live in the gospel age when salvation is preached to the Gentiles as never before. Isaiah 60:1-4 is being fulfilled today, 'Arise, shine; for your light has come! And the glory of the LORD is risen upon you. For behold, the darkness shall cover the earth, and deep darkness the people; but the LORD will arise over you, and his glory will be seen upon you. The Gentiles shall come to your light, and kings to the brightness of your rising. Lift up your eyes all around, and see: they all gather together, they come to you; your sons shall come from afar, and your daughters shall be nursed at your side.'

THINGS TO DISCUSS WITH YOUR FAMILY

1. Why was the gospel extended worldwide? Read Romans 11:7-11.
2. Why did the centurion believe Jesus could heal his servant from a distance?
3. What do we see of Christ's human nature in Luke 7:9?

Meditation

Meditate upon God's goodness to the Gentiles.

Wise Words

Christ often gives encouraging answers to his praying people, when they are interceding for others.

Matthew Henry

'Then fear came upon all, and they glorified God, saying, "A great prophet has risen up among us"; and, "God has visited his people"' (Luke 7:16).

Read: Luke 7:11-16

Death is the consequence of sin and causes sorrow. Funerals are times of sadness, especially for those who have lost someone they loved dearly. Many tears are shed, not for the person who has died, but for themselves — they have suffered the loss of someone precious to them.

Christ lived a busy life and the day after healing the centurion's servant in Capernaum he made his way the forty kilometres to Nain where he met a funeral procession wending its way to the burial ground that was outside the city boundary. As he approached the weeping widow and the men carrying the open coffin he was surrounded by a great number of people. Jesus was accompanied by his disciples and crowds of people from the surrounding area who had come along to hear his teaching and witness any miracles he performed.

The boy's mother was greatly distressed, not only because her only son had died, but because she now had no one to care for her in her old age or to carry on the family name.

Christ's presence that day was no matter of chance. He was there in accordance with God's plan to help a poor widow and once again display his compassion and almighty power. Our God tells us to show compassion to those in need. James wrote: 'Pure and undefiled religion before God and the Father is this: to visit orphans and widows in their trouble' (James 1:27).

No one asked Christ for help, but he saw the widow's sorrow. Telling her not to weep, he touched the coffin containing the dead body and said, 'Young man, I say to you, arise.' At once the young man sat up and spoke to his mother. This miracle was a demonstration of the power of One who said elsewhere, 'I am he who lives, and was dead, and behold, I am alive for evermore. Amen. And I have the keys of Hades and of Death' (Revelation 1:18).

Daily Christ, through the Holy Spirit, raises the spiritually dead, which is a tremendous miracle. Every Christian has experienced this miracle in their own lives. Once dead and without hope, we were made alive in Christ and became adopted children of the living God.

The people who witnessed this miracle saw something happen that filled them with awe. The words of Zacharias were being fulfilled — 'Blessed is the Lord God of Israel, for he has visited and redeemed his people...' (Luke 1:68).

The Apostle Paul wrote that the last enemy to be defeated is death (1 Corinthians 15:26). Christ showed his power over death in his miracles, the greatest being his own resurrection. The day is coming when Christ will return in power and glory and death's icy grip on mankind will be gone for ever. In Paradise there will be no tears, sin or death.

Those who witnessed the raising of the widow's son spread the news of the miracle far and wide. Now the Pharisees had to deal with Jesus, because he was giving every evidence that he was the Messiah. This they could not tolerate.

THINGS TO DISCUSS WITH YOUR FAMILY

1. What can you and your church do to help widows in their times of distress?
2. It is right to weep when we lose one who was special to us. However, what did Paul teach in 1 Thessalonians 4:13?
3. How can you prepare for your own death?

Meditation

John Wesley said, 'My people die well.' Will you 'die well'?

Wise Words

To be familiar with the grave is prudence.

C. H. Spurgeon

'Jesus answered and said to them, "Go and tell John the things you have seen and heard: that the blind see, the lame walk, the lepers are cleansed, the deaf hear, the dead are raised, the poor have the gospel preached to them"' (Luke 7:22).

Read: Matthew 11:2-6

I feel sure that being in prison would be most unpleasant, and more so if you were innocent of the crime for which you were being punished.

John the Baptist was in prison because he had spoken out against the immorality of King Herod Antipas and the woman he married. He knew that because Herod's wife wanted him killed, his future on earth was very bleak. However, in prison he had been able to receive visitors who told him about the preaching and miracles of the Lord Jesus. All Christians suffer times of uncertainty concerning their faith and John began to have some doubts concerning Jesus — 'Was he the Christ who was foretold in the Scriptures?'

Some time beforehand John had said of Jesus, 'Behold! The Lamb of God who takes away the sin of the world!' (John 1:29), and 'No one has seen God at any time. The only begotten Son, who is in the bosom of the Father, he has declared him' (John 1:18). John saw his role as the one to announce the appearance of the Messiah, 'I have been sent before him. He who has the bride is the bridegroom; but the friend of the bridegroom, who stands and hears him, rejoices greatly because of the bridegroom's voice. Therefore this joy of mine is fulfilled. He must increase, but I must decrease. He who comes from above is above all; he who is of the earth is earthly and speaks of the earth. He who comes from heaven is above all' (John 3:28-31).

While in prison, cut off from the world and facing death, John may have thought that the Christ was to establish his kingdom in Israel and act with great power and majesty. The Jesus who was reported to him was humble, compassionate and gentle and he wanted to know if he was the anticipated Messiah.

Jesus simply told the disciples to tell John what was happening. His words reflected Isaiah's prophecies concerning the Messiah, 'Then the eyes of the blind shall be opened, and the ears of the deaf shall be unstopped. Then the lame shall leap like a deer, and the tongue of the dumb sing... The Spirit of the LORD GOD is upon me, because the LORD has anointed me to preach good tidings to the poor; he has sent me to heal the broken-hearted, to proclaim liberty to the captives, and the opening of the prison to those who are bound' (Isaiah 35:5-6; 61:1).

This report would have strengthened John's faith considerably.

Jesus concluded with words that were a mild rebuke to his imprisoned friend, 'And blessed is he who is not offended because of me.' While our faith sometimes doubts, we should never be shamed by our Saviour nor offended by the gospel we love. By God's grace we will stand firm despite our circumstances, and so bring honour to the Saviour we love and serve.

THINGS TO DISCUSS WITH YOUR FAMILY

1. Find out why Herod's wife hated John.
2. How do we cope when our faith is tried?
3. How would John and his disciples have felt when they discussed Christ's reply?

Meditation

Meditate upon John's courage in calling Herod and his 'wife' to repentance.

Wise Words

He who would believe, let him reconcile himself to the fact that his faith will not stay untempted.

Martin Luther

'This is he of whom it is written: "Behold, I send my messenger before your face, who will prepare your way before you"' (Luke 7:27).

Read: Luke 7:24-30

Frequently those who courageously preach God's truth are the objects of criticism from the world and sadly from some who profess to be Christians. If you want to experience this, start telling people of their need of a Saviour because they are sinners. Very soon they will start making sly comments, degrading you in the eyes of their friends.

Christ had just given John a mild rebuke for questioning if he was truly the expected Messiah. Now however, Jesus defends the character and teaching of the one who had prepared the way for his coming. The Pharisees, like Herod, hated John and his teaching, believing they were the true teachers concerning the way of salvation. May we never be like that and bear hatred to faithful ministers and the truth they preach.

First Jesus reminded them that John was not a luxury-loving person. He was not a man of the world in any way. Of John we read, '[He] was clothed in camel's hair, with a leather belt around his waist; and his food was locusts and wild honey' (Matthew 3:4).

Second, Jesus reminded the people that they went out to hear John because they believed him to be a prophet with a commission from God, who came to bear witness that Jesus was the Christ: 'For this is he of whom it is written: "Behold, I send my messenger before your face, who will prepare your way before you"' (Matthew 11:10). Isaiah prophesied John's work and he in turn prepared the way for the One whose coming was foretold by the same prophet. He was the 'Elijah' prophesied by Malachi (Matthew 11:14).

In the days of his initial preaching John was a popular figure despite his humble appearance and courageous words demanding repentance and faith in God's salvation, but things had changed. Jesus never fails his people and in our day of trial he has promised, 'I will never leave you nor forsake you' (Hebrews 13:5). We have that satisfying assurance of eternal security in Christ: 'I am persuaded that neither death nor life, nor angels nor principalities nor powers, nor things present nor things to come, nor height nor depth, nor any other created thing, shall be able to separate us from the love of God which is in Christ Jesus our Lord' (Romans 8:38-39).

All New Testament saints are greater than John with regard to our knowledge of Christ and his salvation. We know more than John and the Old Testament people ever knew. We are a privileged people.

John's preaching had been rejected by the proud Pharisees, but the sinners and tax collectors who believed, 'justified' God — they acknowledged justice, mercy, love and God's way of salvation through faith in his Son. Millions today are like those Church leaders of old, and reject Christ and the gospel of salvation.

THINGS TO DISCUSS WITH YOUR FAMILY

1. Why did the Pharisees hate John and his message of repentance?
2. In what way could John be likened to Elijah?
3. Discuss the meaning of Matthew 11:11.

Meditation

Thank God for his many material blessings.

Wise Words

The faith that saves reposes in the person of Christ; it leads at once to a committal of the total being to Christ, an act impossible to natural man. To believe rightly is as much a miracle as was the coming forth of dead Lazarus at the command of Christ.   *A. W. Tozer*

'But wisdom is justified by all her children' (Luke 7:35).

Read: Luke 7:24-30

Have you quietly sat and watched a group of children at play? So often what started off as a quiet, pleasant game ends up in disputes and arguments over the next game that should be played. Some say what they like while others object to the suggestion and demand something entirely different.

Jesus had been praising John the Baptist and turned to condemn the fickle thoughts of the Pharisees and their disciples. He must have seen children playing in the market place and likened their arguments to the ways of the Pharisees.

From the start the Pharisees were suspicious of John and his teaching. They saw him as being so unlike themselves. He was a very humble, austere man, who lived an isolated life, ate locusts and honey and certainly didn't dress as they did. While the tax collectors and sinners flocked to hear him preach the need of repentance before God, the Pharisees strongly objected. They were self-righteous people who saw themselves as holy in God's sight. To the proud Pharisees, John's ways were unacceptable.

The same men who condemned John for his ways condemned Jesus, only this time it was because he mixed with all sorts of people, even tax collectors and sinners. Jesus took an active part in social activities, attending feasts and even drinking wine. Unlike John, whom they considered to be insane, Jesus was to them 'a glutton and a winebibber'.

Things have not changed as the world will always condemn spiritual truth no matter who it is that preaches the gospel. It doesn't matter if the godly person comes from a particular social order where they mix freely with others or live a simple life with a degree of isolation from the world and its sinful ways. Paul summed it up as follows, '… the carnal mind is enmity against God; for it is not subject to the law of God, nor indeed can be. So then, those who are in the flesh cannot please God' (Romans 8:7-8). To these people the truth and the true church is open to criticism and hatred. God's people are always a small despised flock!

Jesus went on to say the words of our text, 'But wisdom is justi-fied by all her children.' It is the spiritually wise of this world who by God's grace recognize God's wisdom in his way of salvation. It is God's children, chosen for salvation in eternity and 'born again' in time who see Christ as the only way of salvation. This is the wis-dom of God, yet in the eyes of the world it is all foolishness. What Paul wrote of Timothy is true of all Christians, '… you have known the Holy Scriptures, which are able to make you wise for salvation through faith which is in Christ Jesus' (2 Timothy 3:15).

Who were the wise of Christ's day? It was mainly the tax collec-tors and sinners who turned to the Lord for salvation. Are you one of God's wise people?

THINGS TO DISCUSS
WITH YOUR FAMILY

1. What are we told is 'the beginning of wisdom'? Read Proverbs 9:10.
2. In what way were the Pharisees like children at play?
3. Can you think of anyone like that today — in the way they speak about Jesus our Saviour and godly ministers?

Meditation

Meditate upon Proverbs 9:10 — 'The fear of the LORD is the beginning of wisdom, and the knowledge of the Holy One is understanding.'

Wise Words

It is better to get wisdom than gold. Gold is another's, wisdom is our own; gold is for the body and time, wis-dom for the soul and eternity. *Matthew Henry*

'But the house of Israel will not listen to you [Ezekiel], because they will not listen to me; for all the house of Israel are impudent and hardhearted' (Ezekiel 3:7).

Read: Matthew 11:20-24

There are occasions when people are caught doing the wrong thing. When this happens they usually begin to fear that punishment might follow. I'm sure every one of my readers has experienced this at some time or other.

Jesus warned the Pharisees that their sinful ways would lead them to hell unless they repented. Now Jesus turns his attention to the people who lived in the region about Capernaum. There he had performed mighty miracles and preached powerful sermons calling them to repent of their sins and trust in him for their eternal security. Despite their great privileges, very few turned to him with saving faith. Now the cities of Capernaum, Chorazin and Bethsaida, all big cities with much industry and wealth, would suffer the judgement of an angry God. The basic teaching of Christ's words are summarized in his words recorded in Luke 12:48: 'For everyone to whom much is given, from him much will be required.'

This is a warning to us all because we have so many spiritual blessings poured out upon us. Most homes have more than one Bible, there good churches in our townships, and some families conduct daily worship. Yet the vast majority of people turn their backs upon Christ and walk the broad way which ends in hell.

We are also told by Christ that there are degrees of punishment in hell which should fill with horror every person who has spurned their spiritual privileges — 'And that servant who knew his master's will, and did not prepare himself or do according to his will, shall be beaten with many stripes. But he who did not know, yet committed things deserving of stripes, shall be beaten with few' (Luke 12:47-48).

The children of Israel were hard hearted in their dealings with Jesus and very few believed in him. This has been the same throughout the ages. Isaiah recorded a parable where God likened Israel to a vineyard: 'What more could have been done to my vineyard that I have not done in it? Why then, when I expected it to bring forth good grapes, did it bring forth wild grapes? And now, please let me tell you what I will do to my vineyard: I will take away its hedge, and it shall be burned; and break down its wall, and it shall be trampled down. I will lay it waste...' (Isaiah 5:4-6).

Jesus told the people that if the wicked people of Tyre and Sidon had heard him preach and seen his miracles they would have repented. Their sincerity would have been shown by wearing sackcloth and covering themselves with ashes. Both were symbols of humble, repentant hearts.

May every one of my readers have Christ as their Saviour and not face condemnation on the Day of Judgement.

THINGS TO DISCUSS WITH YOUR FAMILY

1. What is the gospel's effect on people who hear it preached? Read 2 Corinthians 2:14-17.
2. What is 'the Day of Judgement'?
3. What gospel privileges have you experienced? How do you treat them?

Meditation

Meditate upon the words of Hebrews 10:31, 'It is a fearful thing to fall into the hands of the living God.'

Wise Words

Apostasy must be called what it is — spiritual adultery.

Francis Schaeffer

'The LORD replied, "My Presence will go with you, and I will give you rest"' (Exodus 33:14, NIV).

Read: Matthew 11:25-30

Today many churches have a very full calendar. To attend all activities can become a burden to members of the congregation. Christianity was never meant to be like this.

Having rebuked the Pharisees and people generally, Jesus was able to thank his heavenly Father for revealing the truth to some humble, ordinary people whom he called 'babes'. They were like little children who were unable to care for themselves and depended upon their parents for all they needed. So also sinners who want to be saved must look away from themselves to God, because he alone made salvation possible and that is through faith in Christ. The proud Pharisees who believed that they were the wise men of their age had it all wrong.

They taught that the way of salvation was obedience to God's law. This they believed placed God under the obligation to bless and save them. This requirement placed a great burden upon the people and try as they did they could never perfectly keep the law of God and the Pharisees. This meant they had no spiritual peace because they had no assurance of salvation.

Why had God revealed the truth to some and not others? I don't know the answer to this question, but trust God's word in Deuteronomy 29:29, 'The secret things belong to the LORD our God, but those things which are revealed belong to us and to our children for ever, that we may do all the words of this law.'

The law of God has a place in the life of the Christian — obedience is not to win favour with God, but a sign that we love God. Jesus said, 'If you love me, keep my commandments' (John 14:15).

Our Saviour invited those who were weary of trying to earn their salvation to come to him as the way of salvation was simple — it was faith in Christ himself. Saving faith gives rest and peace of heart to all believers. The Apostle Paul wrote, 'There is therefore now no condemnation to those who are in Christ Jesus, who do not walk according to the flesh, but according to the Spirit' (Romans 8:1). In Christ alone there is rest, peace and joy for sin-sick souls. And what Christ said to the people those many years ago stands true today.

Another truth expressed in our reading is that Christ is God. He alone 'knows' the heavenly Father and the Father knows the Son. With the Holy Spirit we have what Paul called 'the Godhead', three Persons constituting One God. When Christ took upon himself our humanity he was still God. This is a mystery which we must believe because it is taught in the Scriptures.

Let none of us feel that in some way we have contributed something towards our salvation — we have not. When the 'Pharisee' within us raises its head may we turn to Christ in repentance and declare that we are what we are only by the grace of God (1 Corinthians 15:10).

THINGS TO DISCUSS WITH YOUR FAMILY

1. What does Matthew 11:30 mean? — 'For my yoke is easy and my burden is light.'
2. What do your spiritual works prove to you, God and other people?
3. Where particularly do we see the glory of God? Read 2 Corinthians 4:6, NIV — 'For God, who said, "Let light shine out of darkness," made his light shine in our hearts to give us the light of the knowledge of the glory of God in the face of Christ.'

Meditation

Meditate upon the spiritual rest you have in Jesus.

Wise Words

Faith is the starting-post of obedience.

Thomas Chalmers

'Therefore, as God's chosen people, holy and dearly loved, clothe yourselves with compassion, kindness, humility, gentleness and patience' (Colossians 3:12, NIV).

Read: Luke 7:36-39

As we study through the Gospels we learn of the Savour's gracious compassion to those who were in need. He mixed with unbelievers. This same compassion should be found in the heart of all of Christ's people. In today's reading we see a woman displaying her love of Jesus in a most unusual way.

Jesus had been asked to the home of Simon, a Pharisee, where they would eat a meal together. In those hot regions of the world rooms often had open wall areas to allow the gentle breezes to circulate cool air. It meant that passers by could see and hear what was happening during the meal. People didn't sit on chairs around a table, but sat on cushions with their feet behind them slightly.

When important guests arrived for a meal it was the custom to provide water and towels so that hot, dusty feet could be washed. Sometimes oil was provided to rub on the visitors face and body, but Simon made no effort to make Christ feel welcome. Possibly he was using the occasion to gather some evidence that could be used to condemn Jesus at the next meeting of the Sanhedrin.

Much to the horror of Simon and other 'religious' leaders who may have been present, a woman who had a very bad reputation entered the room and stood behind Jesus. Simon knew the woman's notoriety and wondered what Christ would do. He thought to himself, 'If this Jesus is truly a prophet he will know all about the woman and have nothing to do with her. He should have known Isaiah's warning, "Do not come near me, for I am holier than you"' (Isaiah 65:5). His secret thoughts were known to Jesus.

Yet Jesus knew the woman standing behind him to be a believer whose heart was filled with love for her Saviour. She had found forgiveness and knew that God loved her. With a heart of love towards Christ, tears of gratitude dropped from her eyes and splashed upon the feet of her beloved Redeemer. Immediately she knelt behind the seated Christ and dried the Lord's feet with her long hair. Letting her hair down was not the done thing! Then she opened a bottle of fragrant oil and after kissing her Saviour's feet poured the precious substance on them. We are told that the oil was 'precious' and possibly had been purchased from the earnings of her immorality. But what did that matter now that she had peace with God through faith in Christ?

Every Christian must display their love of Christ through the compassion they show to others, despite the cost and social 'embarrassment'. Our Lord humbled himself for us, even to death upon the cross. We can never repay our debt of gratitude, but can show our love in what we do.

THINGS TO DISCUSS WITH YOUR FAMILY

1. What does it mean to have your sins forgiven?
2. What should be your attitude towards God, Father, Son and Holy Spirit when you are saved?
3. What did Jesus mean when he said, 'Those who are well have no need of a physician, but those who are sick' (Matthew 9:12)?

Meditation

Meditate upon Paul's words in Galatians 6:10 — 'as we have opportunity, let us do good to all, especially to those who are of the household of faith'.

Wise Words

It would tire the hands of an angel to write down all the pardons God bestows upon penitent believers.

William Bates

'And he said to her, "Your sins are forgiven"' (Luke 7:48).

Read: Luke 7:40-50

We sometimes hear of people who claim the power to read our thoughts, but they are plain fakes as are all 'fortune tellers'. On the other hand frequently Jesus showed that he knew the thoughts of others and this should be a warning to you and me — make sure our thoughts are pure as they will be exposed on Judgement Day.

Yesterday we saw that Simon gave no sign of love for Jesus as he failed to show him even the common courtesies normally extended to visitors. Simon, a Pharisee, was about to learn that Jesus was the 'Messiah' who had the authority to forgive sins. Now sin is a debt that we owe God. We are born sinful and daily commit many sins, even though we confess our faith in Christ. Some people however are greater sinners than others and the woman in this story was guilty of 'many' sins. Simon on the other hand had always done his best to obey both the law of God and the Scribes and Pharisees.

Following the short parable Christ asked which of the two people loved their kind creditor the most. Simon's answer was correct. Jesus then went on to explain that the sinful woman's actions were nothing more than the display of her love of God for the gift of salvation. She is a wonderful example of John's words, 'We love him because he first loved us' (1 John 4:19).

The woman had been humbled by God granting her an aware-ness of her sins and making her understand that salvation was to be found in Jesus. Her heart was bursting with a joyful love for her Sav-iour and she showed it by what she did. This love is the fruit of the Spirit and should be found in the heart of every person confessing faith in Christ.

Simon was a lost Pharisee. He had shown no love for Jesus and when Christ announced to the woman, 'Your sins are forgiven,' Si-mon and his friends started to ask one another, 'Who is this who even forgives sins?' Those present knew that Christ's words, if true, were a claim to divinity. Previously, when Christ healed the paralytic man and said that his sins were forgiven, the Scribes said, 'This Man blasphemes!' (Matthew 9:3). Those present still looked upon Jesus as the son of a carpenter who had great powers, but to them he was not the Son of God.

Jesus told the woman her faith had saved her and she could leave with peace in her heart. The same is true of every Christian. Paul wrote: 'Therefore, having been justified by faith, we have peace with God through our Lord Jesus Christ' (Romans 5:1). Our saving faith is the gift of God to a renewed heart. We are justified by faith in Christ, and like the forgiven woman show our love of God by our works of righteousness.

THINGS TO DISCUSS WITH YOUR FAMILY

1. How do you show that you love Jesus?
2. Will you be judged for sins you have confessed?
3. What are the two basic ingredients of 'justification'?

Meditation

Meditate upon the words of 1 John 1:9 — 'If we confess our sins, he is faithful and just to forgive us our sins and to cleanse us from all unrighteousness.'

Wise Words

Release! Signed in tears, sealed in blood, written on heavenly parchment, recorded in eternal archives. The black ink of the indictment is written all over with the red ink of the cross: 'The blood of Jesus Christ cleanseth us from all sin.' *T. De Witt Talmage*

'For the wisdom of this world is foolishness with God' (1 Corinthians 3:19).

Read: Luke 8:1-3; Matthew 12:22-24

It is always hurtful when people make unjust accusations about your
character. We like to be respected by those who know us because
of our kindness. Jesus was truly human and was frequently attacked in
a most unjust manner. He would have felt the hurt when his motive
for what he did was questioned in the harshest manner.

Jesus, with his disciples, had commenced his second tour of Galilee. He was again doing good works, preaching saving truth and revealing God to the people. This time he was accompanied by some
kindly women who had experienced his mercy. They took care of
the Lord and the disciples, buying food and whatever else was needed, out of their own funds. The Creator was showing his humility by
giving others the privilege to serve him.

As they journeyed about the Lord healed the sick and on this
occasion he was confronted by a poor man who was indwelt by a
wretched demon. Satan and his demons have always done all they
could to harm people, and this man was in a pitiable state — he
was blind and dumb. Jesus is the most compassionate person to have
walked the earth and we can completely agree with Isaiah 53:4,
'Surely he has borne our griefs and carried our sorrow.'

Jesus was about to perform another great act of healing, but again
the Pharisees present were watching closely hoping to find some
evidence to use against him. Some Scribes were also present, having come all the way from Jerusalem hoping to catch Jesus out in
something he said or did. They knew his background, that he was a
carpenter. They recognized him as just a carpenter's son, and despite
his wonderful healings did not accept that he was the prophesied
Messiah. Others had performed wonders but the One they expected
was to be a king who would re-establish the throne of David and
by force of arms drive out the Roman overlords and free the nation
from foreign dominion.

They could not accept the fact that this carpenter's son could forgive sins and bring about reconciliation with God. To them he was an imposter. To them he was an 'antichrist'.

The Lord was unconcerned about the thoughts and words of those Scribes and Pharisees who hated him. He was the Son of God of whom the Prophets and John the Baptist bore witness. Now those present would see him fulfil the words of Isaiah 42:7 with this deaf and dumb man — he would 'open blind eyes' and rescue the one who was trapped in Satan's prison.

The man was healed, but this was not the proof the Scribes and Pharisees wanted to confirm that Jesus was the Messiah. This carpenter, they thought, was 'mad'. They even made the ridiculous accusation, 'This fellow does not cast out demons except by Beelzebub, the ruler of the demons.'

Often humble Christians face similar accusations. May we support believers who are undergoing trials.

THINGS TO DISCUSS WITH YOUR FAMILY

1. Not all 'mad' people are demon possessed. Some are just mentally ill. How should we treat these unfortunate people?
2. What acts of kindness can you do for people who are in need?
3. Discuss the teaching of today's text.

Meditation

Meditate upon the blessings of a sound mind and good health. Remember that upon Christ's return the saints will be made perfect in every respect — mentally, physically and spiritually.

Wise Words

A man's heart is what he is.   *R. B. Kuiper*

'He who is not with me is against me,
and he who does not gather with me
scatters abroad' (Matthew 12:30).

Read: Matthew 12:24-30

In the light of our text we should put a muzzle on our mouth to prevent uncharitable words being spoken. The Scribes and Pharisees had just accused the Lord of casting out a demon by the power of Beelzebub. This was a very serious accusation because it inferred that not only was Jesus mad, but the very power he used to perform miracles and cast out demons was that of Satan. They believed that Satan indwelt Jesus! This was blasphemy, because the power of Christ on earth was that of the Holy Spirit who was poured out upon him, without measure, at the time of his baptism.

Christ's reply was simple — Satan doesn't fight against his demons who carry out his bidding to destroy humanity and where possible inhabit the body of a person. The Lord also reminded the church leaders that some of their friends — 'sons' — also cast out demons. They needed to consider by what power they performed such works.

Jesus rejected the cruel accusation by saying that it was by the power of the indwelling Holy Spirit that Satan's kingdom was being attacked, which proved that the kingdom of God had come in its fullness. Sinners were being taken from Satan's kingdom to the kingdom of God. In the wilderness temptation, Christ had proved himself victorious over the evil one. On the cross Satan's power was further destroyed as Paul wrote: 'Having disarmed principalities and powers, he made a public spectacle of them, triumphing over them in it' (Colossians 2:15). When our Saviour ascended into heaven we read of war taking place and Satan being cast out and confined to the earth where he 'walks about like a roaring lion, seeking whom he may devour' (1 Peter 5:8).

Satan is now very much restricted in his ability for we read in Revelation 20:2-3 — 'He laid hold of the dragon, that serpent of old, who is the Devil and Satan, and bound him for a thousand years; and he cast him into the bottomless pit, and shut him up, and set a seal on him, so that he should deceive the nations no more till the thousand years were finished. But after these things he must be released for a little while.' Satan is like a dog on a chain, having limited power.

Christ concluded with the words of our text in which we are taught that the Lord's servants will take the gospel throughout the world and gather new citizens for God's kingdom. All Christians are reapers, using the gospel as their reaping hook. Satan and his henchmen scatter the sheep just like the hireling in Christ's parable of the Good Shepherd (John 10:12-13).

Today the gospel has reached into the remotest corners of the earth and the kingdom of God continues to grow. Satan is truly a defeated foe. Christians exercise spiritual power in this world because our bodies are the temple of the Holy Spirit. We have the power of God at our disposal. Praise the Lord!

THINGS TO DISCUSS WITH YOUR FAMILY

1. Read and discuss Proverbs 11:30-31.
2. For whom was the gospel? Read Romans 1:16 — 'For I am not ashamed of the gospel of Christ, for it is the power of God to salvation for everyone who believes, for the Jew first and also for the Greek.'
3. Why did the Scribes and Pharisees accuse Christ of being 'mad'?

Meditation

Consider Satan's devices to trap us.

Every sin is an election of the devil to be our Lord.
Stephen Charnock

Wise Words

'Therefore I say to you, every sin and
blasphemy will be forgiven men, but the
blasphemy against the Spirit will not be
forgiven men' (Matthew 12:31).

Read: Matthew 12:31-37

Sometimes people believe they are in a hopeless spiritual situation
because they have committed the unforgivable sin. Have you ever
thought this? Jesus told some Scribes and Pharisees that they were
guilty of this terrible sin.

We read the wonderful truth that sins against other people,
against Christ and blasphemy against God and man will be forgiven
when sinners confess and seek pardon. These are words of encouragement to all who come to Christ seeking forgiveness and salvation.
King David had committed adultery and murder. Paul before repentance on the road to Damascus had tried to destroy the church and
had been involved in the murder of Stephen. Peter had denied his
Saviour, but upon repentance had found pardon.

Those men had not committed the unforgivable sin, and indeed
everyone who turns to Jesus with a truly repentant heart and seeks
forgiveness will find pardon because they have not sinned against the
Holy Spirit.

The Pharisees had claimed that Christ was indwelt by Satan and
all of his miracles, including the casting out of demons, was done by
the power of the evil one. They attributed the workings of the Holy
Spirit to Beelzebub — Satan. Despite all the evidence to the contrary
they refused to turn away from this vile sin. They did not cry out
for mercy and their hearts became harder in their attitude towards
Christ. They rejected the pleading of the Holy Spirit to repent and
turn to Jesus.

There are steps in the sin called 'the unforgivable sin'. First there
is the deliberate resisting of the calling of the Holy Spirit just as Stephen said of the Jews before his martyrdom: 'You stiff-necked and
uncircumcised in heart and ears! You always resist the Holy Spirit;
as your fathers did, so do you' (Acts 7:51). This is followed by the
quenching of the Holy Spirit. Paul warned against this sin, 'Do not

312

quench the Spirit' (1 Thessalonians 5:19). This is where unbelievers harden their hearts against the gospel. We are warned against this sin in Hebrews 3:15: 'Do not harden your hearts as in the rebellion.' The writer then went on to say, 'they could not enter in because of unbelief' (Hebrews 3:19). This is the unforgivable sin — dying in unbelief.

Christ then said that godly works came from those with a renewed heart; and Christ's works were from the heart of God due to the power of the Holy Spirit. It was the Pharisees and Scribes who spoke words that would bring them to a judgement of condemnation. We should be concerned with Christ's warning that we will have to give an account of every 'idle' word; this is frightening, but what about those deliberately spoken hard, cruel words? May the words found in James 3:6 concerning the speech of the ungodly never be said of us: 'And the tongue is a fire, a world of iniquity. The tongue is so set among our members that it defiles the whole body, and sets on fire the course of nature; and it is set on fire by hell.'

THINGS TO DISCUSS WITH YOUR FAMILY

1. How do you know that the Holy Spirit is in your heart?
2. Read James 3:1-12. What are you taught there?
3. What sin is never forgiven?

Meditation

If you are a Christian thank God that you have not committed the unforgivable sin.

Wise Words

He who has the Holy Spirit in his heart and the Scriptures in his hands has all he needs.   *Alexander MacLaren*

'For as Jonah was three days and three nights in the belly of the great fish, so will the Son of Man be three days and three nights in the heart of the earth' (Matthew 12:40).

Read: Matthew 12:38-45

We like to be loved by others and by our actions show that we care for and respect them. The majority of Jews were showing no sincere love for Jesus despite all of his acts of compassion. He was looked upon by most people as just the carpenter's son who had a gift of healing — even the ability to cast out demons. Most people rejected his claim to be the Messiah.

The Scribes and Pharisees who led the opposition to Jesus asked him to give them a 'sign' that would prove to their satisfaction that he was who he claimed to be. They even sarcastically called him 'Teacher'.

Jesus gave them a reply that must have mystified them — 'no sign will be given [this generation] except the sign of the prophet Jonah'. We know that our Lord was saying that just as Jonah had been three days in the belly of that great fish before being disgorged up on the beach, he also after three days of death and burial would rise from the dead. This would be the greatest sign of all, yet even this was unacceptable to them. The people of Israel were known for their hard hearted ways and their continual spiritual harlotry. Centuries before, they had suffered captivity in Babylon for seventy years because they turned away from the living God and disobeyed his law. Upon their return they repented, but this did not last as their religious leaders led them along a pathway that was worse than before the captivity. Jesus told them the parable of the demons who after being removed from a person returned creating a worse situation than before. This was what was happening at that very time. The people had rejected Jesus as Messiah, declaring that he was demon possessed.

The nation had not changed; her spiritual life in Christ's time was as it had been before. Jeremiah wrote of their spiritual harlotry: '"Surely, as a wife treacherously departs from her husband, so have you dealt treacherously with me, O house of Israel," says the LORD'

(Jeremiah 3:20). Very soon the generation that rejected the Saviour would suffer horrific judgement from the Roman armies when in AD 70 Jerusalem would be destroyed and the people scattered throughout the nations.

Jesus rebuked the Scribes and Pharisees by reminding them that when Jonah preached a very simple message of repentance, the people of Nineveh turned from their ways and found forgiveness with God. He also spoke of the Queen of Sheba who travelled a great distance to see and hear Solomon and his great kingdom, yet the Scribes, Pharisees and people had God's Son with them, preaching and performing great wonders and they rejected him. The repentant Ninevites would agree with Christ's condemnation of Israel on the Day of Judgement.

Our salvation requires regeneration by the sovereign power of the Holy Spirit and a God-given faith in the Lord Jesus. Israel had neither.

THINGS TO DISCUSS WITH YOUR FAMILY

1. Why did the Jews refuse to acknowledge Jesus as the Messiah?
2. Who was the Queen of Sheba?
3. What was Jonah's sermon to the people of Nineveh?

Meditation

Think about the foolish attitude of the Scribes, Pharisees and people concerning Jesus. If you are a believer thank God that you are not like them.

Wise Words

The devil is the most diligent of preachers.

Hugh Latimer

'For whoever does the will of my Father in heaven is my brother and sister and mother' (Matthew 12:50).

Read: Matthew 12:46-50

We are all members of a family although they differ in their make-up. The usual household consists of parents and children but at the moment mine is just three — husband, wife and Tootsie the dog. Jesus was part of a family. His mother was Mary and his foster father was Joseph. He had half brothers and sisters born to Mary and Joseph and we know the names of several brothers — 'James, Joses, Simon, and Judas' (Matthew 13:55).

Jesus had just been rebuking the Scribes and Pharisees and with his disciples went to a house followed by crowds of onlookers. The religious leaders had openly said that Christ was demon-possessed and his family had heard what was said. They also knew that Jesus was working very hard, even to the extent that he was missing his meals. Possibly they began to believe that there was some truth in what was being said about him for we read that they said, 'He is out of his mind' (Mark 3:21).

When Mary and her sons arrived at the house in which he was preaching they sent a message asking to speak with him. What they wanted to say we can only guess, but Jesus understood that they were going to interrupt the work that the Father had given him to carry out. Once before he had reminded his mother, 'Did you not know that I must be about my Father's business?' (Luke 2:49).

Jesus now took the opportunity to teach the truth that spiritual ties are more important and lasting than physical ones. Turning to his disciples and other faithful believers he said, 'Here are my mother and my brothers! For whoever does the will of my Father in heaven is my brother and sister and mother.'

The Apostle John had written of Christ's family: 'But as many as received him, to them he gave the right to become children of God, to those who believe in his name: who were born, not of blood, nor of the will of the flesh, nor of the will of man, but of

God' (John 1:12-13). Christians make up 'the household of faith' (Galatians 6:10).

From the Saviour's words to his family we notice that in God's family neither gender, race nor colour matter. Paul wrote precious words to all Christians, 'For you are all sons of God through faith in Christ Jesus. For as many of you as were baptized into Christ have put on Christ. There is neither Jew nor Greek, there is neither slave nor free, there is neither male nor female; for you are all one in Christ Jesus' (Galatians 3:26-28). All members of Christ's family are bound together in love of their heavenly Father and show that love by obedience to God's law. Yet those who were so close to Jesus — the Scribes and Pharisees failed to trust their eternal security to him.

Let us always remember that our closest ties are with those who are 'born again'. We will spend eternity with them and together sing the praises of our heavenly Father.

THINGS TO DISCUSS WITH YOUR FAMILY

1. Who did Jesus say made up his family?
2. Read and discuss Hebrews 2:10-11.
3. How do sinners become members of God's family?

Meditation

Meditate upon Galatians 4:6-7 — 'And because you are sons, God has sent forth the Spirit of his Son into your hearts, crying out, "Abba, Father!" Therefore you are no longer a slave but a son, and if a son, then an heir of God through Christ.'

Wise Words

Adoption gives us the privilege of sons, regeneration the nature of sons.   *Stephen Charnock*

'But blessed are your eyes for they see, and your ears for they hear' (Matthew 13:16).

Read: Matthew 13:10-17

We have come to a new section in the life of Jesus which is our Lord's use of parables to teach biblical truth. And what is a parable? Some describe it as an earthly story with a heavenly meaning. Jesus told stories that his listeners could easily understand, but not everybody could understand the truth that he was teaching. We are not to look for meaning in every part of a parable as most teach just one or two important truths.

Parables were not something new as we read some in the Old Testament. You might like to read the one found in Judges 9:7-15. The disciples asked their Teacher why he taught in parables and we find him quoting a passage from Isaiah 6 which Jesus said was being fulfilled that day. The Pharisees and others had stony hearts and believed that Christ was demon-possessed. The Lord thus taught in parables so they could not understand what great truths were being taught. Salvation is all of grace and so is understanding of the words of Christ.

Paul wrote: 'But the natural man does not receive the things of the Spirit of God, for they are foolishness to him; nor can he know them, because they are spiritually discerned' (1 Corinthians 2:14). Spiritual understanding is the gift of God to his believing people. The disciples, who asked him the question concerning his teaching by means of parables, were told that to them was given the ability to understand great mysteries. They would know the wonder of salvation and the Person of Christ. They would be guided by the Holy Spirit to write the New Testament, and despite the fact that at that time their knowledge was limited, it would increase. Jesus was their teacher and he would give them greater knowledge to be used as they preached the gospel.

Not so the cold, hard-hearted Pharisees and their friends. The Lord had called them to repentance, but their hearts were hardened and they showed more and more hatred towards the Son of God.

They were well described in Psalm 58:4-5: 'Their poison is like the poison of a serpent; they are like the deaf cobra that stops its ear, which will not heed the voice of charmers, charming ever so skilfully.'

In the Old Testament we find many prophecies concerning Christ and we are told that the prophets longed to see their prophecies fulfilled. Possibly they didn't have an understanding of what they prophesied. Peter wrote of them: 'Of this salvation the prophets have inquired and searched carefully, who prophesied of the grace that would come to you, searching what, or what manner of time, the Spirit of Christ who was in them was indicating when he testified beforehand the sufferings of Christ and the glories that would follow' (1 Peter 1:10-11). The disciples came to fully understand what the prophets had said concerning the Messiah. The same is true of all Christians of this latter age. We have the Word of God and the indwelling Holy Spirit who gives us understanding of the Scriptures. Ours is an age of opportunity. Prayerfully read your Bible and thank God for daily unveiling to you more of his truth.

THINGS TO DISCUSS
WITH YOUR FAMILY

1. What is meant when we are told that God hardens men's hearts?
2. Why did Jesus use parables to teach the truth?
3. What causes spiritual growth?

Meditation

Meditate upon Psalm 119:105: 'Your word is a lamp to my feet and a light to my path.'

Wise Words

The perfect Christian is the one who, having a sense of his own failure, is minded to press towards the mark.

Ernest F. Kevan

'Therefore, my brethren, you also have
become dead to the law through the
body of Christ, that you may be married
to another — to him who was raised
from the dead, that we should bear fruit
to God' (Romans 7:4).

Read: Matthew 13:3-9, 18-23

This is probably the best known of Christ's parables, often known
as the 'Parable of the Soils'. It follows the Lord's rebuking of the
Scribes and Pharisees for their satanic hatred. The disciples were not
sure of the meaning of the parable and needed an explanation from
their Teacher.

The sower was Christ and all who preach the gospel, the soil is
the human heart and the seed the word of God.

The seed that fell on the wayside was removed immediately by
the hungry birds. This represented all those who reject Christ and his
message. They were unwilling to even give serious consideration to
what Christ was doing and saying. Jesus' message meant nothing to
them. This is so much like the hard hearts of people today — they are
totally unconcerned with spiritual reality and live for themselves and
personal happiness.

The seed that fell on the stony places referred to those who heard
and accepted the gospel for a short time, but soon returned to their
old ways. Some seed fell amongst thorns and this spoke of those who
heard the gospel and received it with joy. Yet soon worldly cares and
love of the world replaced the pleasure they had in Christ. This is like
so many today. They hear the gospel and receive it with an emotional
impulse, but the affairs of life soon become all important. We all need
to take notice of the message of Proverbs 30:8,9: 'Give me neither
poverty nor riches — feed me with the food allotted to me; lest I be
full and deny you, and say, "Who is the LORD?" Or lest I be poor and
steal, and profane the name of my God.'

The final soil to receive the seed is that person which has been
prepared by the Holy Spirit to accept the gospel with a great spiritual
hunger. Nicodemus was told of the necessity of being born again
— 'Most assuredly, I say to you, unless one is born again, he cannot
see the kingdom of God' (John 3:3). The new birth is the sovereign

work of a God of grace. It is God who gives the ability and desire to believe in Jesus. The Psalmist wrote: 'Your people shall be volunteers in the day of your power' (Psalm 110:3). They submit to Christ when they experience the saving power of the Holy Spirit. It is these people who bear spiritual fruit, just like the plants that grew in the good soil. In Psalm 1:1-3 we read of these people: 'Blessed is the man who walks not in the counsel of the ungodly, nor stands in the path of sinners, nor sits in the seat of the scornful; but his delight is in the law of the LORD, and in his law he meditates day and night. He shall be like a tree planted by the rivers of water, that brings forth its fruit in its season.' This should be you and me.

THINGS TO DISCUSS WITH YOUR FAMILY

1. Give some examples of things that snatch away the 'Word'.
2. What is the new birth and who brings it about?
3. Worldliness is a great sin. What are we taught in 1 Timothy 6:10?

Meditation

Meditate upon the 'fruit of the Spirit' in your Christian life — 'But the fruit of the Spirit is love, joy, peace, long-suffering, kindness, goodness, faithfulness, gentleness, self-control' (Galatians 5:22-23). What does it mean to you? Is your faith the genuine thing?

Wise Words

If you are wise, let the world pass, lest you pass away with the world. *Augustine*

'Let your light so shine before men, that they may see your good works and glorify your Father in heaven' (Matthew 5:16).

Read: Mark 4:21-25

It is so easy to flip the switch when we want light in a room. Times certainly have changed. My wife remembers her young days when electricity wasn't connected to their home and each night the lamps had to be lit. In Christ's age oil lamps were used to lighten darkened rooms.

Following the parable of the sower we move on to several more that give extra meaning to 'the kingdom of God'. We are told that when the 'seed' falls into good soil something happens — the plant grows and produces more seed. In other words the redeemed heart responds to the new birth.

The church leaders of Christ's day had hidden the truth from unbelievers. The Scribes and Pharisees had buried the way of salvation under a mountain of their manmade laws. Elsewhere Jesus had rebuked them saying, 'Why do you transgress the commandment of God because of your tradition?' (Matthew 15:3). Jesus accused them of 'teaching as doctrines the commandments of men' (Matthew 15:9). Now he exhorts believers to shine like lights.

All who are born again are to let the light of their salvation shine brightly in this sin darkened world, testifying to God's amazing grace. We are to be like the Psalmist who wrote: 'I will declare what [God] has done for my soul' (Psalm 66:16). The apostle Paul gave Timothy a charge that applies to all ministers of the gospel: 'Preach the word! Be ready in season and out of season. Convince, rebuke, exhort, with all long-suffering and teaching' (2 Timothy 4:2). We are commanded to confess Christ before our neighbours, friends, work mates — all with whom we have contact. If this is done then Christ will confess us before his heavenly Father (Matthew 10:32).

The day is coming when everything will be revealed for all to see. The sins of the hypocrites will be exposed. We must make sure that our faith is genuine.

We are also reminded that in making judgements we must be scrupulously fair. This was taught in the Sermon on the Mount where we read, 'Judge not, that you be not judged. For with what judgement you judge, you will be judged; and with the measure you use, it will be measured back to you' (Matthew 7:1-2). This is what Jesus was teaching in verse 24.

Our Saviour went on to say that we must make good use of our spiritual gifts and the gospel. Do we hide it? Later he told the parable of the talents concluding, 'For to everyone who has, more will be given, and he will have abundance; but from him who does not have, even what he has will be taken away' (Matthew 25:29). If we don't use our God given gifts we will lose everything.

In our reading Jesus said, 'If anyone has ears to hear, let him hear.' The Pharisees and Scribes refused to hear and obey. May you and I listen to every word of Christ and carry out the Lord's commands because we love him and want to see him glorified and his name honoured.

THINGS TO DISCUSS WITH YOUR FAMILY

1. How can you show others that you are a Christian?
2. Christians forgive those who hurt them. Why?
3. Discuss Romans 2:5-6: 'But in accordance with your hardness and your impenitent heart you are treasuring up for yourself wrath in the day of wrath and revelation of the righteous judgement of God, who "will render to each one according to his deeds".'

Meditation

Meditate upon the way you can glorify God by your works of Christian love.

Wise Words

God calls people to worship him with their obedience, and instead they try to fob him off with their religion.

John Hercus

How does your garden grow?

 'I planted, Apollos watered, but God gave the increase. So then neither he who plants is anything, nor he who waters, but God who gives the increase' (1 Corinthians 3:6-7).

Read: Mark 4:26-29

How many times have you been called upon by your minister to repent of your sins and exercise saving faith in the Lord Jesus Christ? Many times you would have heard this call, but the question really is, 'What can you do to be saved?' The answer is very plain, 'Nothing at all!'

There are some ministers who give the impression that we can do something which will result in our salvation, but this short parable tells us something very different. Christ describes the situation known to all farmers where they plant their crops and somehow what appears to be a dead seed bursts into life. The farmer sees the plant growing and its growth is a real mystery to him. Eventually his crop is ready to be harvested.

Jesus is describing the kingdom of God and speaks of himself being the farmer who scatters the good news. This is the work of our ministers today, and indeed every person who confesses faith in Christ. We can invite people to turn from their sins in true repentance and believe in Jesus as their Saviour, but we can't make this happen as it is the work of God. The saving of sinners is a mystery. First, we must be born again — we need a new heart and this is the sovereign work of the Holy Spirit. When this takes place we are enabled to repent and believe in Christ. Nicodemus couldn't understand how this could be and the Lord told him it was all a mystery to mankind: 'The wind blows where it wishes, and you hear the sound of it, but cannot tell where it comes from and where it goes. So is everyone who is born of the Spirit' (John 3:8).

Next is the sanctifying work of the Holy Spirit by which the sinner turns from his sins to a life of holiness. He is being moulded into the likeness of his Saviour until perfection is reached when he meets the Lord face to face. We read in 1 John 3:2 — 'we know that when he is revealed, we shall be like him, for we shall see him as he is'. This again is a mystery to us all but in Proverbs 4:18 the work of sanctification is beautifully described: 'But the path of the just is like the shining sun, that shines ever brighter unto the perfect day.'

Once given saving faith we do all things to the praise of God just as Paul wrote: 'For you were bought at a price; therefore glorify God in your body and in your spirit, which are God's' (1 Corinthians 6:20).

By the grace of God, the kingdom of God grows. This is a mystery, but we are to continue to preach Christ and bear witness to his salvation, praying that God might bless those who hear. There is power in the word, but God alone gives the power.

In Deuteronomy 29:29 we read words that we should take to heart, 'The secret things belong to the LORD our God, but those things which are revealed belong to us and to our children for ever, that we may do all the words of this law.' Remember to thank God for your salvation.

THINGS TO DISCUSS WITH YOUR FAMILY

1. What are we taught in the words of Isaiah 1:18? '"Come now, let us reason together," says the LORD. "Though your sins are like scarlet, they shall be as white as snow; though they are red as crimson, they shall be like wool."'
2. Two people hear the same sermon, one comes to saving faith in Christ and the other goes away unconcerned. Why?
3. If we can't save people what should we do with the good news concerning the Saviour?

Meditation

Meditate upon this question — 'Why did God save me?'

Wise Words

For of him and through him and to him are all things, to whom be glory for ever. Amen.   *Apostle Paul*

June

'His winnowing fan is in his hand, and he will thoroughly clean out his threshing floor, and gather the wheat into his barn; but the chaff he will burn with unquenchable fire' (Luke 3:17).

Read: Matthew 13:24-30; 36-43

I spend time digging weeds out of the garden. Unfortunately I am occasionally told that I have killed a good plant in the process and that I need to be more careful. We have been looking at a series of parables concerning the kingdom of God and now we see something new about God's kingdom on earth. Christ's words are easy to read, but like the disciples we need help to know exactly what Jesus, 'the Son of Man' (Daniel 7:13), is teaching us. After he told the parable, he sent the people away so he could privately explain to the disciples the meaning of his story.

Satan's great desire is to destroy the church which is the Bride of Christ. He made use of the hypocritical teachers within the nation — and still does. The Apostle Paul wrote of these people: 'For such are false apostles, deceitful workers, transforming themselves into apostles of Christ. And no wonder! For Satan himself transforms himself into an angel of light' (2 Corinthians 11:13-14). When church members are suspected of being evil some people want them removed from membership. There are occasions when this must be done, but the main object of discipline is to bring sinners to repentance.

There are times when there is a desire just to rid the church of those who appear to be troublemakers, when we should rather seek to strengthen their faith.

Jesus taught that Christians should treat as brothers and sisters of the visible church all who give evidence of saving faith despite the fact that some are unsaved. We cannot see into the heart of all who profess faith in Christ and except in cases of open sin we should show Christian love and tolerance to everyone.

The Lord said that because of the danger of hurt to the church, all professing Christians should live together in peace because there is a day coming when the all-knowing Christ will separate the sheep from the goats. Christ will return to earth with his mighty angels to gather together all mankind for judgement. The ungodly will be cast into the eternal fires of hell, the place of 'shame and everlasting contempt' (Daniel 12:2). Of their punishment John wrote: 'And the smoke of their torment ascends for ever and ever; and they have no rest day or night, who worship the beast and his image, and whoever receives the mark of his name' (Revelation 14:11). Eternity without God is real!

However, all of Christ's people 'shall shine like the brightness of the firmament' (Daniel 12:3). We will shine forth in our new, resurrected bodies that are like that of our Saviour. Having been made perfect in holiness we will occupy the new heavens and earth and there forever enjoy the company of God in Christ. Are you ready for Christ's return? I pray you are.

THINGS TO DISCUSS WITH YOUR FAMILY

1. When a church member commits open, wicked sin what is the church to do? Read Matthew 18:15-20.
2. Discuss Galatians 6:1 — 'Brethren, if a man is overtaken in any trespass, you who are spiritual restore such a one in a spirit of gentleness, considering yourself lest you also be tempted.'
3. This parable concludes with, 'He who has ears to hear, let him hear!' What does Christ mean by this?

Meditation

Meditate upon the glory that awaits God's people when Christ returns.

Wise Words

Hell is truth seen too late.   *H. G. Adams*

 'I will open my mouth in a parable; I will utter dark sayings of old' (Psalm 78:2).

Read: Matthew 13:31-33

Many years ago when our children were young we made our own bread. This was great fun especially as we watched the effect of the yeast in the mixture. The bread was always delicious to eat. We have now read two short parables again about the kingdom of God and its growth.

Jesus said that the birth of the Christian church could be likened to the very small mustard seed. Before the Day of Pentecost we read that just one hundred and twenty people were at prayer. This was the congregation of believers, but on the Day of Pentecost, following Peter's sermon about three thousand people were added to the church number (Acts 2:41). Within a short time the Apostle Paul could tell the Colossians that the gospel had spread worldwide (Colossians 1:6).

The disciples knew their Scriptures and looked forward to the day when the name of Christ would be glorified in all nations. They knew God's promise to Abraham, 'In your seed all the nations of the earth shall be blessed, because you have obeyed my voice' (Genesis 22:18). Later Habakkuk had prophesied: 'For the earth will be filled with the knowledge of the glory of the LORD, as the waters cover the sea' (Habakkuk 2:14).

We have seen this parable become a reality as the church now contains people from all ages and nationalities. It has grown like that mustard tree. Those who come into the church also have a small beginning. They are born again and they grow in their faith and love of Christ. Our Saviour deals gently with his new converts so they become useful citizens of the kingdom of God, bringing glory to the Saviour.

There are times when the church is small, but let us never become discouraged. The 'King of kings and Lord of lords' rules this earth and the church will grow as he sees fit.

The second short parable compares the kingdom of God to leaven used in cooking bread. God's kingdom grows under Christ's kingship, the Holy Spirit acting like leaven in the hearts of the saints. Wherever the gospel is preached unbelievers are being saved because there is power in the word. The writer to the Hebrews said, 'For the word of God is living and powerful, and sharper than any two-edged sword, piercing even to the division of soul and spirit, and of joints and marrow, and is a discerner of the thoughts and intents of the heart' (Hebrews 4:12).

As the disciples preached the good news concerning a resurrected Christ their opposition complained that they had 'turned the world upside down' (Acts 17:6).

Despite the efforts of many to force conversions using the sword, the Holy Spirit alone changes hearts. This is done throughout the world, bringing sinners to salvation through a God-given faith in Christ.

Let each one of us confess Christ to those about us and pray for their salvation. Then we must leave it to God to bring them to the Saviour.

THINGS TO DISCUSS
WITH YOUR FAMILY

1. What are you taught in Luke 12:8? — 'Also I say to you, whoever confesses me before men, him the Son of Man also will confess before the angels of God.'
2. What can you and your local congregation do to expand the kingdom of God?
3. Should we be discouraged by the smallness of the church?

Meditation

Think upon the work God would have you do to extend his kingdom.

Wise Words

The kingdom of God does not exist because of your effort or mine. It exists because God reigns. Our part is to enter this kingdom and bring our life under his sovereign will. *T. Z. Koo*

'But seek the kingdom of God, and all these things shall be added to you' (Luke 12:31).

Read: Matthew 13:44-46

We have things which we treasure and usually take care that they are not lost or damaged. However our most valuable possessions in no way compare with the treasure we have in our Saviour, the Lord Jesus Christ. Today we have two short parables about things of great value.

The first parable is about a person who accidentally discovered a treasure hidden in the ground. In ages past when there were no banks in which to place valuables, people often placed their valuables in a metal container and hid them in a hole in the ground. In this instance the owner must have died before revealing where his fortune could be found. Later, possibly a tenant who worked the land came across the hidden container. He wanted it for himself and sold everything he had to buy the field so he could call what he found his own.

Jesus was teaching his disciples that sometimes sinners hear the gospel and with a God-given realization of its spiritual value, decide to make it theirs. They willingly sacrifice everything in order to be saved. The Apostle Paul was such a person. On the way to Damascus he was confronted by the majestic and all-precious Lord Jesus Christ. With a changed heart he willingly sacrificed everything he once held precious to become a disciple of the One whose followers he was trying to kill. Paul's changed attitude recorded in Philippians 3:3-9 are summarized in verses 7 to 9 — 'But what things were gain to me, these I have counted loss for Christ. Yet indeed I also count all things loss for the excellence of the knowledge of Christ Jesus my Lord, for whom I have suffered the loss of all things, and count them as rubbish, that I may gain Christ and be found in him, not having my own righteousness, which is from the law, but that which is through faith in Christ, the righteousness which is from God by faith.' The Gentiles weren't waiting for the coming of Christ, but Isaiah prophesied, 'I was found by those who did not seek me' (Isaiah 65:1).

The second parable was about a man who was looking for lovely pearls which were rare in Christ's day. He found one of great value and, like the man who accidentally found the hidden treasure, sold everything he had to raise the money to buy that precious pearl, which symbolizes Christ and his salvation. Many people know that something is missing in their life and make a genuine search to discover what it is. This was like the Ethiopian eunuch who wanted to know the person described in Isaiah 53. He was looking for spiritual peace, as were the Philippian jailer, the Bereans, the rich young ruler and Cornelius. This is God calling his people to faith in Christ. Isaiah (55:11) wrote of this — 'So shall my word be that goes forth from my mouth; it shall not return to me void, but it shall accomplish what I please, and it shall prosper in the thing for which I sent it.'

We must be ready to sacrifice everything for Christ. Jesus said, '... there is no one who has left house or brothers or sisters or father or mother or wife or children or lands, for my sake and the gospel's, who shall not receive a hundred fold now in this time ... and in the age to come, eternal life' (Mark 10:29-30). Have you?

THINGS TO DISCUSS WITH YOUR FAMILY

1. What is the most valuable thing in this world?
2. What are you willing to sacrifice for the sake of the Lord Jesus?
3. Do we behave as if salvation has little value to us?

Meditation

Meditate upon Ecclesiastes 3:11: 'He has made everything beautiful in its time. Also he has put eternity in their hearts, except that no one can find out the work that God does from beginning to end.'

Wise Words

The poor man's hand is Christ's bank.   *John Trapp*

'So those servants went out into the highways and gathered together all whom they found, both bad and good. And the wedding hall was filled with guests' (Matthew 22:10).

Read: Matthew 13:47-50

I used to spend a lot of time fishing. This was my sport which I enjoyed greatly, especially since we could eat our catch. Jesus had some ex-fishermen as his disciples and often we find Jesus speaking about fish.

This parable reinforces what the disciples had already been told. It is similar to the parable of the wheat and the tares (Matthew 13:24-30; 36-43) and is one of the final parables in the group about the kingdom of God. Jesus is teaching us not to neglect the prize, no matter what it costs.

When fishermen brought their catch to the shore not all of the catch was kept. The Old Testament defined clean and unclean fish and it was the first job of the fishermen to dispose of all the fish classified as 'unclean'. We read, 'These you may eat of all that are in the water: whatever in the water has fins and scales, whether in the seas or in the rivers — that you may eat … Whatever in the water does not have fins or scales — that shall be an abomination to you' (Leviticus 11:9,12).

This parable tells us that the sea represents the world and the fishermen are the disciples and all who confess Christ. The kingdom of God on earth consists of all who respond to the call of the gospel for a variety of reasons. All are under the impression that they are secure in Christ, but many are not. In the church there are many who believe they are saved because they have been baptized, sit at the Lord's table, or have made a confession of faith. Others believe they are 'good' people who continually have done their best and thus are right with God. Christ warned such people about the coming judgement, 'Not everyone who says to me, "Lord, Lord," shall enter the kingdom of heaven, but he who does the will of my Father in heaven. Many will say to me in that day, "Lord, Lord, have we not prophesied in your name, cast out demons in your name, and done many wonders in your name?" And then I will declare to them, "I never knew you; depart from me, you who practise lawlessness"' (Matthew 7:21-23). These are frightening words!

When Christ returns with his mighty, holy angels they will separate the saints from those who are citizens of Satan's kingdom. We know that the righteous will inherit the kingdom which Christ has prepared for his people, but the unrighteous will be condemned to the fire of eternal hell. We are told there will be 'wailing', which speaks of the effects of punishment. The 'gnashing of teeth' speaks of the everlasting anger and hatred of God by those confined to the pit.

We must make sure that we are secure in Christ or else his return and the Day of Judgement will be a day of horror for each one of us.

Let each one of us confess Christ to those about us and pray for their salvation. Then we must leave it to God to bring them to the Saviour.

THINGS TO DISCUSS WITH YOUR FAMILY

1. For what purpose were some creatures called 'unclean' and not to be eaten?
2. What is a spiritual hypocrite?
3. When will this world come to an end?

Meditation

Meditate upon your situation on the Day of Judgement.

Wise Words

You threaten me with the fire that burns for an hour and in a little while is put out, for you do not know about the fire of the judgement to come and the fire of eternal punishment reserved for the ungodly. *Polycarp*

'How beautiful are the feet of those who preach the gospel of peace, who bring glad tidings of good things!' (Romans 10:15).

Read: Matthew 13:51-53

It is always pleasant to visit people who take care of their home and prepare tasty foods and drink for meals. Some drinks keep for many years during which time they mature and are delicious to taste. When growing up on the farm we would put pumpkins on the roof in the sun and that preserved them for the following year, giving a better taste than some just pulled from the vine.

Jesus had concluded his series of parables about the kingdom of God and asked the disciples if they understood what he had taught. When they indicated that they had, the Lord told them they were to be teachers — 'scribes' — and teach the truths they had learned. They had a work to do and that was to preach the gospel and see the kingdom of God expand throughout the world. Just as the scribes were the great teachers of his age, so the disciples would become the Lord's scribes. In the Old Testament Ezra was one who is described as doing the work of a scribe. We read, '... Ezra came up from Babylon; and he was a skilled scribe in the Law of Moses, which the LORD GOD of Israel had given ... For Ezra had prepared his heart to seek the Law of the LORD, and to do it, and to teach statutes and ordinances in Israel' (Ezra 7:6,10).

The disciples had much to learn, but the time would come when some of them would prove to be the best scribes the world has known. We only need to read the New Testament to discover this.

When the apostles began preaching it was not just Christ's teaching that was expounded, but like the householder who used things old and new for food, so the apostles used the Old and New Testaments as their source of truth. Paul could say to the Ephesian elders he was meeting for the last time, 'And indeed, now I know that you all, among whom I have gone preaching the kingdom of God, will see my face no more. Therefore I testify to you this day that I am innocent of the blood of all men. For I have not shunned to declare to you the whole counsel of God' (Acts 20:25-27). He had taught the treasures from all sources of truth — the Old Testament and what Christ had taught him.

Today our 'scribes' — ministers of the gospel called to this office — should know and teach the whole Bible because 'All Scripture is given by inspiration of God, and is profitable for doctrine, for reproof, for correction, for instruction in righteousness, that the man of God may be complete, thoroughly equipped for every good work' (2 Timothy 3:16-17).

Our Lord here stresses the importance of teaching and preaching the gospel for this is God's usual way of bringing sinners to faith in Christ. Christ commanded his disciples, 'Go into all the world and preach the gospel to every creature' (Mark 16:15). Paul understood the primary importance of preaching. He wrote, 'For Christ did not send me to baptize, but to preach the gospel ...' (1 Corinthians 1:17).

Let us support by prayer, assistance and finances all faithful ministers who are the 'scribes' of our age. Like the apostles they are God's means of spreading the gospel and increasing the size of the kingdom of God.

THINGS TO DISCUSS WITH YOUR FAMILY

1. In what ways can you assist your pastor?
2. What is the greatest treasure to be found in the Scriptures?
3. Are you a true believer?

Meditation

Meditate upon the expanding kingdom of God in your community.

Wise Words

We have the truth and we need not be afraid to say so.

J. C. Ryle

337

'Behold, he who keeps Israel shall neither slumber nor sleep' (Psalm 121:4).

Read: Mark 4:35-41

There are times when all we want is peace, quietness and rest without interruption. The Lord had had a very busy day. He had told crowds of people a series of parables about the kingdom of God and then spent time privately explaining their meaning to his disciples. Now he wanted to get away from the crowds and rest.

The disciples were asked to obtain a boat and sail across the Sea of Galilee to the region of the Gadarenes. This incident opens our eyes to the true humanity of our Saviour. He was both God and man in one Person. He was weary and soon fell asleep in the stern of the boat. It is encouraging for us to realize that Christ was like us all in some ways — he felt pain, hunger, thirst and the emotions we experience — but all without sin. In Hebrews 4:15-16 we have words to give peace in troubled times — 'For we do not have a High Priest who cannot sympathise with our weaknesses, but was in all points tempted as we are, yet without sin. Let us therefore come boldly to the throne of grace, that we may obtain mercy and find grace to help in time of need.'

Without warning, a squall descended from Mount Hermon, which is about three thousand metres high, and soon the boat was being tossed about on the raging sea. Most of the disciples were sailors and used to rough seas, but these waves were such that they feared the boat would be swamped and they would drown. In their time of need they turned to their Teacher. They had seen his miracles and knew that he alone was their hope.

When wakened, Jesus rebuked the disciples for their weak faith. While they were with him in the boat they were secure. They had been told that he had still much work to do. With Christ on our side we are spiritually secure and no power can pluck us out of his care. Jesus knows our weaknesses and doesn't cast off those who have only little faith. He expects us to go to him in troubled times and ask for help. The psalmist wrote, 'Call upon me in the day of trouble; I will deliver you, and you shall glorify me' (Psalm 50:15).

With a word the winds dropped and instantly the sea became calm. The disciples were safe, but this demonstration of Christ's power terrified them. In holy awe they asked: 'Who can this be, that even the wind and the sea obey him?' This godly fear glorified Christ and we should remember that 'The fear of the LORD is the beginning of wisdom, and the knowledge of the Holy One is understanding' (Proverbs 9:10). Christ's power is almighty and protects us from the evil one. The disciples were learning that the 'carpenter's son' was God in flesh and blood. Is he your God?

There is peace of heart in the psalmist's words — 'For as the heavens are high above the earth, so great is his mercy toward those who fear him' (Psalm 103:11). Remember the words of Romans 5:1 — 'Therefore, having been justified by faith, we have peace with God through our Lord Jesus Christ.'

THINGS TO DISCUSS WITH YOUR FAMILY

1. How did Christ create the world?
2. Discuss Christ's miracles and what they teach you about our Saviour.
3. Why were the disciples filled with fear?

Meditation

Meditate upon the expression — 'With Christ in the vessel we can smile at the storm.'

Wise Words

But what is the fear of the Lord? It is that affectionate reverence, by which the child of God bends himself humbly and carefully to his Father's law.   *Charles Bridges*

'So shall my word be that goes forth from my mouth; it shall not return to me void, but it shall accomplish what I please, and it shall prosper in the thing for which I sent it' (Isaiah 55:11).

Read: Mark 5:1-20

I'm sure most of us have seen 'streakers' who run naked onto a playing field, disrupting the sporting fixture and attracting the attention of everyone to their disgusting behaviour. Many now end up with large fines — and rightly so!

Jesus had crossed the sea to save a man who was possessed by demons. Satan is a cruel taskmaster. When the Lord ordered the demons from the man and demanded their name, the reply came, 'My name is Legion for we are many.' A legion in the Roman army consisted of six thousand men. The demon-possessed man was not suffering from some mental disease, but was controlled by the many vile servants of Satan whose object is to harm men and women in the worst possible ways. The man in this story was unable to be confined or restricted because the demons gave him great strength. The locals kept out of his way because they feared the naked, wild person who lived among the tombs of the dead. People were impotent against Satan's power, but Jesus was acknowledged by the demons to be the 'Son of the Most High God'. He is Jehovah. This we learn when the apostle John gave understanding to Isaiah's majestic vision of Christ sitting upon his heavenly throne of glory (read Isaiah 6:1-4 and John 12:36-41).

One of Jesus' works was to 'destroy the works of the devil' (1 John 3:8). When Satan was forced to face the Lord in the wilderness he was defeated. The miracles performed by Jesus overcame the tragedies caused by sin, and with a word demons were ordered out of people.

Facing God's Son the demons pleaded with him that they might not be sent to hell at that time (Luke 8:28). It is on the Day of Judgement that Satan, his evil fallen angels and all his human followers will find themselves confined to the eternal flames. The demons pleaded that they might be allowed to enter the herd of pigs grazing on a nearby hillside. When Jesus gave them permission they obeyed his command, 'Come out of the man, unclean spirit!'

Instantly the man was freed of the demons, who entered the pigs, causing them to run down the hill and into the sea where they drowned.

The man who was now calm, in his right mind and dressed normally began expressing his love and gratitude to Jesus, asking that he might go with him. Instead Jesus gave him a more important work to do, 'Go home to your friends, and tell them what great things the Lord has done for you, and how he has had compassion on you.' The demoniac had become a missionary.

Satan is real and has great power, so don't trifle with the evil one. He has a kingdom and the majority of this world's people are citizens of that kingdom. Has God adopted you into his family and made you a member of his kingdom? If not, you belong to Satan, and should pray for God's mercy to give you a saving faith in Jesus.

THINGS TO DISCUSS WITH YOUR FAMILY

1. Why did Jesus allow the demons to enter the pigs? Is the answer found in the words of Daniel 4:35?
2. Why did the locals want Jesus out of their region? What should have been their attitude towards him?
3. What does Satan do today? Read 1 Peter 5:8-9.

Meditation

Meditate upon the almighty power of Jesus over the forces of evil.

Wise Words

The devil is a great student in divinity. *William Gurnall*

'And God will wipe away every tear from their eyes; there shall be no more death, nor sorrow, nor crying. There shall be no more pain, for the former things have passed away' (Revelation 21:4).

Read: Mark 5:21-24; 35-43

Death is a curse which we will all face unless the Lord returns before that day. Death is the result of sin just as Adam was warned in the Garden of Eden — 'And the LORD GOD commanded the man, saying, "Of every tree of the garden you may freely eat; but of the tree of the knowledge of good and evil you shall not eat, for in the day that you eat of it you shall surely die"' (Genesis 2:16-17). The death spoken of here was both physical and spiritual. Sin is the cause of every evil that befalls the human race. How we should hate sin and love God!

Jesus and his disciples had returned to the Capernaum side of the sea and again they were surrounded by crowds. Very soon he was confronted by Jairus, a ruler of the Capernaum synagogue. No doubt he had seen the Lord perform great miracles, heard his teaching and realized that he was the hope of the hopeless. Jairus was in desperate need of help as his little daughter was almost dead. He knew of Christ's compassion and asked him to come and just touch the child so that she would be healed.

Death is the king of terrors and despite people not wanting to discuss the subject we are taught, 'It is appointed for men to die once, but after this the judgement' (Hebrews 9:27). Death comes to people of all ages and we must all prepare for the day when we face that sin's wages.

Because of an interruption which we will look at tomorrow, word was received that the little girl had died and it was too late for Christ to visit the home. Yet the compassionate Lord spoke words of encouragement to Jairus, 'Do not be afraid; only believe.'

Arriving at the house, he ordered the wailing people outside and with Jairus and his wife, Peter, James and John he entered the room where the child lay. We can only try and imagine the scene when Jesus commanded the dead child, 'Little girl, I say to you, arise.' Now dead people can't hear those speaking, but this time the child heard Christ's majestic voice. Her heart started beating, she began breathing, her eyes opened and the colour returned to her flesh. The dead lived! The impossible had occurred!

And when Christ returns the 'impossible' will again happen. The dead bodies of every human who ever lived will be raised to life. Jesus said, 'Do not marvel at this; for the hour is coming in which all who are in the graves will hear his voice and come forth — those who have done good, to the resurrection of life, and those who have done evil, to the resurrection of condemnation' (John 5:28-29).

Every Christian has experienced the miracle of life from the dead. We who were dead in our sins have by the new birth been made spiritually alive. Our Saviour has power over death as he showed by his resurrection. In the new heavens and earth death will be gone for ever. Death, the last enemy, will be thrown into hell and we shall live for ever in Paradise! Praise God.

THINGS TO DISCUSS WITH YOUR FAMILY

1. List four ways Jesus showed compassion in the story about Jairus' daughter.
2. When will death be finally gone from humanity?
3. What did Jesus mean when he said, 'The child is not dead, but sleeping'?

Meditation

Think about the almighty power of our Redeemer in raising the dead.

Wise Words

All deaths are solemn events. Nothing in the whole history of a man is so important as his end. *J. C. Ryle*

'God is greatly to be feared in the assembly of the saints, and to be held in reverence by all those around him' (Psalm 89:7).

Read: Mark 5:25-34

There is so much sickness in our world and often doctors take a long time to determine the problem and prescribe the cure. Sickness is a curse because of the unpleasant suffering.

Today we read of a woman who had been ill for many years. She had spent a fortune on doctors, but none had been able to provide a cure. Nevertheless she knew of Christ, his teachings and miracles, and believed that he could do for her what the doctors could not. What stands out about this woman is her strong faith in Jesus which was the gift of God. She was just one of the many who crowded about the Lord as he made his way to Jairus' home. Yet she was determined to touch his clothing because she believed that this would bring about her healing.

One touch and she was healed! Again this shows the almighty power that is at the disposal of our Saviour. At once, Jesus asked, 'Who touched me?' He knew what had happened but wanted the woman to openly confess her faith. Try and imagine how the woman felt as she slowly approached the Lord, trembling with fear. She bowed down before him confessing what she had done. Let us take notice of Christ's gentle reply — 'Daughter, your faith has made you well. Go in peace, and be healed of your affliction.' She hadn't done anything to earn her healing — God's gift of faith was the vehicle through which her blessing came.

Here the Lord was glorified before the watching crowd. Our duty is to glorify God in every aspect of our lives and to let the world know what the Lord has done for us. We are invited to go to God for help, as the psalmist wrote, 'Call upon me in the day of trouble; I will deliver you, and you shall glorify me' (Psalm 50:15). Our Saviour has given us wonderful promises if we believe in him. His words to the Philippian jailer are ours as well — 'Believe on the Lord Jesus Christ, and you will be saved, you and your household' (Acts 16:31).

Jesus told the woman to go in peace. Christians are promised peace of heart in this troubled world. Paul wrote, 'Be anxious for nothing, but in everything by prayer and supplication, with thanksgiving, let your requests be made known to God; and the peace of God, which surpasses all understanding, will guard your hearts and minds through Christ Jesus ... and the God of peace will be with you' (Philippians 4:6-7,9).

Jesus has the same power today as he had when he walked the streets of Capernaum on his way to the home of Jairus. Go to him with your troubles and seek his favour.

THINGS TO DISCUSS WITH YOUR FAMILY

1. Why did Jesus praise the woman's faith?
2. Can Jesus today still heal sickness? How do you know this?
3. Read Isaiah 43:1-2 and discuss what you are being taught there — 'But now, thus says the LORD, who created you, O Jacob, and he who formed you, O Israel: "Fear not, for I have redeemed you; I have called you by your name; you are mine. When you pass through the waters, I will be with you; and through the rivers, they shall not overflow you. When you walk through the fire, you shall not be burned, nor shall the flame scorch you."'

Meditation

Think upon the words of Psalm 50:15 — 'Call upon me in the day of trouble; I will deliver you, and you shall glorify me.'

Wise Words

Do not expect the supernatural when God would have you proceed in the normal, natural course of things.
Vance Havner

'So the LORD said to him, "Who has made man's mouth? Or who makes the mute, the deaf, the seeing, or the blind? Have not I, the LORD?"' (Exodus 4:11).

Read: Matthew 9:27-34

Many of the readers of this book would frequently attend worship where they hear a minister preach from the Scriptures. Imagine what it must have been like to see and hear the Lord Jesus as he went about performing miracles and preaching words that our minister takes for his text. Would we have believed what Jesus said, and trusted our eternal security to him?

We have again read of Christ performing more wonderful miracles, which added to the mountain of proof that he was the Son of God — the Messiah. First we read that two blind men knew who he was and what he could do for them. No doubt they had heard about Christ, possibly being present when he preached and performed miracles. They believed Jesus' claims and knew that they also could be healed by the one they called 'Son of David'. This was a title by which the Messiah was known. Later when approaching Jerusalem for the last time the crowds of people cried out to him, 'Hosanna to the Son of David!' (Matthew 21:15). The Pharisees were furious as they understood the people were declaring that Jesus was the Messiah.

The two blind men made their way to the house where Jesus was, and openly stated that they believed he could give them their sight. Just a touch was all that was necessary and they would be able to see. Despite being told not to talk about their healing they praised God by making it known throughout the countryside. This just gave more reason for the Scribes and Pharisees to hate him. Again they failed to understand what the psalmist had written: 'The LORD opens the eyes of the blind' (Psalm 146:8). And why shouldn't Christ give sight to blind eyes for God told Moses who suffered a speech problem — 'Who has made man's mouth? Or who makes the mute, the deaf, the seeing, or the blind? Have not I, the LORD?' (Exodus 4:11). Christ who created the eye could very easily repair sin's damage to the eye!

This healing was followed by some people bringing a man who was 'mute and demon possessed'. At once another miracle was performed. When the demon was driven from the man, he could speak. Again the Pharisees failed to look at the words of Isaiah 35:5-6 which prophesied of Christ's work — 'Then the eyes of the blind shall be opened, and the ears of the deaf shall be unstopped. Then the lame shall leap like a deer, and the tongue of the dumb sing.' All they could do was accuse Jesus of performing such miracles by the power of Satan.

May we always praise and thank the Lord for all of his blessings. The writer of the Proverbs said, 'To seek one's own glory is not glory' (Proverbs 25:27). We live in an age where proud people are always seeking the attention of others. They want the praise of their community and are no better than the Pharisees of old. We are to be humble people who magnify God as Jesus did.

THINGS TO DISCUSS WITH YOUR FAMILY

1. Why should God be concerned with the healing of any sinner?
2. How do you think Satan felt about his continual defeat by the almighty power of Jesus?
3. Why did Jesus tell the healed man not to tell people about his healing?

Meditation

Meditate upon Revelation 20:10 — 'The devil, who deceived them, was cast into the lake of fire and brimstone where the beast and the false prophet are. And they will be tormented day and night for ever and ever.'

Wise Words

The devil allows no Christian to reach heaven with clean feet all the way. *Martin Luther*

Familiarity breeds contempt

'But Jesus said to them, "Only in his home town and in his own house is a prophet without honour"' (Matthew 13:57, NIV).

Read: Mark 6:1-6

In our reading we learn something that is very true: good people gain the least honour and respect from people living in their own locality. For some reason it is the little known outsiders who are admired and praised. Jesus found this to be true and rebuked the people of his home town for their failure to recognize him as Messiah. They didn't use their privileges.

The people of Nazareth, and his family, saw him grow up and must surely have seen his perfect life of love of Jehovah and obedience to his holy law. Those present at the local synagogue heard him preach his great sermon in which he claimed to be the one fulfilling the prophecy of Isaiah 61:1-2: 'The Spirit of the LORD is upon me, because he has anointed me to preach the gospel to the poor; he has sent me to heal the broken-hearted, to proclaim liberty to the captives and recovery of sight to the blind, to set at liberty those who are oppressed; to proclaim the acceptable year of the LORD.' He then closed the scroll, sat down and commenced his sermon with the words, 'Today this Scripture is fulfilled in your hearing' (Luke 4:18-19,21).

With few exceptions, his family members refused to believe what he said. Everyone knew that he had not attended the 'universities' of his day. He was just a carpenter. They could not accept that the one who grew up in their midst was the Creator of the world. It was only after his resurrection that his brothers and sisters believed that he was the Christ (Acts 1:14).

Unbelief is the worst of sins as it is the pathway to hell. God's spiritual blessings come to us through faith and where there is no faith people are spiritually dead. Because of their unbelief Jesus didn't perform any great miracles in the locality — only a few were healed of illness. Because of their unbelief he moved on.

It was unbelief that resulted in Adam and Eve falling into sin. They doubted God's warning concerning the eating of the forbidden fruit in Eden. Today so many refuse to believe the plain teaching of Scripture, '... he who does not believe will be condemned' (Mark 16:16).

Today, many godly ministers who preach the truth are held in contempt by those who should know better. We must encourage our church office bearers as they do the work of the Lord. In the western world we have so many spiritual privileges. Yet few appreciate them and don't thank God for their blessings. May we not be like those citizens of Nazareth, who saw and heard so much about Jesus and then treated him with contempt. Let us encourage all Christians as they follow the Lord Jesus, living obedient lives. May we each live a godly life and not be surprised when others treat us with scorn.

THINGS TO DISCUSS WITH YOUR FAMILY

1. How can you encourage your minister and his wife in their spiritual work among the congregation?
2. Have you ever prayed for the office bearers of your congregation? If not, start now!
3. When should we do as Christ said in Luke 9:5: 'And whoever will not receive you ... shake off the very dust from your feet as a testimony against them'?

Meditation

Meditate upon the unbelief in your family members. Ask the Lord to bring them to himself.

Wise Words

In all unbelief there are these two things: a good opinion of one's self and a bad opinion of God. *Horatius Bonar*

'Then he said to his disciples, "The harvest truly is plentiful, but the labourers
are few. Therefore pray the Lord of the
harvest to send out labourers into his
harvest"' (Matthew 9:37-38).

Read: Matthew 9:35 – 10:4

After spending many years at school where you were taught a
great deal, the time comes to get a job and use your education.
Your parents teach you about God and a right way to live. When you
leave home you are expected to make good use of what you were
taught in order to be a good citizen of your country and the kingdom of God.

The disciples had been instructed by the Lord and now it was
time for them to make use of what they had been taught. They were
to follow in the footsteps of their Teacher who always went about
doing good, healing people and preaching the truth concerning the
kingdom of God. The Lord gave his disciples the power needed to
cast out demons and heal the sick. They were to preach that entrance into the kingdom of God was through faith in Jesus and not
by obedience to the laws of God and the Pharisees, which were a
burden that weighed heavily upon their hearts. The Pharisees were
confronted with crowds of sinners yet had failed to teach the important salvation truths — 'justice and mercy and faith' (Matthew 23:23).

Jesus pointed out to his disciples that there was a field of unbelievers and they, although only twelve in number, were to get out and
'harvest' people into God's kingdom. We also notice that the Lord
sent the disciples out in pairs (Mark 6:7). This shows the wisdom of
the Saviour because two provide each other with company and encouragement, especially when there are difficulties. We read in Ecclesiastes 4: 9-10: 'Two are better than one, because they have a good
reward for their labour. For if they fall, one will lift up his companion.
But woe to him who is alone when he falls, for he has no one to
help him up.'

The Scribes and Pharisees were supposed to faithfully shepherd
the people, but failed as had Israel's spiritual leaders over the centuries before. In Jeremiah 23:1-2 we read of the false shepherds: '"Woe

to the shepherds who destroy and scatter the sheep of my pasture!"
says the LORD. Therefore thus says the LORD GOD of Israel against the
shepherds who feed my people: "You have scattered my flock, driven
them away, and not attended to them…'"

Now the 'Good Shepherd' was sending out true shepherds to
bring into the kingdom of God 'the lost sheep of the house of Israel'.
Many were won into the kingdom, especially on and after the Day of
Pentecost, but the persecution of Christians by the Jews meant that
the gospel was taken from Israel and given to the Gentiles. After his
resurrection Christ gave his disciples their 'marching orders': "'Go
therefore and make disciples of all the nations, baptising them in the
name of the Father and of the Son and of the Holy Spirit, teaching
them to observe all things that I have commanded you; and lo, I am
with you always, even to the end of the age." Amen' (Matthew 28:19-
20). We live in a wonderful age, an age of great opportunity.

THINGS TO DISCUSS
WITH YOUR FAMILY

1. Find out all you can about the twelve disciples.
2. Who was Christ's betrayer?
3. Who is 'the Good Shepherd'? Read Psalm 23.
4. What factor unified the disciples?

Meditation

Read Ezekiel 34:23-31 and think of what you are taught
about the Lord Jesus.

The key to the history of the world is the kingdom of
God.   *D. Martyn Lloyd-Jones*

Wise Words

'Even so the Lord has commanded that those who preach the gospel should live from the gospel' (1 Corinthians 9:14).

Read: Matthew 10:5-15

We all should be paid for the work we do. At the end of each week workers expect to be paid so that they can provide for their families. Maybe young people expect a regular pocket money for helping about the home. One of my grandsons mows our lawn and we have a contract which means a payment when the work is carried out.

Our reading today indicates what the disciples were to do. They were to preach, cast out demons and heal the sick. The Pharisees and Scribes had failed to carry out their duties. Now the disciples would do as the Lord commanded and by the grace of God extend the kingdom. What was happening was prophesied in Isaiah 49:6 — 'Indeed he [God] says, "It is too small a thing that you should be my Servant to raise up the tribes of Jacob, and to restore the preserved ones of Israel; I will also give you as a light to the Gentiles, that you should be my salvation to the ends of the earth."' Soon there would be no distinction between Jew and Gentile in the sight of God. Paul wrote: 'There is neither Jew nor Greek, there is neither slave nor free, there is neither male nor female; for you are all one in Christ Jesus' (Galatians 3:28).

As with John the Baptist, the Lord Jesus and now the disciples, the call would be to repentance and faith in God's Son.

The twelve were told to set out in pairs, taking no money or spare clothing with them. They were to prayerfully rely upon God for their daily needs. We are told to support our ministers who preach the gospel. Paul's teaching is plain: '… the Lord has commanded that those who preach the gospel should live from the gospel' (1 Corinthians 9:14). This means that Christians must support those God has appointed as their full-time ministers.

The disciples had the most precious commodity of all to preach, and that was the gospel about their Master, Jesus. He would be freely offered to sinners just as he is today. The invitation is the same as is the cost, 'Ho! Everyone who thirsts, come to the waters; and you who have no money, come, buy and eat. Yes, come, buy wine and milk without money and without price. Why do you spend money for what is not bread, and your wages for what does not satisfy? Listen carefully to me, and eat what is good, and let your soul delight itself in abundance. Incline your ear, and come to me. Hear, and your soul shall live; and I will make an everlasting covenant with you — the sure mercies of David' (Isaiah 55:1-3).

The Lord knew that just as he had faced opposition so also would his disciples. Hence they were told to accept the welcome of gracious people, but when opposition reared its head they were to get away and take the good news to others with a more receptive heart. God's judgement upon such wicked people would be worse than that which would fall upon the citizens of Sodom and Gomorrah. We must beware of rejecting the truth and those who bring the good news of salvation.

THINGS TO DISCUSS WITH YOUR FAMILY

1. What are we here taught about our responsibilities to our pastors?
2. In your reading, verse 13 speaks about 'peace' that came from the disciples. What is that 'peace'?
3. Why were the disciples told to go to 'the lost sheep of the house of Israel'?

Meditation

Think upon this expression, 'What we weave in time we wear in eternity.'

Wise Words

I had rather be fully understood by ten than admired by ten thousand. *Jonathan Edwards*

'I have become all things to all men, that I might by all means save some' (1 Corinthians 9:22).

Read: Matthew 10:16-25

No one likes to be unpopular and the object of the contempt of other people. Most people do all they can to win and keep friends. I'm sure that Jesus and the disciples felt this way. Yet life is not always easy and frequently we become the scorn of other people who can't stand what we say or do.

The disciples were sent out to heal, cast out demons and preach the good news and I am sure they wanted to be well received wherever they went, but Jesus gave them a warning: 'They hated me and they will hate you also.' Jesus told his disciples to act wisely in their dealing with sinners and thus make sure they were not persecuted for foolish behaviour. The Apostle Peter said the same in his epistle: 'If you are reproached for the name of Christ, blessed are you, for the Spirit of glory and of God rests upon you. On their part he is blasphemed, but on your part he is glorified. But let none of you suffer as a murderer, a thief, an evildoer, or as a busybody in other people's matters. Yet if anyone suffers as a Christian, let him not be ashamed, but let him glorify God in this matter' (1 Peter 4:14-16).

Just as the world despised Jesus and his disciples so also the world hates Christians. The apostle John warns us, 'Do not marvel my brethren, if the world hates you' (1 John 3:13). Christians are abhorred when they remind people that they are sinners, unable to save themselves. People don't like being told that they must humble themselves, repent of their sins and trust the Lord Jesus in order to be saved. This is not the thinking of proud members of the kingdom of Satan! Wherever the apostles were dragged up before the rulers of the nations they would be given words to use in their defence. The Holy Spirit who gave them the words we have in our Bibles would direct their minds to a godly defence of Christ and the gospel.

The Apostle Paul indicated what the world thought of him and the saints, 'We have been made as the filth of the world, the offscouring of all things until now' (1 Corinthians 4:13). This will be the attitude of the world until Jesus, our Saviour, returns in power and glory to gather his people together. It is only then that we will find perfect rest.

The Lord told them they would find opposition from the Pharisees and Scribes as they preached through Israel. After his resurrection Jesus appeared to his disciples with instructions to take the gospel to the four corners of the world.

Satan still has great power for we are told he goes about as a 'roaring lion' attempting to overthrow the gospel and kill those who preach the truth (1 Peter 5:8). Nevertheless, his power is curtailed. During the gospel age he cannot totally deceive the nations as he did before Christ's entrance into this world. We must persevere to the end of our lives if we would be saved, and thank God, he will give us the grace to do so despite the world's hatred.

THINGS TO DISCUSS WITH YOUR FAMILY

1. How do we 'endure' to the end? (Matthew 10:22).
2. How did Paul become 'all things to all men' (1 Corinthians 9:22)?
3. Why do humans want to be liked by others?

Meditation

Meditate upon the expression, 'The blood of the martyrs is the seed of the church.'

Wise Words

Persecution is one of the surest signs of the genuineness of our Christianity. *Benjamin E. Fernando*

'And do not fear those who kill the body but cannot kill the soul. But rather fear him who is able to destroy both soul and body in hell' (Matthew 10:28).

Read: Matthew 10:26-31

Nobody likes to be hurt and the disciples were people like you and me. They felt pain and weren't happy when they were persecuted. Jesus had just been telling them that they would suffer opposition as they went about doing good and preaching the good news of salvation through faith in himself. This cruelty wasn't going to end when their Master died upon a cross, but would become worse. They were being told to fearlessly tell sinners of their need of salvation. We are going to consider four outcomes in all which have application to every Christian when they proclaim the gospel of Christ.

First, the fierce opposition faced wouldn't stop the spread of the gospel through faith in Christ (verses 26-27). Jesus had privately taught the disciples and now they were to let the world know what was once a mystery. It would be as if the disciples stood on the top of a tall building and with a loudspeaker preached for all to hear. On the Judgement Day the secrets of men's hearts, especially those who opposed the gospel, will be revealed for all to see. Paul spoke of that day and of the glory that would be poured out upon the saints — 'Therefore judge nothing before the time, until the Lord comes, who will both bring to light the hidden things of darkness and reveal the counsels of the hearts. Then each one's praise will come from God' (1 Corinthians 4:5).

Secondly, when we courageously bear witness to Christ we should not fear what ungodly people can do. Yes, they can hurt our bodies and that is unpleasant, but the worst that they can do is kill us. They cannot destroy our soul. Jesus reminded his disciples that God can eternally destroy both body and soul in hell. Gehenna is the hell of eternal separation from God and everlasting punishment. The lake of fire is reserved for all whose names were 'not found written in the Book of Life' (Revelation 20:15). This means that all who have no saving faith in Jesus are punished for ever.

We should fear God and not cruel humans. Millions of Christians have died in preference to denying their Saviour. In the sermon on the mount Jesus gave a special promise to all who suffered persecution because of their love for him. He said, 'Blessed are those who are persecuted for righteousness' sake, for theirs is the kingdom of heaven. Blessed are you when they revile and persecute you, and say all kinds of evil against you falsely for my sake. Rejoice and be exceedingly glad, for great is your reward in heaven, for so they persecuted the prophets who were before you' (Matthew 5:10-12).

May we all be courageous disciples of the Lord Jesus.

THINGS TO DISCUSS WITH YOUR FAMILY

1. Discuss the two outcomes the disciples were to expect when they preached the gospel.
2. What are the reasons why you should witness to the saving work of Jesus in your life?
3. Discuss Hebrews 4:16 — 'Let us therefore come boldly to the throne of grace, that we may obtain mercy and find grace to help in time of need.'

Meditation

Pray that the Lord will give you courage to speak to others about your love of Jesus Christ.

From every story wind that blows,
From every tide of rising woes,
There is a calm, a sweet retreat;
'tis found beneath the mercy seat.

Thomas Hastings

Wise Words

'We love him because he first loved us'
(1 John 4:19).

Read: Matthew 10:26-33

I'm sure that all of us have done things of which we are truly ashamed. There are times when we have to go to the person we have offended and say, 'Sorry'. There are some things we have done that we hope no one ever finds out about, as our shame would be more than we could bear, but Christians should never be ashamed of having faith in the Lord Jesus, despite what people might think of us.

Further to our last meditation the Lord gave his disciples two more results of fearlessly proclaiming the gospel. We read — 'Are not two sparrows sold for a copper coin? And not one of them falls to the ground apart from your Father's will. But the very hairs of your head are all numbered. Do not fear therefore; you are of more value than many sparrows.'

The little brown sparrows were of no great significance to people. Sometimes they were bought and cooked to be eaten, but they cost next to nothing. However, our God cares for the sparrows. He provides them with the seed they need for food and not one dies without God's knowledge and determination. Jesus told his disciples that they were of much greater value than the sparrows God cared for each day. In fact even the hairs on their heads were known to God. These are encouraging words to believers for they tell us that God loves us, body and soul. We are chosen in eternity to be recipients of God's saving love and our destiny is heaven.

In Psalm 116:15 we read very encouraging words, 'Precious in the sight of the LORD is the death of his saints.' All Christians can speak courageously of their Saviour because God cares for us all and we can rest easy in the words of the apostle Paul: 'And we know that all things work together for good to those who love God, to those who are the called according to his purpose' (Romans 8:28).

The Lord's final reason given to the disciples for confessing him before the Jews is found in verses 32 and 33 — 'Therefore whoever confesses me before men, him I will also confess before my Father who is in heaven. But whoever denies me before men, him I will also deny before my Father who is in heaven.' We should never be ashamed to confess our love of Jesus. Some people have a special gift of witnessing about the Saviour, but every Christian should make a stand for our Lord when opposition raises its ugly head.

Jesus is the only Mediator between God and man. Whilst on earth, as Mediator, he prayed for Peter — 'But I have prayed for you, that your faith should not fail' (Luke 22:32). Today Jesus continues his work as Mediator for we read in Hebrews 7:25, 'Therefore he is also able to save to the uttermost those who come to God through him, since he always lives to make intercession for them.' This should thrill our hearts. In heaven the God/man Jesus Christ speaks to his heavenly Father on behalf of his people. And on the great Judgement Day when one by one we stand before Christ the Judge, he will speak to his Father on behalf of each one of his faithful people. Christ honours those who honour him. Hallelujah!

THINGS TO DISCUSS WITH YOUR FAMILY

1. How can you bear witness to your Saviour?
2. Does Satan play a part in preventing us witnessing for Christ? How?
3. What is the warning in Matthew 10:32-33 to believers?

Meditation

Meditate upon Revelation 20:12b — 'And the dead were judged according to their works, by the things which were written in the books.'

Wise Words

Human tribunals deal with crime; they have punishments but no rewards. The divine tribunal has both.

A. Plummer

'For son dishonours father, daughter rises against her mother, daughter-in-law against her mother-in-law; a man's enemies are the men of his own household' (Micah 7:6).

Read: Matthew 10:34-39

It is sad when we find households torn apart over some issue, often of little consequence. I know of some families where members have not spoken to each other for many years and never intend to do so — their hearts are filled with contempt. It is a blessing to be a member of a family where love binds all members together, despite the occasional argument.

The Lord Jesus is called 'Prince of Peace' (Isaiah 9:6). It is through his sacrificial death upon the cross that he won peace for his people. No longer did God look upon his people as those to be condemned to eternal hell.

Jesus praised those who went out of their way to establish peace. We read, 'Blessed are the peacemakers, for they shall be called sons of God' (Matthew 5:9).

Christ's work of salvation was to establish peace between God and man. The very moment a sinner trusts the Lord Jesus for his salvation he is justified in the court of heaven, and of this great event Paul wrote: 'Therefore, having been justified by faith, we have peace with God through our Lord Jesus Christ, through whom also we have access by faith into this grace in which we stand, and rejoice in hope of the glory of God' (Romans 5:1-2). All unbelievers who are convicted of their sins by the Holy Spirit and find Christ as Saviour can say with Paul, 'O wretched man that I am! Who will deliver me from this body of death? I thank God through Jesus Christ our Lord!' (Romans 7:24-25).

Once a person becomes a Christian he is adopted into the family of God; he is a son or daughter of the living God. The Apostle John wrote: 'But as many as received him, to them he gave the right to become children of God, to those who believe in his name: who were born, not of blood, nor of the will of the flesh, nor of the will of man, but of God' (John 1:12,13).

Yet, how often the words of Christ in our reading become a reality — unconverted sinners hate Christ and his followers. They dislike the family member who loathes sin and loves righteousness. They are bitter towards the one reading his Bible, praying, going to church and speaking of his love of Christ. Often the Christian is told to make his home elsewhere. In some ungodly countries the one who becomes a Christian is killed. May we all take comfort in the words of Jesus: 'Blessed are you when they revile and persecute you, and say all kinds of evil against you falsely for my sake. Rejoice and be exceedingly glad, for great is your reward in heaven' (Matthew 5:11-12).

Every day we are to take up our God-given cross and follow Christ. If we are martyred because of our faith in the Saviour we are assured of eternal life. Failure to stand firm for Jesus invites God's anger and is an indication that our faith may not be genuine. May God give us all spiritual courage in the face of the world's opposition.

THINGS TO DISCUSS WITH YOUR FAMILY

1. We are told to take up our 'cross'. What did Jesus mean by this?
2. What rewards does Christ have for his persecuted people?
3. Discuss Matthew 10:39 — 'He who finds his life will lose it, and he who loses his life for my sake will find it.'

Meditation

Think upon the spiritual truth that our sacrifice for Christ and his cause must be total.

Wise Words

The easiest place in which to be spiritual is in public; the most difficult is at home.   *Charles Ryrie*

'For God is not unjust to forget your work and labour of love which you have shown toward his name, in that you have ministered to the saints, and do minister' (Hebrews 6:10).

Read: Matthew 10:40-42

Often when we lived in the manse there was a knock on our front door and when we opened it we found someone in need of help. Sometimes the person wanted a place to sleep for the night. We had arrangements made for these people to be accommodated in a local motel, but sometimes we provided the person with bed and breakfast. We often thought of the words of Hebrews 13:2, 'Do not forget to entertain strangers, for by so doing some have unwittingly entertained angels.' Then there were times when the congregation was able to give substantial support to our Christian friends.

God had sent his Son into a hostile world and very few people welcomed him with love and open arms. The big majority of the children of Israel reviled him and rejoiced to see him crucified. Jesus was sending his disciples out into a hostile world and after giving them instructions in what they were to do and how they were to re-act when people ignored their message, he indicated that some would receive them with gladness.

The words of Christ remind us that the motive for what we do is so important. All we do should be the result of a heart that has been born again and is indwelt by the Holy Spirit. Christians see things differently to the worldly person. Our acts of kindness are motivated by our love of God and gratitude to him for what he has done for us.

The disciples were told that when they were welcomed by other believers it was as if the one who sent them was being welcomed. Later Jesus told a parable in which the same thought was repeated. We read of the Lord blessing those who gave help to their brethren, 'And the King will answer and say to them, "Assuredly, I say to you, inasmuch as you did it to one of the least of these my brethren, you did it to me"' (Matthew 25:40). To welcome a disciple was to welcome Christ and in turn to welcome the heavenly Father into their company.

While Saul (later the Apostle Paul) was on the road to Damascus to persecute Christians, 'he fell to the ground, and heard a voice saying to him, "Saul, Saul, why are you persecuting Me?"' (Acts 9:4). To harm a Christian is considered as an attack upon their Saviour.

Jesus promises great rewards to those who treat his messengers with kindness and respect. They will receive the reward given to a prophet or a righteous man. These recompenses are spiritual — everlasting life, peace of heart and eternal blessings on the Day of Judgement. Our text summarizes what the Lord said to his disciples, and those words apply to all of his faithful people. God does not forget anything done for his people, whether good or bad, especially during times of persecution as it is risky. He has kept a record of all that everyone has done and we read that on Judgement Day: 'And the dead were judged according to their works, by the things which were written in the books' (Revelation 20:12). May we show love and compassion to all of Christ's people, especially those who preach the gospel.

THINGS TO DISCUSS WITH YOUR FAMILY

1. What is the reward of Christ to those who give help to their Christian brothers and sisters?
2. What acts of kindness does your church do to help their less fortunate brethren?
3. Do you pray for suffering Christians throughout the world? If not, start now.

Meditation

Think upon 1 Corinthians 15:58 — 'Therefore, my beloved brethren, be steadfast, immovable, always abounding in the work of the Lord, knowing that your labour is not in vain in the Lord.'

He is too busy who is too busy to be kind.

James Alexander

Wise Words

Herod has a problem

'"But I say to you that Elijah has come already, and they did not know him but did to him whatever they wished. Likewise the Son of Man is also about to suffer at their hands." Then the disciples understood that he spoke to them of John the Baptist' (Matthew 17:12-13).

Read: Mark 6:14-29

Every day in the news we hear of terrible atrocities. If God did not rule this world we would be in the most hopeless situation imaginable. Your reading today is largely about the murder of the godly John the Baptist by the despicable, weak Herod and his obnoxious wife, Herodias. She was in some ways like Jezebel, the wife of Ahab, who also hated godliness and truth.

Herod had a problem — he believed that Jesus was the resurrected John whom he had murdered. Herod tolerated John's preaching until he touched a very sore point — he had married his brother Philip's wife while Philip was still alive. The law of God did not permit this marriage, making Herod and Herodias guilty of adultery. Herodias hated John and wanted him dead, but he continued to speak out courageously against their sin. John the Baptist was a godly man who always preached the truth, ignoring the consequences his preaching would bring.

This should be the attitude of every minister, and indeed every Christian. We are to be bold in rebuking sin. The world hates the gospel and the truth of God, but regardless of the persecution and hatred it brings we are called to be faithful witnesses of God's revelation.

You have read why John was murdered, but now Herod was filled with fear as he believed that Jesus was really John the Baptist, whom he had had put to death. Many people were questioning who Jesus was, some believing he was a resurrected Elijah or the prophet prophesied by Moses (Deuteronomy 18:15-18).

Herod had committed that terrible crime to placate his wife after making a foolish promise. It was his birthday party and possibly having drunk too much strong drink he promised Herodias' daughter anything she wanted up to half of his kingdom. John's head on a platter was the request. The outcome of sin can be very gruesome!

It wasn't long before Herod began to hate Jesus and his preaching and wanted him put to death. On one occasion some Pharisees came to Jesus with a warning, 'Get out and depart from here, for Herod wants to kill you' (Luke 13:31).

Faithful ministers of the gospel will never be popular outside their circle of Christian friends, but great promises are made to faithful saints who suffer the disdain of the world. Paul wrote: 'For I consider that the sufferings of this present time are not worthy to be compared with the glory which shall be revealed in us' (Romans 8:18).

There are times when we are rebuked by a Christian friend for some sinful behaviour. If so, we should thank God for such a good friend. In Proverbs 27:6 we read, 'Faithful are the wounds of a friend.' We should hate sin and be ready to expose it wherever it is found, our aim being to bring about repentance or a turning to Christ for salvation.

THINGS TO DISCUSS WITH YOUR FAMILY

1. Why do people detest God's law?
2. Why did Herod hate Jesus?
3. What are you to do when you see a Christian friend involved in sinful behaviour?

Meditation

Think upon the expression, 'Silence sin or sin will silence the conscience.'

Wise Words

Persecution and opposition ought to encourage rather than discourage us, for we are faithfully warned by our Lord that the natural man and the religionist will not receive the gospel of the grace of God. *Henry Mahan*

'There remains therefore a rest for the people of God' (Hebrews 4:9).

Read: Mark 6:30-34

I'm sure that everyone of us have on occasions been working so hard that we just had to stop and rest; we couldn't go on any further. Some people work without a break and end up having a forced rest in hospital. We live in an age where much of our day is devoted to work of one kind or another.

The disciples had been out and about preaching the good news concerning Christ, healing the sick and casting out demons. Life had been very busy for all of the 'apostles' as the disciples were called. They were a group of weary men who had not been eating regularly and were in need of rest.

They had spent time telling Jesus what they had done and how taxing their work had been, but now it was time to recuperate in preparation for the next preaching tour. Jesus told them, 'Come aside by yourselves to a deserted place and rest a while.' This was very good advice which we also need to heed.

Today in the ministry we read of so much 'burnout'. Too many ministers have the impression that they must be on the go all the time, day and night. Often they do not have their one day of rest each week and before long they are physically and spiritually sick. Our bodies were not created for continual work and the Lord instructed that we have one day in seven away from work as God did after creation. Ministers of the gospel give themselves to feeding their congregations with spiritual food and never seem to realize that they also need to sit in a pew and be fed with the word of God.

In the early church the apostles found themselves doing much work that interfered with what they were called to carry out. The result was the election of deacons to look after the material concerns of the congregation. The apostles then said, '… we will give ourselves continually to prayer and to the ministry of the word' (Acts 6:4).

Jesus saw that crowds of people were following them to the desert place where they hoped to rest and he was concerned that the crowds were like sheep without a faithful shepherd. Later he said of the Pharisees, '… they are blind leaders of the blind. And if the blind lead the blind, both shall fall into the ditch' (Matthew 15:14).

Ministers must realize that they are responsible to God to preach the truth which involves the prayerful study of the Scriptures which takes time and effort. Congregations and ministers should notice the words: 'Obey them that have the rule over you, and submit your-selves: for they watch for your souls, as they that must give account, that they may do it with joy, and not with grief: for that is unprofit-able for you' (Hebrews 13:17).

Care for your minister, pray for him and make sure his physical needs are met. And ministers, make sure you regularly take a rest. Burnout is a widespread reality in the Christian ministry.

THINGS TO DISCUSS WITH YOUR FAMILY

1. In what way did God 'rest' after completing cre-ation?
2. Discuss the meaning of today's text.
3. Is your leisure time spent wisely? What do you do during your time of rest?

Meditation

Meditate upon the ways your pastor is able to rest from his labours.

Wise Words

No man should stand before an audience who has not first stood before God.   *A. W. Tozer*

'Then those men, when they had seen
the sign that Jesus did, said, "This is truly
the Prophet who is to come into the
world"' (John 6:14).

Read: John 6:1-14

My wife likes picnics, but I find them disturbing. Too quickly the ants and flies appear and I wish I was having lunch at home away from those pests. Today you have read about a great miracle performed by the Lord, possibly the greatest of all his miracles.

It was soon Passover time and Christ was not going up to Jerusalem. He had more work to do and the Scribes and Pharisees in Jerusalem wanted him dead. We have read that Jesus wanted the disciples to get away for a while and rest from their labours, yet they were followed by the crowds who wanted to hear more preaching and see more miracles performed. The day was nearly over and the suggestion was made that the people be sent to their homes as there was not sufficient food to feed the huge crowd that numbered five thousand men plus women and children.

The disciples had seen the Lord perform many great miracles — demons were cast out, the sick were healed, the wind and the waves had been calmed and now he asked Philip, one of his disciples, 'Where shall we buy bread, that these may eat?' This was to test Philip, who should have responded stating that Jesus could perform a miracle and produce the food necessary to feed the crowd. All Philip could do was think about the money that Judas had in the money bag and suggest they could never buy sufficient food for the crowd. The money necessary for such an amount of food would take the wages for about two hundred days of work. Philip was at a loss about what should be done.

Being told of the young boy with five barley loaves and two small fish (probably dried fish ready to be eaten) Jesus told the disciples to have the people sit ready for a meal. Our Saviour knew beforehand what he was going to do and taking the food he gave thanks to God for what he held. This giving of thanks was done in anticipation of the food to be eaten, although it was common to give thanks at the conclusion of meals. This was taught in Deuteronomy 8:10: 'When you have eaten and are full, then you shall bless the LORD your God for the good land which he has given you.' Today in some parts of the Christian world 'grace' is said both before and after a meal. What about your family? Do you give thanks to God for your daily food? You should, because more than half the world goes to bed each night hungry. Starvation is widespread yet we have so much in the western world. May we enjoy our God-given food, but always give thanks for what we have on our table.

Following the 'picnic' twelve baskets of fragments were collected showing that in this miracle Christ had created food out of very little. There was not very much with which to start but so much was left over. This is our Saviour — God in flesh and blood. He is concerned about us, body and soul. Always thank God for both your spiritual food and what is on your plate each day.

THINGS TO DISCUSS WITH YOUR FAMILY

1. Why has the western world such an abundance of food while people in other countries face starvation?
2. What makes the feeding of the five thousand such an amazing miracle?
3. The people acknowledged Jesus as the prophet foretold by Moses. Read Deuteronomy 18:15-18 and discuss the passage.

Meditation

Meditate upon Christ's creative power; so much from so little.

Wise Words

To strip Christianity of the supernatural is to destroy Christianity.   *R. B. Kuiper*

'Yet I have set my King on my holy hill of Zion' (Psalm 2:6).

Read: Matthew 14:22-36

There are very few kings of this world who proved themselves worthy of their title. The vast majority were and still are power hungry, wealthy rulers who are filled with pride and treat their subjects with little respect. This is not just so of kings and queens, but of rulers generally.

Jesus Christ is called 'KING OF KINGS AND LORD OF LORDS' (Revelation 19:16). In Psalm 2 we read our text where the psalmist tells us that God has appointed his Son to be king over the nations of the earth and he is to rule them 'with a rod of iron' (Revelation 12:5).

The citizens of Israel expected their Messiah, who is the greatest son of the great King David, to establish a kingdom in Israel. He would overthrow the Roman armies and make Israel a great nation once again. However, they failed to comprehend the nature of the Lord's kingdom. When Christ was arrayed before Pilate he was asked, 'Are you the king of the Jews?' Part of Christ's reply was an explanation of his kingdom, 'My kingdom is not of this world. If my kingdom were of this world, my servants would fight, so that I should not be delivered to the Jews; but now my kingdom is not from here.'

When Pilate asked again: '"Are you a king then?" Jesus answered, "You say rightly that I am a king"' (John 18:36-37).

The kingdom of the Lord Jesus is worldwide and has in it people of all ages, but it is in the hearts of his people. Membership in the kingdom of God is the result of the new birth.

Following the feeding of the five thousand Jesus sent his disciples to Capernaum by boat while he went up on a mountainside to spend time in prayer. He often did this and we should do the same — get away by ourselves to talk with our heavenly Father, who has an open ear to the prayers of his people.

Meanwhile his disciples were valiantly rowing their boat across the sea having gone only about three kilometres because of the rough weather, when suddenly they saw what they believed to be a phantom coming towards them. It was early morning between 3.00am and 6.00am and in the dim light what they saw filled them with fear until Jesus spoke to them, 'Be of good cheer! It is I; do not be afraid.' At once Peter asked the Lord to bid him to walk across the water. When he heard Christ say, 'Come,' he stepped out and walked a few steps towards his Lord. However, the waves were turbulent and when he took his eyes off Jesus he began to sink. When he called for help Christ lifted him up saying, 'O you of little faith, why did you doubt?' At once the wind dropped and all in the boat worshipped Jesus saying, 'Truly you are the Son of God.' Do you believe this about our Redeemer?

There are times when our faith is very weak, but the writer to the Hebrews gives us good advice — to look 'unto Jesus the author and finisher of our faith; who for the joy that was set before him endured the cross, despising the shame, and is set down at the right hand of the throne of God' (Hebrews 12:2). Always keep this in mind when the going gets difficult.

THINGS TO DISCUSS WITH YOUR FAMILY

1. How could Jesus walk upon water?
2. Why did Peter's attempt to do the same end in failure?
3. What are we to do when our faith is tested? Read James 1:2.

Meditation

Meditate upon Psalm 104:1 — 'Bless the LORD, O my soul! O LORD my God, you are very great: you are clothed with honour and majesty.'

Wise Words

The more you think about Christ, the more you think of him.   *H. C. Trumbull*

'Do not labour for the food which perishes, but for the food which endures to
everlasting life, which the Son of Man
will give you, because God the Father
has set his seal on him' (John 6:27).

Read: John 6:22-29

Every Christian acknowledges that Jesus Christ is their King —
their 'KING OF KINGS AND LORD OF LORDS' in every part of their
life (1 Timothy 6:15). His kingdom has been growing for several
thousand years, but there is still plenty of room for more citizens.

In our last devotion we saw that the Jews wanted Jesus to be
their King. He would be a great king for their nation as there would
be no need to spend money educating doctors or building hospitals.
No longer would droughts cause starvation as Jesus could produce
all the food that was necessary to feed the nation. The people also
believed that with the almighty power at his disposal the Roman
armies could be driven from Israel and the nation once again would
gain its independence. What a King!

Jesus had returned to the area near Capernaum and soon found
himself surrounded by crowds who wanted to see the great miracle
worker. They brought their sick to him in order that they might be
healed. Again we see the compassion of our Saviour, who showed
mercy to all who asked for help. Yet the crowds sought him for the
wrong basic reason. He was not looked upon as the Saviour of sinners, the One who could establish peace with God.

Jesus rebuked the misguided attitude of the people towards him
and spoke the precious words we have in our text: 'Do not labour
for the food which perishes, but for the food which endures to everlasting life, which the Son of Man will give you, because God the
Father has set his seal on him.'

At once the people asked the most important question that
could be asked, 'What shall we do, that we may work the works
of God?' It was similar to that asked by the Philippian jailer, 'Sirs,
what must I do to be saved?' (Acts 16:30); or that asked by the rich
ruler, 'Good Teacher, what shall I do to inherit eternal life?' (Luke
18:18).

The reply that Jesus gave is that which has stood the test of
time and is the only way by which sinners might be saved, 'This

is the work of God, that you believe in him whom he sent.' Again Jesus proclaimed that he had come from heaven, having been sent by God himself. The way of salvation was not that set out by the Scribes and Pharisees — obey the hundreds of commandments to win God's favour — but faith in himself as the Saviour of sinners.

Read and reread John 3:16 and let the teaching of that sentence fill your heart. If you realize you are an unbeliever and the sword of God's anger is above you ready to fall, go to Jesus with a repentant heart, confess your unworthiness and trust your eternal security to him alone — then salvation is yours. Do you believe this? I pray you do and that you have a God-given saving faith in Christ, God's Son.

THINGS TO DISCUSS
WITH YOUR FAMILY

1. Why did the people want Jesus to be their king?
2. Do you want him to be your King? Why?
3. Discuss John 6:29: 'This is the work of God, that you believe in him whom he sent.'

Meditation

Meditate upon the words of John 3:16. What do they mean to you? 'For God so loved the world that he gave his only begotten Son, that whoever believes in him should not perish but have everlasting life.'

Wise Words

Whatever we need for the relief of our hungering souls, Christ is ready and willing to bestow.   *J. C. Ryle*

'And Jesus said to them, "I am the bread of life. He who comes to me shall never hunger, and he who believes in me shall never thirst"' (John 6:35).

Read: John 6:30-40

I'm sure that we all like bread with most of our meals. Today we have a great variety of foods but in the time of Christ bread was eaten with almost every meal. The Jews saw Christ perform great miracles, all of which testified that he came from heaven and was the prophesied Messiah. The Scriptures spoke of him; John the Baptist announced that he was the Son of God; our Lord told the people who he was; and at his baptism God spoke from heaven declaring that Jesus was his Son. Yet still the crowds wanted some special sign that would make it possible for them to believe his claims. I wonder what we would have been thinking about Christ if we had lived at that time?

Jesus reminded the people that their ancestors had eaten what was called 'bread from heaven'. Although they pointed to Moses as being the one to have provided the manna for the people, it came from God as the psalmist wrote: '[God] rained down manna on them to eat, and [gave] them of the bread of heaven. Men ate angels' food; He sent them food to the full' (Psalm 78:24-25). Having just told the people they must believe in him for salvation, Jesus declared that he was 'the true bread from heaven' given to Israel by his heavenly Father. Jesus himself was the 'sign' they requested!

The Apostle John wrote words for all of us to note, 'And this is the testimony: that God has given us eternal life, and this life is in his Son. He who has the Son has life; he who does not have the Son of God does not have life' (1 John 5:11-12). Jesus had thus declared to the people that eternal life was to be found in him, the true heavenly bread. Christ's words 'I am the bread of life' pointed to the truth that he is God, the One who spoke to Moses out of the burning bush and called himself, 'I AM WHO I AM' (Exodus 3:14). The Pharisees knew what this expression meant and at a later incident were furious and wanted Jesus put to death for blasphemy.

Jesus told the people they simply had to come to him to satisfy their spiritual hunger and thirst. Again he was talking about 'believing' in him. Yet the people wouldn't come and the Lord told them why: 'All that the Father gives me will come to me, and the one who comes to me I will by no means cast out.'

Here was their problem — they were not among that great number who were his gift from his heavenly Father. They were not the elect of God whose names were written in the Lamb's book of life. Jesus then gave all his listeners hope for he said, 'and the one who comes to me I will by no means cast out.' Christ had come from heaven to carry out his Father's will which was to save his people from eternal death. Jesus concluded this section of his address by saying that not one of those given to him by his heavenly Father would be lost, but on the Day of Judgement would be glorified and take their place in the new heavens and earth. Truly, the best is yet to be.

THINGS TO DISCUSS WITH YOUR FAMILY

1. Jesus said, 'I have come down from heaven' (John 6:38). What does this teach us?
2. What was manna?
3. In what way was Jesus like manna?

Meditation

Think upon the way you can feast upon Christ, the true bread from heaven.

Wise Words

Not one lamb of his flock shall ever be left behind in the wilderness. He will raise to glory, in the last day, the whole flock entrusted to his charge, and not one shall be found missing. *J. C. Ryle*

'No one can come to me unless the Father who sent me draws him; and I will raise him up at the last day' (John 6:44).

Read: John 6:41-59

Jesus continues his sermon, describing himself as heavenly bread that must be 'eaten' in order to be saved. Now Christians frequently sit at the Lord's Table and there drink wine and eat bread in remembrance of his sacrificial death, shed blood and a broken body. However, we should not think that here Christ is talking about the Lord's Supper which had not yet been instituted. No, he is talking about saving faith which is found in the heart of all of his people.

Much of what Jesus had been saying was confusing to the people surrounding him and they began to talk among themselves — 'How can he say he came from heaven and that God is his Father? We know that his mother is Mary and his father [they thought] is Joseph. He is just like us, born of ordinary parents. He grew up amongst us just as our children did. Who does he think he is?' They judged Jesus on a human level alone.

Jesus went on to tell the crowds that he was 'the living bread which came down from heaven'. Then he said, 'If anyone eats of this bread, he will live for ever; and the bread that I shall give is my flesh, which I shall give for the life of the world.' The people were more disturbed, especially when he continued: 'Most assuredly, I say to you, unless you eat the flesh of the Son of Man and drink his blood, you have no life in you. Whoever eats my flesh and drinks my blood has eternal life, and I will raise him up at the last day.'

To many who heard this, Christ appeared to be talking about cannibalism, eating his flesh and drinking his blood. Jesus was not talking about a carnal eating, but a spiritual act of the heart resting in Christ and his sacrificial blessings. It was a trusting in Jesus Christ, the Son of God for eternal life. And this would be a continual 'feasting' upon Christ for the grace to faithfully follow him to life's end.

In the time of the Old Testament the people were taught by God through the prophets, but now the greatest prophet of all was in their presence and that was God himself. The prophets of old wrote of this time: 'All your children shall be taught by the LORD, and great shall be the peace of your children' (Isaiah 54:13); and in Jeremiah 31:33-34 we read, '"But this is the covenant that I will make with the house of Israel after those days," says the LORD; "I will put my law in their minds, and write it on their hearts; and I will be their God, and they shall be my people. No more shall every man teach his neighbour, and every man his brother, saying, 'Know the LORD,' for they all shall know me, from the least of them to the greatest of them, says the LORD. For I will forgive their iniquity, and their sin I will remember no more."'

Few believed what Jesus said because they were not his people. Those given to Christ by his heavenly Father would be drawn to him by the almighty power of the Holy Spirit, enabling them to repent and trust in his atoning sacrifice for sin. Do you?

THINGS TO DISCUSS WITH YOUR FAMILY

1. How do sinners become members of God's family?
2. Discuss the way God called you to believe in Jesus.
3. What are the differences between the 'manna' that fell in the desert and Christ, 'the bread of life'?

Meditation

Meditate upon the saving work of the Holy Spirit in your life '… according to his mercy he saved us, through the washing of regeneration and renewing of the Holy Spirit…' (Titus 3:5).

Wise Words

The food of this world, for which so many take thought, will perish in the using, and not feed our souls. He only that eats of 'the bread that came down from heaven' shall live for ever.   *J. C. Ryle*

26 June   A grave error of misunderstanding

'It is the Spirit who gives life; the flesh profits nothing. The words that I speak to you are spirit, and they are life' (John 6:63).

Read: John 6:60-66

We all make mistakes and often misunderstand what people say to us. Usually these errors don't make a great difference to the way we live, but we now come to a situation where many who misunderstood what Christ had said turned away from him and went back to their former way of living and thinking. There could be no greater mistake they ever made because it meant the loss of eternal life. They had seen and heard so much, yet misconstrued what Jesus meant when he said it was necessary to eat his flesh as he was the true 'bread' that came down from heaven.

All they saw and heard meant nothing and they were not going to become involved in eating Christ's flesh. We can only wonder how they expected to eat the flesh of the Son of God. Things have not changed, for people at large please themselves and reject the claims of Christ to be the Son of God and the only way to eternal life. The Apostle John wrote: 'We are of God. He who knows God hears us; he who is not of God does not hear us. By this we know the spirit of truth and the spirit of error' (1 John 4:6). We who are Christians can only thank God for calling us to Jesus and giving us the saving faith that unites us to the Saviour. It is the work of the Holy Spirit that took away our cold heart of stone and gave us a new heart of flesh upon which God has written his law. Our God of grace has given us a love for himself and our neighbour.

Yet many disciples turned away from Jesus no doubt hoping that obedience to God's law would open heaven's doors for them, just as the Pharisees had taught. These were the ones spoken of by Jesus in his parable of the sower. They were described as the seed that fell on the stony places, 'But he who received the seed on stony places, this is he who hears the word and immediately receives it with joy; yet he has no root in himself, but endures only for a while. For when tribulation or persecution arises because of the word, immediately he stumbles' (Matthew 13:20-21).

Only those who are born again remain faithful to the very end. It must have been a disappointment for the Saviour when many left him, yet he was aware that only those given grace to believe would remain faithful.

It is better to be one of small faith than a hypocrite with no saving faith. We must all examine ourselves to ensure that our faith is the real thing. If it is, we will see the fruit of the Spirit shining in our lives — the 'love, joy, peace, long-suffering, kindness, goodness, faithfulness, gentleness, self-control' (Galatians 5:22-23). Can you see the fruit of the Spirit in your life? Are you living a life of humble trust in Christ, the Redeemer?

THINGS TO DISCUSS WITH YOUR FAMILY

1. We must pray for all professing Christians that they might truly be 'born again'.
2. What is the work of the heavenly Father in our salvation?
3. Discuss today's text.

Meditation

How do you know your faith is genuine?

'Also we have come to believe and know that you are the Christ, the Son of the living God' (John 6:69).

Read: John 6:67-71

It is comforting to read the words of our text and be able to say, 'That's exactly what I believe!' We know that there is no salvation outside of the Lord Jesus Christ. Many of the Saviour's disciples were proved to be hypocrites despite giving evidence for some time that they loved the One they called 'Master'.

In Hebrews 10:26-29 we read of these people: 'For if we sin wilfully after we have received the knowledge of the truth, there no longer remains a sacrifice for sins, but a certain fearful expectation of judgement, and fiery indignation which will devour the adversaries. Anyone who has rejected Moses' law dies without mercy on the testimony of two or three witnesses. Of how much worse punishment, do you suppose, will he be thought worthy who has trampled the Son of God underfoot, counted the blood of the covenant by which he was sanctified a common thing, and insulted the Spirit of grace?' Here we are plainly taught that if we turn away from Christ there is no other to whom we might go to find salvation. To turn from the Lord means all is lost and life is wasted, other than to display the justice and anger of God against sin and sinners.

Peter's confession that Christ is the 'Son of God' was not something he dreamed up because of what he saw Jesus do and what his Master had said. The disciples who turned away had the same experiences. Jesus explained why it was that Peter and ten other disciples truly believed savingly that he was the Saviour, the Son of God: 'Blessed are you, Simon Bar-Jonah, for flesh and blood has not revealed this to you, but my Father who is in heaven' (Matthew 16:17).

Now what does this say to all you who have trusted Christ for your eternal security, believing that he is God's Son? It means that the Holy Spirit who has taken up residence in your heart has revealed to you the truth concerning Jesus.

What about any readers who are not Christians and would like to know Jesus as their personal Saviour? Read Luke 11:11-13: 'If a son asks for bread from any father among you, will he give him a stone? Or if he asks for a fish, will he give him a serpent instead of a fish? Or if he asks for an egg, will he offer him a scorpion? If you then, being evil, know how to give good gifts to your children, how much more will your heavenly Father give the Holy Spirit to those who ask him!'

Here is God's promise to everyone who sincerely seeks a saving faith in the Lord Jesus — ask honestly and continue to ask until God answers your prayer. May God bless you all.

THINGS TO DISCUSS WITH YOUR FAMILY

1. Judas didn't believe despite all he saw and heard. Why not?
2. What is the Christian life believers are to live?
3. Discuss Isaiah 55:1-2: 'Ho! Everyone who thirsts, come to the waters; and you who have no money, come, buy and eat. Yes, come, buy wine and milk without money and without price. Why do you spend money for what is not bread, and your wages for what does not satisfy? Listen carefully to me, and eat what is good, and let your soul delight itself in abundance.'

Meditation

Meditate upon Romans 5:8: 'But God demonstrates his own love toward us, in that while we were still sinners, Christ died for us.'

Wise Words

Faith is not a once-done act, but a continuous gaze of the heart at the triune God.   *A. W. Tozer*

'The heart is deceitful above all things, and desperately wicked; who can know it? I, the LORD, search the heart, I test the mind, even to give every man according to his ways, according to the fruit of his doings' (Jeremiah 17:9–10).

Read: Matthew 15:1-20

Both my wife and I have heart problems and each morning one of our first jobs is to take our medication. While our tablets help control our blood pressure, every person who has ever lived, except the Lord Jesus, has an even greater heart problem — our hearts are sick with sin. But thank God there is a medication freely available to correct our heart disease, and that cure is found in the Person of our Saviour, the Lord Jesus Christ.

Some Scribes and Pharisees had come down from Jerusalem to verbally attack Jesus by accusing his disciples of failing to follow the laws of God and the Pharisees, namely that they should wash before eating. The Scribes and Pharisees were not concerned about hygiene, but of the likelihood that unclean hands meant spiritual uncleanness because dust from a Gentile might be eaten or disciples might have touched some 'unclean' food. By attacking the Lord's disciples they also accused the Lord Jesus of sin.

Jesus quoted Isaiah 29:13 to the church leaders: 'Inasmuch as these people draw near with their mouths and honour me with their lips, but have removed their hearts far from me, and their fear toward me is taught by the commandment of men...' The Jews had gone full circle. In Isaiah's day the commandments of men were considered as coming from God and this was what the Scribes and Pharisees taught.

These church leaders were hypocrites and a spiritual danger to the people as they were spiritually blind and lead the people along the broad way that emptied into hell. Ezekiel wrote of such people: 'So they come to you as people do, they sit before you as my people, and they hear your words, but they do not do them; for with their mouth they show much love, but their hearts pursue their own gain' (Ezekiel 33:31). Using their own law they nullified the plain teaching of the fifth commandment. Instead of helping their parents when requested, they said that their property was 'dedicated to the temple'. As it belonged to God it could not be used to alleviate their parents' need.

Jesus plainly told the Scribes and Pharisees that food does not spiritually harm a person, but the outpouring of the sinful hearts was what defiled a man. The Apostle Paul wrote words instructing us how to live: 'Therefore do not let your good be spoken of as evil; for the kingdom of God is not eating and drinking, but righteousness and peace and joy in the Holy Spirit' (Romans 14:16-17).

What sinners need is a new heart with which to praise God: 'Therefore by him let us continually offer the sacrifice of praise to God, that is, the fruit of our lips, giving thanks to his name' (Hebrews 13:15).

THINGS TO DISCUSS WITH YOUR FAMILY

1. In Jeremiah 13:23 we read: 'Can the Ethiopian change his skin or the leopard its spots? Then may you also do good who are accustomed to do evil.' What does this mean?
2. The Pharisees were blind leaders of the blind. Who are today's spiritually blind leaders?
3. In what way does God uproot the plants he has not planted? (Matthew 15:13).

Meditation

Meditate upon Romans 8:1: 'There is therefore now no condemnation to those who are in Christ Jesus, who do not walk according to the flesh, but according to the Spirit.'

Wise Words

If you are never born again, you will wish you had never been born at all. *Derek Cleave*

'It was good for me that I have been afflicted, that I may learn your statutes' (Psalm 119:71).

Read: Matthew 15:21-28

I like being at home; in fact there are times when I'm told that I'm becoming a recluse, but I haven't reached that stage yet. As I have been reading the life of Jesus he was anything but a recluse. He was out and about, ever doing the will of his heavenly Father. He and the disciples walked many miles preaching and performing miracles. We now find the Lord in the region of Tyre and Sidon — Gentile territory.

As Jesus traversed Israel he found very few who came to believe in him as the Messiah, the Saviour of sinners. The church leaders were already plotting his death. But the Old Testament prophets spoke of a day when Gentiles would flood into the kingdom of God. The sinful Rahab had been saved by the grace of God as had been Ruth and the many repentant sinners of Nineveh. Isaiah had prophesied of Messiah's work: 'It is too small a thing that you should be my Servant to raise up the tribes of Jacob, and to restore the preserved ones of Israel; I will also give you as a light to the Gentiles, that you should be my salvation to the ends of the earth' (Isaiah 49:6). When old Simeon held the baby Jesus in his arms he said, 'Lord, now you are letting your servant depart in peace, according to your word; for my eyes have seen your salvation which you have prepared before the face of all peoples, a light to bring revelation to the Gentiles, and the glory of your people Israel' (Luke 2:29-32).

Jesus was confronted by a Canaanite mother whose dearly loved daughter was demon-possessed. This woman recognized that Jesus was Messiah for she gave him the title 'Son of David', a Messianic name. She heard of Jesus' great compassion and love as shown in his preaching and healing ministry. To her, the Son of David was her only hope for her daughter's healing. She believed all she had heard about the Lord and came begging for his compassionate help.

Jesus appears to have ignored her cry for help, but he was strengthening her faith for the woman did not give up asking, even when she was told that Christ was sent to 'the lost sheep of the house of Israel'. He told her it was not proper to 'take the children's bread and throw it to the little dogs'. These were the pet dogs that sat beside their masters as they ate, and gobbled up the crumbs thrown to them. The woman was not offended at being called a 'dog' and pleadingly indicated that she was willing to eat just the tiny crumbs that fell from the 'Master's table'.

Jesus admired her faith and humility and healed her daughter. From this healing we note that the woman persevered in her pleading for help — so should we when we are in need of the Lord's assistance.

THINGS TO DISCUSS WITH YOUR FAMILY

1. Read Matthew 7:7-11. What are we taught there?
2. What is a Jew?
3. I have listed several Gentiles who were saved before the coming of Christ. Make a list of others we read about in the Old Testament.

Meditation

Thank God for his salvation to the Gentiles. I'm a Gentile and can never thank God enough that I live in the gospel age.

Wise Words

Christ is the mine of mercy and the gold-ore of grace and salvation. *Anonymous*

'So the LORD said to him, "Who has made man's mouth? Or who makes the mute, the deaf, the seeing, or the blind? Have not I, the LORD?"' (Exodus 4:11).

Read: Mark 7:31-37

Following the birth of one of our daughters we noticed that she was having difficulty sucking. Upon a close examination we could see that she was slightly tongue-tied. A trip to the doctor soon had the problem fixed, and drinking became easy as it should have been. Had the skin which held her tongue tight not been snipped, she would have experienced speaking difficulties as well.

Jesus left Tyre and went to the Sea of Galilee into the region of Decapolis, beside the Sea of Galilee. Surrounded by many sick people he again commenced his healing ministry and no doubt preached the need of the new birth and a saving faith in himself, the Son of God. Mark records one special healing at this time, that of a man who was deaf and with a speech impediment, probably tongue-tied or a stammer. For several reasons this healing was unusual.

First, Christ took the man away from the crowds and placed his fingers in the man's ears indicating that he would do something to his ears. Then Jesus spat on his own finger and put it on the man's tongue, signifying that it would be cleansed — healed. Maybe the deaf man could have read Christ's lips, but what the Lord did showed that he was about to perform a great healing miracle which was once again proof that he was God's appointed Messiah. We read in Isaiah 35:4-6: 'Say to those who are fearful-hearted, "Be strong, do not fear! Behold, your God will come with vengeance, with the recompense of God; he will come and save you." Then the eyes of the blind shall be opened, and the ears of the deaf shall be unstopped. Then the lame shall leap like a deer, and the tongue of the dumb sing.'

Looking heavenward, denoting that the healing was the work of God, Jesus sighed and said, 'Be opened.' Again there was immediate healing. Now the man could plainly praise God and clearly hear Christ's preaching. Matthew records that the crowds were astounded at Christ's amazing miracles 'and they glorified the God of Israel' (Matthew 15:31). Many present that day must have been

Gentiles. The crowds spoke well of Jesus, saying, 'He has done all things well.' This is our God! He always does all things perfectly. I don't know about you, but I long to be able to speak with these people and get firsthand information about the events that occurred. This miracle was done quietly, modestly and graciously.

Jesus told the man to keep the healing a secret, but again he didn't do as the Lord had commanded. We are the same. We read the commandments of God and so often fail to be obedient. We should always remember the words of Christ, 'If you love me, keep my commandments' (John 14:15).

Has the Holy Spirit opened your spiritual ears so you can believe the gospel? If so, praise God.

THINGS TO DISCUSS
WITH YOUR FAMILY

1. In what way did Christ deal differently with the man he healed on this occasion?
2. Why did Jesus sigh?
3. Why did Jesus want the miracle kept secret?

Meditation

Meditate upon the wise use of your speech. Remember the words of James 3:1-12.

Wise Words

As there is no mercy too great for God to give, so there is no mercy too little for us to crave. *Thomas Brooks*

July

'The eyes of all look expectantly to you, and you give them their food in due season. You open your hand and satisfy the desire of every living thing' (Psalm 145:15-16).

Read: Matthew 15:32-38

We all need a daily supply of food to keep our bodies healthy. In the western world we have an abundance of edibles. When we sit down to eat we should give sincere thanks to God for our daily sustenance. In the Lord's Prayer we ask for our daily food and we should realize what a great debt of gratitude we owe God for it.

Crowds, numbering four thousand men plus women and children, had been with Jesus and the disciples for three days in the desert region. They were keen to see Christ performing miracles and hear what he had to say. They must have brought some food with them, but after three days nothing was left and the people were hungry and weakened.

It is worth comparing the attitude of those people who were eager to hear the good news, to people today. How often do people complain of the time taken for the worship service? If the minister preaches for more than thirty minutes complaints are made. Worship should delight our hearts as it is both a time of learning and a time to praise God with like-minded people who confess that they love the Lord Jesus.

We should notice a marked difference between Jesus and the disciples. Our compassionate Saviour wanted to have the people fed before sending them to their homes, but all the disciples could think of was the difficulty of obtaining food in the desert region. Only a short time before they had seen Christ provide food for a much larger group of people, but now they seem to have forgotten the almighty power at his disposal. What the Lord had done once he could do again. They failed to comprehend that they were to be involved in 'distributing to the needs of the saints, [and] given to hospitality' (Romans 12:13). May you and I remember this great truth and always be ready to give to those in genuine need.

Jesus asked what food was available — just seven small loaves of bread and some small fish. This was all the Lord needed, and after having the people sit he thanked God for the provision of the food. Do you always thank God for his gracious provision of your daily food? In Psalm 104:15 we read that God provided '...wine that makes glad the heart of man, oil to make his face shine, and bread which strengthens man's heart'. Our God is good. He makes the rain fall on both the just and unjust (Matthew 5:45). Our God is a God of grace.

Following their meal the scraps were collected — seven large hamper bags were filled.

This great miracle again displayed the awesome power at Christ's disposal. It was also a demonstration of his sympathy for the hungry people.

The psalmist tells us that we are to eat the labour of our own hands (Psalm 128:2). We are to work and earn wages to buy food. Paul warns those who will not work and expect a free handout — 'If anyone will not work, neither shall he eat' (2 Thessalonians 3:10). However, the best food of all is that free bread that comes from God — eternal life through spiritually feasting upon Christ who is 'the bread of life' (John 6:48).

THINGS TO DISCUSS WITH YOUR FAMILY

1. What can we learn from the ant? Read Proverbs 6:6-11.
2. Can you think of a greater miracle than the one you have read today? Discuss why it is greater.
3. If you do not give thanks to God for your daily food, start now.

Meditation

Give thanks to God for his provision of your daily food.

Wise Words

Nothing that is God's is obtainable by money.

Tertullian

'Now the LORD had prepared a great fish
to swallow Jonah. And Jonah was in the
belly of the fish three days and three
nights' (Jonah 1:17).

Read: Matthew 16:1-4

To be swallowed by a huge fish would be a fearful happening, but
to spend three days and nights in the stomach of that fish would
be disastrous. Jonah experienced that punishment and it brought him
to his senses. Our reading today is of a short confrontation between
Jesus and a group of Pharisees and Sadducees who had come to
question him, hoping to hear him say something that could be used
against him.

They were a strange alliance as they held very different beliefs.
The Sadducees did not believe in an afterlife nor the existence of
angels. The Pharisees believed in life after death and the unseen realm
of spiritual beings, but with a common enemy, Jesus, they joined
forces and demanded of him a 'sign from heaven' that would prove
he was the Christ of God.

Now, these 'theologians' had seen and heard about Christ's miracles and claims, but this was not enough as they wanted a special 'sign
from heaven'. As they stood before Jesus and asked for such a sign
they failed to realize that Christ himself was the 'sign from heaven'.
He was the Second Person of the Godhead, sent into the world by his
heavenly Father and filled with the Holy Spirit on a mission to save
sinners. Everything about Jesus was proof that he was God's Son.

The Lord then ridiculed the Pharisees and Sadducees by telling
them they could discern the weather by looking at the sky. His words
remind me of a saying most people have today:

> *A red sky in the morning — a shepherd's warning;*
> *A red sky at night is a shepherd's delight.*

They couldn't however interpret the signs of the times! The
leaders of the Jewish church failed to realize that the advent of Christ
meant the end of worship as they knew it and that soon the gospel
would be taken from Israel and sent to the Gentiles, worldwide. They
failed to understand that Israel's age was about to end and Satan's

kingdom defeated. Satan was about to suffer his greatest defeat through the crucifixion and resurrection of the Redeemer. Despite Christ's resurrection the church leaders refused to acknowledge that he was the Messiah. The One they said was demon-possessed was God in flesh and blood, and as a consequence of his saving work we read: 'Therefore God has highly exalted him and given him the name which is above every name...' (Philippians 2:9).

Jesus gave the Pharisees and Sadducees a sign they could not understand — 'the sign of Jonah the prophet'. This was not the first time Christ had given this sign, but we know that it meant that he would die and his body placed in a tomb for three days, after which he would rise again.

Christ's miracles were not his most important work. His first priority was the salvation of his people. Thank God for such a wonderful Saviour.

Let each one of us confess Christ to those about us and pray for their salvation. Then we must leave it to God to bring them to the Saviour.

THINGS TO DISCUSS WITH YOUR FAMILY

1. What proof was there for the Pharisees and Sadducees that Jesus was the Messiah?
2. Find out what you can about the Sadducees.
3. Read Proverbs 26:4-5. Discuss this as it applied to Christ's answer to the question of the Pharisees and Sadducees.

Meditation

Meditate upon the greatest proof that Jesus is the Messiah — his resurrection and ascension to heaven to sit upon the throne of God.

Christ is not only the Saviour but salvation itself.

Matthew Henry

Wise Words

'But as it is written: "Eye has not seen, nor ear heard, nor have entered into the heart of man the things which God has prepared for those who love him." But God has revealed them to us through his Spirit' (1 Corinthians 2:9-10).

Read: Mark 8:13-21

As we read our Bibles we come to many passages we find hard to understand. Some people don't read some books of the Bible because they believe them to be too difficult to comprehend. This is nothing new. The Apostle Peter had some difficulty when he read the writings of Paul. In 2 Peter 3:15-16, he wrote of his 'beloved brother Paul, according to the wisdom given to him, has written to you … some things hard to understand, which untaught and unstable people twist to their own destruction, as they do also the rest of the Scriptures'.

In today's reading we find the disciples somewhat confused with Christ's words. The Lord had taught them much and displayed his almighty power, but still they didn't understand.

After speaking to the Pharisees and Sadducees the Lord and the disciples boarded a boat to go to Bethsaida. As they were settling down there was the realization that they had not purchased enough food for all on board. All they had with them was just one loaf. When Jesus began to teach them about the false doctrine of the Pharisees which he called 'the leaven of the Pharisees' the disciples believed they were being rebuked for not getting sufficient bread for all on board.

Jesus accused the disciples of still being blind to all they had seen and been taught. Christ had produced enough bread to feed more than five thousand hungry people on one occasion and over four thousand on a second occasion. Surely the twelve could have believed that if food was really necessary the Lord could have miraculously used the one loaf to feed everyone on the boat.

Jesus was warning his disciples to beware of the false teaching of the Pharisees who taught that the way of salvation was to be found through obedience to the law of God and the traditions of men. This the Pharisees believed was the way to win God's favour. The Pharisees were self-righteous, proud church leaders who wanted Christ out of the way. The Sadducees were the same. They were worldly men who couldn't stand Christ's call to living a holy life.

Today things are no different. The Church of Rome claims its own manmade rules must be believed in order to be saved. They teach that faith in Christ is not sufficient for salvation. It is taught that Mary was born without sin and is co-mediatrix with Jesus; priests are forbidden to marry and the Pope, in certain situations, claims the authority to speak with the authority of God in matters of faith and doctrine. The Mormons and the Jehovah's Witnesses claim salvation is only to be had by following their dogmatic teachings. There are many church leaders today who make the same claim.

You and I have God's revealed will freely available to us in the Old and New Testaments. Prayerfully read these writings and believe what you are taught. Trust your eternal security to the Lord Jesus and as a sign of your love for him, obey his commandments.

THINGS TO DISCUSS WITH YOUR FAMILY

1. What did Jesus mean when he spoke of hearts being 'hardened'?
2. To what did Jesus refer when he said, 'What comes out of a man, that defiles a man'?
3. Why did Christ use the example of 'leaven' (i.e., yeast)?

Meditation

Consider Romans 7:12 — 'Therefore the law is holy, and the commandment holy and just and good.'

Wise Words

If a thousand old beliefs were ruined in our march to truth we must still march on.   *Stopford A. Brooke*

'I was eyes to the blind, and I was feet to the lame' (Job 29:15).

Read: Mark 8:22-26

Blindness is a terrible affliction. One girl I remember from my teaching days was going blind. At school we were making every effort to help prepare her for the day when she was totally without sight. Today you have read about a man who was blind whose friends brought him to Jesus hoping that he would be healed.

As we read about this man we are given the impression that he was born with sight, and later became blind. In the process of giving him his sight he said that he saw 'men like trees, walking'. He could hardly have said this if he had never seen trees or people walking about. However, there are some unusual aspects of this miracle.

First Jesus led the man outside the town and away from the crowd. This is like our text from Job, who said that he also as an act of kindness led about the blind. Second, Jesus spat upon the man's eyes. Why? I don't know, but it certainly made the man concentrate his attention on his eyes that needed healing. Third, when Jesus touched him he had partial sight. He saw 'men like trees, walking'.

Jesus then touched him a second time and the man's sight returned to what it once had been and he could see clearly. This is a most unusual method of healing, but it shows that Jesus was able to use many ways to heal people — a word, a touch, spit, finger in ears and touching a tongue with his wet finger, through his disciples and by someone just touching him — a variety of methods, but one power, that of Almighty God.

Giving sight to the blind was one sign of Jesus being the Messiah. He had told the disciples of John, 'The blind see and the lame walk; the lepers are cleansed and the deaf hear; the dead are raised up and the poor have the gospel preached to them' (Matthew 11:5).

Following this miracle Jesus told the man to go home, no doubt there to give thanks to God for what had been done and to cope with his healing.

We might learn from this healing that Jesus gives spiritual sight to spiritually blind people. Sinners are blind to spiritual truth and until the Holy Spirit brings about the new birth there is no salvation. Many are the ways Jesus uses to bring people to saving faith — many are convicted of their sins, others are amazed by God's love, some are given a fear of hell and some turn to God in times of calamities. But once Jesus begins the work of calling his elect to himself, we can be assured that he will complete the work. The Apostle Paul wrote, '... he who has begun a good work in you will complete it until the day of Jesus Christ ...' (Philippians 1:6). At first our faith might be weak, but soon the Lord will have us eating solid spiritual food.

As the blind man was healed in stages so also are the saints sanctified. The writer to the Hebrews said, 'For by one offering he has perfected for ever those who are being sanctified' (Hebrews 10:14). Thank God for the daily sanctifying work of the Holy Spirit.

THINGS TO DISCUSS WITH YOUR FAMILY

1. What is unusual about this healing of a blind man?
2. Make a list of the methods Jesus used in his miraculous healings.
3. What does Psalm 146:8 mean? 'The LORD opens the eyes of the blind; the LORD raises those who are bowed down; the LORD loves the righteous.'

Meditation

Meditate upon Christ's compassion in coming to this poor sick world to seek and save the lost.

Wise Words

Every day we see some new thing about Christ. His love has neither brim nor bottom. *Samuel Rutherford*

'Simon Peter answered and said, "You are the Christ, the Son of the living God"' (Matthew 16:16).

Read: Matthew 16:13-20

I find it very difficult to mix with a crowd of people who have no idea of my name or who I am. It's hard to make conversation and usually I get away with one or two people and talk politely. It is much easier to be with a group of people I know.

Jesus faced a similar situation. The people of Israel had many ideas who the Lord was. When Christ asked Peter who people said he was, he was given a variety of answers. Then he asked, 'But who do you say that I am?' There came a reply on behalf of the other eleven disciples, 'You are the Christ, the Son of the living God.'

The disciples had been with Christ for many months and were assured that their Lord and Master was the Son of God, the Messiah. This was not something they had worked out for themselves, but it had been revealed to them by Christ's heavenly Father. The disciples understood that Jesus, the son of Mary, was the Anointed One, the Mediator between God and man, the One who was filled with the Holy Spirit, the Christ who was prophet, priest and king.

The Lord's reply to Peter has caused confusion amongst Christians. The Roman Catholic Church see Christ's words to Peter — 'you are Peter, and on this rock I will build my church' — as the appointment of Peter as the head of the church, the first Pope.

To understand what Jesus was saying it is worth looking at other inspired statements concerning the foundation of the church. The Apostle Paul wrote of building the kingdom of God and said, 'For no other foundation can anyone lay than that which is laid, which is Jesus Christ' (1 Corinthians 3:11). It is the Christ described by Peter who is the foundation of the church. Elsewhere Paul wrote of the church being a unified body of Jews and Gentiles 'having been built on the foundation of the apostles and prophets, Jesus Christ himself being the chief cornerstone' (Ephesians 2:20).

The church of God has an enemy, Satan, who is always doing all he can to destroy this holy temple, but we have Christ's promise that the gates of hell will not be victorious. We read in Revelation

12:13-17 of his warfare with the saints, but Christ will be victorious despite the persecution of Christians.

The disciples were given the 'keys' to the kingdom of God that they used with great success. The Book of Acts records the tremendous expansion of the church after the outpouring of the Holy Spirit. On the day of Pentecost Peter preached his first great sermon with the result that the keys for entrance into the kingdom of heaven opened doors for some three thousand people.

Finally Jesus asked his disciples to refrain from telling people that he acknowledged he was the Messiah. Such would only antagonize the Pharisees and other church leaders more than ever. Christ's timetable for his work and death were according to the will of God.

THINGS TO DISCUSS WITH YOUR FAMILY

1. How do you understand Peter's great confession concerning Christ?
2. On what 'rock' was the church built?
3. Who today has the keys to the kingdom of God and how are they used?

Meditation

Think about all that the Word of God has revealed to you about the Person of the Lord Jesus.

Wise Words

Stating it in just about the most simple terms we know, the Christian church is the assembly of redeemed saints.

A. W. Tozer

'For you know the grace of our Lord Jesus Christ, that though he was rich, yet for your sakes he became poor, that you through his poverty might become rich' (2 Corinthians 8:9).

Read: Matthew 16:21-23

I remember the day my doctor phoned, asking that I urgently visit his surgery as he had the results of some tests that had been carried out. He spoke to my wife and told her to bring all that I needed for a stay in hospital. I was very ill and when he told me the news I was very concerned. I found it hard to believe what he said.

The disciples had been with Jesus for many months listening to his preaching, watching his miracles and being privately taught many truths, although some were taught in a veiled manner. They had heard Christ speak about the sign of the prophet Jonah, but had failed to understand what it meant.

The time had come for Christ to reveal to the twelve the main reason for his coming to the earth, that being to save sinners.

Like most Jews they anticipated that the Christ would re-establish the kingdom of Israel and sit upon the throne of David. They saw the establishment of a throne where they would be given positions of power. Their idea of the Messiah was a 'crown' and certainly didn't include a 'cross'. Jesus was to explain to them the meaning of Isaiah 53.

The disciples were shocked when their Master spoke about his forthcoming death. It seemed impossible that their Lord would be killed in Jerusalem, for this city Christ had said was 'the city of the great King' (Matthew 5:35). Yet, the greatest surprise was that Jesus would be put to death after suffering at the hands of the church rulers. The prophets of old had searched the Scriptures to gain an understanding of what Christ was now revealing. John the Baptist had said of Christ, 'Behold! The Lamb of God who takes away the sin of the world' (John 1:29).

Jesus was to be the sacrificial lamb who would die bearing the sins of his people. Before that cruel death he would be humiliated and abused terribly by Jews and Roman soldiers. Why? Because he was the sacrificial substitute for all those given to him by his heavenly Father. He would bear their hell. This was an open display of God's love for the elect. Paul wrote: 'But God demonstrates his own love toward us, in that while we were still sinners, Christ died for us. Much more then, having now been justified by his blood, we shall be saved from wrath through him' (Romans 5:8-9). The disciples were told that death could not hold him, but that he would be resurrected on the third day.

Peter could not accept what he heard and expressed his doubt. In return, Christ rebuked Peter calling him 'Satan'. At that moment he was spiritually blind to the teachings of the Old Testament concerning the death of Jesus, but soon the Holy Spirit would open his spiritual eyes to behold the truth of what had been taught. When this happened he then preached a crucified and risen Christ. Do you truly believe this about the Lord Jesus?

THINGS TO DISCUSS WITH YOUR FAMILY

1. Who was responsible for Christ's death?
2. Discuss the suffering of the Saviour which lead to his death upon a cross.
3. Read and discuss Galatians 2:20: 'I have been crucified with Christ; it is no longer I who live, but Christ lives in me; and the life which I now live in the flesh I live by faith in the Son of God, who loved me and gave himself for me.'

Meditation

Meditate upon the sufferings of Christ which he took willingly and lovingly.

Wise Words

The cross of Christ will always be an offence to the natural man. *Anonymous*

401

What is your greatest treasure

 'For what profit is it to a man if he gains the whole world, and loses his own soul? Or what will a man give in exchange for his soul?' (Matthew 16:26).

Read: Matthew 16:24-28

What is the most valuable of all your possessions? I have some treasures that I care for very much and I have taken out insurance against breakages, theft and destruction by fire or flood. But when all is said and done the day is coming when I, through death or the return of Christ, will leave them all behind. God is my most important possession. My church and family are extremely important, but not the most important.

Jesus now tells his disciples that they will suffer because they follow him. Each day every Christian must take up his cross and follow the Lord. The Jews of that day knew exactly what Christ was saying. When a person took up their cross it was to carry it to the place of their execution. Jesus is telling us that we will suffer because we are his disciples, and possibly that suffering might end in martyrdom. We enter heaven through tribulation, as a writer once said: 'No cross, no crown.' We all must bear the reproach of Christ.

The Apostle Paul wrote of our union with the Saviour which leads to eternal life: 'I have been crucified with Christ; it is no longer I who live, but Christ lives in me; and the life which I now live in the flesh I live by faith in the Son of God, who loved me and gave himself for me' (Galatians 2:20).

Jesus told the disciples that their most precious possession was their soul which was worth more than anything the world could offer. The things of the world are attractive, but Moses made the right choice when he chose a life of godliness instead of the crown of Egypt. We read, 'By faith Moses, when he became of age, refused to be called the son of Pharaoh's daughter, choosing rather to suffer affliction with the people of God than to enjoy the passing pleasures of sin, esteeming the reproach of Christ greater riches than the treasures in Egypt; for he looked to the reward' (Hebrews 11:24-26).

The Apostle John has written some very wise words: 'Do not love the world or the things in the world. If anyone loves the world, the love of the Father is not in him. For all that is in the world — the lust of the flesh, the lust of the eyes, and the pride of life — is not of the Father but is of the world. And the world is passing away, and the lust of it; but he who does the will of God abides for ever' (1 John 2:15-17). Eternal life, the love of Christ and the ability to glorify God is of more value than anything we can ever imagine.

Christ will return to reward his faithful people, not because they have earned it but because of God's amazing grace. On Judgement Day the books will be opened and our works will be used to determine our eternal rewards.

Jesus then said that some of the disciples would not die before they saw him 'coming in his kingdom'. Obviously this didn't refer to his second coming, but his coming in power when he rose from the dead and gave the Holy Spirit to empower the disciples to preach the gospel and win citizens into the kingdom of God. Are you a member of his kingdom?

THINGS TO DISCUSS WITH YOUR FAMILY

1. In order of value, make a list of what things you consider to be most important to you.
2. Can you think of anything you have sacrificed for the Lord and your salvation?
3. What did Paul sacrifice when he became a Christian? See Philippians 3:1-9.

Meditation

Meditate upon the cross you take up daily as commanded by Jesus.

Wise Words

We must not conceal from ourselves that true Christianity brings with it a daily cross in this life, while it offers us a crown of glory in the life to come. *J. C. Ryle*

'Therefore God also has highly exalted him and given him the name which is above every name, that at the name of Jesus every knee should bow, of those in heaven, and of those on earth, and of those under the earth, and that every tongue should confess that Jesus Christ is Lord' (Philippians 2:9-11).

Read: Matthew 17:1-8

It is good to receive encouragement especially when it comes from an unexpected person. In your reading today you have read one of the most strengthening events in the life of Jesus and three of his disciples. The disciples had been told of their Lord's impending sacrificial death at the hands of the church leaders and the Romans. They were despondent as this was most unexpected news to them. However, Peter, James and John experienced a vision of Christ in his majestic glory.

These three disciples witnessed the majesty of Christ's divine holiness and were told not to speak of what they saw until after his resurrection — not even to their fellow disciples. Later Peter wrote: 'For we did not follow cunningly devised fables when we made known to you the power and coming of our Lord Jesus Christ, but were eyewitnesses of his majesty. For he received from God the Father honour and glory when such a voice came to him from the Excellent Glory: "This is my beloved Son, in whom I am well pleased." And we heard this voice which came from heaven when we were with him on the holy mountain' (2 Peter 1:16-18).

Christ had three witnesses to his transfiguration which was in keeping with the number of witnesses needed to prove a historical fact (Deuteronomy 19:15). The three disciples saw the Lord's face shining with the brightness of the sun and his clothing as white as light.

Elijah and Moses, representing the law and the prophets, appeared and spoke to Christ showing us the safe and continued life of believers. While the bodies of the saints might rest in the earth until Jesus returns, their souls are with God, having been made perfect (Hebrews 12:23). Our God is the God 'of the living and the dead' (Acts 10:42). Death is not the end of our existence. We all live for ever, but where we will be is dependent upon our attitude to the Lord Jesus.

We must obey God's command given on the Mount of Transfiguration, 'This is my beloved Son, in whom I am well pleased. Hear him!' The three disciples were so fearful of what they saw and heard that they fell to the ground. Jesus lifted them up, telling them not to fear what had happened. You and I need to put into practice God's words to the disciples concerning his Son — 'Hear him!' We must read our Bibles, believe in Christ as our Saviour and obey all that the Scriptures ask of us, for the Bible is God's infallible Word to mankind. We read in Hebrews 1:1-2: 'God, who at various times and in various ways spoke in time past to the fathers by the prophets, has in these last days spoken to us by his Son.' We must hear him and obey.

THINGS TO DISCUSS
WITH YOUR FAMILY

1. Why do you think the disciples wanted to build three 'tabernacles'?
2. How were the disciples encouraged by the events of that day?
3. Do you think the transfiguration was an encouragement to Jesus? How?

Meditation

Meditate upon the transfigured glory of Christ as seen by the disciples and Malachi 4:2 — 'The Sun of Righteousness shall arise with healing in his wings.'

No man ever errs on the side of giving too much honour to God the Son.   *J. C. Ryle*

Wise Words

'Behold, I will send you Elijah the prophet before the coming of the great and dreadful day of the LORD' (Malachi 4:5).

Read: Matthew 17:9-13

I'm sure we all have difficulty understanding various sections of the Bible, but it is wise to interpret difficult passages in the light of other passages which are easy to understand. Sometimes it is better to read on without giving a passage of Scripture a meaning that is totally incorrect. We have now come to another section of Scripture where Elijah features prominently.

The disciples had been taught that Jesus would die at the hands of the church leaders and then be resurrected by the almighty power of God. From our last devotion you should remember that three disciples had witnessed his transfiguration on the mountain, where Moses and Elijah had appeared and spoken to him. The voice of God had been heard and the three disciples were filled with awe and fear.

Now the disciples had a question: 'Why do the scribes say that Elijah must come first?' The scribes and others knew what Malachi had written concerning Elijah: 'Behold, I will send you Elijah the prophet before the coming of the great and dreadful day of the LORD. And he will turn the hearts of the fathers to the children, and the hearts of the children to their fathers, lest I come and strike the earth with a curse' (Malachi 4:5-6). Jesus answered their question by agreeing with what the scribes had said, because they simply quoted what Malachi had written. However, they failed to grasp the meaning of that prophecy.

Earlier John had denied that he was Elijah. This was true as Elijah was in Paradise. When John the Baptist's father, Zacharias, was told of his son's impending birth the angel said to him, 'He will also go before him [Jesus] in the spirit and power of Elijah, "to turn the hearts of the fathers to the children", and the disobedient to the wisdom of the just, to make ready a people prepared for the Lord' (Luke 1:17). Later Jesus spoke of John the Baptist and said of him, 'This is he of whom it is written: "Behold, I send my messenger before your face, who will prepare your way before you"' (Luke 7:27).

John the Baptist was the 'Elijah' prophesied by Malachi. He came in the spirit and power of the Elijah of old and preached repentance as he prepared the way for the coming of Christ, the Son of God.

Jesus then told the disciples that, just as the authorities through Herod had murdered John, so also they would do the same to himself, 'the Son of man'. As John was hated, so also Christ was hated by the church authorities. Everyone would be involved in having Christ put to death — the scribes, the Pharisees, the Sadducees, the priests, King Herod, the unbelieving Jews, Pilate as the local head of the Roman empire and all of the saints whose sins nailed Christ to the cross.

At last the disciples understood what Christ was saying about John the Baptist being Elijah in the work he did preparing the way for the advent of Christ.

THINGS TO DISCUSS WITH YOUR FAMILY

1. Make a list of the ways in which John the Baptist was like Elijah.
2. What was John's main work?
3. What did Jesus mean when he said, 'Elijah truly is coming first and will restore all things'?

Meditation

Meditate upon the self-sacrificing work of John the Baptist and ask God how you can serve the Lord Jesus better than you are doing today.

Wise Words

I thirst for truth, but shall not reach it till I reach the source. *Robert Browning*

'Be sober, be vigilant; because your adversary the devil walks about like a roaring lion, seeking whom he may devour' (1 Peter 5:8).

Read: Mark 9:14-29

Many are the times when I have felt elated by the teaching of a sermon, a book I have read or some happy event, only to find myself later troubled and feeling uneasy. I'm sure this must have been the case with the disciples, especially the three who had seen Jesus transfigured. They all had witnessed Christ's great power and they themselves had been on a preaching and healing tour returning with exciting stories of what had happened.

When Jesus and the three disciples came down from the mountain they found the nine being ridiculed by some scribes. The very embarrassed disciples had attempted to cast a demon out of a boy but had failed. The scribes who were present with a crowd of people immediately began mocking the disciples and through them their Master, the Lord Jesus.

The disciples needed Christ's help and when he appeared they must have heaved a sigh of relief. Jesus rebuked the scribes and all those who refused to believe that he was God's Son with almighty, heavenly power. At once he turned to the boy and his distressed father, and after discussing the boy's plight heard the father say, 'But if you can do anything, have compassion on us and help us.' The father's faith was weak as his words contained 'But if…' On many other occasions the cry for assistance came from people who knew that Christ could help; they knew he had the power of heaven at his disposal. This father was unsure if Christ could do anything to heal his child.

When Jesus asked the weeping man to believe, he replied, 'Lord, I believe; help my unbelief.' Christ then commanded the unclean spirit to leave the boy which it did immediately. What the disciples could not do, Christ did immediately.

What are we taught from this incident? We must beware of attempting to do the Lord's work in our own power. The church and Christians individually make plans to implement various programmes, but find they come to nothing because they do not have the power of Christ. Jesus said to his disciples and through them to all of his people, 'I am the vine, you are the branches. He who abides in me, and I in him, bears much fruit; for without me you can do nothing' (John 15:5).

Many times we fail in our discipleship and fall into sin. Always remember Peter's denial of his Saviour which was followed by repentance and forgiveness.

When the disciples asked why they had failed in their attempts to heal the boy Jesus reminded them that great miracles required fasting and prayer. Our enemy Satan is still very powerful and as our text reads, he 'walks about like a roaring lion, seeking whom he may devour'. The demon within the boy was a most powerful one and great power was needed to oust him from the child. The power needed to defeat the evil one comes through time devoted to prayer. Fasting gives us more time for our devotions and we have Paul's assurance: 'And the God of peace will crush Satan under your feet shortly' (Romans 16:20). Christians, pray on!

THINGS TO DISCUSS WITH YOUR FAMILY

1. How do you know Satan still has great power at his disposal?
2. Why were the disciples unable to free the boy from his demon possession?
3. True or false: Little faith is better than no faith? Why?

Meditation

Pray for the children in your family and the church family. Jesus shows mercy to the young.

Wise Words

If you don't believe in the devil's existence, just try resisting him for a while.   *Charles G. Finney*

'Even my own familiar friend in whom I trusted, who ate my bread, has lifted up his heel against me' (Psalm 41:9).

Read: Mark 9:30-32

It is very distressing when you are let down by someone you considered to be a close friend. Unfortunately, this is very prevalent in today's world. Think of all the marriages that have fallen apart because one party has proved to be a false 'friend'. What happens so frequently in the world today is common to all ages, and the Saviour was no exception, for we read his words to the disciples as recorded in Matthew 17:22 — 'The Son of Man is about to be betrayed into the hands of men...'

We know that Judas Iscariot was chosen to be one of the Lord's disciples, but we also know that Jesus knew that he was the one who would betray him.

Today our reading is an outline of what Christ taught his disciples concerning the reason for his entrance into this world of sin and rebellion against God. Recently we saw that Jesus told the disciples quite plainly that he must die a violent death, be buried and rise again. He said that the fulfilment of the sign of Jonah the prophet would add to the proof that he was Messiah. Nevertheless, as school children must have constant revision, so that they might understand what is being taught, so also the disciples needed to be taught the same facts again and again, especially as they had preconceived ideas of the kingdom of God. They expected Jesus to sit upon the throne of David and rule Israel in glory and with almighty power and wisdom.

The Lord took his disciples aside and again told them of what was soon to happen to him. They were told that he would be handed over to cruel men. These men were the church leaders who hated him, considering him to be a false Messiah and one in whom Satan was dwelling. The very people who should have been rejoicing with the advent of the Christ were planning his death. Yet as a result of their merciless actions, unbelievers would be saved. His death was to be no ordinary death, but that of the Saviour dying a sacrificial death on behalf of his people.

Christ's words, recorded by the Apostle John, explain perfectly what was to take place: 'Therefore my Father loves me, because I lay down my life that I may take it again. No one takes it from me, but I lay it down of myself. I have power to lay it down, and I have power to take it again. This command I have received from my Father' (John 10:17-18).

Clearly, Jesus foretold his resurrection. The Apostle Paul wrote that Jesus 'was delivered up because of our offences, and was raised because of our justification' (Romans 4:25). The resurrection was the result of the almighty power of the triune God, Father, Son and Holy Spirit, and that same almighty power will one day be used to raise the dead when Christ returns to this sin-ridden world. What a day that will be!

THINGS TO DISCUSS WITH YOUR FAMILY

1. The disciples were slow learners for we are told, 'But they did not understand this saying, and were afraid to ask him.' What made them such slow learners?
2. What is the significance of the name 'the Son of Man'? See Daniel 7:13-14.
3. Why did Jesus come to this sin-ridden world?

Meditation

'Because the sinless Saviour died, my sinful soul is counted free. For God the just is satisfied to look on him and pardon me.' Is this true of you?

Wise Words

If Jesus Christ be God and died for me, then no sacrifice can be too great for me to make for him.   *C. T. Studd*

12 July — Paying the temple tax

'And you shall take the atonement money of the children of Israel, and shall appoint it for the service of the tabernacle of meeting, that it may be a memorial for the children of Israel before the LORD, to make atonement for yourselves' (Exodus 30:16).

Read: Matthew 17:24-27

We hear a lot of complaints when taxation time comes around each year. For some reason most people don't like paying taxes to the government despite the good use made of most of the money. We have hospitals, the police service, an army to protect the nation against forces of evil, schools, pensions for the aged and those in need, roadways, a postal department and many other essential services, all because we pay our taxes. Tax time should be a time of gratitude to those who pay their dues.

No sooner had the Lord returned to Capernaum than Peter was approached by the temple tax collector and asked, 'Does your teacher not pay the temple tax?' Peter's reply would indicate that Jesus had paid the tax before, but this time the Lord raised the matter of his necessity to do so. This particular tax was a tax paid by sinners, 'a ransom for himself to the LORD' (Exodus 30:12). The money collected was used to maintain the temple and meet the cost of the temple services to the people.

Jesus asked Peter if kings who established the taxes, and their families, paid taxes, or whether it was ordinary citizens who paid these taxes. The answer was obvious: kings and their families didn't pay taxes. Jesus then said to Peter, 'Then the sons are free.'

Jesus was 'born under the law' and as such was liable to obey the law of God and the nation. The Lord also knew that to refuse to pay the tax would invite even greater hatred, thus he instructed Peter to make the payment for both of them. Jesus and the disciples were not wealthy, but Christ's Father had unlimited resources at his disposal. The universe had been created through Christ. Paul wrote of Christ: 'He is the image of the invisible God, the firstborn over all creation' (Colossians 1:15). As 'firstborn' he has supreme authority and power to ensure creation functions as it should. He also has all power over all life, even the fish of the sea. Peter, as instructed by his Lord, went to the sea and caught a fish with the correct tax money in its mouth.

What do we learn from this amazing event? First, our Lord paid his taxes, identifying himself with the ordinary person. We should also pay the duties set by the state. Paul said, 'Render therefore to all their due: taxes to whom taxes are due, customs to whom customs, fear to whom fear, honour to whom honour' (Romans 13:7).

Second, we see the almighty power of our Saviour which should encourage all of his people living in a world that despises Christ and the church.

Third, Christ could have refused to pay a tax. The temple was his, as we read in Malachi 3:1: 'Behold, I send my messenger, and he will prepare the way before me. And the Lord, whom you seek, will suddenly come to his temple...' As King of creation he was not obligated to pay the temple tax, but for the sake of peace the tax was paid. Too often disputes come about because people demand their 'rights'. Are you one such person?

THINGS TO DISCUSS WITH YOUR FAMILY

1. Read and discuss Romans 13:5-7.
2. Why should you pay government taxes?
3. In the light of Matthew 12:6 should Christ have paid the temple tax?

Meditation

Think about your obedience to the legitimate laws of your country.

Gospel liberty is a liberty from sin, not to sin.

Thomas Hall

Wise Words

'Pride goes before destruction, and a haughty spirit before a fall' (Proverbs 16:18).

Read: Mark 9:33-37

There's a little bit of pride in the heart of the finest Christians alive, even pride because of their humility. When I attended Primary School I wasn't a great student, but I was very proud of my marble playing ability. I considered myself the best marble player in the school of about one hundred pupils. I can still outplay my adult children and grandchildren!

Now the disciples had just been told that their Lord was to be crucified and would die. Continually they had been taught that the kingdom of God existed in the hearts of his people which was totally different from the kingdoms of the world. But, the disciples were slow to learn as they had pre-conceived ideas of what God's kingdom was to be. They still believed that Jesus would re-establish the kingdom of David, with his throne and government in Jerusalem. As the disciples walked along they began to discuss who would occupy the positions of authority and more particularly who would, under Christ, hold the office of greatest supremacy.

The sin of this discussion was pride. This is one of the great problems of the world today. The world respects, or envies or hates, those who exercise authority, those with great wealth, the mental giants or the sporting heroes. Generally, the world looks up to these people and parents use them as examples of what their children should aim to become.

The world's concept of greatness was not what Jesus had been teaching. He himself was the perfect example of true greatness which we must emulate. Paul wrote: 'Let this mind be in you which was also in Christ Jesus, who, being in the form of God, did not consider it robbery to be equal with God, but made himself of no reputation, taking the form of a bondservant, and coming in the likeness of men, and being found in appearance as a man, he humbled himself and became obedient to the point of death, even the death of the cross' (Philippians 2:5-8).

In Isaiah 40:10-11 we read of God's almighty power and humility in dealing with the helpless: 'He will feed his flock like a shepherd; he will gather the lambs with his arm, and carry them in his bosom, and gently lead those who are with young.'

Jesus took a young person in his arms and said that true greatness was to be found in helping the weak and needy in society, to forget self and bring joy to the downcast, needy and weakest people. Those who receive the greatest rewards in the kingdom of God are those who are the most humble and helpful in this world. In Galatians 6:2 we read, 'Bear one another's burdens, and so fulfil the law of Christ.'

Jesus washed the disciples' feet, which was the work of the lowest servant, and told his disciples to do likewise. This is true greatness in God's sight. Jesus summarized this teaching when he said, 'For who is greater, he who sits at the table, or he who serves? Is it not he who sits at the table? Yet I am among you as the One who serves' (Luke 22:27). May we all be 'great' members of Christ's kingdom. Remember, 'A person wrapped up in himself makes a very small parcel.'

THINGS TO DISCUSS WITH YOUR FAMILY

1. What can you do to show your 'greatness' in the kingdom of God?
2. What is humility?
3. What are we taught in 1 Peter 5:5? 'Yes, all of you be submissive to one another, and be clothed with humility, for "God resists the proud, but gives grace to the humble."'

Meditation

Can you say, 'As a disciple of Christ I desire nothing more than that my Saviour be exalted'?

Wise Words

A bishop's office is a name of labour rather than honour; so that he who covets pre-eminence rather than usefulness may understand that he is not a bishop. *Augustine*

'Then Moses said to him, "Are you zealous for my sake? Oh, that all the LORD's people were prophets and that the LORD would put his Spirit upon them!"' (Numbers 11:29).

Read: Mark 9:38-41

There are many shortages in this world and one of them is tolerance. So much harm is caused because of lack of tolerance of other people because they are different to us or do things we find objectionable, even though what they do doesn't cause any harm. Our reading today is about the Apostle John who at that time showed himself to be somewhat intolerant of another follower of Christ.

John approached Jesus with the news that the disciples had seen another person casting out demons in his name. This they found objectionable and when they tried to stop the man from his good work, he refused and went on with what he was doing. Jesus' answer was to say that the man was a disciple, not someone making a name for himself using his name to perform miracles. Christ's disciples are found everywhere and we must respect them even though we may not agree with everything they do or believe. Paul wrote some wise words that we should take to heart: 'For if we live, we live to the Lord; and if we die, we die to the Lord. Therefore, whether we live or die, we are the Lord's' (Romans 14:8).

The miracle worker was a Christian brother to John, and Christ was being glorified through his actions. The Apostle John had something to learn about tolerance. He, with his brother James, were known as 'Boanerges, that is, "Sons of Thunder"' (Mark 3:17). The sanctifying work of the Holy Spirit brought about a change in John and he became known as 'the disciple whom Jesus loved' (John 21:20). We need to learn the same and show tolerance to Christ's people who are different to us in church practice and some minor matters of doctrine.

Jesus went on to say that the man and indeed anyone who from the heart carried out works of love in his name would be rewarded by his heavenly Father.

A similar incident is recorded in Numbers 11:16-30, where Moses had chosen seventy elders to assist him in the government of Israel as the people made their way to the Promised Land. The seventy were to present themselves to him at the tabernacle, where God would pour out his Spirit upon them. Two were still in the camp when this happened, and when Joshua heard that Eldad and Medad were prophesying he ran to Moses asking that they be prevented from doing this. Joshua was jealous of Moses' reputation and thought that the two men were detracting from his leader's honour. Moses rebuked him saying, 'Are you zealous for my sake? Oh, that all the LORD's people were prophets and that the LORD would put his Spirit upon them!' (Numbers 11:29).

Paul faced a similar problem when some brethren in Rome preached the gospel, hoping to hurt him, but his reply was, 'Some indeed preach Christ even from envy and strife, and some also from good will ... What then? Only that in every way, whether in pretence or in truth, Christ is preached; and in this I rejoice, yes, and will rejoice' (Philippians 1:15,18).

May we all be tolerant Christians.

THINGS TO DISCUSS WITH YOUR FAMILY

1. What is Christian tolerance?
2. What is your attitude to believers in other denominations?
3. What is the 'reward' mentioned by Jesus in Mark 9:41?

Meditation

Meditate upon your Christian love for Christians who hold different beliefs than you.

One loving heart sets another on fire.   *Augustine*

Wise Words

'And the smoke of their torment ascends for ever and ever; and they have no rest day or night, who worship the beast and his image, and whoever receives the mark of his name' (Revelation 14:11).

Read: Mark 9:42-50

Often we hear a foolish person tell another, 'Go to hell!' Such a statement is foolish because the speaker has neither the authority nor the power to carry out his threat. Hell is an unpleasant subject and people are more ready to discuss heaven than the place that burns with unquenchable fire. Jesus, however, spoke more about hell than heaven.

Today's reading is really a warning to everyone that we must be willing to sacrifice everything, especially those things that are important to us in order to gain a home in Paradise. First, there is a terrible warning to anyone who causes a child to sin — 'it would be better for him if a millstone were hung around his neck, and he were thrown into the sea'.

Then Christ turns to body parts that are most valuable to us all: our eyes, feet, hands, and says that if these cause us to sin it would be better to get rid of them than end up in the eternal flames of hell. Our Saviour's warning must not be taken literally, but rather as the Apostle Paul inferred when he wrote, 'Therefore, brethren, we are debtors — not to the flesh, to live according to the flesh. For if you live according to the flesh you will die; but if by the Spirit you put to death the deeds of the body, you will live' (Romans 8:12-13).

Job saw the danger of lust coming through his eyesight and did something about it. He didn't pluck out his eyes but we read, 'I have made a covenant with my eyes; why then should I look upon a young woman?' (Job 31:1).

We are to avoid putting ourselves in situations that are temptations to sin. If necessary turn off the TV and don't read immoral literature. Don't go to those places that cause sin to rise in the heart but rather behave as did Paul who wrote, 'But I discipline my body and bring it into subjection, lest, when I have preached to others, I myself should become disqualified' (1 Corinthians 9:27).

Hell was likened to Gehenna which was the constantly burning Jerusalem garbage dump. This spot had been used by Manasseh and

Ahaz to sacrifice their children to the false god, Moloch (2 Kings 16:3; 21:6). Hell is the place of eternal punishment for all who are not saints. It is described in our text as the place of eternal torment where there is nothing good or pleasant. Gone are earth's joys, hopes and riches, for it is the place of 'no hope'.

It is wise to make sacrifices now in order to gain eternal life and the joy of being with Christ and the saints in the new heavens and earth in which there will be perfect righteousness.

We suffer fiery trials, but these like salt purify us. Christians are the salt of the world and as such we purify and preserve society. This 'salt' produces the fruit of the Spirit in our lives and floods our soul with spiritual peace. God is at peace with us because of Christ's sacrificial life and death in the place of his people. We in turn live at peace with all others. Let us live to the glory of our Saviour.

THINGS TO DISCUSS WITH YOUR FAMILY

1. What did Jesus mean when he said, 'Salt is good'? (Mark 9:50).
2. How can you avoid spending eternity in a place where God is absent?
3. Find out what you can about Ahaz and Manasseh sacrificing their children to Moloch.

Meditation

Meditate upon the wonder of your rescue from hell by the Lord Jesus.

Wise Words

Could every damned sinner weep a whole ocean, yet all those oceans together would never extinguish one spark of eternal fire. *Thomas Brooks*

'Obey those who rule over you, and be submissive, for they watch out for your souls, as those who must give account. Let them do so with joy and not with grief, for that would be unprofitable for you' (Hebrews 13:17).

Read: Matthew 18:15-20

Frequently people are involved in disputes with others. This even occurs within the church and does great damage to the cause of Christ. Newspapers are only too happy to sensationalize church problems. In today's reading we find the Lord acknowledging that there will be times when Christians fall out with each other, but he outlines a course of action that can restore harmony.

Jesus stresses that the ideal way to settle an argument is to do so gently. The Apostle Paul wrote: 'Brethren, if a man is overtaken in any trespass, you who are spiritual restore such a one in a spirit of gentleness' (Galatians 6:1). The first step in re-establishing harmony is to approach the brother causing the offence and privately try to reach a settlement. In Proverbs 25:9 we read wise words, 'Debate your case with your neighbour, and do not disclose the secret to another…'

If this fails then witnesses are required to be present at the next attempt to sort out the dispute. The two or three friends may be able to give wise advice when necessary. If the trouble is not solved they will be needed as witnesses when the issue is taken to the church for investigation.

If step two does not bring about a resolution then the church — the meeting of the elders, must be called to hear the evidence and make a decision. When the decision is announced both parties should accept the outcome, realizing the truth of our text, 'Obey those who rule over you, and be submissive, for they watch out for your souls, as those who must give account.'

If the guilty party refuses to accept the decision of the church he is to be expelled until he repents and seeks forgiveness. Nevertheless, we must remember that he is a fallen brother. Paul indicates what is to be done: 'And if anyone does not obey our word in this epistle, note that person and do not keep company with him, that he may be ashamed. Yet do not count him as an enemy, but admonish him as a brother' (2 Thessalonians 3:14-15).

Christ gave the church the keys to the kingdom of heaven, with the authority to make decisions in matters of discipline (Matthew 16:19). When the church meets to make decisions in matters of discipline they have the promise that Christ is present, giving guidance to make sound judgements.

One precious promise to the church is found in the last verse of today's reading: 'For where two or three are gathered together in my name, I am there in the midst of them.' When we meet for worship, in our Bible study groups or around the table as a family, Christ is present by his Spirit. The world despises small congregations, but Christ does not, for he is with every meeting of his people. Ensure you attend worship services, for Christ is there also.

THINGS TO DISCUSS WITH YOUR FAMILY

1. How does the church deal with troublemakers outside the church? Read 1 Corinthians 5:12-13.
2. Why should Christians obey those God has placed over them?
3. What is the purpose of church discipline?

Meditation

How does the church deal with persistent troublemakers? Consider Paul's teaching in Titus 3:10-11: 'Reject a divisive man after the first and second admonition, knowing that such a person is warped and sinning, being self-condemned.'

Wise Words

When we take God for our God, we take his people for our people. *Matthew Henry*

'Wash me thoroughly from my iniquity, and cleanse me from my sin' (Psalm
51:2).

Read: Matthew 18:21-35

There are many times during our life when another Christian
hurts us. What are we to do? When Peter raised this question he
believed he was being very generous in saying he would forgive an
offending brother seven times. He was probably shocked when he
heard the Lord's reply.

In this parable Jesus tells us that we are to forgive the sinning
brother who asks for forgiveness, just as the compassionate king forgave his servant who owed him a great amount of money.

The servant, not being able to make the repayment, appealed to
the king for mercy, which resulted in his debt being forgiven. The
man then demanded the repayment of a small amount another servant owed him. When the poor person couldn't make the repayment
his creditor had him thrown into prison until the debt was paid. The
man who had received mercy from his king refused to show mercy
to another who begged for time to repay the small amount that he
owed.

The king represents our God who is a God of great mercy. We
are great sinners just as David wrote in Psalm 40:12: 'My iniquities
have overtaken me, so that I am not able to look up; they are more
than the hairs of my head; therefore my heart fails me.' All who do
not believe in the Lord Jesus Christ should beware for the Apostle
John wrote, 'He who does not believe the Son shall not see life, but
the wrath of God abides on him' (John 3:36). We are God's debtors
and cannot personally repay him any part of what we owe.

We are invited to go to him through the Lord Jesus Christ and
seek forgiveness. Christ has paid the debt owing to God for the sins
of his people. When we approach God with true repentance we are
forgiven. In Isaiah 43:25 we read wonderful words about God's forgiveness, 'I, even I, am he who blots out your transgressions for my
own sake; and I will not remember your sins.'

In Micah 7:19 we read, 'You will cast all our sins into the depths
of the sea.' David wrote of God's mercy in dealing with his people's

sins: 'For as the heavens are high above the earth, so great is his mercy toward those who fear him; as far as the east is from the west, so far has he removed our transgressions from us' (Psalm 103:11-12).

If we believe in the Lord Jesus Christ, eternal life is God's free gift to us. Remember that a mark of a Christian is that he freely forgives those who have offended him. James warns that a failure to show mercy invites God's anger. He wrote, 'For judgement is without mercy to the one who has shown no mercy. Mercy triumphs over judgement' (James 2:13). Paul tells us how we are to treat our sinning brother: 'And be kind to one another, tender-hearted, forgiving one another, just as God in Christ forgave you' (Ephesians 4:32).

An unforgiving spirit will close heaven's door to you. There are times when we have been offended and must leave the issue in the hands of God who on Judgement Day will right all wrongs. Do you have a forgiving heart? If not, pray for one.

THINGS TO DISCUSS WITH YOUR FAMILY

1. Does true forgiveness include forgetting the offence?
2. What did Jesus mean when he said we are to forgive our offending brother 'seventy times seven'?
3. God does not forgive the unrepentant — should we?

Meditation

Meditate upon your standing with God if you have found forgiveness with him.

Wise Words

Even as Christ forgave you, so you also must do.
Apostle Paul

'When he had called the people to himself, with his disciples also, he said to them, "Whoever desires to come after me, let him deny himself, and take up his cross, and follow me"' (Mark 8:34).

Read: Luke 9:57-62

I thank God that I live in Australia as it is still a peaceful nation. We have freedom of religion and speech which means that the gospel can be preached throughout the land. Recently some institutions rejected the Gideon's placing Bibles in their rooms and this included our local hospital; after some letter writing, gentle approaches and prayer, the decision was reversed, and now a Bible is beside every bed. God does answer prayer and we still do have the right to arbitrate for changes to foolish laws — and praise God, leaders do on occasions have a change of heart.

It is easy to be a Christian in Australia as no one really cares what people believe. Yet, to become a Christian in some countries invites cruel opposition, even death. During the time Christ went about healing and preaching the kingdom of God, persecution followed. Today you have read about several people who wanted to become disciples of our Lord, but had not counted the cost of such a change in their life. The same still applies to anyone who is contemplating following the Redeemer. Paul's instruction to Timothy applies to every person who is a Christian, 'You therefore must endure hardship as a good soldier of Jesus Christ' (2 Timothy 2:3).

When a scribe asked to be allowed to follow Jesus he was told that his life would be very hard as Christ moved about preaching the gospel, and had no permanent home. Frequently he slept in the open, unlike the animals that had dens or nests in which to live. Jesus experienced rejection.

A second person was told by the Lord, 'Follow me.' Jesus and his disciples were about to move on, but the man wasn't willing to do that. He wanted to go home and bury his father. Maybe his father was aged and it meant he wanted to remain with him until he died. The man was unwilling to follow Christ because his family came first. Christians are people who obey their Saviour's commands. Jesus had said, 'You are my friends if you do whatever I command you' (John 15:14). The spiritual family is of more importance than our blood relations, just as Jesus once said to this mother and siblings, 'My mother and my brothers are these who hear the word of God and do it' (Luke 8:21).

Another prospective disciple wanted time to return home and bid farewell to his parents. This man had not really decided what he wanted to do as he still had a divided heart, Christ or home. Once we commence following Christ there can be no turning back. Lot's wife discovered the danger of such an action (Genesis 19:26). No, Christ is first in the life of the Christian just as Paul wrote, 'And he [Christ] is the head of the body, the church, who is the beginning, the firstborn from the dead, that in all things he may have the pre-eminence' (Colossians 1:18). Are you able to say with the Apostle Paul, 'I press toward the goal for the prize of the upward call of God in Christ Jesus' (Philippians 3:14). Be willing to sacrifice everything for the Lord your Saviour.

THINGS TO DISCUSS WITH YOUR FAMILY

1. What have you suffered because of your discipleship of the Lord Jesus?
2. Is there anything you wouldn't give up for Jesus? Discuss this.
3. What did Jesus mean when he said, 'Let the dead bury their own dead'? (Luke 9:60).

Meditation

Meditate upon the sacrifices Christ made to save sinners.

Wise Words

Ministry that costs nothing accomplishes nothing.

J. H. Jowett

'I have become a stranger to my brothers, and an alien to my mother's children'
(Psalm 69:8).

Read: John 7:1-13

Many of us live in countries where we can move about quite safely, but this was not so with Jesus. There was a growing number of groups that wanted him dead. We know, as he did, that his main purpose in life was to die and so pay the penalty owed by his people for their sins. His family members didn't understand this. In fact they were not sure what Jesus was to do, other than he was a great worker of miracles who claimed to be the Messiah. At times they thought he was out of his mind, but now they wanted him to go with them to Jerusalem to celebrate the Feast of Tabernacles. This was a happy feast time as it was both a harvest celebration and a time to remember God's care of their ancestors as they wandered through the wilderness on their way to the Promised Land. In Jerusalem, many families built 'booths' out of palm fronds and lived in these shelters during the feast. It must have been a very happy time for the children.

Christ's family wanted Jesus to accompany them to Jerusalem and there perform miracles in the hope that the crowds would support any claim he made to become King of the Jews, re-establishing the throne of King David.

Jesus was not ready to do as his brothers asked. He told them that his life was in danger and his time had 'not yet fully come'. It was not yet the time for his death, hence he had to take care. He told his family that he was hated just as would be everyone who followed him. The Apostle John, writing to Christians said, 'Do not marvel my brethren, if the world hates you' (1 John 3:13). In fact, in the Sermon on the Mount Christ had warned his disciples: 'Woe to you when all men speak well of you, for so did their fathers to the false prophets' (Luke 6:26).

Jesus and his disciples of all eras are despised when they reveal the sins of humanity. This was what he told Nicodemus: 'And this is the condemnation, that the light has come into the world, and men loved darkness rather than light, because their deeds were evil. For everyone practising evil hates the light and does not come to the light, lest his deeds should be exposed' (John 3:19-20). This was the attitude of the King of Israel concerning the godly prophet Micaiah: '... but I hate him, because he does not prophesy good concerning me, but evil' (1 Kings 22:8).

Jesus knew what it is to be tempted and hurt. The writer to the Hebrews gives us comfort when we read: 'Therefore, in all things he had to be made like his brethren, that he might be a merciful and faithful High Priest in things pertaining to God, to make propitiation for the sins of the people. For in that he himself has suffered, being tempted, he is able to aid those who are tempted' (Hebrews 2:17-18).

The attitude of Jesus' brothers and sisters was a disappointment, but things changed, for we read that at the prayer meeting following his ascension into heaven those present included his mother and 'his brothers' (Acts 1:14).

THINGS TO DISCUSS WITH YOUR FAMILY

1. Why did Christ's family want him to accompany them to the feast of Tabernacles?
2. Why did the Jews despise the Lord Jesus?
3. Why do people today hate the Christian church?

Meditation

Pray for your family members that they all might know Christ as Lord and Saviour.

Wise Words

The family altar would alter many a family.

Anonymous

'Be hospitable to one another without grumbling' (1 Peter 4:9).

Read: Luke 9:51-56

Christians are to be hospitable to everyone, especially to fellow believers in Christ. In the western world we tend to have an abundance of food which we should use to help those in true need. Yet, too often most people, including Christians, look upon their possessions as their own, and only grudgingly use them to help others.

Jesus' family had set off for Jerusalem, probably angry that he had not accompanied them. Nevertheless, the Lord was soon to leave, but at his own time and travelling ways that would not attract the attention of people who abhorred him. The Apostle John said he went up 'in secret' (John 7:10). He knew what the not too distant future held for him — persecution, whipping, a mock trial, a crown of thorns, spitting, abuse and finally crucifixion. He was ready to die for sinners just as the writer to the Hebrews said, '… who for the joy that was set before him endured the cross, despising the shame, and has sat down at the right hand of the throne of God' (Hebrews 12:2).

His mind was fixed upon the cross and he set off for the capital city fully aware of God's promise to him, 'For the Lord GOD will help me; therefore I will not be disgraced; therefore I have set my face like a flint, and I know that I will not be ashamed' (Isaiah 50:7).

Some disciples had gone ahead to make arrangements for an overnight stay in a township of Samaria, but they returned with the news that he was not welcome and would not be accommodated anywhere. The Samaritans hated the Jews. They argued over the correct place to worship and while both nations looked for the arrival of the Messiah, the Samaritans had no place for Jesus in their theology or township.

When James and John, 'sons of thunder', heard the report they showed their true colours by asking the Lord to punish such inhospitable people. They were jealous of their Lord's honour and asked for lightning from heaven to wipe them out, just as Elijah had called upon fire from heaven to destroy the troops sent by Ahaziah, the king of Samaria, to take him prisoner (2 Kings 1).

Jesus rebuked 'the sons of thunder' for their violent outburst. They had been taught to love their enemies, to preach peace and goodwill to the people and to bless those who cursed them. Their request was contrary to Christ's teaching of showing compassion and mercy.

Jesus reminded them that his coming to earth was not to destroy men but to save people from their sins. He had continually shown himself as a compassionate Saviour. Christ and his disciples wiped the dust of that uninviting town from their feet and moved on to another village where they were given accommodation.

May we show our Christian love by being hospitable people. Wouldn't it be wonderful if what the writer to the Hebrews wrote was true of us: 'Let brotherly love continue. Do not forget to entertain strangers, for by so doing some have unwittingly entertained angels' (Hebrews 13:1-2).

THINGS TO DISCUSS WITH YOUR FAMILY

1. In what ways have you shown Christian hospitality?
2. Why do you think the Samaritans refused to accommodate Christ and his disciples?
3. Discuss the Samaritan who met Jesus at Jacob's well.

Meditation

Consider the ways that you can show hospitality to others, especially to non-Christians.

Wise Words

The only time a miser puts his hand in his pocket is during cold weather. *Anonymous*

'Jesus said to them, "If God were your Father, you would love me, for I proceeded forth and came from God; nor have I come of myself, but he sent me"' (John 8:42).

Read: John 7:11-24

If you have attended a school reunion, I am sure you have looked for friends you made many years ago. Jesus had finally arrived in Jerusalem where there was an air of expectation that he would be present. People were talking about him, discussing who they thought he was. Some believed he was a good man while others believed he was leading people astray. However, no one spoke too openly about him because they feared the leaders of the church.

When he arrived, Jesus made his way to the temple where he began to teach the people about the kingdom of God.

This upset the Pharisees and Scribes because he spoke with authority and demonstrated a vast knowledge of the Scriptures. He could read and write (see John 8:6 and Luke 4:16) but he didn't have a 'theology degree' from the great educational institutions of his day.

When he was questioned about his teaching he told the people that he taught what was given him by his heavenly Father. Later he said, 'For I have not spoken on my own authority; but the Father who sent me gave me a command, what I should say and what I should speak. And I know that his command is everlasting life. Therefore, whatever I speak, just as the Father has told me, so I speak' (John 12:49-50). This was in keeping with what we read in Deuteronomy 18:18-19 concerning the Messiah: 'I will raise up for them a Prophet like you from among their brethren, and will put my words in his mouth, and he shall speak to them all that I command him. And it shall be that whoever will not hear my words, which he speaks in my name, I will require it of him.'

Jesus told his hearers that he was not seeking his own glory but the honour and glory of the One who sent him — God, his heavenly Father! Moses had given them God's law which they didn't keep. Now they wanted to kill the One who came in the name of Jehovah.

Jesus reminded them that they wanted him put to death because the rulers believed he had broken God's law; he had healed on the

Sabbath. This the church rulers said was work and the punishment for working on the Sabbath was death. The Lord rebuked them by saying that the priests, in accordance with the law of Moses, on occasions circumcised a baby on the Sabbath which was not considered sin. He was teaching that works of mercy and necessity could be carried out on the Sabbath that was made for man.

Christ concluded by telling the Jews to make righteous judgements as he did. In Isaiah 11:3,4 we read: 'His delight is in the fear of the LORD, and he shall not judge by the sight of his eyes, nor decide by the hearing of his ears; but with righteousness he shall judge the poor, and decide with equity for the meek of the earth.' Christ can see into the mind, something we cannot do. May we make careful, compassionate judgements concerning others.

THINGS TO DISCUSS WITH YOUR FAMILY

1. Read and discuss 1 Samuel 16:7: 'For the LORD does not see as man sees; for man looks at the outward appearance, but the LORD looks at the heart.'
2. Why did Jesus say, 'My doctrine is not mine, but his who sent me' (John 7:16)?
3. Was Christ wise in going up to Jerusalem? Discuss.

Meditation

Meditate upon the judgements you make of others. Have they been righteous and fair?

Wise Words

Never throw mud. You may miss your mark; but you must have dirty hands. *Joseph Parker*

　　　From where does this Man come?

'No one has ascended to heaven but he who came down from heaven, that is, the Son of Man who is in heaven' (John 3:13).

Read: John 7:25-36

Recently I received an e-mail from a person whose name I recognized, but that was all. I asked some friends if they knew who he was and received a variety of replies. Jesus had arrived in Jerusalem unbeknown to his family, but when some Jews saw him they questioned if he was the person the priests and Pharisees wanted to kill. Others heard him speak with authority, showing great knowledge, and suggested that the church leaders were treating him with respect because they acknowledged that he was the Messiah. Some people said they knew where Jesus was born, but that no one knew from where the Christ would come.

The people should have known from the Scriptures that Christ would be born in Bethlehem (Micah 5:2), having been sent into this sinful world by his heavenly Father. Jesus reminded the people that they did not know his Father. Elsewhere the Lord spoke to the people about the same matter: 'All things have been delivered to me by my Father, and no one knows the Son except the Father. Nor does anyone know the Father except the Son, and the one to whom the Son wills to reveal him' (Matthew 11:27).

The rulers decided to arrest Christ, but we read, 'but no one laid a hand on him, because his hour had not yet come'. God had foreordained all that was to happen to his Son, and his almighty power frustrated the evil plans of the church authorities.

We should be comforted by this. Every day when we hear of the violence and hatred in the world, we know that God rules all events to his own glory. Nothing happens but what God has ordained. David knew what it was to be despised by many people who would have been delighted to have him dead. Yet, as we read his words in Psalm 31:14-15 we should be comforted: 'But as for me, I trust in you, O Lord; I say, "You are my God." My times are in your hand; deliver me from the hand of my enemies, and from those who persecute me.'

When Pilate wanted to put Christ to death, the Lord told him that God ruled the affairs of this world: 'You could have no power at all against me unless it had been given you from above' (John 19:11).

Despite the opposition there were some who believed that Jesus was the Messiah and trusted their eternal security to him. The Lord told the people that soon he would return to his Father in heaven and then those who looked for him would not find him.

We must remember that the day of grace will one day end and unbelievers will have lost all hope of salvation. The writer of Proverbs warns every unrepentant person: 'Then they will call on me, but I will not answer; they will seek me diligently, but they will not find me' (Proverbs 1:28). May this never happen to you.

THINGS TO DISCUSS WITH YOUR FAMILY

1. Where did the Jews think Jesus might have been going? Why there?
2. Why were the officers unable to take Jesus a prisoner?
3. Why did Jesus know God intimately?

Meditation

Meditate upon God's control of the inhabitants of the earth. Consider Daniel 4:35: 'All the inhabitants of the earth are reputed as nothing; he does according to his will in the army of heaven and among the inhabitants of the earth. No one can restrain his hand or say to him, "What have you done?"'

Wise Words

Christ's consciousness of deity was not suspended during his earthly life. *Marvin R. Vincent*

'Blessed are those who hunger and thirst
for righteousness, for they shall be filled'
(Matthew 5:6).

Read: John 7:37-39

Recently, two young men left their workplace on a cattle sta-
tion to drive to a town several hundred miles away. When
they didn't arrive a search party was sent out. Sadly their bodies
were found several miles away from their broken-down car. Apparently, after the breakdown, they set out to walk along a rough track
hoping they would be found, but they had insufficient water with
them and died of thirst.

It was the final day of the Feast of Tabernacles and people were
getting ready to leave for their homes, no doubt disappointed as
Jesus had done nothing nor said anything to demonstrate that he
was the Messiah. The sacrifices were completed, the altar had been
washed clean of the blood and ash of the many sacrificed animals;
booths were pulled down and many family groups prepared to depart. Then Jesus stood up and began to speak with great authority.
Previously he had told the people he had come from heaven and
would soon return to his Father, but now there was a special invitation offered to the people: 'If anyone thirsts, let him come to me
and drink.' Obviously he was not talking about physical thirst, but
a thirst of the soul for salvation.

The Lord was inviting wayward people to turn to him and they
would find spiritual satisfaction. Before our conversion we are all
spiritually dead and need the gracious work of the Holy Spirit to
enliven our dead souls. The Philippian jailer is a good example of
one who was awakened to his sinful state and called out to Paul and
Silas, 'Sirs, what must I do to be saved?' (Acts 16:30). He had the
spiritual thirst about which Christ was now speaking.

In the Old Testament, sinners were directed to the water of
salvation. In Isaiah 12:3 we read, 'Therefore with joy you will draw
water from the wells of salvation.' Now One stood up and said, 'If
you want spiritual salvation don't go to some place where you think
you will find salvation, but come to me.'

Jesus Christ is the fountain of life to all who believe. The water of which he spoke was a saving faith, the work of the Holy Spirit, who while present in the world, awakening sinners to their need and bringing about the new birth, was soon to be poured out in a greater way than ever before. When born again the Christian longs for purity of heart and a growing Christ likeness. Consistent prayer and study of the Scriptures will help produce holiness of life and the longing to see Christ glorified in the world. The Christian's spiritual thirst will find perfect satisfaction in heaven when the redeemed are with their Saviour and made perfect in righteousness.

Not only does the Holy Spirit bring about a new heart, but he causes the new saint to bear such a witness to his salvation that the same Holy Spirit who indwelt him captures other prodigals for Christ. May God be pleased to use you to bring others to the Lord.

THINGS TO DISCUSS WITH YOUR FAMILY

1. Why is the Holy Spirit likened to water?
2. List some spiritual blessings that are given to those who go to Christ and 'drink'.
3. What makes people 'hunger and thirst for righteousness'?
4. In what way was the Holy Spirit active in Old Testament days?

Meditation

Think of the words of Isaiah 44:3: 'For I will pour water on him who is thirsty, and floods on the dry ground; I will pour my Spirit on your descendants, and my blessing on your offspring.'

Wise Words

The Holy Spirit is the great beautifier of souls.

John Owen

'But you, Bethlehem Ephrathah, though
you are little among the thousands of Judah, yet out of you shall come forth to
me the One to be ruler in Israel, whose
goings forth are from of old, from everlasting' (Micah 5:2).

Read: John 7:40-53

Many of us, especially as we age, see someone and then begin to wonder who the person is. We can usually remember
things about the person, where he lives and a few other facts, but try
as we might we still cannot recall the person's name.

Jesus was well known to the Jews. The people rejoiced to see
him in Jerusalem at the Feast of Tabernacles. They heard him speak
and knew the attitude of the church leaders to the compassionate
miracle healer. Yet the question still was, 'Who is this man, Jesus?
Is he the Messiah sent from God?'

There can be no doubt that Israel expected Christ to appear
at that time. They knew the prophecy of Daniel which indicated
a time period when Christ would appear (Daniel 9:24-27). Some
believed that if Jesus was the Messiah he would re-establish David's throne. Others saw the Lord as the great prophet prophesied
by Moses (Deuteronomy 18:15,18). Some who knew the Scriptures
said that the Christ would be born in Bethlehem, but believed that
Jesus was born in some other village. It was a pity they didn't bother
to ask Mary where her son, Jesus, was born.

There was much discussion concerning Christ, but the chief
priests and Pharisees sent officers to arrest him. These men failed to
take him into custody, saying to their masters, 'No man ever spoke
like this man!'

Jesus had been openly teaching in the temple and he did so
with authority, revealing a deep understanding of God's word. The
ordinary people could understand what he was saying. We need
ministers today who speak in the same way! However, the church
authorities had closed their minds to the truth. They saw Christ as
a demon-possessed imposter who had to be put to death. Despite
his teaching and compassionate treatment of the sick and hurting,
the church leaders wanted him out of the way. He had been working and preaching for about eighteen months and only one Pharisee
openly defended him.

When the rulers began to condemn Jesus it was Nicodemus who spoke up in his defence, 'Does our law judge a man before it hears him and knows what he is doing?' Throughout history only a few of the world's great ones have become followers of Christ. Paul wrote, 'But God has chosen the foolish things of the world to put to shame the wise, and God has chosen the weak things of the world to put to shame the things which are mighty; and the base things of the world and the things which are despised God has chosen, and the things which are not, to bring to nothing the things that are, that no flesh should glory in his presence' (1 Corinthians 1:27-29). Thank God for your salvation.

THINGS TO DISCUSS WITH YOUR FAMILY

1. Some church intellectuals said that no prophet came from Galilee. Were they correct? Read 2 Kings 14:25.
2. Discuss some features of the prophet spoken of in Deuteronomy 18:15-18.
3. Why did Nicodemus defend Jesus?

Meditation

The people were confused over the identity of Jesus. Meditate upon your understanding of Christ.

Wise Words

It is not always those who begin suddenly in religion, and profess themselves rejoicing Christians, who continue steadfast to the end.   *J. C. Ryle*

 'Marriage is honourable among all, and the bed undefiled; but fornicators and adulterers God will judge' (Hebrews 13:4).

Read: John 8:1-11

We live in an age where many people do not honour their marriage vows. Almost fifty percent of first marriages end in divorce and so many children grow up in homes with just one parent. We should take very seriously all oaths we make, and that includes marriage vows made before God, friends and relatives.

The Feast of Tabernacles had concluded and people were returning to their homes. Jesus had no home so he spent the night on the Mount of Olives resting and no doubt in prayer with his heavenly Father. The next morning he made his way to the temple where he again began to teach the people concerning the kingdom of God.

It wasn't long before he was interrupted by some scribes and Pharisees who dragged a poor, humiliated and frightened woman into his presence. They said, 'Teacher, this woman was caught in adultery, in the very act. Now Moses, in the law, commanded us that such should be stoned. But what do you say?' I have always wondered where was the man involved in this sin. We know that the scribes and Pharisees weren't really concerned about the woman's adultery but were trying to trap Jesus into saying something that could be used to bring him to trial.

Those with the woman called Jesus, 'Teacher', although the day before they had called him a deceiver. Everyone knew that the law of God stated that the death penalty for both parties was the punishment for adultery: 'The man who commits adultery with another man's wife, he who commits adultery with his neighbour's wife, the adulterer and the adulteress, shall surely be put to death' (Leviticus 20:10). For Jesus to have said this law was to be carried out would have caused the Roman authorities to arrest him, as they alone had the power to inflict capital punishment. To have said, 'Let her go free,' would have denied the authority of the law of Moses. Jesus knew the intention of the woman's accusers and made no reply to their question. He knelt down and began to write something in the dirt while more questions were asked of him.

Finally he said, 'He who is without sin among you, let him throw a stone at her first.' The law of Moses required, 'The hands of the witnesses shall be the first against him to put him to death, and afterward the hands of all the people. So you shall put away the evil from among you' (Deuteronomy 17:7). Jesus had not come to act as judge but to save sinners. He had taught that marriage was honourable and that the marriage vow was to be kept, except for one reason, sexual immorality.

The consciences of the woman's accusers were so powerful that they walked silently away, leaving the fearful, embarrassed woman standing before Jesus and the spectators. Jesus told the woman to go and show true repentance by sinning no more. May we never become involved in such a wicked scheme of trying to trap a person by his words.

THINGS TO DISCUSS WITH YOUR FAMILY

1. What are we taught in the seventh commandment?
2. How can you tell that the scribes and Pharisees were hypocrites?
3. Discuss Ephesians 5:3-4 — 'But fornication and all uncleanness or covetousness, let it not even be named among you, as is fitting for saints; neither filthiness, nor foolish talking, nor coarse jesting, which are not fitting, but rather giving of thanks.'

Meditation

Meditate upon what makes a good marriage partner.

Wise Words

The Christian married couple can be a powerful weapon in the hand of Jesus. *John Benton*

'In him [Christ] was life, and the life was the light of men. And the light shines in the darkness, and the darkness did not comprehend it' (John 1:4-5).

Read: John 8:12-20

Light is very important to us, although I knew a blind man who after worship went home, made a cup of tea, showered and went to bed without turning on the light. It all seemed so strange, but it saved on his electricity account.

Jesus now made one of his great 'I AM' statements — 'I am the light of the world.' This was one of Christ's claims that he was God in flesh and blood. He was the great 'I AM' who spoke to Moses at the burning bush (Exodus 3:14).

Many times we read that Jesus was God's light to the Gentiles, 'I will also give you as a light to the Gentiles, that you should be my salvation to the ends of the earth' (Isaiah 49:6). The Gentile nations had lived in spiritual darkness for thousands of years but now, as Isaiah wrote, something great was about to happen, 'Arise, shine; for your light has come! And the glory of the LORD is risen upon you. For behold, the darkness shall cover the earth, and deep darkness the people; but the LORD will arise over you, and his glory will be seen upon you. The Gentiles shall come to your light...' (Isaiah 60:1-3).

The Lord Jesus is God's remedy for the darkness of sin. To follow him is to believe in him and this means eternal life. As Jesus preached, the light of the truth showed sin for what it was and clearly lit up the pathway to Paradise. All of the elect are called from spiritual darkness into the Lord's glorious light. Peter wrote of the church, the bride of Christ, 'But you are a chosen generation, a royal priesthood, a holy nation, his own special people, that you may proclaim the praises of him who called you out of darkness into his marvellous light' (1 Peter 2:9).

We who follow Christ can rejoice in the words of the Apostle Peter: 'But if we walk in the light as he is in the light, we have fellowship with one another, and the blood of Jesus Christ his Son cleanses us from all sin' (1 John 1:7). This is salvation: forgiven by God because Christ bore our sin and shame upon that cursed cross, and walked that narrow pathway of holiness. Jesus, the light of life, leads the way, driving darkness out of our life.

Many didn't understand Jesus or what he was saying. They accused him of bearing false witness about himself. However, John the Baptist had openly declared him to be the Son of God, the Messiah, as did the disciples and others who believed in him. Jesus had a greater witness than just a few humans, as we are told in 1 John 5:9: 'If we receive the witness of men, the witness of God is greater; for this is the witness of God which he has testified of his Son.' As well, God had spoken from heaven that Jesus was his beloved Son and people had heard his voice (Mark 1:11; Matthew 17:5).

Jesus was one with his Father and for lost sinners to find their way to heaven they had to go through him. He said, 'I am the way, the truth, and the life. No one comes to the Father except through me' (John 14:6). Are you following the One who said, 'I am the light of the world'?

THINGS TO DISCUSS WITH YOUR FAMILY

1. Make a list of the times Jesus said 'I am...' With what did he compare himself each time?
2. Read and discuss 2 Corinthians 4:6.
3. What did Jesus mean when he told people to follow him? (John 8:12).

Meditation

Meditate upon 1 John 1:5: 'God is light and in him is no darkness at all.' How is Jesus the light of the world?

Wise Words

To follow Christ is to commit ourselves wholly and entirely to him as our only leader and Saviour, and to submit ourselves to him in every matter both of doctrine and practice. *J. C. Ryle*

'Do you not believe that I am in the Father, and the Father in me? The words that I speak to you I do not speak on my own authority; but the Father who dwells in me does the works' (John 14:10).

Read: John 8:21-30

I remember attending a mathematical lecture which left me totally confused; and I'm sure there were times when after a lesson there were some children who had little real understanding of what I was teaching. We come now to a passage of Christ's teaching that is difficult to comprehend.

Jesus told those with him that soon he would be leaving them. He would be going to a place where they could not find him. They would be left to die in their sins. Some of the Jews deduced from his words that he was going to commit suicide, but Jesus quickly rejected that idea. He stated that he came from above and was not of this world.

He warned his hearers that one day people would seek him, but fail in their search. In Proverbs 1:28-30: 'Then they will call on me, but I will not answer; they will seek me diligently, but they will not find me. Because they hated knowledge and did not choose the fear of the LORD, they would have none of my counsel.' Later the Jews, when cast off by God because they killed the King of Glory, found God's ear closed when they cried for mercy. They still would not believe that Jesus was the Christ. What a tragedy. Don't make a mess of your life by living for the things of the world and rejecting Christ's call to repentance.

All who believe in Jesus as Lord and Saviour are not of this world, and the victory is theirs: 'Who is he who overcomes the world, but he who believes that Jesus is the Son of God?' (1 John 5:5). All unbelievers are of this world and hate the truth. Jesus is from above and is one with his heavenly Father. He spoke the words that God gave him and carried out God's foreordained works that would lead to the salvation of unbelievers.

The God and Father of Jesus is described in Micah 7:18: 'Who is a God like you, pardoning iniquity and passing over the transgression of the remnant of his heritage? He does not retain his anger for ever, because he delights in mercy.' This describes the Lord Jesus perfectly, but the Pharisees and church officials rejected him. Their god was a harsh cold god who demanded salvation by keeping the law, which was an impossibility. These people, who believed they were God's elect, would crucify Jesus.

We are warned to escape the judgement of God by faith in his Son, the Lord Jesus. He warned all unbelievers of their perilous plight — 'he who does not believe will be condemned' (Mark 16:16). This is the condemnation of eternal hell, where 'their worm does not die and the fire is not quenched' (Mark 9:46). May you be on the pathway that leads to Paradise.

THINGS TO DISCUSS WITH YOUR FAMILY

1. Discuss J. C. Ryle's words: 'Hell is truth known too late.'
2. Why is there a Paradise?
3. Discuss Psalm 66:18: 'If I regard iniquity in my heart, the Lord will not hear.'

Meditation

Meditate upon the words of Acts 1:9: 'Now when he had spoken these things, while they watched, he was taken up, and a cloud received him out of their sight.'

Wise Words

God is transcendent above all his works even while he is immanent within them. He is here and the whole universe is alive with his life! *A. W. Tozer*

'Stand fast therefore in the liberty by which Christ has made us free, and do not be entangled again with a yoke of bondage' (Galatians 5:1).

Read: John 8:31-36

It is hard to believe that today slavery still exists in parts of the world. It is a wonderful privilege to live in a country where there is freedom to speak, move about and openly worship God. Today our reading is about freedom, but a freedom that comes from faith in Christ our Saviour.

When Jesus said that the truth he spoke freed sinners, the Jews misinterpreted him and claimed that as God's elect, descendants of Abraham, they had never been in bondage to anyone. They conveniently overlooked the times when they were slaves in Egypt and Babylon, and they were then subject to the rule of the Roman Empire.

Jesus had to correct their understanding of what he was teaching. He said that to be his disciples it was necessary to believe in him as the Son of God and the Saviour of the spiritually lost. This faith broke the power of Satan in their lives and gave them a spiritual freedom by which they could worship and serve God. When Jesus commenced his preaching he read from Isaiah 61:1-2, which spoke of his work of setting free prisoners of sin: 'The Spirit of the LORD is upon me, because he has anointed me to preach the gospel to the poor; he has sent me to heal the broken-hearted, to preach deliverance to the captives and recovery of sight to the blind, to set at liberty those who are oppressed; to preach the acceptable year of the LORD' (Luke 4:18,19).

Many times we read of the spiritual freedom that comes from faith in Christ. The Apostle Paul wrote, 'Do you not know that to whom you present yourselves slaves to obey, you are that one's slaves whom you obey, whether of sin leading to death, or of obedience leading to righteousness?' (Romans 6:16).

A God-given saving faith in the Lord Jesus means you are justified, forgiven and clothed in the righteousness of Christ; no longer are you a member of Satan's kingdom, but a citizen of the kingdom of God with the freedom to worship and glorify God your Saviour. No one can lay a charge against you, just as Paul wrote, 'Who shall bring a charge against God's elect? It is God who justifies' (Romans 8:33).

Even death and the grave cannot hold us captive. Our Saviour died and his body was placed in a tomb, but on the third day he rose again. We read words of encouragement to us: 'O Death, where is your sting? O [grave], where is your victory?' (1 Corinthians 15:55). Christ's victory over death is ours also.

Christians have every reason to rejoice in Christ, for we read, 'And because you are sons, God has sent forth the Spirit of his Son into your hearts, crying out, "Abba, Father!" Therefore you are no longer a slave but a son, and if a son, then an heir of God through Christ' (Galatians 4:6,7). We are free from sin's dominion, praise the Lord!

THINGS TO DISCUSS WITH YOUR FAMILY

1. What is meant by 'liberty of conscience'?
2. What is spiritual freedom?
3. How can you gain spiritual freedom?

Meditation

If you are a Christian think upon the words of Galatians 4:6-7: 'And because you are sons, God has sent forth the Spirit of his Son into your hearts, crying out, "Abba, Father!" Therefore you are no longer a slave but a son, and if a son, then an heir of God through Christ.'

Wise Words

Opinions alter, but truth certified by God can no more change than the God who uttered it.   *C. H. Spurgeon*

'For he is not a Jew who is one out-wardly, nor is circumcision that which is outward in the flesh; but he is a Jew who is one inwardly; and circumcision is that of the heart, in the Spirit, not in the letter...' (Romans 2:28-29).

Read: John 8:37-47

The Jews were proud of their ancestry as are most people. To-day many people spend years researching their family history. Sometimes exciting discoveries are made concerning famous fore-bears; at other times findings are seemingly insignificant.

While acknowledging that in the flesh the Jews were descend-ed from Abraham, by their behaviour and thoughts they showed their spiritual father was Satan, the great enemy of Christ. It was he who wanted Christ put to death and that was something Abraham would never have wanted. Jesus stated that Lucifer was both a liar and murderer from the very beginning. With all the false accusa-tions the Jews made of Jesus, he challenged them: 'Which of you convicts me of sin?' Of course there was no reply, despite the Phari-sees believing he had broken their Sabbath regulations.

In the Garden of Eden, Satan deceived Eve by saying God was a liar. Having been told that to eat the fruit of the tree of the knowl-edge of good and evil would cause death, he said, 'You will not surely die' (Genesis 3:4). No sooner had they tasted the forbidden fruit than they died spiritually and their bodies commenced a jour-ney that would end in the grave. Today Satan stalks about 'like a roaring lion, seeking whom he may devour' (1 Peter 5:8), and doing all he can to have people walk the broad way that leads to eternal death.

Christians, we are to fight against the evil one just as James wrote: 'Resist the devil and he will flee from you' (James 4:7). Our assurance of victory is 'because he who is in you is greater than he who is in the world' (1 John 4:4). The Holy Spirit who dwells in believers is all powerful.

The Jews thought that with Abraham as their ancestor and citizenship in God's elect nation, they were assured of eternal life. There are people today who think the same way. They look back to godly ancestors, their own church attendance, baptism, sitting at the Lord's table, having a sound knowledge of the Scriptures, and consider that they are spiritually secure. Friends, it is a saving relationship with Jesus Christ that gives eternal life and security.

Jesus outlined the marks of a Christian and we should look carefully at them to ensure we are numbered amongst his people. Do you believe what Christ is teaching us? You have your Bibles! Don't just read them, but believe what you read, as it is the Word of the living God. Jesus asked the Jews if God was their heavenly Father because a mark of this would be seen in their love of his Son. Do you love the Lord Jesus? Do you love God with all your heart?

May God fill you with love for himself and love for your fellow man. May your life be filled with works of righteousness, always aimed at honouring the Saviour.

THINGS TO DISCUSS WITH YOUR FAMILY

1. Can Christians claim to have Abraham as their father? Discuss Romans 4:11-12 and Galatians 3:29.
2. Jesus said that the Jews didn't listen to the truth he taught. What about you?
3. What two marks of a Christian are given in John 10:27?

Meditation

Consider Christ's words in John 8:44: 'You are of your father the devil, and the desires of your father you want to do. He was a murderer from the beginning, and does not stand in the truth, because there is no truth in him. When he speaks a lie, he speaks from his own resources, for he is a liar and the father of it.'

He who gives over never truly began.   *William Jenkyn*

Wise Words

 'And God said to Moses, "I AM WHO I AM." And he said, "Thus you shall say to the children of Israel, 'I AM' has sent me to you'" (Exodus 3:14).

Read: John 8:48-59

It is most unpleasant when people attack our character and make us out to be the worst type of person. When this happens our prayer should be that of the psalmist: 'Deliver my soul, O LORD, from lying lips and from a deceitful tongue' (Psalm 120:2).

From today's reading you can see that Jesus was again under attack by the Jews who had heard his preaching and witnessed all his compassionate miracles. Again he was accused of being demon-possessed while others called him a 'Samaritan'. The Jews hated the Samaritans and used the name as a derogatory term about another person. The woman to whom Jesus spoke at Jacob's well had said, 'Jews have no dealings with Samaritans' (John 4:9). Jesus showed the most patient nature just as the apostle Peter wrote: '...when he was reviled, he did not revile in return; when he suffered, he did not threaten, but committed himself to him who judges righteously' (1 Peter 2:23).

Jesus was being dishonoured by the very people who should have welcomed him and thanked God for his coming. However, he was more concerned about the veneration of his heavenly Father who was being dishonoured when he was being ridiculed. Jesus reminded the Jews that he received the greatest recognition possible, that from his heavenly Father. Our aim as Christians must be to glorify God. In turn he will honour us because we love his Son and faithfully obey his laws.

Christ spoke words of encouragement to all his suffering people: 'Most assuredly, I say to you, if anyone keeps my word he shall never see death.' Obviously he was speaking of the second death — eternal hell. Hell is a fearful home for all those who do not have a saving faith in him; we read that all such people 'have their part in the lake which burns with fire and brimstone, which is the second death' (Revelation 21:8).

Many times Jesus had said that those who believed in him had eternal life. What a joy! Because of his sacrificial death for his people he freed 'those who through fear of death were all their lifetime subject to bondage' (Hebrews 2:15).

The Jews objected to Christ saying that those who believed him should not die. They pointed to Abraham, saying that he was dead. Yet Jesus stated plainly that Abraham had looked forward to the day of his saving work and, although seeing it dimly, had rejoiced at what was to take place. Christ, as the Angel of Jehovah, the Second Person of the Godhead, had spoken to Abraham before the destruction of Sodom, and with Abraham had established an eternal covenant, part of which promised that through his 'Seed' great blessings would come to the world.

When the Jews laughed at what he was saying, Jesus said, 'Most assuredly, I say to you, before Abraham was, I AM.' Here was Jesus' claim that he was God in flesh and blood. For this claim the Jews took up stones to throw at him, but by a miracle he passed safely from them.

THINGS TO DISCUSS WITH YOUR FAMILY

1. What does the name 'I AM' mean?
2. Why was Abraham so greatly respected by the Jews? Read Hebrews 11:8-19.
3. Read and discuss Colossians 1:17: 'And he is before all things, and in him all things consist.'

Meditation

Meditate upon the eternity of God, the great 'I AM.' Read John 11:7 — 'Can you search out the deep things of God? Can you find out the limits of the Almighty?'

God is not the great 'I WAS'; he is the great 'I AM.'

Eric Alexander

Wise Words

A blind man healed

'In that day the deaf shall hear the words of the book, and the eyes of the blind shall see out of obscurity and out of darkness' (Isaiah 29:18).

Read: John 9:1-12

During my teaching days there were times when I had to go over some lessons many times so that everyone could understand. In fact, even now I have to read some articles several times before I understand what the author is saying.

The Pharisees, other religious groups, and the people generally had seen so much proof that Jesus was their Messiah, and yet it did not penetrate their cold, hard hearts. Your reading from John was another proof that Jesus is the Christ, yet the Pharisees refused to believe.

A short time before this, Jesus had said that he was the light of the world, and now he was about to perform a miracle that would give a man both physical and spiritual sight. The disciples wanted to know why the man was born blind, as they thought it must have been punishment for his sins or that of his parents. All of our sicknesses, diseases and death are the result of sin. In the Garden of Eden, Adam was warned that he would die if he broke God's law. Of course, some sicknesses are the result of particular sins. I have read of a thief who climbed a ladder to break into a house. With his bag of stolen goods he slipped while descending the ladder and broke his leg when he hit the ground. He knew which sin had caused his broken leg!

Jesus told the disciples that the man's blindness would be used to glorify God. Soon his day of carrying out the work that his Father had given him to do would come to an end. He would be crucified, and after his resurrection would ascend to heaven to govern the world for the benefit of the saints and the glory of God. You and I need to remember this, for our days will be completed and we will die. As Christians, we must do the good works that God would have us do and so bring glory to our Saviour. In his letter to the Philippians, Paul told the saints: '...work out your own salvation with fear and trembling; for it is God who works in you both to will and to do for his good pleasure' (Philippians 2:12-13).

Jesus carried out this healing in an unusual manner. He made some clay, which he placed over the man's eyelids, and told him to wash it away in a local pool, the pool of Siloam. The man obeyed; when he washed away the clay he could see. Do you remember Elisha telling Naaman, who had leprosy, to wash seven times in the Jordan River and he would be healed? Naaman thought this was a stupid prescription, but when his servants encouraged him to go and wash, he did so and was healed. Naaman and the blind man had something in common — they obeyed the one responsible for their healing. We should take note of God's blessing for obedience.

The blind man was healed and people were amazed. They wanted to know who was responsible for this miracle, but all the man could say was, 'A Man called Jesus...'

Do you know this 'Man called Jesus'? I pray that you do.

THINGS TO DISCUSS WITH YOUR FAMILY

1. How did the blind man get money to buy food?
2. What is spiritual blindness?
3. Again we read of Christ's almighty power. Read and discuss Matthew 28:18.

Meditation

Meditate upon the almighty power of God and 'Praise him for his mighty acts; praise him according to his excellent greatness!' (Psalm 150:2).

Wise Words

Grant me God and miracles take care of themselves.

A. W. Tozer

August

'I am the LORD, that is my name; and my glory I will not give to another' (Isaiah 42:8).

Read: John 9:13-25

Once, in discussion with another Christian about the right use of the Lord's Day, I suggested that the man use the day for good works. He had outlined to me a list of things I should not do, but I suggested that he could spend some time writing letters to overseas missionaries. He replied, 'There are better days than the Lord's Day for that sort of thing.' To him the Lord's Day was a day for worship and rest — not works of necessity and mercy.

The Pharisees had the same problem. People found it hard to believe that one born blind could have his sight restored in such a way, and the Pharisees considered the healing a great sin because it had been carried out on the Sabbath. They argued that Jesus was not the Christ because he did not obey God's commandments. What they really meant was that Jesus had not obeyed the rules and regulations they had made. The Pharisees permitted medical attention on the Sabbath, but only in cases of extreme urgency. They believed this did not fit the case of the man who had been blind for a lifetime — another day would have been more suitable for such a healing.

When the Pharisees found the man, they demanded to know what he knew about Jesus. They were told that he believed Jesus to be 'a prophet'. Possibly this was a reference to the prophet foretold by Moses — 'I will raise up for them a Prophet like you from among their brethren, and will put my words in his mouth, and he shall speak to them all that I command him and it shall be that whoever will not hear my words, which he speaks in my name, I will require it of him' (Deuteronomy 18:18-19).

The Pharisees were greatly disturbed that the healed man was giving glory to Jesus for what had happened so they demanded of him that he give the glory to God, not this supposed demon-possessed healer. However, every word spoken honouring Christ glorifies God who gave his Son to save sinners. Jesus had clearly said, '...all should honour the Son just as they honour the Father. He who does not honour the Son does not honour the Father who sent him' (John 5:23). Our text tells us that praise must be given to Jehovah, and as Jesus Christ is the Second Person of the Godhead, he is Jehovah. In Isaiah 6:3 we read of the holy angels surrounding the heavenly throne upon which Christ sat, calling out, 'Holy, holy, holy is the LORD of hosts; the whole earth is full of his glory!' The Apostle John said that this was a vision Isaiah had of Jesus before he entered the world (John 12:35-41).

The Pharisees were blind leaders of the blind, yet when the parents of the healed man were called to give an account of their son and his blindness, they were afraid and said they should speak to him. No doubt they feared spiritual isolation from the local synagogue if they dared to speak out against the Pharisees who were greatly respected by the people.

Let us be on guard against spiritual error and always stand firm for Christ and his majesty. He still performs miracles. Every Christian has experienced the miracle of receiving a new heart. Have you?

THINGS TO DISCUSS WITH YOUR FAMILY

1. Why did the Pharisees object to Christ's healing of the blind man on the Sabbath?
2. What was wrong with the Pharisees telling the healed blind man to give God the glory for the healing? Read John 9:24.
3. Why did the healed man say that Jesus was a prophet? Read John 9:17.

Meditation

Think upon the words of Exodus 15:11.

Wise Words

The Day of the Lord is likely to be a dreadful day to them that despise the Lord's Day. *George Swinnock*

'You number my wanderings; put my
tears into your bottle; are they not in
your book?' (Psalm 56:8).

Read: John 9:26-41

W hen you enter your church building, look about you and notice those who have gathered with you to worship God. I
am sure you will find that most are ordinary, middle and lower-class
working people. I do not think you will find too many of the well-
known, important people sitting with you. The Apostle Paul gives us a
reason for this: 'For you see your calling, brethren, that not many wise
according to the flesh, not many mighty, not many noble, are called.
But God has chosen the foolish things of the world to put to shame
the wise, and God has chosen the weak things of the world to put to
shame the things which are mighty ... that no flesh should glory in
his presence' (1 Corinthians 1:26-29). For some reason known only
to God, the majority of sinners he has chosen for salvation are the
nobodies of this world.

The majority of the proud Pharisees, who were greatly respected
by the Jews, had no place in the kingdom of God. They were very
harsh in their treatment of the healed man. Instead of praising Jesus
they spoke of him with contempt. When the healed man believed in
Jesus, the Son of God, and aligned himself with the despised disciples,
the Pharisees expelled him from the synagogue. This meant he was
a spiritual and social outcast. He was suffering persecution from the
cruel Pharisees, who should have been showing kindness and compassion to the man in need.

The healed blind man believed the truth, but the rich, proud
Pharisees who had a great say in the affairs of the church, were strangers to the grace of God and the truth concerning Jesus. They rebuked
the man saying, that while he was a disciple of Jesus, they were disciples of the great lawgiver — Moses. However, Jesus indicated that it
was the Pharisees who were spiritually blind. They claimed that Jesus
did not come from God.

All of Christ's disciples suffer persecution because they believe in him, but today's text has words of comfort. God does not forget the hurt done to his people. The psalmist asked God to collect all of his tears in a bottle, which could be used on the Day of Judgement as proof in the Lord's righteous condemnation of those who had persecuted him because of his faith in God.

When you are being tormented for being a Christian remember God's words in Isaiah 41:10, 13: 'Fear not, for I am with you; be not dismayed, for I am your God. I will strengthen you, yes, I will help you, I will uphold you with my righteous right hand ... For I, the LORD your God, will hold your right hand, saying to you, "Fear not, I will help you."'

Let us trust Jesus in all circumstances of life; he has promised never to forsake his people (Hebrews 13:5). In our Saviour we are eternally secure.

THINGS TO DISCUSS WITH YOUR FAMILY

1. How should we deal with those who persecute us?
2. Was it fair that the healed man should have been expelled from the synagogue?
3. Discuss Isaiah 50:6 — 'I gave my back to those who struck me, and my cheeks to those who plucked out the beard; I did not hide my face from shame and spitting.'

Meditation

Think upon John 9:31 — 'Now we know that God does not hear sinners; but if anyone is a worshipper of God and does his will, he hears him.'

Wise Words

Let us use diligently whatever religious knowledge we possess, and ask continually that God would give us more. *J. C. Ryle*

'For he is our God, and we are the people of his pasture, and the sheep of his hand' (Psalm 95:7).

Read: John 10:1-9

In Australia, where flocks of sheep number thousands, shepherds don't lead them about nor do they know them all by name. They are rounded up by dogs and men on motorbikes. Life for the sheep is tough as they have no secure sheepfold in which to spend the night in safety from dingoes and the cold.

Our reading is a continuation of Christ's talk to the Pharisees, who were very critical of him because of his healing of the blind man on the Sabbath. Here Christ again rebukes them as false leaders of the Jewish people. The Pharisees were unsure of what Christ was saying to them, despite being students of the Old Testament and descendants of godly Abraham.

Christ likened believing Jews to sheep within a sheepfold who were cared for by God's prophets and godly 'shepherds'. Now to be a true leader of God's sheep, it was essential that they enter the sheepfold through the God-appointed Door — the Lord Jesus Christ. When Jesus said, 'I am the door,' he was again claiming to be God. He used the name of God given to Moses at the burning bush — 'I AM' (Exodus 3:14).

To enter the fold by some other way — climbing over or crawling under the fence — was the behaviour of a thief who wanted to steal the sheep. This was like the Pharisees who had rejected Christ as the Son of God and Saviour of sinners. To them he was not a mediator between God and man, as they considered that they, with the church priests, occupied that spiritual position.

Jesus said that the 'sheep' within the sheepfold, the elect, took no notice of the voice of the false guides. They knew the true Shepherd. After all they had heard his words many times and listened when he called them by name. These sheep followed their trusted guide through the doorway as they knew they were safe with him. Moses had asked God for such a protector: 'Let the LORD, the God of the spirits of all flesh, set a man over the congregation, who may go out before them and go in before them, who may lead them out and bring them in, that the congregation of the LORD may not be like sheep which have no shepherd' (Numbers 27:16-17). The immediate answer to this prayer was Joshua, who was a type of the great Shepherd, the Lord Jesus.

All Christians should understand this. Christ is not only the true guide of the sheep but the 'Door' which leads to eternal spiritual security. Jesus said, 'I am the way, the truth, and the life. No one comes to the Father except through me' (John 14:6).

We must also ensure that we attend a church that has a true spiritual elder as its pastor. We want a minister who is converted, loves Jesus and wants to see people won into the kingdom of God. We want a pastor whose great desire is to see our Saviour glorified. May God bless us with such a man.

THINGS TO DISCUSS WITH YOUR FAMILY

1. Why did the sheep not follow false spiritual guides?
2. In what way is Jesus the 'true shepherd' of his sheep?
3. What are the marks of God's 'sheep'?

Meditation

Meditate upon Psalm 100:3 — 'We are his people and the sheep of his pasture.'

Wise Words

Unconverted ministers are the dry-rot of the church.

J. C. Ryle

'He will feed his flock like a shepherd; he will gather the lambs with his arm, and carry them in his bosom, and gently lead those who are with young' (Isaiah 40:11).

Read: John 10:10-21

In the time of the white settlement in Australia, shepherds accompanied their flocks, living with them in the open fields, protecting them from attack by dingoes and eagles. They would be considered good shepherds. Today in our reading we read of the best Shepherd the universe has, the Lord Jesus Christ.

Jesus said, 'I am the good shepherd' because he is the One who ensures the security of those he calls his 'sheep'. Christ's 'sheep' are the elect — those given to him by his heavenly Father. He tells all who listen that he came into the world to ensure that they would have eternal life. However, he went beyond simply teaching that his people would live for ever, but said their life would be abundant. Eternal life will be an eternity with God displaying his glory, love and majesty.

Sadly, the Jews were being taught spiritual falsehood by blind shepherds. They led the people along the broad road that leads to hell. In Isaiah 56:11 we read a description of the false shepherds: 'Yes, they are greedy dogs which never have enough. And they are shepherds who cannot understand; they all look to their own way, every one for his own gain, from his own territory'.

Those false shepherds despised the 'good Shepherd' and wanted him put to death. Zechariah prophesied of this situation: '"Awake, O sword, against my Shepherd, against the Man who is my Companion," says the LORD of hosts. "Strike the Shepherd, and the sheep will be scattered"' (Zechariah 13:7).

Jesus said that he was loved by his Father. He was the Second Person of the Godhead and one with his Father and the Holy Spirit. At the time of his baptism the Father had spoken of his love for his Son: 'This is my beloved Son, in whom I am well pleased' (Matthew 3:17). Jesus had perfectly obeyed his heavenly Father and was to be greatly rewarded. Paul wrote, 'Therefore God also has highly exalted him and given him the name which is above every name' (Philippians 2:9).

Jesus' sacrificial life and death was not just to save God's chosen 'sheep' of Israel but those from another fold, the Gentile nations. When the Jews crucified the Lord, the gospel was taken to the surrounding nations, again a fulfilment of the words of Malachi, '"For from the rising of the sun, even to its going down, my name shall be great among the Gentiles; in every place incense shall be offered to my name, and a pure offering; for my name shall be great among the nations," says the LORD of hosts' (Malachi 1:11).

After listening to Jesus many said that he was demon-possessed. Others replied that a demon-possessed person couldn't open the eyes of the blind.

One message from our reading is to ensure that the earthly shepherd of our souls is one who loves Christ and longs to see wayward people saved.

THINGS TO DISCUSS WITH YOUR FAMILY

1. Who are the 'other sheep' spoken of by Christ in John 10:16?
2. Who today are the false shepherds? How can you tell?
3. Why is Jesus loved by his heavenly Father?

Meditation

Meditate upon the love of God and his compassion being beyond your comprehension.

Wise Words

We are not chosen because we are good; we are chosen that we may be good.   *B. B. Warfield*

'Two are better than one, because they have a good reward for their labour. For if they fall, one will lift up his companion. But woe to him who is alone when he falls, for he has no one to help him up' (Ecclesiastes 4:9-10).

Read: Luke 10:1-16

Most congregations today have one pastor, yet so often we read in the New Testament that disciples went about their preaching duties in pairs. Is there something that we can learn from this?

The Lord now had seventy disciples who had been well taught and were ready to undertake the work of preaching the gospel to the people of Israel. As there were many souls to be 'harvested' and so few to carry out this work, Jesus told the disciples to pray that 'the Lord of the harvest' might send out many more labourers. All Christians are to be involved in harvesting unbelievers into the kingdom of God, but few have the necessary speaking gifts to be pastors; nevertheless, we can all pray and witness. Prayer has been the means of accomplishing many great works. In James 5:16 we read encouraging words, 'The effective, fervent prayer of a righteous man avails much.'

The apostles were so involved in their many duties that they found their prayer time limited. Consequently they had deacons elected to carry out physical work such as ensuring that all widows received help. This was a great spiritual benefit to the apostles who said, 'We will give ourselves continually to prayer and to the ministry of the word' (Acts 6:4).

As the twelve disciples had been sent out on a similar work, the seventy were told to depend upon good people for their support. They were not to carry money or spare clothing with them. Where they received a welcome to stay with a family, they were to bless and pray the peace of God upon all the household.

This meant there was to be no show of worldliness, but a complete dependence upon those who were believers. We must also remember this when we receive our wages, for we have a responsibility to support our minister and his family and the work of the church. The Apostle Paul wrote, 'Even so, the Lord has commanded that those who preach the gospel should live from the gospel' (1 Corinthians

9:14). Yes, 'the labourer is worthy of his wages' (1 Timothy 5:18).

The seventy were warned of the opposition they would face when they preached the gospel. Jesus said he was sending them out as 'lambs among wolves'. John told us the same: 'Do not marvel, my brethren, if the world hates you' (1 John 3:13). If the welcome mat was not extended, the disciples were told to move on to another township. Jesus told them that on Judgement Day the eternal punishment imposed upon sinful Sodom and Tyre would be mild compared to that handed down to the local towns and cities that turned their backs upon the Son of God and his message of salvation.

And the message to be preached was, 'The kingdom of God has come near you.' Messiah had come and entrance into the kingdom was through faith in him.

THINGS TO DISCUSS WITH YOUR FAMILY

1. Discuss Luke 10:16: 'He who hears you hears me, he who rejects you rejects me, and he who rejects me rejects him who sent me.'
2. Read and discuss Luke 12:47–48.
3. Why did Jesus send the disciples out in pairs?

Meditation

Consider Christ's words to his disciples: 'Behold, I send you out as lambs among wolves' (Luke 10:3).

Wise Words

When men try to extinguish the light of the gospel it burns more brightly. *Henry T. Mahan*

'There shall come forth a Rod from the stem of Jesse, and a Branch shall grow out of his roots. The Spirit of the LORD shall rest upon him, the Spirit of wisdom and understanding, the Spirit of counsel and might, the Spirit of knowledge and of the fear of the LORD' (Isaiah 11:1-2).

Read: Luke 10:17-24

Do you remember those days when you had to hand your school report to your parents? During my school days we had to take an envelope to school and then take it home for mum and dad to open. Many were the times I carefully sneaked a look before handing it to my parents. In those days steam from the boiling jug softened the glue, making it possible to open an envelope undetected — it does not work now!

We read that the seventy disciples returned to Christ with great rejoicing. They had found that they could perform miracles in the Lord's name, even casting out demons. The good news of the kingdom of God had been preached and some hearers had become true believers. For the first and possibly only time in the New Testament we read: 'Jesus rejoiced.' There were occasions when Jesus wept, but this time we read that he rejoiced. Why?

He was glad because he could see that Satan's power was being destroyed and God was being glorified. In the wilderness temptations, Satan retreated a defeated foe; demons were being cast out of people and citizens of his evil kingdom were being won into the kingdom of God. Jesus could see that after his resurrection and ascension the devil would be thrown out of heaven by the great archangel Michael (Revelation 12:7-9).

Despite the power of the seventy over Lucifer and his demons, the Lord told them they had a greater reason to rejoice, and that was because their names were 'written in heaven'. All Christians have this reason for thanking God, for it is a declaration that they are the elect of God and have their names 'written in the Lamb's Book of Life' (Revelation 21:27).

Jesus rejoiced because of his salvation of sinners, and praised God that so many believers were not the great ones of the earth, but the poor, the hated tax collectors and vile sinners. The ordinary people were looked down upon by those who believed themselves to be the wise of the world. Isaiah records God's words upon this subject: 'For thus says the high and lofty One who inhabits eternity, whose name is Holy: "I dwell in the high and holy place, with him who has a contrite and humble spirit, to revive the spirit of the humble, and to revive the heart of the contrite ones"' (Isaiah 57:15).

Again Jesus spoke of the perfect relationship that existed in the Godhead. The Father had given his Son all power in heaven and on earth (Matthew 28:18), the authority to be judge of mankind (John 5:27) and the right to give eternal life to all those given to him (John 17:2). In his teaching with his disciples and believers generally Jesus was revealing the majestic truths about his heavenly Father, truths that you and I should know through our reading of the Scriptures. The disciples had firsthand knowledge of the great prophecies made by the prophets of old who foretold the coming of Christ to save the lost. We now know the reality of what they wrote. We live in a golden spiritual age!

THINGS TO DISCUSS WITH YOUR FAMILY

1. Discuss any Old Testament prophecy you know concerning the kingdom of God.
2. Why was Satan cast out of heaven as recorded in Revelation 12?
3. Why did Jesus rejoice when he heard the reports from the seventy disciples?

Meditation

Meditate upon Christ's victory over Satan and what you are doing in the battle.

Wise Words

The word 'Trinity' is not found in the Bible, but the truth of this doctrine is in every part of the book.

Donald Grey Barnhouse

'To the law and to the testimony! If they do not speak according to this word, it is because there is no light in them' (Isaiah 8:20).

Read: Luke 10:25-28

Even though our children are grown up and Val, Tootsie and I have the house to ourselves, we still have some rules that we carry out — if we remember. Before coming inside we take off our shoes to save the carpet from becoming dirty. Tootsie ignores this rule, however!

Our God has given us a book containing his laws which if obeyed would make the world a much better place. Sadly there are professing Christians who believe they can have Christ as Saviour, but not as Lord. This is not so as Christians acknowledge Jesus as both Lord and Saviour. Paul wrote of God's law in glowing terms — '... the law is holy, and the commandment holy and just and good' (Romans 7:12).

You and I need to read our Bibles, believe what we read and practise the truth we find. The apostle Paul wrote to Timothy, '... from childhood you have known the Holy Scriptures, which are able to make you wise for salvation through faith which is in Christ Jesus' (2 Timothy 3:15).

In our reading, a Jewish lawyer, a student of the Old Testament, approached Jesus to ask what is probably the most important question that any person can ask: 'Teacher, what shall I do to inherit eternal life?' Do you know the answer to this question? If not go and speak to a Christian pastor or friend and find out the answer as your eternal salvation depends upon your relationship with Christ. The lawyer who asked this question had a wrong motive for what he did. He was trying to get Jesus to reply in a way that could be used against him.

When Jesus asked the man to answer his own question the lawyer quoted two passages from the Old Testament: 'You shall love the LORD your God with all your heart, with all your soul, with all your strength, and with all your mind,' and 'your neighbour as yourself' (Deuteronomy 6:5 and Leviticus 19:18). Elsewhere Jesus said of this statement concerning the law — 'On these two commandments hang all the Law and the Prophets' (Matthew 22:40).

The lawyer knew his Bible and what he said was so true. Jesus said to him, 'You have answered rightly; do this and you will live.' But his problem was that he was unable to perfectly keep the commandments as God required. Today most people are like that lawyer and walk the broad way that leads to eternal punishment. They believe that by doing their best they will win God's favour and eternal life, but this cannot be.

Before Jesus could add to his words the lawyer had another question which showed that he had a problem concerning the interpretation of the term 'neighbour.' He needed to hear Christ's call, 'Come to me, all you who labour and are heavy laden, and I will give you rest. Take my yoke upon you and learn from me, for I am gentle and lowly in heart, and you will find rest for your souls' (Matthew 11:28,29).

Do you love God and your neighbour? Is Jesus Christ your Lord and Saviour?

THINGS TO DISCUSS WITH YOUR FAMILY

1. How do you know the lawyer was not sincere in the question he asked Jesus?
2. What did Christ mean when he said, 'Take my yoke upon you' (Matthew 11:29)?
3. What is meant by 'eternal life'?

Meditation

Meditate upon Proverbs 9:10: 'The fear of the LORD is the beginning of wisdom, and the knowledge of the Holy One is understanding.'

Wise Words

Love to God and obedience to God are so completely involved in each other that any one of them implies the other too. *F. F. Bruce*

467

'Then the Jews answered and said to him, "Do we not say rightly that you are a Samaritan and have a demon?"' (John 8:48).

Read: Luke 10:29-37

I can remember the days after the second world war when many migrants came to Australia. At school we called them 'Balts' as many came from the Baltic region. This usually happened when we were angry. It was then a derogatory name. In our text Jesus was called a 'Samaritan' which was a name of those the Jews abhorred.

Now Jesus had agreed with the lawyer who repeated the great Old Testament laws of God, but Jesus knew that he had not kept them. Having said that he was to love his neighbour he asked, 'And who is my neighbour?' As a student of the Old Testament he should have known the answer to his question for we read in Leviticus 19:34: 'The stranger who dwells among you shall be to you as one born among you, and you shall love him as yourself; for you were strangers in the land of Egypt: I am the LORD your God.' In Exodus 23:4,5 we read that help was even to be given to an enemy: 'If you meet your enemy's ox or his donkey going astray, you shall surely bring it back to him again. If you see the donkey of one who hates you lying under its burden, and you would refrain from helping it, you shall surely help him with it.'

Despite the law of God, the Jews treated the Samaritans with contempt. When Jesus spoke to the woman from Sychar she was surprised at Christ's request for a drink. She said, 'For Jews have no dealings with Samaritans' (John 4:9). When Jesus asked for accommodation in a Samaritan village, while on his way to Jerusalem he was refused (Luke 9:52,53). There was no love between the Jews and the Samaritans.

Jesus told the lawyer the parable you have read and you will have seen the lack of compassion shown to the dying man. The priest and Levite, more than anyone, should have shown compassion to the assaulted man, but for their own reasons they went on their way. They were like many people today who refuse to help those in distress because they don't want to become involved.

The Samaritan was the one to show compassion and give the injured man the help he needed, even at considerable cost to himself. When the lawyer was asked, 'So which of these three do you think was neighbour to him who fell among the thieves?' he gave the reply, 'He who showed mercy on him.' Correct! However, I notice he didn't say 'the Samaritan' — I wonder if it would have hurt him to say the name of the people he despised.

He was then told to 'go and do likewise'. So must you and I, especially if we are Christians. We are commanded to do unto others as we would have them do unto us. Jesus has set the example for you and me. He has shown his compassion for dying sinners by coming to this world and bearing the anger of God in their place. We have a wonderful, merciful Saviour!

THINGS TO DISCUSS WITH YOUR FAMILY

1. In what way is Jesus like the Good Samaritan?
2. How can you be like the Good Samaritan? Read 1 John 4:7-12.
3. Try to find out why the Jews hated the Samaritans.

Meditation

Meditate upon the words of Isaiah 61:1: 'The Spirit of the Lord GOD is upon me, because the LORD has anointed me to preach good tidings to the poor; he has sent me to heal the broken-hearted, to proclaim liberty to the captives, and the opening of the prison to those who are bound...'

Wise Words

Biblical orthodoxy without compassion is surely the ugliest thing in the world. *Francis Schaeffer*

'For what will it profit a man if he gains the whole world, and loses his own soul?' (Mark 8:36).

Read: Luke 10:38-42

Good friends are very valuable and should be treated with loving respect. I thoroughly enjoy spending time with my 'mates' as we have much in common and find joy in talking about the good times of the past and our hopes and plans for the future. Often our families get together for a meal and talk. Jesus was a true man, although without sin, but he enjoyed friendship with others.

Today's short reading is about some of his dear friends whom he loved (John 11:5) — Mary, Martha and Lazarus who lived at Bethany, a small village not far from Jerusalem. Mary and Lazarus lived in the house owned by their sister Martha who it seems was rather 'house proud.' They were converted people who believed that Jesus was the Messiah who had come to earth to save his people, making them sons and daughters of God and members of his kingdom. They were indwelt by the same Holy Spirit and saved by the same Saviour in whom they had faith. They loved God's holiness and loathed sin.

When Jesus and his twelve disciples arrived, Mary went to where the Lord was sitting as she wanted to hear every word he spoke. Jesus was not a frequent visitor and she wanted to learn as much as she could about the way of salvation. Martha on the other hand saw Jesus as a most important guest, with his twelve disciples, who had to be given the very best meal possible. She set about preparing for her guests, but grew weary of doing everything herself and complained to the Lord asking that he send Mary to give her some help.

Jesus, however, gently rebuked Martha by telling her that Mary was doing what was best — she was sitting at his feet, listening to everything he said. Martha should have been doing the same as there was no assurance that Jesus would ever again visit their home. Instead of preparing a delicious meal it would have been better to sit beside Mary, absorb Christ's teaching and then provide a simple meal which could be quickly prepared without much fuss.

There is a message here for us all — Christians differ in many ways, despite having a common Saviour and being members of God's kingdom. We all detest sin and love righteousness, but we have different likes and dislikes which must be tolerated. We all have many responsibilities, including preparing the daily meal, but we must never let the cares of the world interfere with our spiritual responsibilities. Our private devotions should not be pushed aside on a regular basis because of the time needed for work or play.

The day will come when the preparation of meals and sweeping the floor means nothing and all that matters is our relationship with the Saviour. We will die and leave behind all our earthly treasures. May we all make sure our relationship with Christ is most secure.

THINGS TO DISCUSS WITH YOUR FAMILY

1. Discuss Proverbs 27:6: 'Faithful are the wounds of a friend, but the kisses of an enemy are deceitful.'
2. Meals are important. What was Martha's problem as seen by Jesus?
3. Make a list of those things that interfere with your Christian life. How do you deal with them?

Meditation

Meditate upon the ways you can encourage others to 'sit at Jesus' feet'.

Wise Words

A worldly Christian is spiritually diseased.

C. H. Spurgeon

'Every good gift and every perfect gift is from above, and comes down from the Father of lights, with whom there is no variation or shadow of turning' (James 1:17).

Read: Luke 11:1-13

We often read of the hours spent in prayer by great saints. They claimed that they were unable to carry out their Christian duties in a right way until they spent time with the Lord. Martin Luther spent about four hours each morning in private devotions with his Saviour. And what about us? Prayer is hard work, but we must give time each day to read the Scriptures for that is how God speaks to us, and in prayer with our heavenly Father.

Once again we have read the Lord's Prayer, but we need to be constantly reminded of having a disciplined prayer life. After Jesus had been praying, a disciple asked that the twelve might be taught how to pray, just as John the Baptist had taught his disciples.

Jesus told the twelve that first they should praise their heavenly Father, as he was the One they normally approached in prayer. The psalmist rightfully said, 'Not unto us O Lord, not unto us, but to your name give glory' (Psalm 115:1). Jesus was concerned that God's name should be glorified and later said to his disciples, 'Father, glorify your name' (John 12:28).

Jesus then told the disciples to pray for the growth of God's kingdom. The twelve knew that they had a part to play in that great work which God himself had stated would happen — 'My name shall be great among the Gentiles ... for my name shall be great among the nations' (Malachi 1:11). We should be praying for the return of Christ which will mean the new heavens and new earth, in which will be perfect righteousness.

Jesus told the disciples to pray that God would ensure their daily supply of food and forgive their sins. It is most encouraging to read the words of 1 John 1:9 — 'If we confess our sins, he is faithful and just to forgive us our sins and to cleanse us from all unrighteousness.' Every saint is justified but daily needs to have his feet washed just as Jesus told Peter: 'He who is bathed needs only to wash his feet, but is completely clean' (John 13:10).

Jesus told two short parables both teaching the value of genuine, persistent prayer. In the first parable the man in bed responded to his friend's request for bread, because of his persistent knocking and asking. Here we are taught to pray on and never give up. We are told to 'ask', 'seek' and 'knock' and God will respond.

In the second short parable Jesus reminds us that when our children come seeking help, despite the fact that we are sinful, selfish beings, we will help them. Then came words of encouragement to the disciples and to each one of us who has unconverted loved ones, 'If you then, being evil, know how to give good gifts to your children, how much more will your heavenly Father give the Holy Spirit to those who ask him!' This is the greatest gift that God can give to any sinner — salvation, eternal life, a love of himself, a tongue to glorify him and spiritual peace!

Remember Paul's words, 'Pray without ceasing' (1 Thessalonians 5:17).

THINGS TO DISCUSS WITH YOUR FAMILY

1. Why does God forgive us our sins?
2. Who is the Holy Spirit?
3. I work for my daily food. In what way does God provide it for us?

Meditation

Meditate upon the wonder of being indwelt by the Holy Spirit. 1 Corinthians 3:16 says, 'Do you not know that you are the temple of God and that the Spirit of God dwells in you?'

The Holy Spirit may be had for the asking.

R. B. Kuiper

Wise Words

'But even if we, or an angel from heaven, preach any other gospel to you than what we have preached to you, let him be accursed' (Galatians 1:8).

Read: Luke 11:14-28

It is always time for rejoicing when a war is ended and peace established. During the days of warfare times are troubled and much damage is done to people and property. Ever since Adam fell into sin there has been spiritual warfare taking place on this earth. The consequences of Adam's sin are horrendous — death surrounds us on every side and the world itself has been greatly spoilt. How we should be praying for Christ's return so that the reality of his victory will be visible to everyone.

Already Satan is a defeated foe, but we are told that he 'walks about like a roaring lion, seeking whom he may devour' (1 Peter 5:8). In our reading Jesus was again faced with a demon-possessed man who had been made dumb by God's cruel enemy. The Lord healed the dumb man, but once again some people accused him of casting out the demon by the power of Satan (Beelzebub). Such an argument is not logical. Never become involved in attributing wrong motives to those godly ministers of Christ who stand firm for the truth. A man once said to me that ministers lived a good, upper class life because they 'fleeced their flock'. This was a very cruel comment!

We should always remember that Satan is the 'strong man' spoken of by Christ and always be on our guard to walk life's pathway in the power of the Holy Spirit. There can be no neutrality in our Christian life. We must take up our cross and courageously follow Jesus. Division within the church brings ridicule, and despite standing firm for the truth we must never let minor matters split the body of Christ. We have seen churches divide over minor issues that have assumed great proportions in the minds of some. There are some truths that are non-negotiable, for example justification by faith alone. Why should a congregation divide over the issue of women wearing head coverings in worship? We must be loving, tolerant people. The apostle Paul said, 'For though I am free from all men, I have made myself a servant to all, that I might win the more ... I have become all things to all men, that I might by all means save some' (1 Corinthians 9:19, 22).

Jesus then warned those who decided to follow him, yet were not truly converted. These are people who decide 'to turn over a new leaf' and begin living a life of obedience to the law. They might attend church and give the appearance that all is well with their soul — but without the indwelling Holy Spirit their soul is left open for the return of Satan and his demons who will make the person's situation worse than before.

When someone in the crowd praised Christ's mother there came a reply that we must believe, 'Blessed are those who hear the word of God and keep it!' We must read our Bibles and live the life of faith, all to the praise and honour of God.

THINGS TO DISCUSS WITH YOUR FAMILY

1. Can you be a prayerless Christian?
2. Why should church divisions cause ridicule by non-Christians?
3. Make a list of non-negotiable spiritual truths and discuss them.

Meditation

Meditate upon Christ's victory over Satan — 'Then I saw an angel coming down from heaven, having the key to the bottomless pit and a great chain in his hand. He laid hold of the dragon, that serpent of old, who is the Devil and Satan, and bound him for a thousand years; and he cast him into the bottomless pit, and shut him up, and set a seal on him, so that he should deceive the nations no more till the thousand years were finished' (Revelation 20:1-3).

Wise Words

If God were not my friend, Satan would not be so much my enemy. *Thomas Brooks*

 'So the people of Nineveh believed God, proclaimed a fast, and put on sackcloth, from the greatest to the least of them' (Jonah 3:5).

Read: Luke 11:29-36

It is so important to keep a good check on your eyesight as blindness is a terrible affliction. There was a time when I could see very well, but now I need to wear my spectacles when I shave or tidy the few hairs still growing on my head.

Jesus was surrounded by a large crowd of unbelieving Jews and he took the opportunity to preach a sermon. Earlier he had been asked to produce 'a sign from heaven' that would prove that he was the Christ. Standing before them was the sign from heaven — Jesus, the Son of God. However, he again gave them a sign that they would soon see and still not believe — the sign of Jonah. He was saying that just as Jonah had been in the belly of the large fish for three days, so also he would die and be buried in a tomb for three days and then would rise from the dead. This happened but it made no difference to the unbelieving majority.

Jesus warned his hearers that the people of Nineveh, who repented at the preaching of the prophet Jonah, would be involved in their judgement just as the Apostle Paul wrote, 'Do you not know that the saints will judge the world' — even the fallen 'angels'? (1 Corinthians 6:2-3).

The Queen of Sheba travelled many hundreds of miles to hear the great King Solomon's wisdom. The Jews had a greater prophet than Solomon for we read: 'God, who at various times and in various ways spoke in time past to the fathers by the prophets, has in these last days spoken to us by His Son' (Hebrews 1:1,2).

You and I have the words of God's greatest prophet, the Lord Jesus Christ. We must read and obey his word.

Our Saviour also told the short parable that you have read which teaches that all who have the gospel should make it known to the world. Christians must speak the truth and live godly lives that bear witness to the grace of God in their heart. We who believe have the gospel that Christ described as a 'pearl of great price' (Matthew 13:46). Show it to your friends and neighbours.

Jesus then spoke of a seeing eye being an essential part of the body. A good eye helps us walk without falling. It guides our hand when we reach out to pick up something and it makes possible the discovery of the truth through reading the word of God. The person with the good 'spiritual eye' is one whose life is centred upon the Saviour and has the desire to press on in his Christian life. Paul's good spiritual eye made it possible for him to write, 'Brethren, I do not count myself to have apprehended; but one thing I do, forgetting those things which are behind and reaching forward to those things which are ahead, I press toward the goal for the prize of the upward call of God in Christ Jesus' (Philippians 3:13,14). We can say with King David, 'One thing I have desired of the LORD, that will I seek: that I may dwell in the house of the LORD all the days of my life, to behold the beauty of the LORD, and to inquire in his temple' (Psalm 27:4).

If you have a dark spiritual eye your eternal life will be that place of outer darkness.

THINGS TO DISCUSS WITH YOUR FAMILY

1. Why is hell described as 'outer darkness'? See Matthew 22:13.
2. Who was the prophet to Nineveh? What was his message to the people? Read Jonah 3:4.
3. To have a good spiritual 'eye' what must happen to your heart? Read John 3:3-8.

Meditation

Think upon, 'But now Christ is risen from the dead, and has become the firstfruits of those who have fallen asleep' (1 Corinthians 15:20).

Wise Words

The Christian's task is to make the Lord Jesus visible, intelligible and desirable. *Len Jones*

'Keep your heart with all diligence, for out of it spring the issues of life' (Proverbs 4:23).

Read: Luke 11:37-44

Mealtimes are normally happy times where those sitting around the table discuss the issues of the day, laugh and joke and show kindness and love for one another. Jesus was invited to a meal by a Pharisee who was not one of his disciples. The invitation was accepted as the Saviour had a sacred message for his host and all who were listening. Jesus is teaching us that we must mix with non-Christians and use some of our time to speak of the kingdom of God. We are not to be spiritual hermits and live in our own holy huddle.

Christ's host was very surprised that Jesus had not washed his hands before eating his meal. Normally we do this to get rid of the germs that may be lurking on them. The Pharisees, however, washed their hands to avoid becoming spiritually unclean. They thought they may have been touched by a Gentile or have some dust on their hands that had come from one who was not of the covenant of Israel. To eat contaminated dust would make them ceremonially unclean.

Jesus at once took up the issue by saying that the Pharisees should pay special attention to the state of their heart. While they could claim to be living an upright life without any great visible sins they were corrupt internally. The Pharisees were most concerned about outward appearances and this was wrong for Samuel quoted what God had said, 'For the LORD does not see as man sees; for man looks at the outward appearance, but the LORD looks at the heart' (1 Samuel 16:7).

The God they claimed to worship made both the body and the soul but they failed to understand that what mattered in the final analysis was the state of the heart. Nicodemus had been told he needed to be born again if he wanted membership in the kingdom of God. The new birth is the sovereign work of the Holy Spirit. With purified hearts their works would be pure, because they came from a correct motive just as Paul wrote, 'To the pure all things are pure, but to those who are defiled and unbelieving nothing is pure' (Titus 1:15). Sadly, this was the state of Christ's host.

Jesus rebuked the pride of the Pharisees for failing in their religious duties. They tithed, even where it was not necessary, but failed to carry out God's commandments concerning their relationship with others. All of us should heed the Lord's words in Micah 6:8: 'And what does the LORD require of you but to do justly, to love mercy, and to walk humbly with your God?' Does this describe you and me?

Jesus finally said that the Scribes and Pharisees were such hypocrites that they were like well-kept graves that concealed corrupting bodies beneath the lovely green grass. People looked at the Pharisees and Scribes as the spiritual giants of the day, but their external show of righteousness simply concealed unbelieving, corrupt hearts. They were leading people to hell.

I wonder how the Pharisee host thought his meal was progressing?

THINGS TO DISCUSS WITH YOUR FAMILY

1. What was a 'scribe'?
2. Why did Jesus call the Pharisees 'hypocrites', because, after all, they displayed a godly life?
3. Who are today's 'spiritual' hypocrites?

Meditation

Think about Christ's words recorded in Matthew 15:18 — 'But those things which proceed out of the mouth come from the heart, and they defile a man.'

Wise Words

Piety outside and corruption inside is a revolting mixture. *Michael Green*

'The things which you learned and received and heard and saw in me, these do, and the God of peace will be with you' (Philippians 4:9).

Read: Luke 11:45-54

It is rather unpleasant when serious arguments develop amongst guests. When this happens most people want to bring the visit to an end and show their guests to the door. It is then that peace prevails.

I feel sorry for the Pharisee who had invited Jesus to his home for a meal. His motive was possibly wrong, but soon he heard his guest speaking some very plain truths about the Scribes and Pharisees. Christ's words must have infuriated those present for no sooner had he finished speaking of the hypocrisy of the Pharisees than a lawyer who was present said, 'Teacher, by saying these things you reproach us also.'

Jesus responded by outlining their religious sins. The lawyers knew the Scriptures but failed to have a true understanding of what was being taught. Jesus accused them of making rules and regulations which they expected the people to obey, yet did nothing to help the people cope with their spiritual burden. There were hundreds of man-made laws that they were expected to obey and this to them was an impossibility. The kingdom of God must have seemed closed to them because of the burden placed upon their heart by the church rulers. Jesus was the answer to their burden of sin. He had said, 'Come to me, all you who labour and are heavy laden, and I will give you rest. Take my yoke upon you and learn from me, for I am gentle and lowly in heart, and you will find rest for your souls. For my yoke is easy and my burden is light' (Matthew 11:28-30).

The church leaders spoke in a way which indicated that they honoured their prophets of old. Some had built monuments to remember them while others ensured their tombs were well cared for and kept tidy. The well-kept tombs were monuments to hatred. Like their ancestors they rejected the teachings of the prophets of God. Yet at that very moment, there stood before them the greatest prophet of all ages, the one prophesied by Moses: 'I will raise up for them a

Prophet like you from among their brethren, and will put my words in his mouth, and he shall speak to them all that I command him. And it shall be that whoever will not hear my words, which he speaks in my name, I will require it of him' (Deuteronomy 18:18,19). In all ages the saints have been subject to persecution — things haven't changed!

Jesus told those who were listening that the punishment for the killing of the prophets would fall upon their generation. This happened in AD 70 when the Roman armies destroyed Jerusalem and the temple and drove the people from Israel to the four corners of the earth.

The lawyers, Scribes and Pharisees furiously verbally attacked Jesus, hoping to hear him say something they could use against him if he were brought to trial. I guess the Pharisee's meal with Christ was one he would never forget.

THINGS TO DISCUSS WITH YOUR FAMILY

1. Read our text. In what way was the Apostle Paul unlike the lawyers in our reading today?
2. Who was Abel and why was he murdered?
3. What did Jesus mean when he said, 'You load men with burdens hard to bear' (Luke 11:46)?

Meditation

Think about Christ's words in Luke 11:52 — 'Woe to you lawyers! For you have taken away the key of knowledge. You did not enter in yourselves, and those who were entering in you hindered.' Have you the 'key of knowledge'?

Wise Words

Precious in the sight of the LORD is the death of his saints.

The psalmist

'I will speak your testimonies also before kings, and will not be ashamed' (Psalm 119:46).

Read: Luke 12:1-12

When I was a teacher everyone in the class was quiet when I spoke and at least pretended they were listening. We made some rules on our first day and they were to be obeyed. I made several concessions to the children. No one needed to ask for permission to leave the room and go to the toilet or have a drink of water. I told them I wasn't really interested in their toilet problems and if they were thirsty they should have a drink. They knew I kept watch on their comings and goings and we didn't have any problems. They treated me fairly as I did each class member.

Jesus was now instructing his disciples, but the crowd about them was so great that they were pushing and trampling upon each other. Teaching was difficult for the Lord at that time, but he courageously denounced the hypocrisy of the Pharisees. He had come to save unbelievers and that was the prime purpose of everything he said and did.

He said that everything done in secret, and the thoughts of the mind would one day be revealed. Sometimes this happens during our lifetime when someone discovers something we were certain was well hidden. When we ask how the person found out our secret we are often told, 'A little bird told me' — read Ecclesiastes 10:20. Yet there is a coming day of judgement when 'God will bring every work into judgement, including every secret thing, whether it is good or whether it is evil' (Ecclesiastes 12:14).

Jesus warned his disciples that they would suffer great persecution, even death from the Pharisees and others who hated Christianity. This became a reality when our Saviour was crucified and the young church began to suffer violent opposition. Jesus promised that when the disciples and his people were dragged up before wicked rulers, the Holy Spirit would give them the appropriate replies to their cruel accusations. All such wicked people have limited power. The worst they can do is kill the body, but it is God who can destroy the body and then cast the eternal soul into hell. The punishment of these rebellious people is fearful for we read, 'And the smoke of their torment ascends for ever and ever; and they have no rest day or night, who worship the beast and his image, and whoever receives the mark of his name' (Revelation 14:11).

Our God is all powerful. He holds the affairs of the world in his hands. All Christians can take comfort in Paul's words: 'And we know that all things work together for good to those who love God, to those who are the called according to his purpose' (Romans 8:28). We are of more value than the little sparrows. God will ensure the salvation of every one of his people. Jesus warned all those listening that sin against the Holy Spirit will never be forgiven. This is the rejection of the call of the Holy Spirit to repentance and faith in the Son of God.

The disciples and all Christians are called upon to confess Jesus Christ as their Lord and Saviour. On Judgement Day he then will confess us as his people before God and the holy angels.

THINGS TO DISCUSS WITH YOUR FAMILY

1. How can Christians survive the wicked persecution that comes from the world?
2. How does God demonstrate his awesome power today?
3. What is the end of all those who ignore the gospel?

Meditation

Meditate upon God's care of his people, and in particular his care of you.

Wise Words

Life is sweet and death is bitter. But eternal life is more sweet, and eternal death is more bitter. *Bishop Hooper*

'Let your conduct be without covetousness; be content with such things as you have. For he himself has said, "I will never leave you nor forsake you"' (Hebrews 13:5).

Read: Luke 12:13-21

Covetousness is a terrible sin and frequently it is not obvious. Many people are greedy and spend a great deal obtaining as much of the world's goods as they can. Others who are poor will never obtain much, but within their heart they want what others have. This is covetousness — envy. We are to have the same attitude to possessions as that of the Apostle Paul — 'I have learned in whatever state I am, to be content' (Philippians 4:11).

Jesus was asked by a greedy man to have his brother divide the inheritance equally between them. Obviously the elder brother had received double from his father's estate, which was in accordance with Old Testament law (Deuteronomy 21:15-17), and the second son was not pleased. Christ refused to become involved in the dispute as God had not appointed him to be a judge in civil matters. He had entered the world as God's Prophet, Priest and King of the heavenly kingdom.

Those who are ministers of the church should take notice of Christ's refusal and avoid becoming entangled in civil disputes. Paul warned Timothy of such involvement when he wrote, 'No one engaged in warfare entangles himself with the affairs of this life, that he may please him who enlisted him as a soldier' (2 Timothy 2:4).

Jesus told the parable about the rich man who decided to increase the value of his property by erecting additional buildings and storing away more possessions. He then thought he would be able to retire and enjoy his life to the fullest. He failed to see his plans materialize as that very night he died. His life had been spent piling up his possessions but he failed to ensure that he had treasure in heaven. He didn't have a saving faith in God. When we make plans for the future we should remember the words of James 4:15 — 'If the Lord wills, we shall live and do this or that.'

He was a worldly man and worldliness is a danger to every person. The Apostle John gave us all a warning: 'Do not love the world or the things in the world. If anyone loves the world, the love of the Father is not in him. For all that is in the world — the lust of the flesh, the lust of the eyes, and the pride of life — is not of the Father but is of the world. And the world is passing away, and the lust of it; but he who does the will of God abides for ever' (1 John 2:15-17).

Our worldly possessions are not safe. They can be stolen, the house or storage sheds can burn to the ground, or our investments can suddenly lose their value. Certainly when we die we lose them all and who knows what will happen to them. We should all note the wise words found in Ecclesiastes 2:18,19: 'Then I hated all my labour in which I had toiled under the sun, because I must leave it to the man who will come after me. And who knows whether he will be wise or a fool? Yet he will rule over all my labour in which I toiled.'

We must lay up treasure in heaven — faith in Christ, love of God, the fruit of the Spirit and richness in good works. This is the treasure that will count on the day of judgement — all that flows from our love of God and faith in Christ.

THINGS TO DISCUSS WITH YOUR FAMILY

1. Read and discuss 1 Timothy 6:10.
2. Thank God for all that you possess. Read Deuteronomy 8:17,18.
3. What is the best treasure that any person can have?

Meditation

Think about the words of Proverbs 23:5 — 'Will you set your eyes on that which is not? For riches certainly make themselves wings; they fly away like an eagle toward heaven.'

Worldly possessions have ruined many people but redeemed none. *Anonymous*

Wise Words

First things first!

 'Give me neither poverty nor riches —
feed me with the food allotted to me'
(Proverbs 30:8).

Read: Luke 12:22-34

Tension! This is the cause of much illness today. How often we spend much time worrying about something that doesn't eventuate and all the anxiety has proved a waste of time and energy. Always remember that God's grace is freely available to us, enabling us to cope in the difficult times.

Our Saviour has been talking about the foolishness of living for the things of the world when the most important thing is to live at peace with God if he has blotted out your sins. The 'rich fool' had his priorities all wrong. He lost his material possessions and eternal life in Paradise. He lost everything! Now the Lord gave advice to his disciples — advice that we should take to heart — 'Life is more than food, and the body is more than clothing.' We don't need an abundance but sufficient for our needs.

All of us have daily needs. In the 'Lord's Prayer' he told the disciples to pray, 'Give us this day our daily bread' (Matthew 6:11). We need food, clothing, a roof over our heads, and the Lord now tells the twelve that they were not to become overly anxious about satisfying those needs. He pointed to the birds and said that God provided their daily food. Then he spoke about the flowers and grasses growing in the field, indicating that God clothed them in beauty.

Next came the Lord's plain teaching about food and clothing, 'If then God so clothes the grass, which today is in the field and tomorrow is thrown into the oven, how much more will he clothe you, O you of little faith?' Surely we can say with David, 'The Lord is my shepherd; I shall not want' (Psalm 23:1). When Israel wandered through the desert regions on their way to the Promised Land God provided food from heaven called manna. He also ensured that their clothing did not wear out. We should be content with what God has given us and not spend time worrying. This doesn't mean that we don't visit a doctor who can use his God-given skills to help overcome medical problems.

God knows our needs before we ask and assures us that they will be provided. There may be times when our finances are gone and we must depend upon others to satisfy our needs, but God will provide for his people. All Christians are to be on the lookout for those in need for we are commanded, 'Therefore, as we have opportunity, let us do good to all, especially to those who are of the household of faith' (Galatians 6:10).

We have obligations to provide for our families just as Paul told Timothy, 'But if anyone does not provide for his own, and especially for those of his household, he has denied the faith and is worse than an unbeliever' (1 Timothy 5:8). We must not sit and worry about what we need for our family, but be like the ant and work (Proverbs 6:6-11).

Membership in God's kingdom comes first and then comes the rest. Let us all be sure that our real treasure is not to be found on earth, but in heaven, cared for by our loving Saviour. Good things are in store for those who have treasure in heaven. Peter wrote, '... when the Chief Shepherd appears, you will receive the crown of glory that does not fade away' (1 Peter 5:4).

THINGS TO DISCUSS WITH YOUR FAMILY

1. Make a list of your concerns and what you can do to overcome them.
2. God calls the disciples a 'little flock' (Luke 12:32). Why?
3. Should we take Luke 12:33 literally? What does it mean?

Meditation

Think of Christ's words, 'Life is more than food, and the body is more than clothing' (Luke 12:23).

Wise Words

God's promises are like the stars; the darker the night the brighter they shine.   *David Nicholas*

487

'But of that day and hour no one knows, not even the angels of heaven, but my Father only' (Matthew 24:36).

Read: Luke 12:35-48

After a loved one has been away for some time there is always excitement when we receive word that they are on their way home. We usually make special preparations and if their return is expected to be during the night we leave an outside light turned on.

Our reading today speaks of the return of the Lord Jesus Christ after his resurrection and ascension into heaven. We have the assurance of his return, but do not know the time. This means we must always be ready. Paul wrote: 'For our citizenship is in heaven, from which we also eagerly wait for the Saviour, the Lord Jesus Christ, who will transform our lowly body that it may be conformed to his glorious body' (Philippians 3:20,21).

Jesus had been speaking about living for the glory of God and membership in the kingdom of heaven and now he speaks of living a life of godliness. You have read two parables which teach important truths of how we must live.

We must live with our Christian profession brightly burning so that others might be attracted to the Lord and also be prepared for his return. Our faith in him must grow stronger, our love deepen, the fruit of the Spirit sweeten and we must fulfil works of love to all people.

A day is coming when the heavens will be divided and Christ will break into history again. This time he will come as the majestic King of kings and Lord of lords, accompanied by his mighty angels, and the souls of his people who have been with him in Paradise, ready to be united with their resurrected bodies. Yet, it is about two thousand years since Christ revealed that he is coming again. Many now treat this truth as a joke and laugh at us for holding fast to what our Lord has taught. Peter wrote of these people: '... scoffers will come in the last days, walking according to their own lusts, and saying, "Where is the promise of his coming? For since the fathers fell asleep, all things continue as they were from the beginning of creation'" (2 Peter 3:3,4). In the second parable Christ spoke of these people and warned them that they would face the anger of the Lamb of God as he is the appointed judge of mankind.

There are degrees of punishment in hell for we read, 'And that servant who knew his master's will, and did not prepare himself or do according to his will, shall be beaten with many stripes. But he who did not know, yet committed things deserving of stripes, shall be beaten with few. For everyone to whom much is given, from him much will be required; and to whom much has been committed, of him they will ask the more.'

Much is expected of each one of us who have Bibles, know the truth and profess our faith in the Lord Jesus Christ. We must ask ourselves the question, 'Am I producing spiritual fruit?' On the day of judgement may it not be shown that we are spiritual hypocrites.

THINGS TO DISCUSS WITH YOUR FAMILY

1. What does Luke 12:37 mean? 'Blessed are those servants whom the master, when he comes, will find watching.'
2. Discuss the teaching of Luke 12:47,48.
3. Read and discuss 2 Peter 3:10-13.

Meditation

Think about your preparation for the Lord's return.

Wise Words

There shall be no time for parting words or a change of mind when the Lord appears.   *J. C. Ryle*

'But as for me and my house, we will serve the LORD' (Joshua 24:15).

Read: Luke 12:49-59

There are many Christians who daily pray for the conversion of members of their family — as well as others. It is saddening to watch loved ones turn their back upon what they have been taught when young and begin living for self, pleasure and the world. Jesus now tells his disciples that faithfully following him was going to cost them much. The same is true for every Christian.

Jesus had come to the world to carry out God's plan of salvation and so save all those his heavenly Father had given him. He had stepped down from the throne of his glory and clothed himself in sinless flesh and blood to carry the sins of all believers. Finally the Messiah would die upon a Roman cross and experience God's anger for sin.

In our reading we find him expressing the wish that the anticipated day of his death might soon come for he knew the awesome punishment he would bear for his people. The psalmist described his punishments in fearful terms, one of which reads, 'All your [God's] waves and billows have gone over me' (Psalm 42:7). His sacrificial death would bring peace between God and those people given to him by his heavenly Father. Paul wrote: 'Therefore, having been justified by faith, we have peace with God through our Lord Jesus Christ' (Romans 5:1).

We are told that the Christian faith will bring about division between family members, societies and nations. Becoming a disciple of Christ means facing the opposition of those who hate both the Lord and the church. 'We must through many tribulations enter the kingdom of God' (Acts 14:22). Families are able to rejoice if they can say with Joshua the words of our text: 'But as for me and my house, we will serve the LORD.'

Jesus then rebuked the people who stood before him. They were well able to forecast the weather by what they saw in the sky, but were unable to correctly interpret what was happening in Israel at that time. They saw Jesus performing great miracles and preaching the gospel of repentance and saving faith in himself. They had the book of Daniel that accurately told of the time of his coming (Daniel 9:24-27). The prophecy found in Genesis 49:10 was fulfilled — 'The sceptre shall not depart from Judah, nor a lawgiver from between his feet, until Shiloh comes.'

Jesus called upon the people to look away from the false teaching of the Pharisees and other church leaders and follow him. They needed the new birth and saving faith in order to be able to faithfully obey the Word of God. The people were warned to be reconciled with God or face eternal punishment. They had heard so much from the Lord yet turned away from the revealed truth. How do you stand concerning the revealed truth of God? Remember that Paul wrote: 'There is therefore now no condemnation to those who are in Christ Jesus, who do not walk according to the flesh, but according to the Spirit' (Romans 8:1).

THINGS TO DISCUSS WITH YOUR FAMILY

1. What did Jesus mean when he said, 'Do you suppose that I came to give peace on earth? I tell you, not at all, but rather division' (Luke 12:51)?
2. Discuss today's text.
3. What did Jesus mean when he said, 'I have a baptism to be baptized with' (Luke 12:50)?

Meditation

Pray for spiritual unity between members of your family.

Wise Words

Out of the wealth of his resources, God has paid debts which were no concern of his.   *J. A. Motyer*

The curse of sin

'For man also does not know his time: like fish taken in a cruel net, like birds caught in a snare, so the sons of men are snared in an evil time, when it falls suddenly upon them' (Ecclesiastes 9:12).

Read: Luke 13:1-9

Death is all about us. Some people know well in advance that they have a terminal illness while others die without any warning. We do know the cause of death. It is not always due to ageing, but sin, for we read, 'For the wages of sin is death, but the gift of God is eternal life in Christ Jesus our Lord' (Romans 6:23).

There must have been a lot of discussion throughout Israel about some Galileans who had been killed by Pilate's soldiers at the time they were offering a sacrifice. The blood of the men had mixed with that from the sacrificial animals. Like many people it was thought that such a violent death must have been the result of God's anger because of some terrible sin they had committed.

Jesus warned the crowd that the death of the Galileans was not the most important issue, but preparations for their own deaths. Plainly the Lord told those present of their need to repent of their sins or they would perish in an unsaved state. The prophets of old, John the Baptist and the disciples had all preached the same message that Christ preached — repentance!

Repentance is an admission to God that you have sinned, with a plea for forgiveness. Godly repentance involves a turning from sin, a hatred of sin and a love of righteousness. It may also involve putting things right with someone you have offended. Every time we become conscious of sinning we should repent and seek God's forgiveness.

Jesus then told the parable about an unproductive fig tree. The owner of that tree had planted it in the good soil found in his vineyard. It received the best care but at harvest time there was no fruit. When he ordered it to be cut down a servant pleaded that it be given another year of tender care and then if no fruit was to be found it should be removed. This was a parable about Israel, God's covenant nation, which he had cared for, for many years. Yet despite his prophets teaching the truth and calling the nation to repentance, Israel was fruitless. The Jews had not evangelized the Gentile nations and the leaders of the church had lead the people astray. The Pharisees of Christ's time taught that salvation was to be earned by obedience to the laws of God and the church authorities. The nation was being given time to repent, even after they killed the Prince of Glory, God's beloved Son.

Finally God had had enough of Israel's hypocrisy and spiritual adultery, and the nation was destroyed by the Roman armies in AD 70 — the fig tree was cut down! There is a warning in this parable to everyone who calls himself a Christian, and for churches professing to teach the truth. We are all called to repentance and a saving faith which produces 'fruit'.

THINGS TO DISCUSS
WITH YOUR FAMILY

1. Read and discuss Isaiah 5:1-7.
2. What is repentance?
3. In what way did the fig tree symbolize Israel?

Meditation

Consider the statement by John Calvin — 'A man is acceptable to God only if he brings him holiness of heart.'

Of all acts of man repentance is the most divine. The greatest of all faults is to be conscious of none.

Thomas Carlyle

Wise Words

'But he was wounded for our transgressions, he was bruised for our iniquities; the chastisement for our peace was upon him, and by his stripes we are healed' (Isaiah 53:5).

Read: Luke 13:10-17

Our world is filled with sickness which is the consequence of sin. We must continually thank the Lord for giving us people with great medical skills to cure many diseases and relieve the symptoms of others. Yet, there is no medical cure for the greatest sickness of all — death. However, there is One who has by his own sacrificial death destroyed the power of death. Because of that saving work he also healed those suffering physical and mental sicknesses. On one occasion after healing many ill people Matthew records that he did so 'that it might be fulfilled which was spoken by Isaiah the prophet, saying: "He himself took our infirmities and bore our sicknesses"' (Matthew 8:17). This will be completely fulfilled in heaven.

We learn some important truths from Jesus healing the crippled woman in the synagogue on the Sabbath Day. First, despite being crippled she still attended worship for she was a true believer, 'a daughter of Abraham'. Second, she faithfully attended worship, no doubt to have her faith strengthened and to be blessed by God. Had she not been at her place of worship she would not have met Christ and been healed.

You and I must have the same attitude towards worship each Lord's day and be able to say with the Psalmist, 'How lovely is your tabernacle, O LORD of hosts! My soul longs, yes, even faints for the courts of the LORD; my heart and my flesh cry out for the living God' (Psalm 84:1, 2). Today so many spend Sunday mowing the lawn, watching television, attending sporting activities — anything but worshipping the Lord of glory. What a tragedy it would be if we were absent from our place of worship on that very day the blessings of the Lord were poured out on the congregation.

Jesus healed the crippled woman with a word and a touch. After eighteen years of physical distress she could stand upright. This healing was the literal fulfilment of what we read in Psalm 146:8 — 'The

LORD raises those who are bowed down.' Nothing is too difficult for our Saviour to perform. Having saved his people, he brings about the new birth through the work of the Holy Spirit. If you are a Christian you will have experienced this divine miracle.

Sadly the synagogue ruler was offended by what the Lord had done. He believed that Jesus had worked on the Sabbath and so broken God's commandment. Jesus plainly told the man that he was a hypocrite as their law allowed them to feed their animals on the Sabbath — an act of necessity and mercy. The ruler had overlooked the commandment, 'And what does the LORD require of you but to do justly, to love mercy, and to walk humbly with your God?' (Micah 6:8). The synagogue ruler believed that man was made for the Sabbath, not as Christ said, 'The Sabbath was made for man' (Mark 2:27,28).

The Lord rebuked the man for his lack of compassion for a woman whose illness was caused by Satan. Let us use the Lord's day to magnify God with worship and works of righteousness.

THINGS TO DISCUSS WITH YOUR FAMILY

1. Discuss the attitudes of the witnesses to the miracle (Luke 13:17).
2. Why did the Lord call the synagogue ruler a hypocrite?
3. How can you honour God in your daily life?

Meditation

Think upon Matthew 8:17 — 'He himself [Jesus] took our infirmities and bore our sicknesses.'

Wise Words

Break down Sunday, close the churches, open the bars and the theatres on that day, and where would value be? What was real estate worth in Sodom?   *H. L. Wayland*

'And it shall come to pass in the place where it was said to them, "You are not my people," there it shall be said to them, "You are sons of the living God"' (Hosea 1:10).

Read: Luke 13:18-21

It has just turned to spring as I write these words. Outside the trees are budding and our maple tree is about to open its leaves. When it does, many birds will come and rest on its branches. Once it was just a small tree about fifty centimetres tall, but care and time has seen it grow to a height of about eight metres.

We have read two very short parables told by Jesus, the first being about the growth of the kingdom of God which he likened to a growing mustard tree. At the time of speaking, the church was very small as there were only a few believers in the land of Israel. Christ had come to save the lost and establish the kingdom of God in this new era. After his death and ascension to his heavenly Father we read of just one hundred and twenty Christians meeting for prayer (Acts 1:15). They were largely uneducated people, but were filled with a zeal to win converts to the Lord. Following the outpouring of the Holy Spirit on the day of Pentecost the gospel was preached with power and Peter saw about three thousand people added to the kingdom of God.

The disciples received a specific command from Jesus concerning their work — 'Go into all the world and preach the gospel to every creature' (Mark 16:15). Soon the gospel was being preached to Jews everywhere, but without any great success as they refused to believe that Jesus, whom they crucified, was their Messiah. Christians were scattered throughout the surrounding regions where they gossipped the gospel, winning Gentiles into the kingdom. With the conversion of Paul and his persecution by the Jews he declared, 'Your blood be upon your own heads; I am clean. From now on I will go to the Gentiles' (Acts 18:6).

The church was growing just as Paul wrote, 'Now thanks be to God who always leads us in triumph in Christ, and through us diffuses the fragrance of his knowledge in every place' (2 Corinthians

2:14). He also wrote to the Colossians of the gospel 'which has come to you, as it has also in all the world, and is bringing forth fruit' (Colossians 1:6). Missionaries have taken the gospel to the four corners of the earth and today the church is a mighty kingdom which 'shall stand for ever' (Daniel 2:44).

In the second short parable Jesus likened spiritual growth, especially in the newly converted believer, to the work of leaven mixed with flour. Gradually the leaven changes the flour until the dough is ready for cooking. The action of the leaven is not seen. The first work of God in bringing a sinner to membership in the kingdom of God is the new birth, which is the work of the Holy Spirit. Then follows the sanctifying work of the same Spirit of God. All who are born again have an assurance from God 'that he who has begun a good work in you will complete it until the day of Jesus Christ' (Philippians 1:6). We have every reason to praise God.

THINGS TO DISCUSS
WITH YOUR FAMILY

1. What is leaven and what is its use?
2. What is meant by the term 'born again'? Read John 3:3ff.
3. What is the work of missionaries? Who was Hudson Taylor?

Meditation

Meditate upon the ways God enlarges his kingdom and what part you play in the process.

Wise Words

Ten million roots are pumping in the streets: do you hear them? Ten million buds are forming in the axles of the leaves: do you hear the sound of the saw or the hammer? All next summer is at work in the world: but it is unseen by us. And so 'the kingdom of God comes not with observation.'   *Henry Ward Beecher*

'The angel of the LORD encamps all around those who fear him, and delivers them' (Psalm 34:7).

Read: John 10:22-30

In many communities there is an annual celebration of something of importance to the people. In Australia, ANZAC Day is set aside to give thanks to all those men and women who have been involved in the defence of our nation. On 25 April 1915 the Australian and New Zealand military forces were involved in the landing on the beaches at Gallipoli.

Jesus was in Jerusalem for the Feast of Dedication where the rededication of the temple by Judas Maccabee in 165 BC was remembered. While walking in the temple section known as Solomon's Porch, which was the only section of Solomon's temple still standing, Jesus was asked, 'If you are the Christ, tell us plainly?' He had often answered this question in a variety of ways, especially by fulfilling the prophecies made concerning the Messiah. He had also told many parables that taught the same thing, but now the Jews wanted a plain answer — Yes or No — 'Are you the Christ?'

Christ's reply was a rebuke. He said that they had been told in word and his actions, and they still refused to believe. And why wouldn't they believe? They preferred darkness to light.

Jesus spoke of his own people whom he called his 'sheep'. The sheep were his because they were given to him by his heavenly Father. Some time before he had said, 'All that the Father gives me will come to me, and the one who comes to me I will by no means cast out' (John 6:37). Christ's sheep were precious for we read, 'For you were bought at a price; therefore glorify God in your body and in your spirit, which are God's' (1 Corinthians 6:20). Christians are totally dependent upon Christ for everything and while the world despises him, his 'sheep' love him. We are God's children, members of the kingdom of heaven, and we follow our Lord and Saviour wherever he leads us.

We are given eternal life, peace of heart, righteousness, and daily we bask in God's majestic grace. The saints are eternally loved by God and on their way to Paradise. Jesus said that no one, not even the malignant Satan, can pluck us out of his hands because God has hold of us. The first step in our salvation is the gracious work of the Holy Spirit. Jude assures us that our end is eternal life with God: 'Now to him who is able to keep you from stumbling, and to present you faultless before the presence of his glory...' (Jude 24). Paul traced the work of salvation in Christ's people when he wrote: 'Moreover whom he predestined, these he also called; whom he called, these he also justified; and whom he justified, these he also glorified' (Romans 8:30).

Jesus then declared that he and his Father were 'one'. In the Godhead there are three distinct Persons — Father, Son and Holy Spirit, each playing a different part in the salvation of sinners, but one in essence. This is a wonderful mystery, but is a guarantee of our salvation.

THINGS TO DISCUSS WITH YOUR FAMILY

1. Why are the saints eternally secure?
2. In what way does God reward his people?
3. What was the 'Feast of Dedication'?

Meditation

Meditate upon the mystery of the Godhead — one God, three Persons.

Wise Words

There are three persons in the Godhead: the Father, the Son, and the Holy Spirit; and these three are one God, the same in substance, equal in power and glory.

Shorter Catechism Question 6

'For God so loved the world that he gave his only begotten Son, that whoever believes in him should not perish but have everlasting life' (John 3:16).

Read: John 10:31-39

Throwing stones was banned when I was young — as it is today — but we had many great mud fights. We made our supply of mud missiles and when the battle was ended we were filthy; but it was good fun.

Jesus had just declared to the Jews that he and his Father were 'One'. To those present this was blasphemy, so they started gathering stones to throw at him in accordance with the law: 'And whoever blasphemes the name of the LORD shall surely be put to death. All the congregation shall certainly stone him' (Leviticus 24:16). The mob wanted to execute the merciful, compassionate, sinless Son of God.

When Jesus asked why they were about to act this way they declared, 'For a good work we do not stone you, but for blasphemy, and because you, being a man, make yourself God.'

Jesus then referred to the Scriptures which they held to be God's word to the nation and made reference to Psalm 82:6 where we read: 'I said, "You are gods, and all of you are children of the Most High."' The Scriptures referred to the nation's rulers and judges as 'gods' which was acceptable to the people. Thus Jesus asked, 'What's your problem if I use the same word with reference to myself?' The Lord had been very specific in calling himself the Son of God when he spoke to Nicodemus. The problem the Jews had with Jesus was that he was not what they expected of their Messiah. He wasn't establishing a mighty, glorious earthly kingdom centred upon the throne of David. He had spoken against the false teaching of the church leaders, especially the hypocrisy of the Pharisees who were held in high regard by the people. The people should have noted that Christ's works were those his heavenly Father said Messiah would carry out.

The disciples were learning that just as their Master was despised, so also they would suffer hatred. To the twelve he said, 'If the world hates you, you know that it hated me before it hated you' (John 15:18).

We should notice that Jesus used the Scriptures to defend himself against false accusations. He had done the same when he faced Satan in the wilderness. We also must hold the Scriptures to be the precious, inspired, infallible word of the living God. Paul wrote to Timothy on this subject and we should take notice of his thoughts, 'All Scripture is given by inspiration of God, and is profitable for doctrine, for reproof, for correction, for instruction in righteousness, that the man of God may be complete, thoroughly equipped for every good work' (2 Timothy 3:16,17). Make sure you read your Bible on a regular basis and give some time and effort to memorization of important texts. One day they will prove useful.

When Jesus concluded his speaking by declaring that 'the Father is in me, and I in him' the angry mob again tried to take him by force, but failed.

THINGS TO DISCUSS WITH YOUR FAMILY

1. What does it mean that the Bible is the inspired word of God?
2. Discuss Paul's words to Timothy found above (2 Timothy 3:16,17).
3. What did Jesus mean when he said, 'I and my Father are one' (John 10:30)?

Meditation

Meditate upon the words of Psalm 119:11 — 'Your word I have hidden in my heart, that I might not sin against you!'

Wise Words

Unconverted men would kill God himself if they could only get at him.   *Quoted by J. C. Ryle*

'...I looked, and behold, a great multitude which no one could number, of all nations, tribes, peoples, and tongues, standing before the throne and before the Lamb ... crying out with a loud voice, saying, "Salvation belongs to our God who sits on the throne, and to the Lamb!"' (Revelation 7:9,10).

Read: Luke 13:22-30

When we attend worship we usually find our congregations are small and in many places those attending services are older people. Many of our young people are forced to leave their homes and move to areas where they can find work. Frequently this results in them drifting into the ways of the world, and church attendance is forgotten. Quite often Christ then plays no part in their lives.

While making his way to Jerusalem, Jesus attracted crowds of onlookers, and on this occasion he was asked, 'Lord, are there few who will be saved?' Jesus, in his sermon on the mount answered this question when he said, '... narrow is the gate and difficult is the way which leads to life, and there are few who find it' (Matthew 7:14). The wonderful truth is that God is willing to save all who come to him through the Lord Jesus. The apostle Peter wrote that the Lord is '... not willing that any should perish but that all should come to repentance' (2 Peter 3:9).

In our reading Jesus stresses that the doorway to heaven will not be open for ever, but that the day is coming when God will close that door and then it will be too late for any sinner to enter. Do you remember that Noah built the ark just as God commanded and after the animals and his family had entered, God closed the door? For over one hundred years Noah had called upon people to repent and enter through the doorway, but nobody believed what he said. Consequently when the rain fell and the flood waters lifted the ark off the earth, unbelieving humanity perished.

This was Christ's message to the Jews of his day — repent and trust in him and be saved. When the door is closed it will be too late and unbelievers will experience the 'wrath of the Lamb' (Rev. 6:16). The unbelieving Jews would acknowledge the truth of the words of Proverbs 1:28: 'Then they will call on me, but I will not answer; they will seek me diligently, but they will not find me.'

Despite their pleas for acceptance, even claiming personal knowledge of the Saviour, the Lord will reply, 'I tell you I do not know you, or where you come from. Depart from me, all you workers of iniquity.' Instead of sorrow at their predicament, the hearts of those cast into hell will be filled with hatred towards God. They will watch as the patriarchs and the despised prophets pass into Paradise, accompanied by their most detested 'neighbours' — the Samaritans and Gentiles from the four corners of the world.

Many of those who enter God's kingdom will be given great rewards because of their faithful service of their Lord and Saviour. I pray that all who read this book have a place in glory reserved for you.

THINGS TO DISCUSS WITH YOUR FAMILY

1. When is the doorway into heaven closed for people?
2. What did Jesus mean when he said, 'There are last who will be first, and there are first who will be last' (Luke 13:30)?
3. Will we know one another in heaven? Read Luke 13:28.

Meditation

If you are a Christian thank God that the doorway to heaven was opened to you.

Wise Words

The entrance fee into the kingdom of God is nothing; the annual subscription is all that we possess.

Henry Drummond

26 August   Tears shed over the city of God — Jerusalem

 "'But if you will not hear these words, I swear by myself,'" says the LORD, "that this house shall become a desolation'" (Jeremiah 22:5).

Read: John 10:40-42; Luke 13:31-35

We all like to think our homes and townships are safe and secure. Once, when I was young we had a flood. Often floodwater had surrounded our house, but never had the muddy water come into the house. On this occasion the unbelievable happened. We watched the water rise until at last it seeped through the floorboards. After some hours it was several metres deep. While we lost our possessions there was no loss of life in our immediate region.

I'm sure the Jews felt that their beautiful city of Jerusalem, the 'city of God' (Psalm 87:3), would last for ever. The city with Solomon's glorious temple had been largely destroyed by King Nebuchadnezzar's armies, but they couldn't imagine it happening again.

Jesus had moved away from Jerusalem to the region where John the Baptist had carried out a faithful ministry. When King Herod heard that Jesus was there he let it be known that he wanted him killed. Jesus sent word back to the King indicating that he still had work to do and nothing would prevent him completing his Father's plans. We also must remember that God rules this world and our times are in his hands, not those of our enemies. Paul's words to the Roman Christians should comfort us: 'And we know that all things work together for good to those who love God, to those who are the called according to his purpose' (Romans 8:28).

Jesus was soon to return to Jerusalem where he would be crucified. All of God's prophets had been killed in that region and his place of death would be the same. Christ was the greatest and the last of God's prophets to Israel (Hebrews 1:1,2).

God had no desire to see Jerusalem and its citizens destroyed. Ezekiel wrote, "'As I live,'" says the Lord GOD, "I have no pleasure in the death of the wicked, but that the wicked turn from his way and live. Turn, turn from your evil ways! For why should you die, O house of Israel?'" (Ezekiel 33:11). When his Son was murdered God's patience came to an end. Forty years later the Romans would destroy Jerusalem and the Israelites scattered throughout the world. This was a distressful end to the great city and the people. Jesus had spent years calling the people to repentance, but they refused. He had said, 'But you are not willing to come to me that you may have life' (John 5:40). Now their blood was upon their own heads.

Following his death, many ungodly Jews would not see Jesus again until he returned in majestic power. Then, '... every knee [will] bow, of those in heaven, and of those on earth, and of those under the earth, and that every tongue ... confess that Jesus Christ is Lord, to the glory of God the Father' (Philippians 2:10,11). On that day every eye will see him, even the Pharisees and others who condemned him. Are you prepared for that day?

THINGS TO DISCUSS
WITH YOUR FAMILY

1. Why does the world today remember the city of Jerusalem?
2. The Jews generally refuse to acknowledge Jesus as their Messiah. Are you praying for their conversion? Why? Read Romans 11.
3. Why did Jerusalem deserve to be destroyed by the Roman army?

Meditation

Meditate upon the spiritual state of the Jews today. Pray that God might open their eyes to recognize Jesus as their Messiah.

Wise Words

The resurrection and the judgement will demonstrate before all worlds who won and who lost. We can wait.

A. W. Tozer

'Therefore the LORD said: "Inasmuch as these people draw near with their mouths and honour me with their lips, but have removed their hearts far from me ..."' (Isaiah 29:13).

Read: Luke 14:1-6

We like people to speak well of us, but sometimes wonder if they really mean what they say. We may never know what they really think because we have no way of looking into their mind. The Pharisees as a group despised Jesus, but there were some like Nicodemus who loved him and when able tried to protect him. We now have a leading Pharisee inviting the Lord to a meal. On the surface this seems to be a socially pleasant invitation, but on this occasion we know what was going on in the hearts of those present. We read the reason for the invitation, '... that they watched him closely.' They were doing all they could to catch Jesus out in what he did or said, that it might be used against him if and when he was paraded before the Sanhedrin.

Jesus accepted the invitation as he took every opportunity to mix with unbelievers that he might preach the truth to them and point them to the only way of salvation — through faith in himself. We must learn from this event that we are not to shut ourselves off from the world and become spiritual hermits. Only religious cowards do this. We must mix with people and speak to them of Christ and their need of eternal life. Paul wrote to the Corinthians, 'I wrote to you in my epistle not to keep company with sexually immoral people. Yet I certainly did not mean with the sexually immoral people of this world, or with the covetous, or extortioners, or idolaters, since then you would need to go out of the world' (1 Corinthians 5:9,10).

The host and his friends were trying to catch Jesus out in what happened. The people of the world know how Christians should live and are always watching, hoping to see us fall into sin so they can point the finger of scorn at us. We must always be on guard.

Jesus healed the man who had dropsy. We don't know if he was brought to the meal hoping that Christ would heal him, thus giving his enemies a reason to accuse him of breaking the Sabbath regulations. Jesus knew their thoughts and asked the question they refused to answer, 'Is it lawful to heal on the Sabbath?' Immediately Jesus healed the man.

They knew that it was God's law to do good on the Sabbath Day. They went out of their way to rescue an animal that had fallen into a hole in the ground and knew in their hearts that it was also right to do good to a helpless, sick man on any day of the week.

We should also carry out works of necessity and mercy on the Lord's Day. Certainly it is a day of rest from our weekly work, but we must be careful that it does not end up like all other days — lawn mowing day, a time for sport and other worldly activities. Christians must not relax the sanctity of the Christian Sabbath. The Lord's Day is given to us for our benefit — to worship God, for rest and for acts of compassion. May it always be used to the glory of God.

THINGS TO DISCUSS
WITH YOUR FAMILY

1. Did Jesus sin when he healed the man with dropsy? Discuss your answer.
2. Why is the Christian Sabbath on the first day of the week?
3. What acts of necessity and mercy should you carry out on the Lord's Day?

Meditation

Meditate upon the significance of the Lord's Day.

Wise Words

Show me a nation that has given up the sabbath [Lord's Day] and I will show you a nation that has got the seed of decay.   *D. L. Moody*

'A man's pride will bring him low, but
the humble in spirit will retain honour'
(Proverbs 29:23).

Read: Luke 14:7-14

We all have some pride within our hearts despite the effort we
make to live a humble life. Some people are proud of the fact
that they are so humble. Pride is a curse and Isaiah records that it
was Satan's sin in heaven — 'For you have said in your heart: "I will
ascend into heaven, I will exalt my throne above the stars of God; I
will also sit on the mount of the congregation on the farthest sides of
the north; I will ascend above the heights of the clouds, I will be like
the Most High"' (Isaiah 14:13,14).

In Eden, Adam was tempted by Satan's words, which questioned
God's truthfulness and the temptation to 'be like God' (Genesis 3:5).
Pride played its part in Adam's sin.

As the guests were taking their seats at the Pharisee's home Jesus
again saw pride dictating where the guests sat. Most were making
sure they gained the most socially acceptable seat. They didn't want
to be seated at the lowest place.

Jesus then told a parable which was a rebuke to them. The Pharisees and other church leaders were proud men who looked down
upon others, especially those they saw as sinners and tax collectors.
Jesus, in his parable, said that people should take the lower seat so
that when the host began to seat his close friends near to him, some
would have to be moved to a position of less importance — what an
embarrassment!

The Pharisees should have known the teaching of Scripture.
Proverbs 25:6,7 says, 'Do not exalt yourself in the presence of the
king, and do not stand in the place of the great; for it is better that
he say to you, "Come up here," than that you should be put lower ...'

Christians must say with the Apostle Paul, 'But by the grace of
God I am what I am' (1 Corinthians 15:10). We have nothing of
which to be proud and should agree with Paul in his words to Timothy, 'This is a faithful saying and worthy of all acceptance, that Christ

Jesus came into the world to save sinners, of whom I am chief' (1 Timothy 1:15). We are fallen men and women, and commanded '... in lowliness of mind let each esteem others better than himself' (Philippians 2:3).

The great saints — Moses, Job, Paul and others — were noted for their humility. They saw themselves as sinners totally dependent upon God for everything. This should be our attitude as well.

Jesus then told his host that while he had every right to invite his friends to a meal, he should also extend an invitation to people who could never repay him. We are to remember the poor and be given to hospitality, expecting nothing in return. Like Jesus, when we are dining with friends or strangers we should take the opportunity to speak of Christ and the kingdom of God. Jesus did so at this meal. If we do the same, there are blessings in store when Christ returns and the judgement takes place.

THINGS TO DISCUSS WITH YOUR FAMILY

1. What does Paul mean in Romans 12:13 where we are told we must be 'given to hospitality'?
2. In what way does God bless humble people? Read James 4:6.
3. How did Christ humble himself?

Meditation

Meditate upon James 1:27 — 'Pure and undefiled religion before God and the Father is this: to visit orphans and widows in their trouble, and to keep oneself unspotted from the world.'

Wise Words

God abhors them worst who adore themselves most.
William Secke

'All that the Father gives me will come
to me, and the one who comes to me I
will by no means cast out' (John 6:37).

Read: Luke 14:15-24

As I write this section I have received a phone call from a friend
asking to be excused from a Bible study meeting. The reason
was very legitimate. A close friend had died and was to be buried the
following day making it impossible to be in two places at the same
time.

Jesus heard one of the guests at the Pharisee's meal remark,
'Blessed is he who shall eat bread in the kingdom of God!' Jesus took
this comment as an opportunity to tell another parable which was a
rebuke to all those who heard him preach the gospel but turned their
back upon salvation.

The parable is the story of people who were invited to a wonderful gathering. They had indicated they would be present, but when
they were sent a reminder that it was time to attend, out came a set
of very lame excuses. This was the attitude of the Jews to Jesus and
the gospel he preached. Down through the ages they had longed for
Messiah's coming, but now that he was present they refused his invitation to membership in the kingdom of God. Again and again Jesus
had invited unbelievers to come to him and gain eternal life. He said
in John 6:35, 'I am the bread of life. He who comes to me shall never
hunger, and he who believes in me shall never thirst.'

With the crucifixion of their Messiah and the rejection of the
gospel, the good news of a risen Saviour was taken to the Gentiles.
The nations of the world were evangelized and unbelievers won into
the kingdom of God. In the parable, the host sent his servants to find
anyone who would come to fill his tables. The same happened with
the gospel when it was taken to the Gentiles. Paul instructed Timothy,
'Preach the word! Be ready in season and out of season. Convince,
rebuke, exhort, with all long-suffering and teaching' (2 Timothy 4:2).

With such a wonderful gospel invitation, unbelievers were won
into the kingdom. Again we read precious words spoken by Christ,

'All that the Father gives me will come to me, and the one who comes to me I will by no means cast out' (John 6:37). This parable reminds us of God's love of sinners who are saved by his Son's sacrificial work on the cross. All of God's people will be brought into the kingdom and sit at his table. Isaiah spoke of this feast, 'The LORD of hosts will make for all people a feast of choice pieces, a feast of wines on the lees, of fat things full of marrow, of well-refined wines on the lees' (Isaiah 25:6).

Following the Judgement Day all the saints who make up the church — the bride of Christ — will be greatly blessed. We read in Revelation 19:7-9, '"Let us be glad and rejoice and give him glory, for the marriage of the Lamb has come, and his wife has made herself ready." And to her it was granted to be arrayed in fine linen, clean and bright, for the fine linen is the righteous acts of the saints. Then he said to me, "Write: 'Blessed are those who are called to the marriage supper of the Lamb!'"'

Today, accept Christ's invitation to become a citizen in the kingdom of God.

THINGS TO DISCUSS WITH YOUR FAMILY

1. If you are not a Christian, what is your excuse for rejecting Christ's invitation?
2. How do you accept Christ's invitation to sit at his feast?
3. In what way do Christians never 'hunger' or 'thirst' (John 6:35)?

Meditation

Pray for God's blessing upon all faithful pastors.

Wise Words

Holiness indeed is perfected in heaven: but the beginning of it is invariably confined to this world.   *John Owen*

'For if, after they have escaped the pollutions of the world through the knowledge of the Lord and Saviour Jesus Christ, they are again entangled in them and overcome, the latter end is worse for them than the beginning' (2 Peter 2:20).

Read: Luke 14:25-35

Most sensible people count the cost before undertaking a new venture. Before buying a house it is necessary to make sure you have sufficient money in order to get a loan from a lending institution. If you are building a house you need to be certain that you have sufficient finance to meet all the expenses.

Jesus had often told his disciples and others that to become a disciple would be at great cost — even the possible loss of life. In the Sermon on the Mount Jesus warned of persecution: 'Blessed are you when men hate you, and when they exclude you, and revile you, and cast out your name as evil, for the Son of Man's sake. Rejoice in that day and leap for joy! For indeed your reward is great in heaven, for in like manner their fathers did to the prophets' (Luke 6:22,23). You notice that those who suffered persecution for the Lord Jesus would be greatly rewarded.

Jesus was now being followed by a great crowd, some of whom were considering becoming one of his disciples. He knew it was important that they gave serious consideration to this as it would cost them dearly.

Jesus was teaching a fundamental truth of discipleship — he was to have the pre-eminence in every aspect of their lives. Paul wrote of Christ, 'And he is before all things, and in him all things consist. And he is the head of the body, the church, who is the beginning, the first-born from the dead, that in all things he may have the pre-eminence' (Colossians 1:17, 18). Jesus told two parables, each one teaching the necessity of 'counting the cost' of becoming a disciple. Every Christian must take up their God-given cross and follow the Lord. Carrying a cross in that era meant crucifixion at the end of the road.

Today in most western countries people couldn't care less who became a Christian; but to do so in a Moslem country most likely means death. We are all warned of trials if we become a follower of

Christ. Paul wrote to Timothy, 'Yes, and all who desire to live godly in Christ Jesus will suffer persecution' (2 Timothy 3:12).

In the parable about the king with a small army, he counted the cost of going to war and possibly suffering defeat. He thus sent a delegation to discuss peace. Again the teaching is — count the cost of becoming Christ's disciple.

All disciples are to act as salt in the community. Salt preserves and flavours food. We must influence people to turn to Christ and by living a holy life bring about godly, socially beneficial living that preserves the community from falling into chaos. This is happening throughout the world today, and in those communities where Christian influence is dying, social problems are increasing.

May we all learn what Christ is teaching in these short parables and faithfully live out their teaching.

THINGS TO DISCUSS WITH YOUR FAMILY

1. If you are a Christian what has this cost you?
2. Discuss the meaning of the two short parables.
3. What did Jesus mean when he said, 'Whoever does not bear his cross and come after me cannot be my disciple' (Luke 14:27)?

Meditation

Meditate upon the ways you can give Christ the pre-eminence in your daily life.

Wise Words

It costs to follow Jesus Christ, but it costs more not to.

Anonymous

'I will seek what was lost and bring back what was driven away, bind up the broken and strengthen what was sick...' (Ezekiel 34:16).

Read: Luke 15:1-10

I don't know about you but often I misplace something I value and waste much time looking until I have found my prized possession.

Jesus was again surrounded by people, but this time the Scribes and Pharisees were very critical of our Saviour: 'This Man receives sinners and eats with them.' This was true as our Lord had come into the world to save the lost. Not only were his people to be forgiven but they were to be prepared for heaven. They were to live holy lives as was commanded in the Old Testament and this should have been known by the Pharisees and other church leaders. God had told Moses, 'Speak to all the congregation of the children of Israel, and say to them: "You shall be holy, for I the LORD your God am holy"' (Leviticus 19:2).

Without the saving work of the Holy Spirit we cannot be saved. Jesus had come to redeem the spiritually lost and told three parables about things that were missing. You have read about a lost sheep and a lost coin, both of which were of value to their owners. Every effort was made to find them and when they were found there was great rejoicing.

Unbelievers are lost people, but praise God, Jesus saves everyone given to him by his father. Unbelievers have no desire to find their way to the Saviour. They need the gracious work of the Holy Spirit to bring them to repentance and saving faith.

Again we are taught of the love and compassion of our God who desires that no one should perish. He has determined to save his people and this salvation is a work of grace. Isaiah describes the lost state of sinners, 'All we like sheep have gone astray; we have turned, every one, to his own way; and the LORD has laid on him the iniquity of us all' (Isaiah 53:6).

When he finds his lost 'sheep' he deals with them in a most kindly way. Isaiah wrote, 'He will feed his flock like a shepherd; he will gather the lambs with his arm, and carry them in his bosom, and gently lead those who are with young' (Isaiah 40:11). Christians are to look 'unto Jesus, the author and finisher of our faith, who for the joy that was set before him endured the cross, despising the shame, and has sat down at the right hand of the throne of God' (Hebrews 12:2).

The parable tells us of the joy when the missing item was found. Likewise there is great joy in heaven when a sinner repents and turns to the Lord Jesus with a God-given faith. Even the holy angels who do not need a Saviour are involved in the rejoicing as they show a great interest in the saving work of the God they love and serve.

A lesson for all Christians is that we should also rejoice and praise God when a sinner is converted. When the greatly feared Saul was converted, he, as the Apostle Paul, wrote that those who heard the news 'glorified God in me' (Galatians 1:24).

Let us pray for those who do not believe in Jesus, and rejoice when our prayers are answered.

THINGS TO DISCUSS WITH YOUR FAMILY

1. In Luke 15:7 we read of those 'just persons who need no repentance'. Who are they?
2. Why do humans need a Saviour?
3. Why do you think that one lost coin caused such an upset?

Meditation

Consider the value God places upon the human soul.

Wise Words

God gets more out of your salvation than you ever will.
David Shepherd

September

'Because you say, "I am rich, have become wealthy, and have need of nothing" – and do not know that you are wretched, miserable, poor, blind, and naked...' (Revelation 3:17).

Read: Luke 15:11-24

I'm sure you have seen many people who were just like the sons in the parable you have read. How many times do we meet broken hearted parents whose children have turned their backs upon the Saviour they love and serve? The sons in the parable speak of two groups of people. The younger son can be likened to the tax collectors and sinners amongst the Jews and the elder son depicts particularly the Pharisees. In some ways the younger son is like the Gentiles who are descended from Noah, that godly man who served God and taught his family the way of salvation.

We are all like both sons in the parable for we were all sinners from the start, just as David wrote, 'Behold, I was brought forth in iniquity, and in sin my mother conceived me' (Psalm 51:5). Because of this we sin. We have no desire to repent of our iniquities and turn to God for salvation. No, without God's intervention we will happily walk that broad way that leads to eternal hell.

With his bag of money the younger son set off to enjoy the world. He made sure he was a long way from his home so that his father would not hear of his disgraceful conduct. He was just like the church at Laodicea which said of itself, '"I am rich, have become wealthy, and have need of nothing" — and do not know that you are wretched, miserable, poor, blind, and naked' (Revelation 3:17). Soon, because of the son's wasteful living, he ended up working in a pigsty. He learned the truth of Isaiah's words, '"There is no peace," says my God, "for the wicked"' (Isaiah 57:21).

There in the pigsty the young man saw his sin and the consequences of his rebellion against both his father and God. As his repentance was genuine he stood up and set off for his father's home. He had been 'born again' and his cry to God was 'God, be merciful to me a sinner!' (Luke 18:13).

518

The great truth we must recognize is that God welcomes home repentant people. All who see their sins must not only show repentance and hatred of sin, but must trust their eternal security to the Lord Jesus. With joy the young son was welcomed home, but before he could enter the house he had to be dressed in the clothing of a son. For repentant people to enter heaven they also need clothing from God, just as described by Isaiah, '...For he has clothed me with the garments of salvation, he has covered me with the robe of righteousness' (Isaiah 61:10). This righteousness is the gift of the Lord Jesus. Never will we boast of any self uprightness for our salvation is all of God. Paul put this truth plainly: 'For by grace you have been saved through faith, and that not of yourselves; it is the gift of God, not of works, lest anyone should boast' (Ephesians 2:8, 9).

As in the parable of the lost sheep and the lost coin there was great joy at the younger son's return. Heaven rejoices when a sinner repents and claims Christ as his Saviour.

THINGS TO DISCUSS WITH YOUR FAMILY

1. How do unbelievers become aware of the fact that they are sinners in God's sight?
2. Read and discuss 1 John 1:9 — 'If we confess our sins, he is faithful and just to forgive us our sins and to cleanse us from all unrighteousness.'
3. Why do we need Christ's righteousness to enter heaven?

Meditation

Meditate upon Proverbs 15:10 — 'Harsh discipline is for him who forsakes the way, and he who hates correction will die...'

Wise Words

The confession of evil works is the first beginning of good works. *Augustine*

 'A people who provoke me to anger ... who say, "Keep to yourself, do not come near me, for I am holier than you"' (Isaiah 65:3,5).

Read: Luke 15:25-32

I'm sure you all know people who consider they belong to a superior social class to you. These people have proud hearts and are like the elder son in Christ's parable.

The proud, elder son represented the Pharisees of Christ's day. They were self-righteous and refused to have anything to do with those they looked upon as outcasts of heaven — tax collectors and sinners. As he approached home the elder son heard the rejoicing and when he discovered the reason for the festivities he was furious. He was angry with his father for his obvious joy. He would not call his brother by an affectionate term, but simply said to his father, 'this son of yours'.

The scribes and Pharisees believed that faithful obedience to the law of God, as they understood it, would result in God welcoming them into the celestial city. When the compassionate Jesus invited spiritual outcasts to repent of their sins and trust themselves to him they were furious. The apostle John wrote of these people, 'He [Jesus] came to his own, and his own did not receive him' (John 1:11). Our Lord came to save unbelievers, including the arrogant Pharisees. The ex-Pharisee, Paul knew this and wrote, 'This is a faithful saying and worthy of all acceptance, that Christ Jesus came into the world to save sinners, of whom I am chief' (1 Timothy 1:15).

Like the Pharisees the elder brother was unwilling to talk with such a brother, even a repentant, sinful brother.

The Pharisees and all unbelievers need a change of heart. Nicodemus, a well-known Pharisee, had been told by Christ, 'Most assuredly, I say to you, unless one is born again, he cannot see the kingdom of God' (John 3:3). This was not some strange new doctrine that Christ was teaching for the prophet Ezekiel had quoted God, 'I will give you a new heart and put a new spirit within you; I will take the heart of stone out of your flesh and give you a heart of flesh. I will

put my Spirit within you and cause you to walk in my statutes...'
(Ezekiel 36:26,27).

This the Pharisees needed — to be born from above. They needed to put behind them their false teaching and follow faithfully all
that Christ was saying. They required a complete change in their
lifestyle which would come from a changed heart. Paul wrote of
their need: 'Therefore, if anyone is in Christ, he is a new creation;
old things have passed away; behold, all things have become new' (2
Corinthians 5:17).

When a person is born again, the law of God becomes a delight,
not a hardship. Obedience to God's law is a sign that we love him.
Jesus said, 'You are my friends if you do whatever I command you.'
One basic command was '...that you love one another as I have loved
you' (John 15:14, 12). This love was not found in the heart of the
Pharisees and other church leaders. They hated Jesus and wanted him
dead. Without repentance and a saving faith in the Lord Jesus you are
eternally lost.

THINGS TO DISCUSS WITH YOUR FAMILY

1. Describe the character of the elder brother. Read
   Proverbs 30:12.
2. Discuss Hebrews 12:2.
3. Read Luke 15:32. What did Jesus mean when he
   said this?

Meditation

Search your heart for any pride. If you find any, get rid of
it and ask God for forgiveness.

Wise Words

You might as well talk about a heavenly devil as talk
about a worldly Christian.   *Billy Sunday*

3 September   Parable of the unjust worker

 'For all things come from you, and of your own we have given you' (1 Chronicles 29:14).

Read: Luke 16:1-13

As we read our Bibles we frequently come to parts that are difficult to understand. The passage you have read might raise problems as you try to work out what Jesus was teaching his disciples. We know that the Pharisees were also listening to what was being said because after hearing the parable they mocked the Lord.

The parable is about a worker called 'the unjust steward'. This man was a thief and not to be imitated by anyone, especially people who call themselves Christians. As we read the parable we must remember it is about a wicked man. The rich man and the 'unjust steward' don't represent any particular group of people, but the parable has an important teaching that everyone should take to heart which is — make preparations for that time in the future when you will stand before Christ on the Day of Judgement.

In the parable, the manager of the property was to be called before the owner to explain the manner in which things were being done. Knowing that he was going to be dismissed for something underhand, he called all the owner's debtors together and had them rewrite their accounts so they had less to pay. This was theft! When the owner of the property discovered what had been done he realized that his manager, who was a thief, had shown human wisdom in preparing for the day when he was dismissed.

Christ is not telling us to act like the 'unjust steward', but to show spiritual wisdom in preparing for the day of our death. Obviously the only wise preparation we can make for that day is a saving faith in the Lord Jesus, repentance, a hatred of sin and living a life of holiness. Since our Lord was talking about money he warned his disciples that they were to use their possessions wisely. Paul wrote, 'For the things which are seen are temporary, but the things which are not seen are eternal' (2 Corinthians 4:18). Our text tells us that all we have has come from God and Jesus tells us to use it wisely to advance the kingdom of God.

The Lord teaches that to receive greater gifts from God we must show ourselves faithful in the wise use of lesser gifts. Again, since money is spoken about we must use our God-given finances not just for ourselves but to help the poor and those in need. If we do not prove faithful in caring for the property and finances of others, God will not give us money of our own to waste. Remember Paul's warning, 'Moreover it is required in stewards that one be found faithful' (1 Corinthians 4:2). Is this you?

Some people live for their money, pleasure and the world, but the saints live for God and his glory. They show that their faith is genuine by using God's gifts to help the needy and to extend the work of the gospel. We must understand that we cannot serve God and wealth, but should use our wealth for his praise and honour.

THINGS TO DISCUSS WITH YOUR FAMILY

1. Discuss 1 Timothy 6:10 — 'For the love of money is a root of all kinds of evil, for which some have strayed from the faith in their greediness.'
2. What did Jesus mean when he said, 'You cannot serve God and mammon' (Luke 16:13)?
3. Make a list of how you can use your money wisely.

Meditation

Consider Psalm 69:30 — 'I will praise the name of God with a song, and will magnify him with thanksgiving.'

Wise Words

If men do not put the love of the world to death, the love of the world will put them to death. *Ralph Venning*

'Make me walk in the path of your commandments, for I delight in it. Incline my heart to your testimonies, and not to covetousness' (Psalm 119:35,36).

Read: Luke 16:14-18

When we open our newspapers we find them filled with advertisements for everything we need to make life more comfortable — or so they claim. Jesus had been talking about the Pharisees who loved their wealth and made no real effort to help those in need.

Jesus had been speaking to his disciples, but when the Pharisees overheard what was said they mocked him because they considered what was being taught was just foolishness. Our Saviour rebuked the proud Pharisees by telling them that God knew what their hearts were really like, despite their outward show. Paul wrote, 'For not he who commends himself is approved, but whom the Lord commends' (2 Corinthians 10:18). Again it is what God knows of the human heart that matters.

Jesus then taught that the Old Testament ceremonial ways were ending. Until the time of John the Baptist the Jews had been told to look for the coming of Christ, but now he was present and calling unbelievers to faith in himself. Entrance into the kingdom of God required effort as it does today. In Christ's day to become a follower of Jesus meant persecution and hatred from the church leaders and often friends and family members. Today when a member of an unfaithful church is converted, persecution usually commences, and harsh criticism comes from those who should know better.

Despite persecution, membership in the kingdom of God means joy and peace within the heart. Two statements from Paul give the Christian every reason to praise God and calmly rest in the Saviour — 'There is therefore now no condemnation to those who are in Christ Jesus, who do not walk according to the flesh, but according to the Spirit'; and '...a man is not justified by the works of the law but by faith in Jesus Christ, even we have believed in Christ Jesus, that we might be justified by faith in Christ and not by the works of the law; for by the works of the law no flesh shall be justified' (Romans 8:1; Galatians 2:16).

Salvation by faith alone does not mean the law is put aside. The ceremonial law was perfectly fulfilled in Christ's saving work, but the moral law is ours to obey. Jesus said, ' You are my friends if you do whatever I command you' (John 15:14). This law was summarized: '"You shall love the LORD your God with all your heart, with all your soul, and with all your mind." This is the first and great commandment. And the second is like it: "You shall love your neighbour as yourself"' (Matthew 22:37-39).

Jesus then pointed to the law of marriage which the Pharisees had undermined. Divorce, according to some, was permissible for almost any reason the husband had — just or unjust. Isaiah wrote truly of Christ, 'He will magnify the law and make it honourable' (Isaiah 42:21). Are you able to say with the Apostle Paul, 'I delight in the law of God according to the inward man' (Romans 7:22)?

THINGS TO DISCUSS WITH YOUR FAMILY

1. Today what things make it difficult to enter the kingdom of God?
2. Why is divorce so common in today's world?
3. What is the difference between God's moral law and the ceremonial law?

Meditation

Meditate upon the law of God and its value to our sinful world.

Wise Words

The law reflects the nature and character of God just as surely as does the gospel. *Douglas Macmillan*

'For the wages of sin is death, but the gift of God is eternal life in Christ Jesus our Lord' (Romans 6:23).

Read: Luke 16:19-31

Rarely in Australia do we see people begging as our government provides financial help for those in need. However, on a trip to Asia some years ago I saw people begging and found this distressing.

Jesus now tells us of two men — one a very rich man who would have been respected by those who knew him, and a needy man who was probably a cripple and had to beg for his daily food. In the eyes of those who passed by he would have been a nobody. Yet, we very soon discover in this story that God viewed these men differently. Wealth is not necessarily a sign of God's blessing. If you read Psalm 73 you will discover this truth. Jeremiah quoted God: 'Let not the wise man glory in his wisdom, let not the mighty man glory in his might, nor let the rich man glory in his riches; but let him who glories glory in this, that he understands and knows me, that I am the LORD, exercising loving kindness, judgement, and righteousness in the earth. For in these I delight' (Jeremiah 9:23,24). The rich man failed to use his wealth wisely and had no treasure in heaven.

Soon both men died as we read in Ecclesiastes 3:20: 'All go to one place: all are from the dust and all return to dust.' All who profess faith in the Lord Jesus should daily live in the knowledge that they will one day die and face judgement. This story, told by Jesus, plainly teaches that following death, while the body is buried and returns to dust, the soul returns to God and is very much alive.

However we notice the difference between the death of the rich man and that of Lazarus. Godly Lazarus was carried by God's angels to Abraham's bosom — another name the Jews had for heaven. How true are the psalmist's words, 'Precious in the sight of the LORD is the death of His saints' (Psalm 116:15). There he enjoyed the blessings of God and the company of the believers who had gone before him. The rich man died and his soul was turned into hell to suffer eternal punishments as we read in Revelation 14:11: 'And the smoke of their torment ascends for ever and ever; and they have no rest day or night, who worship the beast and his image, and whoever receives the mark of his name.' This is the end for all who do not have saving faith in the Lord Jesus.

The man in hell pleaded for relief, but that was impossible. He then asked that Lazarus might return and warn his brothers of hell, but Jesus said that even if one returned from death they would not believe. Jesus returned from the grave and the Jews laughed and persecuted anyone who believed this to be true and became one of his disciples.

Reader, all I can say to you is — don't die in your sins as your destiny will be hopeless and you will frequently say, 'If only...'

THINGS TO DISCUSS WITH YOUR FAMILY

1. What can believers expect when they die?
2. Why does God have a hell?
3. Jesus suffered hell for his people. What was the worst aspect of his suffering?

Meditation

Meditate upon Mark 8:36 — 'For what will it profit a man if he gains the whole world, and loses his own soul.'

Wise Words

As surely as God is eternal, so surely is heaven an endless day without night and hell and endless night without day.
J. C. Ryle

'Give no offence, either to the Jews or to
the Greeks or to the church of God, just
as I also please all men in all things, not
seeking my own profit, but the profit of
many, that they may be saved' (1 Corinthians 10:32,33).

Read: Luke 17:1-4

It is very easy to put stumbling blocks before sinners that cause
them to turn away from Christ and salvation. One of the most
common is when we hear Christians being critical of the church or
their minister. When our children hear these comments their natural
inclination is to want nothing to do with a faith that causes such re-
marks from those they love.

Jesus knew that this sin would be found everywhere in society.
After all, the Pharisees and others were doing all they could to prevent people believing in him. One great example of this in the Old
Testament was that of David and his adultery with Bathsheba and
the murder of her husband, Uriah. When confronted by Nathan the
prophet, he was told, '... because of this deed you have given great
occasion to the enemies of the LORD to blaspheme' (2 Samuel 12:14).

Following the resurrection of the Lord, the Pharisees and church
leaders went out of their way to prevent the gospel being taken to the
Gentiles. Paul in his letter to the Romans rebuked those wicked Jews:
'The name of God is blasphemed among the Gentiles because of you'
(Romans 2:24). The Apostle Paul had the correct attitude which all
Christians should adopt. This is our text for today.

Jesus spoke of such offences against 'little ones', referring to those
who were 'babes in Christ' (Matthew 18:6). Christians are to grow in
the Lord and not remain spiritual babes for ever. All who love Jesus
should continually feed new Christians with the solid food of the
Word of God and pray that they might grow spiritually.

We can put stumbling blocks before others by laughing at filthy
jokes, watching and discussing approvingly the immoral television
shows that many people watch, or by pilfering the boss's property.

Jesus then told his disciples that they were to forgive those who
offended them. He instructed them to approach the one who caused
the hurt and seek his repentance and then forgive him — as often as

the person repents. We forgive others as God forgives us (Matthew 6:12).

The Scripture clearly teaches how we are to act when hurt by another, 'Do not say, "I will do to him just as he has done to me; I will render to the man according to his work"' (Proverbs 24:29). Obviously if there is no repentance, true reconciliation is not possible, but we must show Christian love to everyone, even the person who will not repent. The Apostle John wrote a great deal on the subject of Christian love, as did the Apostle Paul. John says that Christian love is a sign of the new birth — 'We know that we have passed from death to life, because we love the brethren. He who does not love his brother abides in death'; and 'If someone says, "I love God," and hates his brother, he is a liar; for he who does not love his brother whom he has seen, how can he love God whom he has not seen? And this commandment we have from him: that he who loves God must love his brother also' (1 John 3:14; 4:20,21).

THINGS TO DISCUSS WITH YOUR FAMILY

1. If there are people you should forgive, what are you doing about it?
2. Discuss — 'There is nothing wrong with holding grudges.'
3. 'Proud people do not forgive.' Is this true?

Meditation

Meditate upon your acts of Christian love to those who have offended you.

Wise Words

Nothing causes us to so nearly resemble God as the forgiveness of injuries.   *Chrysostom*

'But God forbid that I should boast except in the cross of our Lord Jesus Christ, by whom the world has been crucified to me, and I to the world' (Galatians 6:14).

Read: Luke 17:5-10

Often people ask for help and we do what we can to solve the person's problem. The disciples made a most thoughtful request of the Lord Jesus, and one that we should also make — 'Increase our faith.'

Saving faith is not something that we can somehow create within our own heart, as it is a gift of God. The Apostle Paul put it plainly — 'For by grace you have been saved through faith, and that not of yourselves; it is the gift of God, not of works, lest anyone should boast. For we are his workmanship, created in Christ Jesus for good works, which God prepared beforehand that we should walk in them' (Ephesians 2: 8-10). Salvation is all of God's grace from beginning to end and we must ever praise him for that wonderful work.

Some time before, the disciples had been involved in a situation where they could not cast out a demon. Jesus told them that they lacked the faith to carry out such a great miracle (Matthew 17:14-21).

Faith is fundamental to our salvation for it is our link to God. In Hebrews 11:6 we read, 'But without faith it is impossible to please him, for he who comes to God must believe that he is, and that he is a rewarder of those who diligently seek him.' Sinners must approach God and pray for saving faith and then pray that it will grow. In verse 6 Jesus used what appears to be a proverb to explain the growth of faith. The Apostle Paul used a similar expression (1 Corinthians 13:2).

Jesus told the parable of the servant and his relationship with his master. Our faith, being the sovereign gift of God means that we become his willing servants. As such we cannot expect to be treated as an equal to God or to our Saviour Christ. Jesus set the example of servanthood for we read that he '...made himself of no reputation, taking the form of a bondservant, and coming in the likeness of men. And being found in appearance as a man, he humbled himself and became obedient to the point of death, even the death of the cross' (Philippians 2:7,8). He perfectly obeyed his Father and showed his disciples that they also were to act as servants. On one occasion after washing his disciples' feet he told them, 'If I then, your Lord and Teacher, have washed your feet, you also ought to wash one another's feet. For I have given you an example, that you should do as I have done to you' (John 13:14,15).

The teaching of this parable is summed up in Christ's words, 'So likewise you, when you have done all those things which you are commanded, say, "We are unprofitable servants. We have done what was our duty to do"' (Luke 17:10). Even though our salvation is all of grace, God does reward his servants for their faithfulnesss. On Judgement Day our Lord will say, 'Well done, good and faithful servant; you were faithful over a few things, I will make you ruler over many things. Enter into the joy of your lord' (Matthew 25:21). Then we will sit with him at the great wedding feast (Revelation 19:7-9). We have a glorious Saviour and Lord.

THINGS TO DISCUSS WITH YOUR FAMILY

1. What can you do to increase your faith?
2. How do you boast in the cross of the Lord Jesus Christ? Read your text — Galatians 6:14.
3. Discuss Eliphaz's words to Job found in Job 22:1-3.

Meditation

Meditate upon your servant-hood to Jesus and all that you owe your Lord and Saviour.

Wise Words

There is such a thing as pride which wears the cloak of humility. *J. C. Ryle*

'Behold, I tell you a mystery: We shall not all sleep, but we shall all be changed - in a moment, in the twinkling of an eye, at the last trumpet. For the trumpet will sound, and the dead will be raised incorruptible, and we shall be changed' (1 Corinthians 15:51,52).

Read: John 11:1-27

In life we are surrounded by sickness, distress and death. This world is a sad place due to sin — both original sin that we have inherited from Adam, and our own personal sin.

Lazarus lived with his sisters Mary and Martha at Bethany which was about two miles from Jerusalem where the Pharisees and priests were plotting to get rid of Jesus as soon as they could. Mary and Martha sent a message to Jesus, 'Lord, behold, he whom you love is sick.' After some discussion Jesus told his disciples plainly that Lazarus had died, but not before he had described death as a 'sleep'. He also told his disciples that Lazarus' death was not permanent, but that through the events that would occur he (Jesus) would be glorified, and through him God also.

Today's text does the same. It paints a picture of the body peacefully sleeping in the grave awaiting the day when Christ returns in majestic power and glory to raise the bodies of the dead and reunite them with their souls which have been with him in the heavenly realms.

The disciples were afraid to return to the region of Jerusalem as they feared Christ's enemies would kill him and they would be martyred. Yet, we read the courageous words of 'doubting' Thomas, 'Let us also go, that we may die with him.' Jesus knew that he would not die as it was still 'daytime' for him. He had much to do before he would die and no one could take his life until God's providence gave his enemies permission to do so.

When Jesus and the twelve arrived in Bethany Lazarus had been dead for four days. Martha met him and said that had he come earlier he could have healed her brother. Jesus told her that her brother would rise again and spoke some of the most comforting words in the Scriptures, 'I am the resurrection and the life. He who believes in me, though he may die, he shall live. And whoever lives and believes in me shall never die.'

Here Jesus tells us that despite the fact that our body dies, those who trust in him, like Lazarus in the parable, will be in 'Abraham's bosom' (Luke 16:22) — heaven. All who believe in Christ will never die spiritually, but will in their resurrected body eternally live with Jesus in the new heavens and new earth.

When Martha was asked if she believed Christ's words that he was 'the resurrection and the life' her reply was a statement of her saving faith, 'Yes, Lord, I believe that you are the Christ, the Son of God, who is to come into the world.'

If you have put your saving faith in the Lord Jesus, eternal death cannot touch you. You will live eternally with him who is Saviour and Lord of all his people.

THINGS TO DISCUSS WITH YOUR FAMILY

1. What was the special purpose for the death of Lazarus?
2. Why did Jesus describe death as a 'sleep'?
3. When will the resurrection take place and what will happen on that day?

Meditation

Meditate upon 'Christ's delays are not his denials.'

Wise Words

God fits our souls here to possess a glorious body after; and he will fit the body for a glorious soul.

Richard Sibbes

'Let us therefore come boldly to the throne of grace, that we may obtain mercy and find grace to help in time of need' (Hebrews 4:16).

Read: John 11:28-44

In most societies, crowds of friends and relatives gather to comfort those who are grieving the death of a dear one. Funerals are events where most people meet others they haven't seen for many years.

It was the same at Bethany. Crowds had gathered to grieve with Martha and Mary and to give them some comfort. We should do the same when death takes one loved by a friend or relative. In such times our text tells us what we should do — go to Jesus Christ, our great High Priest, our Lord and Saviour, who is merciful to all of his people. The compassion he showed while on earth to those in need he shows today by comforting the heart of those distressed by tragic events.

We grieve when we lose a loved one, but Christians are given hope, for the apostle wrote, 'But I do not want you to be ignorant, brethren, concerning those who have fallen asleep, lest you sorrow as others who have no hope. For if we believe that Jesus died and rose again, even so God will bring with him those who sleep in Jesus. For this we say to you by the word of the Lord, that we who are alive and remain until the coming of the Lord will by no means precede those who are asleep. For the Lord himself will descend from heaven with a shout, with the voice of an archangel, and with the trumpet of God. And the dead in Christ will rise first. Then we who are alive and re-main shall be caught up together with them in the clouds to meet the Lord in the air. And thus we shall always be with the Lord. Therefore comfort one another with these words' (1 Thessalonians 4:13-18).

When the Lord observed the distress caused by sin, and felt the pain caused by the death of his friend, 'Jesus wept' — the shortest verse in the Bible. After asking some of those present to remove the big tombstone, Martha warned him that Lazarus' body would have an unpleasant odour, as it was four days since he died. Jesus told her what he had told his disciples, 'Did I not say to you that if you would believe you would see the glory of God?' Then he looked heavenward and prayed aloud so everyone could hear him acknowledge that God had sent him into the world.

There could be no doubting that Jesus was the Messiah, the Son of God, who was God and man in the one Person and what he was about to do would bring glory to his heavenly Father. Then in a loud voice he gave the command, 'Lazarus, come forth!' Lazarus, wrapped in his burial clothes, gently stepped out of the tomb. Here was another demonstration of Christ's power. Some Christians believe that this was his greatest miracle.

Can you say with Paul, 'I know whom I have believed and am persuaded that he is able to keep what I have committed to him until that Day' (2 Timothy 1:12)? Death is not the end of existence. May God grant us all grace to prepare for our death and the Day of Judgement which will surely follow.

THINGS TO DISCUSS WITH YOUR FAMILY

1. What effect should this miracle have had upon everyone present that day?
2. What did this miracle prove about the Christ?
3. How can you comfort people who mourn the death of loved ones?

Meditation

Meditate upon Paul's words that Jesus is 'the eternally blessed God' (Romans 9:5).

Wise Words

Let us pray for such stores of inward faith, that when our turn comes to suffer, we may suffer patiently and believe all is well.   *J. C. Ryle*

'If they do not hear Moses and the prophets, neither will they be persuaded though one rise from the dead' (Luke 16:31).

Read: John 11:45-57

Had I been present that day, by the grace of God I would have given myself to Jesus who was God and man in one Person — the Son of God who exercised almighty power in all that he did. Sadly however, not all thought that way.

Our text comes from Christ's parable of the rich man and Lazarus and reinforces a truth we find fulfilled when Lazarus rose from the dead. Following the resurrection of our Saviour only small numbers have come to saving faith.

In Jerusalem when the Pharisees and priests heard what had happened they plotted Jesus' death. Having acknowledged that he had performed miracles they should have reassessed their conclusions concerning his claim to be the Son of God, the Messiah. But no, they wanted him killed. Later they even wanted Lazarus put to death to get rid of the evidence of the great miracle. Those church leaders were students of the Scriptures and knew the eighth commandment — 'You shall not murder' (Exodus 20:13). They expected Christ to establish the kingdom of God in Israel, but again they misunderstood that God's kingdom is within the heart of his people. Jesus told the Pharisees, 'The kingdom of God does not come with observation; nor will they say, "See here!" or "See there!" For indeed, the kingdom of God is within you' (Luke 17:20,21).

Caiaphas, the high priest, called a meeting to plan Christ's death. This partially fulfilled Psalm 2:2,3 — 'And the rulers take counsel together, against the LORD and against his Anointed, saying, "Let us break their bonds in pieces and cast away their cords from us."' Caiaphas argued that if Pilate and Caesar heard Christ's claim to be King of Israel the Roman armies would destroy the nation. He then made a statement, implanted in his mind by the Holy Spirit, '... it is expedient for us that one man should die for the people, and not that the whole nation should perish.' This was a politically expedient reason for what he wanted done. Governments today are no different. Little did Caiaphas know that the murder of Jesus would bring God's fierce anger upon them and the nation would be destroyed.

How true were those words — Jesus would die for sinful people and sinners would be saved. The whole nation would not be cast into hell. The Apostle John recorded that the Lord would not only die for repentant Jews, but those members of God's kingdom 'scattered abroad'. This means elect Jews and Gentiles living throughout the world and in all ages.

Having agreed to murder Jesus, the church leaders went about their religious duties to ensure they were purified and able to take part in the forthcoming Passover festivities. What they needed was a heart made pure by the Holy Spirit. Jesus was aware of their plans and moved away from Jerusalem for he had work to carry out before he was sacrificed for his people.

Are you born again or are you just carrying out your spiritual activities as a matter of form?

THINGS TO DISCUSS WITH YOUR FAMILY

1. Why did Caiaphas want Jesus put to death?
2. Discuss Matthew 5:8 — 'Blessed are the pure in heart, for they shall see God.'
3. Following the raising of Lazarus what should the church leaders have done?

Meditation

Meditate on the evidence that should have caused the church leaders to recognize Jesus as Messiah.

Wise Words

The hideous inconsistency of the Jewish formalists in our Lord's time has never been without a long succession of followers. *J. C. Ryle*

Ten lepers

'Be anxious for nothing, but in everything by prayer and supplication, with
thanksgiving, let your requests be made
known to God; and the peace of God,
which surpasses all understanding, will
guard your hearts and minds through
Christ Jesus' (Philippians 4:6,7).

Read: Luke 17:11-19

Most people enjoy making a trip to their nation's capital city to
see all the important buildings and monuments. Often people
gather in these cities for important festivities. The Royal Easter Show
in Sydney, Australia, is annually visited by several million people.

Jesus was setting out for Jerusalem to take part in the Passover
activities. It was not to be a joyful occasion for him, but his death
upon a Roman cross. Following the raising of Lazarus he had left the
Jerusalem area. Now we find him on the border between Samaria
and Galilee. There as he was about to enter a village he saw ten lepers
standing at a distance and calling for help, 'Jesus, Master, have mercy
on us!' These men were outcasts as required by God's law — 'He
shall be unclean. All the days he has the sore he shall be unclean. He
is unclean, and he shall dwell alone; his dwelling shall be outside the
camp' (Leviticus 13:46).

Leprosy is a terrible disease and is likened to sin. The sinner is
a spiritual leper who is living outside the kingdom of God. He has
no way of entrance into that kingdom until he is cleansed of his sin.
This was achieved by the Lord Jesus when he was sacrificed for the
sins of his people. He won God's forgiveness and cleansed us with his
imputed righteousness. In God's sight we are holy as he is holy.

Jesus told the ten lepers to go and show themselves to the priests
as specified by God's law (Leviticus 14:1ff). At that moment they
were lepers, but as they moved off in obedience to his command
they were healed. Nine continued on their way, but one, realizing
what a great miracle had occurred, turned about to thank the Lord.
The unusual thing about this man was that he was one of the hated
Samaritans. His fellow lepers, who were Jews, had not bothered to
return with him to praise God for their healing.

The Samaritan 'glorified God' and fell down before Jesus and
thanked him.

Gratitude is a rare commodity in our world today. People demand their rights and accept what is given as something they deserve. Humility is not found in many hearts, but we must all understand that in God's sight we are all sinners deserving his wrath — eternal hell.

Jesus has done so much for his people that we must continually offer 'the sacrifice of praise' (Hebrews 13:15). We must be like the psalmist and show our appreciation to God for all his goodness. We must, '...proclaim with the voice of thanksgiving, and tell of all [his] wondrous works...' (Psalm 26:7). Our text reminds us to appreciate all God's gifts. Paul wrote: 'Continue earnestly in prayer, being vigilant in it with thanksgiving' (Colossians 4:2). In heaven above the inhabitants praise God with wondrous words of love, 'Amen! Blessing and glory and wisdom, thanksgiving and honour and power and might, be to our God for ever and ever. Amen' (Revelation 7:12). May these words be always on our lips.

THINGS TO DISCUSS
WITH YOUR FAMILY

1. Discuss Christ's words in Luke 17:19 — 'Your faith has made you well.'
2. What was Naaman told to do by Elisha in order to be healed of leprosy? See 2 Kings 5:10ff.
3. How can you thank your minister for all the work he carries out for your congregation?

Meditation

Give thanks to God for all that he has done for you — physically, mentally and spiritually.

Wise Words

Thankfulness is a flower which will never bloom well excepting upon a root of deep humility.   *J. C. Ryle*

'Behold, I am coming as a thief. Blessed is he who watches, and keeps his garments, lest he walk naked and they see his shame' (Revelation 16:15).

Read: Luke 17:20-37

I'm sure we all have many questions to ask the Lord Jesus when we get to heaven. The well-educated Pharisees certainly asked a lot when he came into this world two thousand years ago. Christ was making his way to Jerusalem for the Passover and was met by some Pharisees who asked him when they could expect the appearance of the kingdom of God. Jesus warned them about people who would declare that he had come and was building his earthly kingdom.

We know that the kingdom of God is established in the hearts of men and women when they are born again. The visible kingdom of God will be seen when Christ returns in power and majestic glory as 'KING OF KINGS AND LORD OF LORDS' (Revelation 19:16). Jesus told the Pharisees that his return would be sudden and at a time unexpected by the majority of the world's population. Yet they were told that when he returned he would be seen by everyone just as lightning is visible as it flashes across the heavens. Elsewhere we are told that his return will not only be seen by those still living, but 'every eye will see him, even they who pierced him' (Revelation 1:7).

The Lord likened his return for his people to that day when Noah and his family entered the ark and God shut the door. Then condemnation fell upon the ungodly. He also likened the day of judgement to the day when Lot and his family left Sodom to escape God's anger. He made special mention of Lot's wife who disobeyed God and looked back to the place she loved. Before this, Christ warned people not to live for the world, because his coming meant the loss of everything they held dear. In the book of Revelation we read of their 'loss' — 'For in one hour such great riches came to nothing ... The sound of harpists, musicians, flutists, and trumpeters shall not be heard in you anymore. No craftsman of any craft shall be found in you anymore, and the sound of a millstone shall not be heard in you anymore. The light of a lamp shall not shine in you anymore, and the voice of bridegroom and bride shall not be heard in you anymore' (Revelation 18:17, 22,23).

For the ungodly at Christ's sudden return, there will be the loss of all their worldly possessions and the noise of joyful activities silenced. For God's beloved people it will be a day of great rejoicing and praise for we shall see our Saviour face to face and receive our glorified bodies. Then the kingdom of God will be an eternal, visible reality in the new heavens and new earth.

How can you prepare for Christ's sudden return when the world mocks you for believing this truth? The Apostle Peter tells us, 'Therefore, beloved, looking forward to these things, be diligent to be found by him in peace, without spot and blameless ... [growing] in the grace and knowledge of our Lord and Saviour Jesus Christ' (2 Peter 3:14,18).

THINGS TO DISCUSS WITH YOUR FAMILY

1. How can you prepare for Christ's return?
2. When speaking to the Pharisees, why did the Lord mention Lot's wife?
3. Why is Christ's return described as being like a 'thief in the night' (1 Thessalonians 5:2)?

Meditation

Meditate upon Psalm 47:2 — 'For the LORD Most High is awesome; he is a great King over all the earth.'

Wise Words

I never preach a sermon without thinking that possibly the Lord may come before I preach another.

D. L. Moody

'Rejoice always, pray without ceasing, in everything give thanks; for this is the will of God in Christ Jesus for you' (1 Thessalonians 5:16-18).

Read: Luke 18:1-8

This parable speaks of something we have all experienced one way or another. How often have we given in to the persistent demands of others? How often have we made the same request many times to get something we really wanted? I'm sure the Pharisees and others who were listening understood what Christ was teaching.

Prayer is our lifeline to God. When we come to our heavenly Father in Christ's name and merit, he listens to what we have to say. He will answer our prayers for his own glory and the good of his people. Christ had been talking about his second coming and the establishment of the kingdom of God. He had many times told his disciples that they would suffer persecution with the possible loss of their life because of their faithfulness to him. In this context Jesus was telling his followers that they were to continually knock on heaven's door pleading for God's blessings and for justice upon their enemies. Even in heaven the saints, many who had been martyred, cried out, 'How long, O Lord, holy and true, until you judge and avenge our blood on those who dwell on the earth?' (Revelation 6:10).

Throughout the ages the saints have been persecuted, martyred and mocked. People laugh at the idea that Christ will return. Peter wrote, '...scoffers will come in the last days, walking according to their own lusts, and saying, "Where is the promise of his coming? For since the fathers fell asleep, all things continue as they were from the beginning of creation"' (2 Peter 3:3,4). Intolerance will grow more violent as the day of Christ's return gets nearer. In fact it will seem to many that the church is dead. In Revelation 11 we read of the church under the symbol of two prophets lying dead in the streets while the godless rejoice. However, Jesus said of his church that 'the gates of Hades [hell] shall not prevail against it' (Matthew 16:18).

Our Saviour has promised preserving grace to all his people. We read that promise in Isaiah 43:2,3 — 'When you pass through the waters, I will be with you; and through the rivers, they shall not over-flow you. When you walk through the fire, you shall not be burned, nor shall the flame scorch you. For I am the LORD your God, the Holy One of Israel, your Saviour.'

God has loved his people 'with an everlasting love' (Jeremiah 31:3), but there is a day of condemnation coming for all who have no saving faith in Christ.

Jesus asked the question whether there would be saints living when he returned. The answer is, 'Yes.' In 1 Thessalonians 4:15-17 Paul states this truth clearly, '…we who are alive and remain until the coming of the Lord will by no means precede those who are asleep. For the Lord himself will descend from heaven … And the dead in Christ will rise first. Then we who are alive and remain shall be caught up together with them in the clouds to meet the Lord in the air. And thus we shall always be with the Lord.'

Persecuted saints, pray on. God listens and is ready to answer to the praise of his glory.

THINGS TO DISCUSS WITH YOUR FAMILY

1. What is prayer?
2. What is required for our prayers to be answered?
3. Will there be a Christian church in existence when Christ returns? How do you know?

Meditation

Meditate upon persevering prayer e.g. 'Elijah was a man with a nature like ours, and he prayed earnestly that it would not rain; and it did not rain on the land for three years and six months' (James 5:17).

Wise Words

God does not keep office hours.   *A. W. Tozer*

 'Blessed is he whose transgression is forgiven, whose sin is covered. Blessed is the man to whom the LORD does not impute iniquity' (Psalm 32:1,2).

Read: Luke 18:9-14

Do you ever feel that you are much better than certain other people because you have greater ability, are more intelligent, or because you go to church? If so, beware. The parable you have read is about a man who thought he was far better than the tax collector beside him. In fact he believed that he was so good that God should bless him. In Proverbs 20:6 we read something true about most people, 'Most men will proclaim each his own goodness.'

The self-righteous Pharisee had never been born again. He saw things through his natural sinful heart. He didn't believe what David had written, 'Behold, I was brought forth in iniquity, and in sin my mother conceived me' (Psalm 51:5). He failed to understand that as an unrepentant sinner he would die and suffer God's eternal anger.

As you read the words spoken by the Pharisee, I'm sure you will say, 'That doesn't sound like a prayer but a speech comparing himself to the tax collector beside him when he should have compared himself to God.' Moses recorded God's words to the people of Israel — 'You shall be holy, for I the LORD your God am holy' (Leviticus 19:2). The Pharisee didn't understand that he was a spiritual leper in God's sight — unclean! His 'prayer' came from his proud brain.

The tax collector knew that he had nothing to offer God to gain mercy. He was humbled by his sins and couldn't look upwards towards heaven. He beat his chest in despair because of his sins and did the only thing he could — plead for God's forgiveness and mercy. He knew that God was a God of mercy who forgave those who are truly repentant.

This man's prayer came from his 'born again' heart of which David said, 'The sacrifices of God are a broken spirit, a broken and a contrite heart — these, O God, you will not despise' (Psalm 51:17). That man went to his home no doubt with his heart full of praise because God's peace filled his heart. He was justified — pardoned because of Christ's sacrificial death on the cross and clothed in the imputed righteousness of his Saviour.

Today when sinners are convicted of their sins they are drawn to the Lord Jesus where with a repentant heart they will find mercy. Jesus came into this world to save sinful humans — not fallen angels. The writer to the Hebrews said of our Lord, 'in all things he had to be made like his brethren, that he might be a merciful and faithful High Priest in things pertaining to God, to make propitiation for the sins of the people' (Hebrews 2:17).

Praise God for our wonderful, compassionate Saviour.

THINGS TO DISCUSS WITH YOUR FAMILY

1. What was a tax collector and why were they so hated by the Jews?
2. Why did the tax collector 'beat his breast'?
3. Why should God have mercy on you?

Meditation

Meditate upon Romans 3:28 — 'Therefore we conclude that a man is justified by faith apart from the deeds of the law.'

The tax collector confessed plainly that he was a sinner. This is the very ABC of saving Christianity; we never begin to be good till we can feel and say that we are bad.

J. C. Ryle

Wise Words

'Therefore a man shall leave his father and mother and be joined to his wife, and they shall become one flesh' (Genesis 2:24).

Read: Matthew 19:1-12

We live in a world where marriage vows are frequently not kept. Divorce is common causing much heartache and often great anger. Jesus lived in a society where divorce was common for a great variety of reasons, even burning the toast for breakfast. Today in many countries divorce needs no reason, just separation for a period of time. Many couples today don't bother to go through any marriage ceremony.

Our text reminds us that men and women marry and live together as husband and wife. Divorce was not part of God's plan, but when sin entered the world, marriages began to break down. To give some protection to a divorced woman, God's law demanded that a certificate of divorce be given, which in effect declared the marriage to be finished. But in the days of Malachi, God spoke out against this practice which had become very common. We read, '...let none deal treacherously with the wife of his youth ... For the LORD God of Israel says that he hates divorce' (Malachi 2:15,16).

The Pharisees questioned Jesus about his attitude towards divorce, hoping he would say something they could later use against him. Maybe they hoped he would speak out against King Herod's divorce and remarriage which was contrary to God's law. Herod had John the Baptist killed because of this. The leading scholars of the day had differing opinions about the problem, but here our Saviour gave one reason for a legitimate breakdown of a marriage — 'sexual immorality.' Later he gave further grounds for ending a marriage (1 Corinthians 7:10-16).

When the disciples heard their Master's narrow teaching on the subject they concluded 'it is better not to marry.' But this conclusion was wrong. Again he gave a sound reason for marriage, '...if they cannot exercise self-control, let them marry. For it is better to marry than to burn with passion' (1 Corinthians 7:9). Jesus said that some people were given the gift of remaining single. Some took action to remove any desire for marriage, but let us remember, 'Marriage is honourable among all, and the bed undefiled; but fornicators and adulterers God will judge' (Hebrews 13:4). The Apostle Peter was married and his wife often accompanied him on his preaching journeys (1 Corinthians 9:5).

Paul wrote some beautiful words about marriage which we should take to heart: 'Wives, submit to your own husbands, as to the Lord. For the husband is head of the wife... Husbands, love your wives, just as Christ also loved the church and gave himself for her...' (Ephesians 5:22,23,25).

Always remember that divorce and remarriage are not unforgiveable sins.

THINGS TO DISCUSS WITH YOUR FAMILY

1. Discuss Peter's words in 1 Peter 3:7: 'Husbands, likewise, dwell with them with understanding, giving honour to the wife, as to the weaker vessel, and as being heirs together of the grace of life, that your prayers may not be hindered.'
2. What are some of the responsibilities that come with marriage?
3. Marriage should be a happy institution. Read and discuss Psalms 127 and 128.

Meditation

Pray that God will make you a sexually moral Christian.

Wise Words

Try praising your wife, even if it does frighten her at first.
Billy Sunday

'For the unbelieving husband is sanctified by the wife, and the unbelieving
wife is sanctified by the husband; otherwise your children would be unclean,
but now they are holy' (1 Corinthians
7:14).

Read: Mark 10:13-16

We should love our children dearly for they are God's gift to
us. He has given us the responsibility of teaching them how
to live in society, but of more importance is that they are taught the
way of salvation. We, and the congregation, should pray for our young
people who find it difficult growing up in this sinful world.

Jesus was confronted by parents and others caring for little covenant children, asking that he might touch and bless them. The children didn't need the healing of their bodies, but rather that they
might be awakened spiritually to their need of a Saviour.

Today we bring our children to the Lord in prayer that he might
touch them spiritually and bring them to repentance and saving faith.
God's promise to Abraham that he would be God to him and his
children (Genesis 17:7) applies today. In Peter's Pentecost sermon he
said, 'Repent, and let every one of you be baptised in the name of
Jesus Christ for the remission of sins; and you shall receive the gift of
the Holy Spirit. For the promise is to you and to your children, and
to all who are afar off, as many as the Lord our God will call' (Acts
2:38,39). The children of Christians are not to be treated as little
pagans, for the Apostle Paul wrote, 'For the unbelieving husband is
sanctified by the wife, and the unbelieving wife is sanctified by the
husband; otherwise your children would be unclean, but now they
are holy' (1 Corinthians 7:14).

The disciples couldn't tolerate being bothered by the little ones
and wanted to send them away, but the compassionate Jesus said, 'Let
the little children come to me, and do not forbid them; for of such is
the kingdom of heaven.' The children were special to our Lord. They
looked to him with a trust in their eyes and he blessed them. This
reminds me of the words of Isaiah 40:11: 'He will feed his flock like
a shepherd; he will gather the lambs with his arm, and carry them in
his bosom, and gently lead those who are with young.'

Oh, how we should care for the spiritual well-being of our children. The Apostle Paul tells the head of the Christian family — 'do not provoke your children to wrath, but bring them up in the training and admonition of the Lord' (Ephesians 6:4).

Parents must pray for their family and teach them the things of God. We must take our children to worship and involve them in family devotions. We must set them a godly witness as parents who love the Lord and delight in obedience to his word.

Jesus finally told his disciples that those who wanted citizenship in the kingdom of God had to believe in him like the small children who were before them.

THINGS TO DISCUSS WITH YOUR FAMILY

1. What responsibilities do we have to our children and grandchildren?
2. If you don't have family worship, why not commence this with your family at once?
3. Discuss Christ's words in Mark 10:15 — '...Whoever does not receive the kingdom of God as a little child will by no means enter it.'

Meditation

Meditate upon God's promise to his people, 'I will pour my Spirit on your descendants, and my blessing on your offspring' (Isaiah 44:3).

Wise Words

The best way to beat the devil is to hit him over the head with a cradle. *Billy Sunday*

'For the love of money is a root of all kinds of evil, for which some have strayed from the faith in their greediness, and pierced themselves through with many sorrows' (1 Timothy 6:10).

Read: Matthew 19:16-26

The words of our text are so true. Most people love money and want more and more so they can purchase more of the world's treasures. The young man who met the Lord Jesus was one of these people and his love of money was leading him to a Christless eternity.

However, the young man was concerned about his relationship with God. He believed he had kept God's commandments, but his heart told him that this was not enough. He had failed to take serious notice of Abraham and his relationship with God. When God promised him descendants in number like the stars in heaven, despite being unable to have children he believed God's promise and we read, 'And he believed in the LORD, and he accounted it to him for righteousness' (Genesis 15:6).

The man failed to understand the spiritual nature of the commandments and that obedience has to come from a renewed heart. He lacked belief in the promises of God concerning salvation through faith. This young man's sin was covetousness, for when Jesus asked him to give away his possessions to help the poor, he could not obey. His love of money and his worldly goods stood in the way of his salvation. Jesus was telling him to do as he said and he would have treasure in heaven that would stand him in good stead on the Day of Judgement.

What about us? What is our darling sin? Are we willing to make the supreme sacrifice and get rid of that much loved precious 'idol' in order to be united with our merciful Saviour, the Lord Jesus? The rich young man turned away from Christ with great sorrow. We never again read of this man but I often wonder if he was amongst those three thousand converted to Christ on the day of Pentecost.

The Apostle John plainly warns everyone who is born again, 'Little children, keep yourselves from idols' (1 John 5:21). There are rich saints in all ages, and their possessions are not sinful — it is the 'love' of these things that is the sin.

When the disciples heard the discussion between Christ and the rich young man, especially his words, 'Assuredly, I say to you that it is hard for a rich man to enter the kingdom of heaven. And again I say to you, it is easier for a camel to go through the eye of a needle than for a rich man to enter the kingdom of God,' they asked, 'Who then can be saved?'

Thank God for Christ's answer of mercy to sinners. Salvation comes from God through the Holy Spirit who brings about the new birth. The renewed heart puts Christ first, making possessions of much less importance.

Let us make sure that Christ has the pre-eminence in our lives and we live a life of faith in him.

THINGS TO DISCUSS WITH YOUR FAMILY

1. Discuss the wise use of your money.
2. What did Jesus mean when he said, '...it is easier for a camel to go through the eye of a needle than for a rich man to enter the kingdom of God' (Matthew 19:24)?
3. What was the rich young man's sin? Read the text.

Meditation

Search your heart for any 'idols' hidden there and ask God to remove them.

Wise Words

It is possible to love money without having it, and it is possible to have it without loving it. *J. C. Ryle*

 'Now he who plants and he who waters are one, and each one will receive his own reward according to his own labour' (1 Corinthians 3:8).

Read: Matthew 19:27-30

We all like to be thanked for what we do. Peter spoke to Jesus on behalf of the other disciples for they were concerned with what they heard him say to the rich young ruler. Salvation is totally of God and Peter asked Jesus to assure the disciples of their salvation. He reminded the Lord that they had forsaken everything to be with him.

They must have rejoiced with Christ's reply that they would receive great rewards in the kingdom of God. The twelve (Judas later being replaced) were promised that they would sit on twelve thrones as rulers in the new heavens and earth. In his reply to Peter, Jesus called himself the 'Son of Man' which was a direct claim to be the Messiah spoken of by Daniel using the same title (Daniel 7:13).

Jesus went on to tell the twelve that anyone who had made sacrifices for him would be rewarded greatly and be given everlasting life. Great things are in store for the saints — rewards beyond anything we could imagine. Do you know that we will be involved in the judgement of the fallen angels? Read 1 Corinthians 6:3.

In Matthew 25:34 we read of the Judgement Day scene where Christ the King says to his people, 'Come you blessed of my Father, inherit the kingdom prepared for you from the foundation of the world.' There are differing rewards for faithfulness as we are taught in the parable of the talents (Matthew 25:14-30). For their faithful use of God's various gifts they were rewarded. We read, 'For to everyone who has, more will be given, and he will have abundance.'

In all of our activities we are to work as serving the Lord. Paul wrote, 'Servants, obey in all things your masters according to the flesh, not with eye service, as men-pleasers, but in sincerity of heart, fearing God. And whatever you do, do it heartily, as to the Lord and not to men, knowing that from the Lord you will receive the reward of the inheritance; for you serve the Lord Christ' (Colossians 3:22-24).

We must all look and pray for the return of the Lord Jesus who said, 'My reward is with me, to give to every one according to his work' (Revelation 22:12). The Lord who can see into the heart and observe the motive for what we do reminds us that many who give the appearance of being great Christians will be eclipsed by others who appear insignificant disciples. The reason for this is that they have been faithful with all that God has given them.

We must not have the attitude of the Pharisees who believed that they earned their reward, but acknowledge that salvation is all of grace, as are the rewards God gives his faithful people.

THINGS TO DISCUSS WITH YOUR FAMILY

1. Why should God reward anyone for following Jesus?
2. For what reason should we become disciples of the Saviour, Jesus Christ?
3. What did Jesus mean when he said, 'Many who are first will be last, and the last first' (Matthew 19:30)?

Meditation

Meditate upon what reward you expect God to give you when you reach heaven — and whether you deserve it.

Wise Words

No grace is stronger than humility. *Richard Sibbes*

'So likewise you, when you have done all those things which you are commanded, say, "We are unprofitable servants. We have done what was our duty to do"' (Luke 17:10).

Read: Matthew 20:1-16

There are some people who always leave everything to the last minute and this is not always the best practice. Before we get away for a couple of days break from our normal routine, packing our bags is one of the final things we do. Other people I know have their suitcases ready a week before they leave.

Jesus told his disciples a parable which speaks of the amazing grace of God in salvation. It is a warning not to leave spiritual matters too late in your life. The Lord had told his disciples that they would sit on thrones in the coming kingdom of God. This was a reward of grace for faithful service. Now he speaks to them about the fundamental matter of salvation.

We are all in the same situation, born in sin and sinners without hope in the world to come. Yet God has his people scattered throughout society. The call of the gospel goes out and some, early in life respond when the Holy Spirit brings about the new birth. Paul writes of these people, '...if anyone is in Christ, he is a new creation; old things have passed away; behold, all things have become new' (2 Corinthians 5:17).

Others are called to salvation at God's time late in life, again an act of his glorious grace. We must remember that humanly speaking we are called to repent every time we hear the call of the gospel. We must never reject Christ and leave our salvation to a more convenient time. That saving call might never come again.

Our parable tells us that after the day's work all the workers received the same pay. Here Jesus was teaching us that every believer will receive eternal life, even those brought into the kingdom at the last moment, as was the thief on the cross. This wonderful truth can give comfort to a dying person. Yet many close to death are unable to comprehend what is being said as their attention is upon the distress of pain and leaving loved ones.

Young people, you are never too young to trust your eternal security to the Lord Jesus. The Apostle Paul wrote, 'Behold, now is the accepted time; behold, now is the day of salvation' (2 Corinthians 6:2). Remember that our salvation is all of God's grace through faith in the Lord Jesus as Paul wrote, 'Therefore we conclude that a man is justified by faith apart from the deeds of the law' (Romans 3:28). We know, saving faith is the gracious gift of God.

God has every right to do as he pleases concerning salvation in Christ which he freely bestows on unbelievers. To think otherwise is to accuse God of injustice. On the Day of Judgement we will find that many we thought to be the least of the saints will have a larger crown than we receive. Again, this is in the hands of our God of grace. Praise him for his gracious salvation.

THINGS TO DISCUSS WITH YOUR FAMILY

1. What is the danger of delaying belief in Christ until tomorrow?
2. Is it fair that every saint receives salvation despite their length of service to the Lord?
3. Discuss the teaching of this parable.

Meditation

Think upon Christ's words to the thief on the cross — 'Assuredly I say to you, today you will be with me in Paradise' (Luke 23:43).

Wise Words

Few are ever saved on their deathbeds. One thief on the cross was saved, that none should despair; but only one, that none should presume. A false confidence in those words, 'the eleventh hour', has ruined thousands of souls.

J. C. Ryle

'And walk in love, as Christ also has loved us and given himself for us, an offering and a sacrifice to God for a sweet-smelling aroma' (Ephesians 5:2).

Read: Mark 10:32-34

We all like to know what the future holds for us, but despite all of our plans and hopes we can never be sure because we can't control what will happen. I knew a man who planned to retire and go on a world trip, but he died before he boarded the plane.

Jesus knew what was soon to happen to him. He and the disciples were making their way up to Jerusalem where he would be murdered. Try and imagine the scene — Jesus leading the way along a dusty road while the disciples followed, afraid of what was going to happen. They knew of the hatred the church leaders had for their Lord and believed that they were likely to be killed with him. Jesus stopped walking and, gathering the twelve about him, told them what was soon to take place. Twice before he had spoken to them of his forthcoming death (Mark 8:31; 9:31). Yet what they once thought was an impossibility if he was the Christ, was now becoming more real and they were fearful.

Jesus gave the twelve more detail than before, but he called himself 'the Son of Man' to remind them who he was. This was the name that Daniel had called the Messiah.

This time Jesus told them that he would be condemned by the ruling body of the church, the Sanhedrin. The very people who should have welcomed him as the Messiah because of all he did and said, and the witness of those who heard God speak from heaven confirming that he was his beloved Son, wanted him dead. They would be guilty of killing 'the king of glory' (Psalm 24:7-10).

Those who considered themselves the great biblical teachers of the time had completely misunderstood the teaching of Isaiah 53 and other passages that foretold what would happen. This time Jesus revealed that after a trial resulting in his condemnation to death he would be handed over to the Gentiles who would carry out the sentence. Again we should look at Psalm 2:1-3 because what was about to happen was prophesied by David. Jesus spoke of some specific parts of his ill treatment — the mocking, the whipping and the spitting, all which were prophesied as we will discover in later devotions.

Despite the cruelty and his death, the situation would end in triumph, for on the third day he would rise from the grave. Obviously from the events that took place this teaching wasn't understood by his followers. We know the truth for we have the record of the witnesses to the Lord's resurrection. Believe it and trust yourself to Jesus and his sacrificial death on the cross. It is the display of God's love for sinners — 'For God so loved the world that he gave his only begotten Son, that whoever believes in him should not perish but have everlasting life' (John 3:16). Praise God for such a love!

THINGS TO DISCUSS WITH YOUR FAMILY

1. Knowing that he would be killed, why did Jesus continue on his way to Jerusalem?
2. What is the Sanhedrin?
3. Discuss 1 John 4:9 — '...the love of God was manifested toward us, that God has sent his only begotten Son into the world, that we might live through him.'

Meditation

Meditate upon the feeling of the disciples when Jesus again revealed what was soon to happen.

Wise Words

God was the master of ceremonies at the cross.

Ernest Reisinger

'Let nothing be done through selfish ambition or conceit, but in lowliness of mind let each esteem others better than himself' (Philippians 2:3).

Read: Mark 10:35-45

Most people enjoy exercising power over others. They like to rule! Watch today's politicians as they struggle to gain the places of importance in parliament. Few politicians are content to carry out the job of just representing their constituents.

Now we come to a situation where James and John, encouraged by their mother (Matthew 20:20), approached Jesus asking an open-ended question: 'Teacher, we want you to do for us whatever we ask.' Jesus could not agree with this request so he asked what they wanted. There is something here for us to notice — don't make any promise until you know what is being asked of you.

Peter, James and John were the inner circle of the disciples. They had a closer relationship with Jesus than the other nine. Of these three we are told that John was the disciple whom Jesus loved in a special, tender way. Later he would ask him to care for his mother. However, it was just John and James who asked for the positions of importance in the kingdom of God. They had been told that the disciples would reign on thrones and, being ambitious, decided to ask for the positions of greatest importance.

This was after being taught that membership in the kingdom of God was for humble servants. Jesus reminded them both of his own servanthood, despite being the Son of God. At that stage they must have believed that immediately after Christ's resurrection the kingdom would become a reality. His final word on the subject should have a place in your heart and mine — 'And whoever of you desires to be first shall be slave of all for even the Son of Man did not come to be served, but to serve, and to give his life a ransom for many.' Jesus demonstrated by his death that the gospel was hated and Christians would suffer for his sake. Peter tells all suffering Christians to 'rejoice to the extent that you partake of Christ's sufferings, that when his glory is revealed, you may also be glad with exceeding joy' (1 Peter 4:13).

Jesus asked them if they were willing to suffer for his sake. They said they would, but at the time of the Passover, they ran away fearing they might also be killed. Things later changed and they willingly suffered for the Lord they loved. Of James we read, 'Then he [Herod] killed James the brother of John with the sword' (Acts 12:2). John was finally confined to prison on the island of Patmos.

Both men were told that God would give the thrones of importance to the ones he had chosen. God rewards his people as he sees fit, for he can see into the heart and mind and can determine who are the most humble servants of all. When the other disciples heard what had happened they were very angry with both men, and their mother.

May we have the same attitude as the psalmist who wrote, 'I would rather be a doorkeeper in the house of my God than dwell in the tents of wickedness' (Psalm 84:10).

THINGS TO DISCUSS
WITH YOUR FAMILY

1. In our reading we find the word 'baptism'. What does it mean here?
2. Discuss the following comment — 'The disciples were looking for a crown without a cross, glory without suffering and honour without humility.'
3. Read and discuss Matthew 5:10-12.

Meditation

Think upon Psalm 145:1 — 'I will extol you, my God, O King; and I will bless your name for ever and ever.'

Wise Words

The itch for the pre-eminence is one disease for which no natural cure has ever been found.   *A. W. Tozer*

'Then the eyes of the blind shall be opened, and the ears of the deaf shall be unstopped' (Isaiah 35:5).

Read: Mark 10:46-52

Many people have physical handicaps. Only recently I had a hearing test and will need a new hearing aid. I wear spectacles, but my difficulty is nothing compared to those who are physically blind. You have read Mark's account of the healing of blind Bartimaeus, but should notice that he was just one of two blind men who begged (Matthew 20:30). One reason I love this story is because of three words we have read — 'Jesus stood still.'

Bartimaeus was blind and had never seen Christ perform any miracle, but he could hear and must have heard many accounts of the Lord's healings. Being aware that Jesus was about to pass by he saw this as his only hope for physical healing. He called for help, and from his words we can tell that despite his physical blindness he very much could see spiritually. When he called Jesus 'Son of David' he was saying that he recognized him as the Messiah, the King of Israel.

Today we have not seen Jesus, but know about him and like blind Bartimaeus I pray that you believe in him. The Apostle Peter wrote of people like us, 'whom having not seen you love. Though now you do not see him, yet believing, you rejoice with joy inexpressible and full of glory, receiving the end of your faith — the salvation of your souls' (1 Peter 1:8,9).

When the people told the blind men to be quiet they called out even louder, for they believed that Jesus could do what no other could do — restore their sight. Then we read those words of compassion and mercy — 'Jesus stood still.' Healing followed and we read that Bartimaeus immediately stood up wanting to follow the Lord. He was 'glorifying God' (Luke 18:43). The watching crowd also praised God for what had taken place. It was a very happy incident on Christ's journey to Jerusalem.

What about you? Are you spiritually blind and unable to see your need of a Saviour because of your unbelief? You need to be 'born again' by the Holy Spirit. Jesus has told us what to do — pray, 'If you then, being evil, know how to give good gifts to your children, how much more will your heavenly Father give the Holy Spirit to those who ask him!' (Luke 11:13). Here is God's promise to those who see their need of the new birth. Think of God's promise in Psalm 50:15: 'Call upon me in the day of trouble; I will deliver you, and you shall glorify me.'

Pray, read your Bibles, repent of your sins, confess you sinfulness, ask for forgiveness and associate with God's people. Attend a Christian church where the truth is preached and ask God for saving faith. If your faith is genuine you will see the radical difference in your thinking and life, and you will have no difficulty in glorifying God in Christ. May God bless you.

THINGS TO DISCUSS WITH YOUR FAMILY

1. What is encouraging in the words, 'Jesus stood still' (Mark 10:49)?
2. In what way was God's healing of Bartimaeus the result of his faith in Jesus?
3. What is the significance of the term, 'Son of David' (Mark 10:47)?

Meditation

Meditate upon the words of today's text — 'Then the eyes of the blind shall be opened, and the ears of the deaf shall be unstopped' (Isaiah 35:5).

Wise Words

Sovereign grace can make strangers into sons.

C. H. Spurgeon

'I was sought by those who did not ask
for me; I was found by those who did
not seek me' (Isaiah 65:1).

Read: Luke 19:1-10

This is a wonderful story as it teaches us that God saves the worst
of sinners, even a sinner who, to see the Saviour, had to climb a
tree because he wasn't very tall.

Zaccheus was a rich, powerful tax collector, hated by his fellow
Jews because he worked for the Roman army of occupation. The
tax collectors had a reputation for corruption. He was like that rich
young ruler, only Zaccheus didn't go to Christ seeking salvation.
Christ called him from his spiritual darkness to discover 'the light of
life' (John 8:12).

Zaccheus answered Christ's call while in an unusual place — he
was perched up a tree. This reminds me of the prodigal son who came
to himself whilst in a pigsty. They both answered Christ's call. If you
feel within your heart the Holy Spirit's call to repentance and faith in
Christ, then pray for saving grace. Zaccheus needed a changed heart
which happened to him while he was sitting on the limb of a tree.

Unbelievers need to understand that salvation is impossible without the new birth which is the sovereign work of the Holy Spirit.
Nicodemus was told, 'You must be born again' (John 3:7) and so must
every sinner who wants salvation in Christ.

In Zaccheus' salvation, we see the grace of God poured out
upon an unbeliever. He was one of God's elect, loved eternally, predestined, called, justified, adopted, sanctified and at the end of his life,
glorified. He didn't seek salvation, but God gave him saving faith.
This incident is like that told by Christ in the parable of the man
who found some valuable treasure (Matthew 13:44). When Christ
told him to get down from the tree and prepare for a visit, Zaccheus
obeyed instantly — a mark of a Christian.

If you confess to be a Christian do you obey Christ's commandments? Of course you frequently fall into sin, but do you confess
when you do? We see that Zaccheus was a changed person. He was

ready and willing to make restitution to everyone from whom he had taken more taxes than he should. God's law demanded double repayment in some cases of theft (Exodus 22:4). In other situations a person convicted of stealing was required to repay what he had stolen plus a fine of an additional one fifth. Zacchaeus was going to repay fourfold. He also promised to give half of his possessions to the poor. How unlike that rich young ruler who loved his money.

We must be like Zacchaeus and reach out to help those in need; not of necessity but willingly and from the heart.

That very day salvation had come to the home of Zacchaeus. I'm sure all the family became aware of what had happened and, God willing, all members of the family came to saving faith in Jesus. There is hope for the worst of sinners.

THINGS TO DISCUSS WITH YOUR FAMILY

1. Why were the people critical of Jesus having a meal at the home of Zacchaeus?
2. Discuss Isaiah 65:1: 'I was sought by those who did not ask for Me; I was found by those who did not seek Me. I said, "Here I am, here I am," to a nation that was not called by My name.'
3. James 2:26 tells us that 'faith without works is dead'. What does this mean?

Meditation

Think about the commandment, 'You shall not steal' (Exodus 20:15).

Wise Words

Family life is a school for character.   *Martin Luther*

24 September   The parable of the ten minas

'The kings of the earth set themselves, and the rulers take counsel together, against the LORD and against his Anointed, saying, "Let us break their bonds in pieces and cast away their cords from us"' (Psalm 2:2,3).

Read: Luke 19:11-28

Some people are slow learners. I met children at school who despite being told something many times never seemed to remember. This time it was the disciples who were in this category. They had been told many times that the kingdom of God was not then going to be a reality for the world to see, but was to be found in the hearts of believers throughout the world and in all ages. Jesus reminded them that when he came a second time the kingdom would be visible to everyone, with himself seated upon the throne of his glory.

Soon the disciples would witness his death. Again he told them by means of a parable, what to expect. You have read the parable so let us look at what Jesus was teaching them.

The nobleman represents the Lord Jesus who after his crucifixion ascended to heaven where as King he is building the kingdom of God. The heavenly Father said of his Son, 'I have set my King on my holy hill of Zion' (Psalm 2:6). During the period between his ascension into heaven and his return, the kingdom is growing as the Holy Spirit calls people to citizenship in it. In the meantime our Saviour's disciples are serving him by speaking of his majesty and saving power. Jesus has given his people a variety of gifts which they are to use in his service. Paul described these abilities in a humorous way: 'For in fact the body is not one member but many. If the foot should say, "Because I am not a hand, I am not of the body," is it therefore not of the body? ... If the whole body were an eye, where would be the hearing? If the whole were hearing, where would be the smelling? But now God has set the members, each one of them, in the body just as he pleased' (1 Corinthians 12:14,15,17,18).

In the parable, the ungodly citizens despised their ruler who had gone to receive his kingdom. They faced a terrible judgement upon the nobleman's return which is a clear warning to unbelievers of all ages. The message to all professing Christians is that we are to make use of our God-given skills so that people might be saved and the Lord glorified. Some time before, Jesus had said, 'For everyone to whom much is given, from him much will be required' (Luke 12:48).

How can we prepare for the day of our Lord's return? Peter tells us: 'Therefore, beloved, looking forward to these things, be diligent to be found by him in peace, without spot and blameless' (2 Peter 3:14). Always remember the words of Paul, 'For I consider that the sufferings of this present time are not worthy to be compared with the glory which shall be revealed in us' (Romans 8:18).

THINGS TO DISCUSS WITH YOUR FAMILY

1. Discuss Paul's thoughts of 1 Corithians 4:2 — 'Moreover it is required in stewards that one be found faithful.'
2. What was the punishment given to the unprofitable servant?
3. Why did the people say, 'We will not have this man to rule over us' (Luke 19:14)?

Meditation

Meditate upon the ways you should be using your God-given gifts to produce spiritual fruit and honour God.

Wise Words

God never tires of giving.   *William Still*

'No one can serve two masters; for either he will hate the one and love the other, or else he will be loyal to the one and despise the other. You cannot serve God and mammon' (Matthew 6:24).

Read: John 11:55 – 12:11

It is so true that in our world most people live for money and possessions. This is not something new, because in our study of the life of Christ we discover that money was a god to many people. In today's reading we find out something about Judas — he loved money and was a thief!

The events you have read took place on the Friday before the Passover week. People were making their way to Jerusalem for the feast and there was an air of anticipation — 'Will Jesus come to Jerusalem for the Passover?' Some people truly believed that Jesus was the Messiah, but the Sanhedrin wanted him arrested and put to death for blasphemy, because he claimed that he was the Son of God.

Jesus and the disciples had arrived in Bethany and were staying at the home of his friends, Mary, Martha and Lazarus whom he had raised from the dead. Many people were calling at their home to see Lazarus who was living proof of Christ's great miracle. No doubt they wanted to make sure he was not a spirit being, but a man whose body was made of flesh and blood capable of talking and eating food like everyone else.

The family had made a meal for their guests and as they sat down, probably on cushions, Mary approached Jesus with a bottle of very costly, perfumed oil. She wanted to show everyone present of her great love of her Saviour who had raised her brother to life from the tomb. From the writings of the Apostle Paul we know that often women washed the feet of the saints (1 Timothy 5:10).

What Mary did was not the washing of the Saviour's feet, but the act of anointing his feet with the valuable oil. She then wiped off the excess oil with the hair of her head — no doubt she had long hair which was required of godly women. Later Paul wrote, '...if a woman has long hair, it is a glory to her; for her hair is given to her for a covering' (1 Corinthians 11:15).

Immediately Judas spoke out against Mary's loving act, 'Why was this fragrant oil not sold for three hundred denarii and given to the poor?' The reason for his statement was that he was a thief and had stolen from the money bag for which the Lord had made him responsible. We should take care not to steal, especially from what belongs to our Lord.

The words of Jesus, 'She has kept this for the day of my burial', reminds us that following Christ's death the ladies had put aside oil to anoint the Lord's body.

May we all support the work of the Christian church in spreading the gospel, and at the same time give encouragement to those facing death. There are many seriously ill unbelievers in our community and our witness may be used by the Holy Spirit to bring them to true repentance and saving faith.

THINGS TO DISCUSS WITH YOUR FAMILY

1. How did Jesus know that Judas was a thief?
2. What is our responsibility to people who are poor and those facing imminent death?
3. How can you show your love of the Lord Jesus?

Meditation

Meditate upon the love and humility Mary showed to Jesus.

Wise Words

No labour is servile when the Lord's approval is the paramount consideration. *Geoffrey B. Wilson*

26 September   The King of kings approaches Jerusalem

'Rejoice greatly, O daughter of Zion! Shout, O daughter of Jerusalem! Behold, your King is coming to you; he is just and having salvation, lowly and riding on a donkey, a colt, the foal of a donkey' (Zechariah 9:9).

Read: Luke 19:29-40

When our Prime Minister makes a visit to a community he comes in his official car which flies the Australian flag. He is accompanied by police and security men who are there to ensure his safety. The same happens in other countries and is really a display of power and authority.

Jesus was about to make his triumphal entry into the capital city of his nation. The manner of his entry was the fulfilment of the prophecy which is our text for today. We learn a lot from these few verses. First, God not only knows the future but has the power to bring it to pass as he has ordained. Secondly we learn that Jesus foresaw that a man had a colt which would be made available to him. In fact the Lord told the disciples who went to get the animal exactly what would be said by the man and how they were to answer him. What does this tell us about Jesus? It tells us that he is God just as the Apostle Paul wrote, saying he is 'the eternally blessed God' (Romans 9:5).

Because he is God, his eyes can see into all parts of the world at the same moment and he can see into the very depths of our mind. Hypocrites of all ages can fool people as to their standing before God, but they can't deceive Jehovah.

As Jesus set out for Jerusalem, riding the colt, the disciples began to shout out his praise saying, '"Blessed is the King who comes in the name of the LORD!" Peace in heaven and glory in the highest!' The crowds joined in, cutting branches from the palm trees and spreading them on the roadway in front of the Lord. They also cried out, acknowledging that Christ was their King, 'Hosanna to the Son of David! "Blessed is he who comes in the name of the LORD!" Hosanna in the highest!' (Matthew 21:9).

No longer was Christ's Messiahship to be kept secret. It was now openly displayed, filling the hearts of the members of the Sanhedrin and the other church leaders with hatred. They couldn't stand such praise being shouted out to Jesus and demanded that the disciples keep quiet. They refused to believe the prophecies concerning Christ and the evidence of his miracles which testified that he was the Son of God. Jesus told them that if people didn't praise him then the stones would do so.

The time had come for the people to acknowledge Jesus as the Messiah, who had come to save his people. Let the Sanhedrin carry out their vile plans, for in so doing salvation was perfected and their destruction assured. Let us all note that one day the whole world will acknowledge who Jesus is, for we read of that coming time when 'at the name of Jesus every knee should bow, of those in heaven, and of those on earth, and of those under the earth, and that every tongue should confess that Jesus Christ is Lord, to the glory of God the Father' (Philippians 2:10,11).

THINGS TO DISCUSS WITH YOUR FAMILY

1. Why did the church leaders demand that the crowds stop praising Jesus as the King of glory?
2. What do you think went through the minds of the people that day?
3. Why did Jesus enter Jerusalem riding a donkey?

Meditation

Think about the majestic glory of Christ as he rode into Jerusalem on the donkey.

Wise Words

Christ is the most sparkling diamond in the ring of glory.
Thomas Brooks

'Most assuredly, I say to you, he who believes in me, the works that I do he will do also; and greater works than these he will do, because I go to my Father. And whatever you ask in my name, that I will do, that the Father may be glorified in the Son' (John 14:12,13).

Read: Mark 11:12-14; 20-26

Only a few days ago I dug out two small trees because they had not flowered. It is not much use having trees that don't produce the expected fruit.

After his triumphal entry into Jerusalem Jesus, with his disciples, returned to Bethany for the night. The next morning he again set out for Jerusalem and on the way became hungry. Seeing a fig tree near the roadway, covered in leaves, he decided to pull a fig to eat. Normally if fig trees had leaves it meant that it was bearing fruit. Arriving at the tree he found it was just a show of leaves but bore no fruit. Consequently he said, 'Let no one eat fruit from you ever again.' The disciples heard this curse upon the tree. During the day our Saviour had work to do which we will look at later, but in the evening he and his disciples left the city.

The following day as they made their way back to Jerusalem they saw that the fig tree was already dead from the root up. When Peter pointed this out to Jesus he told his disciples that they were to have faith in God for the time was coming when they would do great miracles in his name. It is possible that the expression concerning the mountain being thrown into the sea was a common expression of that age.

Let us always remember that we are saved through faith alone as Paul wrote, 'For by grace you have been saved through faith, and that not of yourselves; it is the gift of God, not of works, lest anyone should boast' (Ephesians 2:8,9).

The faithful eleven, Judas' replacement Matthias (Acts 1:26) and Paul carried out great works and miracles in the name of Christ.

Our text tells us that when we pray we do so through the only God-given Mediator, 'the Man Christ Jesus, who gave himself a ransom for all' (1 Timothy 2:5,6). Paul's words to the Romans are an encouragement to every Christian: 'Therefore, having been justified by faith, we have peace with God through our Lord Jesus Christ' (Romans 5:1). Justification is through faith alone and not the reward for any works we might have done (Romans 3:28).

Jesus reminds us all that when we pray we must 'ask in faith, with no doubting, for he who doubts is like a wave of the sea driven and tossed by the wind' (James 1:6).

The cursing of the fig tree was a warning to hypocritical Israel. God had cared for them but they were bringing doom upon themselves. Soon the nation would be scattered throughout the world, the temple destroyed and Jerusalem torn apart for they produced no spiritual fruit, but were hypocrites of the first order. It is dangerous to play about with God's offer of mercy. Jesus also reminded his disciples once again that they were to forgive anyone who had offended them. Do you forgive freely and willingly? I pray you do.

THINGS TO DISCUSS WITH YOUR FAMILY

1. Who is the only Mediator between God and man?
2. Does Jesus teach that God will answer every request Christians make in their Lord's name? Discuss.
3. What did the fig tree symbolize?

Meditation

Thank God for answered prayers.

Wise Words

The Christian should resemble a fruit tree, not a Christmas tree. *John Stott*

'The Lord is not slack concerning his promise, as some count slackness, but is long-suffering toward us, not willing that any should perish but that all should come to repentance' (2 Peter 3:9).

Read: Luke 19:41-44

If you have access to the history of the Jews written by Josephus, read his description of the judgement of God upon Jerusalem. God would punish his covenant people because they had killed their Messiah, God's only begotten Son. God had cared for his covenant people over the centuries. He sent them prophets whom they rejected and killed. They distorted the way of salvation from faith in God to salvation by works, and threw off humility to wear a cloak of self-righteous hypocrisy.

The nation was ready for judgement just as Isaiah had prophesied: '"What more could have been done to my vineyard that I have not done in it? Why then, when I expected it to bring forth good grapes, did it bring forth wild grapes? And now, please let me tell you what I will do to my vineyard: I will take away its hedge, and it shall be burned; and break down its wall, and it shall be trampled down. I will lay it waste; it shall not be pruned or dug, but there shall come up briers and thorns. I will also command the clouds that they rain no rain on it." For the vineyard of the LORD of hosts is the house of Israel, and the men of Judah are his pleasant plant. He looked for justice, but behold, oppression; for righteousness, but behold, weeping' (Isaiah 5:4-7).

Jesus was looking over the city where people were busily preparing for the Passover feast. Knowing what was to happen to the people because he would be rejected and crucified, our compassionate Saviour wept. He pitied his sinful, lost people. Our God loves this ruined world and our text tells us that it is not the Lord's desire that anyone should perish, but that all should see their sinful state, repent and turn to him for forgiveness and saving faith. Despite all that was done for the nation, God's judgement would soon fall.

Jesus wept, and so should we as we see our nation merrily walking the broad way that ends in hell. Regardless of all the evidence, the

Jews refused to believe. It is no different today. The evidence of God is everywhere about us, but people refuse to believe.

Christ's words were a warning that the armies of Rome would surround the city and totally destroy everything. The nation would go out of existence for many centuries. However, the people didn't take any notice of the Lord's warning. Before he was crucified Pilate attempted to have Jesus released but the people demanded he be put to death, saying, 'His blood be on us and on our children' (Matthew 27:25).

Don't reject God's call to repentance, for that call may never again come. May God bless you with salvation.

THINGS TO DISCUSS WITH YOUR FAMILY

1. There were three occasions recorded in the Scriptures where Jesus wept. Can you remember them?
2. Why was Jerusalem to be destroyed by God?
3. What does Christ's warning to Jerusalem teach us?

Meditation

Consider God's hatred of sin. 'God is a just judge, and God is angry with the wicked every day' (Psalm 7:11).

Wise Words

Those who will not deliver themselves into the hand of God's mercy cannot be delivered out of the hand of his justice. *Matthew Henry*

'Because zeal for your house has eaten me up' (Psalm 69:9).

Read: Mark 11:15-19

Despite the fact that our church buildings are just timber and brick, they are used by the saints as they worship God. In time they are knocked down and replaced, as they are just convenient places for worship. However, even in our age those buildings are special as many will tell you that it was during a time of worship in that place that they were converted. Others respect the building as it was where they were baptized or married — or it was there that a service was conducted for a loved one who died.

The Jews had a great respect for the tabernacle and later the temple, for it was there in the Holy of Holies that God met with his people. Solomon's temple was built as God had instructed and he blessed the completed building by a display of his divine presence. We read in 2 Chronicles 7:1,2: 'When Solomon had finished praying, fire came down from heaven and consumed the burnt offering and the sacrifices; and the glory of the LORD filled the temple. And the priests could not enter the house of the LORD, because the glory of the LORD had filled the LORD's house.' This was no ordinary building, but 'the LORD's house'.

When Jesus entered Herod's temple, he discovered that traders were using as a saleyard the area set aside for the Gentiles. In the holy place there were bankers exchanging local currency for foreign coins as only the money of Israel was acceptable in worship. Traders were also selling animals for sacrifice. Try to imagine the scene in the heat of the day — stinking birds with the floor covered with their droppings, the shouting of sellers encouraging visitors to buy their creatures — and all of this in 'the LORD's house'.

The Son of God was furious with the desecration of his Father's temple and at once made his way through the crowds, overturning the tables of the bankers and those who sold doves. He also drove out of the temple the people who were walking about with their purchases.

Jesus then gave the crowd the reason for what he had done. As in his battle with Satan in the desert he quoted Scripture — 'My house shall be called a house of prayer for all nations' (Isaiah 56:7; and words from Jeremiah 7:11 which read, "'Has this house, which is called by my name, become a den of thieves in your eyes? Behold, I, even I, have seen it," says the LORD.'

When the church leaders saw that the people were showing a great interest in the Lord's words they made more specific plans to have Jesus arrested and put to death — and these scribes and priests were the church rulers! May we never fall into their evil thinking, but always give Christ the pre-eminence in every aspect of our lives.

May we also treat the place where we worship God with respect. It is not God's house as was the temple because God meets with his people anywhere. Nevertheless the church building is not just an ordinary place.

THINGS TO DISCUSS WITH YOUR FAMILY

1. What is the 'church'?
2. Where does God meet with his people today?
3. How should we treat the building where we meet for worship?

Meditation

Why is the place where the congregation meets for worship important to you?

Wise Words

Worship is the adoring contemplation of God as he has revealed himself in Christ and in his Word.

J. Oswald Sanders

'Then Jesus said to his disciples, "If anyone desires to come after me, let him
deny himself, and take up his cross, and
follow me"' (Matthew 16:24).

Read: John 12:20-26

Several years ago some local people had visitors from New Zealand. They had read some of my books and knowing I lived nearby they asked to meet me. It proved to be a very pleasant time. No
doubt Jesus was used to people struggling through the crowds to see
him face to face, but it was Passover time and in Jerusalem there were
many visitors from the surrounding countries who had come in obedience with God's law to celebrate the feast.

You have read of some visiting Greeks who had heard of Jesus
and wanted to see for themselves if he was indeed the Messiah. They
spoke to Philip who had the Greek name and the message eventually
reached Jesus who gave them his full attention, explaining the purpose of his coming to the earth.

Plainly he told the Greeks and anyone who was listening that
the time had arrived 'that the Son of Man should be glorified'. He
likened what was going to happen to him to a seed falling into the
ground and dying. After a short time the plant appeared and grew tall
producing much seed. We know that it was only through the sacrificial death of our Saviour that sinners can be saved. Without his death,
bearing the sins of his people, no one would be saved. His death,
instead of being a tragedy for his people, was glorious, for through it
we pass from death to life.

Those Greeks and every believer knows the truth of the words
found in Hebrews 12:1,2 — 'Let us run with endurance the race
that is set before us, looking unto Jesus, the author and finisher of
our faith, who for the joy that was set before him endured the cross,
despising the shame, and has sat down at the right hand of the throne
of God.' Spiritual life flows from Christ through the sovereign work
of the Holy Spirit bringing about the new birth and sanctification.

We are told that Christ must be first in our life, even before life
itself. As our text says, we are to take up the cross that God has given

us and faithfully follow Jesus. This means we do not live for an earthly, worldly life, but 'according to the Spirit, [and] the things of the Spirit' (Romans 8:5).

The Greeks and every Christian can rejoice in Paul's words, 'The Spirit himself bears witness with our spirit that we are children of God, and if children, then heirs — heirs of God and joint heirs with Christ, if indeed we suffer with him, that we may also be glorified together' (Romans 8:16,17).

To follow Jesus means eternal life in his presence. We must be like the trusting sheep that follow their shepherd. This should encourage us in our daily walk along that narrow way, following the 'Good Shepherd' who leads to Paradise. There may be many thorns along the way that cause us to stumble, but we will never fall eternally. Such is the grace of God to his people. Let us praise God for his goodness to us.

THINGS TO DISCUSS WITH YOUR FAMILY

1. What did Jesus mean when he said, 'The hour has come that the Son of Man should be glorified' (John 12:23)?
2. How does God 'honour' Christ's faithful servants (John 12:26)?
3. Why do you think the Greeks wanted to meet Jesus?

Meditation

Think of how Jesus, the 'Son of Man', could be glorified by dying on a cross.

Wise Words

It is as true of Christians as it is of Christ, there can be no life without death, there can be no sweet without bitter, there can be no crown without a cross. *J. C. Ryle*

October

'Having disarmed principalities and powers, he made a public spectacle of them, triumphing over them in it' (Colossians 2:15).

Read: John 12:27-33

I'm sure that there are many times when our hearts are troubled by what is happening. Tension is the cause of much illness.

Jesus knew that the purpose of his incarnation was about to take place and in his sacrificial, substitutionary death he would suffer hell for his people. He would feel for a time the absence of his Father's presence because he was the sin bearer, being punished for his people's sins. Christ's death was not that of a martyr for his cause, but the death of a Saviour who became 'a curse for us' (Galatians 3:13).

Our Lord continued speaking to the Greeks and said, 'My soul is troubled.' Again we have a clear indication that Jesus was truly man with a soul. He knew what lay before him and was suffering conflict in his mind. In Romans 7:13-25 we read of a spiritual conflict that Paul had suffered. This type of conflict in the heart is not sin, but as man Jesus drew back from the terror that lay before him. Nevertheless, our Saviour lived a life of perfect submission to his heavenly Father. He would not ask to be saved from the cross, but rather, as in everything he did he could say, 'Father, glorify your name.'

Then for the third time it is recorded in the Scriptures that God spoke from heaven, 'I have both glorified it and will glorify it again.' We can only imagine what went through the minds of those present that day. Some thought it was thunder while others believed it was an angel speaking to the Lord. It was yet another reason for people to believe that Jesus was the Christ.

Jesus now indicated that he would be lifted up to die on a Roman cross and through his death Satan's power and kingdom would be defeated. Later he said of Satan, 'the ruler of this world is judged' (John 16:11). Satan's power over the human heart was overthrown, and the Holy Spirit was using his divine power to remove sinners from Satan's domain and into the kingdom of heaven.

When Jesus ascended into heaven and took his place upon the throne of God we read of two great, powerful events. First, there was 'war' in heaven and Satan was cast down to the earth (Revelation 7:7-17). No more could he accuse God of saving sinners without the saving death of Christ. Secondly the evil one's power was severely restricted for we read, 'And I saw an angel come down from heaven, having the key of the bottomless pit and a great chain in his hand. And he laid hold on the dragon, that old serpent, which is the Devil, and Satan, and bound him a thousand years, And cast him into the bottomless pit, and shut him up, and set a seal upon him, that he should deceive the nations no more, till the thousand years should be fulfilled' (Revelation 20:1-3). Now the gospel would have a world-wide congregation.

THINGS TO DISCUSS WITH YOUR FAMILY

1. In this age how is Satan's power restricted? Read Revelation 20:1-3.
2. Jesus was to be crucified. How did he know this?
3. What did Jesus mean when he said, 'My soul is troubled' (John 12:27)?

Meditation

Thank God that Jesus, our Saviour, defeated Satan and his demons.

Satan, as in his first temptation, is still on the losing side.
William Gurnall

Wise Words

'Behold, the Lord God shall come with
a strong hand, and his arm shall rule for
him' (Isaiah 40:10).

Read: John 12:34-43

As I write I am well aware of my inability to foretell the future. Val
and I had made plans for a four days' break away from home and
the computer, only to receive word that an aged member of my past
congregation had died. He had asked that I conduct his funeral. James
gives us good advice when we begin making our plans acknowledging — 'If the Lord wills, we shall live and do this or that' (James 4:15).

With Jesus it is different, for he as God knows the end from the
beginning. He has ordained all that is to happen and has the power to
bring to fruition everything he has planned. In today's reading Jesus
clearly revealed the way he would die. He also told his audience that
the hatred of the Pharisees, the church leaders and the majority of
the covenant people would reject him. He quoted Scripture to show
that this was prophesied.

Jesus had said that he was the 'light of the world', and now he
told the people that the light would be taken from them. If they did
not believe they would stumble along through life in spiritual darkness, only to be lost in hell — 'outer darkness; [where] there [would]
be weeping and gnashing of teeth' (Matthew 22:13).

Jesus quoted Isaiah 53:1 which foretold that very few would believe what was revealed about God's 'Servant'. The proud students of
the Bible had failed to comprehend the teaching of Isaiah 53 and in
their foolishness brought everything there prophesied to pass.

He also quoted a passage from Isaiah 6 which John noted came
from Isaiah, revealing Jesus as Jehovah seated upon the throne of
heaven. It is a glorious scene and worth reading over and over — 'I
saw the Lord sitting on a throne, high and lifted up, and the train of
his robe filled the temple. Above it stood seraphim; each one had six
wings: with two he covered his face, with two he covered his feet,
and with two he flew. And one cried to another and said: "Holy, holy,

holy is the LORD of hosts; the whole earth is full of his glory!"' (Isaiah 6:1-3).

John records, 'These things Isaiah said when he [Isaiah] saw his [Jesus'] glory and spoke of him [Jesus].' Let all who deny that Jesus is Jehovah meditate upon these passages of the Word of God.

The Greeks had been well taught in their short time with the Lord, but I often wonder if they believed that he was the Messiah. The Pharisees and others were blinded by God to the truth concerning Jesus because of their hard, cold unbelief. They, except for God's remnant, would stagger along in spiritual darkness to their eternal doom.

How about you? Do you believe from the heart that Christ is your Lord and Saviour? I pray you do.

THINGS TO DISCUSS WITH YOUR FAMILY

1. With all the evidence before them, why didn't the Jews believe that Jesus was their Messiah?
2. How do you know that Isaiah 6:1-5 referred to the holiness and majesty of Jesus?
3. How do people become 'sons of light' (John 12:36)?

Meditation

Meditate upon the words of Isaiah 6:1-3 — 'I saw the Lord sitting on a throne, high and lifted up, and the train of his robe filled the temple. Above it stood seraphim ... And one cried to another and said: "Holy, holy, holy is the LORD of hosts; The whole earth is full of his glory!"'

Wise Words

They [the members of the Sanhedrin] were not willing to part with their great places in the magistracy, which brought them respect, honour, and applause from men. They valued this more than God's praise.   *M. Poole*

'For God did not send his Son into the world to condemn the world, but that the world through him might be saved' (John 3:17).

Read: John 12:44-50

In many aspects of our life Val and I think as one. We know how we think, what are our likes and dislikes, but in some issues we have differences of opinion. We have now come to another piece of Scripture which records the unity that exists in the Godhead — this time particularly between the Father and Son.

There was never a time when God's eternal Son did not exist. He was before he entered this world to die and save the lost. The Apostle John clearly teaches that Jesus Christ is God. He wrote, 'In the beginning was the Word, and the Word was with God, and the Word was God. He was in the beginning with God' (John 1:1,2). Jesus entered this world as 'the light of men' (John 1:4) to save unbelievers. Several times we read of our Saviour telling people that he had not come to judge the world. That would happen when he comes a second time.

Facing a crowd, some of whom were involved in making plans for his death, Jesus said that to reject him as Lord and Saviour was to show their disbelief in God, his Father who had sent him into the world. The Lord told the people that the unity between himself and God was such that the very words he spoke were given to him by his heavenly Father. Jesus was God's greatest prophet, prophesied by Moses: 'I will raise up for them a Prophet like you from among their brethren, and will put my words in his mouth, and he shall speak to them all that I command him' (Deuteronomy 18:18). Christ's words (verse 49) were a claim to be that prophet.

To believe the truth spoken by Christ would result in eternal life with all its gracious blessings. Paul wrote wonderful words of encouragement to all who have trusted their eternal security to Jesus — 'There is therefore now no condemnation to those who are in Christ Jesus, who do not walk according to the flesh, but according to the Spirit' (Romans 8:1).

The vast majority of the Jews that day still lived in spiritual darkness, despite hearing Jesus preach the truth, witnessing his tremendous miracles and hearing God's spoken words of approval concerning his only begotten Son. What more was necessary before they believed? Soon they would be confronted with his resurrection, when many would believe all of his claims concerning his deity; yet, it would still only be a remnant of the nation. The result would be great blessings for the Gentiles.

Writing of the Jews and their rejection of Jesus Paul said, 'I say then, have they stumbled that they should fall? Certainly not! But through their fall, to provoke them to jealousy, salvation has come to the Gentiles' (Romans 11:11).

On Judgement Day the very words spoken by Christ and rejected by the unbelieving Jews and Gentiles will result in their eternal condemnation. May you not be numbered among them.

THINGS TO DISCUSS WITH YOUR FAMILY

1. Why is Jesus coming to earth a second time?
2. In what way can Christ's teaching be our judge?
3. Why could Jesus say that he spoke the words given to him by his heavenly Father?

Meditation

Meditate upon the significance of Christ's words — 'I and my Father are one' (John 10:30).

Wise Words

The trinity is (not are) God the Father, God the Son, God the Holy Spirit. *Donald Grey Barnhouse*

4 October   From where does your authority come?

'Then Jerusalem, all Judea, and all the region around the Jordan went out to him and were baptised by him in the Jordan, confessing their sins' (Matthew 3:5,6).

Read: Matthew 21:23-32

There are many times when we are asked to explain why we behave as we do. Often I found it necessary to ask members of my class why they acted as they did. Usually the reasons made good sense while others did things without knowing why.

Jesus, now in the temple, was confronted by the chief priests and elders who demanded to know on whose authority he was acting. They knew of his many miracles, had heard his teaching and claims to be the Messiah, had heard the people shouting out 'Hosanna!' to him and more recently witnessed him drive out from the temple precincts the money changers and those who sold doves. Their question was an effort to trap him into making a public statement that could be used against him. Thus they asked, 'Show us your authority for what you are doing!'

If Jesus had replied that God gave him the authority for what he did there would be the cry of, 'Blasphemy!' If he said he acted on his own authority then again the cry would be blasphemy because he, a man, did that which belonged to God alone.

Jesus replied by asking them a question, 'The baptism of John, where is it from? From heaven or from men?' The church leaders were in a dilemma. To admit that John's baptism was from heaven would have invited further questions from the Lord — 'Why then didn't you believe what he taught concerning me? He said of me, "Behold! The Lamb of God who takes away the sin of the world!" ... He who sent me to baptise with water said to me, "Upon whom you see the Spirit descending, and remaining on him, this is he who baptises with the Holy Spirit." And I have seen and testified that this is the Son of God' (John 1:29,33,34).

Jesus then told the parable of the two sons who symbolized the two groups in their society. One son typified the Pharisees and church leaders who made a pretence of serving God but did not. Isaiah wrote of these people, 'Therefore the LORD said: "Inasmuch as these people draw near with their mouths and honour me with their lips, but have removed their hearts far from me"' (Isaiah 29:13).

The other son represented the sinners who were despised by the church leaders — the tax collectors and immoral people. They saw their sins, repented and turned to believe in Jesus. John's preaching had seen unbelievers converted as our text indicates. They had been born again and now obeyed God's law from their changed heart.

Christ's words indicate that the door into Paradise was still open. There was still plenty of room in the Kingdom of God, and not only for Jews. The Samaritan woman and people from Sychar had come to acknowledge Jesus as the Christ (John 4:39-42). God still calls unbelievers to salvation for the Apostle John wrote, 'If we confess our sins, he is faithful and just to forgive us our sins and to cleanse us from all unrighteousness' (1 John 1:9). Have you done so?

THINGS TO DISCUSS WITH YOUR FAMILY

1. Which of the two sons was obedient?
2. Jesus baptizes with the Holy Spirit. What does this mean?
3. '...to obey is better than sacrifice' (1 Samuel 15:22). What does this mean?

Meditation

Meditate upon the way Jesus handled the questions from the chief priests and elders of the people — he answered a question with a question!

Wise Words

The price of hating other human beings is loving oneself less. *Eldridge Cleaver*

'Kiss the Son, lest he be angry, and you perish in the way, when his wrath is kindled but a little. Blessed are all those who put their trust in him' (Psalm 2:12).

Read: Matthew 21:33-46

None of us likes to hear others saying unkind things about us, especially when what they say is false. Sometimes what we hear is true and brings repentance and a change in how we behave.

Jesus was constantly reminding the Jews and in particular their church leaders of their sinful rejection of him. The Pharisees and others were arrogant, self-righteous people who despised the many blessings God had given them. Jesus then told the parable of the owner of the vineyard who expected fruit from his vines. Isaiah had written a parable with similar teaching, 'Now let me sing to my Well-beloved a song of my Beloved regarding his vineyard: my Well-beloved has a vineyard on a very fruitful hill. He dug it up and cleared out its stones, and planted it with the choicest vine. He built a tower in its midst, and also made a winepress in it; so he expected it to bring forth good grapes, but it brought forth wild grapes. And now, O inhabitants of Jerusalem and men of Judah, judge, please, between me and my vineyard. What more could have been done to my vineyard that I have not done in it? Why then, when I expected it to bring forth good grapes, did it bring forth wild grapes? ... let me tell you what I will do to my vineyard: I will take away its hedge, and it shall be burned; and break down its wall, and it shall be trampled down. I will lay it waste; it shall not be pruned or dug, but there shall come up briers and thorns. I will also command the clouds that they rain no rain on it. For the vineyard of the LORD of hosts is the house of Israel, and the men of Judah are his pleasant plant. He looked for justice, but behold, oppression; for righteousness, but behold, weeping' (Isaiah 5:1-7).

Nothing had changed! The very ones who had received such tender care from God, even sending them his one and only beloved Son, were planning his murder. In Christ's parable the church leaders, symbolized by the vine dressers, '...said among themselves, "This is the heir. Come, let us kill [God's Son] and seize his inheritance." So they took him and cast him out of the vineyard and killed him.'

The chief priests and Pharisees knew Christ was speaking about them and despite wanting to have him arrested then and there, they were afraid of the people who still listened intently to what he was teaching. The people looked upon Jesus as one of God's prophets. At least they had that correct, but they would soon be calling for the Saviour's death. Nevertheless, Christ would be triumphant, just as the Lord's quote from Isaiah 8:14,15 taught. He was the stone of judgement that would eventually crush into powder all who conspired to his death. How do you stand in relation to Christ the judge?

THINGS TO DISCUSS WITH YOUR FAMILY

1. Discuss the meaning of the text.
2. Discuss Matthew 21:42: 'Jesus said to them, "Have you never read in the Scriptures: 'The stone which the builders rejected has become the chief cornerstone. This was the LORD's doing, and it is marvellous in our eyes'?"'
3. To whom was the gospel given when Jesus was rejected by Israel as their Lord and King? Read Romans 11:11.

Meditation

Think upon Christ's words in Matthew 21:44 — 'And whoever falls on this stone will be broken; but on whomever it falls, it will grind him to powder.'

Wise Words

The law is what we must do; the gospel is what God will give.   *Martin Luther*

         The wedding breakfast

'Therefore judge nothing before the time, until the Lord comes, who will both bring to light the hidden things of darkness and reveal the counsels of the hearts. Then each one's praise will come from God' (1 Corinthians 4:5).

Read: Matthew 22:1-14

Marriage ceremonies are usually happy events not just for the bride and groom, but for all the guests who meet friends and relatives they normally only see at funerals and weddings. Jesus told a parable about a wedding feast to the Pharisees, chief priests and anyone who bothered to listen. The normal practice was for invitations to be sent out well in advance of the wedding and a reminder as the day drew closer.

This parable was once again a rebuke to the leaders of the church and the people of Israel who were plotting to kill God's Son. In the parable Jesus prophesied judgement upon the nation and the sending of the gospel to the hated Gentiles.

The salvation of both Jew and Gentile is in exactly the same way. The Apostle Paul wrote, 'For there is no distinction between Jew and Greek, for the same Lord over all is rich to all who call upon Him. For "whoever calls on the name of the LORD shall be saved"' (Romans 10:12,13).

The Apostle John wrote wonderful words of salvation, 'In this the love of God was manifested toward us, that God has sent his only begotten Son into the world, that we might live through him. In this is love, not that we loved God, but that he loved us and sent his Son to be the propitiation for our sins' (1 John 4:9,10).

God invites the spiritually lost to come to him just as Jesus said, 'All that the Father gives me will come to me, and the one who comes to me I will by no means cast out' (John 6:37). To Christ we must go in humble repentance seeking forgiveness and cleansing. God will have a feast for his Son and his people. The Church, the bride of Christ, is precious and all the elect will be irresistibly drawn to the Saviour by the Holy Spirit.

In the parable all the guests were given the same clothing, representing the righteousness of the Lord Jesus. This is the holiness we need to enter the celestial city and see God. Paul said, 'For as many of you as were baptised into Christ have put on Christ' (Galatians 3:27). In Revelation 19:7,8 we read of clothing that comes from our works of righteousness, purified by the Redeemer — 'Let us be glad and rejoice and give him glory, for the marriage of the Lamb has come, and his wife has made herself ready. And to her it was granted to be arrayed in fine linen, clean and bright, for the fine linen is the righteous acts of the saints.' Our righteousness is all of Christ.

But one was present wearing his own clothing, which was the way of salvation taught by the Pharisees and most members of the Sanhedrin. This man wore his own self-righteousness and was cast into outer darkness — hell. There he gnashed his teeth in anger at God for even in hell there is no humility, repentance and love of God.

The gospel call has gone far and wide and is savingly heard only by the elect — those who will repent and believe. Are you one of them?

THINGS TO DISCUSS WITH YOUR FAMILY

1. How is it that 'bad' people can go to heaven?
2. Why is hell spoken of as 'outer darkness' (Matthew 22:13)?
3. What does the wedding garment symbolize?

Meditation

If you are a Christian praise God for your election, calling and future glorification.

Wise Words

Those that love darkness rather than light shall have their doom accordingly. *Matthew Henry*

'Let every soul be subject to the governing authorities. For there is no authority except from God, and the authorities that exist are appointed by God' (Romans 13:1).

Read: Matthew 22:15-22

Most people dread tax time, which usually means finding receipts and other financial papers in order to fill in the form. There is also the payment of taxes on everything we purchase. So much money goes to the government to provide what we need to make life more secure and easy.

Jesus now found himself being questioned by some self-righteous Pharisees and worldly Herodians. They used flattering words hoping to encourage him to answer them — 'Teacher, we know that you are true, and teach the way of God in truth; nor do you care about anyone, for you do not regard the person of men. Tell us, therefore, what do you think? Is it lawful to pay taxes to Caesar, or not?' No matter what Christ answered they believed they could use it against him. The Herodians believed that the poll tax should be paid, but the Pharisees objected to the Roman coinage which carried the imprint of the Emperor stating he was the 'Highest priest' and 'Son of the divine Augustus'. This the Pharisees believed to be blasphemous.

Jesus knew their intentions and that they were again showing their hypocrisy. They acknowledged the Emperor as their ruler every time they used a Roman coin. However, Jesus answered their question in a manner that could not leave him open to any accusations of blasphemy or rebellion against the Emperor.

He simply acknowledged that there are two kingdoms and that in the kingdom of this world we must pay our taxes and show respect to those God has appointed to rule over us. We are not to give them the honour due to God. Paul, writing to the Christians in Rome, told them to respect the government of the day, evil though it was. This is what is taught in our text. Paul also wrote, 'Therefore you must be subject, not only because of wrath but also for conscience' sake. For because of this you also pay taxes, for they are God's ministers attending continually to this very thing. Render therefore to all their due: taxes to whom taxes are due, customs to whom customs, fear to whom fear, honour to whom honour' (Romans 13:5-7).

There is another kingdom, and that is the kingdom of God whose supreme Ruler is Jehovah. It is to him that we all must give honour and glory. David wrote in Psalm 29:1,2 words that we should take to heart: 'Give unto the Lord, O you mighty ones, give unto the Lord glory and strength. Give unto the Lord the glory due to his name; worship the Lord in the beauty of holiness.'

Paul tells us the same and gives the reason — 'For you were bought at a price; therefore glorify God in your body and in your spirit, which are God's' (1 Corinthians 6:20). Where there is a conflict between the state and God's law the Apostle Peter tells us what to do — 'We ought to obey God rather than men' (Acts 5:29). May we be faithful Christians.

THINGS TO DISCUSS WITH YOUR FAMILY

1. Why should we pay taxes?
2. Why should we obey the government? Read Romans 13:1-4.
3. What must Christians do when the law of the land conflicts with God's law?

Meditation

Examine your honesty in your payment of your taxes. Do you have a clear conscience?

Wise Words

It is certain that the church must not swallow up the state; it is no less certain that the state must not swallow up the church. *J. C. Ryle*

'Beloved, now we are children of God; and it has not yet been revealed what we shall be, but we know that when he is revealed, we shall be like him, for we shall see him as he is' (1 John 3:2).

Read: Luke 20:27-40

It is amazing the lengths people will go to in order to hurt others. Some people spread false rumours hoping to damage the character of the person they dislike.

Jesus faced the same behaviour of his enemies and today's reading shows the hypocrisy of the Sadducees in questioning Jesus about marriage in the afterlife. Those wicked people denied an afterlife, believing that the soul died with the body. They rejected the resurrection and the existence of angels, yet they asked Jesus a question about marriage in a state they didn't believe existed. Paul said of them, 'For Sadducees say that there is no resurrection — and no angel or spirit; but the Pharisees confess both' (Acts 23:8).

There are many in the church today who believe that death and the grave are victorious and that there is no afterlife. Indeed there are people in the pulpits of today's churches who deny the inspiration of the Scriptures, reject the idea of Christ's resurrection and the existence of heaven and hell. Many have the attitude of 'Many paths — one heaven' — believe anything, and if it is a sincere belief all will be well. This is the blind leading their blind followers on the broad way that leads to damnation.

Jesus answered those who questioned him saying that there is no marriage between the resurrected saints. There is of course the loving relationship between Christ and his bride — the church (Ephesians 5:22-29). The greatest joy of heaven is seeing God in Christ and when we see him we are told that we will be like him. Our attention first and foremost will be centred upon our Saviour.

The psalmist wrote words that would have been known by the Sadducees — 'Therefore my heart is glad, and my glory rejoices; my flesh also will rest in hope. For you will not leave my soul in Sheol, nor will you allow your Holy One to see corruption. You will show me the path of life; in your presence is fullness of joy; at your right hand are pleasures for evermore' (Psalm 16:9-11). Job also looked forward to the resurrection, 'For I know that my Redeemer lives, and he shall stand at last on the earth; and after my skin is destroyed, this I know, that in my flesh I shall see God, whom I shall see for myself, and my eyes shall behold, and not another' (Job 19:25-27).

The God and Father of the Lord Jesus is the God of the living and the dead. Jesus declared him to be the God of Abraham, Isaac and Jacob who lived many centuries before. The patriarchs looked forward to the heavenly Jerusalem where they would be very much alive and in the presence of God (Hebrews 11:10-16).

I trust you believe in the life to come in the presence of God, and have prepared for the day when your earthly life is ended.

THINGS TO DISCUSS WITH YOUR FAMILY

1. In Luke 20:36 Jesus said of his people, '...nor can they die anymore, for they are equal to the angels and are sons of God, being sons of the resurrection'. What did he mean?
2. How can God be the God of his people who have died?
3. What are the joys of heaven?

Meditation

Meditate upon the wonder of God's dwelling place — heaven.

Wise Words

This is my coronation day. I have been looking forward to it for years. *D. L. Moody*

 'For God so loved the world that he gave his only begotten Son, that whoever believes in him should not perish but have everlasting life' (John 3:16).

Read: Mark 12:28-34

It is wonderful when you find someone who is of a good character, trustworthy and shows a genuine interest in what you are doing. Jesus didn't find many people like that amongst the church rulers. However, a scribe who had heard the Lord speak the truth to the Sadducees who were plainly out to cause trouble, approached him with an important question. He asked a sincere question and from Christ's reply to him it would appear that he was a man of good character and truly interested in the kingdom of God.

What commandment do you think is the most important?

Jesus answered the scribe by quoting words from the Scriptures which he had studied. We must remember that then people only had the Old Testament and the Saviour's reply is worth reading and rereading, 'The first of all the commandments is: "Hear, O Israel, the LORD our God, the LORD is one. And you shall love the LORD your God with all your heart, with all your soul, with all your mind, and with all your strength." This is the first commandment. And the second, like it, is this: "You shall love your neighbour as yourself." There is no other commandment greater than these.' (These words come from Deuteronomy 6:4,5; 10:12; 30:6; and Leviticus 19:18.)

Why should you love God? Most would answer, 'Because he loved us and sent his Son to die and save sinners.' True, this is a great reason for loving God, especially if you have tasted his love. There is another reason and that is because of his Person. In Australia a visit to Ayers Rock will fill your mind with majestic wonder. It is a spectacular sight. Think of God and his Person — a God of infinite grace, love, mercy; he is all wise and powerful, and he is omnipresent and omniscient. We know many more aspects of God's character and these should fill us with a love coming from a redeemed heart. He is majestic and glorious beyond anything we can imagine. Just read John's description of God on his throne in heaven found in Revelation 4. John could only describe his vision in words of majestic wonder.

God's 'royal law' is 'You shall love your neighbour as yourself' (James 2:8). Do you?

Christ's reply was what the scribe wanted to hear. He totally agreed with what Jesus had said and understood that love of God and man was far more important than animal sacrifices. He knew God's words found in Hosea 6:6: 'For I desire mercy and not sacrifice, and the knowledge of God more than burnt offerings.'

Jesus told this scribe that he was 'not far from the kingdom of God.' He needed to be born again and place his faith in the One who answered his question. I sometimes wonder if he was amongst those who turned in repentance to Jesus as a result of Peter's great sermon on the day of Pentecost. I pray that you are a member of God's kingdom.

THINGS TO DISCUSS WITH YOUR FAMILY

1. Why is James 2:8 called 'the royal law'? — 'You shall love your neighbour as yourself.'
2. How can you show your love of God?
3. What did Jesus mean when he told the scribe, 'You are not far from the kingdom of God' (Mark 12:34)? Is this a dangerous position in which to be?

Meditation

Meditate upon the reasons for your love of God e.g. 'I love the LORD, because he has heard my voice and my supplications' (Psalm 116:1).

Wise Words

Love of the creature toward the Creator must include obedience or it is meaningless. *Francis Schaeffer*

Christ — a descendant of King David

'I, Jesus, have sent my angel to testify to you these things in the churches. I am the Root and the Offspring of David, the Bright and Morning Star' (Revelation 22:16).

Read: Matthew 22:41-46

Many people today spend a lot of time tracing their 'family tree'. A friend once told me of the many picnics his parents had beside cemeteries. They had spent many hours searching for the graves of relatives. My brother-in-law has traced his family on both sides and his research is interesting. One of his ancestors came to Australia as a convict on the second fleet.

Jesus took the advantage of speaking to a group of Pharisees who hated him and wanted him dead. He asked a simple question: 'What do you think about the Christ? Whose Son is he?' The reply was very biblical — 'The Son of David'.

God had made many promises to David. He recorded the Lord's words concerning his throne — 'Once I have sworn by my holiness; I will not lie to David: his seed shall endure for ever, and his throne as the sun before me; it shall be established forever like the moon, even like the faithful witness in the sky' (Psalm 89:35-37).

When Jesus was performing many miracles the people asked one another, 'Could this be the Son of David?' (Matthew 12:23). Jesus did not reject the title when some used it of him. Blind Bartimaeus had said, 'Jesus, Son of David, have mercy on me!' (Mark 10:47).

The Pharisees believed the Christ would be a man — a descendant of David who would, by God's power, establish David's throne once again and drive out the Roman armies. Yet this was not all the truth concerning Christ, for he was the Son of God, God and man in one Person.

Hence Jesus asked the Pharisees how it was that David, inspired by the Holy Spirit, could call the Messiah, 'Lord'. He then quoted words from the Messianic Psalm 110:1 — 'The Lord said to my Lord, "Sit at my right hand, till I make your enemies your footstool."' In this passage Jehovah is speaking of Christ, the Mediator between God and man, and seating him on the divine throne. In other words,

Messiah was God, not just a physical descendant of David through his mother, Mary.

Isaiah wrote of Christ, ' There shall come forth a Rod from the stem of Jesse, and a Branch shall grow out of his roots. The Spirit of the LORD shall rest upon him, the Spirit of wisdom and understanding, the Spirit of counsel and might, the Spirit of knowledge and of the fear of the LORD ... And in that day there shall be a Root of Jesse, who shall stand as a banner to the people; for the Gentiles shall seek him, and his resting place shall be glorious' (Isaiah 11:1,2,10).

Christ was God's King over his kingdom which is in the hearts of his people. Is he your King?

Christ's answer confounded the Pharisees because they could not comprehend how the Christ could be both David's son and David's Lord. Christ is God and man in one Person!

THINGS TO DISCUSS
WITH YOUR FAMILY

1. In what way is Jesus the 'son of David'?
2. Read and discuss Philippians 2:5-11.
3. Why do you think the Pharisees gave up asking Jesus any more 'trick' questions?

Meditation

Meditate upon the mystery of Christ being God and yet the 'Son of David' in one Person.

Wise Words

If Jesus Christ is not true God, how can he *help* us? If he is not true man, how can he help *us*?   *Dietrich Bonhoeffer*

'How can you believe, who receive honour from one another, and do not seek the honour that comes from the only God?' (John 5:44).

Read: Matthew 23:1-13

There were times when I was a school teacher that I had to speak harshly to children who were causing problems for both teachers and students. I always spoke plainly in order to be clearly understood. I avoided using hurtful words.

Matthew 23 contains some very plain speaking by the Lord concerning the Pharisees. His disciples needed to be well aware of their sinful teaching and living. These people were considered by the ordinary citizens of Israel to be the most godly of people. They were amongst the few who stood firm in their opposition to Roman rule, but they were leaders of the opposition to Jesus, wanting him dead.

In Matthew 23 we have a record of Christ's last words spoken in the temple and we should note them carefully. The Pharisees instructed the people concerning the law of Moses and in many synagogues they sat in a special seat called 'Moses' seat'. Jesus told his disciples to listen to their teaching and obey the truth when it was taught, but they were not to behave as the Pharisees did when they acted contrary to the law of God. They held an important place in the religious life of the nation and their office was to be held in respect. Today, while we may object to the actions and morality of our political rulers, we must respect their position. When Paul spoke harshly of a person whom he did not know was the high priest, he repented saying, 'I did not know, brethren, that he was the high priest; for it is written, "You shall not speak evil of a ruler of your people"' (Acts 23:5).

Jesus told the disciples of the heavy burdens the Pharisees placed upon the people. They demanded obedience to hundreds of laws, both God's law and the laws they had made. They were proud, demanded the best seats, asked to be called by titles that belonged to God and wore clothing with very large 'phylacteries' containing

God's law. (Read Exodus 13:8,9,16; Deuteronomy 11:18.) They also had very wide fringes on their clothing to show they were godly people. (Read Numbers 15:37-41.) The Pharisees wanted the preeminence in everything and expected the ordinary people to look up to them.

Humility is one mark of a Christian. Peter gives us a clear teaching and warning, 'Likewise you younger people, submit yourselves to your elders. Yes, all of you be submissive to one another, and be clothed with humility, for "God resists the proud, but gives grace to the humble." Therefore humble yourselves under the mighty hand of God, that he may exalt you in due time...' (1 Peter 5:5,6).

Paul had once been a proud Pharisee, but when he was converted he said of those things of which he was once so proud, that they were 'rubbish' (Philippians 3:8). Are you a humble person, giving thanks to God for all your talents?

THINGS TO DISCUSS WITH YOUR FAMILY

1. What is a 'phylactery'?
2. What special spiritual names belong to God alone?
3. What heavy burdens did the Scribes and Pharisees place upon the people (Matthew 23:4)?

Meditation

Think on Christ's words — 'And whoever exalts himself will be abased and he who humbles himself will be exalted' (Matthew 23:12).

Wise Words

Until a man is nothing God can make nothing of him.
Martin Luther

'And what does the LORD require of you but to do justly, to love mercy, and to walk humbly with your God?' (Micah 6:8).

Read: Matthew 23:13-33

None of us has any reason to be proud for all we are and all we have are gifts from God. Many times we have read of the Pharisees who considered themselves better than everyone else and lived such holy lives that God was indebted to them. There are many people today who think the same. Do you?

The Pharisees were spiritually blind, who through their false teaching of the way of salvation, closed the door of heaven to sinners. The key to heaven's doorway is Jesus Christ and yet the words and influence of the Pharisees and Scribes prevented people from believing in 'the Son of David'. God had called the nation of Israel to evangelize the world with the knowledge of the living God, but they failed miserably. When they won a convert it was nearly always to their religious beliefs and thus to hell. They used their religiosity to cheat widows and foolish people out of their money, for they were lovers of wealth. Today, many TV 'evangelists' do the same. They preach their own gospel and are always after money. Friends, beware of these people!

In Zechariah 7:9-10 we are told how to live: 'Thus says the LORD of hosts: "Execute true justice, show mercy and compassion everyone to his brother. Do not oppress the widow or the fatherless, the alien or the poor. Let none of you plan evil in his heart against his brother." But they refused to heed, shrugged their shoulders, and stopped their ears so that they could not hear.' Is this not a true statement concerning those self-righteous Pharisees?

They tithed, but not according to the teaching of Scripture. Nowhere were they told to tithe mint, anise or cummin, but this tithing must have sounded very religious to those who looked kindly upon the Pharisees.

Jesus said that the Pharisees made every effort to appear religious people — didn't their clothing show this? However, they were internally corrupt. Their hearts were satanic, needing the new birth and cleansing by the Saviour they were about to kill. But what was different? Hadn't their like-minded ancestors persecuted and killed God's prophets? They had built monuments to the prophets yet had taken no notice of what they taught. They enjoyed their popularity, but should have taken notice of Job's words, '...the triumphing of the wicked is short, and the joy of the hypocrite is but for a moment' (Job 20:5).

Jesus had pronounced eight woes upon the Pharisees. Today's Bible reading concluded with, 'Serpents, brood of vipers! How can you escape the condemnation of hell?' These are fearful words, but they are spoken to all self-righteous hypocrites. May God bless you all with godly humility and a genuine love of the Lord and your fellow man — even your enemy.

THINGS TO DISCUSS WITH YOUR FAMILY

1. What is needed for a person to do good in God's sight?
2. What was the Pharisees' greatest sin?
3. Discuss today's text.

Meditation

Search your heart and root out any sin of the Pharisees you find there.

Wise Words

I have read of many wicked popes, but the worst pope I ever met with is Pope *Self.*   *John Newton*

'Say to them: "As I live," says the Lord GOD, "I have no pleasure in the death of the wicked, but that the wicked turn from his way and live. Turn, turn from your evil ways! For why should you die, O house of Israel?"' (Ezekiel 33:11).

Read: Matthew 23:34-39

Our courts are flooded with people who have broken the laws of the land, and most people consider their punishments are too light. People who break the law must pay their debt to society.

Jesus has been speaking about the sinful activities and teaching of the Pharisees. God's punishment was soon to fall upon them and the covenant nation, a punishment that was horrific. We all must remember Paul's words of warning, 'Do not be deceived, God is not mocked; for whatever a man sows, that he will also reap' (Galatians 6:7). The nation had murdered many of God's prophets and now were about to murder God's Son, the greatest prophet of all.

Jesus told his audience that he was to send out a new group of prophets and wise church leaders, but they would treat them just as the prophets of old had been treated. Saul (later the Apostle Paul) confessed to cruelly treating Christians: 'This I also did in Jerusalem, and many of the saints I shut up in prison, having received authority from the chief priests; and when they were put to death, I cast my vote against them. And I punished them often in every synagogue and compelled them to blaspheme; and being exceedingly enraged against them, I persecuted them even to foreign cities' (Acts 26:10,11). Later Stephen was stoned to death, Peter was crucified, Paul was beheaded and many faithful Christians were killed in very cruel ways. Just think of mad Nero who had Christians thrown into the arena to be mauled by wild animals, and all this for the entertainment of the people. Yet in all their persecutions the Christians were victorious. Soon the covenant nation would be punished for its ungodly behaviour.

Divine punishment would be poured out on the Jews. Jerusalem and the temple would be destroyed and the people scattered throughout the nations where they would continue to hear salvation in Christ preached.

As Jesus looked over the city and with a compassionate heart he reminded the people that he often wanted to gather them to himself like a hen did with her chickens when a hawk appeared. However, the people rejected him, the Son of David, God's Son, the long awaited Messiah. The day of reckoning was about to come because of the nation's ill treatment of the prophets and God's Son. After his death the nation would see him no more until he returned in power and glory as 'KING OF KINGS AND LORD OF LORDS' (Revelation 19:16). Then every person would pay him homage as Paul had written, 'at the name of Jesus every knee should bow, of those in heaven, and of those on earth, and of those under the earth, and that every tongue should confess that Jesus Christ is Lord, to the glory of God the Father' (Philippians 2:10,11).

Have you bowed the knee before the divine Jesus Christ? One day, whether you want to or not, you will do so! Remember God said, "'I have no pleasure in the death of one who dies ... Therefore turn and live!'" (Ezekiel 18:32).

THINGS TO DISCUSS WITH YOUR FAMILY

1. When and how did God punish his covenant people?
2. For what reason will God punish sinners?
3. What did Jesus mean when he said, 'See! Your house is left to you desolate' (Matthew 23:38)?

Meditation

Meditate upon the day when you will meet Christ, the Judge.

Wise Words

Let justice be done though the world perish.   *Augustine*

'So let each one give as he purposes in his heart, not grudgingly or of necessity; for God loves a cheerful giver' (2 Corinthians 9:7).

Read: Mark 12:41-44

There's a saying that goes something like this: 'Misers have deep pockets.' Many rich people are like that rich young ruler who so loved his wealth that he put it before his salvation. What a tragedy! Then there are others who have given till it hurts. Many who supported Hudson Taylor, the founder of the China Inland Mission, gave from a heart that was in love with God and wanted to play a part in the salvation of sinners. Where do we fit into this picture?

In the temple there was a section known as 'The women's court'. In this room there were thirteen containers into which ladies placed their giving to support the work of the priests and Levites. Now of our Saviour we know, '... there is no creature hidden from his sight, but all things are naked and open to the eyes of him to whom we must give account' (Hebrews 4:13), but he was present and saw what happened through an archway or another opening.

Many women must have been milling about as it was the time of the Passover festival and there were many visitors in Jerusalem. No doubt everyone made an effort to visit the temple and make their annual offering to support God's work. Jesus obviously saw rich women tossing their coins into the containers, but from his comments few if any gave as they should have — from a renewed heart.

He took special notice of a widow who tossed in two very small coins — mites — which humanly speaking were worthless, yet in the Lord's eyes was a priceless gift. She gave her all and Jesus drew the attention of his disciples to this loving act. She had given every coin she had, trusting in God to provide for her in the future. This was the only recorded commendation made by Jesus while in the temple.

God has a special interest in widows, orphans and those in humble circumstances. Of him the psalmist wrote, 'A father of the fatherless, a defender of widows, is God in his holy habitation' (Psalm 68:5). The early church appointed deacons to give special attention to widows (see Acts 6:1-3).

James stated: 'Pure and undefiled religion before God and the Father is this: to visit orphans and widows in their trouble, and to keep oneself unspotted from the world' (James 1:27). The Apostle Paul wrote about giving to the Lord's work: 'But this I say: He who sows sparingly will also reap sparingly, and he who sows bountifully will also reap bountifully. So let each one give as he purposes in his heart, not grudgingly or of necessity; for God loves a cheerful giver' (2 Corinthians 9:6,7).

Let us show our love for God and our fellow man by having shallow pockets where our money can be easily reached. Remember that God is no man's debtor. Also remember that God accused the Jews of stealing money that was rightfully his (Malachi 3:8-10). We should consider this matter seriously.

THINGS TO DISCUSS WITH YOUR FAMILY

1. Why do Christians put their money on the plate each Lord's Day?
2. Why was the widow's giving so priceless in Christ's eyes?
3. How are we to determine our giving to support the Lord's work?

Meditation

Think about Jesus' comment when he saw the widow give so generously to the work of the LORD. Someone said, 'The Lord measures not what we give, but what we keep.'

Wise Words

All believers are taught to give — but there is such a thing as a special gift of giving.   *A. W. Tozer*

'...there will be false teachers among you, who will secretly bring in destructive heresies, even denying the Lord who bought them, and bring on themselves swift destruction. And many will follow their destructive ways, because of whom the way of truth will be blasphemed' (2 Peter 2:1,2).

Read: Matthew 24:1-14

The first time I saw the Sydney Opera House I just stood and looked in awe at the amazing building. It looked like a ship about to sail away on the Sydney Harbour. My wife, Val, and I spent a long time observing the building, both outside and inside. The disciples had pointed out to their Lord the amazing temple building which was the centre of worship for the nation. It was there in the Holy of Holies, above the ark of the covenant, that God met with his people in a special way. They were surprised to hear Jesus say, 'Assuredly, I say to you, not one stone shall be left here upon another, that shall not be thrown down.'

When Jesus and the disciples had made their way from the temple to the Mount of Olives they asked him several questions — 'Tell us, when will these things be? And what will be the sign of your coming, and of the end of the age?' We now look at the first part of the Lord's answer that deals with the end of the 'age' which involved both the destruction of the temple and Jerusalem. The old age was soon to end and the Messianic age begin. The disciples were learning that Christ's second coming did not correspond with the end of the 'age'.

Your reading is a portion of Christ's teaching concerning the state of the nation before the Roman armies came and carried out the destruction of all that the Jews held precious. Rome, which was experiencing a degree of peace, would find rebellion breaking out in parts of its empire and even some internal revolution. There would be earthquakes culminating in the explosion of Mount Vesuvius in AD 79.

Many would stand up claiming to be Christ and attract a following. Josephus, the Jewish historian of that age, described many of the false prophets who claimed to be speaking God's words.

Persecution of the Christian church would become more violent. We know that Saul the Pharisee (later the Apostle Paul) was involved in having Christians imprisoned and in some cases put to death. He held the coats of the men who stoned the godly deacon, Stephen (Acts 7:58 – 8:1). Such terrible persecution caused some to abandon their faith in Christ. In some places the initial love the saints had for Christ grew cold. This was the case of the church at Ephesus (Revelation 2:4).

Also to be fulfilled before the destruction of Jerusalem and the temple was that the gospel had to be preached throughout the inhabited world. When the Christians in Jerusalem were forced to escape persecution, they told people everywhere they went of Christ the Saviour. Paul and the other disciples tramped the known world preaching faith in a resurrected Jesus. Paul urged the Colossian church to remain faithful to the gospel 'which was preached to every creature under heaven' (Colossians 1:23). Then the end of the age came.

THINGS TO DISCUSS WITH YOUR FAMILY

1. What did Jesus mean by 'then the end will come' (verse 14)?
2. What was the cause of Saul becoming a Christian? Read Acts 9:1-8.
3. How was the gospel spread so quickly throughout the world?

Meditation

Consider the Lord's righteous anger towards those who reject the gospel and persecute Christians.

Wise Words

Take care if the world does hate you that it hates you without cause.   *C. H. Spurgeon*

'But when you see Jerusalem surrounded by armies, then know that its desolation is near' (Luke 21:20).

Read: Matthew 24:15-22

Every age has witnessed the destruction of cities in time of war.
Property is destroyed and people killed. This was to happen to
Jerusalem and the nation of Israel and our reading deals specifically
with that historical event.

Jesus referred his disciples to a prophetic statement made by
Daniel which was to be fulfilled during the days preceding the final
destruction of Jerusalem. Several times Daniel mentioned 'the abomination of desolation' (Daniel 11:31; 12:11) which happened when
the vile Antiochus Epiphanes offered a pig on the temple altar and
for a time prohibited worship in the temple. However, Christ was
referring to a passage found in Daniel 9:27 which he said was soon
to occur. This was a warning for Christians to escape from the city
before its destruction.

Because of Israel's rebellion against Rome, the Emperor sent
down his army that surrounded the city. The soldiers carried the
'standards' which pictured their 'divine' emperor who was worshipped as god. When the army appeared in AD 68 the Christians
realized the implications of Christ's words and escaped from the city
during a lull in fighting. They quickly made their way to the safety
of the mountains. We again see the compassion of the Lord who was
concerned for Christian mothers with babies still at the breast. He
knew that the time of escape would be made more difficult if it was
winter or on the Sabbath when they would be given no help by the
church authorities to leave the city.

There are times when Christians have every right to escape
from those who want them killed for their faith. The Apostle Paul's
conscience did not prevent him escaping from the governor of
Damascus who wanted him arrested. We read, 'I was let down in a
basket through a window in the wall, and escaped from his hands' (2

Corinthians 11:33). There are times of course when we must stand firm for the truth of our Saviour and suffer whatever evil people do.

Jesus went on to tell the disciples that the time of the destruction of Jerusalem would cause horrific suffering that would never be equalled. When the city was sealed off from the outside, those trapped ran out of food and frequently parents murdered their children and ate their flesh. Factions developed in the city which caused much infighting, but for the sake of the 'elect' destruction would be swift. These 'elect' were Jews, chosen by God to turn to Christ as their Lord and Saviour.

Rome's destruction of the nation was complete just as Jesus had foretold: 'And they will fall by the edge of the sword, and be led away captive into all nations. And Jerusalem will be trampled by Gentiles until the times of the Gentiles are fulfilled' (Luke 21:24).

THINGS TO DISCUSS WITH YOUR FAMILY

1. Why did God inflict such a terrible punishment upon Israel?
2. Who was Antiochus Epiphanes?
3. What did Jesus mean when he said that 'Jerusalem will be trampled by Gentiles until the times of the Gentiles are fulfilled' (Luke 21:24)?

Meditation

Pray that many more Jews will recognize Jesus as their Messiah.

Wise Words

If men refuse to be taught by precept they must be taught by punishment.   *T. V. Moore*

'Behold, the day of the LORD comes, cruel, with both wrath and fierce anger, to lay the land desolate; and he will destroy its sinners from it. For the stars of heaven ... will not give their light; the sun will be darkened ... and the moon will not cause its light to shine' (Isaiah 13:9,10).

Read: Matthew 24:23-36

There are parts of God's word that are difficult to interpret. Often this is due to the fact that, unlike the Jews, we are unfamiliar with the wording of the Old Testament. Many people see our reading as relating to both the destruction of Jerusalem and the second coming of our Saviour. I understand it to continue teaching the end of the pre-Messianic age and the start of the last age of human history where the kingdom of God spreads throughout the Gentile nations.

Jesus told the disciples to take no notice of people who said he could be found in various places, because his return would be visible for all to see just as we can see lightning flashing through the sky. Christ's return will not be a secret coming. Just as circling eagles signify some dead carcass they are about to eat, so also the Roman armies would signify death and destruction to Israel because the nation was ripe for judgement.

Jesus used words from the Old Testament describing his coming in judgement upon Israel. Our text is one and it concerns the destruction of the great Babylonian empire. The Lord foretold judgement upon Egypt where he is described as 'coming' — 'The burden against Egypt. Behold, the LORD rides on a swift cloud, and will come into Egypt; the idols of Egypt will totter at his presence...' (Isaiah 19:1). Jesus used a similar expression when speaking to Caiaphas, the high priest who asked if he was the Christ. He replied, 'I am. And you will see the Son of Man sitting at the right hand of the Power, and coming with the clouds of heaven' (Mark 14:62).

Jesus was to send out his 'messengers' to call unbelievers to saving faith. With Jerusalem's destruction many would acknowledge this judgement of God as the 'sign' that Christ was in heaven. The short parable about the fig tree is of a tree about to bloom and bear fruit which, unlike the barren fig tree which referred to Israel, indicated

612

the glorious Messianic age of the worldwide spread of the gospel.

God's judgement was about to fall upon an apostate nation and Christ's words indicated that the generation then living would bear witness to the events he had described — 'Assuredly, I say to you, this generation will by no means pass away till all these things take place.' The old age was ending and the glorious new one was about to begin, but let us always remember Paul's words, 'For I am not ashamed of the gospel of Christ, for it is the power of God to salvation for everyone who believes, for the Jew first and also for the [Gentile]' (Romans 1:16).

THINGS TO DISCUSS WITH YOUR FAMILY

1. What did the 'end of the age' signify?
2. What is the new age of the church?
3. Make a list of the different ways God has 'come' to this world.

Meditation

Meditate upon the birth of the new age of the church and what it means to you.

Wise Words

These events, while they signify the end of the departing age, have a positive function; they introduce the 'birth' of a new age, the age of the church. *John Legg*

'And what I say to you, I say to all: "Watch!"' (Mark 13:37).

Read: Matthew 24:37-51

I hope that you all pray for the Lord's return to this world of sin and heartache. You often pray 'Your kingdom come,' (Matthew 6:10) but do you understand what you are asking from God?

Jesus now moves from talking about the end of the age to his second coming. We should take note of his words, 'But of that day and hour no one knows, not even the angels of heaven, but my Father only.' The Saviour did not know when he would come a second time. This information was not revealed to him by God during his life on earth, but, throughout the centuries since Jesus said these words many have attempted to set the date for his return, some even to the very hour. Beware of such false prophets.

The Lord told his disciples that when he returned the world would be going along as usual, just as it was when Noah built the ark. There is no sin in the activities outlined by Christ, but what is missing is a saving love of God. People will be doing their own thing without any concern for Christ or their eternal well-being. The gospel will be preached, but only a remnant will take any notice. This happened in the days of Noah, that 'preacher of righteousness' (2 Peter 2:5). Everyone went about their own business ignoring his warning. Then at the appointed moment God closed the ark's door and soon the rain began to fall. With the door shut it was too late for those outside to be saved. The same will happen when Christ returns in power and glory to gather his people together. It will be too late to repent when the Lord appears.

One will be taken to be with the Lord and another left to face the judgement of an angry God. Christ's warning to us all is, 'Be ready all the time for you don't know when I will return.' The disciples had been given signs foretelling Jerusalem's destruction, but there is no sign given to indicate the Lord's imminent return. Just as a thief does not advertise when he is to commit a robbery, so the Lord does not reveal the exact time of his coming. Paul warned the Thessalonians, 'Therefore let us not sleep, as others do, but let us watch and be [self-controlled]' (1 Thessalonians 5:6).

The Lord's parable about the two servants is a reminder to all Christians to get on with the work of confessing and glorifying God in Christ. Peter wrote of the preparation needed by the saints for the Lord's return, '...what manner of persons ought you to be in holy conduct and godliness...?' (2 Peter 3:11). Many hypocritical, professing Christians will ridicule believers concerning their love of the Lord and their longing for his return. Peter records their mocking words, 'Where is the promise of his coming? For since the fathers fell asleep, all things continue as they were from the beginning of creation' (2 Peter 3:4).

May we be faithful Christians who can say with the Apostle Paul, 'For our citizenship is in heaven, from which we also eagerly wait for the Saviour, the Lord Jesus Christ' (Philippians 3:20).

THINGS TO DISCUSS WITH YOUR FAMILY

1. When will Jesus return to planet earth?
2. What will the ungodly lose when Jesus returns? Read Revelation 18:22,23.
3. When will 'the earth ... be filled with the knowledge of the glory of the LORD' (Habakkuk 2:14)?

Meditation

Think about Christ's words — 'Watch therefore for you do not know what hour your Lord is coming' (Matthew 24:42).

Wise Words

When Christ comes again, the remains of ignorance shall be rolled away.   *J. C. Ryle*

'None of them can by any means redeem his brother, nor give to God a
ransom for him...' (Psalm 49:7).

Read: Matthew 25:1-13

Weddings are times when families get together for an exciting celebration. Everyone is very interested to see the arrival of the bride and groom and have a close look at what is being worn, especially by the bride. Throughout the world wedding customs vary but what stands out in Christ's parable is that the bridesmaids were waiting for the arrival of the groom whom they would escort to the bride's home for the wedding feast.

The parable was spoken to his disciples as the Lord sat on the Mount of Olives overlooking Jerusalem. He had told them of the forthcoming destruction of the temple, the city and the scattering of the people to the four corners of the earth. They had been told that no one knew the exact time of his second coming. This parable is another teaching of the unexpected nature of his appearance — it will be sudden and many will not be prepared to meet the Redeemer.

The ten virgins represent the church which has always been a mixture of believers and those who are strangers to God's saving grace. Jesus spoke of the people who were convinced of their salvation only to discover on the Day of Judgement that they were hypocrites of the first order. Jesus had plainly said, 'Not everyone who says to me, "Lord, Lord," shall enter the kingdom of heaven, but he who does the will of my Father in heaven ... And then I will declare to them, "I never knew you; depart from me, you who practice lawlessness!"' (Matthew 7:21,23).

When Christ returns the world will be going about as usual without any concern for his visible intervention into history. Even the church will largely be asleep. However, at our Lord's appearance we shall all be changed in the twinkling of an eye and rise to meet him in the air. It will be terrible for those hoping that all was well with them spiritually, when they hear Christ's words, 'I do not know you.' Praise God he knows his people and none will be overlooked.

Paul wrote very comforting words to the saints, 'The Lord knows those who are his' (2 Timothy 2:19). Jesus said, 'I am the good shepherd; and I know my sheep, and am known by my own' (John 10:14).

In the parable, the foolish virgins asked the wise ones for their oil of salvation, but this could not be. Our text is a reminder that we cannot give God's saving grace to another as it is the gift of God given in accordance with his electing love. When the Lord returns the earth's history will be completed. It will also mean that the day of grace to unbelievers is ended. There are no second chances. To which group of the ten virgins do you belong?

THINGS TO DISCUSS WITH YOUR FAMILY

1. Can you say with the Apostle Paul, 'I live by faith in the Son of God, who loved me and gave himself for me' (Galatians 2:20)?
2. How can you live in a state of readiness for the Lord's return?
3. In this parable how does Christ describe hell?

Meditation

Think upon Paul's words: 'I live by faith in the Son of God, who loved me and gave himself for me' (Galatians 2:20).

Wise Words

The brightness of Christ's advent will reveal the true character of those things which were previously hidden by darkness.

Geoffrey B. Wilson

 'Now there are diversities of gifts, but the same Spirit' (1 Corinthians 12:4).

Read: Matthew 25:14-30

There is no doubt that God has given wonderful gifts to mankind generally. As we look about us we see the great variety of skills that people have and we must remember that they are all the sovereign gift of God. The same is true in the church. The Lord has distributed a great variety of talents to his people so that the church can function as a living body. In 1 Corinthians 12 Paul devoted a chapter to these gifts. We are all different, but when working properly the church of God is a bright, living, holy organization where every believer can say with the Apostle Paul, 'But by the grace of God I am what I am' (1 Corinthians 15:10). We all have a work to do, so let us use our God-given skills to his glory.

Christ told a parable about the kingdom of heaven where the owner gave gifts to his labourers. We should note that the owner didn't give every servant the same amount of talents, but distributed them according to their capacity to use the money correctly. Some were given great responsibilities while others had less expected of them. Nevertheless, they all knew they were to wisely use the money given to them and produce an income.

When the master returned he rewarded those servants who had used their talents wisely to produce an income. However, one servant was lazy, despite knowing what was expected of him. He even said to his master, 'Lord, I knew you to be a hard man, reaping where you have not sown, and gathering where you have not scattered seed. And I was afraid, and went and hid your talent in the ground. Look, there you have what is yours.' What a fool!

Elsewhere Jesus spoke words that we should all note: 'And that servant who knew his master's will, and did not prepare himself or do according to his will, shall be beaten with many stripes' (Luke 12:47). Lazy people are told to take notice of the hard-working ant (Proverbs 6:9-11). God observes the way we use the gifts he has given us. The writer to the Hebrews gives us comforting words, 'For God is not unjust to forget your work and labour of love which you have shown toward his name, in that you have ministered to the saints, and do minister' (Hebrews 6:10).

The Scriptures have much to say about the wise use of God's gifts. Peter records, 'As each one has received a gift, minister it to one another, as good stewards of the manifold grace of God. If anyone speaks, let him speak as the oracles of God. If anyone ministers, let him do it as with the ability which God supplies, that in all things God may be glorified through Jesus Christ, to whom belong the glory and the dominion for ever and ever' (1 Peter 4:10,11).

Are you ready to give an account to the Lord for the wise use of the talents God has given you? Always remember, 'For as the body without the spirit is dead, so faith without works is dead also' (James 2:26).

THINGS TO DISCUSS WITH YOUR FAMILY

1. What does James 4:17 mean? — 'Therefore, to him who knows to do good and does not do it, to him it is sin.'
2. What are we taught of a servant's responsibility to his master? Read Ephesians 6:5.
3. How do you use your talents to glorify God and help the church?

Meditation

Meditate upon God's goodness — 'Every good gift and every perfect gift is from above, and comes down from the Father of lights...' (James 1:17).

Let us beware of a do-nothing Christianity: such Christianity does not come from the Spirit of God.   *J. C. Ryle*

Wise Words

619

21 October   The sheep and goats judgement

'For we must all appear before the judgement seat of Christ, that each one may receive the things done in the body, according to what he has done, whether good or bad' (2 Corinthians 5:10).

Read: Matthew 25:31-46

In Australia many parts of the countryside are covered with an attractive yellow flower which is a pest. I remember as a youngster on the farm spending many hours digging out these plants. Nevertheless, the weeds won the day and in parts of the country in spring time the fields look lovely, covered with 'fireweed' flowers. Yet, a lover of fireweed is the goat. They enjoy eating the plant and many people make use of these animals to control the weed.

Our parable doesn't speak very highly of goats. They refer to all those people who on Judgement Day stand condemned by the Lord because they did not believe in him. They are the hypocrites in the church, the ungodly outside the church — anyone who has lived without a saving faith in the 'Son of Man'. This group of people face the anger of an offended God and will suffer eternal damnation.

Here on earth people are divided into many groups — male and female, rich and poor, slave and free, workers and retired, and on we could go; but on Judgement Day there are just two groups — saved and lost — sheep and goats. And every person who has ever lived will be there to face judgement. They will give an account of their life and the use they have made of God's wonderful gifts.

All who have lived a life trusting their eternal well-being to the Lord Jesus can face judgement rejoicing, for the Apostle Paul has told us, 'There is therefore now no condemnation to those who are in Christ Jesus, who do not walk according to the flesh, but according to the Spirit' (Romans 8:1). Instead of fearing judgement we know that 'having been justified by faith, we have peace with God through our Lord Jesus Christ' (Romans 5:1).

In this judgement, true faith is evidenced in the works of righteousness done by the saints. Today's text points this out clearly as does the verse quoted in our last devotion: 'For as the body without the spirit is dead, so faith without works is dead also' (James 2:26).

There is a very close union between Christ and his people. The Lord looks upon the help given to a Christian as help given to himself. Paul was taught that to harm a saint was to hurt Christ. On the road to Damascus to persecute believers he came face to face with the Lord who said, 'Saul, Saul, why are you persecuting me?'

May we all go out of our way to help fellow believers who are in need. Christ looks upon such help as being given to himself and rewards his people accordingly; failure brings eternal destruction. Have you a faith in Christ that shines through the works you do? If not, then note the psalmist's warning, 'Kiss the Son, lest he be angry, and you perish in the way, when his wrath is kindled but a little. Blessed are all those who put their trust in him' (Psalm 2:12).

THINGS TO DISCUSS WITH YOUR FAMILY

1. Who are the sheep in Christ's parable?
2. What caused some people to be classified as 'goats' in the Lord's parable?
3. What does it mean 'Kiss the Son'? (Psalm 2:12).

Meditation

Meditate upon your place in the judgement scene described by Christ in this parable.

Wise Words

Our separations will avail us nothing, unless we take care to be found in the number of Christ's sheep, when he comes to judgement. *Sherlock*

'For I am God, and there is no other; I am God, and there is none like me, declaring the end from the beginning, and from ancient times things that are not yet done, saying, "My counsel shall stand, and I will do all my pleasure"' (Isaiah 46:9,10).

Read: Matthew 26:1-5

Many times I have made plans to do something, but they came to nothing because I could not control everything that happened. God is so different. He rules the world and as our text tells us he knows the 'end from the beginning'. God knows all events because he controls the world and brings all of his plans to pass.

Jesus had been teaching his disciples wonderful things, but now he again turns their attention to the immediate future of his death and resurrection. Very soon God's prophecy made in the garden of Eden would be brought to pass, 'I will put enmity between you and the woman, and between your seed and her Seed; he shall bruise your head, and you shall bruise his heel' (Genesis 3:15). That prophecy pointed to Christ's sacrificial death on the cross being the defeat of Satan's efforts to destroy God's plans for mankind. Christ would crush his head and institute a new and living way to heaven for his believing people. The prophets had written of Christ's atoning death on behalf of his people whereby he would pay their penalty for sin. John the Baptist clearly said of Jesus, 'Behold! The Lamb of God who takes away the sin of the world!' (John 1:29).

Blood had to be shed for 'according to the law almost all things are purified with blood, and without shedding of blood there is no remission' (Hebrews 9:22). The Old Testament sacrificial system pointed to the death of the Saviour. The shedding of blood signified a brutal death which was so true concerning the death of Christ. God's plan of salvation was to come to pass. If you have time, read Isaiah 53 for there we are told what was to happen to God's Servant, the Lord Jesus Christ.

Meanwhile the members of the Jewish council — the Sanhedrin — were planning Christ's death. These people were the heads of the church and murder should have been nowhere in their thoughts.

Such was against the law of the God they professed to love and serve. They had seen the miracles, the raising of Lazarus, the voice of God speaking from heaven and heard the loving words spoken by Jesus.

Really they were driven by Satan in everything they planned, but God is always victorious. He is the One 'who works all things according to the counsel of his will' (Ephesians 1:11). Our text teaches us the same truth. Jesus is 'our Passover ... sacrificed for us' (1 Corinthians 5:7).

On earth wicked men were making their plans to kill God's only begotten Son, but during all their planning the psalmist tells us, 'He who sits in the heavens shall laugh; the LORD shall hold them in derision' (Psalm 2:4). Foolish people cannot defeat God's purposes any more than an ant can successfully attack an elephant. Where do you fit into this picture?

THINGS TO DISCUSS WITH YOUR FAMILY

1. Why did the Sanhedrin want Jesus killed?
2. How did their plans fit into God's plans?
3. Read and discuss Daniel 4:35 — 'All the inhabitants of the earth are reputed as nothing; he does according to his will ... No one can restrain his hand or say to him, "What have you done?"'

Meditation

Try to imagine the scene as the Sanhedrin met to discuss the judicial killing of the Lord Jesus.

Wise Words

In the wounds of Christ alone is predestination found and understood.   *Martin Luther*

'And let us not grow weary while doing good, for in due season we shall reap if we do not lose heart. Therefore, as we have opportunity, let us do good to all, especially to those who are of the household of faith' (Galatians 6:9,10).

Read: Mark 14:3-9

Some people think that this anointing of Christ was the one we considered when Mary anointed the Lord's feet at Bethany, six days before the Passover (John 12:1-11), but there are some significant differences. The fact that Martha was serving implies that the meal was in their home at Bethany, and on that occasion Mary is recorded as anointing Jesus' feet. Today's reading indicates that this happened just two days before the Passover meal.

This time the meal was in the home of Simon the leper, most likely a leper who had been healed by the Lord, but whose name was still used. We are not told who it was who entered the room where the meal was being eaten, but the person carried with her 'an alabaster flask of very costly oil of spikenard'. There must have been quite a crowd at the meal as Christ was normally accompanied by his disciples. All those present witnessed what the woman did to the Lord. She broke open the flask of oil which was valued at just under a year's wages and poured the contents over the Lord's head. As the sweet fragrance filled the room, someone — was it Judas? — asked, 'Why was this fragrant oil wasted? For it might have been sold for more than three hundred denarii and given to the poor.' Others who were present agreed, but not our Saviour.

He saw the woman's behaviour as one of great love. Such anointings were not uncommon in the Middle East and were actions of great respect. Possibly this woman had heard Christ say that he was soon to die, and obviously she believed that Jesus was both Messiah and Saviour. To her nothing was too good for the One who loved her and was soon to die carrying her sins to the cross.

To many that day, the woman was a religious fanatic, but not to the Lord. He immediately spoke up and silenced all criticism. One thing he said was important, 'She has come beforehand to anoint my body for burial.' The disciples seemed largely unconcerned with Christ's warning that he was to die. Jesus reminded them they always had the poor and should fulfil their obligations to those in need. God's law demanded that this be done (see Leviticus 19:10).

We should remember that God is honoured through our good words done in his name. In Proverbs 14:31 we read, 'He who oppresses the poor reproaches his Maker, but he who honours him has mercy on the needy.'

For this good work an unknown woman who loved Jesus is remembered this day — nearly two thousand years after the event. Christ highly esteemed her for what she did. Now what are our acts of love that our Lord remembers in some special way? Remember Paul's words, 'Therefore, as we have opportunity, let us do good to all, especially to those who are of the household of faith' (Galatians 6:10).

THINGS TO DISCUSS WITH YOUR FAMILY

1. What is 'spikenard'?
2. What was the significance of the woman's actions that day?
3. The poor are always with us. What can you do to help them?

Meditation

Meditate upon Christ words — 'If you love me, keep my commandments' (John 14:15).

Wise Words

The true, living faith, which the Holy Spirit instils into the heart, simply cannot be idle. *Martin Luther*

'For the love of money is a root of all kinds of evil, for which some have strayed from the faith in their greediness, and pierced themselves through with many sorrows' (1 Timothy 6:10).

Read: Matthew 26:14-16

Most people in the world love money whether they have a little or a lot. Everyone who works earns wages which they use for a variety of purposes, most of which are legitimate; but there are those who just want to build up a big bank account. Many poor people are jealous of the wealthy and wish they had more. Money is a useful tool if it is used wisely, remembering that it is the gift of God who gave us the skills and ability to earn our wages. Moses wrote a clear warning to all who falsely believe: 'My power and the might of my hand have gained me this wealth.' He continued: 'And you shall remember the LORD your God, for it is he who gives you power to get wealth' (Deuteronomy 8:17,18).

The writer of Proverbs gives good advice: 'Give me neither poverty nor riches — feed me with the food allotted to me; lest I be full and deny you, and say, "Who is the LORD?" Or lest I be poor and steal, and profane the name of my God' (Proverbs 30:8,9).

Judas loved money and we are told that he was a thief. He was the treasurer of the money belonging to the disciples and pilfered it for himself. He was Satan's man for a vile work — he would betray his Master. Luke wrote of Judas' plans, 'Then Satan entered Judas, surnamed Iscariot, who was numbered among the twelve. So he went his way and conferred with the chief priests and captains, how he might betray him to them' (Luke 22:3,4).

He knew that the Sanhedrin wanted to capture Jesus and kill him, and saw the opportunity to betray the Lord for a sum of money. The church leaders weren't keen to have Christ arrested during daylight hours, fearing the crowds who believed he was a prophet. It had to be a night betrayal and Judas, unbeknown to the other disciples, accepted thirty pieces of silver for the terrible work he was soon to carry out.

Zechariah had prophesied what price was to be put upon Christ's betrayal and what would later happen with the money: 'And the LORD said to me, "Throw it to the potter" — that princely price they set on me. So I took the thirty pieces of silver and threw them into the house of the LORD for the potter' (Zechariah 11:13).

From the very start of his public ministry, when Jesus selected his twelve disciples John recorded, 'For Jesus knew from the beginning who they were who did not believe, and who would betray him' (John 6:64). Later Jesus would say of Judas, 'It would have been good for that man if he had never been born' (Mark 14:21).

It doesn't appear that Judas hated Jesus — at least he didn't show it openly — he just loved money. Our prayer should be, 'Search me, O God, and know my heart; try me, and know my anxieties; and see if there is any wicked way in me, and lead me in the way everlasting' (Psalm 139:23,24).

THINGS TO DISCUSS WITH YOUR FAMILY

1. Is there any sin in having money in your bank account?
2. How should Christians use their money?
3. Why didn't Judas believe in Jesus as Saviour?

Meditation

Think upon Paul's words in 1 Timothy 6:7-9 — 'For we brought nothing into this world, and it is certain we can carry nothing out. And having food and clothing, with these we shall be content. But those who desire to be rich fall into temptation and a snare, and into many foolish and harmful lusts which drown men in destruction and perdition.'

Wise Words

Make money your god, and it will plague you like the devil. *Henry Fielding*

25 October   Preparations for the Passover meal

'Your lamb shall be without blemish, a male of the first year. You may take it from the sheep or from the goats' (Exodus 12:5).

Read: Mark 14:12-16

Australia is one of the world's greatest producers of lamb and mutton for the dining-room table. Maybe you have sat down to a meal of Australian lamb. One important food at the Passover was the cooked flesh of a lamb or kid goat. Over the years it became the custom to kill and eat a lamb.

The time had arrived for the disciples to make preparations for the Passover meal, which would be the last meal they had with Jesus before he was crucified. The lamb would have been selected on 10 Nisan ready to be killed on 14 Nisan as required by God's law. The passover was a celebration of the last night before the children of Israel left Egypt where they had been slaves, working for Pharaoh. Moses had given them instructions, just as God had given them to him. The lamb was to be killed and its blood smeared on the doorposts, and the wood above the door, so that the angel of death which was to kill the eldest child in each house, would pass over those homes where the blood could be seen.

The Passover pointed to the sacrificial work of the Lord Jesus who would die for lost people. His blood would be shed like that of the Passover lamb, after all he was 'The Lamb of God who takes away the sin of the world!' (John 1:29). Paul later wrote of our Saviour, 'For indeed Christ, our Passover, was sacrificed for us' (1 Corinthians 5:7).

When the disciples asked Christ what they were to do to prepare for the Passover, Jesus gave instructions that give us another glimpse of the divinity of our Redeemer. How could Jesus know that the disciples would meet a man carrying a pitcher of water? It would be easy for them to find this man as he was doing the work normally done by the women. How could Jesus know exactly what was going to happen when Peter and John met the man? It was because he was God and man in one Person. As God he had divine foreknowledge of what would happen.

The two disciples were shown to a furnished upper room where they made all the necessary preparations. They had to have a cooked lamb, unleavened bread, bitter herbs, wine, cushions on which to sit, bowls for the food and anything else that was needed.

We must remember that the Passover celebrated freedom from slavery. Through Christ's shed blood we are freed from slavery to sin. Christ's atonement means forgiveness for everyone who believes in him as Lord and Saviour. The writer to the Hebrews rightly said, '... according to the law almost all things are purified with blood, and without shedding of blood there is no remission' (Hebrews 9:22). May Christians always remember that they belong to Christ. Paul said, 'For you were bought at a price; therefore glorify God in your body and in your spirit, which are God's' (1 Corinthians 6:20).

THINGS TO DISCUSS WITH YOUR FAMILY

1. Of what event did the Passover remind the Jews?
2. Why is Jesus called 'our Passover'? (1 Corinthians 5:7).
3. In whose place did the Passover lamb die in Egypt?

Meditation

Meditate upon Peter and John preparing the Passover meal and what it meant.

Wise Words

Jesus became as like us as God can be.   *Donald English*

'Better to be of a humble spirit with the lowly, than to divide the spoil with the proud' (Proverbs 16:19).

Read: Luke 22:14-18; 24-30

When we have guests to a meal there are no special seats allocated for them. I usually sit in the seat which has always been mine — next to the window so I can get fresh air. Val sits in the seat closest to the kitchen making it easier for her to distribute food. We usually invite visitors to sit where they like.

It was Passover time and the disciples were ready to sit down, but before they were seated problems arose. Who was to sit in the places of importance? Despite all the Lord's teaching about humility and servanthood, the disciples still wanted to occupy the places of greatest importance. Maybe it was a question of sitting beside the Lord at the meal, as well as thinking about the future when they would sit on heavenly thrones. None seemed to have the attitude of John the Baptist who said of Christ, 'He must increase, but I must decrease' (John 3:30). There was pride at the Lord's table!

Jesus had set the greatest example of humility they would ever see and this is recorded by Paul, 'Let this mind be in you which was also in Christ Jesus, who, being in the form of God, did not consider it robbery to be equal with God, but made himself of no reputation, taking the form of a bondservant, and coming in the likeness of men. And being found in appearance as a man, he humbled himself and became obedient to the point of death, even the death of the cross' (Philippians 2:5-8).

The disciples were reminded that they were not to think of themselves as did the rulers of the Gentile nations who were looked upon as benefactors, but in reality were proud tyrants who did as they pleased. Jesus then drew attention to himself whom they knew to be the Son of God, the Creator of the universe, yet had taken the role of a servant. He told the disciples that they were to act as the young people who showed their humility in their relationship with their elders. Yes, they would one day sit on thrones, but they were to be servants of God.

Jesus reminded them that he had a kingdom, given to him by his Father as recorded by David in Psalm 2:6: 'Yet I have set my King on my holy hill of Zion.' Despite all the glory and honour he deserved, he was still to complete his role as a servant. Following his sacrificial death and resurrection he would sit on his heavenly throne. Paul wrote of Christ's glorification: 'Therefore God also has highly exalted him and given him the name which is above every name, that at the name of Jesus every knee should bow, of those in heaven, and of those on earth, and of those under the earth, and that every tongue should confess that Jesus Christ is Lord, to the glory of God the Father' (Philippians 2:9-11).

May we do as Paul said, '... in lowliness of mind let each esteem others better than himself' (Philippians 2:3). Amongst themselves the disciples were arguing who was the greatest. David wrote, 'Behold, how good and how pleasant it is for brethren to dwell together in unity!' (Psalm 133:1). Humility and unity should be found in every congregation of Christ's church.

THINGS TO DISCUSS WITH YOUR FAMILY

1. Discuss — 'A man wrapped up in himself makes a very small parcel.'
2. Why were the disciples arguing over seating arrangements?
3. Discuss Proverbs 29:23 — 'A man's pride will bring him low, but the humble in spirit will retain honour.'

Meditation

Consider the sin of pride and how unbecoming it is of Christ's people.

Wise Words

If God has made us men, let us not make ourselves gods.
Richard Sibbes

'Yes, all of you be submissive to one another, and be clothed with humility...'
(1 Peter 5:5).

Read: John 13:1-17

There have been times when I found washing my own feet unpleasant, especially when I was young. In those days when I
walked about barefoot I often had filthy, smelly feet, but after a wash
in soapy water and a dusting with talcum powder they smelled like a
rose. I would not like the job of washing the feet of someone else, unless it was someone special who for some reason was unable to do it.

Jesus was very near to his death on the cross and was giving his
disciples their final teaching. The twelve had been squabbling over
who was to be the greatest in God's kingdom and who should sit
beside the Lord at the Passover meal. Again he called their attention
to the need of humility as a prime characteristic of a saint. He then
did something that demonstrated 'the love of Christ which passes
knowledge' (Ephesians 3:19). He stripped off his outer clothing, and,
dressed in a loin cloth, took a basin of water, indicating that he was
going to wash the disciples' feet, including those of Judas who was
still present. This was the work usually given to the lowest slave in a
household.

Jesus wanted his disciples to understand that they were to be
humble servants, willing to do the most menial tasks in his name. He
had shown them by his incarnation that he had undertaken the greatest work of humility the world would ever know. Now the disciples
were to understand the life they were to live.

At first Peter said that he would never allow Christ to wash his
feet, but later wrote, 'Likewise you younger people, submit yourselves
to your elders. Yes, all of you be submissive to one another, and be
clothed with humility, for "God resists the proud, but gives grace to
the humble". Therefore humble yourselves under the mighty hand
of God, that he may exalt you in due time' (1 Peter 5:5,6). He had
learned the lesson well!

When Christ told the disciples that they were 'clean' he did not include Judas because the cleansing of which he spoke was spiritual. The disciples were to be washed from their sins through the shed blood of their Redeemer. Paul said the same of all who believe in the Lord Jesus Christ, 'But you were washed, but you were sanctified, but you were justified in the name of the Lord Jesus and by the Spirit of our God' (1 Corinthians 6:11). It is the blood of Jesus Christ that cleanses us from all of our sins.

The Lord told Peter that he still needed to wash his feet, teaching believers that we must go to the Redeemer seeking forgiveness for the sins of the day, praying that we might be cleansed — forgiven and clothed in his righteousness. May we daily seek forgiveness through the cleansing that comes from our Saviour. We have a wonderful God of all grace.

THINGS TO DISCUSS WITH YOUR FAMILY

1. Discuss Proverbs 27:21 — 'The crucible for silver and the furnace for gold, but man is tested by the praise he receives.'
2. What are we taught from today's reading?
3. Discuss the teaching found in John 13:16,17.

Meditation

Think upon the words of Micah 6:8 — 'And what does the LORD require of you but to do justly, to love mercy, and to walk humbly with your God?'

Wise Words

The devil allows no Christian to reach heaven with clean feet all the way. *Martin Luther*

'Even my own familiar friend in whom I
trusted, who ate my bread, has lifted up
his heel against me' (Psalm 41:9).

Read: John 13:18-30

During our lifetime we have many people we call 'friends', but
very few who are 'soul mates'. One great example in the Scriptures is the close friendship that existed between David and Jonathan.
Read 1 Samuel 18:1-3. Jesus had friends, some closer than others,
and of all the disciples it was John who was described as 'the disciple
whom Jesus loved' (John 21:20).

Jesus taught the disciples that when they went out to do the
work of an apostle, those people who welcomed them into their
midst were in fact welcoming the One who sent them — Christ
himself. This also meant they accepted the God and Father of the
Lord Jesus who had sent him into the world. Again we are being
taught the wonderful unity that exists between God, the Lord Jesus
and his people.

However, Jesus was 'troubled in spirit' as he was becoming increasingly aware of what was soon to take place. He also knew that
Judas, one of the twelve, would betray him. This betrayal was the
fulfilment of the prophecy made in Psalm 41:9 which is today's text.

The disciples began to ask the question, 'Is it I?' (Mark 14:19).
Obviously Judas had been very secretive in what he had done and no
one at that time suspected him of selling the Lord for thirty pieces of
silver. Peter then asked John who sat beside Christ to find out who
the betrayer was. It is worth noting that John sat in the place of importance, not Peter. The Lord responded by telling him, but no one
else at the meal heard what was said.

Long before speaking to the disciples he had said, '"Did I not
choose you, the twelve, and one of you is a devil?" He spoke of Judas
Iscariot, the son of Simon, for it was he who would betray him, being
one of the twelve' (John 6:70,71). Judas was Satan's man right from
the start.

Having indicated to John that it was Judas who would betray him, Jesus told Judas to quickly carry out his wickedness. Judas then left the group, giving the impression that he was going to give some money to the poor.

Peter's warning concerning Satan should be taken to heart, 'Be sober, be vigilant; because your adversary the devil walks about like a roaring lion, seeking whom he may devour' (1 Peter 5:8). Satan is our enemy. Yes, he was defeated by Christ, but today fights a rearguard action in an attempt to destroy the church and ruin the witness of believers. James tells us, 'Therefore submit to God. Resist the devil and he will flee from you' (James 4:7). We can be victorious over Satan's temptations, but we must walk closely with God. Read your Bible, pray, mix with other Christians and attend worship. Walk in the pathway of righteousness and do all you can, by God's grace, to be a faithful servant of the Lord Jesus.

THINGS TO DISCUSS WITH YOUR FAMILY

1. What time of the day was it when Judas left the Passover meal?
2. Read and discuss Psalm 1:1.
3. How could the psalmist write the accurate prophecy of Psalm 41:9 a thousand years before it came to pass?

Meditation

Consider the attitude of Judas to the Lord and why he betrayed him. Search your own heart for any Satanic influences and get rid of them seeking God's forgiveness. Think about Psalm 139:23,24 — 'Search me, O God, and know my heart; try me, and know my anxieties; and see if there is any wicked way in me, and lead me in the way everlasting.'

Wise Words

Satan does far more harm as an angel of light than as a roaring lion. *Vance Havner*

"'Awake, O sword, against my Shepherd, against the Man who is my Companion," says the LORD of hosts. "Strike the Shepherd, and the sheep will be scattered...'" (Zechariah 13:7).

Read: John 13:31-38

All Christians should be willing to lay down their life for the Lord Jesus, although in most western countries we are not called upon to suffer this way. However, in many countries Christians are being murdered simply because they are Christians and live a humble, godly life.

Our reading is of events that took place at night time. Judas had left the group as they sat at the Passover meal — he had to earn his thirty pieces of silver! Very soon the Lord would die upon a Roman cross, bearing the sins of repentant people. His sacrificial, atoning death would glorify God and himself. He would die a horrific death hanging naked upon that cross, forsaken by God and his disciples.

Our Saviour was obeying his Father implicitly and through his obedience he would save his sinful people. His death would be a perfect demonstration of compassion, love, mercy and wisdom, and result in the overthrow of Satan's power. We are to look 'unto Jesus, the author and finisher of our faith, who for the joy that was set before him endured the cross, despising the shame, and has sat down at the right hand of the throne of God' (Hebrews 12:2).

Soon Jesus would be going home, to heaven where he would be with his heavenly Father and sit upon his throne of glory.

Jesus gave the disciples a 'new' commandment, '...that you love one another; as I have loved you, that you also love one another. By this all will know that you are my disciples, if you have love for one another.' The Old Testament taught brotherly love, but now love was to be on a higher plane. We are to love as Christ loved, giving his life for his people. Where necessary we are to exhibit a love that costs. The exhibition of this love will encourage unbelievers to investigate the reason for our behaviour. Is this love seen in your life, family and congregation? It should be!

The Apostle John wrote words we need to read carefully: 'We know that we have passed from death to life, because we love the brethren. He who does not love his brother abides in death ... By this we know love, because he laid down his life for us. And we also ought to lay down our lives for the brethren' (1 John 3:14,16).

A boasting Peter told the Lord that he would go with him wherever he went and would willingly die for him. Then came the Lord's prophecy that he would deny him three times before the rooster crowed in the early morning. There is a warning here to each Christian — 'Therefore let him who thinks he stands take heed lest he fall' (1 Corinthians 10:12).

Then the Lord told Peter he would one day follow him, referring to Peter's death upon a cross also.

THINGS TO DISCUSS WITH YOUR FAMILY

1. Discuss the love that Jesus requires of his disciples.
2. Why should I love my enemies?
3. How could Jesus know that Peter would deny him three times? Does Jesus control crowing roosters? How?

Meditation

Meditate upon the words of our text and the power of God to bring his prophecies to pass.

Wise Words

No man is weaker than a proud man. For a proud man rests on nothing. *Richard Sibbes*

"For as often as you eat this bread and drink this cup, you proclaim the Lord's death till he comes' (1 Corinthians 11:26).

Read: Mark 14:22-25

I am sure your congregation frequently remembers the Lord's death by the celebration of the Lord's Supper. This is a solemn meeting for we recall all that Jesus did to ensure our salvation. It is good to have non-Christians present at this time, for it is an opportunity to present the gospel in a very visible way. The Lord's Supper will continue as a church ordinance until our Saviour returns in majestic glory with his mighty angels and the souls of the saints who died before his return.

The disciples had eaten well — lamb, unleavened bread and wine being the basic food. After the Passover meal the Lord introduced them to the meal of remembrance, to ensure they would never forget his sacrificial, substitutionary, atoning death for all those who repent and believe. His shed blood would be the seal of the new covenant ensuring the salvation of all those given to him by his heavenly Father.

As we come to the Lord's table we should remember the words of John 3:16 — 'For God so loved the world that he gave his only begotten Son, that whoever believes in him should not perish but have everlasting life.' Here we are clearly told that not everyone will be saved, but only those who believe in Christ the Son of God. Only those who are Christians should come and partake of the Lord's Supper. The Apostle Paul warns us that we must examine our heart because '...he who eats and drinks in an unworthy manner eats and drinks judgement to himself, not discerning the Lord's body' (1 Corinthians 11:29).

In Corinth the saints gathered for their 'love feast' and many were getting drunk before sitting at the Lord's table, not understanding what they were doing. Because of this, God had punished many of them with sickness and in some cases, death (1 Corinthians 11:30-34). All who come to the Lord's table should be at peace with God, at peace with their fellow man and know what they are doing. The meal is for those who are spiritually alive.

The Lord's Supper is a meal for the saints who fellowship with each other as they eat the bread and drink the wine, always remembering that their host is the Redeemer. The bread reminds us of his body abused by Roman soldiers and wicked Jews. The red wine speaks of his shed blood. We are told, 'without shedding of blood there is no remission' (Hebrews 9:22).

The Lord's Supper does not give faith, nor is there anything 'magical' in the elements. It is simply using bread and wine as symbols of the Lord's sacrificial death.

The Passover meal has now ended and in its place is the Lord's Supper which speaks of the cost of our salvation. Another thing to note is that the Lord instructed Christians to remember his death by means of the eating of bread and drinking wine — not the great pagan fuss that takes place in some churches at 'Easter'. It is to be a simple ceremony.

THINGS TO DISCUSS WITH YOUR FAMILY

1. Why do we have the Lord's Supper?
2. What do the bread and wine represent?
3. In what way is the Lord's Supper a 'fellowship' meal?

Meditation

Give some thought to the way you should prepare yourself to sit at the Lord's table.

Wise Words

Both the Passover and the Lord's Supper point to Jesus as the only and all-sufficient sacrifice for the sins of the saints. The Passover pointed forward to this; the Lord's Supper points back to it. *William Hendriksen*

'Yea, though I walk through the valley of the shadow of death, I will fear no evil; for you are with me; your rod and your staff, they comfort me' (Psalm 23:4).

Read: John 14:1-4

There have been times when as a family we have moved houses. Occasionally I went first to make sure all was well for the family when they arrived. In our short reading we find that our Lord told his disciples and Christians of all ages, that he was going to heaven where there would be dwelling places for each one of them.

Jesus had been speaking about his forthcoming death, one of the twelve betraying him, Peter deserting him and the horror that would be inflicted upon him by cruel men, motivated by Satan. The disciples were confused and troubled in their thoughts but Jesus gave them some words of encouragement. Every Christian should also be encouraged by these words.

He reminded the eleven that they believed in the true and living God who had revealed himself to the Jews particularly. They were to look to him as their Redeemer. They were to 'believe' in him. This was something Christ had been teaching, but now the object of saving faith was to be himself. This was Paul's instruction to the Philippian jailer: 'Believe on the Lord Jesus Christ, and you will be saved, you and your household' (Acts 16:31). Saving faith brings peace to the troubled heart. Isaiah also gives advice concerning peace of heart, 'You [the LORD] will keep him in perfect peace, whose mind is stayed on you, because he trusts in you' (Isaiah 26:3).

Christ then comforted his disciples by telling them that in heaven where his Father dwelt there were many permanent dwelling places for all the saints. Life and our earthly homes are very precarious — nothing is permanent. Our soul has a home in which to live, but in heaven there is a glorious spiritual body for our being. Paul wrote, 'For we know that if our earthly house, this tent, is destroyed, we have a building from God, a house not made with hands, eternal in the heavens' (2 Corinthians 5:1).

Preparing our heavenly home doesn't mean that the angels are set to work with hammers and nails to construct buildings in Paradise, but rather through his atoning death such dwelling places are assured for his people. In the new heavens and new earth we will find everlasting perfection. Jesus promised his disciples that one day he would return and gather them together in resurrected bodies to be with him eternally. John wrote of heaven's glory: 'Behold, the tabernacle of God is with men, and he will dwell with them, and they shall be his people. God himself will be with them and be their God. And God will wipe away every tear from their eyes; there shall be no more death, nor sorrow, nor crying. There shall be no more pain, for the former things have passed away' (Revelation 21:3,4). But the greatest thing about Paradise is that we will see Jesus face to face. We will be with our Redeemer for ever.

THINGS TO DISCUSS WITH YOUR FAMILY

1. Why is there no death in heaven?
2. What do you think is best about heaven?
3. Why should you be allowed to enter Paradise?

Meditation

Meditate upon the wonder of heaven. Read Revelation 21:3,4 — "'God ... will dwell with them, and they shall be his people. God himself will be with them and be their God. And God will wipe away every tear from their eyes; there shall be no more death, nor sorrow, nor crying. There shall be no more pain, for the former things have passed away.'"

Wise Words

Heaven is a prepared place for a prepared people.

J. C. Ryle

November

'For there is one God and one Mediator between God and men, the Man Christ Jesus, who gave himself a ransom for all' (1 Timothy 2:5).

Read: John 14:5-11

Have you ever been lost? Even with a map and clear instructions of where to turn I easily become lost when trying to drive through Sydney. I need my talking street directory to guide me — my wife, Val!

Jesus had been telling the disciples of events that were soon to take place, but when he mentioned going away to a place they knew and the way was known to them, they became confused. Thomas asked, 'Lord, we do not know where you are going, and how can we know the way?' Maybe they thought Jesus was going to depart to another part of Israel.

However, Christ's reply is one of the best-known passages of Scripture — 'I am the way, the truth, and the life. No one comes to the Father except through me.' The first thing to notice is the Lord's use of the term 'I am'. This was the name God revealed to Moses from the burning bush — 'I AM WHO I AM' (Exodus 3:14). Jesus went on to say that he was 'the way'. He is the door to Paradise and salvation is only through faith in him.

Jesus is 'the truth'. Do you remember that Pilate asked him the question, 'What is truth?' (John 18:38). Well, here is the answer — Jesus is 'the truth'. He is the totally honest and reliable Saviour of all who seek and find him. He is truth incarnate and speaks only God's truth.

Jesus said that he was 'the life'. In Jesus Christ alone there is eternal life. Later Peter said, 'Nor is there salvation in any other, for there is no other name under heaven given among men by which we must be saved' (Acts 4:12). Jesus said those gracious words, 'For God so loved the world that he gave his only begotten Son, that whoever believes in him should not perish but have everlasting life' (John 3:16).

He then told his disciples that Christianity is an exclusive religion for there is no way into God's presence other than through him. He is the only Mediator between God and man.

Jesus again told his disciples of the oneness that existed between himself and his heavenly Father. He spoke the words God had given him and God performed those many miracles through his Son. This union is beyond our understanding. We must believe what we are told. Peter said of the miracles, 'Jesus of Nazareth, a Man attested by God to you by miracles, wonders, and signs which God did through him in your midst...' (Acts 2:22).

And like the disciples we are called to believe what Jesus said that day. To understand God and the union of the Father, Son and Holy Spirit is beyond our comprehension. We must accept what God has revealed about the Godhead.

THINGS TO DISCUSS WITH YOUR FAMILY

1. What three Persons make the One God?
2. What is wrong with the statement 'Many paths, one heaven'?
3. How are we able to gain an audience with God?

Meditation

Meditate upon the glory of the Godhead — Colossians 2:9: 'For in him [Jesus] dwells all the fullness of the Godhead bodily.'

Wise Words

Love and faith are at home in the mystery of the Godhead. Let reason kneel in reverence outside. *A. W. Tozer*

'Therefore he says: "When he ascended on high, he led captivity captive, and gave gifts to men"' (Ephesians 4:8).

Read: John 14:12-20

It is always nice to receive gifts on special occasions. For my birthday I ask my family for gifts of photocopy paper which I find very useful. I trust you all give serious thoughts to the presents you buy for those people who are special in your life.

Jesus had been revealing to his disciples the terrible events that were soon to take place. He would die, having been betrayed by Judas. Peter had been told that he would deny him and with the other disciples leave him to suffer alone (Matthew 26:31). He was now giving the eleven some words of encouragement, telling them that they would do even greater works than those he had done which would be a sign that he was in heaven with his Father. No one could perform greater miracles than Jesus did, but the disciples would, through the preaching of the good news, have many converts — many more than Jesus had. May we always remember that every conversion is a miracle of God's grace, for to become a Christian the Holy Spirit must bring about the new birth. Without a new heart we cannot love and serve the Saviour. Paul plainly writes, 'Now if anyone does not have the Spirit of Christ, he is not his' (Romans 8:9).

Jesus told his disciples that a sign of their new heart was love shown through obedience to his commands. We must look at our life and check whether we are obedient servants of Christ.

Jesus told the disciples that they should pray in his name and he would answer according to his will for the glory of God and the good of the church.

Now the Lord told the disciples that he was going to give them a heavenly Gift — the Holy Spirit. The Holy Spirit is one Person of the Godhead with all the characteristics of God, because he is God. The disciples were told that the 'Spirit of truth' would be a 'Comforter'. They certainly would need comforting in the immediate future. It is the Holy Spirit who gives his people comfort day by day.

Now the Holy Spirit has always worked in bringing about the new birth and giving a great variety of gifts for the benefit of the saints. This was so in the days of the Old Testament as we learn from the Lord's discussions with Nicodemus (John 3:2-10).

If you are a Christian Paul tells you, '...if anyone is in Christ, he is a new creation' (2 Corinthians 5:17). The Holy Spirit 'bears witness with our spirit that we are children of God' (Romans 8:16). We are also told, 'Likewise the Spirit also helps in our weaknesses. For we do not know what we should pray for as we ought, but the Spirit himself makes intercession for us with groanings which cannot be uttered ... he makes intercession for the saints according to the will of God' (Romans 8:26,27). Christ did not leave us comfortless! Our Saviour is present in our lives through the Holy Spirit.

THINGS TO DISCUSS WITH YOUR FAMILY

1. Who is the Holy Spirit?
2. What is some of the work of the Holy Spirit?
3. What did Jesus mean when he said, 'Most assuredly, I say to you, he who believes in me, the works that I do he will do also; and greater works than these he will do, because I go to my Father' (John 14:12)?

Meditation

Meditate upon the Lord's words in John 14:15 — 'If you love me, keep my commandments.'

Wise Words

The Holy Spirit is God's imperative of life.   *A. W. Tozer*

'But you shall receive power when the Holy Spirit has come upon you; and you shall be witnesses to me in Jerusalem, and in all Judea and Samaria, and to the end of the earth' (Acts 1:8).

Read: John 14:21-26

If someone asked me my nationality I would reply, 'Australian.' If they asked me to prove it I would have to find my birth certificate and passport. It wouldn't matter where in the world I was, I would still be an Australian and could prove it.

Are you a Christian? Could you prove it?

Jesus again told his disciples that one mark of being a Christian was obedience to his commandments. The Apostle John wrote, 'Now by this we know that we know him, if we keep his commandments. He who says, "I know him," and does not keep his commandments, is a liar, and the truth is not in him. But whoever keeps his word, truly the love of God is perfected in him. By this we know that we are in him' (1 John 2:3-5). Like David, God's laws should be precious to us so we can say, 'The law of your mouth is better to me than thousands of shekels of gold and silver ... Oh, how I love your law! It is my meditation all the day' (Psalm 119:72,97).

The Pharisees attempted to keep God's law and their own multitude of laws to win God's favour and ultimately their salvation. The saints keep God's law because they love the Lawgiver and have a renewed heart.

God sets his love upon his faithful people and adopts them into his family. Then they have the assurance: 'Who shall separate us from the love of Christ? Shall tribulation, or distress, or persecution, or famine, or nakedness, or peril, or sword? As it is written: "For your sake we are killed all day long; we are accounted as sheep for the slaughter." Yet in all these things we are more than conquerors through him who loved us. For I am persuaded that neither death nor life, nor angels nor principalities nor powers, nor things present nor things to come, nor height nor depth, nor any other created thing, shall be able to separate us from the love of God which is in Christ Jesus our Lord' (Romans 8:35-39).

Jesus comforted the eleven by telling them that God would live within them. The Holy Spirit would come in a more powerful way than ever before. Paul wrote, '...do you not know that your body is the temple of the Holy Spirit who is in you, whom you have from God, and you are not your own' (1 Corinthians 6:19). Christian friend, God lives in you!

The Spirit taught the apostles God's truth, enabling them to write the Scriptures for us to have and read. Paul told Timothy, 'All Scripture is given by inspiration of God, and is profitable for doctrine, for reproof, for correction, for instruction in righteousness, that the man of God may be complete, thoroughly equipped for every good work' (2 Timothy 3:16,17).

If you are a Christian thank God for the saving work of Jesus Christ that the Holy Spirit has applied to you. Pray for the sanctifying work of the same Spirit that you might become more Christ-like day by day.

THINGS TO DISCUSS WITH YOUR FAMILY

1. Why did David love God's law?
2. Who was the only Person to obey God's law perfectly?
3. What did Paul mean: 'For as many as are led by the Spirit of God, these are sons of God' (Romans 8:14)?

Meditation

Think upon 2 Peter 1:21 where we are told that 'holy men of God spoke as they were moved by the Holy Spirit'.

Wise Words

We may take it as a rule of the Christian life that the more we are filled with the Holy Spirit, the more we shall glorify the Lord Jesus. *Frank Gabelein*

'...that through death he might destroy him who had the power of death, that is, the devil, and release those who through fear of death were all their lifetime subject to bondage' (Hebrews 2:14,15).

Read: John 14:27-31

There are times when I am away from home, but as the time to return gets closer I become excited. I don't like being away from Val, Wags and my Christian friends. Jesus had been away from his heavenly Father for over thirty years and very soon it was to be time to return to heaven where he would sit upon God's throne and rule the universe he had created.

Jesus had been telling his disciples much of what was soon to take place and they were confused. For the next few devotions we will be looking at Christ's bequest to his disciples and Christians of all ages. The disciples were living in a world of hostility to Christ and the gospel, but the Lord comforted them by giving them a peaceful heart. The Apostle Paul wrote of 'the God of peace' who gave 'the peace of God which surpasses all understanding' (Philippians 4:9,7), and this peace is ours if only we ask for it.

Many times the disciples had been told of their Lord's impending death and return to his heavenly Father. Despite their distress he told them they should rejoice because he was going home. He had humbled himself for a time. In taking flesh and blood to become Saviour of his people and Mediator between God and man he could say, 'My Father is greater than I.' Yet as God he was equal with his heavenly Father and the Holy Spirit in glory, majesty, holiness, wisdom, power, omniscience, omnipresence and on we could go. The three Persons of the Godhead are of the one essence constituting one God. We worship One God who is three distinct Persons. This is usually called 'the Trinity'. Hard to understand? Yes, very much so as our brains are finite and God is infinite.

Soon Satan would attempt to destroy Jesus, but there was no sin with which the 'ruler of this world' could charge him. Our Saviour is sinless and by his atoning death has saved his chosen people. We are redeemed 'with the precious blood of Christ, as of a lamb without blemish and without spot' (1 Peter 1:19).

Because Jesus has imputed his righteousness to believers Paul could ask the question, 'Who shall bring a charge against God's elect?' (Romans 8:33). He went on to say that no one could lay such a charge against God's people because they have been justified — forgiven and wear his perfect righteousness. We are sinners, but in God's sight we appear as pure as Christ.

Jesus told the disciples that it was time to leave the upper room, but he had a little more to say first — words of great importance to the disciples and to you and me.

THINGS TO DISCUSS WITH YOUR FAMILY

1. Why could Jesus say 'My Father is greater than I'?
2. Why was Jesus overjoyed to be going home?
3. Why should we be overjoyed that Jesus went home to his heavenly Father?

Meditation

Meditate upon Christ's return to the glory of heaven. Read Revelation 5:1-14.

Wise Words

When Christ left the world, he made his will. His soul he bequeathed to his Father, and his body to Joseph. His clothes fell to the soldiers. His mother he left to the care of John. But what should he leave to his poor disciples, who had left all for him? Silver and gold he had none; but he left them what was far better, his peace.

Matthew Henry

'...you have a name that you are alive, but you are dead' (Revelation 3:1).

Read: John 15:1-11

My wife, Val, loves gardening. She enjoys getting about with her snips, cutting flowers and disposing of dead stalks that have finished flowering. My job is to mow the lawn. Jesus told many parables about farming, and today you have read a parable about a person who had a vineyard. This Person was Jesus' heavenly Father. The vineyard is the church which consists of both 'wheat' and 'tares' (Matthew 13:24-30). I believe that this parable is a parable of the covenant that exists between Christ and his bride, the church.

The picture of the vineyard, painted by Christ, is of the church of all ages, consisting of two basic groups of people — the elect, chosen, born again and justified ones. These are the branches that bear fruit. The fruit that is found in the lives of the saints varies in degree as we are all different. First of all there must be evidence of the fruit of the Spirit as outlined by Paul, '...the fruit of the Spirit is love, joy, peace, long-suffering, kindness, goodness, faithfulness, gentleness, self-control' (Galatians 5:22,23).

Elsewhere Paul said of professing Christians — 'work out your own salvation with fear and trembling; for it is God who works in you both to will and to do for his good pleasure' (Philippians 2:12,13). Witnessing to the grace of God in our hearts also is part of bearing fruit as is doing 'good to all; especially to those who are of the household of faith' (Galatians 6:10).

The second group within the church are those who for a variety of reasons are recognized as church members, yet are strangers to the grace of God. They do not bear spiritual fruit despite having been baptized, having sat at the Lord's table and attended worship. Of them Jesus said, 'Not everyone who says to me, "Lord, Lord," shall enter the kingdom of heaven, but he who does the will of my Father in heaven.' They then will hear Christ's reply, 'I never knew you; depart from me, you who practise lawlessness!' (Matthew 7:21,23).

God 'prunes' those branches that bear fruit so that they might bear even more fruit. A good farmer cuts off all dead branches and throws them into the fire. This reminds us that there is a fearful judgement awaiting every person who is not a Christian. In Revelation 20:15 we read of the destiny of those who turned their back upon Christ — 'And anyone not found written in the Book of Life was cast into the lake of fire.'

Christ's parable teaches us that spiritual life comes as a gift from God which produces a saving union with himself. That union is the work of the Holy Spirit who brings about the new birth and gives a saving faith with true repentance and love of God and mankind.

James tells us what this parable teaches — 'For as the body without the spirit is dead, so faith without works is dead also' (James 2:26). As Christians we keep the Lord's commandments and rejoice in the salvation that is ours in Jesus. Are you a believer?

THINGS TO DISCUSS WITH YOUR FAMILY

1. What is the evidence of saving faith?
2. What is the end of all who are not Christians?
3. What did Jesus mean when he said, 'As the Father loved me, I also have loved you; abide in my love' (John 15:9)?

Meditation

Meditate upon Christ's words — 'I am the vine, you are the branches. He who abides in me, and I in him, bears much fruit; for without me you can do nothing' (John 15:5).

Wise Words

A fruitless person is not a failed Christian, but a false one — in other words, not a Christian at all.   *Anonymous*

'By this we know love, because he laid down his life for us. And we also ought to lay down our lives for the brethren' (1 John 3:16).

Read: John 15:12-17

This sin-ridden world with all its hatred, wars, broken families, drug culture and daily disappointments needs a transfusion of godly love. Jesus had told his disciples that as believers they were to produce fruit in their lives. Now he goes on to outline the greatest of the fruit that must be found in the Christian life — love!

There is nothing new in the commandment that we are to love one another, except the standard we must reach — 'This is my commandment, that you love one another as I have loved you. Greater love has no one than this, than to lay down one's life for his friends.' Paul wrote some wonderful words about God's love of sinners — 'But God demonstrates his own love toward us, in that while we were still sinners, Christ died for us' (Romans 5:8). This is true love!

This is the standard of love that Christ expects of all his people. This is a love that comes from a born-again heart that is in love with the Saviour. This love is to be shown to all people, not just the lovely, but also those who are our enemies.

Those united to Christ by faith are called his friends. What a great privilege it is to be called a friend of the Lord Jesus. The disciples were his friends and as friends he told them what they were to expect in the days that lay ahead. To their Saviour they were not just servants. The same is true of the saints of all ages.

All that we do must be motivated by a love of Christ. Many people do wonderful works that are considered great by the world, but in God's eyes they are worth nothing. Paul wrote, 'Though I speak with the tongues of men and of angels, but have not love, I have become as sounding brass or a clanging cymbal. And though I have the gift of prophecy, and understand all mysteries and all knowledge, and though I have all faith, so that I could remove mountains, but have not love, I am nothing. And though I bestow all my goods to feed the poor, and though I give my body to be burned, but have not love, it profits me nothing' (1 Corinthians 13:1-3).

The wonder of our salvation is that God chose some sinners and gave them to his Son. Paul wrote, 'He chose us in him before the foundation of the world, that we should be holy and without blame before him in love' (Ephesians 1:4). Jesus speaking to the crowds gave the reason why the Pharisees and others didn't turn to him in saving faith: 'All that the Father gives me will come to me, and the one who comes to me I will by no means cast out' (John 6:37).

Isn't this wonderful? If you are a Christian, you are one because God chose you to salvation, and the evidence is seen in the love you have for God and every person. If you are not a Christian go to Jesus now in repentance and pray for saving faith. You have the Lord's promise — 'the one who comes to me I will by no means cast out' (John 6:37).

THINGS TO DISCUSS WITH YOUR FAMILY

1. Why is Christian love so important?
2. What did Jesus mean when he said, 'You did not choose me, but I chose you' (John 15:16)?
3. Can a person ever be sure that God has chosen them?

Meditation

Is your name written in the Book of Life (Philippians 4:3)?

Wise Words

Election is always to sanctification. Those whom Christ chooses out of mankind, he chooses not only that they may be saved, but that they may bear fruit and fruit that can be seen. *J. C. Ryle*

'Yes, and all who desire to live godly in Christ Jesus will suffer persecution' (2 Timothy 3:12).

Read: John 15:18-25

It is tragic but true, but we live in a world of sin and despair. Most governments spend vast sums of money building weapons of destruction which have one basic use — to kill and destroy. Many millions of people have been killed in warfare during the last one hundred years. Yet an even greater tragedy is the expenditure of huge sums of money by governments that want to destroy Christianity from the face of the earth.

Jesus had given his disciples the commandment that they were to love one another in a self-sacrificing manner, and now warns them that just as he was hated and would be killed, so they also were to expect persecution. They, as faithful servants of the Saviour, were to expect the same treatment as their master received. The world only loves like-minded people. They despise righteousness which flows from a heart in love with God in Christ. This is what today's text plainly tells all believers.

The Apostle Peter, who himself was crucified, warned Christians of the hatred of the world. He indicated that when the saints suffered, their Redeemer God is glorified: 'If you are reproached for the name of Christ, blessed are you, for the Spirit of glory and of God rests upon you. On their part he is blasphemed, but on your part he is glorified ... Yet if anyone suffers as a Christian, let him not be ashamed, but let him glorify God in this matter' (1 Peter 4:14,16).

The people who persecute Christians obviously detest God and his Son, the Lord Jesus Christ. It is so hard to believe that the Jews who were waiting for the arrival of their Messiah should murder one who went about doing good — showing compassion by healing the sick and raising the dead. As David wrote of Christ, they 'hated me without a cause' (Psalm 69:4). He told the people of the way to the heavenly Jerusalem, but they wanted nothing to do with him. Today it is no different.

Jesus has promised a great reward for his persecuted people — 'Blessed are those who are persecuted for righteousness' sake, for theirs is the kingdom of heaven' (Matthew 5:10). We have the truth and must use it to glorify Christ. Much is expected of all believers. Failure to produce fruit brings punishment as Jesus said, 'And that servant who knew his master's will, and did not prepare himself or do according to his will, shall be beaten with many stripes. But he who did not know, yet committed things deserving of stripes, shall be beaten with few. For everyone to whom much is given, from him much will be required; and to whom much has been committed, of him they will ask the more' (Luke 12:47,48).

Do you love Christ and are you willing to suffer persecution, even death for his sake?

THINGS TO DISCUSS WITH YOUR FAMILY

1. Why did the people despise Jesus so much?
2. Do you belong to Christ or the world? How do you know?
3. Why did Jesus say, 'He who hates me hates my Father also' (John 15:23)?

Meditation

Meditate upon Christ's words — 'They hated me without a cause' (John 15:25).

Wise Words

Persecution is no novelty ... the offence of the cross will never cease till all flesh shall see the salvation of God.

William S. Plumer

'For we did not follow cunningly devised fables when we made known to you the power and coming of our Lord Jesus Christ, but were eyewitnesses of his majesty' (2 Peter 1:16).

Read: John 15:26 – 16:4

When someone dies there is usually the reading of the person's will where instructions concerning the disposal of property are outlined. Everyone listens very carefully hoping their name is mentioned as receiving something of value. One humorous person wrote of these situations — 'Where there's a will there's relatives.'

Having told the disciples that they would face persecution as all Christians do, he now gave them exciting news. Following his ascension into heaven he would have the Father send the 'Helper' — the Holy Spirit — to them. One work of the Holy Spirit is to testify of Christ. The Holy Spirit is one Person of the Godhead. In the story of Ananias and Sapphira who lied to the disciples about the money they said they gave to the church, Peter said to Ananias, 'Ananias, why has Satan filled your heart to lie to the Holy Spirit? ...You have not lied to men but to God' (Acts 5:3,4). Peter had no difficulty calling the Holy Spirit God.

The giving of the Holy Spirit in majestic, divine power would be another proof that the Redeemer was in heaven fulfilling his role of Mediator. On the day of Pentecost we read that the disciples were 'filled with the Holy Spirit and began to speak with other tongues, as the Spirit gave them utterance' (Acts 2:4).

The Holy Spirit creates the new hearts in sinners. Paul tells us plainly, 'Now if anyone does not have the Spirit of Christ, he is not his' (Romans 8:9). The Spirit gives spiritual life and all who believe are 'sealed with the Holy Spirit of promise' (Ephesians 1:13).

God's Spirit has always been active. We know this because of Christ's words to Nicodemus when he indicated he had no understanding of the Old Testament teaching concerning the new birth: 'Are you the teacher of Israel, and do not know these things?' (John 3:10). It is the Holy Spirit who distributes God's gifts to his people.

David feared that because of his sin he would lose his ruling skills as had happened to Israel's first king, Saul. David prayed, '...do not take your Holy Spirit from me' (Psalm 51:11).

Jesus again warned the disciples that they would suffer the scorn of Jews and Gentiles because they preached the living God and salvation through faith in his Son. The Apostle Paul spoke of his effort to destroy the church of Christ: 'This I also did in Jerusalem, and many of the saints I shut up in prison, having received authority from the chief priests; and when they were put to death, I cast my vote against them. And I punished them often in every synagogue and compelled them to blaspheme; and being exceedingly enraged against them, I persecuted them even to foreign cities' (Acts 26:10,11). Paul thought he was serving God by destroying Christians. He failed, for Jesus said that even the gates of hell could not destroy the bride of Christ. If you are a Christian you are spiritually safe.

THINGS TO DISCUSS WITH YOUR FAMILY

1. What is the special work of the Holy Spirit?
2. Can you think of any group that believed they did God's work by killing Christians?
3. Discuss the thoughts of John 15:26 — 'But when the Helper comes, whom I shall send to you from the Father, the Spirit of truth who proceeds from the Father, he will testify of me.'

Meditation

Meditate upon the effects of the coming of the Holy Spirit on the day of Pentecost.

Wise Words

Unless there is that which is above us, we shall soon yield to that which is about us. *P. T. Forsyth*

'These who have turned the world up-side down have come here too' (Acts 17:6).

Read: John 16:5-15

Recently when I visited the doctor to get the results of some tests he asked me, 'What do you want first, the good news or the bad news?' I asked, 'The good news first please.' His reply was, 'The good news is that there is no bad news.' I guess the bad news was the account I had to pay to hear the good news.

Christ had been giving his disciples good news and bad news. He was soon to die. His disciples would desert him, but he would give them the Holy Spirit to exercise more power than ever before. Now our Lord told the disciples that he was going away which distressed them, but again he reminded them of the coming of the Holy Spirit. The descent of the Holy Spirit was the confirmation that Christ was sitting upon the throne of God, ruling the world and acting as the great High Priest for his people.

Jesus said the Spirit would convict the world of sin. This was pointing to the day when the gospel would be preached throughout the world and people would recognize that they were under con-demnation needing a Saviour. Like the Jews, unbelievers would dis-cover what a terrible sin it is to reject Christ. The Holy Spirit would also convict the world of righteousness and sinners would see their only hope of entering heaven was having the righteousness of Christ put to their account where God would consider it as theirs. Jesus was without sin and that purity would be used to clothe the saints.

The Spirit would convict the world of judgement and Satan, the ruler of the world, would be defeated. In Revelation 12:7-12 we read of the devil being thrown out of heaven, a defeated enemy of God. Unconverted people would be removed from Satan's kingdom and placed in the kingdom of God as brothers and sisters of the Lord Je-sus. The Spirit would also remind the world that there was a coming day of judgement when everyone would stand before the throne of Christ to give an account of their life and hear their eternal sentence handed down.

The Spirit was to guide the disciples and writers of the Scriptures into all truth. This makes it possible for us to read God's words as it came from the pen of the writers, knowing it is the inspired, infallible words of the living God. One magnificent work of the Holy Spirit is to glorify Christ. This is done by showing us his glory through the reading and preaching of God's word. In heaven the saints and holy angels surround the throne of God and sing the praises of the Lamb of God. When we enter heaven and see our Lord face to face, we will be enabled to praise him as never before. Friends, the best is yet to be!

THINGS TO DISCUSS WITH YOUR FAMILY

1. Who was the 'ruler of this world'? When is his final judgement? Read Revelation 20:10.
2. Discuss the meaning of today's text concerning the work of the disciples.
3. Reflect on the message of 2 Timothy 3:16, 17: 'All Scripture is given by inspiration of God, and is profitable for doctrine, for reproof, for correction, for instruction in righteousness, that the man of God may be complete, thoroughly equipped for every good work.'

Meditation

Meditate upon Christ's words in John 16:13 — 'However, when he, the Spirit of truth, has come, he will guide you into all truth; for he will not speak on his own authority, but whatever he hears he will speak; and he will tell you things to come.'

Wise Words

Christ's bodily presence was comfortable, but the Spirit is more intimately a Comforter than Christ in his fleshly presence; because the Spirit can comfort all believers at once in all places, while Christ's bodily presence can comfort but few, and that only in one place at once.

J. C. Ryle

'And these things we write to you, that your joy may be full' (1 John 1:4).

Read: John 16:16-24

It is always pleasant to be looking forward to some happy event. Often there is more joy in the anticipation of what is to happen than there is in the actual occasion. The disciples were being told many things by the Lord and not all were causing sadness. They had been told about the coming of the Holy Spirit who would prove to be God's spokesman on earth, guiding the disciples into the truth and ensuring that the Scriptures were accurate in every respect. We have looked at other activities of the Holy Spirit that help individual Christians and the church.

When the disciples heard Christ saying that for a time they would not see him, then they would see him they became confused, not understanding what he was speaking about. As we read our Bibles we also come to portions that we don't understand. Even Peter, when writing about the Apostle Paul's teaching, said there 'are some things hard to understand' (2 Peter 3:16).

There is no doubt that when Christ died the disciples were distressed. When he left them and ascended to his heavenly Father they were very sorrowful. Today we live by faith in a Saviour we have read about and whose Spirit lives in our hearts. The Apostle Thomas wanted to see Jesus face to face after the resurrection. He simply didn't believe what he had heard and wanted to see the evidence that the Person who appeared to the other disciples was Christ. On the Lord's day after the resurrection Jesus again appeared and said to him, 'Thomas, because you have seen me, you have believed. Blessed are those who have not seen and yet have believed' (John 20:29).

Jesus told the disciples that the time had come when they would pray to God in his name. The gospel age was about to dawn in all its glory and Christ the Mediator would convey to God the prayers of his people. It is interesting to find an example in the Old Testament of Daniel praying in the name of his Lord. We read in Daniel 9:17, 'Now therefore, our God, hear the prayer of your servant, and his supplications, and for the Lord's sake cause your face to shine on your sanctuary, which is desolate.'

Jesus told his disciples — and you and me — that he would come again to establish the reality of the kingdom of God in the new heavens and new earth. This will be perfection because we will be with God. We will see Christ face to face and be Spirit filled. Because there is no sin in the new Jerusalem there will be no death, tears, aches, or pains — just joy. In Isaiah 54:7,8 we read some comforting words, '"For a mere moment I have forsaken you, but with great mercies I will gather you. With a little wrath I hid my face from you for a moment; but with everlasting kindness I will have mercy on you," says the LORD, your Redeemer.' There are good things in store for God's people!

THINGS TO DISCUSS WITH YOUR FAMILY

1. What is meant by the following words from the Lord's Prayer — 'Your kingdom come'? (Matthew 6:10).
2. What will give you joy when Christ returns?
3. What did Jesus mean when he said, 'I go to the Father' (John 16:16)?

Meditation

Meditate upon Jesus' words to his disciples — 'Your sorrow will be turned into joy' (John 16:20).

Wise Words

Prayer is the key to heaven's treasures.   *John Gerhard*

'All things have been delivered to me by my Father, and no one knows the Son except the Father. Nor does anyone know the Father except the Son, and the one to whom the Son wills to reveal him' (Matthew 11:27).

Read: John 16:25-33

My computer works, but I have no idea of the science behind the amazing machine. I have a grandson who works with a computer firm and there are times when he tries to explain to me just what is going on as I type, but I just don't understand. Jesus had been giving his disciples information concerning the future, but they didn't fully comprehend what he was telling them. Now we come to a passage of the Lord's words where they reply, 'See, now you are speaking plainly, and using no figure of speech!'

Jesus again began to speak about the relationship that existed between himself and his Father in heaven. He told the disciples that he came from his Father and for that reason he was able to tell them so much about God. Long before he had told them, 'All things have been delivered to me by my Father, and no one knows the Son except the Father. Nor does anyone know the Father except the Son, and the one to whom the Son wills to reveal him' (Matthew 11:27). The Apostle John wrote of the oneness between the Father and his Son: 'No one has seen God at any time. The only begotten Son, who is in the bosom of the Father, he has declared him' (John 1:18).

Because of the unity between the Father, Son and Holy Spirit, Jesus was able to reveal the Father to his disciples. They were taught of the Father's grace, mercy, love, compassion, eternity, omnipresence, omnipotence, omniscience, wisdom and holiness — and much more. And he told his disciples that he came from his heavenly Father. Just think of John 3:16 where we are told this great truth.

Having heard Christ's words we again read the disciples confession of faith in Christ, 'Now we are sure that you know all things, and have no need that anyone should question you. By this we believe that you came forth from God.'

Jesus then reminded them that very soon they would be scattered away from him, leaving him to die alone on the cross. Yet, they and we are reminded that God's peace is ours. Paul wrote of our Lord, 'For he himself is our peace' (Ephesians 2:14).

If you want spiritual peace you must go to Christ, repenting of your sins and asking for the new birth and saving faith. Then Paul's words will have great meaning to you — 'Therefore, having been justified by faith, we have peace with God through our Lord Jesus Christ' (Romans 5:1). Let Satan do his worst! We are spiritually secure in our Saviour. We can rest easy knowing that our eternal destiny is with Jesus Christ — if we truly believe in Jesus as Lord and Saviour. Do you?

THINGS TO DISCUSS WITH YOUR FAMILY

1. How is it that Jesus knows the Father perfectly?
2. What did Jesus mean when he said, 'These things I have spoken to you, that in me you may have peace. In the world you will have tribulation; but be of good cheer, I have overcome the world' (John 16:33)?
3. Why were the disciples soon to be scattered?

Meditation

Meditate upon the words of Psalm 146:1,2 — 'Praise the LORD! Praise the LORD, O my soul! While I live I will praise the LORD; I will sing praises to my God while I have my being.'

Wise Words

Ungodliness is never at rest; but where faith exists there is a mind 'composed'. *John Calvin*

'And we know that the Son of God has come and has given us an understanding, that we may know him who is true; and we are in him who is true, in his Son Jesus Christ. This is the true God and eternal life' (1 John 5:20).

Read: John 17:1-5

I once asked a Christian if he had ever heard his Christian wife pray and was very surprised when his reply was, 'No.' I then asked him, 'How then do you know if she does pray?' The man and his wife were regular church attenders and the husband conducted a daily family devotion, but he had never asked his wife to pray. The church to which he belonged objected to ladies praying when men were present. Have you ever heard your family members pray?

Jesus had taught his disciples to pray, but we now come to what is sometimes called Christ's 'High Priestly' prayer. This prayer is divided into three sections, the first, which you have read, being his prayer for himself. Often Jesus had told his disciples that his time had not yet come, but now he prays, 'Father, the hour has come.' The day of his crucifixion was at hand. This was the purpose of the incarnation — to pay the penalty for sin by his atoning death.

In his death Jesus would bring praise to his Father, as he was completing the work of salvation given to him by God. His death established the kingdom of God and was a display of his Father's wisdom, majesty, glory, mercy, love and grace. Jesus was also to be exalted when he rose from the dead and ascended into heaven. The writer to the Hebrews said that God 'has in these last days spoken to us by his Son, whom he has appointed heir of all things, through whom also he made the worlds; who being the brightness of his glory and the express image of his person, and upholding all things by the word of his power, when he had by himself purged our sins, sat down at the right hand of the Majesty on high' (Hebrews 1:2,3).

Today Jesus sits upon the throne of God governing the nations and saving all who seek him. He has given the Holy Spirit to effectually call his people to himself and give gifts to the saints so that the church might function in such a way that God is magnified.

Christ humbled himself by leaving his heavenly throne and living amongst humanity in order to save those sinners given him by his Father. His ascension meant magnificent praise. Paul wrote, 'Therefore God also has highly exalted him and given him the name which is above every name, that at the name of Jesus every knee should bow, of those in heaven, and of those on earth, and of those under the earth, and that every tongue should confess that Jesus Christ is Lord, to the glory of God the Father' (Philippians 2:9-11).

Soon the one and only sacrifice for sin would be finished and the salvation of the elect assured. Then Christ would reign in majesty for he is God and man in one Person. Both Father and Son would be glorified in the events about to take place. Please exalt God in everything you do and say.

THINGS TO DISCUSS WITH YOUR FAMILY

1. What did Jesus mean when he said, 'Father, the hour has come' (John 17:1)?
2. Discuss the majesty that now surrounds the Lord Jesus in heaven.
3. How do we approach God in prayer?

Meditation

Meditate upon the magnificence that Jesus brought to his heavenly Father — 'And now, O Father, glorify me together with yourself, with the glory which I had with you before the world was' (John 17:5).

Wise Words

We may see God's glory blazing in the sun and twinkling in the stars. *Thomas Watson*

'And he himself gave some to be apostles, some prophets, some evangelists, and some pastors and teachers, for the equipping of the saints for the work of ministry, for the edifying of the body of Christ...' (Ephesians 4:11,12).

Read: John 17:6-19

For whom do you pray each day? I'm sure you pray for your family members, but always remember that there are people for whom no one prays. Think about this and start to pray for people you know who have no interest in spiritual matters. Jesus had prayed for himself, but as the great High Priest he prayed for the eleven apostles who were with him for the entire Passover meal. His prayer has implications for all of his people, despite it being particularly for his small group of faithful disciples.

He acknowledged that they were God's special gift to him as indeed are all Christians. Why were those eleven set aside to serve the Lord and not other members of the Jewish population? I don't have the answer nor can I give a reason for my salvation or yours. The reason for God's electing love is found in God. Writing to the Ephesians Paul says, 'He chose us in him before the foundation of the world, that we should be holy and without blame before him in love, having predestined us to adoption as sons by Jesus Christ to himself, according to the good pleasure of his will...' (Ephesians 1:4,5).

Jesus told God that he had taught his disciples the truth and prayed that they might have the opportunity to preach the gospel throughout the world. They knew that Jesus was the Messiah, the Saviour of sinners and that not only had he come from God but that he was 'the image of the invisible God, the firstborn over all creation' (Colossians 1:15). Only one had proved unfaithful and Jesus knew this from the start. The actions of Judas fulfilled prophecy — 'Even my own familiar friend in whom I trusted, who ate my bread, has lifted up his heel against me' (Psalm 41:9).

In their persecution Christ prayed that they might be kept from death. Before his conversion the Apostle Paul persecuted Christ's church for he said, 'Lord, they know that in every synagogue I imprisoned and beat those who believe on you. And when the blood of your martyr Stephen was shed, I also was standing by consenting to his death, and guarding the clothes of those who were killing him' (Acts 22:19,20).

Jesus prayed that his apostles might be sanctified. Paul made a similar request for the saints at Thessalonica, 'Now may the God of peace himself sanctify you completely; and may your whole spirit, soul, and body be preserved blameless at the coming of our Lord Jesus Christ' (1 Thessalonians 5:23). May God set you apart for his service. May the Holy Spirit lead you along that pathway of righteousness, all to the glory of our Lord Jesus Christ.

THINGS TO DISCUSS WITH YOUR FAMILY

1. What is sanctification?
2. How can God's word sanctify his people?
3. In verse 15 of your reading mention is made of 'the evil one'. Who is this person and why did Christ give him that name?

Meditation

Thank God for the great missionary work of the disciples who took the gospel to the four corners of the known world.

Wise Words

The light of religion ought not to be carried in a dark lantern. *George Swinnock*

'If it is possible, as much as depends on you, live peaceably with all men' (Romans 12:18).

Read: John 17:20-26

Each Sunday Christians go to worship in one of the many church buildings scattered throughout most towns and cities. Some would never enter another place of worship because they believe they alone have an understanding of the truth and other Christians err. This is a very sad situation as worldly people mock us because of our disunity. They point the finger of scorn at us asking why they should join a church when Christians can't agree what is truth.

Jesus prayed that the church might be unified, but in the early church there was a real division between Jewish Christians and Gentile believers. However, the faithful preaching of the truth made it possible for Paul to write, 'But now in Christ Jesus you who once were far off have been brought near by the blood of Christ. For he himself is our peace, who has made both one, and has broken down the middle wall of division ... Now, therefore, you are no longer strangers and foreigners, but fellow citizens with the saints and members of the household of God, having been built on the foundation of the apostles and prophets, Jesus Christ himself being the chief cornerstone, in whom the whole building, being joined together, grows into a holy temple in the Lord, in whom you also are being built together for a dwelling place of God in the Spirit' (Ephesians 2:13,14,19-22).

Unity in the church should reflect the oneness that exists in the Godhead, between Father, Son and Holy Spirit. Christians should also be conscious of being indwelt by the Spirit of God. Paul wrote, 'Do you not know that your body is the temple of the Holy Spirit who is in you?' (1 Corinthians 6:19). This is something beyond our comprehension, but it is true that God dwells in our bodies.

Jesus prayed that the day would come when the saints would behold his glory. This was the glory he had with his Father before coming into the world. Following his death and resurrection he ascended into heaven again and took his rightful seat on the throne of

God. The Apostle John wrote of his vision of Christ's glory: 'Then I looked, and I heard the voice of many angels around the throne, the living creatures, and the elders; and the number of them was ten thousand times ten thousand, and thousands of thousands, saying with a loud voice: "Worthy is the Lamb who was slain to receive power and riches and wisdom, and strength and honour and glory and blessing!" And every creature which is in heaven and on the earth and under the earth and such as are in the sea, and all that are in them, I heard saying: "Blessing and honour and glory and power be to him who sits on the throne, and to the Lamb, for ever and ever!"' (Revelation 5:11-13).

David wrote of the majesty of God which we will see one day, 'You will show me the path of life; in your presence is fullness of joy; at your right hand are pleasures for evermore' (Psalm 16:11). There we will love God in Christ as never before. Are you ready for this?

THINGS TO DISCUSS WITH YOUR FAMILY

1. How does God dwell in the hearts of his people?
2. Why has Christianity split into so many groups?
3. Is there any way to overcome the divisions that exist between churches?

Meditation

Meditate upon the words of Psalm 27:4 — 'One thing I have desired of the LORD, that will I seek: that I may dwell in the house of the LORD all the days of my life, to behold the beauty of the LORD, and to inquire in his temple.'

Wise Words

In ourselves we are scattered; in Christ we are gathered together. *John Calvin*

'Then an angel appeared to him from heaven, strengthening him' (Luke 22:43).

Read: Matthew 26:36-46

Many people face death with great confidence. Christians have God's grace to face death for it is the doorway into the presence of the Lord Jesus. Many non-Christians face death with fearfulness because they believe that it ends existence, and there is nothing when life is extinguished. Jesus knew he was going home to his heavenly Father through his demise on a Roman cross.

What then caused all the sorrow and distress that flooded Christ's heart when he went to Gethsemane to pray? He knew he was God's Son, the Mediator between God and man, the 'I Am' and the long awaited Messiah, yet was distressed by what he knew lay before him.

Christ's concern commenced when he began to feel the weight of sin upon his sinless soul. We are told that God 'made him who knew no sin to be sin for us, that we might become the righteousness of God in him' (2 Corinthians 5:21). Jesus became sin for his people. Our sins were placed upon him and he foresaw the horror of the cross. His death was not going to be an ordinary one, but in the place of his sinful people. The court of heaven had declared Christ to be guilty, and as the sin bearer he would be punished by God. He would suffer hell in the place of all who trust in him.

He asked God if it were possible to have the penalty for sin paid in some other way, but he submitted to the will of God just as Paul wrote, 'And being found in appearance as a man, he humbled himself and became obedient to the point of death, even the death of the cross' (Philippians 2:8). Christ's death on the cross involved being forsaken by his Father, tormented by Satan and his demons, deserted by his disciples and utter humility before a mocking crowd. Yet the beloved Son of God could say, 'Nevertheless, not as I will, but as you will.' Here was total submission to his heavenly Father's will.

In our dark days we pray, and are encouraged when we know that others are praying for us. Jesus had asked the disciples to pray for him, but they were very weary and fell asleep.

When Jesus prayed we are told that perspiration fell from his body like drops of blood. In his distress his compassionate Father strengthened him by sending a mighty angel into the garden. What was said, if anything, we do not know, but any doubts that may have flooded the Saviour's mind were dispelled. His eyes were then firmly fixed upon the cross and the salvation of his people. We are told to look 'unto Jesus, the author and finisher of our faith, who for the joy that was set before him endured the cross, despising the shame, and has sat down at the right hand of the throne of God' (Hebrews 12:2). Beyond the cross the suffering Saviour could see a large number that no one can count, praising him for his saving work. Then waking the sleeping disciples, Jesus told them that his betrayer was approaching.

Do you ever praise and thank God for his Son's faithful work of salvation?

THINGS TO DISCUSS WITH YOUR FAMILY

1. Why was Jesus so distressed in the Garden of Gethsemane? Read Luke 22:39-44.
2. In what way could the presence of an angel strengthen our Lord?
3. What did Jesus mean when he said, 'If it is possible, let this cup pass from me; nevertheless, not as I will, but as you will' (Matthew 26:39)?

Meditation

Think about the transaction that was about to take place at Calvary — your sins for Christ's righteousness — 2 Corinthians 5:21.

Prayer is the sweat of the soul.   *Martin Luther*

Wise Words

'Men and brethren, this Scripture had to
be fulfilled, which the Holy Spirit spoke
before by the mouth of David concerning Judas, who became a guide to those
who arrested Jesus' (Acts 1:16).

Read: John 18:2-11

At the conclusion of making our wedding vows the minister told
me I was permitted to kiss my wife. I was the first person to do
this in her new status, and that was a sign of love. In Psalm 2:12 David
wrote God's words telling us to 'Kiss the Son' as a sign of thankful
love for our salvation.

We now come to the final hours of Christ's life and our reading today involves Judas, the disciple who, with a kiss, betrayed his
Lord. The disciples had moved from the upper room to the Garden
of Gethsemane where Jesus wanted time for prayer, preparing for
the horror of what lay before him. Judas had been with Jesus for
over three years. He had seen the Lord's miracles, heard his gracious
preaching and had himself performed miracles and preached the
truth, yet for thirty pieces of silver betrayed his Master. It was night
time and we have read that the church officials decided not to arrest
Jesus during daylight hours, fearing a riot. Judas had been paid to lead
the soldiers to the Lord during the night and clearly point him out.
What a terrible misuse of a sign of love.

A large group of soldiers appeared, led by Judas who kissed the
Lord, acknowledging that he was the One they sought. When Christ
said that he was Jesus, those brave, cruel soldiers stepped away and fell
to the ground. They stood in the presence of the great, 'I AM' who
then surrendered himself to them. Jesus was completely in control
of the situation. Months before he had indicated he would willingly
give himself as a sacrifice for his people. He had said, 'I am the good
shepherd. The good shepherd gives his life for the sheep' (John 10:11).

To the very end Jesus cared for his disciples telling the soldiers to
allow them to leave. Boastful Peter carried a short bladed sword and
quickly used it to protect Christ. Yet he only succeeded in cutting off
the ear of Malchus, Caiaphas' servant. Jesus again demonstrated his
divine power by healing the injured man.

Christ's kingdom was not of this world, but was a world-wide kingdom in the hearts of repentant sinners. Let us remember that the gospel is not to be spread with a Bible in one hand and a gun in the other. Converts are not won in this manner, but through witness and prayer and ultimately by the gracious work of God in bringing about the new birth.

Christ was arrested and the disciples fled. Mark records that an unknown disciple who was present, turned and ran away with the eleven — 'Now a certain young man followed him, having a linen cloth thrown around his naked body. And the young men laid hold of him, and he left the linen cloth and fled from them naked' (Mark 14:51,52). I wonder who he was?

May you and I prove to be faithful disciples at all times and not desert our Saviour.

With Jesus securely bound, the soldiers set out for the place where the arrogant, hypocritical Annas would investigate Christ's claims to be the Messiah.

THINGS TO DISCUSS
WITH YOUR FAMILY

1. Who was Annas?
2. Why did the soldiers fall to the ground?
3. Jesus said he would 'drink the cup which my Father has given me'. What does this mean?

Meditation

Meditate upon the scene of Christ's arrest and the miracles that displayed his divine power.

Wise Words

Jesus Christ is no security against life's storms, but he is perfect security in life's storms.   *Wendell Loveless*

'Beloved, do not avenge yourselves, but
rather give place to wrath; for it is written, "Vengeance is mine, I will repay,"
says the Lord' (Romans 12:19).

Read: John 18:12-14,19-24

Often when I was a teacher I had to stop children who were
fighting. Some people know only one way to react when hurt
by another person and that is to return the hurt. We have come to the
final hours before Christ's death and despite all the terrible abuse and
hurt, he did not retaliate. He was the sin bearer suffering the anger of
God for the sins of his people. He was willing to leave vengeance in
the hands of his heavenly Father — so should we.

Jesus was arrested, tied up and dragged off to Annas in the middle
of the night. Our Saviour was commencing a time of suffering of
which Peter wrote, 'For Christ also suffered once for sins, the just for
the unjust, that he might bring us to God, being put to death in the
flesh' (1 Peter 3:18).

Annas demanded to be told the names of Christ's disciples, but
Jesus refused to answer. He was protecting those who believed in
him. We can only imagine what use would be made of a list of the
names of Christ's disciples — not just the eleven. They would have
been hunted down and possibly killed in the hope that Christianity
would be stamped out. Annas may well have handed the names to the
Roman authorities as members of a rebellious sect who wanted to
overthrow Rome's power and establish another kingdom.

Annas also wanted Jesus to outline his teaching, no doubt hoping
that he would say something that could be used in a court hearing.
The Lord suggested that he ask those who had heard him preach and
then he would know. He also reminded the priest that his teachings
were done in public and he had no secret agenda. Writing of 'Wisdom' Solomon had said, 'Wisdom calls aloud in the streets; she raises
her voice in the open squares.' These words were written of Christ,
and of the truth Solomon wrote, 'Fools hate knowledge' (Proverbs
1:20,22).

An officer present then slapped the bound Jesus across the face. This was a cowardly act. Many faithful ministers have suffered the same for the Lord they love. Job also suffered because of his righteousness — 'They strike me reproachfully on the cheek' (Job 16:10).

The soldier had not been ordered to hit Jesus who had not been found guilty of any crime. Yet, that was the first of many such assaults and was the fulfilment of Micah 5:1, 'They will strike the judge of Israel with a rod on the cheek.' The One he struck was 'KING OF KINGS AND LORD OF LORDS' (Revelation 19:16). Jesus didn't retaliate. He could have struck that cruel soldier down but these were the days of his humiliation.

Let us also be humble, following the example set by Christ, and always remember, 'Do not be overcome by evil, but overcome evil with good' (Romans 12:21).

THINGS TO DISCUSS WITH YOUR FAMILY

1. Why did Jesus allow people to abuse him in such a terrible way?
2. Earlier Caiaphas had made a prophetic statement concerning the planned death of Christ. What was it and when was it made? Read John 18:14.
3. Why didn't Jesus reveal the names of his disciples?

Meditation

Meditate upon the wickedness of that soldier who struck Jesus. 'The One who gave us freedom was bound.'

Wise Words

The fullest and best ears of corn hang lowest towards the ground.   *Edward Reynolds*

'...false witnesses have risen against me, and such as breathe out violence' (Psalm 27:12).

Read: Mark 14:53-65

Reports of court cases are to be found in the daily newspapers or heard over the radio and TV. Some are very serious cases, but in Australia capital punishment is not practised. Things were different in the Roman Empire. Citizens of Rome were normally executed by beheading while slaves and people of other nations were crucified. The rulers of Israel didn't have the power to execute offenders. The Sanhedrin, made up of the chief priests, scribes, elders and other church leaders, wanted Christ put to death, but needed the order to be given by Pilate, Rome's ruler in the land.

Annas had sent Jesus to the Chief Priest Caiaphas who quickly gathered all members of the ruling council and attempted to lay a charge against him. This was a 'kangaroo court' and very illegal. There was no charge laid against Jesus, despite many people coming forward to say what he had said. However, there was no agreement between the accusers.

Despite all the questioning Jesus said nothing in his defence. Again prophecy was being fulfilled — 'He was oppressed and he was afflicted, yet he opened not his mouth; he was led as a lamb to the slaughter, and as a sheep before its shearers is silent, so he opened not his mouth' (Isaiah 53:7). The sinless One was now being tried by sinful men.

When the high priest asked Jesus a straightforward question — 'Are you the Christ, the Son of the Blessed?' Jesus replied, 'I am. And you will see the Son of Man sitting at the right hand of the Power, and coming with the clouds of heaven.' This was enough for the Sanhedrin to accuse Jesus of blasphemy. He had plainly said he was the Son of God, and by using the name 'Son of Man' he had used the name Daniel called the Messiah (Daniel 7:13).

The members of the Sanhedrin were infuriated when Jesus claimed he would take his seat beside God in heaven and at a later time they would see him returning to earth. These words would have reminded his accusers of David's words of the Messiah found in Psalm 110:1 — 'The LORD said to my Lord, "Sit at my right hand, till I make your enemies your footstool."'

In Revelation 1:7 the Apostle John recorded of Christ, 'Behold, he is coming with clouds, and every eye will see him, even they who pierced him. And all the tribes of the earth will mourn because of him. Even so, Amen.'

Then came the physical abuse by those who should have been lying prostrate before him and acknowledging him to be Messiah. Again prophecy was being fulfilled in what was happening, 'I gave my back to those who struck me, and my cheeks to those who plucked out the beard; I did not hide my face from shame and spitting' (Isaiah 50:6).

To everyone it must have seemed that Jesus was defeated, but we know that he was victorious, defeating Satan and winning salvation for his people.

THINGS TO DISCUSS WITH YOUR FAMILY

1. Why did the High Priest tear his clothes?
2. How are we to react to those who torment us because of our Christian faith?
3. There were times when Jesus refused to speak. Why was this?

Meditation

Meditate upon Jesus' answer when asked if he was 'the Christ, the Son of the Blessed.' Read Matthew 26:64 — 'It is as you said. Nevertheless, I say to you, hereafter you will see the Son of Man sitting at the right hand of the Power, and coming on the clouds of heaven.'

Wise Words

For the absolutely sinless One to be subjected to a trial conducted by sinful men was in itself a deep humiliation. To be tried by *such* men, under *such* circumstances made it infinitely worse. *William Hendriksen*

'Then he began to curse and swear, saying, "I do not know the Man!" Immediately a rooster crowed' (Matthew 26:74).

Read: John 18:15-18; Matthew 26:69-75

When we have problems it is good to have friends who are willing to lend a helping hand, or just give a word of support. Jesus was suffering, and at the time of his arrest his disciples kept away fearing they would suffer a similar fate. We are told that Peter followed at a distance.

Jesus had told the eleven that they would 'stumble' because of what was to happen, fulfilling the words of Zechariah 13:7 — 'Strike the Shepherd, and the sheep will be scattered.' Outspoken Peter had said that no matter what others might do he 'would never be made to stumble'. Jesus replied, 'Assuredly, I say to you that this night, before the rooster crows, you will deny me three times.' Again proud Peter declared, 'Even if I have to die with you, I will not deny you!' (Matthew 26:33,34,35).

Peter kept his distance but was able to gain admittance to the courtyard of the place where Caiaphas lived. It was cold and when approached by a servant girl he denied that he was in any way associated with Jesus. A second denial soon followed and this time he again lied, backing it up with an oath. He was looking after his own interests while being in the presence of the suffering 'Servant' of God.

Finally, when accused of being a follower of the Lord he answered in the words of today's text. Then the rooster crowed fulfilling Christ's prophecy. When Peter looked towards Christ at that moment, he saw that Jesus was looking at him. The Lord had heard the rooster crow and knew what Peter had done. Peter was overcome with shame and with a repentant heart went outside and wept.

Here we are reminded that the best of saints can fall into sin. However, always remember the words of our Lord, 'Whoever confesses me before men, him the Son of Man also will confess before the angels of God. But he who denies me before men will be denied before the angels of God' (Luke 12:8,9).

We must be wary of keeping close company with unbelievers who so easily can be used by Satan to cause us to rebel against God. When we do sin we must be like David and Peter and repent. All sin is against God, even though someone else may be hurt. To God we must go in humility and true repentance and cry as did David, 'Against you, you only, have I sinned, and done this evil in your sight' (Psalm 51:4). Remember the Lord's promise made through the Apostle John, 'If we confess our sins, he is faithful and just to forgive us our sins and to cleanse us from all unrighteousness' (1 John 1:9).

Peter was truly repentant and later was to hear Christ's words of forgiveness. God forgives the sins of repentant people because he is a God of mercy. For the sake of his Son, Jesus Christ, the believer's sins are removed for ever.

THINGS TO DISCUSS WITH YOUR FAMILY

1. Why did Peter deny knowing Jesus?
2. How could Jesus know that a rooster would crow after Peter had denied him three times?
3. What must you do when you break God's law?

Meditation

Think about Peter's gradual steps leading to his terrible sin of denying his Saviour. Pray that you will never do the same.

Wise Words

You cannot repent too soon, because you do not know how soon it may be too late.   *Thomas Fuller*

'And every creature which is in heaven and on the earth and under the earth and such as are in the sea, and all that are in them, I heard saying: "Blessing and honour and glory and power be to him who sits on the throne, and to the Lamb, for ever and ever!"' (Revelation 5:13).

Read: Luke 22:66-71

Under Australian law when a person is convicted of a crime the matter is concluded unless there has been an infringement of the law concerning the conduct of the trial. If a judge gives incorrect advice to the jury it is possible for the convicted person to appeal against his sentence.

Jesus had been forced to meet with the Sanhedrin during the night and was duly convicted of what was considered to be a capital offence. However, it was contrary to Jewish law to hold trials at night. Other legal laws had also been violated. The Lord was dragged before the Sanhedrin a second time, this time at the break of day. The church authorities wanted to give some legality to what was being done, but nothing they carried out did away with what they had planned some time before — to have Jesus put to death.

The matter of dispute was — 'Is this man the Messiah?' The church leaders and Pharisees in particular claimed he was not. They believed the Messiah would re-establish the throne of David, throw out the Roman forces and once again make Israel an independent nation.

When asked if he was the Christ, Jesus replied that there was no point in answering their question as they would not believe what he said. Little did they know that the Person standing before them, bound and bleeding, would within a short time fulfil the prophecy of Daniel 7:13,14 — 'I was watching in the night visions, and behold, One like the Son of Man, coming with the clouds of heaven! He came to the Ancient of Days, and they brought him near before him. Then to him was given dominion and glory and a kingdom, that all peoples, nations, and languages should serve him. His dominion is an everlasting dominion, which shall not pass away, and his kingdom the one which shall not be destroyed.'

When he was asked, 'Are you then the Son of God?' his reply was plain, 'You rightly say that I am.' Instead of rejoicing and praising God, those cruel, hard-hearted, demon-possessed men believed that what Jesus had said was blasphemous, deserving the death penalty.

Never think as those wicked men did. Always stand firm for the Saviour, remembering Paul's words, '...if you confess with your mouth the Lord Jesus and believe in your heart that God has raised him from the dead, you will be saved. For with the heart one believes unto righteousness, and with the mouth confession is made unto salvation. For the Scripture says, "Whoever believes on him will not be put to shame"' (Romans 10:9-11).

All that was now needed by the Sanhedrin was Pilate's order for this 'impostor' to be crucified. Men were doing their worst, but God's plan of salvation was being perfectly fulfilled. We have a glorious, wise and all-powerful God!

THINGS TO DISCUSS WITH YOUR FAMILY

1. What crime did the members of the Sanhedrin believe Jesus had committed?
2. What is blasphemy?
3. What plan of God was being fulfilled that day in Israel?

Meditation

Meditate upon Christ's patience in his terrible suffering.

Wise Words

Miss Christ and you miss all.   *Thomas Brooks*

'The Son of Man indeed goes just as it is written of him, but woe to that man by whom the Son of Man is betrayed! It would have been good for that man if he had never been born' (Mark 14:21).

Read: Matthew 27:3-10; Acts 1:18,19

All we know about Judas is found in the Scriptures, where we learn that he was a very sinful man. Jesus said of him that it would have been better if he had never been born. He was a thief who betrayed his Lord for thirty pieces of silver, yet he mustn't always have been a wicked person. Like many vicious criminals today, Judas had a mother and father who loved him and had great hopes for their son. They could never have imagined that he would commit such a terrible crime that it would be the subject of discussion for several thousand years.

Judas, in the darkness, identified Jesus to the soldiers with a kiss. If ever proof was needed that Jesus was an innocent person we need only look to Judas. When the Sanhedrin wanted evidence to be used against our Saviour, Judas, who had been with him for over three years, would have been the logical person to step forward and speak, but he didn't. He knew that he had betrayed 'innocent blood'. In Hebrews 7:26 we are told that Jesus 'is holy, harmless, undefiled, separate from sinners, and has become higher than the heavens'.

Judas was to discover the truth of Proverbs 10:2 — 'Treasures of wickedness profit nothing.' You and I need to take these words to heart. We must never become involved in illegal activities in an effort to get money. Such money will rot in our wallets. We should also note the words in Jeremiah 17:11 — '...as a partridge that broods but does not hatch, so is he who gets riches, but not by right; it will leave him in the midst of his days, and at his end he will be a fool.'

Judas was overcome with grief because of what he had done, but his sorrow did not come from a changed heart. Paul wrote of two types of repentance, 'For godly sorrow produces repentance leading to salvation, not to be regretted; but the sorrow of the world produces death' (2 Corinthians 7:10). Worldly sorrow is that which comes from being caught committing the crime. True sorrow comes from a heart that knows sin is against God and involves repentance, confession, seeking forgiveness and making restitution if and where possible.

The hypocritical members of the Sanhedrin refused to accept the thirty pieces of silver. The ones who had planned Christ's murder would not accept blood money. It was used to buy land to be used as a cemetery for foreigners which was a fulfilment of prophecy. Matthew mentions Jeremiah as making the prophecy, although most of it comes from Zechariah. This is no problem as we find quotations in other parts of Scripture that come from several sources with only one writer mentioned. A few come from sources that can't be identified — see Jude 14.

Judas then went away and committed suicide by hanging himself. This was a terrible thing to do and for Judas was unforgivable. However, always remember that some people, even Christians, commit suicide because they are ill. God forgives all of the sins of his people, including suicide.

THINGS TO DISCUSS WITH YOUR FAMILY

1. Discuss today's text.
2. What is genuine repentance?
3. Why was the potter's field called the 'field of blood'?

Meditation

Consider seriously your repentance for breaking God's law. Is it genuine?

Wise Words

Repentance is one of the foundation stones of Christianity. *J. C. Ryle*

'Pilate said to him, "What is truth?" And
when he had said this, he went out again
to the Jews, and said to them, "I find no
fault in him at all"' (John 18:38).

Read: John 18:28-38

Many years ago in Australia there was a world renowned court
case. Lindy Chamberlain was wrongly convicted of killing her
baby. Later, when it was determined that a dingo had taken and killed
the infant, she was exonerated. Hollywood made a film of the story.

We have been reading about the life of the Lord Jesus and know
that he was without sin. Pilate, Rome's representative in Jerusalem,
knew the Lord was innocent of the crimes with which he had been
charged, and many times stated this to be so. However, he was a weak
man who bowed to the demands of the Jews and handed Jesus over
to be put to death by crucifixion. We are now seeing the fulfilment
of the words of Psalm 2:2,3 — 'The kings of the earth set themselves,
and the rulers take counsel together, against the LORD and against his
Anointed, saying, "Let us break their bonds in pieces and cast away
their cords from us."'

The members of the Sanhedrin wouldn't enter Pilate's palace as
that would have made them 'unclean' and unable to take part in the
spiritual ritual associated with the Passover. They felt no guilt in the
murder of an innocent man and telling lies about him. Luke records,
'And they began to accuse him, saying, "We found this fellow per-
verting the nation, and forbidding to pay taxes to Caesar, saying that
he himself is Christ, a King"' (Luke 23:2). There are people today
who claim to love God. They attend church on Sunday and live like
the world for the rest of the week. Are you a Christian seven days a
week?

Jesus spoke openly to Pilate who was searching for the reasons
behind the accusations made by the Jews. The Apostle Paul wrote of
Jesus making a 'good confession before Pontius Pilate' (1 Timothy
6:13). When he asked Jesus if he was 'the King of the Jews' the Lord
clearly stated that he was a King of a kingdom, but not at that time
of an earthly kingdom. The great Roman Empire had nothing to fear
from him and his few disciples.

As we study history we find that God has blessed those nations whose citizens are servants of Christ the King. The British Empire was at its height at the time her missionaries took the gospel to the world. The greatness of the U.S.A. was the result of God's grace to a people, a great number of whom were servants of the Son of God.

Jesus told Pilate he had come into the world to 'bear witness to the truth'. Most people know and mock his question to Christ, 'What is truth?' Little did he realize that 'the Truth' in the Person of the Lord Jesus Christ stood before him. Do you remember Jesus saying, 'I am the way, the truth, and the life. No one comes to the Father except through me' (John 14:6)? You and I must bear witness to the truth — to the glory of Jesus, the Son of God and our Saviour.

Pilate could see through the wickedness of the members of the Sanhedrin and declared for all to hear, 'I find no fault in him at all.'

THINGS TO DISCUSS WITH YOUR FAMILY

1. Why wouldn't the Jews go into the Praetorium?
2. What charge did the Sanhedrin bring against Jesus? Did its members believe what they were saying?
3. In what way is Jesus 'the truth'?

Meditation

Meditate upon the perfect innocence of the Lord Jesus.

Wise Words

Nothing is more common than for persons overzealous about rituals to be remiss about morals. *Matthew Poole*

'At that time Herod the tetrarch heard the report about Jesus and said to his servants, "This is John the Baptist; he is risen from the dead, and therefore these powers are at work in him"' (Matthew 14:1,2).

Read: Luke 23:5-12

I'm sure that often children are like their parents. The Herod we are reading about today was like his father in many ways, as both were involved in attempts to kill Jesus. It was Herod who had given the order to kill the babies in the Bethlehem region in an attempt to kill the infant, Jesus. Now his son, Herod, is about to give his support to the Sanhedrin and Pilate in having Jesus executed. Today's text is about Herod's belief that Jesus was the resurrected John the Baptist whom he had had beheaded.

Herod was rich and powerful, despite being appointed by Rome and subject to the Roman authorities. He had heard a lot about Jesus — what he taught and the miracles he performed. Now he expected the Lord to put on a show for him, by performing some miracles. Jesus had performed many compassionate miracles to help the poor and needy, but was not going to do so for the rich, arrogant king.

When Pilate heard that Herod was in Jerusalem he sent Jesus to him, hoping to avoid making the decision that would see Jesus put to death. He was a coward, despite having the might of Rome at his disposal. Pilate had upset Herod, possibly by having Roman troops kill some Galileans 'whose blood [he] had mingled with their sacrifices' (Luke 13:1). This would have been considered a most blasphemous act, but by sending Jesus to him for judgement he was offering the hand of friendship.

Jesus refused to answer Herod's questioning and the accusations of the chief priests and scribes who were present. 'Then Herod, with his men of war, treated him with contempt and mocked him, arrayed him in a gorgeous robe, and sent him back to Pilate.' The mocking was the commencement of the fulfilment of prophecy — 'But I am a worm, and no man; a reproach of men, and despised by the people. All those who see me ridicule me; they shoot out the lip...' (Psalm 22:6,7).

Jesus had been awake for many hours, abused, mocked, treated with contempt and was feeling the weight of the sins of his people upon his pure soul. Nevertheless, everything that happened was in accordance with God's plan of salvation, just as Peter and John said, 'For truly against your holy Servant Jesus, whom you anointed, both Herod and Pontius Pilate, with the Gentiles and the people of Israel, were gathered together to do whatever your hand and your purpose determined before to be done' (Acts 4:27,28).

Herod, after having the Son of God mocked and abused, returned him to Pilate with the result that the broken relationship between the two men was healed.

THINGS TO DISCUSS WITH YOUR FAMILY

1. Discuss the terrible way Pilate healed the broken relationship between himself and Herod.
2. Jesus was suffering terribly. What does this tell us about our sins in God's sight?
3. Why had Herod hated John the Baptist? See Luke 3:19.

Meditation

Meditate upon the cause for Christ to suffer as he did. Were you to blame in any way?

Wise Words

None but God knows what an abyss of corruption is in my heart.   *Robert Murray M'Cheyne*

'He was oppressed and he was afflicted,
yet he opened not his mouth; he was led
as a lamb to the slaughter, and as a sheep
before its shearers is silent, so he opened
not his mouth' (Isaiah 53:7).

Read: Luke 23:13-16

There are times when we read reports of people being cruelly
hurt by others. The unfortunate victim is often assaulted not just
once but many times and if he lives it takes a long time for him to
recover from his injuries.

Each time you read another section of Christ's suffering you
must add them together to get a full picture of what was happening.
He was our sin bearer, carrying the weight of his people's sins and
suffering the anger of God in their place. Jesus had not had any rest
for at least two days, and before that he had been preaching to crowds
of people as well as speaking privately to his disciples. His body was
tired and was being abused by tough soldiers; he had been deserted
by his disciples; he had been declared guilty of crimes by the Sanhedrin members and King Herod. Despite Pilate knowing that Jesus
was innocent of the charges laid against him he was suffering the vile
abuse, both physical and mental, that came from the Roman soldiers
who hated the Jews.

It was morning and the sun shone hot and bright in a cloudless
sky. The Lord was bound and dragged along the roadway through the
watching crowds of people in Jerusalem for the Passover. Pilate had
gone out to face the populace who had gathered and there before
the chief priests and scribes said, 'I have found no fault in this man
concerning those things of which you accuse him; no, neither did
Herod...' Pilate declared Jesus innocent on five different occasions,
but the Jews began crying out for his blood. Believing him to be a
false prophet the law was clear, 'you shall surely kill him' (Deuteronomy 13:9).

After Lazarus had been raised from the dead Caiaphas began
serious planning to have Jesus killed, claiming 'it is expedient for
us that one man should die for the people, and not that the whole

nation should perish' (John 11:50). He believed that not only was Jesus a false Messiah, but any talk of him establishing a kingdom would bring the wrath of Rome upon them. Thus Christ should die!

Pilate wanted to free Jesus as we will see later, but he was weak and feared he would have a riot on his hands if he allowed Jesus to go. He believed that it would be better to let the Jews have their way. Morality and principle meant little to Pilate. He was only interested in what was politically expedient at that time. The innocent Jesus was to die!

In the court of heaven God looked upon his beloved Son as he would a guilty sinner because he had become sin for his people. In that heavenly court, Jesus stood guilty, and was to bear the penalty for sin.

Having declared him innocent, Pilate then sent Jesus away to be whipped, hoping to win the sympathy of the Jews and so be able to release the King of the Jews. This was not to be.

THINGS TO DISCUSS WITH YOUR FAMILY

1. What do we learn of Pilate's character from the events that took place?
2. Why did Pilate want to release Jesus?
3. Whom did Pilate fear that day?

Meditation

Meditate upon the perfectly holy Son of God becoming sin for his people.

Wise Words

The test by which all conduct must finally be judged is motive. *A. W. Tozer*

'While he was sitting on the judgment seat, his wife sent to him, saying, "Have nothing to do with that just Man, for I have suffered many things today in a dream because of him"' (Matthew 27:19).

Read: John 18:39 – 19:16

When Lindy Chamberlain was jailed for the murder of her daughter, many people saw it as a great injustice done to an innocent woman. They worked hard and eventually Mrs Chamberlain was released from jail and all findings against her were squashed. She was formally declared to be innocent of the charges laid against her.

Jesus was now before Pilate who knew him to be innocent of the trumped-up charges laid against him by the hateful church leaders. He knew the members of the Sanhedrin were envious of Jesus who was gaining a following at their expense.

He made an effort to have Jesus released by offering the freedom of the criminal Barabbas or 'the King of the Jews'. Yet the crowds began calling for the release of Barabbas. Pilate then decided to have Christ whipped. He handed him over to the cruel, rough soldiers who used the whip made of leather thongs with stones, bones or metal attached to the ends of the leather pieces. During the assault upon Christ, Pilate's wife sent him an urgent message, 'Have nothing to do with that just Man, for I have suffered many things today in a dream because of him' (Matthew 27:19). Hoping for some sympathy from the watching crowds Pilate had Christ brought out and announced, 'Behold the man!' The response from the Satanic-inspired Jews was, 'Crucify him, crucify him!' Again Pilate declared, 'I find no fault in him.' Then taking a bowl of water he washed his hands and said, 'I am innocent of the blood of this just Person. You see to it.' The people answered, saying, 'His blood be on us and on our children' (Matthew 27:24,25).

All that took place was in perfect accordance with God's plan of salvation. Our text tells us that the death of Christ was vicarious — he died in the place of his people. Pilate then, pointing to the bleeding and abused Jesus, said mockingly, 'Behold your king!'

We see what a coward Pilate was. He had the army that could have released Jesus and dispersed the mob with force, but he did nothing to save 'the King of the Jews'. He took the easy way out. Never let us be like that. Let every Christian always stand firm for the majesty of their Saviour despite what others might do or say.

Jesus told Pilate that God controlled the situation, despite his belief that he was master of his and Christ's destiny. This was recognized by Nebuchadnezzar many years before: 'All the inhabitants of the earth are reputed as nothing; he does according to his will in the army of heaven and among the inhabitants of the earth. No one can restrain his hand or say to him, "What have you done?"' (Daniel 4:35).

In our troubled days it is comforting to know that God is in control of everything. It is also glorious to know that Christ's shed blood has washed away our sins, and his imputed righteousness has opened heaven's door for believers. Praise the Lord!

THINGS TO DISCUSS WITH YOUR FAMILY

1. Why did Pilate have Jesus whipped?
2. At what time of the day was Jesus handed over to the soldiers to be crucified?
3. Why was Pilate such a coward?

Meditation

Meditate upon Galatians 3:13 — 'Christ has redeemed us from the curse of the law, having become a curse for us...'

Wise Words

He suffered not as God, but he suffered who was God.
John Owen

 'But he was wounded for our transgres-
sions, he was bruised for our iniquities;
the chastisement for our peace was upon
him, and by his stripes we are healed'
(Isaiah 53:5).

Read: Matthew 27:27-34

We have looked briefly at Pilate's attempt to have Jesus released,
but we also saw that the events taking place were those de-
signed by God for the salvation of his people. God's great rescue
plan was well underway and for this study let us look at the treatment handed out to Jesus by those cruel Roman soldiers. Because of
Christ's suffering God 'has delivered us from the power of darkness
and conveyed us into the kingdom of the Son of his love, in whom
we have redemption through his blood, the forgiveness of sins' (Colossians 1:13,14).

Remember that Jesus 'died for our sins according to the Scriptures' (1 Corinthians 15:3) — 'the just for the unjust' (1 Peter 3:18).
Pilate sentenced the innocent Jesus to be 'scourged' with a very cruel
whip which tore the flesh from his body, causing blood to flow. Often such a whipping killed the unfortunate victim, but many times
the stones or bones tied to the leather thongs tore through the skin,
tearing the flesh open. Jesus suffered physically as many did at the
hands of the Roman soldiers, but there was a difference — he was
the pure, innocent God/man. His soul suffered because of the burden
of sin he carried. Paul, writing to the Colossians, said, 'For it pleased
the Father that in him all the fullness should dwell, and by him to
reconcile all things to himself, by him, whether things on earth or
things in heaven, having made peace through the blood of his cross'
(Colossians 1:19-20).

Next came the tormenting. Knowing that Jesus claimed to be the
king of the Jews they plaited a crown of thorns and forced it onto his
head. Then dressing him in an old purple robe, the colour of royalty,
they began mocking and physically abusing the Son of God. Little
did those men realize as they abused Christ the King that the day
would come when they would face him in a different situation. Paul

wrote, 'For we must all appear before the judgement seat of Christ, that each one may receive the things done in the body, according to what he has done, whether good or bad' (2 Corinthians 5:10).

This mocking was aimed at Christ's heart and mind and it came from his arch enemy Satan who used evil men to do his work. Do you remember God's words to Satan in the Garden of Eden following Adam's sin — 'And I will put enmity between you and the woman, and between your seed and her Seed; he shall bruise your head, and you shall bruise his heel' (Genesis 3:15)? At that time Satan was bruising Jesus' 'heel', little realizing that the Saviour was crushing his head.

Blood had to be shed for we are told that 'without shedding of blood there is no remission' (Hebrews 9:22). Our text tells us the same. It is through the terrible abuse of Christ that sinners are saved. I was there when Christ suffered — he carried my sins. Were you there that day?

Having had their fun, the soldiers dressed Christ in his own clothing and led him away to be crucified.

THINGS TO DISCUSS WITH YOUR FAMILY

1. There is no record of Jesus making any noise while being brutalized. Why not?
2. Why was the crown of thorns placed on Jesus' head?
3. Why was it necessary for Christ's blood to be shed?

Meditation

Meditate upon the part you played in Christ's suffering.

Wise Words

If we would live aright it must be by the contemplation of Christ's death.   *C. H. Spurgeon*

'Your wife shall be like a fruitful vine in the very heart of your house, your children like olive plants all around your table' (Psalm 128:3).

Read: Luke 23:26-32

A family usually consists of parents and children. Of course we know that there are different groupings that constitute a family. Our family consists of Val, myself and Wags. As Jesus was being taken to be crucified our compassionate Saviour was concerned about the judgement of God that was soon to fall upon Israel. Families would be torn apart.

An exhausted, bleeding Redeemer, accompanied by two convicted criminals, were being led to the Place of the Skull which was outside the city walls, where they were to be crucified. 'He was numbered with the transgressors' as prophesied in Isaiah 53:12. The words of the hymn that speaks of a 'green hill' where Jesus was put to death is not accurate. All criminals were to be executed outside the city precincts (Leviticus 24:14).

I often wonder what was happening in the unseen world. God's angels who watched the events would have been ready to rescue Christ if he had sought their help. Those innocent beings must have been mystified by what they saw happening to the One who was one with God in heavenly majesty.

When Jesus stumbled under the weight of the cross the soldiers ordered Simon, a visitor from Africa to Jerusalem for the Passover, to carry the Lord's cross. He was probably very embarrassed, but what a privilege he had been given by God.

On the way to be crucified Jesus spoke to the many women who stood around watching what was happening. Those compassionate women mourned and were upset by what they saw. When the Lord saw tears in their eyes he told them not to weep for him, but to do so for themselves and their children, because the day was coming when they would say, 'Blessed are the barren, wombs that never bore, and breasts which never nursed!'

Jesus said this because he foresaw the day when the Romans would sack Jerusalem, slaughtering men, women and children. He also saw the day when those trapped in Jerusalem would kill their children for food. Instead of children being a joy to them, they would be a burden and heartbreak. Earlier Jesus had told his disciples of the forthcoming destruction of the temple and Jerusalem and had said, 'But woe to those who are pregnant and to those who are nursing babies in those days!' (Matthew 24:19).

He told them they would call the mountains to fall on them and cover them from the Lord's anger. This was an expression used when describing judgement and a way of escape. Christ said that what was happening to him could be likened to green wood that doesn't burn. The nation of Israel was like dry wood that would be consumed in the fires of judgement that fell when the Roman Titus and his army destroyed the nation. Jesus suffered terribly for his people. The people of Israel suffered horribly for what they had done to God's beloved Son.

THINGS TO DISCUSS
WITH YOUR FAMILY

1. How do you think Simon felt when ordered to carry Christ's cross?
2. Why was Jesus sympathetic to the women who watched him stumbling towards the Place of the Skull?
3. Are children supposed to be a blessing or a nuisance to parents? Why?

Meditation

Meditate upon the words of today's text and Christ's words to the women as he made his way to Calvary.

Wise Words

The glory of the cross of Christ is bound up with the effectiveness of its accomplishment. *John Murray*

'Then he said to them all, "If anyone desires to come after me, let him deny himself, and take up his cross daily, and follow me. For whoever desires to save his life will lose it, but whoever loses his life for my sake will save it"' (Luke 9:23,24).

Read: John 19:18-22

Had I lived during the days of the Roman Empire and been told to take up my cross, I would have been somewhat horrified, because it meant that at the end of the roadway I would be nailed to the cross I was carrying. Jesus told his disciples, and that means disciples of all times, that we must be willing to suffer for the Lord we love and serve.

Simon had been ordered to carry Christ's cross because the Lord had been brutalized by the rough Roman soldiers. He was so weakened he could not continue stumbling along with its weight upon his shoulders. Eventually Jesus and the two criminals who were to be crucified with him reached the place of execution. For many centuries the Jews had been making sacrifices for sin, but this day the Roman soldiers were to make the final sacrifice when they put Jesus to death. His death meant no more sacrifices were needed.

Jesus was offered some gall and sour wine to drink as this helped ease pain and pacify the convicted person, making it easier for the soldiers to carry out their cruel duty. Jesus refused as he would suffer the entire penalty for the sins of his people. It is interesting that prophecy was being fulfilled in this event. We read in Psalm 69:21: 'They also gave me gall for my food, and for my thirst they gave me vinegar to drink.'

A sign was placed on the cross which mocked both Jesus and the Jews — 'JESUS OF NAZARETH, THE KING OF THE JEWS'. This was written in Greek, Hebrew and Latin. Jesus didn't look like a King, but he is always a King and one day every knee will bow before him, including those who crucified him. Then the Lord was stripped naked, the soldiers fulfilling prophecy by dividing his clothes between them. This was a 'perk' associated with their job. David had written, 'They divided my garments among them, and for my clothing they cast lots' (Psalm 22: 18).

After Christ's hands and feet were nailed to the cross, it was dropped into the prepared hole. Again prophecy was being fulfilled, 'They pierced my hands and my feet' (Psalm 22:16). This would have caused extreme pain. And while they did their work Jesus prayed, 'Father, forgive them, for they do not know what they do' (Luke 23:34). Could you do this? Remember we are to pray for our enemies and those who despise us. Jesus here sets us an example.

There hung our Saviour, between two criminals again fulfilling prophecy — '...he was numbered with the transgressors' (Isaiah 53:12). His body was tortured with pain and his heart and mind suffered the torments of those standing about the cross, laughing and mocking. All of this he suffered that we might live — does this include you?

THINGS TO DISCUSS WITH YOUR FAMILY

1. Why do you think Jesus was nailed to the central cross?
2. Why did the church officials object to the sign Pilate had erected on Christ's cross?
3. Why was the sign written in three different languages?

Meditation

Meditate upon the scene described above.

Wise Words

The cross of Christ runs through the whole of Scripture.
Martin Luther

29 November   A sinner saved at the last hour
of his life

'Now to him who is able to do exceedingly abundantly above all that we ask or think, according to the power that works in us, to him be glory in the church by Christ Jesus to all generations, for ever and ever. Amen' (Ephesians 3:20,21).

Read: Luke 23:39-43

I have never sat beside a dying person who was not a Christian and heard them profess faith in Christ, despite sincere prayer, reading the Scriptures and serious discussion. One person told me very bluntly to 'Forget it.' However, you have just read of a thief being converted in the most terrible circumstances.

Two criminals had been nailed to crosses erected on either side of our Saviour. They had felt the pain of nails tearing through their hands and feet and had possibly felt the whip of the Roman soldiers before their last walk carrying their crosses. They faced the reality of death beside the One called 'The King of the Jews'. They would have heard him pray for the soldiers who had stripped him of his clothes and nailed him to the cross. They listened when he placed his mother into the care of his disciple, John (John 19:25-27).

Both men joined the crowd and Sanhedrin members mocking the Lord, 'He saved others; let him save himself if he is the Christ, the chosen of God ... if you are the King of the Jews, save yourself.' It seemed that everyone present that day was mouthing the words Satan put into their hearts. Yet, a change came over one thief who was dying. He rebuked his dying companion, 'Do you not even fear God, seeing you are under the same condemnation? And we indeed justly, for we receive the due reward of our deeds; but this man has done nothing wrong.'

No doubt both thieves knew about Jesus as everyone had heard about or seen the great miracles he had performed. Everyone was aware of the teaching of this One who claimed to be 'Son of Man' and 'Son of God'.

The repentant thief saw Christ as truly a King, but try and imagine what he saw — a man covered in blood, torn apart from a cruel whipping and being mocked by the leaders of the church.

700

He certainly didn't look like a king, but the repentant thief said, 'Lord, remember me when you come into your kingdom.' A simple request — just remember me when you sit upon the throne of your kingdom. But hear the Lord's reply — more than the man had asked or could even have thought possible — 'Assuredly, I say to you, today you will be with me in Paradise.'

If you are a Christian remember that God will give you the grace you need to die well. And we should all be able to say with the Apostle Paul, 'For to me, to live is Christ, and to die is gain' (Philippians 1:21). Death is our enemy, but Christ defeated death and removed its sting. Because our sins are forgiven we can face death with confidence and say with the Apostle Paul, 'There is therefore now no condemnation to those who are in Christ Jesus, who do not walk according to the flesh, but according to the Spirit' (Romans 8:1).

THINGS TO DISCUSS WITH YOUR FAMILY

1. Why is it foolish to leave making peace with God until the last days of your life?
2. Where is the repentant thief today?
3. Why could Paul say that death was 'gain'?

Meditation

Meditate upon the scene that resulted in the conversion of a thief hanging on a cross.

Wise Words

Affliction is God's shepherd dog to drive us back to the fold. *Anonymous*

'For he made him who knew no sin to be sin for us, that we might become the righteousness of God in him' (2 Corinthians 5:21).

Read: Matthew 27:45-50

Often children are afraid of the dark so some parents leave a light turned on until the child falls asleep. Jesus had been hanging upon the cross for some hours when at midday a strange darkness descended over the land and for three hours Christ suffered the torments of hell in the place of sinners. A great exchange was taking place at Calvary that day as our text tells us. Jesus became sin for his people, bearing their sins in his own innocent body. In return his righteousness was put to their account.

Amos wrote, '"And it shall come to pass in that day," says the Lord GOD, "that I will make the sun go down at noon, and I will darken the earth in broad daylight"' (Amos 8:9). The darkness and events of that day filled the hearts of many with fear (Luke 23:48). Often in the Scriptures darkness is associated with the judgement of God on sin (Joel 2:31). Jesus was on that cross giving 'his life a ransom for many' (Matthew 20:28).

We cannot comprehend the suffering of Jesus Christ that day, yet we catch glimpses in various parts of the Scriptures. Paul wrote, 'Christ has redeemed us from the curse of the law, having become a curse for us (for it is written, "Cursed is everyone who hangs on a tree")' (Galatians 3:13). The climax of the Lord's suffering was that moment when he lost the sense of his Father's presence. We read his cry, '"*Eli, Eli, lama sabachthani?*" that is, "My God, my God, why have you forsaken me?"' (Matthew 27:46).

Jesus was forsaken by his heavenly Father so that his people might never be forsaken by God. Christ's faith never wavered for he could still call out to God. The Father always loved his Son, but Jesus was to experience hell for all those given to him by his Father.

Some mocked him saying that he was calling for Elijah. Jesus knew that death was near as he had almost completed the payment for the sins of his people. Again to fulfil Scripture he said, 'I thirst'

(John 19:28; cf. Psalm 22:15) and one kind person put some sour wine on a stick and pushed it to the Saviour's lips.

Jesus knew his work of redemption was completed. No one could take his life from him, but he willingly laid it down for those he loved. Then came the cry of triumph — 'It is finished!' (John 19:30). This was not the soft voice of a dying man, but the shout of triumph from the Son of God, the King of the Jews. All had been accomplished and Jesus could now die saying, 'Father, into your hands I commit my spirit' (Luke 23:46). Again Jesus sensed the presence of his heavenly Father. Now he could die, not because of the brutal treatment he had received, but because his work of salvation was accomplished.

THINGS TO DISCUSS WITH YOUR FAMILY

1. What did Jesus mean when he said, 'It is finished'?
2. What are sin's wages? Read Romans 6:23.
3. Why did the heavenly Father forsake his Son?

Meditation

Meditate upon the words, 'My God, my God, why have you forsaken me?' (Matthew 27:46).

Wise Words

Hell came to Calvary that day, and the Saviour descended into it and bore its horrors in our stead.

William Hendriksen

December

'Therefore, brethren, having boldness to enter the Holiest by the blood of Jesus, by a new and living way which he consecrated for us, through the veil, that is, his flesh...' (Hebrews 10:19,20).

Read: Matthew 27:51-56

When people die tears flow, and friends and relatives gather to support the ones grieving the loss of someone they loved. Yet, when Jesus died events took place that shook the nation of Israel. It was soon after his death at 3.00pm that the land began to shudder as if it could not bear absorbing the blood of the God-man. The earthquake produced some most unusual occurrences.

In the temple the priests were carrying out the evening sacrifice. The Holy Place that the High Priest entered only once each year had a large veil covering its entrance so no one could see inside. This curtain shielded people from looking upon the majestic shekinah glory of God as it was above the mercy seat on the ark of the covenant. Suddenly the curtain was torn apart from top to bottom making it possible for anyone to look into the holy place. Prior to this anyone daring to look into that room was subject to the death penalty, but with the death of Christ for sin, the old sacrificial system had ended. The Holy Place now had no spiritual importance.

In the local cemetery the quivering earth broke open many graves from which resurrected bodies of some saints came forth. When Christ rose from the dead those people appeared to many citizens in Jerusalem. This resurrection was a foretaste of what will happen when Jesus returns in power and glory to gather his saints to himself. On that day 'all who are in the graves will hear his voice and come forth — those who have done good, to the resurrection of life, and those who have done evil, to the resurrection of condemnation' (John 5:28,29).

At the foot of the cross one Roman centurion who had witnessed all that had happened said in fear, 'Truly this was the Son of God.' This was the confession of a tough soldier who had heard Christ's words and witnessed what had happened.

Large crowds had watched the events of that day. They had been involved in the mocking of the Lord, but with the unusual events happening at the moment of Jesus' death we read that they became afraid. Luke records, 'And the whole crowd who came together to that sight, seeing what had been done, beat their breasts and returned' (Luke 23:48). The sky became light once again and the people returned to their homes unable to understand the reason for what had happened. Many must have asked themselves, 'Was Jesus really the Messiah, the Son of God?' We don't know if they became followers of Christ, but many may have been in the three thousand converted when Peter preached on the Day of Pentecost.

Also mentioned was the fact that many of Christ's acquaintances and the faithful women from Galilee stood back from the cross and the mocking crowd to watch the events that were unfolding.

Satan's kingdom had suffered its greatest blow and now would be under attack from the disciples who preached the gospel of salvation through the living God.

THINGS TO DISCUSS WITH YOUR FAMILY

1. Why was the temple curtain torn in half?
2. What caused the Roman soldier to acknowledge that Jesus was 'the Son of God'?
3. Why did the people 'beat their breasts'?

Meditation

Meditate upon the thoughts that must have flooded the mind of that Roman centurion who acknowledged Jesus as the 'Son of God'.

Wise Words

Christ assumed every consequence of sin which was not itself sinful.   *S. P. Tregelles*

'So when the centurion saw what had happened, he glorified God, saying, "Certainly this was a righteous Man!"' (Luke 23:47).

Read: Isaiah 53

I have a hearing aid which makes it easier for me to hear what is being said. It is very useful. Today's text contains the words of a Roman soldier who heard Christ's words during his dying hours and was convinced that the Person on the cross was 'the Son of God'. We have already read Christ's words while on the cross, but below the seven 'words' have been put together. Read them and think about them. They made an impression on that Roman soldier and they should do the same to you.

The first three 'words' were spoken during the daylight hours and all concerned other people. As always, we see the compassionate nature of Christ, the Son of God. Remember that this is our Saviour who 'is the same yesterday, today, and for ever' (Hebrews 13:8).

First: 'Father, forgive them, for they do not know what they do' (Luke 23:34). Bleeding from a cruel whipping, a crown of thorns and nails through his hands and feet, Jesus asked his Father to forgive the soldiers for what they had done. Do you willingly forgive those who hurt you? A Roman soldier confessed that very day that Jesus was the Son of God. Such a confession required the work of the Holy Spirit in the man's hard heart. On the day of Pentecost three thousand people were brought to repentance. God forgave that great number who came to believe that Jesus was the Christ. God does answer his Son's prayers.

Second: 'Assuredly, I say to you, today you will be with me in Paradise' (Luke 23:43). At the end of his life a thief asked Jesus to remember him when he entered his kingdom. The reply Jesus gave was more than the thief could have expected. He was told that on that very same day he would be with him in heaven. It is never too late to pray and for that thief his prayer was heard by God in heaven. Paul's words are so true, 'For to me, to live is Christ, and to die is gain' (Philippians 1:21). We can face death knowing that our Redeemer has opened the door of heaven for us.

Third: 'Then he said to the disciple, "Behold your mother!" And from that hour that disciple took her to his own home' (John 19:27). Many years before, old Simeon had held the baby Jesus and said to Mary, '...yes, a sword will pierce through your own soul also' (Luke 2:35). That prophecy was being fulfilled at that moment. Mary was watching her Son die in a most brutal way. In the midst of his anguish Jesus saw his mother. He spoke to her and John, the apostle he loved. The Lord placed his mother into the hands of John in order that she might receive good care during the latter portion of her life. John was well to do and was able to ensure that Mary was made comfortable till she died. We should make sure that our parents are cared for when life becomes a burden to them. We read in Proverbs 23:22, 'And do not despise your mother when she is old.'

THINGS TO DISCUSS WITH YOUR FAMILY

1. What do these three 'words' tell us of Christ's nature?
2. Of all the disciples why do you think Jesus gave John the care of his mother?
3. What are our responsibilities to our parents?

Meditation

Meditate upon the compassionate nature of Christ and pray that you might have the same character.

Wise Words

Though our Saviour's passion is over, his compassion is not. *William Penn*

 'And according to the law almost all things are purified with blood, and without shedding of blood there is no remission' (Hebrews 9:22).

Read: Acts 4:5-31

Darkness had fallen and Jesus was suffering the pangs of hell for his people. If you are a Christian every sin you have or ever will commit, was placed upon him. During those dark hours from noon until 3.00pm it appears that Jesus suffered in silence. We now continue from our previous devotion.

Fourth: At about 3.00pm the Saviour cried, "*Eloi, Eloi, lama sabachthani?*" which is translated, "My God, my God, why have you forsaken me?"' (Mark 15:34). This was the cry of our Redeemer suffering hell. He lost the sense of the sweet presence of his Father and hung on that cross all alone so his believing people might never be alone. He certainly suffered physically, but he suffered more so spiritually, being under constant attack from Satan and his demonic hosts. Now he could not sense his Father's presence, but his faith did not fail him for he cried out to his God. This cry fulfilled the words of Psalm 22:1. Remember he was willingly and lovingly suffering for his people. Again I ask, does this include you?

Fifth: 'I thirst' (John 19:28). These words fulfilled a prophecy we find in Psalm 22:15. Christ had had nothing to eat or drink since the Passover meal. He had suffered terrible abuse and then hung upon the cross for hours in the hot weather. No kind person offered him water to drink, but he was given some sour wine from a sponge on a rod of hyssop. Hell is terrible punishment. Do you remember the rich man asking for a drop of water to relieve his suffering? (Luke 16:24). May you never suffer the punishing flames of hell!

Sixth: 'It is finished' (John 19:30). These words should not be taken as coming from a person on the verge of death because of some terrible illness or brutality. They came from the lips of our Saviour who knew that the penalty for sin had been totally paid. The great High Priest had offered himself, the perfect sacrifice for sin, and now the debt owed by the saints was cancelled. Salvation was accomplished and Jesus could shout out for all to hear — 'It is accomplished!'

Seventh: 'Father, into your hands I commend my spirit' (Luke 23:46). These words are found in Psalm 31:5. Having completed the work of salvation as far as meeting sin's debt, our Saviour could lay down his life. Again, he did not die because his heart gave out, but because sin's debt was paid and God's wrath appeased. He could allow death to have his body for a time. As the soul of Lazarus was transported into Paradise by the holy angels (Luke 16:22) we can well imagine God's most mighty and glorious angels gently transporting Christ's soul into the presence of his heavenly Father. Notice that Jesus now uses the word 'Father'. He could sense his Father's presence once again and the sky was becoming light. By passing into heaven the glorification of the Son of God had commenced.

We have looked at precious words spoken by our Saviour, but remember that it is Jesus Christ who is precious. He is our glorious God and Redeemer. Love him with all your heart and soul.

THINGS TO DISCUSS WITH YOUR FAMILY

1. In what way did the heavenly Father forsake his Son?
2. Why was Jesus thirsty?
3. 'For he made him who knew no sin to be sin for us, that we might become the righteousness of God in him' (2 Corinthians 5:21). What does this mean?

Meditation

Meditate upon Christ's absolute control of his final hours as he crushed Satan's head.

Wise Words

Jesus did not die just to give us peace and a purpose in life; he died to save us from the wrath of God.

Jerry Bridges

'He guards all his bones; not one of them
is broken' (Psalm 34:20).

Read: John 19:31-42

I have had many falls, especially when young, but so far I have never
broken a bone in my body. There is no record of Jesus ever having a
bone of his body broken thus fulfilling prophecy. To hasten death on
the cross the soldiers would smash the leg bones of the person nailed
to the cross, causing heart failure. When the soldiers came to break
Jesus' legs they found he was already dead so they didn't carry out the
cruel practice. One soldier plunged his spear into the Lord's side and
water and blood flowed out. There can be no doubt that Jesus died
upon that Roman cross.

Two men approached Pilate and gained permission to remove
the Lord's brutalized body from the cross. One was Joseph of Arimathea, a rich man and member of the Sanhedrin. He had been
a secret believer, but now openly displayed his love for Jesus. With
Nicodemus, who had visited Jesus one night over three years before,
they took Christ's body and placed it in a new rock tomb found in a
nearby garden. No other body had been placed in that tomb. Again
we find prophecy fulfilled. In Isaiah 53:9 we read, 'And they made his
grave with the wicked — but with the rich at his death.' This was a
step in the glorification of our Redeemer.

After anointing his body with about one hundred pounds of
myrrh and aloes, the men had the Lord's body wrapped in clean linen
cloth. This was a mixture of costly powder, but to them nothing was
too good for their Lord. These two men must have been despised
by the other members of the Sanhedrin, when they courageously
stepped out in faith to show their love and respect for Jesus, their
Messiah. What had begun as a weak faith was seen as a courageous
faith in the face of the satanic hatred of Christ and all believers. Never
despise the day of small things. Never fear if your faith is weak, but
grow close to your Lord and as you faithfully serve him your faith
will be strengthened.

One day we will die, if the Lord does not return first. Remember, if you are a believer, your body is 'the temple of the Holy Spirit' (1 Corinthians 6:19). When we die our bodies should be treated with respect and not looked upon as a piece of rubbish as some ungodly people do. Our salvation is not complete until that day when our sanctified soul is united with our glorified body.

Jesus' body was carefully and gently laid to rest. Mary Magdalene and several other women who had followed the Lord from Galilee sat outside the tomb. They were to prepare a mixture of spices and sweet smelling oils to anoint the Lord's body after the Sabbath day ended. No one expected a resurrection of the Redeemer despite all that he had told them.

Death is a curse — the last enemy, but Christ has removed death's sting which is sin. Christians can face death with the assurance that they are precious to God and will never be forsaken.

THINGS TO DISCUSS
WITH YOUR FAMILY

1. Did Jesus' body decay in the tomb in which he was laid? See Acts 2:26-28.
2. Why is death a curse?
3. Why was Jesus so precious to Mary Magdalene? Read Mark 16:9.

Meditation

Meditate upon the courage shown by Joseph and Nicodemus. Pray for a similar courage.

There is a fountain filled with blood,
    Drawn from Immanuel's veins;
And sinners plunged beneath that blood
    Lose all their guilty stains.   *William Cowper*

Wise Words

'An evil and adulterous generation seeks after a sign, and no sign will be given to it except the sign of the prophet Jonah. For as Jonah was three days and three nights in the belly of the great fish, so will the Son of Man be three days and three nights in the heart of the earth' (Matthew 12:39,40).

Read: Matthew 27:61-66; 28:11-15

When the first crossing of the Blue Mountains in Australia was made by the British settlers, the track taken was marked with an easily recognizable sign. Marks were cut into trees every several hundred yards. Signs were important to the explorers. When Jesus was asked for a sign to prove he was the Messiah he said the only sign he would give was that of Jonah as indicated in our text.

Jesus' body had been laid to rest in the garden tomb and the Sanhedrin members remembered that he had said that in three days he would break free from the clutches of death. They didn't believe that Christ would rise from the tomb in a glorified body, but they wanted to prevent someone stealing his body. They approached Pilate with the request that soldiers be placed on guard to prevent this happening. In your reading did you notice those hypocritical religious leaders calling Pilate 'Sir' and Jesus a 'deceiver'?

Pilate told them to set a guard about the tomb and seal the entrance with a huge stone. Little did they realize that by their own craftiness in taking precautions to prevent anything happening to the Lord's body they were giving absolute proof that the resurrection took place. Paul's words are proved so true: 'For the wisdom of this world is foolishness with God. For it is written, "He catches the wise in their own craftiness"' (1 Corinthians 3:19). Later the foolish actions of the Sanhedrin to persecute Christians with the aim of destroying the church, resulted in the gospel being spread far and wide. Satan thought he would be victorious by having Jesus killed, but Christ's death saved his sinful people and destroyed Satan's kingdom. God rules this world.

Early on the first day of the week the guards (and the women who had come to anoint the Lord's body) felt the ground shudder and saw two mighty angels dressed in white move the huge stone covering the entrance to the tomb. At that point there was no body inside the tomb for the Lord had risen in his glorified body.

The 'brave' soldiers turned and ran for their lives and reported to the Chief Priests what had happened. Those priests should have rejoiced and praised God, but they gave the guards a large sum of money and told them to say that the disciples had stolen Jesus' body while they slept. This was rather foolish, for sleeping people do not see what is happening. The soldiers who witnessed the majestic events that morning should have become faithful disciples of the risen Christ.

There is a lot of evidence that Jesus rose from the dead. Do you believe it? Christianity is based upon historical facts.

THINGS TO DISCUSS WITH YOUR FAMILY

1. Why were the soldiers given a large sum of money?
2. In what way did the setting of guards about the tomb help prove the resurrection of our Saviour?
3. Why do you think the two angels appeared at the tomb? Read Matthew 28:2-4.

Meditation

Meditate upon the scene the soldiers saw that morning.

Wise Words

Money is a bait for the blackest temptation; mercenary tongues will sell the truth for it.   *Matthew Henry*

'For I delivered to you first of all that which I also received: that Christ died for our sins according to the Scriptures, and that he was buried, and that he rose again the third day according to the Scriptures...' (1 Corinthians 15:3,4).

Read: Mark 16:2-8

We have read about those Roman soldiers who turned and ran for their lives when faced by an earthquake and the sight of two heavenly beings. It was early on the first day of the week when this occurred.

That morning several women who had cared for Christ and the apostles approached the tomb where their Lord's body had been laid. Four women are mentioned — Mary Magdalene; Mary, the mother of James; Salome; and Joanna. They had come with a supply of spices with which they intended to anoint the Lord's body. This shows us that they didn't believe that Jesus was to rise from the dead. They expected to find his corpse in the tomb and would respectfully anoint it with the spices.

One problem that concerned them was the removal of the huge stone that had been placed over the sepulchre's opening. They knew they were too weak to roll it out of the way. As they approached the tomb they, with the soldiers, felt the ground begin to shudder and looking up saw that the burial chamber was open.

Like the soldiers, they saw an angel resting on the stone, but unlike the soldiers who ran away they heard the angel say, 'Do not be afraid, for I know that you seek Jesus who was crucified. He is not here; for he is risen, as he said. Come, see the place where the Lord lay. And go quickly and tell his disciples that he is risen from the dead, and indeed he is going before you into Galilee; there you will see him' (Matthew 28:5-7).

The women looked inside and saw that Christ's body was not there, but still they were unsure of what had happened. The tomb was certainly empty and everything that had occurred pointed towards a miracle, but still the concept of the Lord's resurrection was not realized. An angel told the fearful women to tell the eleven what they had seen and been told.

Today so many professing Christians doubt the resurrection of the Lord Jesus, despite all the available proof. The resurrection is a fundamental article of the Christian faith. Paul wrote, 'And if Christ is not risen, then our preaching is vain and your faith is also vain. Yes, and we are found false witnesses of God, because we have testified of God that he raised up Christ, whom he did not raise up — if in fact the dead do not rise. For if the dead do not rise, then Christ is not risen. And if Christ is not risen, your faith is futile; you are still in your sins! Then also those who have fallen asleep in Christ have perished. If in this life only we have hope in Christ, we are of all men the most pitiable' (1 Corinthians 15:14-19). May this not be said of you!

THINGS TO DISCUSS WITH YOUR FAMILY

1. Despite the evidence why didn't the women believe in the resurrection of Christ?
2. How do you know that Jesus is alive in his glorified body?
3. Why were the women afraid?

Meditation

Meditate upon the thoughts that must have gone through the minds of the ladies that morning.

Wise Words

The resurrection is the proof of our reconciliation.

Geoffrey B. Wilson

'And if Christ is not risen, your faith is futile; you are still in your sins!' (1 Corinthians 15:17).

Read: John 20:2-10

Graves and tombs are constructed to house dead bodies. The ladies who visited the tomb where Christ's body had been placed found the tomb empty except for the linen in which his body had been wrapped.

Mary Magdalene was there with several other women when the angel rolled away the large stone covering the entrance. The guards ran away in fear, and the ladies were told to tell the disciples that Jesus had risen. Mary, finding John and Peter, neither of whom believed that the Lord was alive in his glorified body, said, 'They have taken away the Lord out of the tomb, and we do not know where they have laid him.'

At once both men ran to see for themselves what had happened. John outran Peter, but when Peter arrived he quickly entered the tomb to discover that what the women had said was true. Nevertheless, they still didn't understand that Christ had been raised from the dead. They did not understand the prophetic words of David found in Psalm 16:10 — 'For you will not leave my soul in Sheol, nor will you allow your Holy One to see corruption.' After the giving of the Holy Spirit in great power on the day of Pentecost, Peter used David's words in his sermon to prove that Jesus was the Christ and had, by the power of God, been resurrected (Acts 2:23-28).

Every person who claims to be a Christian must believe in the resurrection of the Saviour. To deny this fundamental truth is to reject God's only way of salvation. Speaking of Christ's righteousness, Paul wrote, 'It shall be imputed to us who believe in him who raised up Jesus our Lord from the dead, who was delivered up because of our offences, and was raised because of our justification' (Romans 4:24,25).

Our text says quite plainly that if Christ did not rise then our faith in him makes no sense. The Lord's resurrection is the proof that the penalty for sin was accepted by his Father. Christians can thus look forward to that day when Christ returns, for then the resurrection of all the dead will take place. We will have glorified bodies like that of our Redeemer.

Peter and John looked into the empty tomb and then returned to their homes. However, there was a difference in their understanding of the situation. John believed that Christ had been raised, but Peter was still unsure of what had taken place. Soon afterwards Jesus appeared to Peter when he was alone (Luke 24:34).

While they were with Jesus before his crucifixion, he had taught them so much, but the idea of his resurrection proved to be a truth they found hard to believe. Even the initial proof was not enough. Christians worship a risen Lord who today sits upon his heavenly throne. We must praise him, for it is because of his resurrection we are justified.

THINGS TO DISCUSS WITH YOUR FAMILY

1. Why didn't John and Peter believe the women who said that Jesus was raised from the dead?
2. Do you believe in the resurrection of the dead? Why?
3. Why is it necessary for professing Christians to believe in the resurrection of the Lord Jesus?

Meditation

Try to imagine the thoughts that were in Peter's mind as he returned from seeing the empty tomb.

Wise Words

They therefore went home: Peter confounded and perplexed, and unable to account for what he had seen; John convinced and persuaded by what he had seen, that his Master had risen from the dead.   *J. C. Ryle*

'The LORD is near to those who have a broken heart, and saves such as have a contrite spirit' (Psalm 34:18).

Read: John 20:11-18

Only recently Val and I purchased two plots of land. When we told our children they thought we must have been close to death. Yet, unless the Lord returns we will occupy, side by side, the plots we have bought. We told our daughters it is not necessary to visit our graves after we have died as our souls will be with the Lord. Some people make regular visits to the graves of their loved ones as a mark of respect, and for a time to think about the old days.

Mary Magdalene dearly loved the Lord who had cast seven demons out of her. She had also experienced spiritual healing from the Saviour. She knew the Lord's body was no longer in the tomb, but wanted to be near the place where it had been laid. Possibly she may have been expecting a miracle to take place as she had heard Jesus speak of being raised.

She had seen the angel at the tomb and we are told she was weeping. The Lord's body that had been brutally abused could not be found. His body had disappeared and she didn't know where it was. Again she stooped down and looked into the tomb, and this time she saw two angels where Christ's body had been placed. When asked why she was weeping she replied, 'Because they have taken away my Lord, and I do not know where they have laid him.' There is no indication that she believed that the Lord had been raised from the dead.

We read of her speaking to the person she thought was the gardener. Then Jesus replied, 'Mary.' The Lord used her personal Aramaic name, 'Miriam'. Instantly she knew who it was. Her eyes were opened to behold her Saviour and she threw her arms about him in great excitement. Her Lord and Teacher was alive! No one had stolen his body!

She held Jesus tightly as if she would never let him go, but the close familiarity that existed before his death was finished. He told her not to 'cling' to him. The Lord Jesus Christ was now her exalted

Saviour and soon he would be leaving her to return to his heavenly Father. Touching Jesus was not forbidden as later Thomas was invited by the Lord to touch his hands, feet and side in order to prove that he was a living being and not a ghost. Notice the Lord's words to Mary: 'I am ascending to my Father and your Father, and to my God and your God.' The Father and God of the Lord Jesus is the Father and God of all the elect. This is a glorious truth!

Mary was told to find the disciples and tell them that he was alive and she had seen and spoken to him. What a wonderful message she had to deliver to the eleven and any others she met. We have a similar message to tell our friends. Jesus Christ, our Lord and Saviour, lives and welcomes repentant sinners to himself. We have a great reason for spiritual joy!

THINGS TO DISCUSS
WITH YOUR FAMILY

1. Describe how Mary must have felt when she realized that Jesus was alive.
2. What does the living Saviour mean to you?
3. What part did the mighty angels play in the death and resurrection of the Lord Jesus?

Meditation

Meditate upon Acts 3:14,15 — 'But you denied the Holy One and the Just, and asked for a murderer to be granted to you, and killed the Prince of life, whom God raised from the dead, of which we are witnesses.'

Wise Words

Jesus has forced open a door that had been locked since the death of the first man. He has met, fought and beaten the King of Death. Everything is different because he has done so. *C. S. Lewis*

'And these words which I command you today shall be in your heart; you shall teach them diligently to your children, and shall talk of them when you sit in your house, when you walk by the way, when you lie down, and when you rise up' (Deuteronomy 6:6,7).

Read: Luke 24:13-32

It is good advice to use our spare time to talk about the Scriptures. How often after a worship service do people gather to talk about the weather, fishing and the need of rain, yet so little if anything is mentioned about the sermon or the glory of God. The disciples had much to discuss. The body of their Lord was missing and they had no idea what had happened.

The reading for today is about two followers of the Lord, one being Cleopas, who were on their way to Emmaus, a village about seven miles from Jerusalem. Most people were talking about the crucifixion of Jesus who claimed he was the Messiah. I imagine the news was spreading that his body had disappeared from the tomb and the guards were telling everyone that the disciples had stolen his body while they slept.

The two in our reading were talking about the recent events concerning the Lord. We should also take the opportunity to discuss with others the Saviour and his death and resurrection. We have an amazing story to tell. We also need to encourage other Christians by discussing our faith and our wonderful Redeemer. The Apostle Paul writing to the Thessalonians said, 'Therefore, comfort each other and edify one another, just as you also are doing' (1 Thessalonians 5:11). Make good use of family time to discuss eternal matters with one another.

Jesus approached Cleopas and his friend, but they did not recognize him. This was a miraculous action of the Lord. When he questioned their discussions Cleopas asked if he had heard of the events that had occurred in Jerusalem relating to Jesus who claimed to be the Christ.

Jesus rebuked the two saying, 'O foolish ones, and slow of heart to believe in all that the prophets have spoken! Ought not the Christ to have suffered these things and to enter into his glory?' Then Jesus went on to expound the passages of the Old Testament that spoke of him.

Here we are told that the Old Testament has many references to Christ. We should not just read the New Testament, but all of the Scriptures, from Genesis to Revelation, because Christ and his glory is the central feature. The sacrificial system pointed to his great final sacrifice for sin and the fact that he was a greater prophet than Moses.

Arriving at Emmaus the two men invited the Lord to stay with them. When they sat down to eat, Jesus took some bread and after giving thanks, handed each person a piece. Instantly they saw that it was the Lord, but he disappeared from their sight. Now there was proof that Christ was truly alive. He was flesh and blood, but his glorified body was different to his body prior to the resurrection. We have something wonderful awaiting us when our bodies are glorified. The best is truly yet to be!

THINGS TO DISCUSS WITH YOUR FAMILY

1. Why did the disciples decide to return to Jerusalem at once?
2. What is our glorified body going to be like?
3. What do you think Jesus explained to Cleophas and his friend (see Luke 24:27)?

Meditation

Meditate upon the glorious body you are expecting to be given when Christ returns. Read 1 Corinthians 15:49.

Wise Words

Christ was the substance of every Old Testament sacrifice, ordained in the law of Moses. Christ was the true Deliverer and King, of whom all the judges and deliverers in Jewish history were types. Christ was the coming Prophet greater than Moses, whose glorious advent filled the pages of prophets. *Michael Bentley*

723

10 December   Christ's first appearance to his assembled disciples

 'Now this I say, brethren, that flesh and blood cannot inherit the kingdom of God; nor does corruption inherit incorruption' (1 Corinthians 15:50).

Read: Luke 24:33-43

I don't know about you, but each Sunday night I sleep well. My day is devoted to worship and Christian activities and by nightfall I am very weary. Yet, my activities are nothing like those of the disciples on that first Lord's Day when Christ rose from the dead. From your reading you will have seen that the day was drawing to a close. The ten were in a room with a securely closed door having a meal together.

There was still much discussion concerning what had happened to the Lord, despite Christ having revealed himself to both Mary Magdalene and Peter. Suddenly there was knocking on the door and when it was opened the two men who had been with the Lord on the road to Emmaus announced the exciting news that they had been with the risen Saviour. His body that they knew looked like Christ's body, but it was now the majestic body of the risen Saviour.

Suddenly Jesus was in the room with them. He had not entered through the door, but had simply appeared. They all knew that his body was not that of his humiliation, but a glorified body capable of doing the impossible. Despite being told that Christ was risen, the people in that room were terrified as they thought that the One before them was a ghost. Immediately, seeing their fear, Jesus said, 'Peace to you.' He wanted to settle their disturbed hearts and prove that he was not a ghost.

He told them to touch him and look at the nail prints in his hands and feet. He wanted the disciples to acknowledge that he was flesh and blood, but having qualities that he did not have before. He then asked for some food and ate it before them, again proving that he had a real body. Jesus then rebuked them for their failure to believe what he had taught them concerning his resurrection and for not believing the reports of Peter and Mary Magdalene that they had seen his resurrected body that very day.

724

Jesus then explained the Old Testament teaching concerning his life, death and resurrection and gave them the command that they were to be witnesses to his resurrection. They were told to preach the gospel and the forgiveness of sins. This was further proof that the risen Christ was God. Some years before when he had forgiven the sins of a crippled man the Jews had rightly said, 'Who can forgive sins but God alone?' (Mark 2:7). Jesus breathed on those present saying, 'Receive the Holy Spirit' (John 20:22). The great power of the Spirit was needed to carry out the work of world-wide gospel proclamation. His words were the 'down payment' on what was to happen at Pentecost.

Thomas was absent from the group on that Lord's Day.

THINGS TO DISCUSS WITH YOUR FAMILY

1. Discuss this passage from Acts 10:39-41: 'And we are witnesses of all things which he did both in the land of the Jews and in Jerusalem, whom they killed by hanging on a tree. Him God raised up on the third day, and showed him openly, not to all the people, but to witnesses chosen before by God, even to us who ate and drank with him after he arose from the dead.'
2. Why did Jesus say to his disciples, 'Peace to you'?
3. Why did Jesus ask the disciples for some food to eat?

Meditation

Meditate upon the majesty of the risen Redeemer — 'The LORD lives! Blessed be my Rock! Let the God of my salvation be exalted' (Psalm 18:46).

Wise Words

None but he who made the world can make a minister.

John Newton

725

'And let us consider one another in order to stir up love and good works, not forsaking the assembling of ourselves together, as is the manner of some, but exhorting one another, and so much the more as you see the Day approaching' (Hebrews 10:24,25).

Read: John 20:24-31

When a reliable person tells us some news we normally believe what they say, especially if we know them well and they have a reputation for honesty. Yesterday we read that Jesus appeared to the majority of his disciples, but Thomas was absent. Despite being told by his close friends that the Lord had appeared to them he said, 'Unless I see in his hands the print of the nails, and put my finger into the print of the nails, and put my hand into his side, I will not believe.' Thomas was a hard man to convince.

By being absent on that first Lord's Day Thomas missed meeting the risen Lord. Today's text tells us to be regular in our attendance at the means of grace. What a tragedy it would be if the blessing of God fell upon the congregation and you were absent. Don't neglect the meetings of the Lord's people for worship. Remember the Lord said, 'For where two or three are gathered together in my name, I am there in the midst of them' (Matthew 18:20).

The eleven were again together in a room with a securely closed door when Jesus appeared in their midst and asked Thomas to look at the marks the nails had left in his hands, and touch the scar where the spear had torn his side. This tells us that Jesus Christ was more than just a man. He knew what Thomas had said after being told that the disciples had seen the Lord. Christ is God and knows our thoughts. However, he is still the compassionate, loving Lord. He didn't rebuke Thomas for his unbelief but gently opened the eyes of his understanding to behold the truth concerning his resurrection.

Thomas replied in words of glorious praise, 'My Lord and my God!' Jesus didn't rebuke him for saying that he was God, but accepted his words of truth. Do you believe that Jesus Christ is God and man in one Person? I do. Once the Apostle John bowed down before an angel only to be told, 'See that you do not do that. For I am your fellow servant, and of your brethren the prophets, and of those who keep the words of this book. Worship God' (Revelation 22:9).

The day is coming when everyone will acknowledge that Jesus is God and on that day 'every knee [will] bow, of those in heaven, and of those on earth, and of those under the earth, and that every tongue [will] confess that Jesus Christ is Lord, to the glory of God the Father' (Philippians 2:10,11).

Jesus told Thomas that he believed because he had seen the evidence, but he then blessed those who would believe without visible evidence. Peter expressed the same of those 'whom having not seen you love. Though now you do not see him, yet believing, you rejoice with joy inexpressible and full of glory, receiving the end of your faith — the salvation of your souls' (1 Peter 1:8,9). Is this you?

THINGS TO DISCUSS WITH YOUR FAMILY

1. Why didn't Thomas believe what the disciples had told him of Christ's visit?
2. Why was Thomas called 'Didymus'?
3. How do you think the disciples felt now that they had all seen the risen Lord?

Meditation

Think about the words of Hebrews 10:24,25 — 'And let us consider one another in order to stir up love and good works, not forsaking the assembling of ourselves together, as is the manner of some, but exhorting one another, and so much the more as you see the Day approaching.'

The authority for faith is the revelation of God.

G. B. Foster

Wise Words

727

'Then Jesus said to them, "Do not be afraid. Go and tell my brethren to go to Galilee, and there they will see me"' (Matthew 28:10).

Read: John 21:1-14

There have been many times I went fishing and came home with an empty bag. When I was young I knew that it was wise to buy cooked prawns for bait which meant if the fish weren't biting, the prawns could be eaten.

Now Jesus had told the disciples to go to Galilee where he would meet them. This was the third time he was to see a group of the disciples — this time seven of them. Peter and the others had returned to fishing as they were not wealthy people and needed to take up some work to earn money in order to purchase food. They were unsure what lay before them as the Lord was yet to tell them of the missionary labours they were to carry out. All night they had been fishing and caught nothing.

As morning dawned the disciples could see someone on the shore, but no one recognized that it was Jesus. When they called out, telling him they had caught nothing all night, the Lord told them to drop the net on the other side of the boat. When they did, they were surprised to feel the weight of a great catch. John realized that the lone figure was the Lord and at once the impetuous Peter jumped over the side and made his way to greet Jesus. The other disciples hauled in the net and then made their way to the Lord.

The church is made up of different people, yet together they constitute the body of Christ. Peter and John had different personalities, but they both loved the Lord and served him as the Lord determined. We are not to expect every Christian to be like us. We must accept our differences as coming from the Holy Spirit.

Again we see a great miracle performed by Christ. The school of fish was exactly where he wanted them to be at that point in time.

When the disciples gathered about Christ they all knew who it was. They knew he was their victorious Redeemer, just as Peter later wrote, 'Blessed be the God and Father of our Lord Jesus Christ, who according to his abundant mercy has begotten us again to a living hope through the resurrection of Jesus Christ from the dead, to an inheritance incorruptible and undefiled and that does not fade away, reserved in heaven for you' (1 Peter 1:3,4).

But there before them a fire was burning. They found that the Lord had cooked a fish and a piece of bread. Where the food came from they did not ask, but once again they witnessed another miracle. The Lord fed the seven from one fish and one piece of bread. Now there could be no doubt that Jesus had risen from the dead and from this little group of disciples the worldwide kingdom of God would grow. Soon they would become fishers of men.

THINGS TO DISCUSS WITH YOUR FAMILY

1. How many fish were in the haul?
2. How could Jesus know where to lower the net in order to catch the school of fish?
3. List the other two times the Lord had appeared to the disciples as a group.

Meditation

Meditate upon the glory of Christ as shown by the miracles performed that day. 'Many, O LORD my God, are your wonderful works which you have done; and your thoughts toward us cannot be recounted to you in order; if I would declare and speak of them, they are more than can be numbered' (Psalm 40:5).

Wise Words

Christ is the most unique man in history. No man can write a history of the human race without giving first and foremost place to the penniless teacher of Nazareth.

H. G. Wells

'Peter answered and said to him, "Even if all are made to stumble because of you, I will never be made to stumble." Jesus said to him, "Assuredly, I say to you that this night, before the rooster crows, you will deny me three times"' (Matthew 26:33,34).

Read: John 21:15-25

One of the most wonderful experiences in life is to know that God has forgiven your sins. Unforgiven sins can cause tension in your mind, because you know that you have offended God and cannot expect any blessing until you have truly repented and found forgiveness.

The Lord had told boastful Peter that he would deny him three times on the night of his trial. Peter showed no humility when he said that others might desert the Lord and have their faith severely tested, but he would never turn away from him. We know the story of Peter denying Christ three times before the rooster crowed. When he realized what he had done, and saw the Lord looking at him, he went away weeping. He had sinned, his proud heart being humbled by several young women.

There is a warning to each one of us here. Pride does go before a fall. We must always be on guard against making boastful statements in front of witnesses because when we fall our embarrassment is even greater.

Three times the Lord asked Peter if he loved him and three times Peter replied that he did. Three questions because of three denials. Peter was instructed by the Lord to take care of the church which contained members of all ages. He learned the lesson well for later he wrote, 'Shepherd the flock of God which is among you, serving as overseers, not by compulsion but willingly, not for dishonest gain but eagerly; nor as being lords over those entrusted to you, but being examples to the flock' (1 Peter 5:2.3).

Peter was told that he would glorify God in his death which would be by crucifixion. All Christians should bring glory to God in their deaths. We are told by David, 'Precious in the sight of the LORD is the death of his saints' (Psalm 116:15). Knowing this, we can patiently await the Lord's call to come home to be with him. We can endure our physical pains with courage, knowing that we will soon be seeing our Saviour face to face. To those about our bedside we can display our confidence in the saving promises of the Lord and show everyone that we have peace in our heart. With David we can say, 'Yea, though I walk through the valley of the shadow of death, I will fear no evil; for you are with me; your rod and your staff, they comfort me' (Psalm 23:4).

The many millions of faithful Christians who have been martyred for their faith have died bravely testifying to the majesty of God and the reliability of the truth they have believed. May God give us the grace to die bravely.

THINGS TO DISCUSS WITH YOUR FAMILY

1. Why did God forgive Peter's sins?
2. Have your sins been forgiven? Why?
3. Why did the Lord ask Peter three times if he loved him? Do you think he might have been deaf?

Meditation

Thank God if he has blotted out all of your sins. Contemplate on the words of Psalm 51:9 — 'Hide your face from my sins, and blot out all my iniquities.'

Wise Words

Our people die well.   *John Wesley*

'After that he was seen by over five hundred brethren at once, of whom the greater part remain to the present, but some have fallen asleep. After that he was seen by James, then by all the apostles' (1 Corinthians 15:6,7).

Read: Matthew 28:16-20

I remember being appointed to a special 'Demonstration School' where I frequently taught under the watchful eye of groups of students from the local Teachers' College. The Inspector of schools responsible for my appointment gave me some 'marching orders' — 'Jim, if you let me down I will remember it when you apply for promotion!'

The Lord had appeared to his disciples many times, instructing them in the truth they were to take throughout the world. On one occasion he appeared to some five hundred witnesses. Thus there can be no doubt that Jesus was raised from the dead in a glorified body. He had told the disciples that it was for their benefit for him to return to heaven and give them the Holy Spirit in greater power than ever before (John 16:7).

The time had arrived for Christ to ascend to heaven and take his seat beside his heavenly Father, but before he departed he gave 'the Great Commission' to his disciples.

First, he said, 'All authority has been given to me in heaven and on earth.' No longer was he the abused, insulted, seemingly power-less 'Son of Man', but the divine Ruler of heaven and earth for all to see and fear. Paul wrote that God had 'put all things under his feet' (Ephesians 1:22). The Saviour we worship is the ruler of the universe.

Second, he died for his people and rose for their justification. This was the message the disciples had to preach wherever they went throughout the world. All Christians have the obligation to testify to the saving grace of the Lord. Jesus said, '...whoever confesses me before men, him the Son of Man also will confess before the angels of God' (Luke 12:8). The disciples were to teach biblical truth to all who came to saving faith. Today many people scorn doctrine. They have no true comprehension of 'justification' or 'sanctification' or other great divine truths. Christians are to be students of the Word of God and understand what they read. Do you?

All Christians are to keep God's commands — not out of a sense of obligation, but because they love God. Jesus said, 'If you love me, keep my commandments' (John 14:15).

Third, believers are to be baptized 'in the name of the Father and of the Son and of the Holy Spirit'. Notice that here we have baptism in the name of the triune God. That name is singular, yet there are three distinct Persons. This is our God.

Fourth, Christ promised his disciples and every believer that he would be with them always. This is a precious promise, especially during difficult days. The very name our Lord bears — 'Immanuel' — means 'God with us' (Matthew 1:23). He has promised, 'I will never leave you nor forsake you' (Hebrews 13:5).

THINGS TO DISCUSS WITH YOUR FAMILY

1. Why do we say God is triune?
2. In what way does Jesus use his absolute power?
3. How can our Saviour, who is in heaven, be with his people today?

Meditation

Meditate upon the almighty power exercised by the Saviour. Read Jeremiah 32:17 — 'Ah, Lord God! Behold, you have made the heavens and the earth by your great power and outstretched arm. There is nothing too hard for you.'

Wise Words

The Lord who vacated his tomb has not vacated his throne. *G. Beasley-Murray*

'Now it came to pass, while he blessed
them, that he was parted from them and
carried up into heaven' (Luke 24:51).

Read: Acts 1:1-11

All Christians should long for the return of the Lord Jesus. We read about that day in the Scriptures and should all be praying for his return. I yearn to see my Saviour — to look at him and praise him. Today you have read about his ascension into heaven.

During the forty days following his resurrection he had spent a great deal of time with the disciples opening their understanding of the Old Testament. He taught them what they needed to know in order to preach the truth and win disciples for him. They now understood the reason for their Lord's death and resurrection. They clearly saw the only way of salvation which was through Christ. Later Peter said to the people, 'Nor is there salvation in any other, for there is no other name under heaven given among men by which we must be saved' (Acts 4:12).

They were also told of the coming of the Holy Spirit in a greater power than they had ever known. Jesus said, 'But you shall receive power when the Holy Spirit has come upon you; and you shall be witnesses to me in Jerusalem, and in all Judea and Samaria, and to the end of the earth.' This was the great power they needed to carry out the commands of their Lord to take the gospel worldwide. The Holy Spirit would give them the courage they needed when facing persecution because of their faithful service.

When the disciples were with the Lord on the Mount of Olives, which was near Bethany, their last recorded question was, 'Lord, will you at this time restore the kingdom to Israel?' They were not given an answer that satisfied their curiosity. That issue was in the hands of God.

Then as Jesus blessed his disciples, he rose into the air, 'and a cloud received him out of their sight'. We can only imagine the amazement that filled the minds of those standing there that day. Then we read that two angels appeared who said, 'Men of Galilee, why do you stand gazing up into heaven? This same Jesus, who was taken up from you into heaven, will so come in like manner as you saw him go into heaven.' Here we have the promise that the same Lord will return one day. We must always be prepared for the majestic appearing of our Saviour. I often wonder if the Lord will return to that same area from which he left this world (Zechariah 14:4).

The disciples then returned to Jerusalem where they went to the temple and spent time praising God and no doubt preaching of Christ's resurrection and ascension to heaven. They had a great story to tell and so do all Christians. The world generally laughs about the second coming of the Lord, but may every Christian desire his return and pray that the day will be soon.

THINGS TO DISCUSS WITH YOUR FAMILY

1. What emotions do you think the disciples felt as they watched their Lord leave them?
2. Where did the Lord go when he ascended into the sky?
3. What did the disciples do when the Lord departed? (See Luke 24:51-53.)

Meditation

Meditate upon that majestic scene as the Lord left his disciples.

Wise Words

If Christ had not ascended he could have not interceded, as he now does in heaven for us. And do but take away Christ's intercession and you starve the hope of the saints.
John Flavel

'Who is he who condemns? It is Christ who died, and furthermore is also risen, who is even at the right hand of God, who also makes intercession for us' (Romans 8:34).

Read: Revelation 5:1-14

When Val and I are away on holidays we always send cards to our family letting them know how we are and what we are doing. Of necessity it is only possible to write a few words on a small card, but it is enough to whet their appetite for the full story when we get home.

Jesus ascended into heaven but we only have little information of what is happening in God's throne room. The glimpses we have are written in a language we can understand, but the full revelation must wait till we enter heaven. Jesus, the 'King of kings', ascended into heaven in a glorified body. He has all power both in heaven and on earth and, as God, had every right to take his seat on the heavenly throne beside his Father. This truth was prophesied in Psalm 2:6 where the psalmist records God's decree, 'I have set my King on my holy hill of Zion.' From the heavenly Zion Christ rules as King.

In the New Testament we read that Christ is seated on God's throne. Paul wrote that God, 'raised him from the dead and seated him at his right hand in the heavenly places, far above all principality and power and might and dominion, and every name that is named, not only in this age but also in that which is to come' (Ephesians 1:20,21). Peter likewise wrote of his Lord, 'who has gone into heaven and is at the right hand of God, angels and authorities and powers having been made subject to Him' (1 Peter 3:22).

Jesus, when standing before Pilate, had told him he was a king, and when crucified had the sign attached to the cross, 'THE KING OF THE JEWS' (Mark 15:26). The Jews hated that sign, but it spoke the truth and today our Lord wears a robe inscribed with the words, 'KING OF KINGS AND LORD OF LORDS' (Revelation 19:16).

In our reading we see that it was Christ alone who could approach God and take the scroll from his outstretched hand. That scroll was God's historical plan for the last days and only God's King could approach him as he did. However, I hope you noticed that he was given two titles — first 'the Lion of the tribe of Judah, the Root of David'. He was a true descendant of David and had the right to sit on David's kingly throne. Second he was called, 'a Lamb as though it had been slain'.

Christ is both the sacrifice for sin, the great High Priest of God, and King. No earthly priest could be King of Israel as kings and priests came from different tribes. Christ is both King and High Priest in one Person.

Jesus Christ rules the universe. I pray that he is both your King and Saviour.

THINGS TO DISCUSS WITH YOUR FAMILY

1. From what tribe did the kings of Israel come?
2. Why is Christ called 'the Lion of the tribe of Judah' (Revelation 5:5)?
3. Why can Jesus sit upon the throne of God?

Meditation

Meditate upon the words of Revelation 5:12 — 'Worthy is the Lamb who was slain to receive power and riches and wisdom, and strength and honour and glory and blessing!'

Wise Words

Certainly if we are to believe what our eyes see, then the kingdom of Christ seems to be on the verge of ruin. But [the] promise that Christ will never be dragged from his throne but that rather he will lay low all his enemies banishes from us all fear. *John Calvin*

'Now is the judgment of this world; now the ruler of this world will be cast out' (John 12:31).

Read: Revelation 12:7-12

Someone once wrote that war was 'hell on earth'. There is no doubt that war causes horrific harm to people and property. War is one of the results of sin and must surely cause Satan to rejoice.

Today you have read of another war — one in heaven — that resulted in another defeat of Satan, the arch enemy of Christ. In a language we can understand, John describes a heavenly vision where Satan's power is further curtailed. We shouldn't think of armies in heaven with our weapons of war causing havoc and great destruction.

In Job 1:6 we read, 'Now there was a day when the sons of God came to present themselves before the LORD, and Satan also came among them.' Then we read of the evil one accusing God of injustice in his dealings with Job. A similar situation is recorded in Zechariah 3. Satan is the accuser of the saints and this was particularly so before Christ's work of salvation. Prior to the Lord's atoning sacrifice, Satan could accuse God of injustice in allowing sinners into heaven without their sins being punished. He could also accuse God of injustice in blessing unbelievers who appeared to have no imputed righteousness.

Everything changed when Jesus went to the cross to pay sin's debt owed to God. He bore our hell and gave his people his perfect righteousness. Instead of the saints facing the eternal condemnation of God, they are received by him because they are united to Christ, the Saviour. Everything necessary for God's people to enter heaven and live in the presence of the heavenly Father has been accomplished by Jesus. No longer has Satan any right to accuse God of injustice.

The enemy of God and the saints was defeated. It was as if there was a war in heaven for Satan could no longer accuse the saints of the stain of sin that would bar them from entrance into God's presence. Satan's accusing mouth was effectively shut. The great angel Michael and his heavenly host forced Satan from God's presence and now he does his worst on earth. Yet here his power is limited. No longer is he able to deceive the nations (Revelation 20:3) as he did prior to the advent of Jesus. Yet he is still able to get about 'like a roaring lion, seeking whom he may devour' (1 Peter 5:8).

Satan's kingdom is under attack as never before and he is losing his citizens as they turn to Christ in repentance and saving faith. Jesus is victorious. Paul summed up Christ's victory saying, 'And you, being dead in your trespasses and the uncircumcision of your flesh, he has made alive together with him, having forgiven you all trespasses ... Having disarmed principalities and powers, he made a public spectacle of them, triumphing over them in it' (Colossians 2:13,15).

THINGS TO DISCUSS WITH YOUR FAMILY

1. Of what could Satan once accuse the saints living in heaven? Revelation 12:10.
2. What prevented any more accusations being made against God's people?
3. In what way is Satan's power limited today? Read Revelation 20:3.

Meditation

Meditate upon Satan's loss of accusing power against the saints because of Christ's atonement for sin.

Wise Words

Satan is 'hurled down from heaven' in this sense, namely that he has lost his place as an accuser of the brethren.
William Hendriksen

'...Jesus, having become High Priest for ever according to the order of Melchize-dek' (Hebrews 6:20).

Read: Hebrews 4:14 – 5:10

Today many who claim to be ministers of God take to themselves the title 'priest' which sets them apart from the rest of their flock, but the Bible tells us that all of God's people are priests. Peter wrote of the saints that we are 'a holy priesthood, to offer up spiritual sacrifices acceptable to God through Jesus Christ' (1 Peter 2:5). We are to 'continually offer the sacrifice of praise to God, that is, the fruit of our lips, giving thanks to his name' (Hebrews 13:15).

Jesus is our great heavenly High Priest, so unlike the priests of Israel. David wrote of Christ's priesthood, 'You are a priest for ever according to the order of Melchizedek' (Psalm 110:4).

Jesus was appointed Priest by God and was ordained to that position when he was baptized. As priest he is so unlike those priests descended from Aaron. First he is without sin and didn't have to offer a sacrifice for his own transgressions as Israel's high priest did. Unlike the priests of Israel who daily offered sacrifices for the people's sin, Jesus did this 'once for all' (Hebrews 7:27). By his very presence in heaven he is our permanent advocate before his Father.

In Romans 8:34 we read, 'Who is he who condemns? It is Christ who died, and furthermore is also risen, who is even at the right hand of God, who also makes intercession for us.' As our High Priest he understands our situation and needs, and shows love and compassion for those he calls his own. We read, 'For we do not have a High Priest who cannot sympathise with our weaknesses, but was in all points tempted as we are, yet without sin. Let us therefore come boldly to the throne of grace, that we may obtain mercy and find grace to help in time of need' (Hebrews 4:15,16).

Christ knows our needs and when we pray he gives us the grace we need to cope with our situations. What he gives might be so different to what we ask or expect, but he is God and provides blessings perfectly suited to our needs. How Christ intercedes for his people we cannot truly comprehend, but he takes our prayers and presents them to his heavenly Father, who answers according to his glory, our need, and for the sake of his beloved Son, Jesus Christ. Our High Priest is most compassionate so we must approach him with a purified heart and the desire to see God glorified. He told his disciples, 'And whatever you ask in my name, that I will do, that the Father may be glorified in the Son' (John 14:13).

Our High Priest gives gifts to his people and one of the most wonderful is the regenerating power of the Holy Spirit. Indeed one of Christ's first gifts to the infant church on the day of Pentecost was the Holy Spirit.

May Christ, our great High Priest greatly bless you.

THINGS TO DISCUSS WITH YOUR FAMILY

1. Who was Melchizedek? Read Genesis 14:17–20.
2. What is the work of Jesus as High Priest?
3. In what way is Jesus, the High Priest, different to Israel's earthly high priests?

Meditation

Think upon — 'Christ gives mercy for past failure and grace for present and future work.'

Wise Words

Prayer as it comes from the saint is weak and languid; but when the arrow of a saint's prayer is put into the bow of Christ's intercession it pierces the throne of grace.

Thomas Watson

'So Jesus said to them, "Assuredly I say to you, that in the regeneration, when the Son of Man sits on the throne of his glory, you who have followed me will also sit on twelve thrones, judging the twelve tribes of Israel"' (Matthew 19:28).

Read: Acts 1:12-36

I don't know about you, but I always like to replace anything broken or lost as soon as possible. When I discover that a book I need is nowhere to be found, I send off an order for a replacement almost at once.

Our text tells us that the twelve apostles would one day sit upon twelve thrones judging the twelve tribes of Israel. The risen Lord had appeared to the disciples and they had seen him ascend into heaven. The small Christian church in Jerusalem gathered in a large room where much time was spent in prayer, anticipating the promised outpouring of the Holy Spirit.

Judas, who had betrayed his Master, had committed suicide. Peter, knowing the prophecy of Psalm 109:8 — '...let another take his office' — realized that it was necessary to replace him with another who would take Judas' place with the remaining eleven disciples.

He spoke to the one hundred and twenty present, indicating the requirements of the one to replace Judas: 'Therefore, of these men who have accompanied us all the time that the Lord Jesus went in and out among us, beginning from the baptism of John to that day when he was taken up from us, one of these must become a witness with us of his resurrection.' The preaching recorded in the book of Acts included frequent references to the risen Christ. The disciples were living proof that Christ had been raised from the dead and was indeed the Saviour of believers.

Before a choice was made the believers spent time in prayer. This should teach us that before we make important decisions we should spend time on our knees seeking guidance from the Lord. We need sanctified common sense in making decisions. We should seek the advice of godly friends, elders and wise Christians as well as carefully reading the Scriptures, especially those relevant sections.

We are told that 'they cast their lots.' Maybe this means they voted, but it could also mean that the decision was left in the hands of the Lord by throwing two markers, each bearing the name of one man. In Proverbs 16:33 we read, 'The lot is cast into the lap, but its every decision is from the LORD.'

The choice was Matthias, and he was then numbered with the twelve, but we don't find him again mentioned in the Scriptures. Nevertheless, the number of apostles was restored to twelve as required by the Lord.

THINGS TO DISCUSS WITH YOUR FAMILY

1. Why was Judas to be replaced?
2. Name the two men put forward to replace Judas. What were their special qualifications?
3. What are we taught in Proverbs 16:33?

Meditation

Meditate upon Daniel 4:35 — 'All the inhabitants of the earth are reputed as nothing; he does according to his will in the army of heaven and among the inhabitants of the earth. No one can restrain his hand or say to him, "What have you done?"'

Wise Words

To leave all and follow Jesus is the biggest thing that a living soul on this earth can do.   *A. Lindsay Glegg*

'And it shall come to pass afterward that I will pour out my Spirit on all flesh; your sons and your daughters shall prophesy, your old men shall dream dreams, your young men shall see visions. And also on my menservants and on my maidservants I will pour out my Spirit in those days' (Joel 2:28,29).

Read: Acts 2:1-13

Do you recall Nicodemus going to the Lord one night where he was taught the necessity of being born again? He was told that this was the work of the Holy Spirit. The Apostle Paul later wrote comforting words to Christians, '...do you not know that your body is the temple of the Holy Spirit who is in you, whom you have from God, and you are not your own?' (1 Corinthians 6:19). We also are told in 1 Corinthians 3:16, 'Do you not know that you are the temple of God and that the Spirit of God dwells in you?' The Holy Spirit is God, one Person of the Godhead with the Father and the Son.

The Holy Spirit has always brought about the new birth in God's people of all ages and given gifts to people, but with the coming of Jesus, John the Baptist said, 'I indeed baptize you with water unto repentance, but he who is coming after me is mightier than I, whose sandals I am not worthy to carry. He will baptize you with the Holy Spirit and fire' (Matthew 3:11). The special outpouring of the Holy Spirit prophesied by Joel took place on the day of Pentecost which fell on the first day of the week — the resurrection day.

You have read of the noise made by the Spirit and the appearance of tongues of fire, all of which caused alarm in Jerusalem among those who heard the unusual sound. The disciples and the members of the Jerusalem church had been praying for this promised gift of God and now they rejoiced in that they had been given special power and courage to take the gospel worldwide. We read of instances where the disciples needed courage to preach with boldness and they sought extra spiritual power from God — 'And when they had prayed, the place where they were assembled together was shaken; and they were all filled with the Holy Spirit, and they spoke the word of God with boldness' (Acts 4:31).

Initially they were given the gift of speaking in foreign languages which was valuable at that time, for many foreigners were in Jerusalem for the feast of Pentecost. However, without learning the languages of the people, the disciples 'gossiped the gospel' to the people they met.

The Holy Spirit's 'fruit' filled the hearts of all believers — '...love, joy, peace, long-suffering, kindness, goodness, faithfulness, gentleness, self-control' (Galatians 5:22, 23).

Another sovereign work of the Holy Spirit is to give gifts to believers. If you read 1 Corinthians 12 you will be well taught about this subject, but you will notice that the greatest gift of the Spirit is love (1 Corinthians 13:13).

We must examine our hearts to ensure that the fruit of the Spirit is there in some measure. If we are not growing spiritually we might not be indwelt by God's Spirit.

THINGS TO DISCUSS WITH YOUR FAMILY

1. Make a list of the works of the Holy Spirit.
2. How do you know that the Holy Spirit is God?
3. How do you know if you are a Christian?

Meditation

Consider the gifts the Holy Spirit has given you. Are they being used?

Wise Words

The fruit of the Spirit is not excitement or orthodoxy: it is *character*.   G. B. Duncan

'My little children, these things I write to you, so that you may not sin. And if anyone sins, we have an Advocate with the Father, Jesus Christ the righteous. And he himself is the propitiation for our sins...' (1 John 2:1,2).

Read: Romans 4:13-25

You may have heard the saying, 'Commit the crime, then do the time.' When people are charged with a crime, brought before the court and found guilty they are given a sentence. Most accused people have an advocate — a lawyer — to represent them in court and plead their case.

All people are sinners and without Christ will suffer eternal punishment in the place prepared for the devil and his demons. However, all of God's people have an Advocate in heaven — the Lord Jesus Christ, who sits on God's throne. He is the Saviour of sinners and has made it possible for them to become citizens of heaven. Our text tells us that Jesus Christ is 'the propitiation for our sins'. He certainly died bearing the sins of his people and by this atoning sacrifice turned the wrath of God to himself.

If we are believers, he is now our Advocate. How he carries out this work is not revealed, but we are told he intercedes for us in the courtroom of heaven.

The day we believed in Christ as our Lord and Redeemer there was a court hearing in heaven. We were charged with breaking God's law. Satan could point to our guilty conscience and the law that we had defiled and declare, 'That person is guilty and deserves eternal hell.'

However, we have an Advocate, Jesus Christ, who states, 'I have paid the penalty for the sins of that person. He is mine and my righteousness has been put to his account. He is righteous in the sight of God, the Judge.'

Because of the permanent presence of our Advocate, God accepts us as forgiven and righteous, all because of the atoning work of his Son. So Paul could write, 'For he [God] made him [Jesus] who knew no sin to be sin for us, that we might become the righteousness of God in him' (2 Corinthians 5:21).

Now we can say with the apostle, 'Who shall bring a charge against God's elect? It is God who justifies. Who is he who condemns? It is Christ who died, and furthermore is also risen, who is even at the right hand of God, who also makes intercession for us' (Romans 8:33,34). Again Paul wrote comforting words for Christ's people: 'And you, being dead in your trespasses and the uncircumcision of your flesh, he has made alive together with him, having forgiven you all trespasses, having wiped out the handwriting of requirements that was against us, which was contrary to us. And he has taken it out of the way, having nailed it to the cross' (Colossians 2:13,14).

Our Advocate is in heaven assuring us of our eternal security in himself. Praise God!

THINGS TO DISCUSS WITH YOUR FAMILY

1. How can God look upon a sinner as being innocent?
2. In what way is Christ our Advocate?
3. What is justification?

Meditation

Meditate upon the purity of Christ that has been imputed to you.

Wise Words

Justification, therefore, is no other than an acquittal from guilt of him who was accused, as though his innocence has been proved. Since God, therefore, justifies us through the mediation of Christ, he acquits us, not by an admission of our personal innocence, but by an imputation of righteousness; so that we, who are unrighteous in ourselves, are considered as righteous in Christ. *John Calvin*

'Then Jesus said, "Father, forgive them,
for they do not know what they do"'
(Luke 23:34).

Read: Acts 2:14-39

Often after worship we discuss the preacher's sermon. There are
times when we are greatly blessed by the teaching. If there is
little blessing we may be to blame for failing to pray more diligently
for the power of the Holy Spirit to accompany the words we hear.

It was the day of Pentecost, fifty days after the Passover feast, the
first day of the week and the Lord had just sent the Holy Spirit in
awesome power upon the disciples to equip them for the evangelistic
work that lay before them. We should remember that we live in the
age of the Holy Spirit and that same courage and power is available
to every Christian. Our problem often is that we try to solve our
own difficulties and fail to seek the divine help of God's Spirit, the
Comforter, who is God's Advocate on earth.

The disciples were given the gift of speaking in foreign languages, but because of the events surrounding the outpouring of the Spirit
they were accused of being drunk.

Peter, filled with the Spirit and surrounded by the other eleven
disciples, began to explain to the crowd what had happened. He told
his large congregation that the prophecy of Joel had been fulfilled.
Then he rebuked the people for their involvement in the murder of
Jesus, who had proved by his miracles and teaching that he was the
Messiah. He went on to say that the Lord who was 'delivered by the
determined purpose and foreknowledge of God, you have taken by
lawless hands, have crucified, and put to death; whom God raised up,
having loosed the pains of death, because it was not possible that he
should be held by it'.

Peter used the Old Testament to prove that Jesus would rise from
the grave and ascend to heaven to sit upon God's throne. The Holy
Spirit convicted a great number who were listening to him. They saw
their guilt and called out to the disciples, 'Men and brethren, what
shall we do?'

Peter's reply was straightforward, 'Repent, and let every one of you be baptized in the name of Jesus Christ for the remission of sins; and you shall receive the gift of the Holy Spirit.' This is what we must do if we wish to be saved. We must be sincerely repentant of all of our sins, which is only possible if we are born again. The Holy Spirit also gives us saving faith. We are then adopted into God's family and become citizens of the Kingdom of Heaven.

That day about three thousand people were converted and baptized. The Holy Spirit's power was exercised and the small church began to grow. Christ's prayer as he was being crucified was answered and many who wanted him dead now found eternal life in him. Have you?

THINGS TO DISCUSS WITH YOUR FAMILY

1. Where did the new converts hold their worship services? Read Acts 2:46.
2. Why did three thousand people repent of their sins?
3. Where did Peter say that Jesus was?

Meditation

Meditate upon your understanding of repentance. Read 2 Corinthians 7:10 — 'For godly sorrow produces repentance leading to salvation, not to be regretted; but the sorrow of the world produces death.'

Sinners need nothing more than pardon.

William Plumer

Wise Words

'As for Saul, he made havoc of the
church, entering every house, and drag-
ging off men and women, committing
them to prison' (Acts 8:3).

Read: Acts 9:1-19

As I look about our congregation it never ceases to amaze me
those God has called into union with his Son. The greatest surprise is that I am in that group. Some are big, others small, some
brilliant, most average, men and women, boys and girls and people
from a variety of countries and backgrounds. Yet there are very, very
few 'great' people in our churches. Paul wrote about God's election
to salvation: 'For you see your calling, brethren, that not many wise
according to the flesh, not many mighty, not many noble, are called.
But God has chosen the foolish things of the world to put to shame
the wise, and God has chosen the weak things of the world to put
to shame the things which are mighty.' Why is this so? Again Paul
wrote, '...that no flesh should glory in his presence' (1 Corinthians
1:26,27,29).

Saul, who became the Apostle Paul, hated Christianity and as
our text tells us, did all he could to destroy the church. He was a
proud Pharisee (Philippians 3:1-9), a citizen of the Roman Empire
and feared by believers — a most unlikely person to become a Christian, let alone the greatest missionary to the Gentiles there ever was.

Nevertheless, he was God's man and while travelling to Damascus where he intended to arrest Christians he suddenly saw a great
light and heard the risen Christ's voice, 'Saul, Saul, why are you persecuting me?' Here we learn that to persecute and harm a Christian
is the same as attacking the Lord himself. The saints are his body and
united to him by faith. Suddenly the proud Saul was face down on
the ground 'trembling and astonished'. Blinded, he was led to the
home of Judas and there a disciple named Ananias touched him, re-
storing his sight.

Saul now realized his sin and when in the presence of Ananias
he stood up, was baptized and received the Holy Spirit, giving him
courage and strength to fulfil what God said he was to do — '...he is

a chosen vessel of mine to bear my name before Gentiles, kings, and the children of Israel'.

Paul spent time in several countries (Galatians 1:15-22), even being taken into heaven where he saw the risen Christ (2 Corinthians 12:2-4). The compassionate, loving Jesus Christ was ruling the world from God's throne room. Now Saul would be his servant as the Apostle Paul, possibly replacing the martyred James. He would work to spread the good news he had seen concerning the risen Christ.

If you are a Christian, have you ever given God thanks for his electing love in making you one of his disciples? Christ is still ruling this world and one day he will return in splendour and majestic power. Are you ready for that day?

THINGS TO DISCUSS WITH YOUR FAMILY

1. Why did God make Saul an apostle?
2. Why was Saul on the road to Damascus?
3. Read and discuss Matthew 25:45 — 'Then he will answer them, saying, "Assuredly, I say to you, inasmuch as you did not do it to one of the least of these, you did not do it to me."'

Meditation

Meditate upon 1 Corinthians 10:31 — 'Therefore, whether you eat or drink, or whatever you do, do all to the glory of God.'

Wise Words

The saved are singled out not by their own merits, but by the grace of the Mediator. *Martin Luther*

'This same Jesus, who was taken up from you into heaven, will so come in like manner as you saw him go into heaven' (Acts 1:11).

Read: 2 Peter 3:1-14

Many people have made predictions concerning the date when Christ is to return to our planet despite Jesus saying, 'But of that day and hour no one knows, not even the angels in heaven, nor the Son, but only the Father' (Matthew 24:36). Nevertheless he had a lot to say about his second coming. He promised his disciples, and every believer, 'And if I go and prepare a place for you, I will come again and receive you to myself; that where I am, there you may be also' (John 14:3).

Peter prophesied that Christians would be mocked for their belief that Christ will come again — 'Where is the promise of his coming? For since the fathers fell asleep, all things continue as they were from the beginning of creation.'

The words of our text were spoken by the angels who were present when the Lord ascended to heaven. They give us the assurance that Jesus will come again. His return will be sudden just as Peter described — 'as a thief in the night'. We must all be ready for that day, for in the parable of the ten virgins, the Lord taught that it will be too late to beg for salvation when he appears in his majestic glory. In one of his parables Jesus said of his people that they must be ever ready for his return (Matthew 24:45-51). How then should we live in anticipation of the Lord's coming?

We are called to be faithful servants, making good use of the gifts the Holy Spirit has given us. In a parable Jesus said that those who were obedient would be rewarded, but those who hid their 'talent' would suffer the anger of God — 'And cast the unprofitable servant into the outer darkness. There will be weeping and gnashing of teeth' (Matthew 25:30). The world says, 'Eat, drink and be merry for tomorrow you die' but Peter has told us to prepare for the Lord's return by living a life of holiness and godliness. We must beware of Satan's temptations: 'Be sober, be vigilant; because your adversary the

devil walks about like a roaring lion, seeking whom he may devour'
(1 Peter 5:8).

The new heavens and earth is our eternal home 'in which righteousness dwells'. We should be praying continually for the sanctifying
work of the Holy Spirit to make us Christlike.

Our life of obedience must flow from a heart that loves God and
our fellow man. Peter said that we must be 'found by [God] in peace,
without spot and blameless' which means that our faith in Christ
must be genuine. We need the imputed righteousness of Christ in
order to be found 'without spot and blameless', but holy living is our
preparation for God's Paradise.

Are you making preparations for the Lord's return when you
will see your Saviour face to face? Do you pray, 'Even so, come, Lord
Jesus!'? (Revelation 22:20).

THINGS TO DISCUSS
WITH YOUR FAMILY

1. How can you find peace with God?
2. When will Jesus return to planet earth?
3. What can you do to prepare for the Lord's
   return?

Meditation

Think about Paul's words: 'For our citizenship is in heav-
en, from which we also eagerly wait for the Saviour, the
Lord Jesus Christ, who will transform our lowly body
that it may be conformed to his glorious body' (Philippians 3:20,21).

Wise Words

The fact that Jesus Christ is to come again is not a reason
for stargazing, but for the working in the power of the
Holy Spirit. *Charles Spurgeon*

'Little children, it is the last hour; and as you have heard that the Antichrist is coming, even now many antichrists have come, by which we know that it is the last hour' (1 John 2:18).

Read: 2 Timothy 3:1-9

Usually before we visit people we let them know when we will be arriving. If it is in the future we ring to remind them that we will soon be on our way. Jesus gave us all some very clear statements that he would soon return to this world and the Apostle Peter gave us instructions of how we should prepare for that day.

Not everyone agrees with the events that must take place before Christ again breaks into history, but we will look at several. First Peter was told that he would die on a cross (John 21:18) which meant the Lord would not return before he was martyred.

Second, we read that there will arise one named 'Antichrist' who as Satan's representative will do much harm to the church, the bride of Christ. If you read 2 Thessalonians 2:1-12 you will find that this 'man of sin' 'exalts himself above all that is called God or that is worshipped, so that he sits as God in the temple of God, showing himself that he is God' (2 Thessalonians 2:3,4). He wants to do what Satan attempted when he rebelled against God (Isaiah 14:12-15). Daniel wrote of this evil representative of Satan saying that he had 'a mouth speaking pompous words' (Daniel 7:8).

Third, the antichrist will attempt to destroy the church. Daniel wrote that he would 'persecute the saints of the Most High' (Daniel 7:25). The Apostle John wrote of the end of this age, 'It was granted to him to make war with the saints and to overcome them' (Revelation 13:7). However the victory belongs to our Saviour, for we read that a day is coming when 'the lawless one will be revealed, whom the Lord will consume with the breath of his mouth and destroy with the brightness of his coming' (2 Thessalonians 2:8).

Fourth, Paul wrote of the chaotic state of human society during the world's last days. He described this age as 'perilous times'. The gospel will be preached throughout the world by missionaries and other saints energized by the almighty power of the Holy Spirit.

God's people will be gathered from the four corners of the globe. Prior to the first coming of Jesus it was really only the Jews who had a knowledge of the true and living God, but during this age the gospel has been preached to the Gentiles, and for this we should thank God. When Israel rejected the Lord Jesus as Messiah, Paul wrote, '... salvation has come to the Gentiles' (Romans 11:11).

Finally I believe we can look for a time of spiritual blessings upon the descendants of Abraham for again Paul wrote 'that hardening in part has happened to Israel until the fullness of the Gentiles has come in' (Romans 11:25). Such a revival will mean great blessings throughout the world (Romans 11:12). The return of the Lord will certainly come to pass, so keep watching and praying for the arrival of that day.

THINGS TO DISCUSS WITH YOUR FAMILY

1. What will Antichrist do to the true church of God?
2. Why was the gospel preached to the Gentiles?
3. Is there to be any difference in daily Christian living and our behaviour immediately prior to the Lord's return?

Meditation

Meditate upon the events to happen before the Lord returns. Pray for Christ's coming.

Wise Words

I never begin my work in the morning without thinking that perhaps *he* may interrupt my work and begin his own. I am not looking for death, I am looking for him.

G. *Campbell Morgan*

'Behold, he is coming with clouds, and every eye will see him, even they who pierced him' (Revelation 1:7).

Read: Revelation 6:12-17

The world has mocked Christians for believing that their Saviour, the Lord Jesus Christ, will one day return. We are given some glimpses of what that day will be like, but I know it will be far more glorious than any of us can possibly imagine.

One day when everything is going along normally, history will come to an end, because Christ will appear in his majestic glory bearing the title, 'KING OF KINGS AND LORD OF LORDS' (Revelation 19:16). This day will be a day of unimaginable joy for the saints, but horror for the ungodly. It will be a day when the universe begins to fall apart in preparation for the making of the 'new heavens and new earth in which righteousness dwells' (2 Peter 3:13).

The Apostle John was given a vision of the day of the Lord. In our reading we have seen that there will be a great earthquake. Of that earthquake he later described it as being 'such a mighty and great earthquake as had not occurred since men were on the earth' (Revelation 16:18).

The sky will become strangely dark and Isaiah wrote, 'All the host of heaven shall be dissolved, and the heavens shall be rolled up like a scroll; all their host shall fall down as the leaf falls from the vine, and as fruit falling from a fig tree' (Isaiah 34:4). Try and imagine the scene — the blue sky being rolled up like a scroll, a shaking earth, thunder, lightning, stars falling and the moon like a ball of blood hanging in the heavens.

Then, surrounded by his mighty angels (2 Thessalonians 1:7) — the armies of heaven (Revelation 19:14) — the Lord himself will descend. There will be the shout of triumph, 'the voice of an archangel, and ... the trumpet of God' (1 Thessalonians 4:16). This is a picture of terror for those people from all social groups who mocked Christians for many years. John wrote, 'And the kings of the earth, the great men, the rich men, the commanders, the mighty men, every slave and every free man, hid themselves in the caves and in the rocks of the mountains, and said to the mountains and rocks, "Fall on us and hide us from the face of him who sits on the throne and from the wrath of the Lamb.'"

The door of grace will be firmly closed and despite the fearful plea, 'Lord, Lord, open to us!' they will hear the Lord's reply, 'I do not know you' (Matthew 25:11,12).

Another group will accompany the returning Lord for Paul tells us, 'For if we believe that Jesus died and rose again, even so God will bring with him those who sleep in Jesus' (1 Thessalonians 4:14). The Bible doesn't teach 'soul sleep' but the conscious existence of those whose bodies 'sleep in Jesus'. We read of them speaking to God, 'How long, O Lord, holy and true, until you judge and avenge our blood on those who dwell on the earth?' (Revelation 6:10).

Are you ready for the day of the Lord?

THINGS TO DISCUSS WITH YOUR FAMILY

1. Make a list of some of the events that will take place when the Lord returns.
2. Discuss 'Satan aims directly at the throat of the church when he destroys faith in the coming Christ' (John Calvin).
3. What are we taught about the souls of those saints who have died?

Meditation

Meditate upon the scene when the Lord breaks into the affairs of this world a second time.

Wise Words

Oh, that the Lord would come! He is coming! He is on the road and travelling quickly. The sound of his approach should be as music to our hearts.   *C. H. Spurgeon*

'Not only that, but we also who have the firstfruits of the Spirit, even we ourselves groan within ourselves, eagerly waiting for the adoption, the redemption of our body' (Romans 8:23).

Read: I Corinthians 15:35-58

Only yesterday we received a phone call from Christian friends who had purchased two cemetery plots of land next to the ones Val and I had purchased. They were very excited as we would rise together to meet the Lord when he returns. I am very much looking forward to the resurrection day as it will mean I will see and be with my Lord. The saints will have glorified bodies like that of their Saviour and when our souls and resurrected bodies are united, our salvation will be complete. Christ's atoning sacrifice was to redeem his people, body and soul, and we should be eagerly awaiting 'the redemption of our body' (Romans 8:23). Even the world will be changed and there will be a 'new heavens and a new earth in which righteousness dwells' (2 Peter 3:13).

The Scriptures are very clear concerning the resurrection of Christ. Paul wrote, 'He was buried, and ... rose again the third day according to the Scriptures' (1 Corinthians 15:4).

When Jesus returns, he will be accompanied by his army of mighty angels and the souls of the saints who died before the moment of his return. In 1 Thessalonians 4:16 we read, 'For the Lord himself will descend from heaven with a shout, with the voice of an archangel, and with the trumpet of God. And the dead in Christ will rise first.' Try to imagine Christ appearing in majestic glory. Suddenly the busiest place on earth will be the local cemeteries and every place where people have been buried. Every particle of every person's body will be miraculously gathered and changed into a new body, 'some to everlasting life, some to shame and everlasting contempt' (Daniel 12:2).

When the dead bodies come forth from their resting places to be united with their souls, those who are still alive will be changed. In today's reading Paul described the change that will be effected upon the living saints — 'We shall not all sleep, but we shall all be changed — in a moment, in the twinkling of an eye, at the last trumpet. For the trumpet will sound, and the dead will be raised incorruptible, and we shall be changed. For this corruptible must put on incorruption, and this mortal must put on immortality.'

Christians will rise to meet the descending Lord. Our bodies will be glorified — perfect in every respect. All my pains will have gone and I won't need my daily morphine medication. Our bodies will be recognizable and we will know one another. Doubting Thomas recognized Christ by his body, still bearing the nail prints in his hands. Our bodies will have abilities and qualities beyond anything we can imagine.

It will be a glorious time. Are you ready for this day? But remember it will be followed by the day of judgement!

THINGS TO DISCUSS WITH YOUR FAMILY

1. What is the 'resurrection'?
2. What will your resurrected body be like?
3. When can we say that our salvation is complete?

Meditation

Meditate upon John 5:28,29 — 'Do not marvel at this; for the hour is coming in which all who are in the graves will hear his voice and come forth — those who have done good, to the resurrection of life, and those who have done evil, to the resurrection of condemnation.'

Wise Words

Our bodies shall be *like* Christ's glorious body, not *equal* to it.   *Richard Sibbes*

'There is therefore now no condemnation to those who are in Christ Jesus' (Romans 8:1).

Read: Revelation 20:10-15

Those who are to appear in court, having been charged with a crime, usually tremble with fear, especially if they know they are guilty and there is plenty of evidence to be used against them. There are some Christians who at times fear the judgement day, but this should not be so. In today's text Paul tells us plainly — 'There is therefore now no condemnation to those who are in Christ Jesus' (Romans 8:1).

Despite their sins all saints know that they have been forgiven as their Saviour has redeemed them and given them his righteousness, throwing open the door of their heavenly home. However, we must all appear before the judgement seat, upon which is seated our Saviour, the Lord Jesus Christ. We read in Acts 17:31 that God 'has appointed a day on which he will judge the world in righteousness by the Man whom he has ordained. He has given assurance of this to all by raising him from the dead.'

From your reading it is clear that every person who has ever lived will appear before the judgement seat. We are told 'it is appointed for men to die once, but after this the judgement' (Hebrews 9:27). We will all stand before Christ to give an account of our lives. Jesus spoke of the great judgement where the 'sheep' will be separated from the 'goats'. Here it is taught that there are just two groups of people on judgement day — the saved, who are born again, love God and have been faithful servants of the Lord; and the unsaved, who have lived for themselves.

Jesus describes the great dividing line between saved and unsaved: 'Most assuredly, I say to you, he who hears my word and believes in him who sent me has everlasting life, and shall not come into judgement, but has passed from death into life' (John 5:24). It is saving faith in Christ that matters.

We will each hear one of the two sentences — 'Depart from me, you cursed, into the everlasting fire prepared for the devil and his angels' (Matthew 25:41), or, 'Come, you blessed of my Father, inherit the kingdom prepared for you from the foundation of the world' (Matthew 25:34).

We will give an account of the use we have made of God's gifts and all faithful servants will be rewarded (Matthew 25:14-30; 24:45-51). We will be judged according to our deeds and rewarded on the basis of our works of love (Romans 2:6-10). However, we should remember that all those things we have done in secret, hoping that no one knows, will be revealed. Paul wrote of 'the day when God will judge the secrets of men by Jesus Christ' (Romans 2:16). Even the thoughts of our hearts will be examined by God.

Jesus said that 'every idle word men may speak, they will give an account of it in the day of judgement' (Matthew 12:36).

THINGS TO DISCUSS WITH YOUR FAMILY

1. Why should the saints not fear the judgement day?
2. Why should the ungodly fear facing Christ on the day of judgement?
3. In some way the saints will be involved with Christ in judgement. Read and discuss 1 Corinthians 6:2,3a.

Meditation

Meditate upon the words of Ecclesiastes 12:14 — 'For God will bring every work into judgement, including every secret thing, whether good or evil.'

Wise Words

We shall have to render an account of every privilege that was granted to us and of every ray of light that we enjoyed.   *J. C. Ryle*

'But the cowardly, unbelieving, abomi-
nable, murderers, sexually immoral, sor-
cerers, idolaters, and all liars shall have
their part in the lake which burns with
fire and brimstone, which is the second
death' (Revelation 21:8).

Read: Revelation 14:6-11; 18:21-23; 20:10-15

I'm sure you have heard people rudely say to someone they don't
like, 'You can go to hell!' If someone says this to you remember
that they have no authority to say such a thing and they do not have
the power to carry out their threat. There is just one who can carry
out this sentence and that is Jesus Christ, the Judge of all mankind.

We have looked at the day of judgement and those who receive
the sentence, 'Depart from me, you cursed, into the everlasting fire
prepared for the devil and his angels' (Matthew 25:41). They will be
escorted to the place of God's eternal punishment, and there suffer
the eternal anger of an offended God. Satan and his demons will have
their place in the lake of fire as well.

Hell has been described in many ways — 'the lake of fire' (Revelation 20:15), 'outer darkness' (Matthew 25:30), and 'the bottomless
pit' (Revelation 20:3). Hell is endless punishment as is clearly taught
in Revelation 14:11: 'And the smoke of their torment ascends for
ever and ever; and they have no rest day or night, who worship the
beast and his image, and whoever receives the mark of his name.'
Beware of those people who teach that such a place does not exist,
or claim that those who are sentenced there will be given a second
chance to escape the clutches of the eternal flames. Also turn away
from those who claim the Bible teaches annihilation.

I have heard foolish people say that hell won't be too bad as
they'll have a lot of mates there. However, the Scriptures are clear that
there is nothing pleasant in 'outer darkness'. In a vision John noticed
that those things that made life happy were missing — 'The sound of
harpists, musicians, flutists, and trumpeters shall not be heard in you
anymore. No craftsman of any craft shall be found in you anymore,
and the sound of a millstone shall not be heard in you anymore.
The light of a lamp shall not shine in you anymore, and the voice of

bridegroom and bride shall not be heard in you anymore' (Revelation 18:22,23).

Jesus taught that there are degrees of punishment in perdition for he said, 'And that servant who knew his master's will, and did not prepare himself or do according to his will, shall be beaten with many stripes. But he who did not know, yet committed things deserving of stripes, shall be beaten with few. For everyone to whom much is given, from him much will be required; and to whom much has been committed, of him they will ask the more' (Luke 12:47,48).

One aspect of punishment for those confined to 'outer darkness' is that they will see the saints enjoying the presence of Christ. While they gnash their teeth in anger so many will utter those sad words, 'If only...' The only way to escape eternal damnation is a saving faith in the Lord Jesus Christ.

THINGS TO DISCUSS WITH YOUR FAMILY

1. Why are people sentenced to eternal hell?
2. What can you do to escape being sentenced to hell?
3. Discuss the factors that make hell so unpleasant.

Meditation

Meditate upon Christ's words in Luke 16:26 — '...between us and you there is a great gulf fixed, so that those who want to pass from here to you cannot, nor can those from there pass to us.'

There are no agnostics in hell.   *Geoffrey B. Wilson*

Wise Words

'Let us be glad and rejoice and give him glory, for the marriage of the Lamb has come, and his wife has made herself ready' (Revelation 19:7).

Read: Revelation 21:1-7

There are times when people will tell you that life is heavenly or possibly they have returned from visiting some lovely spot which they call 'Paradise'. There is no heaven on earth until Christ returns and remakes this world. Then we will have the new heavens and new earth. This remoulded world will be bliss to all who inhabit it, because sin, the cause of all distress, will be gone for ever.

The most wonderful aspect of the new heavens and earth will be seeing Jesus, our Saviour. We are told that 'when he is revealed, we shall be like him, for we shall see him as he is' (1 John 3:2). In our glorified bodies and souls we will have perfect fellowship with Jesus and the saints from all ages. We will be clothed in the Lord's righteousness and have a vision of the purity, holiness, majesty and love of God in Christ. The great wedding feast speaks of the wonderful fellowship that will take place between the saints and Jesus. What stories we will hear and how we will praise God for his electing love!

Jesus told his disciples that there would be dwelling places for all the saints (John 14:2,3). Many saints have suffered terribly on earth, but in heaven God will give them all they need. Heaven is a place of rest, which does not mean that we will sit about and do nothing, but rather it will be a rest from the battle with sin and the temptations of the world. No longer will persecutors cause distress and murder. There will be peace between all inhabitants and between God and his people. No more will God discipline his children. Peace will extend to the animals for we read, 'The wolf also shall dwell with the lamb, the leopard shall lie down with the young goat, the calf and the young lion and the fatling together; and a little child shall lead them. The cow and the bear shall graze; their young ones shall lie down together; and the lion shall eat straw like the ox. The nursing child shall play by the cobra's hole, and the weaned child shall put his hand in the viper's den' (Isaiah 11:6-8).

All that caused distress and hurt on earth will be gone for we read, 'And God will wipe away every tear from their eyes; there shall be no more death, nor sorrow, nor crying. There shall be no more pain, for the former things have passed away.' Our Saviour will have totally overthrown Satan, the cause of all that is unpleasant.

Just as there are degrees of punishment in hell, so also there are levels of reward in heaven. This is taught in the parable of the talents (Matthew 25:14-30). Paul wrote, 'For we must all appear before the judgement seat of Christ, that each one may receive the things done in the body, according to what he has done, whether good or bad' (2 Corinthians 5:10). Ministers of the gospel will receive differing rewards, according to faithfulness (1 Corinthians 3:8-17).

Despite the level of our reward we will be perfectly happy and eternally enjoy the presence of Christ in the new heavens and new earth. Will this be your destiny?

THINGS TO DISCUSS WITH YOUR FAMILY

1. Who will have a home in heaven?
2. Why should God have a home in heaven for you?
3. Make a list of the wonderful things you will experience in heaven.

Meditation

Meditate upon Christ's words in Matthew 25:34 — 'Then the King will say to those on his right hand, "Come, you blessed of my Father, inherit the kingdom prepared for you..."'

Wise Words

Our hearts must be in tune for heaven if we are to enjoy it.   *J. C. Ryle*

'Now when all things are made subject to him, then the Son himself will also be subject to him who put all things under him, that God may be all in all' (1 Corinthians 15:28).

Read: Revelation 19:1-6

Some people like to read the last page of a book first as they want to know how things turn out in the end. I trust you haven't done this. We have come to the last of our devotions, and I pray you are thrilled by what you have read.

We have traced the life of Jesus our Saviour and seen his defeat of Satan, his arch enemy. His sacrificial work accomplished the salvation of all his people. Satan was defeated, but a work was still to be done — to gather in the elect. When the kingdom of God has been fully established, all enemies will have been defeated, the last enemy being death, and the saints will have taken their place in the new heavens and earth where there is no sin. What will happen then?

Our text tells us that Jesus hands everything over to God and then 'God [will] be all in all.' Christ's heavenly Father had given his Son 'all authority ... in heaven and on earth' (Matthew 28:18). This authority will continue until Satan and all traces of sin are gone for ever. No longer will there be warfare as Christ will have established peace throughout all creation. When this time is reached he will hand back to God that special power. Christ will still rule the kingdom as King of kings and Lord of lords, but over all, God will be the supreme Ruler of all things. His perfect glory will overshadow his people.

John wrote, describing his vision of heaven, 'There shall be no night there: They need no lamp nor light of the sun, for the Lord God gives them light...' (Revelation 22:5). There the glorified saints will stand in Paradise. John writes, 'Then a voice came from the throne, saying, "Praise our God, all you his servants and those who fear him, both small and great!" And I heard, as it were, the voice of a great multitude, as the sound of many waters and as the sound of mighty thunderings, saying, "Alleluia! For the Lord God Omnipotent reigns!"' (Revelation 19:5,6).

One God — Father, Son and Holy Spirit will be glorified by all redeemed citizens of God's kingdom, and the words of David in Psalm 145:1-3 will ring out through the heavens — 'I will extol you, my God, O King; and I will bless your name for ever and ever. Every day I will bless you, and I will praise your name for ever and ever. Great is the LORD, and greatly to be praised; and his greatness is unsearchable.'

God will be 'all in all' and we, his people, will be with him for ever. Then we will experience the truth of the answer to Question 1 of the *Shorter Catechism*: 'Man's chief end is to glorify God and enjoy him for ever.' This we will do eternally — we shall enjoy the God we glorify. May God bless us all.

THINGS TO DISCUSS WITH YOUR FAMILY

1. Why should we glorify God?
2. Why will the Lord Jesus make himself 'subject' to God?
3. Whom should we praise for our salvation? Make a list of the Persons in the Godhead and what each has done in saving sinners.

Meditation

Meditate upon Revelation 7:12 — 'Amen! Blessing and glory and wisdom, thanksgiving and honour and power and might, be to our God for ever and ever. Amen.'

Wise Words

His own glory is the only end which consists with God's independence and sovereignty. *Augustus H. Strong*